Rick Steves

BEST OF
SPAIN

Contents

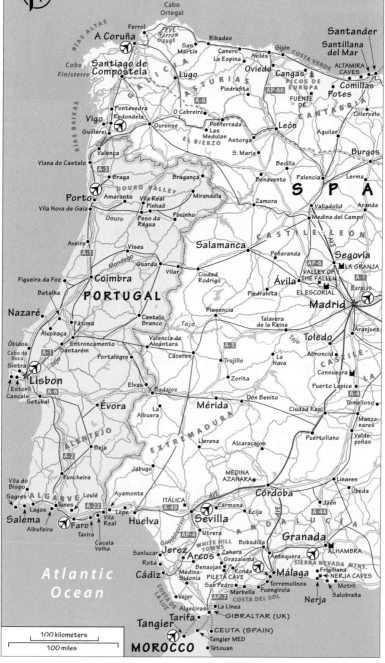

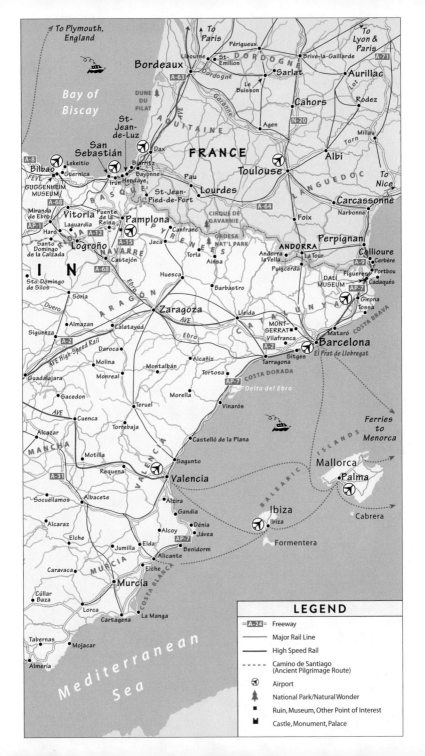

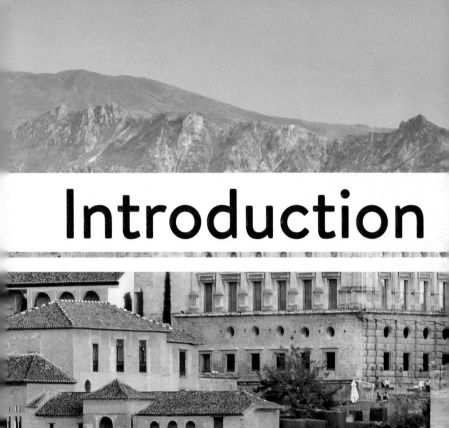

Introduction

Like a grandpa bouncing a baby on his knee, Spain is a mix of old and new, modern and traditional. Spain means massive cathedrals, world-class art, Moorish palaces, vibrant nightlife, whitewashed villages, and glorious sunshine. Spain has a richness of history and culture. From the stirring *sardana* dance in Barcelona to the sizzling rat-a-tat-tat of flamenco in Sevilla, this country creates its own beat amid the heat.

Spain's charm really lies in its people and their unique lifestyle. Even as the Spanish embrace modern times, their daily lives focus on friends and family as they always have. Many still follow the siesta schedule, shutting down work during the midday heat to enjoy the company of loved ones. In the cool of the evening, Spain comes back to life. Whole families stroll through the streets and greet their neighbors—a custom called the paseo. Spaniards are notorious night owls. The antidote for late nights? The next day's siesta.

You can see many European countries by just passing through, but Spain is a destination. Learn its history and accept the country on its own terms. Gain an appreciation for cured ham, dry sherry, and bull's-tail stew. When you go to Spain, go all the way.

THE BEST OF SPAIN

In this book, I've broken Spain down into its top destinations, offering a balanced, comfortable mix of exciting cities and cozy towns—along with the sights and experiences they offer.

The biggies on everyone's list are exuberant Barcelona and bustling Madrid, the nation's capital. Buzzing with energy, Sevilla features flamenco and nightlife that doesn't quit. Granada has Spain's finest Moorish sight—the grand palace of the Alhambra. And no visit to Spain is complete without exploring its smaller towns, from historic Toledo to the sleepy whitewashed hill towns of Andalucía.

Beyond the major destinations, I'll briefly cover what I call the Best of the Rest—great destinations that don't quite make my top cut, but are worth seeing if you have more time or specific interests: the Basque Country, Santiago de Compostela, Córdoba, and the South Coast.

To help you link the top stops, I've included a two-week itinerary (later in this chapter), with tips to help you tailor it to your interests and available time.

Atlantic Ocean

FRANCE

Santiago de Compostela

San Sebastián

Bilbao

Basque Country

ANDORRA

Pamplona

Salamanca

Segovia

El Escorial

Madrid

Toledo

Montserrat

Barcelona

PORTUGAL

Córdoba

Sevilla

Granada

Mediterranean Sea

Arcos

Grazalema

Nerja

Jerez

Ronda

South Coast

Andalucía's White Hill Towns

Gibraltar (UK)

ALGERIA

MOROCCO

100 Kilometers

100 Miles

THE BEST OF BARCELONA

Spain's second city and the proud capital of the Catalan people, Barcelona bubbles with life—from the tangled lanes of the Barri Gòtic to the trendy boulevards of the Eixample. The cradle of modern art, and home to Gaudí, Picasso, and Miró, the city itself is a dynamic work of art in progress, with everything—enthralling sights, man-made beaches, and a fun street scene—continually evolving. Join the parade of people and become part of the show.

❶ The **Ramblas**—Barcelona's grand, tree-lined, pedestrian-friendly boulevard—spills gently down from the heart of the city to the harbor.

❷ The huge, unfinished church of **Sagrada Família,** with its Sequoia-sized columns and fantastical Neo-Gothic decor, feels both medieval and futuristic.

❸ Barcelonans crowd into lively bars to feast on **tapas**—small portions of olives, seafood, meatballs, and all things deep-fried, on a toothpick.

❹ In the shadow of the 700-year-old **cathedral** in the Barri Gòtic neighborhood, locals still join hands in a communal circle to dance the sardana.

❺ **Parc Güell**—with its colorful mosaics, wavy forms, and whimsical statues—is one of several fanciful sights by Antoni Gaudí, the master of Modernisme.

❻ The vibrant and colorful **Boqueria Market** along the Ramblas evokes deep passion among Spain's devout jamón-iphiles.

❼ In the shape of an animal's back with iridescent scales, Gaudí's **Casa Battló** is a magical place.

❽ Near the busy downtown but a world away, the **beach at Barceloneta** is a balmy world of sand, surf, snack shacks, and slow sunsets.

❾ The numerous **street performers** express the spirit of this city—playful, nonconformist, spontaneous, and a bit theatrical.

THE BEST OF MADRID

Lively Madrid, both the nation's capital and its heart, is Spain on a grand scale, with stately squares and modern skyscrapers. The main square, Puerta del Sol, leads west to the lavish Royal Palace and east to the outstanding Prado art museum and Picasso's thought-provoking *Guernica*. With a compact core and a contemporary bar-hopping paseo, this sunny city is intimate, youthful, and welcoming.

❶ The **Plaza Mayor**—Madrid's historic center—is ringed by gloriously symmetrical buildings from the era when the city presided over Spain's Golden Age.

❷ **El Rastro,** Europe's biggest flea market, is a field day for shoppers, browsers, people-watchers, and bar-hopping Madrileños.

❸ Spain's capital city offers a smorgasbord of culinary delicacies from across the country—including **seafood** from the Mediterranean coast.

❹ Escape the brutal Madrid sun in spacious **Retiro Park,** a leafy oasis a stone's throw from the Prado Museum.

❺ Spanish masterpieces (like Las Meninas) hang alongside Italian Renaissance works and more at **the Prado,** arguably Europe's greatest painting museum.

❻ A bear picks berries from a madroño tree—part of the city's coat of arms since medieval times, and now a statue in the city center.

❼ The **Puerta del Sol**—the city's cultural heart and transportation hub—bustles with pedestrians, taxis, neon, demonstrations, and celebrations.

THE BEST OF TOLEDO

The medieval skyline of Toledo, rising atop a hill lassoed by a river, captivated hometown boy El Greco as much as it does travelers today. Its tangled streets are dotted with bakeries making sweet, colorful *mazapán,* and restaurants serving up savory roast suckling pig. Toledo's architecture reflects its Jewish, Moorish, and Christian roots, from the arches of a synagogue and the intricate designs of a mosque to the looming spires of a cathedral—all against the same sky.

❶ The skyline of Toledo looks much the same today as when **El Greco** painted it four centuries ago, when he made the city his home.

❷ **Local cuisine** specializes in game meats from the surrounding countryside—venison, partridge, and wild boar—with almond-sweet mazapán for dessert.

❸ Perched strategically in the geographic center of Iberia along the strategic Tajo River, Toledo grew to become the first capital of Spain.

❹ Here in Spain's capital of **damascene,** artisans inlay gold and silver wires to create intricately patterned bowls, jewelry, and bull-fighting swords.

❺ The magnificent **cathedral** has a collection of priceless paintings, including El Grecos, that would put any museum on the map.

❻ The cathedral's peaceful **cloister** is worth a stroll.

❼ Toledo's many **souvenir shops** sell locally hand-crafted knives, swords, maces, armor, and other nouveau antiques. I buy all my medieval weaponry here.

THE BEST OF GRANADA

Set against a mountainous backdrop, Granada is crowned with the last vestige of Moorish rule in Iberia: the magnificent Alhambra—fortress, palace, and gardens. Beyond that unforgettable sight, Granada offers a historic cathedral and a truly Royal Chapel. Its main square, Plaza Nueva, leads to two distinctive neighborhoods: the Alcaicería with its bustling market streets, and the hilly Albayzín, lined with funky teahouses and graced by the San Nicolás viewpoint where the day ends—and the night begins.

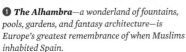

1 *The Alhambra*—a wonderland of fountains, pools, gardens, and fantasy architecture—is Europe's greatest remembrance of when Muslims inhabited Spain.

2 In *flamenco,* the women make graceful turns, the men do the machine-gun footwork, and castanets set the beat.

3 Like an Arabian souk, Granada's **Alcaicería** marketplace is a maze of small shops selling leather purses, scarves, and trinkets.

4 The Alhambra's intricate decoration is rooted in the Moors' reluctance to portray nature—instead, they created with calligraphy and geometric patterns.

5 *Plaza Nueva* is Granada's center, located in a ravine between the hill-topping Alhambra and the hillside neighborhood of Albayzín.

6 The tombs of the "Catholic Monarchs"—Ferdinand and Isabel—are the centerpiece of the **Royal Chapel.**

7 Late-night visits to **the Alhambra** are romantic—and less crowded.

THE BEST OF ANDALUCÍA'S WHITE HILL TOWNS

The meandering "Route of the White Villages" wends through the hilly, windswept landscape of Andalucía, Spain's heartland. Of the many villages worth exploring, tiny Arcos de la Frontera and sturdy Ronda rise above the rest. Slow down and wander their lanes, enjoying the small architectural nuances, the quiet rhythm of life, and the sweeping territorial views.

❶ Whitewashed villages with narrow lanes and timeless traditions, perched atop craggy bluffs—these are Spain's **pueblos blancos.**

❷ Inside the dank **Pileta Cave** you can see some of mankind's oldest creations—paintings of fish, horses, and goats by Paleolithic Michelangelos.

❸ In **Jerez,** you can watch balletic stallions prance and high-step to a classical music soundtrack.

❹ Many hill towns, such as Ronda, have **paradors**—historic luxury inns—where you can sleep with a view (or just settle for a drink on their veranda).

❺ Crowned by its cathedral, **Arcos de la Frontera** is not only quaint—it's also rustic, historic, and real.

❻ Ronda, the birthplace of **bullfighting,** has Spain's first bullring (which still operates), and the best museum on matadors and their craft.

❼ The festive city of Jerez is just a gateway to the White Hill Towns, but it's home to two Andalusian icons: fine horses and **dry sherry.**

THE BEST OF SEVILLA

Spain's most soulful city teems with people day and night. Its top sights are the cathedral and Royal Alcázar. Its top emotion is fervor, whether applied to Holy Week processions, bullfights, or riveting flamenco. Even the paseo goes on past midnight. Museums are plentiful and bars are hopping—but the main attraction is the nonstop city itself.

❶ Elbowing your way through a crowded bar to order **tapas** and a caña of beer is a classic Sevilla dining experience.

❷ Sevilla is home to some of Spain's most "Spanish" traditions, like **flamenco dancing,** which still erupts spontaneously in late-night bars.

❸ Spain's matadors relish showing off their technique in the prestigious Sevillan **bullfighting** arena.

❹ The **cathedral** has the world's biggest church interior, and houses the world's largest altarpiece, a half-ton monstrance, and the tomb of Columbus.

❺ The **Alcázar palace,** with both Christian and Moorish elements, has lavish decor, quiet courtyards, and reminders of Columbus, who sailed from Sevilla.

❻ Graceful statues of the Virgin Mary mourning her crucified son adorn many of **Sevilla's churches**—each one a different variation on sorrow.

❼ Andalusian pride is on display as Sevillans don their traditional outfits—dresses, mantillas, fans, brimmed hats—for the **April Fair.**

❽ Crenellated castle walls surround the **Royal Alcázar,** Sevilla's spectacular 10th-century palace.

THE BEST OF THE REST

If you have the time and interest, splice any of the following destinations into your itinerary. In northeast Spain, the feisty Basque Country features the coastal resort of **San Sebastián,** the famous modern-art museum at **Bilbao,** and bull-running at **Pamplona.** In the far northwest, all roads lead to **Santiago de Compostela,** where pilgrims rejoice at the end of their long journey. **Córdoba** is home to Spain's (and Europe's) only mosque with a cathedral inside. The sunny South Coast boasts the beach town of **Nerja** and British-flavored **Gibraltar.**

❶ Spain's often overlooked progressive side is trumpeted boldly at the Guggenheim modern art museum in the once-gritty now-glitzy city of **Bilbao.**

❷ The **Costa del Sol**—home to sun, sand, and seafood—is heavily touristed, but there are still a few unspoiled beaches and quaint towns.

❸ **Córdoba**'s huge former mosque, with its forest of 800 red and blue columns, attests to the cultural vitality of the Moors' 700-year presence in Spain.

❹ For centuries, pilgrims have trekked across Europe to the Cathedral of **Santiago de Compostela** in Spain's rustic northwest corner.

❺ Apes rule the **Rock of Gibraltar.**

❻ **Nerja** is a relaxed Costa del Sol town, perfect for an evening paseo on its Balcony of Europe promenade.

❼ Locals throughout southern Spain get more excited about their many **festivals** than the tourists do.

❽ The Running of the Bulls in **Pamplona** is like surfing—you hope to catch a good wave and ride it.

TRAVEL SMART

Approach Spain like a veteran traveler, even if it's your first trip. Design your itinerary, get a handle on your budget, line up your documents, and follow my travel strategies on the road.

Designing Your Itinerary

Choose your top destinations. My itinerary (on page 26) gives you an idea of how much you can reasonably see in 14 days, but you can adapt it to fit your own interests and timeframe. Art lovers are drawn to Madrid and Barcelona, which have the greatest concentration of art and the most museums. Historians will want to linger in Granada, Toledo, and Madrid. Connoisseurs of relaxation enjoy the whitewashed hill towns of Andalucía. Night owls nest in Sevilla. If you collect beaches, bask in Barcelona, San Sebastián (Basque Country), and the South Coast.

Rick Steves Audio Europe

My free **Rick Steves Audio Europe app** makes it easy to download audio content to enhance your trip. This includes my

audio tours of many of Europe's top destinations, as well as a far-reaching library of insightful travel interviews from my public radio show with experts from around the globe—including many of the places in this book. The app and all of its content are entirely free. You can download Rick Steves Audio Europe via Apple's App Store, Google Play, or the Amazon Appstore. For more information, see www.ricksteves.com/audioeurope.

Pilgrims head for Montserrat (near Barcelona) and Santiago de Compostela. Photographers want to go everywhere.

Decide when to go. Peak season, July through September, comes with crowds, heat, and higher prices. Spring and fall (April, June, and October) offer the best combination of lighter crowds, moderate prices, good weather, and long days. Off-season, November through March, prices drop, the weather is crisp, and sights have shorter hours.

Connect the dots. Link your destinations into a logical route. Determine which cities in Europe you'll fly into and out of (begin your search at Kayak.com). Decide if you'll be traveling by car or public transportation or a combination. A car is particularly helpful for exploring the hill towns (where public transportation is sparse), but is useless in big cities (park it). Trains are faster and more expensive than buses (which don't run as often on Sundays). To determine approximate transportation times between your destinations, study the driving chart (see page 459) or train schedules (www.renfe.es). Compare the cost of any long train ride with a budget flight (check Skyscanner. com for cheap flights within Europe).

Fine-tune your itinerary. Figure out how many destinations you can comfortably fit in the time you have. Don't overdo it—few travelers wish they'd hurried more. Allow enough days per destination. Avoid visiting a town on the one day a week that its major sight is closed. Check if any holidays or festivals will fall during your trip—these attract crowds and can close sights (for the latest, visit Spain's website, www.spain.info). For detailed suggestions on how to spend your time, I've included suggested day plans for destinations in the chapters that follow.

Balance intense and relaxed days. After a day of hectic sightseeing, plan some downtime. Follow up big cities with laid-back towns. Minimize one-night stands to maximize rootedness; it's worth taking

Average Daily Expenses Per Person: $145/Day

Cost	Category	Notes
$40	Meals	$5 for breakfast, $10 for lunch, and $25 for dinner
$75	Lodging	Based on two people splitting the cost of a $150 double room (solo travelers pay about $100 per room)
$25	Sights and Entertainment	Figure $15-17 per major sight, $5 for minor ones, and $35-50 for splurges like flamenco
$5	City Transit	Buses or Metro
$145	**Total**	Applies to cities; figure on less for towns

a train ride (or a drive) after dinner to get settled in a town for two nights. Staying in a home base (like Madrid) and making day trips can be more time-efficient than changing locations and hotels.

Give yourself some slack. Every trip— and every traveler—needs slack time (laundry, picnics, people-watching, and so on). Many travelers greatly underestimate this. You can't see it all, so pace yourself. Assume you will return.

Ready, set... You've designed the perfect itinerary for the trip of a lifetime.

Trip Costs per Person

Run a reality check on your dream trip. You'll have major transportation costs in addition to daily expenses.

Flight: A round-trip flight from the US to Barcelona or Madrid costs about $1,000-2,000.

Public Transportation: For a two-week trip, allow $300 for second-class trains ($450 for first class) and buses. You'll usually save money buying train tickets in Spain, rather than buying a rail pass before you leave home, and you can save even more with advance-purchase ticket discounts (for info on transportation, see page 450).

Car Rental: Allow roughly $230 per week, not including tolls, gas, parking, and insurance. Rentals and leases are cheapest if arranged from the US.

Budget Tips: It's possible to cut your daily expenses to about $75 per day, particularly outside of the big cities. Cultivate the art of picnicking, stay in hostels or basic hotels, and see only the sights you most want to see. When you splurge, choose something special that you'll always remember (such as a flamenco performance, guided walk, or tapas-tasting tour). Minimize souvenir shopping—focus instead on collecting wonderful memories.

Travel Strategies on the Road

Be your own tour guide. As you travel, get up-to-date info on sights, reserve tickets and tours, reconfirm hotels and travel arrangements, and check transit connections. Upon arrival in a new town, lay the groundwork for a smooth departure; confirm the train, bus, or road you'll take when you leave. You can find out the latest by checking with tourist-information offices (TIs) and your hoteliers, and doing research on your own by phone or online.

Take advantage of deals. You'll find deals throughout Spain (and mentioned in this book). For example, city transit passes (for multiple rides or all-day

THE BEST OF SPAIN IN 2 WEEKS

This unforgettable two-week trip will show you the very best that Spain has to offer. It's geared for public transportation (mainly trains and a few buses), but can be traveled by car. (Ideally, rent a car after you've visited Barcelona, Madrid, and Toledo, which are well-connected by train.)

DAY	PLAN	SLEEP IN
	Arrive in Barcelona	Barcelona
1	Sightsee Barcelona	Barcelona
2	Barcelona	Barcelona
3	Barcelona	Barcelona
4	Travel to Madrid in the morning (3 hours by train)	Madrid
5	Sightsee Madrid	Madrid
6	More Madrid, then head to Toledo in the late afternoon (30 minutes by train, or 1 hour by bus)	Toledo
7	Sightsee Toledo	Toledo
8	Travel to Granada (6 hours by train or bus)	Granada
9	Sightsee Granada	Granada
10	More Granada, then travel to Ronda in the late afternoon (2.5 hours by train)	Ronda
11	Sightsee Ronda	Ronda
12	Travel to Arcos (2 hours by bus), sightsee Arcos	Arcos
13	Travel to Sevilla (2 hours by bus)	Sevilla
14	Sightsee Sevilla	Sevilla
	Linger in Sevilla, or fly out	

FRANCE

Santiago de Compostela

Bilbao
San Sebastián
Pamplona
ANDORRA

Montserrat

Barcelona
4 nights

Salamanca
Segovia
El Escorial

Madrid
2 nights

Toledo
2 nights

Córdoba

Sevilla
2 nights

Arcos
1 night

Grazalema
Jerez
Nerja
Gibraltar (UK)

Ronda
2 nights

Granada
2 nights

PORTUGAL

Mediterranean Sea

ALGERIA

Atlantic Ocean

MOROCCO

100 Kilometers
100 Miles

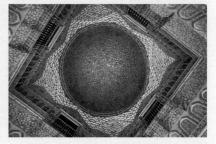

usage) decrease your cost per ride. To take the financial bite out of sightseeing, consider combo-tickets and sightseeing passes that cover multiple museums. Some hotels give a discount for payment in cash and/or longer stays.

Try alternatives to restaurants. Spanish restaurants are often closed when we're hungry. Compared to our standards, Spaniards eat late, having lunch—their biggest meal of the day—around 13:00 to 16:00, and dinner starting about 21:00. To cope, try picnics, sandwich shops, or bars, where you can get a hearty snack or an assortment of tapas (appetizers that can add up to a tasty meal). Consider taking a food-tasting tour; they're pricey, but informative and delicious—filling you in while filling you up.

Beat the summer heat. If you wilt easily, get a hotel with air-conditioning, start your day early, take a midday siesta at your hotel, and resume your sightseeing later. Join the paseo, when locals stroll in the cool of the evening.

Find religion. Churches offer some amazing art (usually free), a respite from heat, and a welcome seat. A modest dress code (no bare shoulders or shorts for anyone, even kids) is enforced at some major cathedrals (like Toledo's), but is often overlooked elsewhere.

Outsmart thieves. Pickpockets abound in crowded places where tourists congregate. Be alert to commotions, such as people bumping into you. Keep your cash, credit cards, and passport secure in a money belt tucked under your clothes; carry only a day's spending money in your front pocket. Don't set valuable items down on counters or café tabletops, where they're easily forgotten or quickly stolen. In case of theft or loss, see page 429.

Be proactive to minimize the effects of potential loss: Keep your expensive gear to a minimum. Bring copies of important documents (passport, debit/credit cards) to aid in replacement if the originals are lost or stolen. While traveling, back up your digital photos and files frequently.

Guard your time, energy, and trip. Taking a taxi can be a good value if it saves you a long wait for a cheap bus or an exhausting walk across town. To avoid long lines, take advantage of the crowd-beating tips in this book (such as making reservations, or arriving at sights early or late). When problems arise (bad food, a run-down hotel, or being overcharged), keep things in perspective. You're on vacation...and you're in Spain!

Attempt the language. Many Spaniards—especially those in the tourist trade and in big cities—speak English. Still, many Spaniards don't. You'll get more smiles and make more friends if you use some key Spanish words. Practice the Survival Phrases near the end of this book, and even better, bring a phrase book.

Connect with the culture. Enjoy the friendliness of the Spanish people. Ask questions—many locals are as interested in you as you are in them. Slow down, step out of your comfort zone, and be open to unexpected experiences. When an interesting opportunity pops up, say *"¡Sí!"*

RICK STEVES' TRAVEL PHILOSOPHY

Travel is intensified living—maximum thrills per minute and one of the last great sources of legal adventure. Travel is freedom. It's recess, and we need it.

Experiencing the real Europe requires catching it by surprise, going casual...

Affording travel is a matter of priorities. (Make do with the old car.) You can eat and sleep—simply, safely, and enjoyably—anywhere in Europe for $100 a day plus transportation costs. In many ways, spending more money only builds a thicker wall between you and what you traveled so far to see. Europe is a cultural carnival, and time after time, you'll find

Before You Go

☐ **Make sure your passport is valid.** If it's due to expire within three months of your ticketed date of return, renew it. Allow up to six weeks to renew or get a passport (www.travel.state.gov).

☐ **Book rooms well in advance,** especially if your trip falls during peak season or any major holidays or festivals. For tips on making hotel reservations, see page 445.

☐ **Reserve or buy advance tickets for major sights,** saving you from long lines: in Granada, for the Alhambra (up to three months in advance at www.alhambra-tickets.es), and in Barcelona, for various Modernista sights, such as the Sagrada Família. Details are in the chapters.

☐ **Consider travel insurance.** Compare the cost of the insurance to the cost of your potential loss. Check whether your existing insurance (health, homeowners, or renters) covers you and your possessions overseas. For tips, see www.ricksteves.com/insurance.

☐ **Call your bank.** Alert your bank that you'll be using your debit and credit cards in Europe; also ask about transaction fees, and get the PIN number for your credit card (see page 430). You won't need to bring euros for your trip—instead, withdraw euros from cash machines in Europe.

☐ **Bringing your phone?** Consider an international plan to reduce the cost of calls, texts, and data (or rely on Wi-Fi). See page 447 for different ways to stay connected in Europe.

☐ **Download apps** to your mobile device to use on the road, such as maps, transit schedules, and my free Rick Steves Audio Europe app (see page 24).

☐ **Watt's up?** Bring an adapter with two round prongs (sold at travel stores in the US) to plug into Europe's outlets. You won't need a convertor, because newer electronics—such as tablets, laptops, and battery chargers—are dual voltage and convert automatically to Europe's 220-volt system. If your old hair dryer isn't dual voltage, buy a cheapie in Europe.

☐ **Buy an International Driving Permit** (sold at AAA offices in the US, www.aaa.com) and bring your driver's license.

☐ **Pack light.** You'll walk with your luggage far more than you think (see packing list on page 465).

☐ **Refer to the Practicalities chapter,** where you'll find everything you need to know to travel smoothly in Spain.

☐ **Get updates** to this book at www.ricksteves.com/update.

that its best acts are free and the best seats are the cheap ones.

A tight budget forces you to travel close to the ground, meeting and communicating with the people. Never sacrifice sleep, nutrition, safety, or cleanliness to save money. Simply enjoy the local-style alternatives to expensive hotels and restaurants.

Connecting with people carbonates your experience. Extroverts have more fun. If your trip is low on magic moments, kick yourself and make things happen. If you don't enjoy a place, maybe you don't know enough about it. Seek the truth. Recognize tourist traps. Give a culture the benefit of your open mind. See things as different, but not better or worse. Any culture has plenty to share.

Of course, travel, like the world, is a series of hills and valleys. Be fanatically positive and militantly optimistic. If something's not to your liking, change your liking.

Travel can make you a happier American, as well as a citizen of the world. Our Earth is home to seven billion equally precious people. It's humbling to travel and find that other people don't have the "American Dream"—they have their own dreams. Europeans like us, but with all due respect, they wouldn't trade passports.

Thoughtful travel engages us with the world. It reminds us what is truly important. By broadening perspectives, travel teaches new ways to measure quality of life.

Globetrotting destroys ethnocentricity, helping us understand and appreciate other cultures. Rather than fear the diversity on this planet, celebrate it. Among your most prized souvenirs will be the strands of different cultures you choose to knit into your own character. The world is a cultural yarn shop, and we're weaving the ultimate tapestry. Join in!

Happy travels! *¡Buen viaje!*

Rick Steves

Key to This Book

Updates

This book is updated regularly—but things change. Once you pin down Spain, it wiggles. For the latest, visit www.ricksteves.com/update.

Abbreviations and Times

I use the following symbols and abbreviations in this book:

Sights are rated:

▲▲▲ Don't miss

▲▲ Try hard to see

▲ Worthwhile if you can make it

No rating Worth knowing about

Tourist information offices are abbreviated as **TI,** and bathrooms are **WCs.** To categorize accommodations, I use a **Sleep Code** (described on page 444).

Like Europe, this book uses the **24-hour clock.** It's the same as ours through 12:00 noon, then keeps going: 13:00, 14:00, and so on. For anything over 12, subtract 12 and add p.m. (14:00 is 2:00 p.m.).

When giving **opening times,** I include both peak-season and off-season hours if they differ. So, if a museum is listed as "May-Oct daily 9:00-16:00," it should be open from 9 a.m. until 4 p.m. from the first day of May until the last day of October (but expect exceptions).

For **transit** or **tour departures,** I first list the frequency, then the duration. So, a train connection listed as "2/hour, 1.5 hours" departs twice each hour and the journey lasts an hour and a half.

Map Legend

⅃⊿ Viewpoint	✈ Airport	Tunnel
↟ Entrance	⊤ Taxi Stand	Pedestrian Zone
🛈 Tourist Info	⯐ Tram Stop	
WC Restroom	Ⓑ Bus Stop	Railway
⚲ Castle	Ⓜ Metro Stop	Ferry/Boat Route
⛪ Church	Ⓡ Rodalies Rail Stop	Tram
✡ Synagogue	Ⓟ Parking	Stairs
▪ Statue/Point of Interest	)(Mountain Pass	Walk/Tour Route
	Park	
⊠ Elevator	◎ Fountain	Trail

Barcelona

Barcelona may be Spain's second city, but it's undoubtedly the first city of the proud and distinct region of Catalunya. Catalan flags wave side by side with Spanish flags, and locals—while fluent in both languages—insist on speaking Catalan first. Joining hands to dance the patriotic *sardana* is a tradition that's going strong. This lively culture is on an unstoppable roll in Spain's most cosmopolitan corner.

The city itself is a work of art. Catalan architects, including Antoni Gaudí, Lluís Domènech i Montaner, and Josep Puig i Cadafalch, forged the Modernista style and remade the city's skyline into a curvy fantasy—culminating in Gaudí's over-the-top Sagrada Família, a church still under construction. Pablo Picasso lived here as a teenager, right as he was on the verge of reinventing painting; his legacy is today's Picasso Museum.

Barcelona bubbles with life—in the narrow alleys of the Barri Gòtic, along the pedestrian boulevard called the Ramblas, in the funky bohemian quarter of El Born, along the bustling beach promenade, and throughout the chic Eixample. The cafés are filled by day, and people crowd the streets at night, popping into tapas bars for a drink and a perfectly composed bite of seafood.

If you surrender to any city's charms, let it be Barcelona.

BARCELONA IN 3 DAYS

Day 1: In the cool of the morning, follow my Barri Gòtic Walk, exploring the winding lanes, unique boutiques, and historic cathedral.

Then take my Ramblas Ramble, strolling down the grand pedestrian boulevard—a festival of people-watching, street performers, and pickpockets. On the Ramblas, duck into La Boqueria Market for fresh produce and unforgettable taste treats. In the afternoon, head to the trendy El Born district to tour the Picasso Museum or Palace of Catalan Music, or both.

On any evening: Have a tapa-hopping dinner in El Born, the Barri Gòtic, or the Eixample. Take in some music (flamenco, guitar, concerts). Zip up to the hilltop of Montjuïc for the sunset, then down to the Magic Fountains (illuminated on weekends). Or stroll the long, inviting beach promenade.

Day 2: Tour the city's fanciful Modernista architecture, championed by Antoni Gaudí. Marvel at the buildings on the

Barcelona Neighborhood Overview

Block of Discord and the street's masterpiece, La Pedrera. Tour Gaudí's soaring church, the Sagrada Família. Then head to Park Güell, with its colorful mosaics, fountains, and stunning city views.

Day 3: Tour the museums on Montjuïc: The Catalan Art Museum displays top medieval sculptures (reservation required), while Fundació Joan Miró features the hometown artist's whimsical work. The hilltop castle ramparts offers sweeping views. You could head back downtown (for museums, shopping, exploring) or take the slow, scenic cablecar from Montjuïc to the port. For a pleasant evening, stroll the beach along Barceloneta, collect another sunset, and find your favorite *chiringuito* (beach bar).

Day Trips: Allot an extra day for a side trip: the holy site of Montserrat, with its dramatic mountain scenery, or Figueres, with its mind-bending Salvador Dalí museum.

Rick's Tip: *Located in the far northeast corner of Spain,* **Barcelona makes a good first or last stop for your trip.** *With the high-speed AVE train, Barcelona is three hours away from Madrid—faster and simpler than flying. If you want to rent a car, start your trip in Barcelona, take the train or fly to Madrid, and see Madrid and Toledo, all before picking up your car—cleverly saving on several days of rental fees.*

ORIENTATION

A large square, **Plaça de Catalunya** at the center of Barcelona, divides the older and newer parts of town. Below Plaça de Catalunya is the Old City, with the Ramblas boulevard running down to the harbor.

The **Old City (Ciutat Vella)** is the compact core of Barcelona—ideal for strolling, shopping, and people-watching. It's a labyrinth of narrow streets, once confined by medieval walls. The lively pedestrian drag called the **Ramblas** goes through the heart of the Old City from Plaça de Catalunya to the harbor. The Old City is divided into thirds by the Ramblas and another major thoroughfare (running roughly parallel to the Ramblas), **Via Laietana.** Between the Ramblas and Via Laietana is the characteristic **Barri Gòtic** (BAH-ree GOH-teek, Gothic Quarter), with the cathedral as its navel. Locals call it "El Gòtic" for short. To the east of Via Laietana is the **El Born** district (a.k.a. "La Ribera"), a shopping, dining, and nightlife mecca centered on the Picasso Museum and the Church of Santa Maria del Mar. To the west of the Ramblas is the **Raval** (rah-VAHL), with a modern-art museum and a university. The Raval is of least interest to tourists (some parts of it are dodgy and should be avoided).

The old harbor, **Port Vell,** gleams with landmark monuments and new developments. A pedestrian bridge links the Ramblas with the modern Maremagnum entertainment complex. On the peninsula across the quaint sailboat harbor is **Barceloneta,** a traditional fishing neighborhood with gritty charm and good seafood restaurants. Beyond Barceloneta, a gorgeous man-made **beach** several miles long leads to the commercial and convention district called the **Fòrum.**

Above the Old City, beyond the bustling hub of Plaça de Catalunya, is the elegant **Eixample** (eye-SHAM-plah) district, its grid plan softened by cutoff corners. Much of Barcelona's Modernista architecture is here—especially along the swanky **Passeig de Gràcia,** an area called **Quadrat d'Or** ("Golden Quarter"). To the east is the **Sagrada Família;** to the north is the **Gràcia** district and Antoni Gaudí's **Park Güell.**

The large hill overlooking the city to the southwest is **Montjuïc** (mohn-jew-EEK), home to some excellent museums (Catalan Art, Joan Miró).

Tourist Information

Barcelona's **TI** has several branches (central tel. 932-853-834, www.barcelona turisme.cat). The primary one is beneath the main square, **Plaça de Catalunya** (daily 8:30-20:30, entrance across from El Corte Inglés department store—look for red sign and take stairs down, tel. 932-853-832); this TI offers a **Picasso walk** (€22, includes museum admission; Tue-Sat at 15:00; 2 hours including museum visit), as well as walks for **gourmets** (€22, Mon-Fri at 10:30, 2 hours) and fans of **Modernisme** (€16; April-Oct Mon, Wed, and Fri at 18:00; Nov-March Wed and Fri at 15:30; 2 hours). Inside the TI is also the privately run **Ruta del Modernisme** desk, which gives out a route map showing all 116 Modernista buildings and offers a sightseeing discount package (€12), with a great guidebook and discounts on many Modernista sights—worthwhile if going beyond the biggies I cover (www.ruta delmodernisme.com).

The TI on **Plaça de Sant Jaume,** just south of the cathedral in the City Hall, offers great guided **Barri Gòtic walks** (€16, daily at 9:30, 2 hours, groups limited to 35, buy your ticket 15 minutes early at the TI desk—not from the guide, in summer stop by the office a day ahead to reserve, Mon-Fri 8:30-20:30, Sat 9:00-19:00, Sun 9:00-14:00, Ciutat 2, tel. 932-853-832, www.barcelonaturisme.cat).

Other convenient branches include a kiosk near the top of the **Ramblas** (#115); near the **cathedral** in the Catalan College of Architects building; inside the base of the **Columbus Monument** at the harbor; at the **airport** (Terminals 1 and 2B); and at the **Sants Train Station.** Smaller kiosks are on **Plaça d'Espanya,** in the park across from the **Sagrada Família** entrance, and on **Plaça de Catalunya.**

At any TI, pick up the free city map (although the free El Corte Inglés map provided by most hotels is better), the small Metro map, the monthly *Barcelona Planning.com* guidebook (with tips

Daily Reminder

SUNDAY: Most sights are open, but the Boqueria and Santa Caterina markets are closed. Some sights close early today, including the Fundació Joan Miró (closes at 14:30), along with the Catalan Art Museum (closes at 15:00). Informal performances of the *sardana* national dance take place in front of the cathedral at noon (none in Aug). Some museums are free at certain times: Catalan Art Museum and Palau Güell (free on first Sun of month), and the Picasso Museum. The Magic Fountains come alive on summer evenings (May-Sept).

MONDAY: Many sights are closed, including the Picasso Museum, Catalan Art Museum, Palau Güell, Casa Lleó Morera, and Fundació Joan Miró. Most major Modernista sights are open today, including the Sagrada Família, La Pedrera, Park Güell, Casa Batlló, and Casa Amatller.

TUESDAY/WEDNESDAY: All major sights are open.

THURSDAY: All major sights are open. Fundació Joan Miró and the Picasso Museum are open until 21:30 year-round, and the Magic Fountains spout on summer evenings (May-Sept).

FRIDAY: All major sights are open. The Magic Fountains light up Montjuïc year-round.

SATURDAY: All major sights are open. Barcelonans occasionally dance the *sardana* on Saturdays at 18:00 in front of the cathedral, and in summer you're likely to see traditional folk activities there at 19:30. The Magic Fountains dance all year. The Catalan Art Museum is free after 15:00.

LATE-HOURS SIGHTSEEING: Sights with **year-round** evening hours (19:30 or later) include La Boqueria Market, Cathedral of Barcelona, Casa Batlló, and Church of Santa Maria del Mar.

Sights offering later hours only in **peak season** (roughly April-Sept) include the Sagrada Família, La Pedrera, Palau Güell, Park Güell, Fundació Joan Miró, Catalan Art Museum, and Gaudí House Museum.

---

on sightseeing, shopping, events, and restaurants), and the quarterly *See Barcelona* guide (with practical information on museums and a neighborhood-by-neighborhood sightseeing rundown). The monthly *Time Out BCN Guide* offers a concise but thorough day-by-day list of events. The monthly *Barcelona Metropolitan* magazine has timely, substantial coverage of local topics and events. All are free.

The **Regional Catalunya TI** can help with travel and sightseeing tips for the entire region and even Madrid (Mon-Sat 10:00-19:00, Sun 10:00-14:00, in Palau Robert building near the intersection of Passeig de Gràcia and Diagonal at Passeig de Gràcia 107, tel. 932-388-091, www.catalunya.com).

Advance Tickets and Sightseeing Passes

To save time, it's smart to **buy tickets in advance online,** especially for the Picasso Museum, Sagrada Família, La Pedrera, and Park Güell's Monumental Zone (advance tickets also available for Casa Batlló and Palau Güell, but less necessary).

Advance tickets are required to tour Casa Lleó Morera (either online or you can buy in Barcelona) and the Palace of Catalan Music.

▲▲▲**The Ramblas** Barcelona's colorful, gritty, tourist-filled pedestrian thoroughfare. **Hours:** Always open. See page 63.

▲▲▲**Picasso Museum** Extensive collection offering insight into the brilliant Spanish artist's early years. **Hours:** Tue-Sun 9:00-19:00, Thu until 21:30, closed Mon. See page 68.

▲▲▲**Sagrada Família** Gaudí's remarkable, unfinished church—a masterpiece in progress. **Hours:** Daily April-Sept 9:00-20:00, Oct-March 9:00-18:00. See page 83.

▲▲**Palace of Catalan Music** Best Modernista interior in Barcelona. **Hours:** 50-minute English tours daily every hour 10:00-15:00, plus frequent concerts. See page 75.

▲▲**La Pedrera (Casa Milà)** Barcelona's quintessential Modernista building and Gaudí creation. **Hours:** Daily March-Oct 9:00-20:00, Nov-Feb 9:00-18:30. See page 81.

▲▲**Park Güell** Colorful Gaudí-designed park overlooking the city. **Hours:** Daily April-Oct 8:00-20:00 (May-Aug until 21:30), Nov-March 8:30-18:15. See page 91.

▲▲**Catalan Art Museum** World-class showcase of this region's art, including a substantial Romanesque collection. **Hours:** May-Sept Tue-Sat 10:00-20:00 (Oct-April until 18:00), Sun 10:00-15:00, closed Mon. See page 93.

▲**La Boqueria Market** Colorful but touristy produce market, just off the Ramblas. **Hours:** Mon-Sat 8:00-20:00, best mornings after 9:00, closed Sun. See page 63.

▲**Palau Güell** Exquisitely curvy Gaudí interior and fantasy rooftop. **Hours:** Tue-Sun 10:00-20:00, Nov-March until 17:30, closed Mon. See page 63.

▲**Cathedral of Barcelona** Colossal Gothic cathedral ringed by distinctive chapels. **Hours:** Generally open to visitors Mon-Fri 8:00-19:30, Sat-Sun 8:00-20:00. See page 66.

▲*Sardana* **Dances** Patriotic dance in which proud Catalans join hands in a circle, often held outdoors. **Hours:** Every Sun at 12:00, sometimes also Sat at 18:00, no dances in Aug. See page 68.

▲**Santa Caterina Market** Fine market hall built on the site of an old monastery and updated with a wavy Gaudí-inspired roof. **Hours:** Mon-Sat 7:30-15:30, Thu-Fri until 20:30, closed Sun. See page 76.

▲**Church of Santa Maria del Mar** Catalan Gothic church in El Born, built by wealthy medieval shippers. **Hours:** Generally open to visitors daily 9:00-20:30. See page 76.

▲**Casa Batlló** Gaudí-designed home topped with fanciful dragon-inspired roof. **Hours:** Daily 9:00-21:00. See page 77.

▲**Casa Lleó Morera** One of the best-preserved Modernista interiors in the city. **Hours:** Tour times vary, open Tue-Sun, closed Mon. See page 77.

▲**Fundació Joan Miró** World's best collection of works by Catalan modern artist Joan Miró and his contemporaries. **Hours:** Tue-Sat 10:00-20:00 (until 19:00 Oct-June), Thu until 21:00, Sun 10:00-14:30, closed Mon. See page 96.

▲**Magic Fountains** Lively fountain spectacle. **Hours:** May-Sept Thu-Sun 21:00-23:00, Oct-April Fri-Sat 19:00-20:30. See page 97.

▲**Barcelona's Beaches** Fun-filled, man-made beach reaching from the harbor to the Fòrum. **Hours:** Always open. See page 97.

"You're Not in Spain, You're in Catalunya!"

You may see this popular nationalistic refrain on T-shirts or stickers around town. Catalunya is *not* the land of bullfighting and flamenco that many visitors envision when they think of Spain (visit Madrid or Sevilla for those).

Catalunya, with Barcelona as its capital, has its own language, history, and culture. Its eight million people have a proud, independent spirit. Historically, Catalunya ("Cataluña" in Spanish, sometimes spelled "Catalonia" in English) has often been at odds with the central Spanish government in Madrid. The Catalan language and culture were discouraged or even outlawed at various times in history, as Catalunya often chose the wrong side in wars and rebellions against the kings in Madrid. In the Spanish Civil War (1936-1939), Catalunya was one of the last pockets of democratic resistance against the military coup of fascist dictator Francisco Franco, who punished the region with four decades of repression. During that time, the Catalan flag was banned—but locals vented their national spirit by flying their football team's flag instead.

Reminders of royal and Franco-era suppression live on in Barcelona's landmarks. Citadel Park (Parc de la Ciutadella) was originally a much-despised military citadel, constructed in the 18th century to keep locals in line. The Castle of Montjuïc has been the site of numerous political executions, including hundreds during the Franco era. Today, many Catalans favor breaking away from Spain, but the central government has vowed to block any referendum on independence.

To see Catalan culture, look for the *sardana* dance or an exhibition of *castellers* (both described on page 67). The main symbol of Catalunya is the dragon, which was slain by St. George ("Jordi" in Catalan)—the region's patron saint. You'll find dragons all over Barcelona, along with the Catalan flag—called the Senyera—with four horizontal red stripes on a gold field.

After the end of the Franco era in the mid-1970s, the Catalan language made a huge comeback. Schools are now required by law to conduct classes in Catalan; most children learn Catalan first and Spanish second. While all Barcelonans still speak Spanish, nearly all understand Catalan, three-quarters speak Catalan, and half can write it.

Consider getting the **Articket BCN pass** if you plan to visit the Picasso Museum, Catalan Art Museum, and Fundació Joan Miró. The pass saves you money and lets you skip the ticket lines (especially helpful at the Picasso Museum). It covers admission to six museums and their temporary exhibits. Just show your Articket BCN (to the ticket taker, at the info desk, or at a special Articket window), and you'll get your entry ticket (€30, valid for three months; sold at participating museums and the TIs at Plaça de Catalunya, Plaça de Sant Jaume, and Sants Station; www.articket bcn.org).

Skip the Barcelona Card and the Barcelona Card Express, which cover public transportation and include free admission to mostly minor sights, with only small discounts on some major sights (Barcelona Card—€45/3 days, €55/4 days, €60/5 days; Barcelona Card Express—€20/2 days; sold at TIs and El Corte Inglés

Here are the essential Catalan phrases:

English	Catalan	Pronounced
Hello	*Hola*	OH-lah
Please	*Si us plau*	see oos plow
Thank you	*Gracies*	GRAH-see-es
Goodbye	*Adéu*	ah-DAY-oo
Long live Catalunya!	*¡Visca Catalunya!*	BEE-skah kah-tah-LOON-yah

When finding your way, these words and place names will come in handy:

exit	*sortida*	sor-TEE-dah
square	*plaça*	PLAS-sah
street	*carrer*	kah-REHR
boulevard	*passeig*	PAH-sage
avenue	*avinguda*	ah-veen-GOO-dah

Here's how to pronounce the city's major landmarks:

Plaça de Catalunya	PLAS-sah duh kah-tah-LOON-yah
Eixample	eye-SHAM-plah
Passeig de Gràcia	PAH-sage duh grass-EE-ah
Catedral	KAH-tah-dral
Barri Gòtic	BAH-ree GOH-teek
Montjuïc	mohn-jew-EEK

department stores, www.barcelona turisme.com).

Tours

The handy **hop-on, hop-off Tourist Bus** (Bus Turístic), which departs from Plaça de Catalunya, offers three multistop circuits in double-decker buses, all with headphone commentary. The two-hour blue route covers north Barcelona (most Gaudí sights, departs from El Corte Inglés). The two-hour red route covers south Barcelona (Barri Gòtic and Montjuïc, departs from the west—Ramblas—side of the square). A short 40-minute green route covers the beaches in summer (1 day-€27, 2 days-€38; buy on bus, from TI, or online; offers small discounts on major sights; daily 9:00-20:00 in summer, off-season until 19:00, buses run every 10-25 minutes, www.barcelonabusturistic.cat).

Reliable **Runner Bean Tours** offer 2.5-hour walks covering the Old City and Gaudí, as well as night tours, family

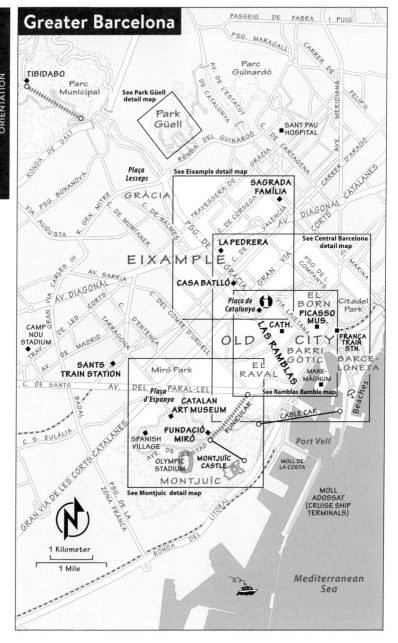

Greater Barcelona

TIBIDABO
Parc Municipal
Parc Guinardó
PASSEIG DE FABRA I PUIG
PSG. MARAGALL
CARRER DE
MERIDIANA
AVE.
FELIP II
See Park Güell detail map
Park Güell
AV. DE L'ESTATUT
DE CATALUNYA
SANT PAU HOSPITAL
RONDA DEL GUINARDÓ
C. DE CARTAGENA
CARRER D'ARAGÓ
RONDA DE DALT
VIA AUGUSTA
PSG. BONANOVA
R. GEN. MITRE
C. DE MUNTANER
C. DE BALMES
Plaça Lesseps
GRÀCIA
See Eixample detail map
TRAVESSERA DE GRÀCIA
SAGRADA FAMÍLIA
C. DE CÓRSEGA
PSG. DE GRÀCIA
VALENCIA
AV. DIAGONAL
CORTS CATALANES
CARRER DE
CI. MARINA
EIXAMPLE
LA PEDRERA
C. DE
CASA BATLLÓ
GRAN VIA
See Central Barcelona detail map
PSG. DE L. COMPANYS
AV. SARRIÀ
AV. DIAGONAL
GRAN VIA CARLES III
DE LES CORTS
C. DE COMTE D'URGELL
C. D'ENTENÇA
TARRAGONA
DE MADRID
Plaça de Catalunya
VIA LAIETANA
EL BORN
PICASSO MUS.
Citadel Park
CATH.
CAMP NOU STADIUM
TRAV.
AV.
SANTS TRAIN STATION
Miró Park
OLD CITY
LAS RAMBLAS
BARRI GÒTIC
FRANÇA TRAIN STN.
BARCE-LONETA
C. DE SANTS
AV.
DEL
Plaça d'Espanya
PARAL-LEL
CATALAN ART MUSEUM
EL RAVAL
MARE-MAGNUM
See Ramblas Ramble map
Beaches
BADAL
C. S. EULÀLIA
CABLE CAR
FUNICULAR
SPANISH VILLAGE
FUNDACIÓ MIRÓ
AVE. DE L'ESTADI
OLYMPIC STADIUM
MONTJUÏC CASTLE
MONTJUÏC
See Montjuïc detail map
Port Vell
MOLL DE LA COSTA
MOLL ADOSSAT (CRUISE SHIP TERMINALS)
GRAN VIA DE LES CORTS CATALANES
PSG. DE LA ZONA FRANCA
RONDA DEL LITORAL
Mediterranean Sea

1 Kilometer
1 Mile
N

walks, and more (tours depart from Plaça Reial daily at 11:00 year-round, plus daily at 16:30 in April-mid-Oct, mobile 636-108-776, www.runnerbeantours.com). **Discover Walks** offers similar tours (suggested tips: €5/person for a bad guide, €10 for a good one, €15 for a great one, daily in summer, Fri-Mon only off-season, www.discoverwalks.com, tel. 931-816-810).

Food tours, lasting about three hours, make several informative, fun stops for tastings in a characteristic neighborhood. Consider **The Barcelona Taste** (€80/person, Tue-Sat, run by US expats, www.thebarcelonataste.com) or **Food Lovers Company** (€90/person Mon-Sat, www.foodloverscompany.com). **Cook & Taste** offers daily cooking classes (€65/person, www.cookandtaste.com).

The **Barcelona Guide Bureau** is a co-op with about 20 local guides. Tour options include day trips outside the city to Montserrat and Figures (customized tours-€102/person for 2, €53/person for 4, Via Laietana 54, tel. 932-682-422, www.barcelonaguidebureau.com).

Helpful Hints

Theft and Safety: You're more likely to be pickpocketed here—especially on the Ramblas—than about anywhere else in Europe. Most crime is nonviolent, but muggings do occur. Leave valuables in your hotel and wear a money belt.

Street scams are easy to avoid if you recognize them. Most common is the too-friendly local who tries to engage you in conversation by asking for the time or whether you speak English. If a friendly man acts drunk and wants to dance, he's a pickpocket. Beware of thieves posing as lost tourists who ask for your help. Don't fall for street-gambling shell games. Beware of groups of women aggressively selling carnations, people offering to clean off a stain from your shirt, and so on.

Some areas feel seedy and can be unsafe after dark. Avoid the southern part of the Barri Gòtic (basically the two or three blocks directly south and east of Plaça Reial—though the strip near the Carrer de la Mercè tapas bars is better). Don't venture too deep into the Raval (just west of the Ramblas).

Internet Access: The free city network, Barcelona Wi-Fi, has hundreds of hotspots around town; look for the blue diamond-shaped sign with a big "W" (see www.bcn.cat/barcelonawifi).

Baggage Storage: Locker Barcelona is located near Hotel Denit. Pay for the day and access your locker as many times as you want. You can also leave bags overnight (€3.50-11 depending on locker size, daily 9:00-21:00, Carrer Estruc 36, tel. 933-028-796, www.lockerbarcelona.com).

BARCELONA WALKS

My two self-guided walks will help you explore the old town—down the main boulevard ("The Ramblas Ramble") and through the cathedral neighborhood ("Barri Gòtic Walk").

The Ramblas Ramble

For more than a century, this walk down Barcelona's pedestrian-only boulevard has drawn locals and visitors alike for the best people-watching in town. Raft the river of Barcelonan life, passing a grand opera house, elegant cafés, flower stands, artists, street mimes, con men, prostitutes, people charging more for a shoe-shine than what you paid for the shoes.

The Ramblas is a one-hour, level stroll that goes from Plaça de Catalunya to the waterfront, with an easy return by the Metro. The word "Ramblas" is plural; the street is actually a succession of five separately named segments. But street signs and addresses treat it as a single long street—"La Rambla," singular.

Be alert for pickpockets. Assume any commotion is a distraction by a team of thieves. Don't be intimidated...be smart. Wear your money belt.

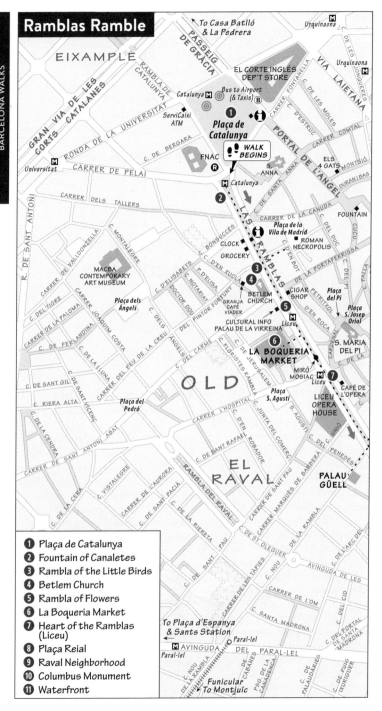

Ramblas Ramble

EIXAMPLE

PASSEIG DE GRÀCIA

To Casa Batlló & La Pedrera

Urquinaona Ⓜ

Urquinaona Ⓜ

DE LES JONQUERES

VIA LAIETANA

RAMBLA DE CATALUNYA

GRAN VIA DE LES CORTS CATALANES

RONDA DE LA UNIVERSITAT

C. DE BERGARA

EL CORTE INGLÉS DEP'T STORE

CARRER FONTANELLA

C. DE LES MOLES

C. DE LES MOLES

Catalunya Ⓜ

Bus to Airport (& Taxis) Ⓑ

ServiCaixi ATM

❶
Plaça de Catalunya

CARRER D'ESTRUC

PORTAL DE L'ANGEL

CARRER COMTAL

WALK BEGINS

ELS 4 GATS

MONTSIÓ

FNAC
Ⓡ

Universitat Ⓜ

CARRER DE PELAI

Ⓜ Catalunya

❷

S. ANNA

C. DE SANTA ANNA

DURAN I BAS

CARRER DELS TALLERS

CARRER DE LA CANUDA

FOUNTAIN

C. DEL DUC

CUCU

R. DE SANT ANTONI

C. DE VALLDONZELLA

C. MONTALEGRE

BONSUCCES

Plaça de la Vila de Madrid ❶

ROMAN NECROPOLIS

DE LA PORTAFERRISSA

C. PETRITXOL

C. PALLA

LAS RAMBLAS

MACBA CONTEMPORARY ART MUSEUM

C. D'ELISABETS

C. D'EN XUCLÀ

CLOCK

GROCERY

❸

P. D'ELISA

C. NOTARIAT

❹

Plaça dels Àngels

DOCTOR DOU

DEL PINTOR FORTUNY

BETLEM CHURCH

CIGAR SHOP

C. DE BONSOT

Plaça del Pi

C. DEL TIGRE

C. DE LA PALOMA

CARRER JOAQUIM COSTA

GRANJA CAFÉ VIADER

❺

D'EN ROCA

Plaça S. Josep Oriol

C. DE FERLANDINA

C. DE LA LLUNA

CARRER DEL PEU DE LA CREU

DELS ÀNGELS

DEL CARME

CULTURAL INFO PALAU DE LA VIRREINA

Liceu Ⓜ

S. MÀRIA DEL PI

C. DE SANT GIL

C. FLORISTES RAMBLA

❻
LA BOQUERIA MARKET

C. DE JERUSALEM

C. DE LA

C. RIERA ALTA

C. DE SANT VICENÇ

Plaça del Pedró

OLD

Plaça S. Agustí

MIRÓ MOSIAC

Liceu Ⓜ ❼

CAFÉ DE L'OPERA

C. DE LA CENDRA

CARRER DE SANT ANTONI ABAT

CARRER L'HOSPITAL

C. D'EN ROBADOR

C. JUNTA DEL COMERÇ

LICEU OPERA HOUSE

C. DE SANT RAFAEL

EL RAVAL

C. D'EN ROBADOR

C. AGUSTÍ

C. DE LA UNIÓ

C. DEL PENEDÉS

C. DE LA CERA

C. VISTALEGRE

CARRER DE L'AURORA

RAMBLA DEL RAVAL

CARRER SANT PAU

CARRER MARQUÉS DE BARBERÀ

PALAU GÜELL

DE L'ARC DEL

C. DE SANT PACIÀ

C. DE LA RIERETA

C. DE SANT PAU

C. DE SANT OLEGUER

AVINGUDA DE LES

C. NOU

DE LA RAMBLA

C. DE SANT

C. DE LES TÀPIES

CARRER SANT PAU

C. SANTA MADRONA

CARRER DE L'OM

C. DEL CID

DEL PORTAL DE SANTA MADRONA

To Plaça d'Espanya & Sants Station

Paral·lel Ⓜ
AVINGUDA DEL PARAL·LEL
Paral·lel

NOU DE LA RAMBLA

C. DE CABANES

PSG. DE LA CANADENCA

C. DE PALAUDÀRIES

C. DEL PUIG XURIGUER

Funicular
To Montjuïc

❶ Plaça de Catalunya
❷ Fountain of Canaletes
❸ Rambla of the Little Birds
❹ Betlem Church
❺ Rambla of Flowers
❻ La Boqueria Market
❼ Heart of the Ramblas (Liceu)
❽ Plaça Reial
❾ Raval Neighborhood
❿ Columbus Monument
⓫ Waterfront

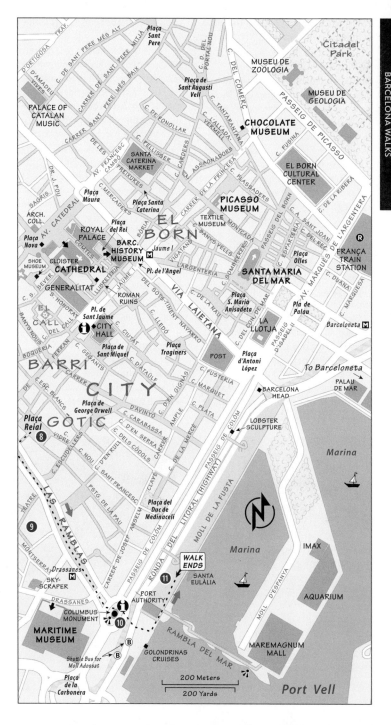

Plaça Sant Pere

Citadel Park

C. D'ORTIGOSA   TRAF.
C. DE SANT PERE MÉS ALT
C. D'AMADEU VIVES
MUSEU DE ZOOLOGIA
C. D. DEL PORTAL NOU
C. DEL COMERÇ

CARRER SANT PERE MÉS BAIX
Plaça de Sant Augusti Vell
C. TANTARANTANA
PASSEIG DE PICASSO

PALACE OF CATALAN MUSIC
CARRER SANT PERE MÉS BAIX
C. DE FONOLLAR
C. L'ALLADA VERMELL
CHOCOLATE MUSEUM

CARRER SANT PERE MÉS BAIX
C. DE LES
AV. FRANCESC CAMBÓ
C. PELLISSER
C. CORDERS
C. ASSAONADORS
C. FUSINA

DR. J. POU
SANTA CATERINA MARKET
FREIXURES
C. FLASSADERS
EL BORN CULTURAL CENTER

SAGRIS...
Plaça Maura
C. MERCADERS
Plaça Santa Caterina
C. DE LA PRINCESA
PASSEIG DEL BORN
C. DE LA RIBERA

ARCH. COLL.
AV. CATEDRAL
Plaça del Rei
BÒRIA
PICASSO MUSEUM
C. A. SANT JOAN

Plaça Nova
ROYAL PALACE
C. COMTES
EL BORN
TEXTILE MUSEUM
MONTCADA
C. DE REC
R

SHOE MUSEUM
CLOISTER
BARC. HISTORY MUSEUM
Jaume I
BANYS VELLS
C. ESPARTERIA
FRANÇA TRAIN STATION

CATHEDRAL
C. VIGATANS
Jaume I
L'ARGENTERIA
SANTA MARIA DEL MAR
C. DUANA

C. S. SEVER
GENERALITAT
LLIBRETERIA
Pl. de l'Angel
C. SOMBRERERS
Plaça Olles
AV. MARQUÉS DE L'ARGENTERA

S. HONORAT
ROMAN RUINS
C. DEL SOTS-TINENT NAVARRO
Plaça S. Maria Anisadeta
C. MARQUESA

EL CALL
Pl. de Sant Jaume
C. CIUTAT
VIA LAIETANA
LA LLOTJA
Barceloneta

BANYS NOUS
CITY HALL
C. LLEDÓ
PASSEIG D'ISABEL II

BOQUERIA
Plaça de Sant Miquel
Plaça Traginers
POST
Pla de Palau

C. DE GEGANTS
C. DATAÜF
C. FUSTERIA
Plaça d'Antoni López

BARRI
CARRER FERRAN
D'AVINYO
C. MARQUET
To Barceloneta

C. ESC. BLANCS
CITY
C. D'EN GIGNÀS
C. PLATA
PALAU DE MAR

Plaça de George Orwell
C. CARABASSA
BARCELONA HEAD

Plaça Reial
GÒTIC
C. D'EN SERRA
AMPLE
LOBSTER SCULPTURE
Marina

8
C. VIDRE
C. NOU
C. D'EN RULL
C. DELS CODOLS
C. DE LA MERCÈ
PASSEIG DE COLOM

C. ESCUDELLERS
C. J. SANT FRANCESC
CLAVÉ
Marina

LAS RAMBLAS
PSTG. DE LA PAU
MOLL DE LA FUSTA
IMAX

TEATRE
9
Plaça del Duc de Medinaceli

MONTSERRAT
Drassanes
CARRER DE JOSEP ANSELM
PASSEIG DE COLOM
RONDA DEL LITORAL (HIGHWAY)
N

SKY-SCRAPER
DRASSANES
WALK ENDS
11
SANTA EULÀLIA
Marina
AQUARIUM

COLUMBUS MONUMENT
PORT AUTHORITY
MOLL D'ESPANYA

MARITIME MUSEUM
10
B

Shuttle Bus for Moll Adossat
B
GOLONDRINAS CRUISES
RAMBLA DEL MAR
MAREMAGNUM MALL

Plaça de la Carbonera
200 Meters
200 Yards
Port Vell

• Start your ramble on Plaça de Catalunya, at the top of the Ramblas.

❶ Plaça de Catalunya

Dotted with fountains, statues, and pigeons, and ringed by grand Art Deco buildings, this plaza is Barcelona's center. The square's straight lines are a reaction to the curves of Modernisme (which predominates in the Eixample district, just north of the square). Plaça de Catalunya is the hub for the Metro, bus, airport shuttle, and Tourist Bus. It's where Barcelona congregates to watch soccer matches on the big screen, to demonstrate, to celebrate, and to enjoy concerts and festivals. More than half of the eight million Catalans live in greater Barcelona; this is their Times Square.

The 12-acre square links the narrow streets of old Barcelona with the broad boulevards of the newer city. Four great thoroughfares radiate from here. The Ramblas is the popular pedestrian promenade. Passeig de Gràcia has fashionable shops and cafés (and traffic). Rambla de Catalunya is equally fashionable but cozier and more pedestrian-friendly. Shopper-friendly and traffic-free Avin-

guda del Portal de l'Angel leads to the Barri Gòtic.

At the Ramblas end of the square, the odd, inverted-staircase **monument** represents the shape of Catalunya and honors one of its former presidents, Francesc Macià i Llussà, who declared independence for the breakaway region in 1931. (It didn't stick.) Sculptor Josep Maria Subirachs, whose work you'll see at the Sagrada Família, designed it.

Venerable Café Zürich, just across the street from the monument, is a popular rendezvous spot. Homesick Americans might prefer the nearby Hard Rock Café. The giant El Corte Inglés department store (on the northeast side) has just about anything you might need.

• Cross the street and head down the Ramblas. To get oriented, pause 20 yards down, at the ornate lamppost with a fountain as its base (on the right, near #129).

❷ Fountain of Canaletes

The black-and-gold fountain has been a local favorite for more than a century. When Barcelona tore down its medieval wall and transformed the Ramblas into an elegant promenade, this fountain was one

Plaça de Catalunya

of its early attractions. Legend says that a drink from the fountain ensures that you'll come back to Barcelona one day. Watch tourists struggle with the awkwardly high water pressure. It's still a popular rendezvous spot.

Get your bearings for our upcoming stroll. You'll see the following features here and all along the way:

The wavy **tile work** of the pavers underfoot represents the stream that once flowed here. *Rambla* means "stream" in Arabic. Look up to see the city's characteristic shallow **balconies.** The **plane trees** lining the boulevard are known for their hardiness in urban settings. These deciduous trees let in maximum sun in the winter and provide maximum shade in the summer.

Nearby, notice the **chairs** fixed to the sidewalk at jaunty angles. At one time, you'd pay to rent a chair for the view of passersby. Enjoy these chairs—you'll find virtually no public benches or other seating farther down the Ramblas, only cafés that serve beer and sangria in just one expensive size: *gigante.*

• *Continue strolling.*

All along the Ramblas are **24-hour newsstands.** Among their souvenirs, you'll see soccer paraphernalia, especially the scarlet-and-blue of FC Barcelona (known as "Barça"). The team is owned by its more than 170,000 "members"— fans who buy season tickets, which come with a share of ownership. Their motto, "More than a club" *(Mes que un club),* suggests that Barça represents not only athletic prowess but the Catalan cultural identity. This comes to a head during a match nicknamed "El Clásico," in which they face their bitter rivals, Real Madrid (whom many fans view as stand-ins for Castilian cultural chauvinism).

Walk 100 yards farther to #115 and the venerable **Royal Academy of Science and Arts building** (now home to a theater). Look up: The clock high on the facade marks official Barcelona time— synchronize. The **TI** kiosk right on the Ramblas is a handy stop for any questions. The **Carrefour** supermarket just behind it (at #113) has cheap groceries (daily 10:00-22:00).

• *You're now standing at the...*

Subirachs sculpture on Plaça de Catalunya

❸ Rambla of the Little Birds

Traditionally, kids brought their parents here to buy pets, especially on Sundays. Today, only one of the traditional pet kiosks survives—there's not a bird in sight. You'll find bird-related pet supplies and recorded chirping.

• *At #122 (the big, modern Citadines Hotel on the left, just behind the pet kiosk), take a 100-yard detour through a passageway marked* Passatge de la Ramblas *to a restored...*

Roman Necropolis: Look down and imagine a 2,000-year-old tomb-lined road. Outside the walls of Roman cities, tombs typically lined the roads leading into town. Emperor Augustus spent time in modern-day Spain conquering new land, so the Romans incorporated Hispania into the empire's infrastructure. This road, Via Augusta, led into the Roman port of Barcino (today's highway to France still follows the route laid out by this Roman thoroughfare).

• *Return to the Ramblas and continue 100 yards or so to the next street, Carrer de la Portaferrissa (across from the big church). Turn left a few steps and look right to see the* **decorative tile** *over a fountain still in use by locals. The scene shows the original city wall with the gate that once stood here. Now cross the boulevard to the front of the big church.*

❹ Betlem Church

This church is dedicated to Bethlehem, and for centuries locals have flocked here at Christmastime to see Nativity scenes.

The church's sloping roofline, ball-topped pinnacles, corkscrew columns, and scrolls above the entrance all identify it as 17th-century Baroque. The Baroque style is unusual in Barcelona because it missed out on several centuries of architectural development. Barcelona enjoyed two heydays: during the medieval period (before the Renaissance) and during the turn of the 20th century (after Baroque). In between those periods, from about 1500 until 1850, the city's importance dropped—first, New World discoveries shifted lucrative trade to ports on the Atlantic, and then the Spanish crown kept unruly Catalunya on a short leash.

For a sweet treat, head around to the narrow lane on the far side of the church (running parallel to the Ramblas) to **Café Granja Viader,** which has specialized in baked and dairy delights since 1870. Step inside to see Viader family photos and early posters advertising Cacaolat—the local chocolate milk Barcelonans love. (For other sugary treats nearby, follow "A Short, Sweet Walk" on page 102.)

• *Continue down the boulevard, through the stretch called the...*

Canaletes fountain

Rambla of Flowers

❺ Rambla of Flowers

This colorful block is lined with flower stands. Besides admiring the blossoms on display, gardeners covet the seeds sold here for varieties of radishes, greens, peppers, and beans seldom seen in the US—including the iconic green Padrón pepper. (If you buy seeds, you're obligated to declare them at US customs when returning home.) On the left, at #100, **Gimeno** sells cigars. Step inside and appreciate the dying art of cigar boxes.

If you want to buy advance required tickets for Casa Lleó Morera, stop by the cultural center at Palau de la Virreina at Ramblas 99, on your right (tickets aren't sold at the actual sight).

• *Continue to the Metro stop marked by the red M. At #91 (on the right) is the arcaded entrance to Barcelona's covered market, La Boqueria. If this main entry is choked with visitors (as it often is), you can skirt around to a side entrance, one block in either direction (look for the round arches that mark passages into the market colonnade).*

❻ La Boqueria Market

This lively market hall is an explosion of chicken legs, bags of live snails, stiff fish, delicious oranges, odd odors, and sleeping dogs. The best day for a visit is Saturday, when the market is thriving. It's closed on Sundays, and locals avoid it on Mondays, when it's open but (they believe) vendors are selling items that aren't necessarily fresh—especially seafood, since fishermen stay home on Sundays.

While tourists are drawn to the area around the main entry (below the colorful stained-glass sign), locals know that the stalls up front pay the highest rent—and therefore inflate their prices and cater to out-of-towners. For example, the juice bars along the main drag charge more than those a couple of aisles to the right.

Stop by the **Pinotxo Bar**—just inside the market, under the sign, and snap a photo of animated Juan giving a thumbs-up for your camera. Juan and his family are busy feeding shoppers. The stools nearby are a fine perch for enjoying both coffee and people-watching.

The market and lanes nearby are busy with tempting little eateries (see page 101). Drop by a café for an *espresso con leche* or *tortilla española* (potato omelet). Once you get past the initial gauntlet, do some exploring.

The produce stands show off seasonal fruits and vegetables. The fishmonger stalls could double as a marine biology lab. Fish is sold whole—local shoppers like to look their dinner in the eye to be sure it's fresh. At meat stands, full legs of *jamón* (ham)—some costing upwards of €200—tempt the Spaniards who so love this local delicacy. You'll see many types of *chorizo* (red spicy sausage). *Huevos del toro* are bull testicles—surprisingly inexpensive... and oh so good.

• *Head back out to the street and continue down the Ramblas.*

You're skirting the western boundary of the old Barri Gòtic. As you walk, glance to the left through a modern cutaway arch for a glimpse of the medieval church tower of **Santa Maria del Pi,** a popular venue for guitar concerts. This also marks Plaça del Pi and a great shopping street, Carrer Petritxol, which runs parallel to the Ramblas.

At the corner directly opposite the modern archway, find the **Escribà** bakery, with its fine Modernista facade and interior (look for the *Antigua Casa Figueras* sign over the doorway). Notice the mosaics of twining plants, the stained-glass peacock, and woodwork. In the sidewalk in front of the door, a plaque dates the building to 1902.

• *After another block, you reach the Liceu Metro station, marking the...*

❼ Heart of the Ramblas

At the Liceu Metro station's elevators, the Ramblas widens into a small, lively square (Plaça de la Boqueria). Liceu marks the midpoint of the Ramblas, half-

- **A** Chinese dragon ornament
- **B** Joan Miró's mosaic
- **C** Plaça Reial
- **D** La Boqueria Market
- **E** Columbus monument
- **F** Palau Güell

way between Plaça de Catalunya and the waterfront.

Underfoot in the center of the Ramblas, find the red-white-yellow-and-blue **mosaic** by homegrown abstract artist Joan Miró. The mosaic's black arrow represents an anchor, a reminder of the city's attachment to the sea. Miró's colorful designs are found all over the city, from murals to mobiles to the La Caixa bank logo. The best place in Barcelona to see his work is in the Fundació Joan Miró.

The surrounding buildings have playful ornamentation typical of the city. The **Chinese dragon** holding a lantern (at #82) decorates a former umbrella shop (notice the umbrella mosaics high up). The dragon is a symbol of Catalan pride for its connection to local patron saint, dragon-slayer St. George (Jordi).

Hungry? Swing around the back of the umbrella shop to **Taverna Basca Irati** (a block up Carrer del Cardenal Casanyes), one of many user-friendly tapas bars in town. Instead of ordering, just grab or point to what looks good on the display platters, then pay per piece.

Back on the Ramblas, a few steps down (on the right) is the **Liceu Opera House** (Gran Teatre del Liceu), which hosts world-class opera, dance, and theater (box office around the right side, open Mon-Fri 13:30-20:00). Opposite the opera house is Café de l'Opera (#74), an elegant stop for an expensive beverage. This bustling café, with Modernista decor and a historic atmosphere, has been open since 1929, even during the Spanish Civil War.

• *We've seen the best stretch of the Ramblas; to cut this walk short, you could catch the Metro back to Plaça de Catalunya. Otherwise, let's continue to the port. The wide, straight street that crosses the Ramblas in another 30 yards (Carrer de Ferran) leads left to Plaça de Sant Jaume, the government center.*

Head down the Ramblas another 50 yards (to #46), and turn left down an arcaded lane (Carrer de Colom) to the square called...

❽ *Plaça Reial*

Dotted with palm trees, surrounded by an arcade, and ringed by yellow buildings with white Neoclassical trim, this elegant square has a colonial ambience. It comes complete with old-fashioned taverns, modern bars with patio seating, and a Sunday coin-and-stamp market (10:00-14:00). Completing the picture are Gaudí's first public works—the two colorful helmeted lampposts. The square is a lively hangout by day or night (though the small streets stretching toward the water from the square can be sketchy). To just relax over a drink, the Ocaña cocktail bar is a good bet.

• *Head back out to the Ramblas.*

Across the boulevard, a half-block detour down Carrer Nou de la Rambla brings you to **Palau Güell** (on the left, at #3), the first of Antoni Gaudí's Modernista buildings, built 1886-1890. The two parabolic-arch doorways and elaborate wrought-iron work signal his emerging nonlinear style. Palau Güell offers an informative look at a Gaudí interior (see page 63).

• *Proceed along the Ramblas.*

❾ *Raval Neighborhood*

The neighborhood on the right-hand side of this stretch of the Ramblas is El Raval. In the last century, this was a rough neighborhood, frequented by sailors, prostitutes, and poor immigrants. Today, it's becoming gentrified, but the back streets can be edgy.

Along this part of the Ramblas, you'll often see surreal **human statues.** These performers—with creative and elaborate costumes—must audition and register with the city government; only 15 can work along the Ramblas at any one time. To enliven your Ramblas ramble, stroll with a pocketful of small change. As you wander downhill, drop coins into their cans (the money often kicks the statues into entertaining gear). But remember, wherever people stop to gawk, pickpockets are at work.

You're also likely to see some old-fashioned **shell games** in this part of town. Stand back and observe these nervous no-necks at work. They swish around their little boxes, making sure to show you the pea. Their shills play and win. Then, in hopes of making easy money, fools lose big time.

Near the bottom of the Ramblas, take note of the Drassanes Metro stop, which can take you back to Plaça de Catalunya when you're ready. The skyscraper to the right of the Ramblas is the Edificio Colón. Built in 1970, the 28-story structure was Barcelona's first high-rise. Near the skyscraper is the Maritime Museum, housed in what were the city's giant medieval shipyards.

• *Up ahead is the...*

⑩ *Columbus Monument*

The 200-foot **column** honors Christopher Columbus, who came to Barcelona in 1493 after journeying to America. It was erected for the 1888 Universal Exposition, an international fair that helped vault a surging Barcelona onto the world stage.

It's ironic that Barcelona celebrates Columbus; his discoveries started 300 years of decline for the city, as Europe began to face West (the Atlantic and the New World) rather than East (the Mediterranean and the Orient). Within a few decades of Columbus, Barcelona had become a depressed backwater, and it didn't rebound until events like the 1888 Expo cemented its comeback.

A tiny elevator ascends to the top of the monument, lifting visitors to an observation area for fine panoramas over the city (€4.50, daily 8:30-20:30, last entry 30 minutes before closing, entrance/ticket desk in TI inside the base of the monument).

• *Scoot across the busy traffic circle to survey the...*

⑪ *Waterfront*

Stand on the boardwalk (between the modern bridge and the kiosks selling harbor cruises), and survey Barcelona's bustling maritime zone. Although the city is one of Europe's top 10 ports, with many busy industrial harbors and several cruise terminals, this low-impact stretch of sea-

Modernista port authority building and the Old Port

front is clean, fresh, and people-friendly.

As you face the water, the frilly yellow building to your left is the fanciful Modernista-style port-authority building. The wooden pedestrian **bridge** jutting straight out into the harbor is a modern extension of the Ramblas. Called La Rambla de Mar ("Rambla of the Sea"), the bridge swings out to allow boat traffic into the marina; when closed, the footpath leads to an entertainment and shopping complex. Just to your right are the *golondrinas*—**harbor cruise boats,** (€7.20-15, daily on the hour 11:30-19:00, more in summer, fewer in winter, tel. 934-423-106, www.lasgolondrinas.com), which can be fun if you love to be out on the water (though the views from the harbor aren't great).

• *Turn left and walk 100 yards along the promenade between the port authority and the harbor.*

This delightful promenade is part of Barcelona's Old Port (Port Vell). The port's pleasant sailboat marina is completely enclosed by a modern complex with the Maremagnum shopping mall, an IMAX cinema, and a huge aquarium. Along the promenade is a moored historic schooner, the *Santa Eulália* (part of the Maritime Museum; €3 for entry without museum visit, Tue-Sun 10:00-20:30 except Sat when it opens at 14:00, Nov-March until 17:30, closed Mon). On a sunny day, it's fun to walk the length of the promenade to the iconic *Barcelona Head* sculpture (by American artist Roy Lichtenstein, not quite visible from here), which puts you right at the edge of El Born.

From here, you can also pick out some of Barcelona's more distant charms. The triangular spit of land across the harbor is **Barceloneta.** This densely populated community was custom-built to house fishermen and sailors whose traditional neighborhood in El Born was razed so Philip V could build a military citadel there in the 18th century. Today's Barceloneta is popular for its easy access to a gorgeous stretch of sandy beaches (on the other side of the Barceloneta peninsula).

Looking back toward the Columbus Monument, you'll see in the distance the majestic, 570-foot bluff of **Montjuïc,** a parklike setting dotted with sights and museums (see page 92; to get there, ride the Metro from Drassanes one stop to the Paral-lel stop, then take the funicular up).

• *Your ramble is over. If it's a nice day, consider strolling the promenade and looping back around on La Rambla del Mar. Or maybe dip into El Born. If you're truly on vacation, walk through Barceloneta to the beach.*

To get to other points in town, your best bet is to backtrack to the Drassanes Metro stop, at the bottom of the Ramblas. Alternatively, you can catch buses #14 or #59 from along the top of the promenade back to Plaça de Catalunya.

Barri Gòtic Walk

The Barri Gòtic (Gothic Quarter) is a bustling world of shops, bars, and nightlife packed into narrow, winding lanes and undiscovered courtyards. This is Barcelona's birthplace—where the ancient Romans built a city, where medieval Christians built their cathedral, where Jews gathered together, and where Barcelonans lived within a ring of protective walls until the 1850s, when the city expanded.

Today "El Gòtic" is a grab bag of grand squares, Art Nouveau storefronts, Thursday flea markets, antique and junk shops, and street musicians. In the center of it all is the cathedral, surrounded by other legacy sights from the city's 2,000-year history. Use this walk to get the lay of the land, then explore the shopping streets nearby.

• *Start on Barcelona's grand main square,* **Plaça de Catalunya.** *From the northeast corner (between the giant El Corte Inglés department store and the Banco de España), head down the broad pedestrian boulevard called...*

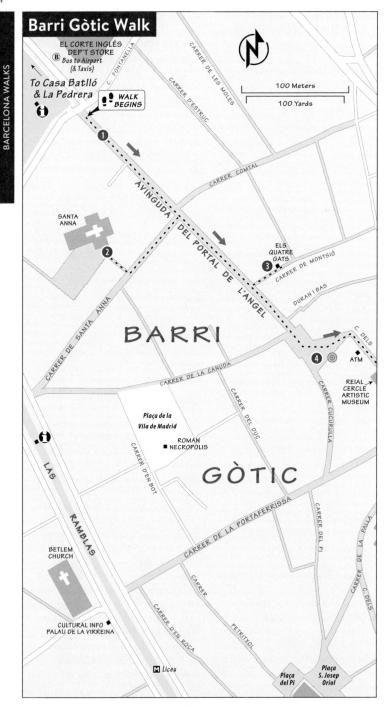

Barri Gòtic Walk

EL CORTE INGLÉS
DEP'T STORE
Ⓑ Bus to Airport
(& Taxis)

*To Casa Batlló
& La Pedrera*

C. FONTANELLA

WALK
BEGINS

CARRER D'ESTRUC

CARRER DE LES MOLES

N

100 Meters

100 Yards

❶

AVINGUDA DEL PORTAL DE L'ANGEL

CARRER COMTAL

SANTA
ANNA

❷

ELS
QUATRE
GATS

❸

CARRER DE MONTSIÓ

DURAN I BAS

C. DELS

CARRER DE SANTA ANNA

BARRI

❹

ATM

REIAL
CERCLE
ARTISTIC
MUSEUM

CARRER DE LA CANUDA

CARRER DEL DUC

CARRER CUCURULLA

*Plaça de la
Vila de Madrid*

ROMAN
NECROPOLIS

GÒTIC

CARRER DEL PI

CARRER DE LA PALLA

C. DELS

LAS

CARRER D'EN BOT

RAMBLAS

BETLEM
CHURCH

CARRER DE LA PORTAFERRISSA

CARRER

CULTURAL INFO
PALAU DE LA VIRREINA

CARRER D'EN ROCA

PETRITXOL

Ⓜ *Liceu*

*Plaça
del Pi*

*Plaça
S. Josep
Oriol*

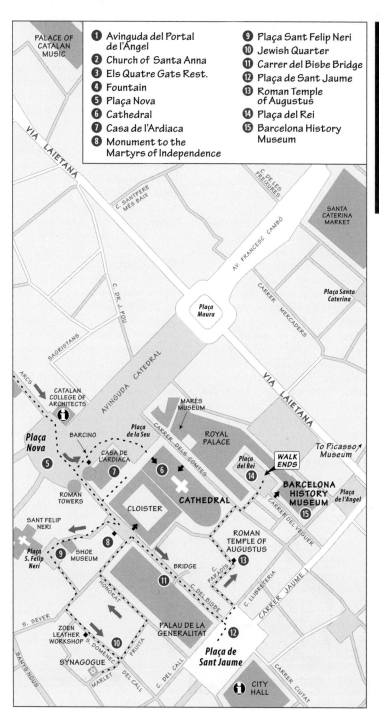

1 Avinguda del Portal de l'Angel
2 Church of Santa Anna
3 Els Quatre Gats Rest.
4 Fountain
5 Plaça Nova
6 Cathedral
7 Casa de l'Ardiaca
8 Monument to the Martyrs of Independence
9 Plaça Sant Felip Neri
10 Jewish Quarter
11 Carrer del Bisbe Bridge
12 Plaça de Sant Jaume
13 Roman Temple of Augustus
14 Plaça del Rei
15 Barcelona History Museum

❶ Avinguda del Portal de l'Angel

For much of Barcelona's history, this was a major city gate. A medieval wall enclosed the city, and there was an entrance here—the "Gate of the Angel" that gives the street its name. It was thought that the angel statue atop the gate kept the city safe from plagues and bid voyagers safe journey as they left the city.

Today, the pedestrians-only street is choked with shoppers cruising through some of the most expensive retail space in town. It's globalized and sanitized, with high-end Spanish and international chains, but a handful of local businesses survive. At the first corner (at #21), a green sign marks **Planelles Donat**—long appreciated for ice cream, sweet *turró* (or *turrón* in Spanish, almond candy), refreshing *orxata* (or *horchata,* almond-flavored drink), and *granissat* (or *granizado,* ice slush).

• *A block farther down, pause at Carrer de Santa Anna to admire the Art Nouveau awning at another El Corte Inglés department store. Take a half-block detour to the right on Carrer de Santa Anna to the doorway at #29 (on the right), which leads into to the pleasant, flower-fragrant courtyard of the...*

❷ Church of Santa Anna

This 12th-century gem, which used to be part of a convent, has a fine cloister—an arcaded walkway around a leafy courtyard (viewable to the left of the church). Climb the modern stairs for views of the bell tower. Inside, you'll see a bare Romanesque interior and Greek-cross floor plan, topped with an octagonal wooden roof. The door at the far end of the nave leads to the cloister (€2, church generally open Mon-Fri 11:00-19:00, closed Sat-Sun).

As you head back to the main drag, you'll pass—a few doors down—a **condom shop** on your left. It advertises (to men with ample self-esteem): *Para los pequeños placeres de la vida* ("For the little pleasures in life").

• *Backtrack to Avinguda Portal de l'Angel. At Carrer de Montsió (on the left), opposite the Zara store, side-trip a half-block to...*

❸ Els Quatre Gats

This restaurant (at #3) is a historic monument, tourist attraction, nightspot, and eatery. It's famous as the bohemian hangout where Picasso nursed drinks with friends and had his first one-man show (in 1900). The building itself, by prominent architect Josep Puig i Cadafalch, is Neo-Gothic Modernisme, inspired by the Paris bohemian intellectual scene. While you can have a snack, meal, or drink here, if you just want to admire the menu cover art—originally painted by Picasso—and take a look around, ask *"Solo mirar, por favor?"*

• *Return to and continue down Avinguda del Portal de l'Angel. In a square on the left is a rack of* **city loaner bikes,** *part of the popular and successful "Bicing" program designed to reduce car traffic (available only*

Architectural details enliven the shopping street.

Fountain with tilework

to Barcelona residents). You'll soon reach a fork in the road and a building with a...

❹ Fountain

The blue-and-yellow tilework, a circa-1918 addition to this even older fountain, depicts ladies carrying jugs of water. In the 17th century, this was the last watering stop for horses before leaving town. As recently as 1940, about 10 percent of Barcelonans got their water from fountains like this.

• You may feel the pull of wonderful little shops down the street to the right. But take the left fork, down Carrer dels Arcs.

Pause after a few steps at the yellow La Caixa ATM (on the right, under the terrace). Touch the screen to see various languages pop up—in addition to English, French, and German, you'll see the **four languages of Spain** and their flags: Català (Catalan; thin red-and-gold stripes), Galego (Galicia, in northwest Spain; white with a diagonal blue slash), Castellano (Español or Spanish; broad red, yellow, and red bands), and Euskara (Basque; red, green, and white). Fiercely proud of its own customs and language, Catalunya is in solidarity with other small ethnic groups.

Just past the ATM, you'll pass the **Reial Cercle Artistic Museum,** a private collection of Dalí's work sculptures that's fun for fans of Surrealism. Don't miss the smaller rooms with additional artworks that are behind the red curtains inside (€10, daily 10:00-22:00).

• Enter the large square called...

❺ Plaça Nova

Two bold Roman towers flank the main street. These once guarded the entrance gate of the ancient Roman city of Barcino. The big stones that make up the base of the reconstructed towers are actually Roman. Near the base of the left tower, modern bronze letters spell out "BARCINO." The city's name may have come from Barca, one of Hannibal's generals, who is said to have passed through during Hannibal's roundabout invasion of Italy. At Barcino's peak, the Roman wall (see the section stretching to the left of the towers) was 25 feet high and a mile around, with 74 towers. It enclosed a population of 4,000.

One of the towers has a bit of reconstructed **Roman aqueduct** (notice the stream bed on top). In ancient times, bridges of stone carried fresh water from the distant hillsides into the walled city.

Opposite the towers is the modern **Catalan College of Architects** building (Collegi d'Arquitectes de Barcelona, TI inside), which is, ironically for a city with so much great architecture, quite ugly. The frieze was designed by Picasso (1962) in his distinctive simplified style, showing Catalan traditions: shipping, music, the *sardana* dance, bullfighting, and branch-waving kings and children celebrating a festival. Picasso spent his formative years (1895-1904, ages 14-23) here in the old town. He frequented brothels a few blocks from here on Carrer d'Avinyó ("Avignon")—which inspired his influential Cubist painting *Les Demoiselles d'Avignon.*

Picasso frieze on the Catalan College building

• Immediately to the left as you face the Picasso frieze, Carrer de la Palla is an inviting shopping street (and the starting point of my "Barri Gòtic Shopping Stroll"; see page 98). But let's head left through Plaça Nova and take in the mighty facade of the...

❻ Cathedral of Barcelona

While this location has been a center of Christian worship since the fourth century, what you see today dates mainly from the 14th century, with a 19th-century Neo-Gothic facade. The facade is a virtual catalog of Gothic motifs: a pointed arch over the entrance, robed statues, tracery in windows, gargoyles, and bell towers with winged angels. This Gothic variation is called French Flamboyant (meaning "flame-like"), and the roofline sports the prickly spires meant to give the impression of a church flickering with spiritual fires. The area in front of the cathedral is where Barcelonans dance the *sardana* (see page 67).

The cathedral's interior—with its vast size, peaceful cloister, and many ornate chapels—is worth a visit (see page 66). If you interrupt this tour and visit the cathedral now, you'll exit from the cloister a block down Carrer del Bisbe. From there you can circle back to the right to visit stop #7—or skip #7 and step directly into stop #8.

• As you stand in the square facing the cathedral, look far to your left to see the multicolored, wavy canopy marking the roofline of the Santa Caterina Market. The busy street between here and the market—called Via Laietana—is the boundary between the Barri Gòtic and the funkier, edgier El Born neighborhood.

For now, return to the Roman towers. Pass between the towers to head up Carrer del Bisbe, and take an immediate left, up the ramp to the entrance of...

❼ Casa de l'Ardiaca

It's free to enter this mansion, formerly the archdeacon's residence and now the

city archives. The elaborate doorway is Renaissance. Enter a small courtyard with a fountain, then step inside the lobby (often featuring free temporary exhibits). Go through the archway at the left end of the lobby and look down into the stairwell at the back side of the ancient Roman wall. Back in the courtyard, climb the balcony for views of the cathedral steeple, gargoyles, and the small Romanesque chapel (on the right)—the only surviving 13th-century bit of the cathedral.

• Return to Carrer del Bisbe and turn left. After a few steps, you reach a small square with a bronze statue ensemble.

❽ Monument to the Martyrs of Independence

Five Barcelona patriots—including two priests—calmly receive their last rites before being strangled for resisting Napoleon's occupation of Spain in the early 19th century. They'd been outraged by French atrocities in Madrid (depicted in Goya's famous *Third of May* painting in Madrid's Prado Museum). According to the plaque marking their mortal remains, these martyrs gave their lives in 1809 *"por Dios, por la Patria, y por el Rey"*—for God, country, and king.

The plaza offers interesting views of the cathedral's towers. Opposite the square is the "back door" entrance to the cathedral (through the cloister; relatively uncrowded and open sporadically).

• Exit the square down tiny Carrer de Montjuïc del Bisbe (to the right as you face the martyrs). This leads to the cute...

❾ Plaça Sant Felip Neri

This square serves as the playground of an elementary school and is often bursting with energetic kids speaking Catalan (just a generation ago, this would have been illegal). The Church of Sant Felip Neri, which Gaudí attended, is still pockmarked with bomb damage from the Spanish Civil War. As a stronghold of democratic, anti-Franco forces, Barcelona

Cathedral of Barcelona

Ⓐ *Roman towers on Plaça Nova*

Ⓑ *Carrer del Bisbe Bridge*

Ⓒ *Church of Sant Felip Neri*

Ⓓ *Monument to the Martyrs of Independence*

Ⓔ *Architectural detail, Casa de l'Ardiaca*

saw a lot of fighting. A plaque on the wall (left of church door) honors the 42 killed—mostly children—in a 1938 aerial bombardment.

The carved reliefs on nearby buildings were paid for by the guilds that powered the local economy. On the corner where you entered the square is the former home of the shoemakers' guild; today it's the home of the fun **Shoe Museum** (€2.50, Tue-Sun 11:00-14:00, closed Mon, Plaça Sant Felip Neri 5, Metro: Jaume I, tel. 933-014-533). Also fronting the square is the colorful **Sabater Hermanos** artisanal soap shop.

• Exit the square down Carrer de Sant Felip Neri. At the T-intersection, turn right onto Carrer de Sant Sever, then immediately left on Carrer de Sant Domènec del Call (look for the blue El Call sign). You've entered the...

❿ Jewish Quarter (El Call)

In Catalan, a Jewish quarter goes by the name El Call—literally "narrow passage," for the tight lanes where medieval Jews were forced to live, under the watchful eye of the nearby cathedral. At the peak of Barcelona's El Call, some 4,000 Jews were crammed into just a few alleys in this neighborhood.

Walk down Carrer de Sant Domènec del Call, passing the **Zoen leather workshop and showroom,** where everything is made on the spot (on the right, at #15). Pass though the charming little square (a gap in the dense tangle of medieval buildings cleared by another civil war bomb) where you will find a rust-colored sign displaying a map of the Jewish Quarter. Take the next lane to the right (Carrer de Marlet). On the right (#5) is the low-profile entrance to what was likely Barcelona's **Old Main Synagogue** during the Middle Ages (Antigua Sinagoga Mayor, €2.50 admission includes a little tour by the attendant if you ask, open Mon-Fri 10:30-18:00, Sat-Sun 10:30-15:00, shorter hours off-season, tel. 931-170-790, www.calldebarcelona.org).

• At the synagogue, start back the way you came, continuing straight as the street becomes Carrer de la Fruita. At the T-intersection, turn left, then right, to find your way back to the Martyrs Statue. From here, turn right down Carrer del Bisbe to the...

⓫ Carrer del Bisbe Bridge

This structure connects the Catalan government building (on the right) with the Catalan president's ceremonial residence (on the left). Though the bridge looks medieval, it was constructed in the 1920s by Catalan architect Joan Rubió, who also carved the ornamentation on the buildings.

The delicate facade a few steps farther down on the right marks the 15th-century entry to the government palace.

• Continue along Carrer del Bisbe to...

⓬ Plaça de Sant Jaume

This stately central square of the Barri Gòtic takes its name from the Church of St. James (in Catalan: Jaume, JOW-mah) that once stood here.

Set at the intersection of ancient Barcino's main thoroughfares, this square was once a Roman forum. In that sense, it's been the seat of city government for 2,000 years. Today it's home to the two top governmental buildings in Catalunya: Palau de la Generalitat and, across from it, the Barcelona City Hall.

For more than six centuries, the **Palau de la Generalitat** (to your immediate right as you enter the square) has housed the offices of the autonomous government of Catalunya. It flies the Catalan flag next to the obligatory Spanish one. Above the doorway is Catalunya's patron saint—St. George (Jordi), slaying the dragon. From these balconies, the nation's leaders (and soccer heroes) greet the people on momentous days. The square is often the site of demonstrations, from a single aggrieved citizen with a megaphone to riotous thousands.

Look left and right down the main

streets branching off the square; they're lined with ironwork streetlamps and balconies draped with plants. Carrer de Ferran, which leads to the Ramblas, is classic Barcelona.

• Facing the Generalitat, exit the square going up the second street to the right of the building, on tiny Carrer del Paradís. Follow this street as it turns right. When it swings left, pause at #10, the entrance to the...

⓭ Roman Temple of Augustus

You're standing at the summit of Mont Tàber, the Barri Gòtic's highest spot. A plaque on the wall reads: "Mont Tàber, 16.9 meters" (elevation 55 feet). A millstone inlaid in the pavement at the doorstep of #10 also marks the spot. Here the ancient Romans founded the town of Barcino around 15 B.C. They built a *castrum* (fort) on the hilltop, protecting the harbor.

Go inside for a peek at the last vestiges of the imposing **Roman Temple of Augustus** (free, daily 10:00-19:00 except Mon until 14:00, good English info on-site, Carrer del Paradís 10, tel. 933-152-311). All

Roman Temple of Augustus

that's left now are four columns and some fragments of the transept and its plinth. The huge columns are as old as Barcelona itself, dating from the late first century B.C. They were part of a temple dedicated to the Emperor Augustus, who was worshipped as a god. These Corinthian columns were the back corner of a 120-foot-long temple that extended from here to Barcino's forum.

• Continue down Carrer del Paridís one block. When you bump into the back end of the cathedral, take a right, and go downhill a block (down Carrer de la Pietat/Baixada de Santa Clara) until you emerge into a square called...

⓮ Plaça del Rei

The buildings enclosing this square exemplify Barcelona's medieval past. The central section (topped by a five-story addition) was the core of the **Royal Palace** (Palau Reial Major). A vast hall on its ground floor once served as the throne room and reception room. From the 13th to the 15th century, the Royal Palace housed Barcelona's counts as well as the resident kings of Aragon. In 1493, a triumphant Christopher Columbus, accompanied by six New World natives and several gold statues, entered the Royal Palace. King Ferdinand and Queen Isabel welcomed him home, honoring him with the title "Admiral of the Oceans." To the right is the palace's church, the 14th-century **Chapel of Saint Agatha,** which sits atop the foundations of a Roman wall.

• From the square, go downhill onto Carrer del Veguer, where you'll find the entrance to the...

⓯ Barcelona History Museum

This museum primarily contains objects from archaeological digs around Barcelona. But the real highlight is underground, where you can examine excavated Roman ruins (€7, free all day first Sun of month and other Sun from 15:00;

open Tue-Sat 10:00-19:00, Sun 10:00-20:00, closed Mon; ticket includes English audioguide). For a peek at the Roman streets, look through the low windows lining the street.

• Your walk is over. Get your bearings by backtracking to either Plaça de Sant Jaume or the cathedral. The Jaume I Metro stop is two blocks away (leave the square on Carrer del Veguer and turn left). Or simply wander and enjoy Barcelona at its Gothic best.

SIGHTS

On or near the Ramblas

▲▲▲THE RAMBLAS

Rife with people-watching opportunities, Barcelona's most famous boulevard meanders through the heart of the Old City, from Plaça de Catalunya, past the core of the Barri Gòtic, to the harborfront Columbus Monument. Boasting a generous pedestrian strip down the middle, the Ramblas features vibrant flower vendors, costumed "human statues," and La Boqueria Market. For a self-guided walk, see page 43.

▲LA BOQUERIA MARKET

Housed in a cool glass-and-steel structure, La Boqueria features a wide variety of edibles that are priced at a premium. Its handy location in the heart of the Old City makes it well worth a visit. For more on the market, see page 49. For a less touristy market, consider Santa Caterina in El Born (page 76).

Cost and Hours: Free, Mon-Sat 8:00-20:00, best on mornings after 9:00, closed Sun, Rambla 91, tel. 933-192-584, www.boqueria.info.

▲PALAU GÜELL

This early mansion by Antoni Gaudí (completed in 1890) shows the architect taking his first tentative steps toward what would become his trademark curvy style. Dark and masculine, with its castle-like rooms, Palau Güell (pronounced "gway") was custom-built to house the Güell clan

and gives an insight into Gaudí's artistic genius. Despite the eye-catching roof (visible from the street), I'd skip touring the interior of Palau Güell if you plan to see the more interesting La Pedrera (see page 81).

Cost and Hours: €12, free first Sun of the month, open Tue-Sun 10:00-20:00, Nov-March until 17:30, closed Mon, last entry one hour before closing, includes audioguide, a half-block off the Ramblas at Carrer Nou de la Rambla 3, Metro: Liceu or Drassanes, tel. 934-725-775, www.palauguell.cat.

Tickets: As with any Gaudí sight, you may encounter lines. Each ticket has an entry time, so at busy times you may have to wait to enter. It's best to buy advance tickets for a set day and time of your choice, either on-site or online (though the predominantly Catalan website is tricky).

Visiting the House: The parabolic-arch **entryways** are the first clue that this is not a typical townhouse. For inspiration, Gaudí hung a chain to create a U-shape, then flipped it upside down. The wrought-iron doors were cleverly designed so that those inside could see out, and light from the outside could get in—but not vice versa.

Once inside, an engaging 24-stop audioguide, included with your admission, fills in the details. The Neo-Gothic **cellar,** with its mushroom pillars, was used as a stable—notice the big carriage doors in the back and the rings on some of the posts used to tie up the horses.

A grand staircase leads to the **living space.** The intricacy of Gaudí's design work evokes the complex patterns that decorate great Moorish palaces. Step onto the terrace out back to take a look at the elaborate (and unmistakably organic-looking) bay window.

The tall, atrium-like **central hall** fills several floors under a parabolic dome. Behind the gilded doors is a personal chapel, which made it easy to convert the

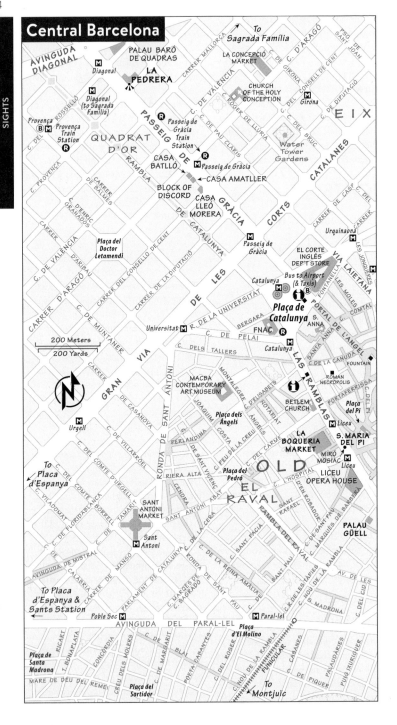

Central Barcelona

To Sagrada Família

AVINGUDA DIAGONAL

PALAU BARÓ DE QUADRAS

LA CONCEPCIÓ MARKET

C. DE GIRONA

C. DE C. D'ARAGÓ

PSG. SANT JOAN

Diagonal

LA PEDRERA

CARRER MALLORCA

CHURCH OF THE HOLY CONCEPTION

CARRER DE CENT

C. DE DIPUTACIÓ

Diagonal (to Sagrada Família)

C. DE VALÈNCIA

C. DE ROGER DE LLÚRIA

Girona

EIX

Provença

ROSSELLÓ

Provença Train Station

PASSEIG DE GRÀCIA

Passeig de Gràcia Train Station

C. DE PAU CLARIS

C. DEL BRUC

Water Tower Gardens

CATALANES

QUADRAT D'OR

RAMBLA

CASA BATLLÓ

Passeig de Gràcia

CASA AMATLLER

C. PROVENÇA

CARRER DE BALMES

BLOCK OF DISCORD

CASA LLEÓ MORERA

GRÀCIA

DE CATALUNYA

CORTS

CARRER DE CASP

C. DEL

C. D'ENRIC GRANADOS

Plaça del Doctor Letamendi

Urquinaona

CARRER DE VALÈNCIA

D'ARIBAU

CARRER DEL CONSELLO DE CENT

CARRER DE LA DIPUTACIÓ

Passeig de Gràcia

EL CORTE INGLÉS DEP'T STORE

VIA LAIETANA

CARRER D'ARAGÓ

C. DE MUNTANER

DE LES

Catalunya

Bus to Airport (& Taxis)

LES JONQUERES

FONTANELLA

C. COMTAL

Plaça de Catalunya

S. ANNA

PORTAL DE L'ANGEL

Universitat

R. DE LA UNIVERSITAT

BERGARA

FNAC

Catalunya

SANTA ANNA

GRAN

VIA

C. DE PELAI

C. DELS TALLERS

LAS RAMBLAS

C.DE LA CANUDA

FOUNTAIN

200 Meters

200 Yards

DE CASANOVA

MONTALEGRE D'ELISABETS

ÀNGELS

MACBA CONTEMPORARY ART MUSEUM

NOTARIAT

ROMAN NECROPOLIS

FORTAFERRISSA

C. DELS

Urgell

C. DE VILLARROEL

JOAQUIM COSTA

Plaça dels Àngels

BETLEM CHURCH

Plaça del Pi

RONDA DE SANT ANTONI

PERLANDINA

DE SANT VICENÇ

C. PEU DE LA CREU

DEL CARME

LA BOQUERIA MARKET

Liceu

S. MARIA DEL PI

To Plaça d'Espanya

C. DEL COMTE D'URGELL

RIERA ALTA

Plaça del Pedró

C. L'HOSPITAL

OLD

MIRÓ MOSIAC

Liceu

LICEU OPERA HOUSE

CENDRA

EL RAVAL

C. DEN ROBADOD

SANT ANTONI MARKET

SANT ANTONI ABAT

SANT RAFAEL

RAMBLA DEL RAVAL

PALAU GÜELL

C. DE FLORIDABLANCA

BORRELL

TAMARIT

SANT ANTONI

SANT PAU

C. MÀRQUES DE BARBERÀ

C. VILADOMAT

Sant Antoni

C. SANT PACIÀ

AVINGUDA DE MISTRAL

CALABRIA

CARRER DE MANSO

PARLAMENT DE CATALUNYA

RONDA DE LA REINA AMÀLIA

SANT PAU

C. NOU DE LA RAMBLA

AV. DE LES

To Plaça d'Espanya & Sants Station

DE

C. MÀRQUES DE C. SAGRADO

RONDA DE SANT PAU

C.DE LESTRIPES

C. MADRONA

C. DEL CID

Poble Sec

AVINGUDA DEL PARAL-LEL

Paral-lel

Plaça d'El Molino

FUNICULAR

Plaça de Santa Madrona

RICART

T. BONAPLATA

CONCÒRDIA

CREU DELS MOLERS

C. DE MARGARIT

BLAI

POETA CABANYES

C. DEL ROSER

C. NOU DE LA RAMBLA

CABANES

C. DE PIQUER

PUIG XURIGUER

PAVADARIES

MARE DE DÉU DEL REMEI

Plaça del Sartidor

To Montjuïc

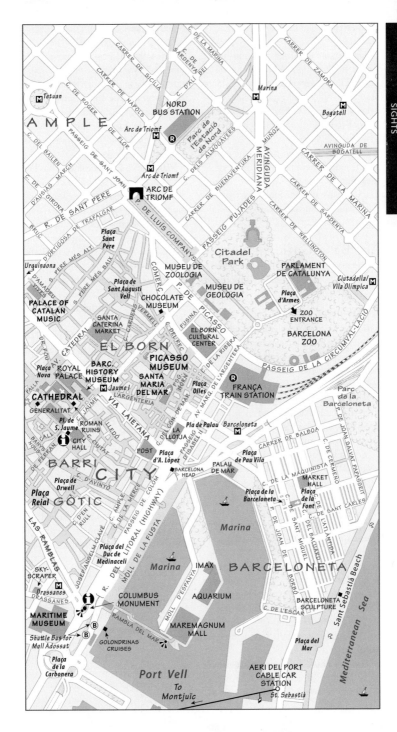

AMPLE

Tetuan

CARRER DE SICILIA

C. DE LA MARINA

C. DE SARDENYA

C. DE NÁPOLS

C. D'ALI-BEI

CARRER DE ZAMORA

CARRER DE LA MARINA

Marina

Bogatell

AVINGUDA DE BOGATELL

C. DEL BAILÈN

C. DE ROGER DE FLOR

PASSEIG DE SANT JOAN

CARRER DE SICILIA

NORD
BUS STATION

Arc de Triomf

Parc de
l'Estació
de Nord

AVINGUDA MERIDIANA

MUÑOZ

CARRER DE BUENAVENTURA

CARRER DE WELLINGTON

CARRER DE SARDENYA

CARRER DE LA MARINA

C. DE AUSIAS MARCH

C. DE GIRONA

R. DE SANT PERE

P. DE SANT JOAN

Arc de Triomf

ARC DE
TRIOMF

P. DE LLUIS COMPANYS

CARRER DE PUJADES

CARRER DE WELLINGTON

DAMADEU

Urquinaona

R. DE SANT PERE

Plaça
Sant
Pere

COMERÇ

Citadel
Park

PARLAMENT
DE CATALUNYA

Ciutadella/
Vila Olímpica

PALACE OF
CATALAN
MUSIC

Plaça de
Sant Agustí
Vell

MUSEU DE
ZOOLOGIA

CHOCOLATE
MUSEUM

MUSEU DE
GEOLOGIA

Plaça
d'Armes

ZOO
ENTRANCE

SANTA
CATERINA
MARKET

CARDERS

VERMELL

G. DEL REC

FUSINA

P. DE PICASSO

EL BORN
CULTURAL
CENTER

BARCELONA
ZOO

EL BORN

Plaça
Nova

ROYAL
PALACE

BARC.
HISTORY
MUSEUM

PICASSO
MUSEUM

SANTA
MARIA
DEL MAR

AV. MARQ. DE L'ARGENTERA

C. DE LA RIBERA

PASSEIG DE LA CIRCUMVAL·LACIÓ

Parc
de la
Barceloneta

CATHEDRAL

GENERALITAT

Jaume I

L'ARGENTERIA

VIA LAIETANA

Plaça
Olles

FRANÇA
TRAIN STATION

Pl. de
S. Jaume

ROMAN
RUINS

CITY
HALL

C. CUITAT

LLEDÓ

LA
LLOTJA

POST

Pla de Palau

Plaça
d'A. López

Barceloneta

CARRER DE BALBOA

BARRI

CITY

Plaça de
Orwell

C. D'AVINYO

C. AMPLE

C. DE LA MERCÈ

BARCELONA
HEAD

PALAU
DE MAR

Plaça
de Pau Vila

C. DE CERMEÑO

C. DE LA MAQUINISTA

MARKET
HALL

Plaça
de la
Font

Plaça
Reial

GÒTIC

LAS RAMBLAS

C. D'EN RULL

PASSEIG DE COLOM

Plaça de la
Barceloneta

C. DE SANT CARLES

C. DE L'ATLANTIDA

Plaça del
Duc de
Medinaceli

MÒLL DE LA FUSTA

LITORAL (HIGHWAY)

Marina

IMAX

BARCELONETA

SKY-
SCRAPER

Drassanes

DRASSANES

JOSEP ANSELM CLAVÉ

R.

Marina

MÒLL D'ESPANYA

Mediterranean Sea

Sant Sebastià Beach

MARITIME
MUSEUM

COLUMBUS
MONUMENT

AQUARIUM

BARCELONETA
SCULPTURE

C. DE L'ESCAR

Shuttle Bus for
Moll Adossat

GOLONDRINAS
CRUISES

RAMBLA DEL MAR

MAREMAGNUM
MALL

Plaça del
Mar

Plaça
de la
Carbonera

Port Vell

To
Montjuïc

AERI DEL PORT
CABLE CAR
STATION

St. Sebastià

hall from a secular space to a religious one.

Upstairs are the Güells' his-and-hers bedrooms, along with a **film** telling the story of the two men behind this building: Gaudí and his patron, Eusebi Güell. At a time when most wealthy urbanites were moving to the Eixample, Güell decided to stay in the Old City.

The most dramatic space is the **rooftop.** Gaudí slathered the 20 chimneys and ventilation towers with bits of stained glass, ceramic tile, and marble to create a forest of giant upside-down ice-cream cones.

The Barri Gòtic

For an interesting route from Plaça de Catalunya to the cathedral neighborhood, see page 53.

▲CATHEDRAL OF BARCELONA

The city's 14th-century, Gothic-style cathedral (with a Neo-Gothic facade) has played a significant role in Barcelona's history—but as far as grand cathedrals go, this one is relatively unexciting. Still, it's worth a visit to see its richly decorated chapels, finely carved choir, tomb of St. Eulàlia, and restful cloister with gurgling fountains and resident geese.

Cost and Hours: Generally open to visitors Mon-Fri 8:00-19:30, Sat-Sun 8:00-20:00. Free to enter Mon-Sat before 12:45, Sun before 13:45, and daily after 17:15, but during free times you must pay to enter the cathedral's three minor sights (museum-€2, terrace-€3, choir-€3). The church is officially "closed" for a few hours each afternoon (Mon-Sat 13:00-17:00, Sun 14:00-17:00), but you can get in to see the interior sights by paying €7. Tel. 933-151-554, www.catedralbcn.org.

Dress Code: The dress code is strictly enforced; don't wear tank tops, shorts, or skirts above the knee.

Getting There: The huge, can't-miss-it cathedral is in the center of the Barri Gòtic on Plaça de la Seu (Metro: Jaume I).

Getting In: The front door is open most of the time. While it can be crowded, the line generally moves fast. Sometimes you can also enter directly into the cloister (through the door facing the Martyrs Statue on the small square along Carrer del Bisbe) or through the side door (facing Carrer dels Comtes).

Services: A tiny, semiprivate WC is in the center of the cloister.

Visiting the Cathedral: This has been Barcelona's holiest spot for 2,000 years, since the Romans built their Temple of Jupiter here. In A.D. 343, the pagan temple was replaced with a Christian cathedral, and in the 11th century, by a Romanesque-style church. The current Gothic structure was started in 1298 and finished in 1450, during the medieval glory days of the Catalan nation. The facade was humble, so in the 19th century the proud local bourgeoisie (enjoying a second Golden Age) renovated it in a more ornate, Neo-Gothic style. Construction was capped in 1913 with the central spire, 230 feet tall.

Inside, the nave is ringed with 28 **chapels.** These serve as interior buttresses supporting the roof (which is why the exterior walls are smooth, without the normal Gothic buttresses outside).

In the middle of the nave, the 15th-century choir (coro) features ornately carved stalls. During the standing parts of the Mass, the chairs were folded up, but VIPs still had those little wooden ledges to lean on. Each was creatively carved and—since you couldn't sit on sacred things—the artists were free to enjoy some secular and naughty fun here.

Look behind the high altar (beneath the crucifix) to find the bishop's chair, or cathedra. To the left of the altar is the organ and the elevator up to the terrace.

The steps beneath the altar lead to the **crypt,** featuring the marble-and-alabaster sarcophagus (1327-1339) containing the remains of St. Eulàlia. The cathedral is dedicated to the 13-year-old Eulàlia, daughter of a prominent Barcelona family,

Circle Dances in Squares and Castles in the Air

From group circle dancing to human towers, Catalans have interesting, unique traditions. A memorable Barcelona experience is watching (or participating in) the patriotic **sardana** dances. Locals of all ages seem to spontaneously appear. For some it's a highly symbolic, politically charged action representing Catalan unity—but for most it's just a fun chance to kick up their heels. Participants gather in circles after putting their things in the center. All are welcome, even tourists cursed with two left feet. The dances are held in the square in front of the cathedral on Sundays at noon (and occasionally on Saturdays at 18:00).

Holding hands, dancers raise their arms—slow-motion, *Zorba the Greek*-style—as they hop and sway gracefully to the music. The band *(cobla)* consists of a long flute, tenor and soprano oboes, strange-looking brass instruments, and a tiny bongo-like drum *(tambori)*. During 36 years of Franco's dictatorship, the *sardana* was forbidden.

Another Catalan tradition is the **castell,** a tower erected solely of people. *Castells* pop up on special occasions, such as the Festa Major de Gràcia in mid-August and La Mercè festival in late September. Towers can be up to 10 humans high. Imagine balancing 50 or 60 feet in the air, with nothing but a pile of flesh and bone between you and the ground. The base is formed by burly supports called *baixos;* above them are the *manilles* ("handles"), which help haul up the people to the top. The *castell* is capped with a human steeple—usually a child—who extends four fingers into the air, representing the four red stripes of the Catalan flag. A scrum of spotters (called *pinyas*) cluster around the base in case anyone falls. *Castelleres* are judged both on how quickly they erect their human towers and how fast they can take them down. Besides during festivals, you can usually see this spectacle in front of the cathedral on spring and summer Saturdays at 19:30 (as part of the Festa Catalana).

One thing that these two traditions have in common is their communal nature. Perhaps it's no coincidence, as Catalunya is known for its community spirit, team building, and socialist bent.

who was martyred by the Romans for her faith in A.D. 304. Legends say she was subjected to 13 tortures.

Exit through the right transept and into the circa-1450 **cloister**—the arcaded walkway surrounding a lush courtyard. It's a tropical atmosphere of palm, orange, and magnolia trees; a fish pond; trickling fountains; and squawking geese. As you wander the cloister (clockwise), check out the coats of arms as well as the tombs in the pavement. These were rich merchants who paid to be buried as close to the altar as possible. Notice the symbols of their trades: scissors, shoes, bakers, and so on. The resident geese have been here for at least 500 years. There are always 13, in memory of Eulàlia's 13 years and 13 torments.

The little museum (at the far end of the cloister) has the six-foot-tall, 14th-century Great Monstrance, a ceremonial display case for the communion wafer that's paraded through the streets during the Corpus Christi festival in June. The next room, the Sala Capitular, has several altarpieces, including a *pietá* (a.k.a. *Desplà*) by Bartolomé Bermejo (1490).

▲ *SARDANA* DANCES

If you're in town on a weekend, you can see the *sardana*, a patriotic dance in which Barcelonans link hands and dance in a circle (see sidebar).

Cost and Hours: Free, Sun at 12:00, sometimes also Sat at 18:00, no dances in Aug, event lasts 1-2 hours, in the square in front of the cathedral.

El Born

Despite being home to the top-notch Picasso Museum, El Born (also known as "La Ribera") feels wonderfully local, with a higher ratio of Barcelonans to tourists than most other city-center zones. Narrow lanes sprout from the neighborhood's main artery, Passeig del Born—the perfect springboard for exploring artsy boutiques, inviting cafés and restaurants,

funky shops, and rollicking nightlife. For tips on shopping streets in El Born, see page 99. The most convenient Metro stop is Jaume I.

▲▲▲ PICASSO MUSEUM (MUSEU PICASSO)

Pablo Picasso may have made his career in Paris, but the years he spent in Barcelona—from age 14 through 23—were among the most formative of his life. Here, young Pablo mastered the realistic painting style of his artistic forebears—and also first felt the freedom that would allow him to leave all that behind and explore his creative, experimental urges. When he left Barcelona, Picasso went to Paris...and revolutionized art forever.

The pieces in this museum capture the moment just before this bold young thinker changed the world. While you won't find Picasso's famous later Cubist works here, you will enjoy a representative sweep of his early years, from the careful crafting of art-school pieces to the gloomy hues of his Blue Period and the revitalized cheer of his Rose Period. You'll also see works from his twilight years, including dozens of wild improvisations inspired by Diego Velázquez's seminal *Las Meninas,* as well as works that reflect the exuberance of an old man playing like a child on the French Riviera. It's the top collection of Picassos in his native country, and the best anywhere of his early years.

Rick's Tip: *To avoid wasting time in ticket-buying lines, buy* **advance tickets** *for the* **Picasso Museum.**

Cost and Hours: €11-14 for timed-entry ticket, cost depends on temporary exhibits and time of year, free all day first Sun of month and other Sun from 15:00; open Tue-Sun 9:00-19:00, Thu until 21:30, closed Mon; audioguide-€5, tel. 932-563-000, www.museupicasso.bcn.cat.

Crowd Control: There's almost always

Picasso Museum—First Floor

Not to Scale

11   4   3

10   5   2

13   9   2

15   11   8   9   Room 1

14   10   7   ELEV.

MAIN   HALLWAY   TOUR BEGINS
Stairs to Ground Floor   Stairs from Ground Floor

16   S   P   G   G-3
16

17   Room 15   N   G-1   G-2
18   TOUR ENDS   18

ENTRANCE
(AT GROUND LEVEL)
CARRER DE MONTCADA

← To Santa Caterina Market
(5 min. walk)

To Church of Santa Maria del Mar →
(5 min. walk)

To Jaume 1 Ⓜ (5 min. walk)
& Cathedral (10 min. walk)

❶ Portraits & Art-School Work
❷ First Communion
❸ Science and Charity
❹ Velázquez Copy
❺ Horta de San Joan
❻ Cancan Dancer
❼ Still Life
❽ The Waiting (Margot)
❾ Motherhood
❿ Rooftops of Barcelona
⓫ Portrait of Bernadetta Bianco
⓬ Woman with Mantilla
⓭ Gored Horse
⓮ Synthetic Cubism
⓯ Las Meninas Studies
⓰ Ceramics
⓱ French Riviera
⓲ Portraits of Jacqueline (2)

a line, sometimes with waits of more than an hour. During peak season, it's possible that tickets, which include an entry time, may sell out altogether. It's best to buy tickets online in advance, or get an **Articket BCN** (see page 40), which lets you go straight to the special Articket window near the main entrance (you'll be allowed in at the next timed-entry slot).

Advance tickets are sold via the museum website (no additional booking fee) and guarantee an entry time with no wait. Note that the ticketing part of the website can be temperamental; if

Pablo Picasso (1881-1973)

Pablo Picasso was the most famous and—OK, I'll say it—greatest artist of the 20th century. He became the master of many styles (Cubism, Surrealism, Expressionism) and many media (painting, sculpture, prints, ceramics, and assemblages). Still, anything he touched looked unmistakably like "a Picasso."

Born in Málaga, Spain, Picasso was the son of an art teacher. At a young age, he quickly advanced beyond his teachers. Picasso's teenage works are stunningly realistic and capture the inner complexities of the people he painted. As a youth in Barcelona, he fell in with a bohemian crowd that mixed wine, women, and art.

In 1904, Picasso moved to the City of Light to paint. When his best friend, Spanish artist Carlos Casagemas, committed suicide, Picasso plunged into a **Blue Period** (1901-1904)—the dominant color in these paintings matches their melancholy mood and subject matter (such as emaciated beggars, and hard-eyed pimps).

In 1904, Picasso got a steady girlfriend (Fernande Olivier) and suddenly saw the world through rose-colored glasses—his **Rose Period.** Picasso played with the "building blocks" of line and color to find new ways to reconstruct the real world on canvas. At his studio in Montmartre, Picasso and his neighbor Georges Braque worked together, in poverty so dire they often didn't know where their next bottle of wine was coming from.

Then, at the age of 25, Picasso reinvented painting. Fascinated by the primitive power of African and Iberian tribal masks, he sketched human faces with simple outlines and almond eyes. He sketched nudes from every angle, then experimented with showing several different views on the same canvas. Nine months and a hundred paintings later, Picasso gave birth to a monstrous can-

Picasso's Portrait of Bernadetta Bianco, *a Rose Period work*

you can't get it to work, try it on another device (such as your mobile phone).

To buy **same-day tickets,** go as early as possible. Upon arrival, check the screen near the ticket office for the day's available entry times (and how many spaces are open for each). Depending upon availability, you can either buy tickets for immediate entry, or purchase tickets to return later that day. You can also buy

same-day tickets online, up to two hours before you want to go. Off-season, you can probably just line up for tickets and get right in.

Note that the museum's busiest times are mornings before 13:00, all day Tuesday, and during the free entry times on Sundays.

Getting There: It's at Carrer de Montcada 15; the ticket office is at #21. From

vas of five nude, fragmented prostitutes with mask-like faces—*Les Demoiselles d'Avignon* (1907).

This bold new style was called **Cubism.** With Cubism, Picasso shattered the Old World and put it back together in a new way. The subjects are somewhat recognizable (with the help of the titles), but they're built with geometric shards ("cubes")—like viewing the world through a kaleidoscope of brown and gray.

In 1918, Picasso traveled to Rome and entered a **Classical Period** (the 1920s) of more realistic, full-bodied women and children, inspired by the three-dimensional sturdiness of ancient statues. While he flirted with abstraction, throughout his life, Picasso always kept a grip on "reality." His favorite subject was people. The anatomy might be jumbled, but it's all there.

Though he lived in France and Italy, Picasso remained a Spaniard at heart, incorporating Spanish motifs into his work. Unrepentantly macho, he loved bull-fights, seeing them as a metaphor for the timeless human interaction between the genders. To Picasso, the horse symbolizes the feminine, and the bull, the masculine. Spanish imagery—bulls, screaming horses, a Madonna—appears in Picasso's most famous work, *Guernica* (1937, on display in Madrid). The monumental canvas of a bombed village summed up the pain of Spain's brutal Civil War (1936-1939) and foreshadowed World War II.

At war's end, Picasso left Paris behind, finding fun in the sun in the **south of France** (1948-1954). Sixty-five-year-old Picasso was reborn, enjoying worldwide fame and the love of a beautiful 23-year-old painter named Françoise Gilot. Bursting with creativity, Picasso cranked out more than one painting a day. His Riviera works set the tone for the rest of his life—sunny, lighthearted, and uncomplicated, using motifs of the sea, Greek myths, and animals. His simple sketch of a dove holding an olive branch became an international symbol of peace.

Picasso also made collages, built "statues" out of wood, wire, ceramics, and papier-mâché, and turned everyday household objects into statues (like his famous bull's head made of a bicycle seat with handlebar horns). **Multimedia** works like these have become so standard today that we forget how revolutionary they were when Picasso invented them. His last works have the playfulness of someone much younger. It's said of Picasso, "When he was a child, he painted like a man. When he was old, he painted like a child."

the Jaume I Metro stop, it's a quick five-minute walk. Just head down Carrer de la Princesa (across the busy Via Laietana from the Barri Gòtic), turning right on Carrer de Montcada.

Services: The ground floor, which is free to enter, has a required bag check, as well as a handy array of other services (bookshop, WC, and cafeteria). For places to eat near the museum, see page 106.

◐ SELF-GUIDED TOUR

The Picasso Museum's collection of nearly 300 paintings is presented more or less chronologically. With the help of thoughtful English descriptions (and guards who don't let you stray), it's easy to follow the evolution of Picasso's work. This tour is arranged by the stages of his life and art. If you don't see a specific piece, it may be out for restoration, on tour, or "sleeping," as the museum guards say. The rooms might be rearranged every so often, but the themes and chronology of the museum remain constant.

• *Begin in Rooms 1 and 2.*

BOY WONDER

Pablo's earliest art (in the first room) is realistic and earnest. Childish pencil drawings from about 1890 quickly advance through a series of technically skilled **art-school works** (copies of plaster feet and arms), to oil paintings of impressive technique. Even at a young age, his **portraits** of grizzled peasants demonstrate surprising psychological insight. Because his father—himself a curator and artist—kept everything his son ever did, Picasso has the best-documented youth of any great painter.

• *In Room 2, you'll find more paintings relating to Pablo's...*

DEVELOPING TALENT

During a summer trip to Málaga in 1896, Picasso dabbles in a series of fresh, Impressionistic-style landscapes (rare in Spain at the time). As a 15-year-old, Pablo dutifully enters art-school competitions. His first big work, **First Communion,** features a prescribed religious subject, but Picasso makes it an excuse to paint his family. His sister Lola is the model for the communicant (notice her exquisitely painted veil), and the features of the man beside her belong to Picasso's father.

Picasso's relatives star in a number of portraits from this time. Find the **portrait of his mother** if it's on view (these portraits are among the works that are frequently rotated). The teenage Pablo is working on the fine details and gradients of white in her blouse and the expression in her cameo-like face. Notice the signature: Pablo Ruiz Picasso. Spaniards keep both parents' surnames, with the father's first, followed by the mother's.

• *Continue into Room 3.*

EARLY SUCCESS

Science and Charity (1897), which won second prize at a fine-arts exhibition, got Picasso the chance to study in Madrid. Now Picasso conveys real feeling. The doctor (modeled on Pablo's father) represents science. The nun represents charity and religion. From her hopeless face and lifeless hand, it seems that Picasso believes nothing will save this woman from death.

Picasso travels to Madrid for further study. He hangs out in the Prado Museum and learns by copying the masters. An example of his mimicry is at the end of this room. Notice young Picasso's nearly perfect copy of a **portrait of Philip IV** by an earlier Spanish master, Diego Velázquez.

• *Head to Room 4.*

BARCELONA FREEDOM

Art Nouveau is all the rage in Barcelona when Picasso returns there in 1900. He falls in with the bohemian crowd, who congregate daily at Els Quatre Gats ("The Four Cats," a popular restaurant to this day). Picasso even created the **menu cover** for this favorite hangout (it's sometimes on view here in Room 4). He paints **portraits** of his new friends, including one of Jaume Sabartés (who later became his personal assistant and donated the works to establish this museum). Still a teenager, Pablo puts on his first one-man show at Els Quatre Gats in 1900.

• *Continue through Room 5. The next few pieces are displayed in Rooms 6 and 7.*

PARIS

In 1900 Picasso makes his first trip to Paris, where he befriends poets, artists, and prostitutes. He paints **cancan dancers** like Toulouse-Lautrec, **still lifes** like Paul Cézanne, brightly colored Fauvist works like Henri Matisse, and Impressionist **landscapes** like Claude Monet. In **The Waiting (Margot),** the subject—with her bold outline and strong gaze—pops out from the vivid, mosaic-like background. It is Cézanne's technique of "building" a

1 *Picasso,* First Communion

2 *Picasso,* Science and Charity

3 *Picasso's menu design for Els Quatre Gats*

4 *Picasso,* La Mujer del Mechón

5 *Picasso,* Woman with Mantilla

6 *Picasso,* Las Meninas

figure with "cubes" of paint that will later inspire Picasso to invent Cubism.

• *Turn right into the hall, then—farther along—right again, to find Rooms 8 and 9.*

BLUE PERIOD

Picasso travels to Paris several times (settling there permanently in 1904). The suicide of his best friend, his own poverty, and the influence of new ideas linking color and mood lead Picasso to abandon jewel-bright color for his Blue Period (1901-1904). He cranks out stacks of blue art just to stay housed and fed. With blue backgrounds and depressing subjects, this period was revolutionary in art history. The artist is painting not what he sees, but what he feels.

Back home in Barcelona, Picasso paints his hometown at night from **rooftops** (in the main part of Room 8). The painting is still blue, but here we see proto-Cubism... five years before the first real Cubist painting.

• *In the left section of Room 8, we get a hint of Picasso's...*

ROSE PERIOD

Picasso is finally lifted out of his funk after meeting a new lady, Fernande Olivier, and moves into his happier Rose Period (1904-1907). For a fine example, see the portrait of a woman wearing a classic Spanish mantilla, **Portrait of Bernadetta Bianco.** Its soft pink and reddish tones are the colors of flesh and sensuality. (This is the only actual Rose Period painting in the museum, but don't be surprised if it is on loan.)

BARCELONA

Picasso spent six months back in Barcelona in 1917 (his girlfriend, a Russian ballet dancer, had a gig in town). The paintings in these rooms demonstrate the artist's irrepressible versatility: He's already developed Cubism (with his friend Georges Braque), but he also continues to play with other styles. In **Woman with Mantilla** (Room 9), we see a little Post-Impressionistic Pointillism in a

portrait as elegant as a classical statue. Nearby, **Gored Horse** has all the anguish and power of his iconic *Guernica* (painted years later).

CUBISM

Pablo's role in the invention of the revolutionary Cubist style is well-known—at least I hope so, since this museum has no true Cubist paintings. A Cubist work gives not only the basics of a subject—it shows every aspect of it simultaneously. The technique of "building" a subject with "cubes" of paint simmered in Picasso's artistic stew for years. In this museum, you'll see some so-called **Synthetic Cubist paintings** (Room 10)—a later variation that flattens the various angles, as opposed to the purer, original "Analytical Cubist" paintings, in which you can simultaneously see several 3-D facets of the subject.

• *Remember that this museum focuses on Picasso's early years. As a result, it has little from the most famous and prolific "middle" part of his career—basically, from Picasso's adoption of Cubism to his sunset years on the French Riviera. Skip ahead more than 30 years and into Rooms 12-14 (at the end of the main hallway, on the right).*

PICASSO AND VELÁZQUEZ

A series of Picasso's works relate to what many consider the greatest painting by anyone, ever: Diego Velázquez's *Las Meninas* (the 17th-century original is displayed in Madrid's Prado Museum). Heralded as the first completely realistic painting, *Las Meninas* became an obsession for Picasso centuries later.

Picasso, who had great respect for Velázquez, painted more than **40 interpretations** of this piece. Picasso seems to enjoy a relationship of equals with Velázquez. Like artistic soul mates, the two Spanish geniuses spar and tease. Picasso deconstructs Velázquez and then injects light, color, and perspective as he improvises on the earlier masterpiece. See the fun Picasso had playing paddleball with Velázquez's tour de force—filtering Velázquez's realism through the kaleidoscope of Cubism.

• *Head back down the hall and turn right, through the* **ceramics** *area (Room 16), to find a flock of carefree white birds in Room 15. Enjoy the palace decoration as it looked before the building became a museum.*

THE FRENCH RIVIERA (LAST YEARS)

Picasso spends the last 36 years of his life living simply in the south of France. He said many times that "Paintings are like windows open to the world." We see his sunny Riviera world: With simple black outlines and Crayola colors, Picasso paints sun-splashed nature, peaceful doves, and the joys of the beach. He dabbles in the timeless art of ceramics, shaping bowls and vases into fun animals decorated with simple, childlike designs. He's enjoying life with his second (and much younger) wife, Jacqueline Roque, whose portraits hang nearby.

Picasso died with brush in hand. Sadly, since he vowed never to set foot in a fascist, Franco-ruled Spain, the artist never returned to his homeland...and never saw this museum (his death came in 1973—two years before Franco's). Picasso continued exploring and loving life through his art to the end.

▲▲PALACE OF CATALAN MUSIC (PALAU DE LA MÚSICA CATALANA)

This concert hall, built in just three years and finished in 1908, features an unexceptional exterior but boasts my favorite Modernista interior in town (by Lluís Domènech i Montaner). Its inviting arches lead you into the 2,138-seat hall, which is accessible only with a tour (or by attending a concert). A kaleidoscopic skylight features a choir singing around the sun, while playful carvings and mosaics celebrate music and Catalan culture. If you're interested in Modernisme, taking this tour is one of the best in town—and helps balance the local fixation on Gaudí as "Mr. Modernisme."

Cost and Hours: €18, 50-minute tours in English run daily every hour 10:00-15:00, tour times may change based on performance schedule, about 6 blocks northeast of cathedral, Carrer Palau de la Música 4, Metro: Urquinaona, tel. 902-442-882, www.palaumusica.cat.

Tour Reservations: You must buy your ticket in advance to get a spot on an English guided tour (tickets available up

Palace of Catalan Music

to 4 months in advance—purchase yours at least 2 days before, though they're sometimes available the same day or day before—especially Oct-March). You can buy the ticket in person at the concert hall box office (open daily 9:30-15:30, less than a 10-minute walk from the cathedral or Picasso Museum); by phone with your credit card (for no extra charge, tel. 902-475-485); or online at the concert hall website (€1 fee).

Concerts: Another way to see the hall is by attending a concert (300 per year, €20-50 tickets, box office tel. 902-442-882, see website for details and online purchases).

▲SANTA CATERINA MARKET

This eye-catching market hall's colorful, rippling roof covers a delightful shopping zone that caters more to locals than tourists. Come for the outlandish architecture, but stay for a chance to shop for a picnic without the tourist logjam of La Boqueria Market on the Ramblas. Besides fresh produce, it has many inviting eateries.

Cost and Hours: Free, Mon-Sat 7:30-15:30, Thu-Fri until 20:30, closed Sun, Avinguda de Francesc Cambó 16, www.mercatsantacaterina.cat.

▲CHURCH OF SANTA MARIA DEL MAR

This "Cathedral of the Sea" was built entirely with local funds and labor, in the heart of the El Born quarter (home to wealthy merchants). Proudly independent, the church features a purely Catalan Gothic interior that was forcibly uncluttered of its Baroque decor by civil war belligerents.

Cost and Hours: Free admission daily 9:00-13:00 & 17:00-20:30, also open 13:00-17:00 with €5 ticket; €8 guided rooftop tours in summer; English tours on the hour Mon-Fri 12:00-16:00, Sat-Sun 11:00-16:00, in summer tours run until 19:00; Plaça Santa Maria, Metro: Jaume I, tel. 933-102-390.

Visiting the Church: On the big front doors, notice the figures of workers who donated their time and sweat to build the church. The stone for the church was quarried at Montjuïc and carried across town on the backs of porters.

Step inside. The church features a purely Catalan Gothic interior. During the Spanish Civil War (1936-1939), Catalan patriots fighting Franco burned the ornate Baroque decoration (carbon still blackens the ceiling), leaving behind this unadorned Gothic. The colorful windows come with modern themes. The tree-like columns inspired Gaudí's work on Sagrada Família. Befitting a church "of the sea," sailors traditionally left models of ships at the altar to win Mary's protection—one remains today.

The Eixample

For many visitors, Modernista architecture is Barcelona's main draw. And at the heart of the Modernista movement was the Eixample, a carefully planned "new town," just beyond the Old City, with wide sidewalks, hardy shade trees, and a rigid

Church of Santa Maria del Mar

grid plan cropped at the corners to create space and lightness at each intersection. Conveniently, all of this new construction provided a generation of Modernista architects with a blank canvas for creating boldly experimental designs.

Block of Discord

At the center of the Eixample is the Block of Discord, where three colorful Modernista facades compete for your attention: Casa Batlló, Casa Amatller, and Casa Lleó Morera (all three are on Passeig de Gràcia—near the Metro stop of the same name—between Carrer del Consell de Cent and Carrer d'Aragó). All were built by well-known Modernista architects at the end of the 19th century. Because the mansions look as though they are trying to outdo each other in creative twists, locals nicknamed the noisy block the "Block of Discord." By the way, if you're tempted to snap photos from the middle of the street, be careful—Gaudí died after being struck by a streetcar.

▲CASA BATLLÓ

While the highlight of this Gaudí-designed residence is its roof, the interior is also interesting—and much more over-the-top than La Pedrera's. Paid for with textile industry money, the house features a funky mushroom-shaped fireplace nook on the main floor, a blue-and-white-ceramic-slathered atrium, and an attic (with parabolic arches). There's barely a straight line in the house. You can also get a close-up look at the dragon-inspired rooftop. Because preservation of the place is privately funded, the entrance fee is steep—but it includes a good (if long-winded) audioguide.

Cost and Hours: €21.50, daily 9:00-21:00, may close early for special events—closings posted in advance at entrance, €3 videoguide shows rooms as they may have been, Passeig de Gràcia 43, tel. 932-160-306, www.casabatllo.cat. Purchase a ticket online to avoid lines, which are especially

fierce in the morning. Your eticket isn't a timed reservation (it's good any time within 3 months of purchase), but it will let you skip to the front of the queue.

CASA AMATLLER

The middle residence of the Block of Discord, Casa Amatller was designed by Josep Puig i Cadafalch in the late 19th century for the Amatller chocolate-making family. It is viewable via guided tour, allowing you to see the modernist interior design, including many original pieces.

Rick's Tip: *If you don't want to pay for a ticket, you can step inside* **Casa Amatller's foyer (free during opening hours)** *to see the Modernist stained-glass door and ceiling, and an elaborate staircase.*

Cost and Hours: €15 for guided tour, daily 11:00-18:00, English tours at 11:00 and 15:00, advance tickets available online, Passeig de Gràcia 41, tel. 934-617-460, www.amatller.org.

▲CASA LLEÓ MORERA

This house, designed by Lluís Domènech i Montaner and finished in 1906, has one of the finest Modernista interiors in town. Access is by guided tour only, which begins with the history of the Lleó Morera family and a look at the paella-like mix of styles on the building's exterior. Inside, you'll marvel at finely crafted mosaics, ceramic work, wooden ceilings and doors, stone sculptures, and stained glass—all of which paint a picture of the life of a Catalan bourgeoisie family in the early 20th century.

Cost and Hours: €15 for 70-minute English tour, €12 for express 45-minute tour (in a mix of English, Spanish, and Catalan); open Tue-Sun, closed Mon; tour times change, so check website for the latest; there is no on-site box office—you must reserve and purchase your ticket online at www.casalleomorera.com, or in person at the cultural center

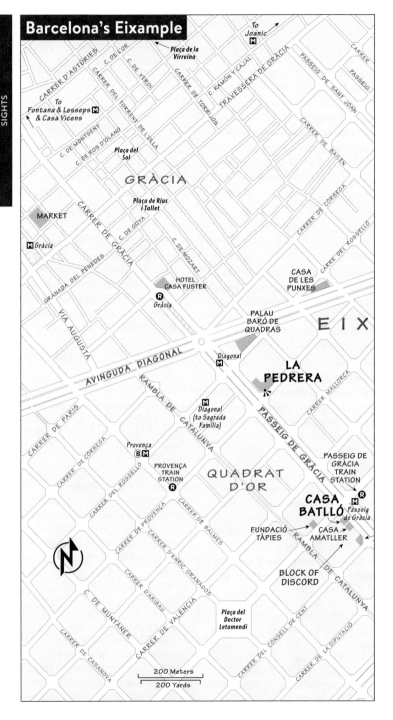

Barcelona's Eixample

To Joanic M

Plaça de la Virreina

CARRER D'ASTÚRIES

C. DE L'OR

C. DE VERDI

CARRER DEL TORRENT DE L'OLLA

CARRER DE TORRIJOS

C. RAMÓN Y CAJAL

TRAVESSERA DE GRÀCIA

PASSEIG DE SANT JOAN

CARRER

PASSEIG

To Fontana & Lesseps M & Casa Vicens

C. DE MONTSENY

C. DE ROS D'OLANO

Plaça del Sol

GRÀCIA

CARRER DE BAILEN

Plaça de Rius i Tallet

MARKET

CARRER DE GRÀCIA

C. DE GOYA

C. DE MOZART

CARRER DE CÒRSEGA

CARRER DEL ROSSELLÓ

M Gràcia

GRANADA DEL PENEDÈS

HOTEL CASA FUSTER

CASA DE LES PUNXES

CARRER DE CÒRSEGA

VIA AUGUSTA

R Gràcia

PALAU BARÓ DE QUADRAS

EIX

AVINGUDA DIAGONAL

Diagonal M

LA PEDRERA

CARRER MALLORCA

RAMBLA DE CATALUNYA

Diagonal (to Sagrada Família) M

PASSEIG DE GRÀCIA

CARRER DE PARÍS

CARRER DE CÒRSEGA

Provença B M

CARRER DEL ROSSELLÓ

PROVENÇA TRAIN STATION R

QUADRAT D'OR

PASSEIG DE GRÀCIA TRAIN STATION

CASA BATLLÓ M R

Passeig de Gràcia

CARRER DE PROVENÇA

CARRER DE BALMES

FUNDACIÓ TÀPIES

CASA AMATLLER

RAMBLA DE CATALUNYA

N

CARRER D'ARIBAU

CARRER D'ENRIC GRANADOS

BLOCK OF DISCORD

C. DE MUNTANER

CARRER DE VALÈNCIA

Plaça del Doctor Letamendi

CARRER DEL CONSELL DE CENT

CARRER DE LA DIPUTACIÓ

CARRER DE CASANOVA

200 Meters

200 Yards

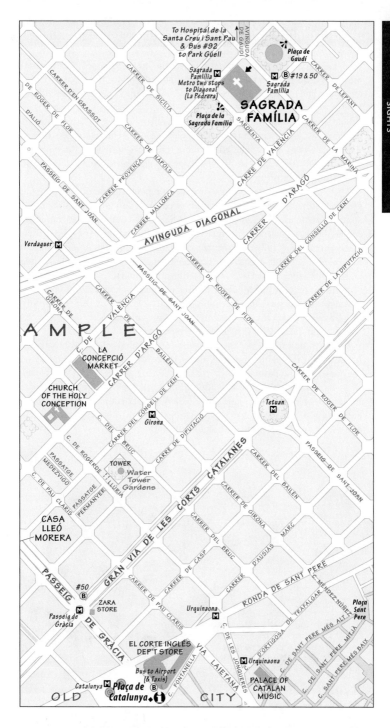

Modernisme and the Renaixença

Modernisme is Barcelona's unique contribution to the European Art Nouveau movement. Meaning "a taste for what is modern"—things like streetcars, electric lights, and big-wheeled bicycles—this free-flowing organic style lasted from 1888 to 1906.

The starting point for the style was a kind of Neo-Gothic, clearly inspired by medieval castles, towers, and symbols—logically, since architects wanted to recall Barcelona's glory days of the 1400s. From the Neo-Gothic look, Antoni Gaudí branched off on his own, adding the color and curves we most associate with Barcelona's Modernisme look.

The aim was to create objects that were both practical and decorative. Modernista architects experimented with new construction techniques, especially concrete, which they could use to make a hard stone building that curved and rippled like a wave. Then they sprinkled it with brightly colored glass and tile. The structure was fully modern, but the decoration was a clip-art collage of nature images, exotic Moorish or Chinese themes, and fanciful Gothic crosses and knights to celebrate Catalunya's medieval glory days.

It's ironic to think that Modernisme was a response to the Industrial Age—and that all those organic shapes were only made possible thanks to Eiffel Tower-like iron frames. The Eixample's fanciful facades and colorful, leafy ornamentation were built at the same time as the first skyscrapers.

Fueling Modernisme was the Catalan cultural revival called the Renaixença. As Europe was waking up to the modern age, downtrodden peoples across Europe—from the Basques to the Irish to the Hungarians to the Finns—were throwing off the cultural domination of other nations and celebrating what made their own cultures unique. Here in Catalunya, the Renaixença encouraged everyday people to get excited about all things Catalan: their language, patriotic dances, art—and their surprising architecture.

Casa Amatller, with stepped roofline, and Casa Batllo, to the right

Palau de la Virreina (Ramblas 99, tel. 933-161-000, www.lavirreina.bcn.cat). The house itself is at Passeig de Gràcia 35, tel. 936-762-733.

▲▲LA PEDRERA (CASA MILÀ)

One of Gaudí's trademark works, this house—built between 1906 and 1912—is an icon of Modernisme. The wealthy industrialist Pere Milà i Camps commissioned it, and while some still call it Casa Milà, most call it La Pedrera (The Quarry) because of its jagged, rocky facade. While it's fun to ogle from the outside, it's also worth going inside, as it's arguably the purest Gaudí interior in town—executed at the height of his abilities (unlike his earlier Palau Güell)—and still contains original furnishings. While Casa Batlló has a Gaudí facade and rooftop, these were appended to an existing building; La Pedrera, on the other hand, was built from the ground up according to Gaudí's plans. Besides entry to the interior, a ticket also gets you access to the delightful rooftop, with its forest of colorful tiled chimneys.

Cost and Hours: €20.50, daily March-Oct 9:00-20:00, Nov-Feb 9:00-18:30, last entry 30 minutes before closing, good audioguide-€4, at the corner of Passeig de Gràcia and Provença (visitor entrance at Provença 261), Metro: Diagonal, info tel. 902-400-973, www.lapedrera.com.

Crowd Control: As lines can be long (up to a 1.5-hour wait to get in), it's best to reserve ahead at www.lapedrera.com (tickets come with an assigned entry time). If you come without a ticket, the best time to arrive is right when it opens.

Rick's Tip: *For a* peek at La Pedrera *without paying for a ticket, find the door directly on the corner, which offers* free entrance to the main atrium. *Upstairs on the first floor are temporary exhibits (generally free, daily 10:00-20:00, closed between exhibitions).*

Nighttime Visits: The building hosts after-hour visits dubbed "The Secret Pedrera." On this pricey visit, you'll get a guided tour of the building with the lights

La Pedrera rooftop

Modernista Masters

Here's a summary of the major players who took part in the architectual revolution of Modernisme:

Antoni Gaudí (1852-1926), Barcelona's most famous Modernista artist, was descended from four generations of metalworkers—a lineage of which he was quite proud. He incorporated ironwork into his architecture and came up with novel approaches to architectural structure and space. His work strongly influenced his younger Catalan contemporary, Salvador Dalí. While Dalí was creating unlikely and shocking juxtapositions of photorealistic images, Gaudí did the same in architecture—using the spine of a reptile for a bannister or a turtle shell design on windows. His best work in Barcelona includes his great unfinished church, the Sagrada Família; several mansions in the town center,

including La Pedrera, Casa Batlló, and Palau Güell; and Park Güell, his ambitious and never-completed housing development.

Lluís Domènech i Montaner (1850-1923), a professor and politician, was responsible for some major civic buildings, including his masterwork, the Palace of Catalan Music (see page 75). He also designed Casa Lleó Morera on the Block of Discord. Although Gaudí is more famous, Domènech i Montaner's work is perhaps more purely representative of the Modernista style.

Josep Puig i Cadafalch (1867-1956) was a city planner who oversaw the opening up of Via Laietana through the middle of the Old City. He was instrumental in the redevelopment of Montjuïc for the 1929 World Expo. He designed Casa Amatller (see page 77). Perhaps most important, Puig i Cadafalch designed the building housing Els Quatre Gats (see page 56), a bar that became a cradle for the Modernista movement.

All architects worked with a team of people who, while not famous, made real contributions. For example, Gaudí's colleague **Josep Maria Jujol** (1879-1949) is primarily responsible for the broken-tile mosaic decorations (called *trencadís*) on Park Güell's benches and Casa Milà's chimneys—which became Gaudí's trademark.

Though not an artist, businessman **Eusebi Güell** (1846-1918) used his nearly $90 billion fortune to bankroll Gaudí and other Modernista masters. Güell's name still adorns two of Gaudí's most important works: Palau Güell (see page 63) and Park Güell (see page 91).

turned down low and a glass of *cava* (€30; English tour offered daily March-Oct at 21:15, but check changeable schedule and offerings online).

Concerts: On summer weekends, La Pedrera has an evening rooftop concert series, "Summer Nights at La Pedrera," featuring live jazz. In addition to the music, it gives you the chance to see the rooftop illuminated (€27, late June-early Sept Thu-Sat at 22:30, book advance tickets online or by phone, tel. 902-101-212, www.lapedrera.com).

Visiting the House: A visit covers three sections—the apartment, the attic, and the rooftop. Enter and head upstairs to the apartment. If it's near closing time, continue up to see the attic and rooftop first, to make sure you have enough time to enjoy Gaudí's works and the views (note that the roof may close when it rains).

The typical bourgeois **apartment** is decorated as it might have been when the building was first occupied by middle-class urbanites (a 7-minute video explains Barcelona society at the time). Notice Gaudí's clever use of the atrium to maximize daylight in all of the apartments.

The **attic** houses a sprawling multimedia exhibit tracing the history of the architect's career, with models, photos, and videos of his work. It's all displayed under distinctive parabola-shaped arches.

From the attic, a stairway leads to the undulating, jaw-dropping **rooftop,** where 30 chimneys and ventilation towers play volleyball with the clouds.

Back at the **ground level** of La Pedrera, poke into the dreamily painted original entrance courtyard.

▲▲▲SAGRADA FAMÍLIA
(HOLY FAMILY CHURCH)
Antoni Gaudí's grand masterpiece sits unfinished in a residential Eixample neighborhood 1.5 miles north of Plaça de Catalunya. An icon of the city, the Sagrada Família boasts bold, wildly creative, unmistakably organic architecture

and decor inside and out—from its melting Glory Facade to its skull-like Passion Facade to its rainforest-esque interior. Begun under Gaudí's careful watch in 1883, the project saw some setbacks in the mid-20th century, but lately the progress has been remarkable. The city has set a goal of finishing by 2026, the centennial of Gaudí's death. For now, visitors get a close-up view of the dramatic exterior flourishes, the chance to walk through the otherworldly interior, and access to a fine museum detailing the design and engineering behind this one-of-a-kind architectural marvel.

The main challenges for this massive undertaking today are to ensure that construction can withstand the vibrations caused by the speedy AVE trains rumbling underfoot, to construct the tallest church spire ever built, and to find a way to buy out the people who own the condos in front of the planned Glory Facade so that Gaudí's vision of a grand esplanade approaching the church can be realized.

Rick's Tip: To avoid wasting time in ticket-buying lines, buy **advance tickets** *for the* **Sagrada Família.**

Cost and Hours: Church-€15, tower elevators-€4.50 each, €18.50 combo-ticket includes church (no towers) and Gaudí House Museum at Park Güell (see page 92); daily April-Sept 9:00-20:00, Oct-March 9:00-18:00.

Advance Tickets: Reserve entry times and buy tickets in advance for both the church and the tower elevators (this is the best way to synch up the timing of your church visit and elevator ride). The easiest option is to book at www.sagrada familia.cat and print tickets at home.

Crowd Control: Waits can be up to 45 minutes at peak times—and occasionally stretch much longer (most crowded in the morning). To minimize waiting, arrive right at 9:00 (when the church opens) or after

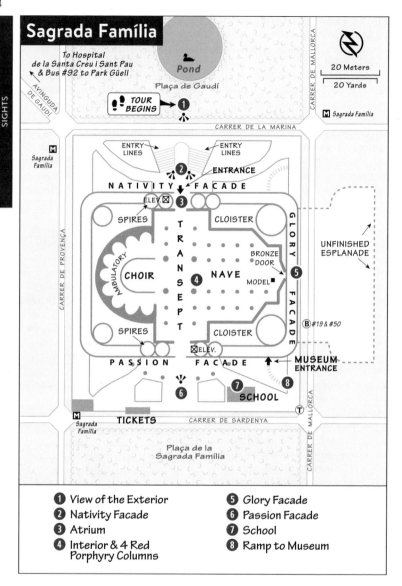

Sagrada Família

To Hospital de la Santa Creu i Sant Pau & Bus #92 to Park Güell

Pond

Plaça de Gaudí

20 Meters

20 Yards

M Sagrada Família

AVINGUDA DE GAUDÍ

TOUR BEGINS ➊

M Sagrada Família

CARRER DE LA MARINA

ENTRY LINES

ENTRY LINES

➋ ENTRANCE

N A T I V I T Y   F A C A D E

ELEV. ☒ ➌

SPIRES

CLOISTER

G L O R Y   F A C A D E

UNFINISHED ESPLANADE

CARRER DE PROVENÇA

AMBULATORY

CHOIR

T R A N S E P T

NAVE

BRONZE DOOR

MODEL ■

➎

➍

B #19 & #50

SPIRES

CLOISTER

☒ ELEV.

P A S S I O N   F A C A D E

MUSEUM ENTRANCE

➏

➐ SCHOOL

➑

CARRER DE MALLORCA

M Sagrada Família

TICKETS

CARRER DE SARDENYA

T

Plaça de la Sagrada Família

➊ View of the Exterior	➎ Glory Facade
➋ Nativity Facade	➏ Passion Facade
➌ Atrium	➐ School
➍ Interior & 4 Red Porphyry Columns	➑ Ramp to Museum

16:00. To skip the line, buy advance tickets, take a tour, or hire a private guide.

Getting There: The church address is Carrer de Mallorca 401. The Sagrada Família Metro stop puts you right on its doorstep.

Getting In: The ticket windows are on the west side of the church, at the Passion Facade (from the Metro, exit toward Plaça de la Sagrada Família). If you already have tickets, head straight for the Nativity Facade (in front of Plaça de Gaudí), where you'll find entry lines for individuals. Show your ticket to the guard, who will direct you to the right line.

Information: Good English information

is posted throughout. Tel. 932-073-031, www.sagradafamilia.cat.

Tours: The 50-minute **English tours** (€4.50) run daily at 11:00, 12:00, 13:00, and 15:00 (no 12:00 tour Mon-Fri in Nov-April; choose tour time when you buy ticket). Or rent the good 1.5-hour **audioguide** (€4.50).

Tower Elevators: Two different elevators take you (for a fee) partway up the towers for a great view of the city and a gargoyle's-eye perspective of the loopy church. Reserve an elevator time when you buy your church ticket.

The easier option is the **Passion Facade elevator,** which takes you 215 feet up and down. You can climb higher, but expect the spiral stairs to be tight, hot, and congested.

The **Nativity Facade elevator** is more exciting and demanding. You'll get the opportunity to cross the dizzying bridge between the towers, but you'll need to take the stairs all the way down.

⊙ SELF-GUIDED TOUR

• Start outside the Nativity Facade (where the entry lines for individuals are located), on the eastern side of the church. Before heading to the entrance, take in the...

❶ View of the Exterior: Stand and imagine how grand this church will be when completed. The four 330-foot spires topped with crosses are just a fraction of this mega-church. When finished, the church will have 18 spires. Four will stand at each of the three entrances. Rising above those will be four taller towers, dedicated to the four Evangelists. A tower dedicated to Mary will rise still higher—400 feet. And in the center of the complex will stand the grand 560-foot Jesus tower, topped with a cross that will shine like a spiritual lighthouse, visible even from out at sea.

The Nativity Facade, where tourists enter today, is only a side entrance to the church. The grand main entrance will be around to the left. That means that the nine-story apartment building will eventually have to be torn down to accommodate it. The three facades—Nativity, Passion, and Glory—will chronicle Christ's life from birth to death to resurrection. Inside and out, a goal of the church is to bring the lessons of the Bible to the world. Despite his boldly modern architectural vision, Gaudí was fundamentally traditional and deeply religious. He designed

Sagrada Família

Sagrada Família nave

the Sagrada Família to be a bastion of solid Christian values in the midst of what was a humble workers' colony in a fast-changing city.

When Gaudí died, only one section (on the Nativity Facade) had been completed. The rest of the church has been inspired by Gaudí's long-range vision but designed and executed by others. This artistic freedom was amplified in 1936, when civil war shelling burned many of Gaudí's blueprints. Supporters of the ongoing work insist that Gaudí, who enjoyed saying, "My client [God] is not in a hurry," knew he wouldn't live to complete the church and recognized that later architects and artists would rely on their own muses for inspiration.

• *Now approach the…*

❷ **Nativity Facade:** This is the only part of the church essentially finished in Gaudí's lifetime. The four spires decorated with his unmistakably nonlinear sculpture mark this facade as part of his original design. Mixing Gothic-style symbolism, images from nature, and Modernista asymmetry, the Nativity Facade is the best example of Gaudí's original

vision, and it established the template for future architects who would work on the building.

The theme of this facade, which faces the rising sun, is Christ's birth. A statue above the doorway shows Mary, Joseph, and Baby Jesus in the manger, while curious cows peek in. It's the Holy Family—or "Sagrada Família"—to whom this church is dedicated. Flanking the doorway are the three Magi and adoring shepherds. Other statues show Jesus as a young carpenter and angels playing musical instruments. Higher up on the facade, in the arched niche, Jesus crowns Mary triumphantly.

The four **spires** are dedicated to apostles, and they repeatedly bear the word "Sanctus," or holy. Their colorful ceramic caps symbolize the miters (formal hats) of bishops. The shorter spires (to the left) symbolize the Eucharist (communion), alternating between a chalice with grapes and a communion host with wheat.

• *Enter the church. As you pass through the* ❸ **atrium,** *look down at the fine porphyry floor (with scenes of Jesus' entry into Jerusalem), and look right to see one of the* **elevators** *up to the towers. For now, continue into the…*

❹ **Interior:** Typical of even the most traditional Catalan and Spanish churches, the floor plan is in the shape of a Latin cross, 300 feet long and 200 feet wide. Ultimately, the church will encompass 48,000 square feet, accommodating 8,000 worshippers. The nave's roof is 150 feet high. The crisscross arches of the ceiling (the vaults) show off Gaudí's distinctive engineering. The church's roof and flooring were only completed in 2010—just in time for Pope Benedict XVI to arrive and consecrate the church.

Part of Gaudí's religious vision was a love for nature. He said, "Nothing is invented; it's written in nature." Like the trunks of trees, these **columns** (56 in all) blossom with life, complete with branches, leaves, and knot-like capitals. The columns are a variety of colors—

Nativity Facade detail

brown clay, gray granite, dark-gray basalt. The taller columns are 72 feet tall; the shorter ones are exactly half that.

Little **windows** let light filter in like the canopy of a rainforest, giving both privacy and an intimate connection with God. The clear glass is temporary and will gradually be replaced by stained glass. High up at the back half of the church, the U-shaped **choir**—suspended above the nave—can seat 1,000. The singers will eventually be backed by four organs (there's one now).

Work your way up the grand nave, walking through this forest of massive columns. At the center of the church stand four **red porphyry columns,** each marked with an Evangelist's symbol and name in Catalan: angel (Mateu), lion (Marc), bull (Luc), and eagle (Joan).

Stroll behind the altar through the **ambulatory** to reach a small chapel set aside for prayer and meditation. Look through windows down at the **crypt** (which holds the tomb of Gaudí). Peering down into that surprisingly traditional space, imagine how the church was started as a fairly conventional, 19th-century Neo-Gothic building until Gaudí was given the responsibility to finish it.

• *Head to the far end of the church, to what will eventually be the main entrance. Just inside the door, find the* **bronze model** *of the floor plan for the completed church. Facing the doors, look high up to see Subirachs' statue of one of Barcelona's patron saints,* **George (Jordi).** *While you can't see it, imagine that outside these doors will someday be the…*

❺ Glory Facade: Study the life-size image of the **bronze door,** emblazoned with the Lord's Prayer in Catalan, surrounded by "Give us this day our daily bread" in 50 languages. If you were able to walk through the actual door, you'd be face-to-face with…drab, doomed apartment blocks. In the 1950s, the mayor of Barcelona, figuring this day would never really come, sold the land destined for the

church project. Now the city must buy back these buildings in order to complete Gaudí's vision: that of a grand esplanade leading to this main entry. Four towers will rise. The facade's sculpture will represent how the soul passes through death, faces the Last Judgment, avoids the pitfalls of hell, and finds its way to eternal glory with God. Gaudí purposely left the facade's design open for later architects—stay tuned.

• *Head back up the nave, and exit through the left transept. Notice the second* **elevator** *up to the towers. Once outside, back up to take in the…*

❻ Passion Facade: Judge for yourself how well Gaudí's original vision has been carried out by later artists. The Passion Facade's four spires were designed by Gaudí and completed (quite faithfully) in 1976. But the lower part was only inspired by Gaudí's designs. The stark sculptures were interpreted freely (and controversially) by Josep Maria Subirachs (1927-2014), who completed the work in 2005.

Subirachs tells the story of Christ's torture and execution. The various scenes—Last Supper, betrayal, whipping, and so on—zigzag up from bottom to top, culminating in Christ's crucifixion over the doorway. The style is severe and unadorned, quite different from Gaudí's signature playfulness. But the bone-like archways are closely based on Gaudí's original designs. And Gaudí had made it clear that this facade should be grim and terrifying.

• *Now head into the small building outside the Passion Facade. This is the…*

❼ School: Gaudí erected this school for the children of the workers building the church. Today it includes exhibits about the design and engineering of the church, along with a classroom and a replica of Gaudí's desk as it was the day he died.

• *Back outside, head down the ramp, where you'll find WCs and the entrance to the…*

Sagrada Família Passion Facade

❽ Museum: Housed in what will someday be the church's crypt, the museum displays Gaudí's original models and drawings, and chronicles the progress of construction over the last 130-plus years.

Upon entering, you'll see **photos** (including one of the master himself) and a **timeline** illustrating how construction work has progressed from Gaudí's day to now. Before turning into the main hall, find **three different visions** for this church.

As you wander, notice how the **plaster models,** used for the church's construction, don't always match the finished product—these are ideas, not blueprints. The Passion Facade model shows Gaudí's original vision, with which Subirachs tinkered freely (see "Passion Facade," earlier). The models also make clear the influence of nature. The columns seem light, with branches springing forth and capitals that look like palm trees.

Turn right up the main hallway, walking under a huge **model of the nave,** and past some original **sculptures** from the different facades (on the left). Farther along, a small hallway on the left leads to some original Gaudí architectural **sketches** in a dimly lit room and a worthwhile 20-minute **movie** (continuously shown in Catalan with English subtitles).

From the end of this hall, you have another opportunity to look down into the crypt and at **Gaudí's tomb.** Gaudí lived on the site for more than a decade and is buried in the Neo-Gothic 19th-century crypt (also viewable from the apse). There's a move afoot to make Gaudí a saint. Gaudí prayer cards provide words of devotion to his beatification. Perhaps someday his tomb will be a place of pilgrimage.

On the right, you can peek into a busy **workshop** still used for making the same kind of plaster models Gaudí used to envision the final product in three dimensions.

• *Our tour is over. From here, you could...*

Visit Park Güell: *The park is nearly two (uphill) miles to the northwest. The easiest way to get there is to spring for a taxi (around €10-12). Or you could reach the park by taking the Metro to the Joanic stop, then hopping on bus #116 (described next, under the "Park Güell" listing).*

Return to Central Barcelona: *You can either hop on the Metro or take one of two handy buses (both stop on Carrer de Mallorca, directly in front of the Glory Facade). Bus #19 takes you back to the* **Old City** *in 15 minutes, stopping near the cathedral and in the El Born district. Bus #50 goes from the Sagrada Família to the heart of the* **Eixample** *(corner of Gran Via de les Corts Catalanes and Passeig de Gràcia), then continues on to Plaça Espanya, where you can get off for* **Montjuïc.**

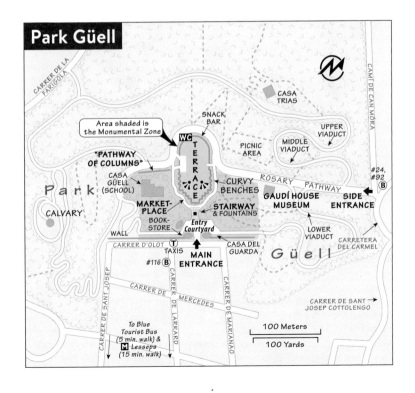

Park Güell

Beyond the Eixample

▲▲PARK GÜELL

Tucked in the foothills at the edge of Barcelona, this fanciful park—designed by Antoni Gaudí as part of an upscale housing development for early-20th-century urbanites—combines playful whimsy, inviting spaces, and a terrace offering sweeping views over the rooftops of the city.

When the entire park was free to enter, it became so popular that it was nearly trampled by tourists, obscuring the very sights they'd come to see. To control crowds, the part of the park with the most popular sights was declared the Monumental Zone, which requires an admission fee and a timed entry to visit. This fairly compact zone contains a pair of gingerbread-style houses, a grand staircase monitored by a colorful dragon, a forest of columns supporting a spectacular view terrace, and an undulating balcony slathered in tile shards.

The park also contains the Gaudí House Museum, Calvary viewpoint, picnic area, and a pleasant network of nature trails. Except for the Monumental Zone

and museum, the rest of the park is free.

No matter where you visit—inside the zone or out—what you're sure to see is Barcelonans and tourists alike enjoying a day at the park.

Cost and Hours: Monumental Zone—€8 at the gate or €7 online, smart to reserve timed-entry tickets in advance, daily April-Oct 8:00-20:00 (May-Aug until 21:30), Nov-March 8:30-18:15, www.parkguell.cat; Gaudí House Museum—€5.50, €18.50 combo-ticket also includes Sagrada Família (church but no towers), daily April-Sept 10:00-20:00, Oct-March 10:00-18:00, www.casamuseu gaudi.org.

Getting There: Park Güell is about 2.5 miles from Plaça de Catalunya, beyond the Gràcia neighborhood in Barcelona's foothills. If asking for directions, be aware that Catalans pronounce it "Park Gway" (sounds like "parkway").

From downtown, a **taxi** will drop you off at the main entrance for about €12. From Plaça de Catalunya, the blue Tourist Bus stops about two blocks downhill from the main entrance, and **public bus** #24 travels from Plaça de Catalunya to the park's side entrance. Or you can ride

Park Güell's entry stairway

the Metro to Joanic, exit toward Carrer de l'Escorial, and find the bus stop in front of #20, where you can catch bus #116 to the park's main entrance. For instructions on linking the Sagrada Família to Park Güell, check page 83 .

Visiting the Park: This tour assumes you're arriving at the front/main entrance.

Entering the park, you walk through a palm-frond **gate** and pass Gaudí's gas lamps (1900-1914), both made of wrought iron. His dad was a blacksmith, and he always enjoyed this medium.

Two Hansel-and-Gretel gingerbread lodges flank the entrance, signaling to visitors that this park is a magical space. One of the buildings houses a good bookshop; the other is home to the skippable **La Casa del Guarda,** a branch of the Barcelona History Museum (MUHBA). The Gaudí House Museum, described later, is more interesting to me.

Climb the grand **stairway,** past the famous ceramic dragon fountain. At the top, dip into the "Hall of 100 Columns," designed to house a produce market for the neighborhood's 60 mansions. The fun columns—each different, made from concrete and rebar, topped with colorful ceramic, and studded with broken bottles and bric-a-brac—add to the market's vitality.

As you continue up (on the left-hand staircase), look left, down the playful **"pathway of columns"** that supports a long arcade. Gaudí drew his inspiration from nature, and this arcade is like a surfer's perfect tube.

Once up top on the **terrace,** sit on a colorful bench—designed to fit your body ergonomically—and enjoy one of Barcelona's best views. Look for the Sagrada Família church in the distance.

As a community development, Park Güell ultimately failed, but it was an idea a hundred years ahead of its time. Back then, high-society ladies didn't want to live so far from the cultural action. Today, the surrounding neighborhoods are some of the wealthiest in town, and a gated community here would be a big hit.

Gaudí House Museum: This pink house with a steeple, standing in the middle of the park (near the side entrance), was Gaudí's home for 20 years (though he didn't design the actual house). It was originally built as a model home to attract prospective residents. His humble artifacts are mostly gone, but the house is now a museum with some quirky Gaudí furniture. Though small, it offers a good taste of what could have been if the envisioned housing development had prospered.

Montjuïc

Montjuïc (mohn-jew-EEK), overlooking Barcelona's hazy port, has always been a show-off. Ages ago, it was capped by an impressive castle. When the Spanish enforced their rule in the 18th century, they built the imposing fortress that you'll see the shell of today. Montjuïc was also prominent during the last century. In 1929, it hosted an international fair, from which many of today's sights originated. And in 1992, the Summer Olympics directed the world's attention to this pincushion of attractions once again.

For art lovers, the most worthwhile sights are the Fundació Joan Miró and Catalan Art Museum. The hilltop castle isn't worth entering, but offers great city views from its ramparts. It serves as a park, jogging destination, and host to a popular summer open-air cinema.

For evening fun, you could drop by the Magic Fountains, and any time of day, you can escalate up to the top of Las Arenas Mall for a view of Montjuïc.

Getting to Montjuïc: You have several choices. The simplest is to take a **taxi** directly to your destination (about €8 from downtown). If you want to visit only the Catalan Art Museum, you can just take the **Metro** to Plaça d'Espanya and ride the escalators up the hill (with some stairs as well).

Buses also take you up to Montjuïc. From Plaça de Catalunya, **bus #55** rides as far as Montjuïc's cable-car station/funicular. If you want to get higher (to the castle), ride the Metro to Plaça d'Espanya, then make the easy transfer to **bus #150** to ride all the way up the hill—then you can do the rest of your Montjuïc sightseeing going downhill. Alternatively, the red Tourist Bus will get you to the Montjuïc sights.

Another option is by **funicular** (covered by Metro ticket, runs every 10 minutes 9:00-22:00). To reach it, take the Metro to the Paral-lel stop, then follow signs for *Parc Montjuïc* and the little funicular icon—you can enter the funicular without using another ticket. From the top of the funicular, turn left and walk gently downhill 4 minutes to the Miró museum or 12 minutes to the Catalan Art Museum. If you're heading all the way up to the castle, you can catch a bus or cable car from the top of the funicular.

For a scenic (if slow) approach to Montjuïc, you could ride the fun, circa-1929 Aeri del Port **cable car** (*telefèric*) from the tip of the Barceloneta peninsula (across the harbor, near the beach) to the Miramar viewpoint park in Montjuïc.

Since the cable car is expensive, loads slowly, and goes between two relatively remote parts of town, it's only worthwhile for its sweeping views or if you'd like to cap off your Montjuïc day with some beach time near Barceloneta (€11 one-way, €16.50 round-trip, 3/hour, daily 11:00-17:30, June-Sept until 20:00, closed in high wind, tel. 934-414-820, www.teleferi codebarcelona.com).

Getting Around Montjuïc: Up top, it's easy and fun to walk between the sights—especially downhill. You can also connect the sights using the red Tourist Bus or one of the public buses: Bus #150 does a loop around the hilltop and is the only bus that goes to the castle; on the way up, it stops at or passes the Catalan Art Museum, Fundació Joan Miró, the lower castle cable-car station/top of the funicular, and finally, the castle. On the downhill run, it loops by Miramar, the cable-car station for Barceloneta. Bus #55 connects only the funicular/cable-car stations, Fundació Joan Miró, and the Catalan Art Museum.

▲▲CATALAN ART MUSEUM (MUSEU NACIONAL D'ART DE CATALUNYA)

This wonderful museum showcases Catalan art from the 10th century through

Montjuïc's Magic Fountains

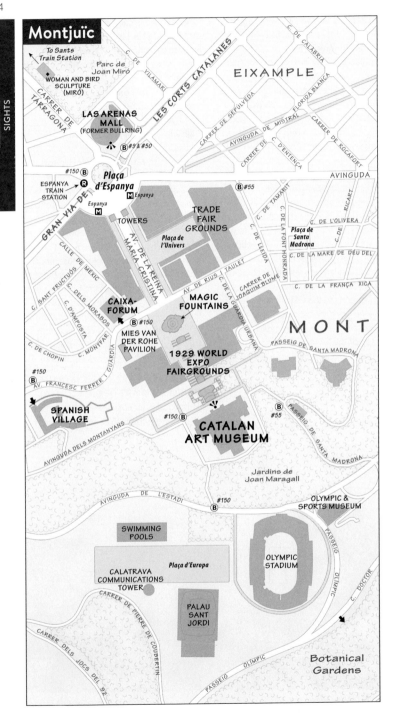

Montjuïc

To Sants
Train Station

Parc de
Joan Miró

WOMAN AND BIRD
SCULPTURE
(MIRÓ)

CARRER DE TARRAGONA

C. DE VILAMARI

C. DE CALABRIA

LES CORTS CATALANES

EIXAMPLE

CARRER DE SEPULVEDA

AVINGUDA DE MISTRAL

FLORIDA BLANCA

CARRER DE ROCAFORT

CARRER DE C. D'ENTENÇA

LAS ARENAS
MALL
(FORMER BULLRING)

B #9 & #50

#150 B

Plaça
d'Espanya

ESPANYA
TRAIN
STATION

R

Espanya

M

Espanya

M

GRAN VIA DE

AVINGUDA

B #55

AV. DE LA REINA MARIA CRISTINA

TOWERS

TRADE
FAIR
GROUNDS

Plaça de
l'Univers

C. DE TAMARIT

C. DE LA FONT HONRADA

C. DE L'OLIVERA

C. DE L'

ELCART

Plaça de
Santa
Madrona

C. DE LA MARE DE DÉU DEL

CALLE DE MEXIC

C. SANT FRUCTUÓS

C. DELS MORABOS

C. D'AMPOSTA

C. DE CHOPIN

C. MONTFAR

CAIXA-
FORUM

B #150

MIES VAN
DER ROHE
PAVILION

AV. DE RIUS I TAULET

C. DE LA GUÀRDIA URBANA

CARRER DE
JOAQUIM BLUME

C. DE LLEIDA

C. DE LA FRANÇA XICA

MAGIC
FOUNTAINS

1929 WORLD
EXPO
FAIRGROUNDS

MONT

PASSEIG DE SANTA MADRONA

#150
B

AV. FRANCESC FERRER I GUÀRDIA

SPANISH
VILLAGE

#150 B

CATALAN
ART MUSEUM

B
#55

PASSEIG DE SANTA MADRONA

AVINGUDA DELS MONTANYANS

Jardins de
Joan Maragall

OLYMPIC &
SPORTS MUSEUM

AVINGUDA DE L'ESTADI

#150
B

SWIMMING
POOLS

Plaça d'Europa

OLYMPIC
STADIUM

PASSEIG OLIMPIC

C. DOCTOR

CALATRAVA
COMMUNICATIONS
TOWER

PALAU
SANT
JORDI

CARRER DE PIERRE DE COUBERTIN

CARRER DELS JOCS DEL 92

PASSEIG OLIMPIC

Botanical
Gardens

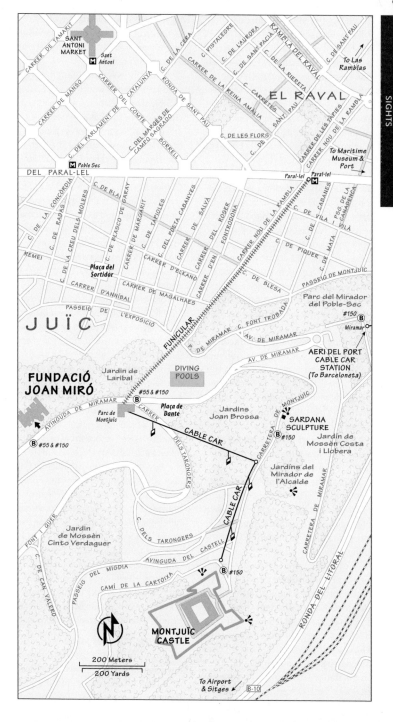

SANT
ANTONI
MARKET

Sant
Antoni

Carrer de Tamarit

Carrer del Comte

Carrer del Parlament de

Carrer de Manso

C. del Marqués de Campo Sagrado

Ronda de Sant Pau

Carrer de la Reina Amàlia

Carrer de la Cera

C. Vistalegre

C. de l'Aurora

C. de Sant Pacia

Rambla del Raval

C. de la Riereta

C. Carretes

Sant Pau

C. de Sant Pau

EL RAVAL

To Las
Ramblas

C. de les Flors

C. de

C. de les Tàpies

Carrer Nou de la Rambla

To Maritime
Museum &
Port

Poble Sec

DEL PARAL-LEL

Paral-lel

Paral-lel

C. de la Concòrdia

C. de Radas

C. de la Creu dels Molers

C. de Blai

C. de Blasco de Garay

Carrer de Margarit

C. del Poeta Cabanyes

Carrer de Salvà

Carrer del Roser

Fontrodona

Carrer Nou de la Rambla

C. de Cabanes

C. de Vila i Vila

Psg. de la Cabanenca

C. de Piquer

C. de Mata

C. de Tàpioles

Carrer d'Elkano

Carrer d'En

Remei

Plaça del
Sortidor

Carrer d'Anníbal

Carrer de Magalhaes

C. de Blesa

Passeig de Montjuïc

Passeig de l'Exposició

JUÏC

FUNICULAR

Parc del Mirador
del Poble-Sec

#150

Miramar

P. de Miramar

C. Font Trobada

Av. de Miramar

Av. de Miramar

AERI DEL PORT
CABLE CAR
STATION
(To Barceloneta)

FUNDACIÓ
JOAN MIRÓ

Jardin de
Laribal

DIVING
POOLS

Avinguda de Miramar

#55 & #150

Parc de
Montjuïc

Plaça de
Dante

Carrer

Jardins
Joan Brossa

Carretera de Montjuïc

SARDANA
SCULPTURE

#150

Jardin de
Mossèn Costa
i Llobera

#55 & #150

CABLE CAR

Dels Tarongers

Jardins del
Mirador de
l'Alcalde

Jardin
de Mossèn
Cinto Verdaguer

CABLE CAR

Font i Quer

C. de Can Valero

C. dels Tarongers

Avinguda del Castell

Passeig del Migdia

Camí de la Cartoixa

#150

Carretera de Miramar

Ronda del Litoral

N

MONTJUÏC
CASTLE

200 Meters

200 Yards

To Airport
& Sitges

B-10

the mid-20th century. Often called "the Prado of Romanesque art" (and "MNAC" for short), it also holds Europe's best collection of Romanesque frescoes. Art aficionados are sure to find something in this diverse collection to tickle their fancy. It's all housed in the grand Palau Nacional, an emblematic building from the 1929 World Expo, with magnificent views over Barcelona, especially from the building's rooftop terrace.

Cost and Hours: €12, includes temporary exhibits and rooftop terrace, rooftop access only—€3.50, museum free Sat from 15:00 and first Sun of month; open May-Sept Tue-Sat 10:00-20:00 (Oct-April until 18:00), Sun 10:00-15:00, closed Mon, last entry 30 minutes before closing; audioguide—€3.10; in massive National Palace building above Magic Fountains, near Plaça d'Espanya—take escalators up; tel. 936-220-376, www.museunacional.cat.

Getting to the Rooftop Terrace: To reach the terrace from the main entrance, walk past the bathrooms to the left and show your ticket to get on the elevator. You'll ride up nearly to the viewpoint, and from there hike up a couple of flights of stairs to the terrace. To take an elevator the whole way, go to the far end of the museum, through the huge dome room, to the far right corner.

Visiting the Museum: As you enter, pick up a map. The left wing is Romanesque, and the right wing is Gothic, exquisite Renaissance, and Baroque. Upstairs is more Baroque, plus modern art, photography, coins, and more.

The MNAC's rare, world-class collection of **Romanesque** (Romànic) art came mostly from remote Catalan village churches. A series of videos shows the process of extracting the frescoes from the churches. The Romanesque wing features a remarkable array of 11th- to 13th-century frescoes, painted wooden altar fronts, and ornate statuary. This classic Romanesque art—with flat 2-D scenes, each saint holding his symbol, and Jesus (easy to identify by the cross in his halo)—is impressively displayed on replicas of the original church ceilings and apses.

Across the way, in the Gothic wing, are vivid 14th-century wood-panel paintings of Bible stories. A roomful of paintings (Room 26) by the Catalan master Jaume Huguet (1412-1492) deserves a look, particularly his *Consecration of St. Agustí Vell.* Also on the ground floor is a selection of **Renaissance** works covering Spain's Golden Age (Zurbarán, heavy religious scenes, Spanish royals with their endearing underbites) and examples of Romanticism (dewy-eyed Catalan landscapes). In addition, you'll find minor works by major—if not necessarily Catalan—names (Velázquez, El Greco, Tintoretto, Rubens, and so on).

For a break, go to the right from the Gothic exit to glide under the huge **dome,** which once housed an ice-skating rink. This was the prime ceremony room and dance hall for the 1929 World Expo.

From the big ballroom, you can ride the glass elevator upstairs to the **Modern Art** section, which takes you on an enjoyable walk from the late 1800s to about 1950, offering a big chronological clockwise circle covering Symbolism, Modernisme, fin de siècle fun, Art Deco, and more. Find the early 20th-century paintings by Catalan artists Santiago Rusiñol and Ramon Casas, both of whom had a profound impact on a young Picasso (and, through him, on all of modern art). Crossing over to the "Modern 2" section, you'll find furniture (pieces that complement the empty spaces you likely saw in Gaudí's buildings—including a Gaudí wooden sofa), Impressionism, the shimmering landscapes of Joaquim Mir, and several distinctly Picasso portraits of women.

▲FUNDACIÓ JOAN MIRÓ

This museum has the best collection anywhere of work by Catalan artist Joan Miró (ZHOO-ahn mee-ROH, 1893-1983). Born in Barcelona, Miró divided his time between Paris and Catalunya (including Barcelona and his favorite village, Montroig del Camp). This building—designed in 1975 by Josep Lluís Sert, a friend of Miró and a student of Le Corbusier—was purpose-built to show off Miró's art.

The museum displays an always-changing, loosely chronological overview of Miró's work (as well as generally excellent temporary exhibits of 20th- and 21st-century artists). Consider renting the wonderful audioguide, well worth the extra charge.

If you don't like abstract art, you'll leave here scratching your head. But those who love this place are not faking it...they understand the genius of Miró and the fun of abstraction. Children probably understand it the best. Eavesdrop on what they say about the art; you may learn something.

Cost and Hours: €11; Tue-Sat 10:00-20:00 (until 19:00 Oct-June), Thu until 21:00, Sun 10:00-14:30, closed Mon; great audioguide-€5, 200 yards from top of funicular, Parc de Montjuïc, tel. 934-439-470, www.fundaciomiro-bcn.org. The museum has a restaurant, café, and bookshop (all accessible without museum ticket).

▲MAGIC FOUNTAINS

These fountains, near the base of Montjuïc, make an artistic, colorful, and coordinated splash some summer evenings, accompanied by music (free 20-minute shows start on the half-hour; almost always May-Sept Thu-Sun 21:00-23:00, no shows Mon-Wed; Oct-April Fri-Sat 19:00-20:30, no shows Sun-Thu, near Plaça d'Espanya).

LAS ARENAS MALL

This mall, on Plaça d'Espanya, was built inside a former bullring. It hosts the usual shops and a food-court basement. Worth ascending, the rooftop terrace offers fine views of Montjuïc (daily 10:00-22:00, small fee for exterior elevator to terrace, but interior escalators are free).

The Beaches and Nearby

▲BARCELONA'S BEACHES

Barcelona has created a summer tourist trade by building a huge stretch of beaches east of the town center. The overall scene is great for sunbathing and for an evening paseo before dinner. A bustling night scene keeps the harborfront busy until the wee hours.

This artificial peninsula, once the home of working-class sailors, is like a resort today—complete with lounge chairs, volleyball, showers, WCs, bike paths, and inviting beach bars called *chiringuitos*. Each beach segment has its own vibe: Sant Sebastià (closest, popular with older beachgoers and families), Barceloneta (with many seafood restaurants), Nova Icària (pleasant family beach), and Mar Bella (attracts a younger crowd, clothing-optional). As you wander the promenade, you'll see Frank Gehry's striking "fish" sculpture shining brightly in the sun.

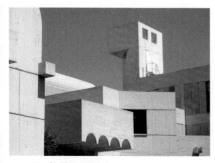

Fundació Joan Miró

Nova Icària beach

Getting There: The Barceloneta Metro stop leaves you blocks from the sand. To get to the beaches without a hike, take the bus. From the Ramblas, bus #59 will get you as far as Barceloneta Park; bus #D20 leaves from the Columbus Monument and follows a similar route. Bus #V15 runs from Plaça de Catalunya to the tip of Barceloneta (near the W Hotel).

Rick's Tip: Biking *is a joy in Citadel Park and along the beachfront. To rent a bike on the beach, try* **Biciclot** *(€5/hour, €10/3 hours, €17/24 hours, daily in summer 10:00-20:00, shorter hours off-season, Passeig Maritime 33, tel. 932-219-778, www.biking inbarcelona.net).*

CITADEL PARK (PARC DE LA CIUTADELLA)

In 1888, Barcelona's biggest, greenest park, originally the site of a much-hated military citadel, was transformed for a Universal Exhibition (world's fair). The stately Triumphal Arch at the top of the park, celebrating the removal of the citadel, was built as the main entrance. Inside you'll find wide pathways, plenty of trees and grass, a zoo, and museums of geology and zoology. Barcelona, one of Europe's most densely populated cities, suffers from a lack of real green space. This park is a haven and is especially enjoyable on weekends, when it teems with happy families. Enjoy the ornamental fountain that the young Antoni Gaudí helped design, and consider a jaunt in a rental rowboat on the lake in the center of the park. Check out the tropical Umbracle greenhouse and the Hivernacle winter garden, which has a pleasant café-bar (Mon-Sat 10:00-14:00 & 17:00-20:30, Sun 10:30-14:00, shorter hours off-season).

Cost and Hours: Park—free, daily 10:00 until dusk, north of França train station, Metro: Arc de Triomf, Barceloneta, or Ciutadella-Vila Olímpica.

EXPERIENCES

Shopping

The streets of the Barri Gòtic and El Born are bursting with characteristic hole-in-the-wall shops, while the Eixample is the upscale "uptown" shopping district. Near Plaça de Catalunya, Avinguda Portal de l'Angel has a staggering array of department and chain stores.

Souvenir Items: In this artistic city, consider picking up art prints, posters, and books. Museum gift shops (Picasso Museum, La Pedrera, and more) offer a bonanza of classy souvenirs. Home-decor shops have Euro-style housewares unavailable back home. Decorative tile and pottery (popularized by Modernist architects) and Modernista jewelry are easy to pack. Foodies might bring back olive oil, wine, spices (such as saffron or sea salts), cheese, or the local nougat treat, *torró*. An *espadenya*—or *espadrille* in Spanish—is the trendy canvas-and-rope shoe that originated as humble Catalan peasant footwear. For a souvenir of Catalan culture, consider a Catalan flag, a dragon of St. Jordi, or a jersey or scarf from the wildly popular Barça soccer team.

Barri Gòtic Shopping Stroll

This route, from the cathedral to the Ramblas, takes you through interesting streets lined with little shops. Avoid the midafternoon siesta and Sundays, when many shops are closed.

Face the cathedral, turn 90 degrees right, and exit Plaça Nova (just to the left of the Bilbao Berria "BB" restaurant) on the tight lane called Carrer de la Palla. This street has a half-dozen antique shops crammed with mothballed treasures. Mixed in are a few art galleries, offbeat shops, and a motorcycle museum. When you reach the fork in the road (where the inviting Caelum café is), you have a choice. If you go left, explore Carrer dels Banys Nous, another great shopping street (with Artesania Catalunya, a city-run market space featuring hand-made items from Catalan artisans).

To carry on toward the Ramblas, take the right fork. You'll pass by the Oro Líquido shop ("Liquid Gold," high-quality olive oils) and soon reach the Church of Santa Maria del Pi, ringed by a charming, café-lined square, Plaça de Sant Josep Oriol. Skirt around the right side of the church to find Plaça del Pi, a delightful square, with Josep Roca, a genteel gentleman's shop. Head up the narrow street, Carrer Petritxol, immediately left of the Josep Roca shop. The street is a fun combination of art galleries, jewelry shops, and simple places for hot chocolate and churros (check out Granja La Pallaresa, just after #11).

You'll dead-end onto Carrer de la Portaferrissa, with its international teen clothing stores. From here, head one block left to reach the Ramblas.

El Born

Although the main streets—Carrer de la Princesa, the perpendicular Carrer de Montcada, and the diagonal Carrer de l'Argenteria—are disappointing for shoppers, if you lose yourself in the smaller back lanes between those arteries, you'll discover a world of artsy, funky little boutiques. Stroll along Carrer dels Flassaders (behind the Picasso Museum), Carrer dels Banys Vells (between Montcada and l'Argenteria), and Carrer del Rec (just south of Passeig del Born)—and all of the little lanes crossing each of these streets.

Plaça de Catalunya and Avinguda Portal de l'Angel

Barcelona natives do most of their shopping at big department stores. You'll find the highest concentration of stores on Avinguda del Portal de l'Angel, which leads south from Plaça de Catalunya to the cathedral.

Plaça de Catalunya hosts the gigantic **El Corte Inglés,** the Spanish answer to one-stop shopping, with clothing, electronics, a travel agency, events box office, a basement supermarket, and a ninth-floor view café (Mon-Sat 10:00-22:00, closed Sun). Across the square is **FNAC**—a French department store that sells electronics, music, books, and tickets for major concerts and events (Mon-Sat

Open-air market in the Barri Gòtic

10:00-22:00, closed Sun).

Along Avinguda Portal de l'Angel, you'll see popular clothing chains such as **Zara**, the Barcelona-based **Mango, Desigual** (with boldly colorful designs), the teen-oriented French chain **Pimkie,** and the more sophisticated **Podivm** and **Blanco.**

The Eixample

This ritzy "uptown" district is home to some of the city's top-end shops. From Plaça de Catalunya, head north up Passeig de Gràcia, which starts out with lower-end international stores (like Zara) and ends up with top-end brands at the top (Gucci, Luis Vuitton, Escada, Chanel). Detour one block west to Rambla de Catalunya for more local (but still expensive) options for fashion, jewelry, perfume, home decor, and more.

Nightlife

For evening entertainment, Barcelonans stroll the streets, greet neighbors, pop into a bar for drinks and tapas, nurse a cocktail on a floodlit square, or enjoy a late meal. Dinnertime is around 22:00, and even families with children can be out well after midnight. If you're near Montjuïc, take in the hilltop view, Magic Fountains, or both.

Neighborhoods for Tapas and Drinks

These neighborhoods party late, but they're also lively for tapas and drinks in the early evening.

El Born: Passeig del Born, a broad park-like strip stretching from the Church of Santa Maria del Mar, is lined with inviting bars and nightspots. Wander the side streets for more options. Miramelindo (Passeig del Born 15) is a favorite for mojitos. La Vinya del Senyor is mellower, for tapas and wine on the square in front of Santa Maria del Mar.

Plaça Reial (in the Barri Gòtic): A block off the Ramblas, this palm-tree-graced square bustles with trendy eateries

charging inflated prices for pleasant outdoor tables—perfect for nursing a drink. Try the Ocaña Bar (€5-14 tapas, reasonable drinks, at #13).

Carrer de la Mercè: This Barri Gòtic street near the harbor is lined with salty tapas bars, with a few trendy ones mixed in.

Barceloneta: The broad beach is dotted with *chiringuitos*—shacks selling drinks and snacks, creating a fun, lively scene on a balmy summer evening.

Performing Arts

Barcelona always has a vast array of cultural events. Pick up the TI's free monthly English-language magazine, *In BCN Culture & Leisure.* Another good source of info is the Palau de la Virreina ticket office (daily 10:00-20:30, Ramblas 99, tel. 933-161-000, www.lavirreina.bcn.cat).

You can buy tickets directly from the venue's website, from box offices at El Corte Inglés or the FNAC store (both on Plaça de Catalunya), from Palau de Verreina, or at www.ticketmaster.es or www.telentrada.com.

The **Palace of Catalan Music,** with one of the finest Modernista interiors in town, offers everything from symphonic to Catalan folk songs to chamber music to flamenco (Palau de la Música Catalana, €20-50 tickets, purchase online or in person, box office open daily 9:30-21:00, Carrer Palau de la Música 4, Metro: Urquinaona, box office tel. 902-442-882).

The **Liceu Opera House** right in the heart of the Ramblas, is a sumptuous venue for opera, dance, and concerts (Gran Teatre del Liceu, tickets from €10, buy tickets online up to 1.5 hours before the show or in person, Ramblas 51, box office just around the corner at Carrer Sant Pau 1, Metro: Liceu, box office tel. 934-859-913, www.liceubarcelona.cat).

"Masters of Guitar" concerts are offered nearly nightly at 21:00 in the Barri Gòtic's **Church of Santa Maria del Pi** (€23 at the door, €4 less if you buy at least 3 hours ahead—look for ticket sellers in front of church and scattered throughout town, Plaça del Pi 7, or sometimes in Sant Jaume Church at Carrer de Ferran 28, tel. 647-514-513, www.maestrosdelaguitarra.com).

Though flamenco music is not typical of Barcelona (it's from Andalucía), **Tarantos** offers entertaining concerts nightly (€10, at 20:30, 21:30, and 22:30; Plaça Reial 17, tel. 933-191-789, www.masimas.com/en/tarantos). **La Pedrera** hosts "Summer Nights at La Pedrera" jazz concerts on its fanciful floodlit rooftop, weekends from June to September (book ahead at tel. 902-101-212 or www.lapedrera.com).

EATING

Barcelona, the capital of Catalan cuisine, offers a tremendous variety of colorful places to eat, ranging from workaday eateries to homey Catalan bistros *(cans)* to crowded tapas bars to avant-garde restaurants. Many eateries serve both stand-up tapas and sit-down meals, often starring seafood.

Basque-style tapas places are popular and user-friendly. Just scan the enticing buffets of bite-size tapas, grab what looks good, order a drink, and save your toothpicks (they'll count them up to tally your bill). I've listed my favorite tapas bars (Taverna Basca Irati, Xaloc, and Sagardi Euskal Taberna), though there are many others (look for *basca* or *euskal;* both mean "Basque").

Budget Meals: Sandwich shops are everywhere, serving made-to-order bocadillos. Choose between bright (mass-produced) chains such as **Bocatta** and **Pans & Company,** or colorful holes-in-the-wall. **Mucci's Pizza** has good, fresh, €2 pizza slices and empanadas (just off the Ramblas, at Bonsuccés 10 and Tallers 75), and **Wok to Walk** has takeaway noodle and rice dishes (€6-9, near the main door of the Boqueria Market). Kebab places are another standby for quick and tasty €3-4 meals. For a fast, affordable lunch with a view, the ninth-floor cafeteria at **El Corte Inglés department store** on Plaça de Catalunya can't be beat. Picnickers can buy groceries at the basement supermarket in El Corte Inglés, or at **La Boqueria Market** on the Ramblas.

The fun Pinotxo Bar at La Boqueria Market

Near the Ramblas

Do not eat or drink at the tourist traps on the Ramblas. Within a few steps of the Ramblas, you'll find handy lunch places, an inviting market hall, and some good vegetarian options.

Taverna Basca Irati serves hot and cold Basque *pintxos* for €2 each. These small open-faced sandwiches are like sushi on bread. Muscle in through the hungry local crowd, get an empty plate from the waiter, and then help yourself. Every few minutes, waiters circulate with platters of new, still-warm munchies. Grab munchies as they pass by...it's addictive (you'll be charged by the number of toothpicks left on your plate). For drink options, look for the printed menu on the wall in the back. Wash down your food with €3 glasses of Rioja (full-bodied red wine), Txakolí (sprightly Basque white wine), or *sidra* (apple wine) poured from on high to add oxygen and bring out the flavor (daily 11:00-24:00, a block off the Ramblas, behind arcade at Carrer del Cardenal Casanyes 17, Metro: Liceu, tel. 933-023-084).

Family-run since 1870, **Café Granja Viader** boasts about being the first dairy business to bottle and distribute milk in Spain. This quaint time capsule—specializing in baked and dairy treats, toasted sandwiches, and light meals—is ideal for a traditional breakfast. Or indulge your sweet tooth: Try a glass of *orxata* (or *horchata*—*chufa*-nut milk, summer only), *llet mallorquina* (Majorca-style milk with cinnamon, lemon, and sugar), *crema catalana* (crème brûlée, their specialty), or *suis* ("Swiss"—hot chocolate with a snow-cap of whipped cream). *Mel i mató* is fresh cheese with honey...very Catalan (Mon-Sat 9:00-13:00 & 17:00-21:00, closed Sun, a block off the Ramblas behind Betlem Church at Xuclà 4, Metro: Liceu, tel. 933-183-486).

Biocenter, a soup-and-salad restaurant popular with local vegetarians, takes its cooking seriously (€8-10 weekday

A Short, Sweet Walk

Here's a dessert walk in three stops—all within a three-minute walk of one another just off the Ramblas (Metro: Liceu). Start at the corner of Carrer de la Portaferrissa midway down the Ramblas. For the best atmosphere, begin your walk at about 18:00.

Torró: Walk down Carrer de la Portaferrissa to #8 (on the right). **Casa Colomina,** founded in 1908, specializes in homemade *torró* (*turrón* in Spanish)—nougat made with almond, honey, and sugar (€2.20 wrapped chunks on counter, daily 10:00-20:30). In summer, try the refreshing *orxata* drink (*horchata* in Spanish).

Churros con Chocolate: Continue down Carrer de la Portaferrissa, taking a right at Carrer Petritxol to #11 to the fun-loving **Granja La Pallaresa,** where you can dip greasy *churros* into cups of hot chocolate pudding for €4.50 (daily 9:00-13:00 & 16:00-21:00).

Chocolate: Continue down Carrer Petritxol to the square, Plaça del Pi, hook left through the two-part square, then left up Carrer del Pi to the corner of Carrer de la Portaferrissa. Founded in 1827, **Fargas,** a traditional chocolate shop, sells even little morsels by weight, so don't be shy (Mon-Sat 9:30-20:30, closed Sun).

lunch specials include soup or salad and plate of the day, €15 dinner specials, otherwise €7-9 salads and €12-13 main dishes, Mon-Sat 13:00-23:00, Sun 13:00-16:00, 2 blocks off the Ramblas at Carrer del Pintor Fortuny 25, Metro: Liceu, tel. 933-014-583).

Try eating at **La Boqueria Market** at least once. It's ringed by colorful, good-value eateries and several good bars—many with enticing seafood options. Lots of stalls sell fun takeaway food—especially fruit salads and fresh-squeezed juices—ideal for **picnics** (Mon-Sat 8:00-20:00). Just to the right as you enter the market, **Pinotxo Bar** is a fun, if touristy, spot for coffee, breakfast (spinach *tortillas*), or tapas. Fun-loving Juan and his family are La Boqueria fixtures. Be careful—this place can get expensive (Mercat de la Boqueria 466, tel. 933-171-731, www.pinotxobar.com). **Kiosko Universal** is popular for its great prices on wonderful fish dishes. As you enter the market from the Ramblas, it's all the way to the left. It's always packed, but less crowded before 12:30. If you see people waiting, go to the cashier to put your name on a list (€8-12 *platos del día* with different fresh-fish options, €8 mixed veggies, €10 mushroom stir-fries, tel. 933-178-286).

In the Barri Gòtic

In the atmospheric Gothic Quarter, you can choose between sit-down meals at restaurants or a string of tapas bars.

Restaurants

If you want to eat outdoors on a convivial, mellow square, **Café de l'Academia** is the place. They serve refined market-fresh Catalan cuisine. The candlelit, air-conditioned interior is rustic yet elegant, with soft jazz, flowers, and modern art. Reservations are smart (€10-15 first courses, €13-20 second courses, fixed-price lunch for €11.50 at the bar or €15 at a table, Mon-Fri 13:00-15:30 & 20:00-23:00, closed Sat-Sun, near the City Hall square, off Carrer de Jaume I, up Carrer de la Dagueria at Carrer dels Lledó 1, Metro: Jaume I, tel. 933-198-253).

Els Quatre Gats was once the haunt of the Modernista greats—including a teenaged Picasso, who first publicly displayed his art here, and architect Josep Puig i Cadafalch, who designed the building. Inspired by Paris' famous Le Chat Noir café/cabaret, Els Quatre Gats ("The Four Cats") celebrated all that was modern at the turn of the 20th century. You can snack or drink at the bar, or go into the back for a sit-down meal (€18 three-course lunch special Mon-Fri 13:00-16:00, €12-28 plates, daily 10:00-24:00, just steps off Avinguda del Portal de l'Angel at Carrer de Montsió 3, Metro: Catalunya, tel. 933-024-140).

Xaloc offers nicely presented gourmet tapas in a woody, modern, and spacious dining room, with fun energy, good service, and reasonable prices. The walls are covered with *Ibérica* hamhocks and wine bottles. They focus on homestyle Catalan classics and serve only one top-quality ham. A gazpacho, plank of ham, *pa amb tomàquet*, and nice glass of wine make a terrific light meal (€3-8 tapas, €6-14 main dishes, open daily, drinks and cold tapas 11:00-23:00, kitchen open 13:00-17:00 & 19:00-23:00, a block toward the cathedral from Plaça de Sant Josep Oriol at Carrer de la Palla 13, Metro: Catalunya, tel. 933-011-990).

Bar del Pi is a simple, hardworking bar serving good salads, sandwiches, and tapas. It has just a handful of tables on the most inviting little square in the Barri Gòtic (daily 9:00-23:00 except closed Tue in winter, Plaça de Sant Josep Oriol 1, Metro: Liceu, tel. 933-022-123).

Restaurant Agut, around since 1924, features a comfortable, wood-paneled dining room that's modern and sophisticated, but still retains a slight bohemian air. The pictures lining the walls are by Catalan artists who are said to have exchanged their canvases for a meal. The menu includes tasty traditional Catalan food (€14 three-course weekday lunch special, €10-15 starters, €13-29 main dishes, Tue-Sat 13:30-16:00 & 20:30-23:30, Sun 13:30-16:00, closed Mon, just up from Carrer de la Mercè and the harbor at Carrer d'En Gignàs 16, Metro: Jaume I, tel. 933-151-709).

La Crema Canela, a few steps above Plaça Reial, feels cozier than the restaurants on that atmospheric square, which

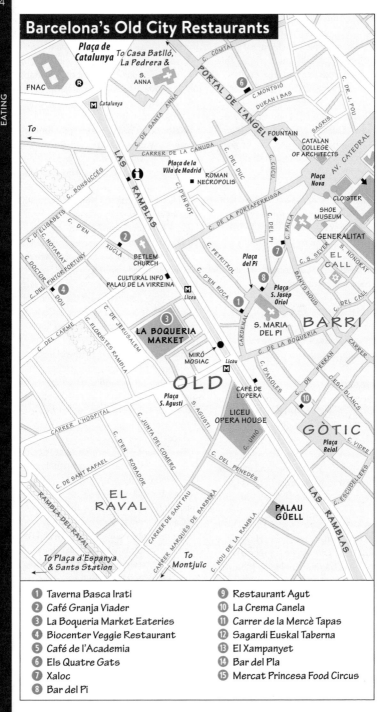

Barcelona's Old City Restaurants

1 Taverna Basca Irati
2 Café Granja Viader
3 La Boqueria Market Eateries
4 Biocenter Veggie Restaurant
5 Café de l'Academia
6 Els Quatre Gats
7 Xaloc
8 Bar del Pi
9 Restaurant Agut
10 La Crema Canela
11 Carrer de la Mercè Tapas
12 Sagardi Euskal Taberna
13 El Xampanyet
14 Bar del Pla
15 Mercat Princesa Food Circus

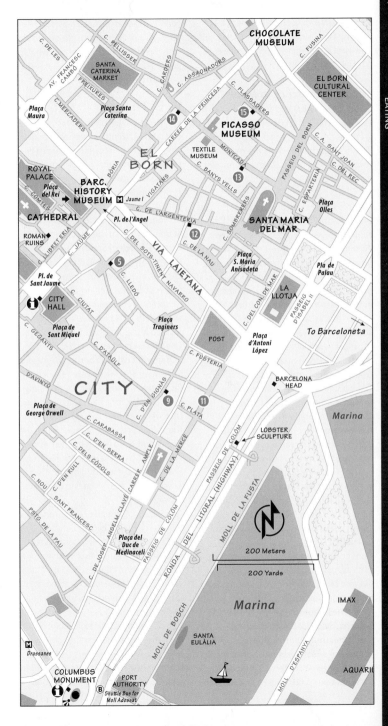

CHOCOLATE
MUSEUM

SANTA
CATERINA
MARKET

EL BORN
CULTURAL
CENTER

C. DE LES
C. PELLISSER
AV. FRANCESC CAMBO
FREIXURES
C. CARDERS
C. ASSAONADORS
C. FUSINA

Plaça
Maura

C. MERCADERS

Plaça Santa
Caterina

CARRER DE LA PRINCESA
C. FLASSADERS

14

EL
BORN

15
PICASSO
MUSEUM

PASSEIG DEL BORN
C. A. SANT JOAN
C. DEL REC

ROYAL
PALACE

BÒRIA

TEXTILE
MUSEUM

MONTCADA

C. ESPARTERIA

Plaça
Olles

BARC.
HISTORY
MUSEUM

Plaça
del Rei

C. VIGATANS

C. BANYS VELLS
13

Jaume I

C. COMTES

CATHEDRAL

C. DE L'ARGENTERIA

SANTA MARIA
DEL MAR

Pl. de l'Angel

ROMAN
RUINS

C. LLIBRETERIA

C. JAUME

12

C. DE LA NAU

Plaça
S. Maria
Anisadeta

Pla de
Palau

Pl. de
Sant Jaume

5

C. LLEDÓ

VIA LAIETANA

C. SOTS-TINENT NAVARRO

C. SOMBRERERS

C. DEL CON. DE MAR

LA
LLOTJA

PASSEIG D'ISABEL II

CITY
HALL

C. CIUTAT

Plaça
Traginers

To Barceloneta

C. GEGANTS

Plaça de
Sant Miquel

C. D'ATAÜLF

POST

Plaça
d'Antoni
López

D'AVINYO

CITY

C. FUSTERIA

BARCELONA
HEAD

Plaça de
George Orwell

C. D'EN GIGNAS

9

11
C. PLATA

Marina

C. CARABASSA

LOBSTER
SCULPTURE

C. D'EN SERRA

PASSEIG DE COLÓM

C. DELS CÒDOLS

C. DE LA MERCE

MOLL DE LA FUSTA

C. NOU
C. D'EN RULL

CARRER AMPLE

ANSELM CLAVE

C. SANT FRANCESC

PSTG. DE LA PAU

RONDA DEL LITORAL (HIGHWAY)

N

200 Meters

Plaça del
Duc de
Medinaceli

PASSEIG DE COLÓM

C. DE JOSEF

MOLL DE BOSCH

200 Yards

Marina

IMAX

Drassanes

SANTA
EULÀLIA

MOLL D'ESPANYA

AQUARIU

COLUMBUS
MONUMENT

PORT
AUTHORITY

B Shuttle Bus for
Moll Adossat

are overrun with tourists. And it takes reservations (Mon-Thu 13:00-23:00, Fri-Sun until 23:30, Passatge de Madoz 6, tel. 933-182-744).

Tapas on Carrer de la Mercè

Carrer de la Mercè lets you experience a rare, unvarnished bit of old Barcelona with great *tascas*—colorful local tapas bars. The neighborhood's dark, the regulars are rough-edged, and you'll get a glimpse of a crusty Barcelona from before the affluence hit.

From the bottom of the Ramblas (near the Columbus Monument, Metro: Drassanes), hike east along Carrer de Josep Anselm Clavé. When you reach Plaça de la Mercè, follow the small street (Carrer de la Mercè) that runs along the right side of the square's church. For a montage of edible memories, wander the next three or four blocks and consider these spots, stopping wherever looks most inviting. Most of these places close down around 23:00. For more refined bar-hopping, skip over to Carrer Ample and Carrer d'En Gignàs, inland streets parallel to Carrer de la Mercè.

Bar Celta (marked *la pulpería,* at #16) has less character than the others, but eases you into the scene with fried fish, octopus, and *patatas bravas,* all with Galician Ribeiro wine. Farther down at the corner (#28), **La Plata** keeps things wonderfully simple, serving extremely cheap plates of sardines (€3), little salads, and small glasses of keg wine (€1). **Tasca el Corral** (#17) serves mountain favorites from northern Spain by the half-*ración,* such as *queso de cabrales,* chorizo *al diablo,* and *cecina* (cured meat, like *jamón* but made from beef)—drink them with *sidra* (hard cider sold by the bottle-€6). **Sidrería Tasca La Socarrena** (#21) offers hard cider from Asturias in €6.50 bottles with *queso de cabrales* and chorizo. At the end of Carrer de la Mercè, **Cervecería Vendimia** slings tasty clams and mussels

(hearty *raciones* for €4-6 a plate). They don't do smaller portions, so order sparingly. Sit at the bar and point to what looks good. The house specialty, *pulpo* (octopus) is more expensive.

El Born

El Born (a.k.a. La Ribera) sparkles with eclectic and trendy as well as subdued and classy little restaurants hidden in the small lanes surrounding the Church of Santa Maria del Mar. Wander around for 15 minutes and pick the place that tickles your gastronomic fancy. Consider starting off your evening with a glass of fine wine at one of the *enotecas* on the square facing the Church of Santa Maria del Mar. Most of my picks are either on Carrer de l'Argenteria (stretching from the church to the cathedral area) or on or near Carrer de Montcada. Many restaurants and shops in this area are, like the nearby Picasso Museum, closed on Mondays. Use Metro: Jaume I.

Sagardi Euskal Taberna offers tempting *pintxos* and *montaditos* (small open-faced sandwiches) at €2 each—along its huge bar. Ask for a plate and graze (just take whatever looks good). You can sit on the square with your plunder for about 20 percent extra. Wash it down with Txakolí, a Basque white wine poured from the spout of a huge wooden barrel into a glass as you watch. Study the two price lists—bar and terrace—posted at the bar (daily 12:00-24:00, Carrer de l'Argenteria 62-64, tel. 933-199-993). Hiding behind the tapas bar is the mod and minimalist restaurant, **Sagardi** (€11-24 first courses for two, €20-28 second courses, plan on €50 for dinner; daily 13:00-16:00 & 20:00-24:00, Carrer de l'Argenteria 62, tel. 933-199-993, www.sagardi.com).

El Xampanyet, a colorful family-run bar with a fun-loving staff (Juan Carlos, his mom, and the man who may be his father), specializes in tapas and anchovies. Don't be put off by the seafood

Catalan Cuisine

Like its culture and language, Catalan food is a fusion of styles and influences. Cod, hake, tuna, squid, and anchovies appear on many menus, and you'll see Catalan favorites such as *fideuà*, a thin, flavor-infused noodle served with seafood—a kind of Catalan paella—and *arròs negre,* black rice cooked in squid ink. *Pa amb tomàquet* is the classic Catalan way to eat your bread—toasted white bread with olive oil, tomato, and a pinch of salt. It's often served with tapas and used to make sandwiches. As everywhere in Spain, Catalan cooks love garlic and olive oil—many dishes are soaked in both.

Catalan cuisine can be heavy for Americans more accustomed to salads, fruits, and grains. A few perfectly good vegetarian and lighter options exist, but you'll have to seek them out. The secret to getting your veggies at restaurants is to order two courses, because the first course generally has a green option. Resist the cheese-and-ham appetizers and instead choose first-course menu items such as creamed vegetable soup, *parrillada de verduras* (sautéed vegetables), or *ensalada mixta.* (Spaniards rarely eat only a salad, so salads tend to be small and simple—just iceberg lettuce, tomatoes, and maybe olives and tuna.)

While the famous cured *jamón* (ham) is not as typically Catalan as it is Spanish, you'll still find lots of it in Catalunya. Another popular Spanish dish is the empanada—a pastry turnover filled with seasoned meat and vegetables. The cheapest meal is a simple *bocadillo de jamón* (ham sandwich on a baguette), sold virtually everywhere.

from a tin: Catalans like it this way. A *sortido* (assorted plate) of *carne* (meat) or *pescado* (fish) with *pa amb tomàquet* makes for a fun meal. It's filled with tourists during the day, but is a local favorite after dark. The scene is great, but it can be tough without Spanish skills. Plan on spending €25 for a meal with wine (same price at bar or table, Tue-Sat 12:00-15:30 & 19:00-23:00, Sun 12:00-16:00, closed Mon, a half-block beyond the Picasso Museum at Carrer de Montcada 22, tel. 933-197-003).

Local favorite **Bar del Pla** is near the Picasso Museum but far enough away from the tourist crowds. Overlooking a tiny crossroads next to Barcelona's oldest church, this brightly lit, classic diner serves traditional Catalan dishes, *raciones,* and tapas. Crispy beef with foie gras (€6) is a highlight. The local IPA on tap is a change of pace from regular Spanish beer. Prices are the same at the bar or at a table, but eating at the bar puts you in the middle of a great scene (€6-15 tapas, Mon-Sat 12:00-23:00, closed Sun; with your back to the Picasso Museum, head right two blocks past Carrer de la Princesa to Carrer de Montcada 2; tel. 932-683-003, www. bardelpla.cat).

Corporate venture **Mercat Princesa Food Circus** fills an old palace with a hive of trendy new bars and eateries sharing a central zone of tables. The energy is great, as is the variety: oysters, sushi, paella, and pizza. It's fun to simply explore, but at busy times, expect to wait in successive slow-moving lines (daily 12:30-24:00, behind the Picasso Museum, Carrer dels Flassaders 21, tel. 932-681-518, www.mer catprincesa.com).

In the Eixample

The people-packed boulevards of the Eixample are lined with appetizing eateries featuring breezy outdoor seating. For the best variety, walk down Rambla de Catalunya.

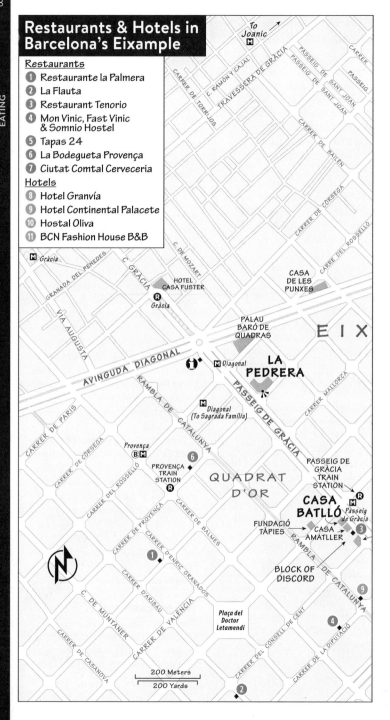

Restaurants & Hotels in Barcelona's Eixample

Restaurants
1. Restaurante la Palmera
2. La Flauta
3. Restaurant Tenorio
4. Mon Vinic, Fast Vinic & Somnio Hostel
5. Tapas 24
6. La Bodegueta Provença
7. Ciutat Comtal Cerveceria

Hotels
8. Hotel Granvía
9. Hotel Continental Palacete
10. Hostal Oliva
11. BCN Fashion House B&B

200 Meters

200 Yards

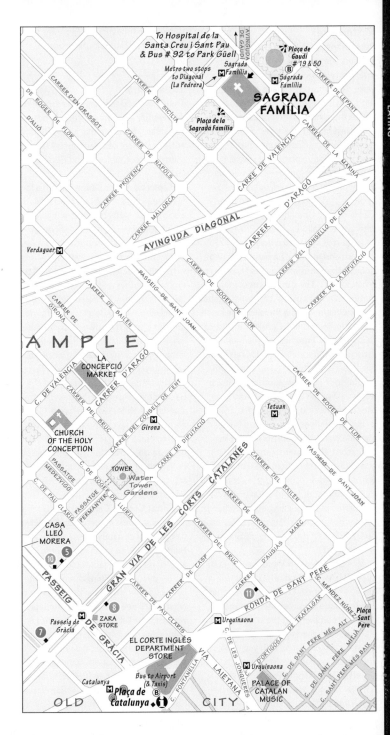

Restaurants

Restaurante la Palmera serves a mix of Catalan, Mediterranean, and French cuisine in an elegant room with bottle-lined walls. This untouristy place offers great food, service, and value. They have three zones: the classic main room, a more forgettable adjacent room, and a few outdoor tables. I like the classic room. Reservations are smart (€12-19 plates, creative €23 six-plate *degustation* lunch—also available during dinner Mon-Wed, open Mon-Sat 13:00-15:45 & 20:00-23:15, closed Sun, Carrer d'Enric Granados 57, at the corner with Carrer Mallorca, Metro: Provença, tel. 934-532-338, www.lapalmera.cat).

Fresh and modern, **La Flauta** fills two floors with enthusiastic eaters (I prefer the ground floor). The fun, no-stress menu features €5 small plates, creative €5 *flauta* sandwiches, and a €13 three-course lunch deal including a drink. Consider the list of *tapas del día*. Order high on the menu for a satisfying, moderately priced meal (Mon-Sat 7:00-24:00, closed Sun, upbeat and helpful staff, no reservations, just off Carrer de la Diputació at Carrer d'Aribau 23, Metro: Universitat, tel. 933-237-038).

Hidden between the famous buildings and clamoring tourists in the Block of Discord, **Restaurant Tenorio** is an actual restaurant (no tapas!). This modern, dressy, and spacious place serves a mix of international and Catalan dishes, concocted in the bustling open kitchen at the back (€10 salads, €15 plates, Passeig de Gràcia 37, Metro: Passeig de Gràcia, tel. 932-720-592).

Sleek, trendy **Mon Vinic** is evangelical about local wines and offers an amazing eating experience. Their renowned chef creates made-to-order Mediterranean dishes to complement the wine (€12-18 starters—designed to share, €8 creative tapas, €25 main dishes with vegetables and potatoes, €20 fixed-price lunch, Diputació 249, Metro: Passeig de Gràcia, tel. 932-726-187, www.monvinic.com). **Fast Vinic** is the associated fast-food and sandwich bar next door (Mon-Sat 12:00-24:00, closed Sun, Diputació 251, tel. 934-873-241).

Tapas Bars

Trendy and touristic tapas bars in the Eixample offer a cheery welcome. These are particularly handy to Plaça de Catalunya and the Passeig de Gràcia artery (closest Metro stops: Catalunya and Passeig de Gràcia).

Tapas 24 makes eating fun. This local favorite, with a few street tables, fills a spot a few steps below street level with happy energy, friendly service, funky decor (white counters and mirrors), and good yet pricey tapas. Along with daily specials, the menu has all the typical standbys and quirky inventions (such as the tiny McFoie burger—order it well-done if you don't want it to moo on your plate). The owner, Carles Abellan, is one of Barcelona's hot chefs; although his famous fare is pricey, you can enjoy it without going broke. Prices are the same whether you dine at the bar, a table, or outside. Figure about €50 for lunch for two with wine. Come early or wait; no reservations are taken (€4-14 tapas, €12-18 plates, Mon-Sat 9:00-24:00, closed Sun, just off Passeig de Gràcia at Carrer de la Diputació 269, tel. 934-880-977, www.carlesabellan.es/restaurantes-tapas-24).

Ciutat Comtal Cerveceria brags that it serves the best *montaditos* (€2-4 little open-faced sandwiches) and beers in Barcelona. It's an Eixample favorite, with an elegant bar and tables plus good seating for people-watching out on the Rambla de Catalunya. It's packed 21:00-23:00, when you'll need to put your name on a wait list. The list of tapas and *montaditos* is easy and fun, with great variety (including daily specials, most tapas around €4-10, daily 8:00-24:00, facing the intersection of Gran Via de les Corts Catalanes and Rambla de Catalunya at Rambla de Catalunya 18, tel. 933-181-997).

SLEEPING

Although Barcelona is Spain's most expensive city, it still has reasonably priced rooms. Book well in advance. Cheap places are more crowded in summer. Business-class hotels fill up in winter and offer discounts in summer (and on weekends)—when you can often get modern comfort in a centrally located business hotel for about the same price (€100) as you'll pay for ramshackle charm.

Near Plaça de Catalunya

These hotels are on big streets within two blocks of Barcelona's exuberant central square, where the Old City meets the Eixample. Expect shiny reception areas, modern bedrooms, and air-conditioning. As business-class hotels, they have hard-to-pin-down prices that fluctuate with demand. I've listed the average rate you'll pay. Most of these are located between two Metro stops: Catalunya and Universitat; if arriving by Aerobus, note that the bus stops at both places. For hotels on busy Carrer Pelai, request a quieter room in back.

$$$ Hotel Catalonia Plaça Catalunya has four stars, an elegant old entryway with a modern reception area, splashy public spaces, slick marble and hardwood floors, 140 comfortable but simple rooms, and a garden courtyard with a pool a world away

from the big-city noise (Db-€200 but can swing much higher or lower with demand, extra bed-€38, breakfast-€19, air-con, elevator, a half-block off Plaça de Catalunya at Carrer de Bergara 11, Metro: Catalunya, tel. 933-015-151, www.hoteles-catalonia.com, catalunya@hoteles-catalonia.es).

$$ Hotel Denit is a small, stylish, 36-room hotel on a pedestrian street two blocks off Plaça de Catalunya. It's chic, minimalist, and fun: Guidebook tips decorate the halls, and the rooms are sized like T-shirts ("small" Sb-€79-109, "medium" Db-€99-119, "large" Db-€119-144, "XL" Db-€149-164, more on Fri-Sat, includes breakfast when you book directly with the hotel, air-con, elevator, Carrer d'Estruc 24, Metro: Catalunya, tel. 935-454-000, www.denit.com, info@denit.com).

$$ Hotel Inglaterra has 60 rooms, a more traditional style, a rooftop terrace, and mini swimming pool (Sb-€119, Db-€139, higher rates Fri-Sat, €20-40 more for bigger "deluxe" rooms, breakfast €15, air-con, elevator, Carrer de Pelai 14, Metro: Universitat, tel. 935-051-100, www.hotel-inglaterra.com, reservas@hotel-inglaterra.com).

$$ Hotel Reding, on a quiet street a 10-minute walk west of the Ramblas and Plaça de Catalunya action, is slick and sleek, renting 44 mod rooms at a reasonable price (Db-€130, €15-30 more for deluxe rooms, extra bed-€33, €15 breakfast, prices go up during trade fairs, air-con, elevator, Carrer de Gravina 5, Metro: Universitat, tel. 934-121-097, www.hotelreding.com, recepcion@hotelreding.com).

$$ Hotel Lleó (YAH-oh) is well-run, with 92 big, bright, and comfortable rooms; a great breakfast room; a generous lounge; and a small rooftop pool (Db-€140 but varies with demand, extra bed-about €30, breakfast-€13, air-con, elevator, Carrer de Pelai 22, midway between Metros: Universitat and Catalunya, tel. 933-181-312, www.hotel-lleo.com, info@hotel-lleo.com).

Sleep Code

Abbreviations: S=Single, D=Double/Twin, T=Triple, Q=Quad, b=bathroom

Price Rankings for Double Rooms: $$$** Most rooms €150 or more, **$$** €100-150, **$ €100 or less

Notes: Some hotels include the 10 percent IVA tax in the room price; others add it to your bill. Prices change; verify rates online or by email. For the best prices, book directly with the hotel.

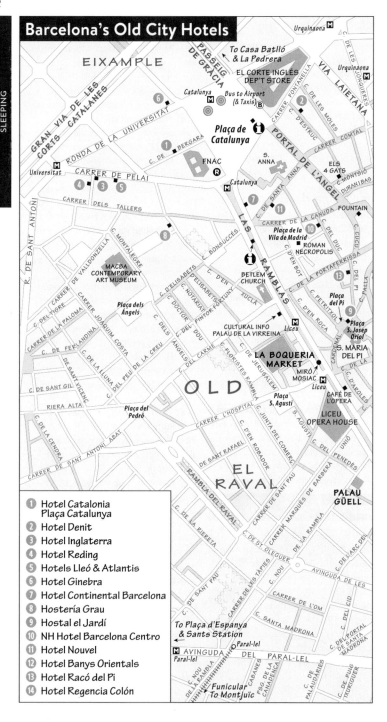

Barcelona's Old City Hotels

1. Hotel Catalonia Plaça Catalunya
2. Hotel Denit
3. Hotel Inglaterra
4. Hotel Reding
5. Hotels Lleó & Atlantis
6. Hotel Ginebra
7. Hotel Continental Barcelona
8. Hostería Grau
9. Hostal el Jardí
10. NH Hotel Barcelona Centro
11. Hotel Nouvel
12. Hotel Banys Orientals
13. Hotel Racó del Pi
14. Hotel Regencia Colón

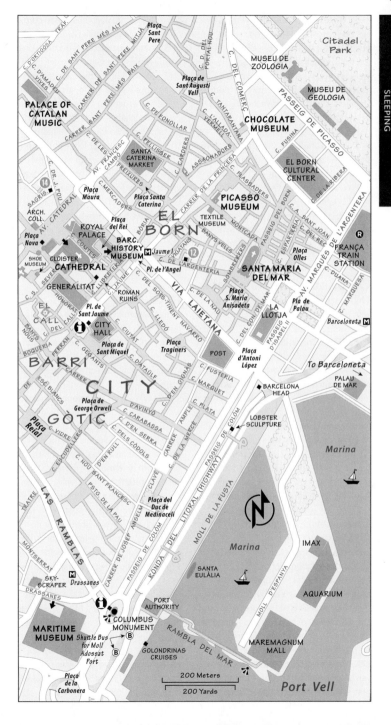

$$ Hotel Atlantis is solid, with 50 big, nondescript, modern rooms and fair prices for the location (Sb-€80, Db-€120, Tb-€150, check website for deals, includes breakfast, air-con, elevator, Carrer de Pelai 20, midway between Metros: Universitat and Catalunya, tel. 933-189-012, www.hotelatlantis-bcn.com, inf@hotelatlantis-bcn.com).

$ Hotel Ginebra is a modern, fresh version of the old-school *pension* in a classic, well-located building at the corner of Plaça Catalunya (Sb-€50-120, Db-€70-150, Tb-€80-180, Qb-€90-240, breakfast-€8, laundry, air-con, elevator, Rambla de Catalunya 1, Metro: Catalunya, tel. 932-502-017, www.barcelonahotelginebra.com, info@barcelonahotelginebra.com).

On or near the Ramblas

These places are generally family-run, with ad-lib furnishings, more character, and lower prices.

$$ Hotel Continental Barcelona, in a building overlooking the top of the Ramblas, has 40 comfortable but faded rooms that come with clashing carpets and wallpaper. Choose between your own little Ramblas-view balcony or a quieter back room. The free breakfast and all-day snack-and-drink bar are a plus (Sb-€110, Db-€130, twin Db-€140, Db with Ramblas balcony-€150, extra bed-€40/adult or €20/child, air-con, elevator, quiet terrace, Ramblas 138, Metro: Catalunya, tel. 933-012-570, www.hotelcontinental.com, barcelona@hotelcontinental.com).

$$ Hostería Grau is homey, family-run, and eco-conscious (LEED-certified). It has 24 cheery rooms a few blocks off the Ramblas in the colorful university district—but double-glazed windows keep it quiet (Db-€115-135, €20 more for superior Db, €50 more for family room, 5 percent discount for booking directly, breakfast extra, strict cancellation policy, air-con, elevator, some rooms with balcony, 200 yards up Carrer dels Tallers from the Ramblas at Ramelleres 27, Metro: Catalunya,

tel. 933-018-135, www.hostalgrau.com, bookgreen@hostalgrau.com, Monica).

$ Hostal el Jardí offers 40 tight, plain, comfy rooms on a breezy square in the Barri Gòtic. Many of the rooms come with petite balconies (for an extra charge) and enjoy an almost Parisian ambience. Book well in advance, as this family-run place has an avid following (small interior Db-€75, nicer interior Db-€90, outer Db with balcony or twin with window-€95, large outer Db with balcony or square-view terrace-€110, no charge for extra bed, breakfast-€6, air-con, elevator, some stairs, halfway between Ramblas and cathedral at Plaça Sant Josep Oriol 1, Metro: Liceu, tel. 933-015-900, www.eljardi-barcelona.com, reservations@eljardi-barcelona.com).

In the Old City

These accommodations are buried in Barcelona's Old City, mostly in the Barri Gòtic. The Catalunya, Liceu, and Jaume I Metro stops flank this tight tangle of lanes; I've noted which stops are best for each.

$$$ NH Hotel Barcelona Centro, with 156 rooms and tasteful chain-hotel predictability, is professional yet friendly, buried in the Barri Gòtic just three blocks off the Ramblas (Db-€160, but rates fluctuate with demand, €25 more for bigger superior rooms, breakfast-€15, air-con, elevator, pay guest computer, Carrer del Duc 15, Metro: Catalunya or Liceu, tel. 932-703-410, www.nh-hotels.com, barcelonacentro@nh-hotels.com).

$$$ Hotel Nouvel, in an elegant, Victorian-style building on a handy pedestrian street, offers more character than the others, boasting royal lounges and 78 comfy rooms (Sb-€75-100, Db-€110-165, online deals can be far cheaper, extra bed-€35, includes breakfast, €20 deposit for TV remote, air-con, elevator, pay Wi-Fi, Carrer de Santa Anna 20, Metro: Catalunya, tel. 933-018-274, www.hotelnouvel.com, info@hotelnouvel.com).

\$\$ Hotel Banys Orientals, a modern, boutique place, has refreshingly straightforward prices. Its 43 restful rooms are located in El Born on a pedestrianized street between the cathedral and Church of Santa Maria del Mar (Sb-€96, Db-€116, breakfast-€14, air-con, Carrer de l'Argenteria 37, 50 yards from Metro: Jaume I, tel. 932-688-460, www.hotelbanysorientals. com, reservas@hotelbanysorientals. com). They also run the adjacent, recommended El Senyor Parellada restaurant.

\$\$ Hotel Racó del Pi, part of the H10 hotel chain, is a quality, professional place with generous public spaces and 37 modern, bright, quiet rooms. It's located on a wonderful pedestrian street immersed in the Barri Gòtic (Db-often around €130-145, can be as low as €80, cheaper for booking "nonrefundable" online, breakfast-€16, air-con, around the corner from Plaça del Pi at Carrer del Pi 7, 3-minute walk from Metro: Liceu, tel. 933-426-190, www. h10hotels.com, h10.raco.delpi@h10.es).

\$\$ Hotel Regencia Colón, in a handy location one block in front of the cathedral, offers 50 slightly older but solid, classy, and well-priced rooms (Db-€120-155 but fluctuates with demand, extra bed-€37, breakfast-€13, air-con, elevator, Carrer dels Sagristans 13, Metro: Jaume I, tel. 933-189-858, www.hotelregencia colon.com, info@hotelregenciacolon. com).

In the Eixample

For an uptown neighborhood, sleep in the Eixample, a 10-minute walk from the Ramblas action. Most of these places use the Passeig de Gràcia or Catalunya Metro stops. Because these stations are so huge—especially Passeig de Gràcia, which sprawls underground for a few blocks—study the maps posted in the station to establish which exit you want before surfacing.

\$\$ Hotel Granvía, filling a palatial, brightly renovated 1870s mansion, offers a large, peaceful sun patio, several comfortable common areas, and 58 spacious modern rooms (Sb-€75-185, Db-€90-180, superior Db-€105-225, family room-€150-260, breakfast €14, air-con, elevator, Gran Via de les Corts Catalanes 642, Metro: Passeig de Gràcia, tel. 933-181-900, www. hotelgranvia.com, hgranvia@nnhotels. com).

\$\$ Hotel Continental Palacete, with 22 small rooms, fills a 100-year-old chandeliered mansion. With flowery wallpaper and ornately gilded stucco, it's more gaudy than Gaudí, but it's also friendly, quiet, and well-located. Guests have unlimited access to the outdoor terrace and the fruit, veggie, and drink buffet (Sb-€114, Db-€153, €35-45 more for bigger and brighter view rooms, extra bed-€55/adult or €40/child, includes breakfast, air-con, 2 blocks northwest of Plaça de Catalunya at corner of Rambla de Catalunya and Carrer de la Diputació, Rambla de Catalunya 30, Metro: Passeig de Gràcia, tel. 934-457-657, www.hotelcontinental. com, palacete@hotelcontinental.com).

\$ Hostal Oliva, family-run with care, has 15 spartan but bright and high-ceilinged rooms and no breakfast or public spaces. It's on the fourth floor of a classic old Eixample building in a perfect location, just a couple of blocks above Plaça de Catalunya (S-€41, Sb-€55, D-€71, Db-€95, elevator, corner of Passeig de Gràcia and Carrer de la Diputació, Passeig de Gràcia 32, Metro: Passeig de Gràcia, tel. 934-880-162, www.hostaloliva.com, hostal oliva@lasguias.com).

\$ BCN Fashion House B&B has 10 basic rooms, a peaceful lounge, and a leafy backyard terrace on the first floor of a nondescript old building (S-€36-56, D-€56-83, bigger "veranda" D-€73-93, Db-€90-125, 2-night minimum, includes breakfast, between Carrer d'Ausiàs Marc and Ronda de Sant Pere at Carrer del Bruc 13, just steps from Metro: Urquinaona, mobile 637-904-044, www.bcnfashion house.com, info@bcnfashionhouse.com).

Hostels

$ Somnio Hostel, an innovative smaller place, has nine simple, clean rooms (S-€49-75, D-€57-84, Db-€65-99, air-con, self-service laundry, Carrer de la Diputació 251, second floor, Metro: Passeig de Gràcia, tel. 932-725-308, www.somniohostels.com, info@somniohostels.com). They have a second location that's five blocks farther out.

TRANSPORTATION

Getting Around Barcelona

Barcelona's Metro and bus system is run by **TMB**—Transports Metropolitans de Barcelona. Ask for TMB's excellent Metro/bus map at the TI, larger stations, or the TMB information counter in the Sants Train Station. Metro maps are often included on tourist maps as well (tel. 902-075-027, www.tmb.cat).

By Metro

The city's Metro, among Europe's best, connects just about every place you'll visit. A **single-ride ticket** (*bitllet senzill*) costs €2.15. The **T10 Card** is a great deal—€9.95 gives you 10 rides (cutting the per-ride cost more than in half). The card is shareable, even by companions traveling with you the entire ride (insert the card in the machine once per passenger). The back of your T10 Card will show how many trips were taken, with the time and date of each ride. One "ride" covers you for 1.25 hours of unlimited use on all Metro and local bus lines, as well as local rides on the RENFE and Rodalies de Catalunya train lines (including rides to the airport and train station) and the suburban FGC trains. Transfers made within your 1.25-hour limit are not counted as a new ride, but you still must revalidate your T10 Card whenever you transfer.

Multiday **"Hola BCN!" passes** are also available. Machines at the Metro entrance have English instructions and sell all types of tickets (€14/2 days, €20.50/3 days, €26.50/4 days, €32/5 days; most machines accept credit/debit cards as well as cash).

Enter the Metro by inserting your ticket into the turnstile (with the arrow pointing in), then reclaim it. Follow signs for your line and direction. On board, most trains have handy lighted displays that indicate upcoming stops. Because the lines cross one another multiple times, there can be several ways to make any one journey. (Keep a general map with you—especially if you're transferring.) Hang onto your ticket until you have exited the subway. You don't need the ticket to exit, but inspectors occasionally ask to see it. When riding the Metro, watch your valuables.

Barcelona has several color-coded lines. Most useful for tourists and pickpockets is the **L3 (green)** line, with handy city-center stops:

Sants Estació—Main train station

Espanya—Plaça d'Espanya, with access to the lower part of Montjuïc and trains to Montserrat

Paral·lel—Funicular to the top of Montjuïc

Drassanes—Bottom of the Ramblas, near Maritime Museum and Maremagnum mall

Liceu—Middle of the Ramblas, near the heart of the Barri Gòtic and cathedral

Plaça de Catalunya—Top of the Ramblas and main square with TI, airport bus, and lots of transportation connections

Passeig de Gràcia—Classy Eixample street at the Block of Discord; also connection to L2 (purple) line to Sagrada Família and L4 (yellow) line (described below)

Diagonal—Gaudí's La Pedrera

The **L4 (yellow)** line, which crosses the L3 (green) line at Passeig de Gràcia, is also useful. Helpful stops include **Joanic** (bus #116 to Park Güell), **Jaume I** (between the Barri Gòtic/cathedral and El Born/Picasso Museum), and **Barceloneta** (at the south end of El Born, near the harbor action).

By Bus

Given the excellent Metro service, it's unlikely you'll spend much time on buses. Buses are useful for reaching Park Güell, connecting the sights on Montjuïc, and getting to the beach (also €2.15, covered by T10 Card, insert ticket in machine behind driver).

Also consider using the hop-on, hop-off Bus Turístic for transportation; it's far pricier than public transit, but it stops at the main sights (see page 41).

By Taxi

Barcelona is one of Europe's best taxi towns. Taxis are plentiful and honest. The light on top shows which tariff they're charging; a **green light** on the roof indicates that a taxi is available. **Cab rates** are reasonable (€2.10 drop charge, about €1/kilometer, these "*Tarif 2*" rates are in effect 8:00-20:00, pay higher "*Tarif 1*" rates off-hours, €2.10 surcharge to/from train station, €3.10 surcharge for airport or cruise port, other fees posted in window). Figure €10 from Ramblas to Sants Station.

Arriving and Departing
By Plane

Most international flights arrive at **El Prat de Llobregat Airport,** eight miles southwest of town. Some budget airlines, including Ryanair, fly into **Girona-Costa Brava Airport,** 60 miles north of Barcelona near Girona.

EL PRAT DE LLOBREGAT AIRPORT

Barcelona's **El Prat de Llobregat Airport** is eight miles southwest of town (airport code: BCN, info tel. 913-211-000, www.aena-aeropuertos.es). Its two large terminals are linked by shuttle buses. **Terminal 1** serves Air France, Air Europa, American, British Airways, Delta, Iberia, Lufthansa, United, US Airways, Vueling, and others. EasyJet and minor airlines use the older **Terminal 2,** which is divided into sections A, B, and C.

Terminal 1 and the bigger sections of Terminal 2 (A and B) each have a post office, a pharmacy, a left-luggage office, plenty of good cafeterias in the gate areas, and ATMs—use the bank-affiliated ATMs in the arrivals hall.

Getting Downtown: To reach central Barcelona cheaply and quickly, take the bus or train (about 30 minutes on either).

The **Aerobus** (#A1 and #A2, corresponding with Terminals 1 and 2) stops immediately outside the arrivals lobby of both terminals (and in each section of Terminal 2). In about 30 minutes, it takes you downtown, where it makes several stops, including Plaça d'Espanya and Plaça de Catalunya—near many of my recommended hotels (departs every 5 minutes, from airport 6:00-1:00 in the morning, from downtown 5:30-24:15, €5.90 one-way, €10.20 round-trip, buy ticket from machine or from driver, tel. 934-156-020, www.aerobusbcn.com).

The **RENFE train** (on the "R2 Sud" Rodalies line) leaves from Terminal 2 and involves more walking. Head down the long orange-roofed overpass between sections A and B to reach the station (2/hour at about :08 and :38 past the hour, 20 minutes to Sants Station, 25 minutes to Passeig de Gràcia Station—near Plaça de Catalunya and many recommended hotels, 30 minutes to França Station; €4.10 or covered by T10 Card). If you are arriving or departing from Terminal 1, you will have to use the airport shuttle bus to connect with the train station, so leave extra time.

A **taxi** between the airport and downtown costs about €35 (including €3.10 airport supplement). For good service, you can round up to the next euro on the fare—but keep in mind that the Spanish don't tip cabbies.

GIRONA-COSTA BRAVA AIRPORT

Some budget airlines, including Ryanair, use **Girona-Costa Brava Airport,** located 60 miles north of Barcelona near Girona (airport code: GRO, tel. 972-186-600, www.aena-aeropuertos.es). Ryanair runs

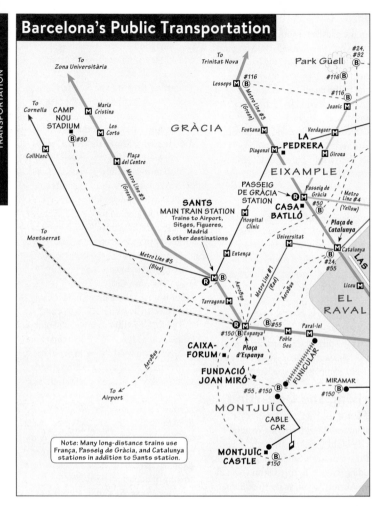

Barcelona's Public Transportation

To Zona Universitària

To Trinitat Nova

Park Güell

#24, #92

Lesseps

#116

#116

#116

Joanic

To Cornella

CAMP NOU STADIUM

#50

Maria Cristina

Les Corts

Collblanc

Plaça del Centre

Metro Line #5 (Green)

GRÀCIA

Fontana

Metro Line #5 (Green)

Diagonal

LA PEDRERA

Verdaguer

Girona

EIXAMPLE

PASSEIG DE GRÀCIA STATION

Passeig de Gràcia

#50

Metro Line #4 (Yellow)

SANTS MAIN TRAIN STATION
Trains to Airport, Sitges, Figueres, Madrid & other destinations

CASA BATLLÓ

Hospital Clínic

Plaça de Catalunya

To Montserrat

Metro Line #5 (Blue)

Entença

Universitat

Catalunya

#24, #55

LAS

Tarragona

Metro Line #1 (Red)

AeroBus

AeroBus

Liceu

EL RAVAL

#150

Espanya

#55

Paral·lel

To Airport

AeroBus

CAIXA-FORUM

Plaça d'Espanya

Poble Sec

FUNICULAR

FUNDACIÓ JOAN MIRÓ

#55, #150

MIRAMAR

#150

MONTJUÏC

CABLE CAR

Note: Many long-distance trains use França, Passeig de Gràcia, and Catalunya stations in addition to Sants station.

MONTJUÏC CASTLE

#150

a **bus,** operated by Sagalés, to the Barcelona Nord bus station (€16, departs airport about 20-25 minutes after each arriving flight, 1.5 hours, tel. 902-361-550, www.sagales.com). You can also take a Sagalés bus (hourly, 25 minutes, €2.75) or a taxi (€25) to the town of Girona, then catch a train to Barcelona (at least hourly, 1.5 hours, €15-20). A taxi between the Girona airport and Barcelona costs at least €120.

By Train

Virtually all trains arrive at Barcelona's Sants Train Station, west of the Old City. AVE trains from Madrid go only to Sants Station. But many trains also pass through other stations en route, such as França Station (between the El Born and Barceloneta neighborhoods), or the downtown Passeig de Gràcia or Plaça de Catalunya stations (which are also Metro stops—and close to most of my recommended hotels). Ask the conductor where your train stops and get off at the station most convenient to your hotel.

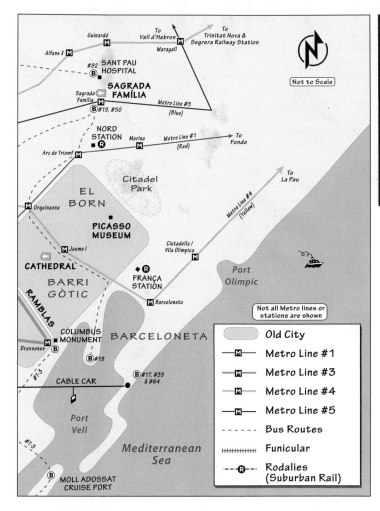

Not to Scale

Not all Metro lines or stations are shown

Old City	
—Ⓜ—	Metro Line #1
—Ⓜ—	Metro Line #3
—Ⓜ—	Metro Line #4
—Ⓜ—	Metro Line #5
- - - - -	Bus Routes
┼┼┼┼┼┼	Funicular
- -Ⓡ- -	Rodalies (Suburban Rail)

SANTS TRAIN STATION

Barcelona's main **Sants Train Station** is vast and sprawling, but manageable. In the large lobby area under the upper tracks, you'll find a TI, ATMs, handy shops and eateries, car-rental kiosks, and, in the side concourse, a classy, quiet Sala Club lounge for travelers with first-class reservations (TV, free drinks, coffee bar). Sants is the only Barcelona station with **luggage storage** (big bag–€5.20/day, requires security check, daily 5:30–23:00, follow signs to *consigna*, at far end of hallway

from tracks 13-14).

In the vast main hall is a long wall of ticket windows. Figure out which one you need before you wait in line. Generally, **windows 1-7** (on the left) are for **local commuter** and **media distancia trains,** such as to Sitges. **Windows 8-21** handle advance tickets for **long-distance** *(larga distancia)* **trains** beyond Catalunya. **Windows 22-26** offer **general information**. **Windows 27-31** sell tickets for **long-distance trains** leaving today. These window assignments can shift during the off-season. The **information booths** by windows 1 and 21 can help you find the right line and provide train schedules. Scattered nearby are two types of train-ticket vending machines. The **red-and-gray machines** sell tickets for local and media distancia trains within Cat unya. The **purple machines** are for nat RENFE trains (you may have difficu using a US credit card). These mac 5 can also print out prereserved tickets you have a confirmation code.

Getting Downtown: To reach the center of Barcelona, take a train or the Metro. To ride the subway, follow signs for the **Metro (red M),** and hop on the **L3 (green)** or **L5 (blue)** line; both link to useful points in town. Purchase tickets for the Metro at touch-screen machines near the tracks.

To zip downtown in just five minutes, take any **Rodalies de Catalunya suburban train** from **track 8 (R1, R3, or R4)** to Plaça de Catalunya (departs at least every 10 minutes). Your long-distance RENFE train ticket comes with a complimentary ride on Rodalies, as long as you use it within three hours before or after your travels. Look for a code on your ticket labeled Combinat Rodalies or Combinado Cercanías. Go to the red-and-gray commuter ticket machines, touch Combinat Rodalies, type in your code, and the machine will print your ticket.

TRAIN CONNECTIONS

Unless otherwise noted, all of the following trains depart from Sants Station; however, remember that some trains also stop at other stations more convenient to the downtown tourist zone: França Station, Passeig de Gràcia, or Plaça de Catalunya. If your train stops at these stations, you can board there, saving yourself the trip to Sants.

If departing from the downtown Passeig de Gràcia Station, where three Metro lines converge with the rail line, you might find the underground tunnels confusing. You can't access the RENFE station

directly from some of the entrances. Use the northern entrances to this station—rather than the s rhern "Consell de Cent" entrance, ch is closest to Plaça de Catalunya (t 02-320-320, www. renfe.com).

From Barcelona by Train to Madrid: The AVE train to Madrid is faster than flying (you're zipping from downtown to downto wn). The train departs at least hourly. T nonstop train is a bit pricier but faster urs) than the train that makes a f ops (3 hours).

Regular reserved AVE tickets can be prepurchased (often with a discount) at www.renfe.com and picked up at the station. If you have a rail pass, you'll pay only a reservation fee of €23 for first class, which includes a meal on weekdays (€10 second class, buy at any train station in Spain). Passholders can't reserve online through RENFE but can make a more expensive reservation at www.raileurope. com for delivery before leaving the US.

From Barcelona by Train to: Montserrat (departs from Plaça d'Espanya—not from Sants, hourly, 1 hour, includes cable car or rack train to monastery); **Figueres** (hourly, 1 hour via AVE or Alvia to Figueres-Vilafant; hourly, 2 hours via local trains to Figueres Station); **Sevilla** (8-9/day, 5.5-6.5 hours); **Granada** (1/day, 7.5 hours via AVE and regional train, transfer in Antequera); **Salamanca** (8/day, 6-7.5 hours, change in Madrid from Atocha Station to Chamartín Station via Metro or cercanías train; also 1/day with a change in Valladolid, 8.5 hours); **San Sebastián** (2/day, 5.5-6 hours).

By Bus

Most buses depart from the Nord bus station at Metro: Arc de Triomf, but confirm when researching schedules (www. barcelonanord.com). Destinations served by Alsa buses (tel. 902-422-242, www.alsa. es) include **Madrid** and **Madrid's Barajas Airport** (nearly hourly, 8 hours), and **Salamanca** (2/day, 11 hours). Sarfa buses (tel. 902-302-025, www.sarfa.com) serve many **coastal resorts,** including **Cadaqués** (2-3/day, 3 hours).

The Mon-Bus leaves from the university and Plaça d'Espanya in downtown Barcelona to **Sitges** (4/day, 1 hour, www.monbus.cat). One bus departs daily for the **Montserrat** monastery, leaving from Carrer de Viriat near Sants Station.

By Car

You won't need a car in Barcelona because the taxis and public transportation are so good. Parking fees are outrageously expensive (the lot behind La Boqueria Market charges upwards of €25/day). If you want to rent a car, remember that it's smart to do it after you visit Madrid and Toledo.

NEAR BARCELONA

MONTSERRAT AND FIGUERES

Two fine sights make tempting day trips. Pilgrims (or hikers) head into the mountains for the most sacred spot in Catalunya: Montserrat. Fans of Surrealism make a mind-bending visit to the Dalí Theater-Museum in Figueres.

Montserrat

Montserrat, with its unique rock formations, a dramatic mountaintop monastery, and spiritual connection with the Catalan people, has been Catalunya's most important pilgrimage site for a thousand years. On a day trip, you can view the mountain from its base, ride a funicular up to the top of the world, tour the basilica and museum, touch a Black Virgin's orb, and hike down to a sacred cave.

Getting There

Barcelona is connected to the valley below Montserrat by train. From there, a cable car or rack railway (your choice) takes you up to the mountaintop. Both options are similar in cost and take about the same amount of time (it's roughly 1.5 hours each way from downtown Barcelona to the monastery). Arrive early or late, as tour groups mob the place midday. Crowds are worst on Sundays.

By Train: Trains leave hourly from Barcelona's Plaça d'Espanya. Follow signs for Montserrat to the FGC (Ferrocarrils de la Generalitat de Catalunya) underground station. Once there, check the overhead screens to find the track for train line R5 (direction: Manresa, departures at :36 past each hour).

The train ride is about an hour. Approaching Montserrat, if you've chosen the cable-car ride up the mountain, get out at the Montserrat-Aeri Station, or for the rack railway, continue for a few minutes to the next station—Monistrol de Montserrat. Keep your train ticket; you'll need it to exit the FGC station when you return to Plaça d'Espanya.

By Cable Car, at Montserrat-Aeri Station: Departing the train, follow signs to the cable-car station (covered by your train or combo-ticket; 4/hour, 5-minute trip, daily March-Oct 9:40-14:00 & 14:35-19:00, Nov-Feb 10:10-14:00 & 14:35-17:45, www.aeridemontserrat.com). When leaving the monastery, give yourself enough time to catch the Barcelona-bound trains departing at :48 past the hour.

By Rack Railway (Cremallera), at Monistrol de Montserrat Station: Catch the rack railway up to the monastery (covered by your train or combo-ticket; hourly, 20-minute trip, www.cremalleradementserrat.com). On the return trip, this train departs the monastery at :15 past the hour, allowing you to catch the Barcelona-bound train leaving Monistrol de Montserrat at :45 past the hour. The last convenient connection back to Barcelona leaves the monastery at 19:15 (Sat-Sun at 20:15). Note that there's one intermediate stop on this line (Monistrol-Vila, at a parking garage), but just stay on until the end of the line.

Rick's Tip: *Should you choose the* **cable car or rack railway?** *For scenery and fun, pick the little German-built cable car. If you're afraid of heights, take the rack railway. Paying extra to ride both isn't worth it.*

Tickets: Various combo-tickets cover the train from Barcelona's Plaça d'Espanya and include either the cable car or rack railway—choose when you buy the ticket. The basic option is a **train ticket** to Montserrat (€22.80 round-trip, Eurail pass not valid, tel. 932-051-515, www.fgc.es). The €29.30 **Trans Montserrat** ticket includes your round-trip Metro ride in Barcelona to and from the train station, the trip to Montserrat, and unlimited trips on the two funiculars at Montserrat. The €46.20 **Tot Montserrat** ticket includes all of this, plus the Museum of Montserrat and a

self-service lunch (served daily 12:00-16:00). Both tickets are well-explained in the Barcelona TI's online shop (http://bcnshop.barcelonaturisme.com). You can buy any of these tickets from machines at Barcelona's Plaça d'Espanya Station—if you need help, go to the orange Montserrat info booth (daily 8:00-14:00) or find a tourist official standing by in the morning. To use your included round-trip Metro ride to get *to* the station, buy the ticket in advance at the Plaça de Catalunya TI in Barcelona.

By Bus: For simpler transportation (though perhaps less fun), there's one bus per day that connects downtown Barcelona directly to the Montserrat monastery (departs from Carrer de Viriat near Barcelona's Sants Station daily at 9:15, departs monastery for Barcelona at 18:00 June-Sept or 17:00 Oct-May, €5 each way, about a 1.5-hour trip, Autocares Julià, www.autocaresjulia.es).

Orientation

All of the transit options converge at the big train station. Above those are both funicular stations: one up to the Sant Joan

Montserrat

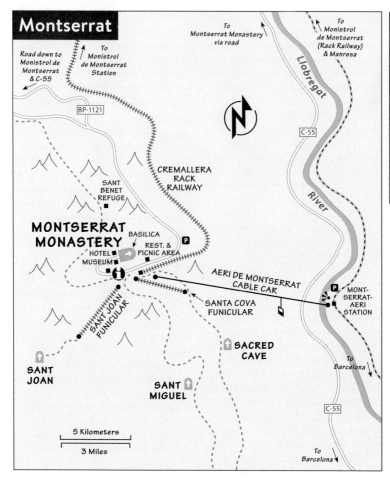

Chapel, the other down to the Sacred Cave trail. Across the street is the **TI**; ask for a hiking map if you're interested (daily from 9:00, closes at 18:45, or 20:15 on weekdays in July-Aug, tel. 938-777-701, www.montserratvisita.com). Above the TI is the main square.

Sights

▲▲BASILICA

Although there's been a church here since the 11th century, the present structure was built in the 1850s, and the facade only dates from 1968. The basilica itself is ringed with interesting chapels, but the focus is on the Black Virgin (La Moreneta) sitting high above the main altar.

Cost and Hours: Free; La Moreneta viewable Mon-Sat 8:00-10:30 & 12:00-18:30, Sun 19:30-20:15; church itself has longer hours and daily services (Mass at 11:00 at the main altar, at 12:00 and 19:30 in side chapels, vespers at 18:45); www.abadiamontserrat.net.

Visiting the Basilica: Pilgrims shuffle down a long, ornate passage leading alongside the church for a moment alone with Montserrat's top attraction, **La Moreneta,** the small wood statue of the Black Virgin, discovered in the Sacred Cave in the 12th century. Legend says she was carved by St. Luke, brought to Spain by St. Peter, hidden in the cave during the Moorish invasions, and miraculously discovered by shepherd children. (Carbon dating says she's 800 years old.)

Join the line of pilgrims, along the right side of the church. Though Mary is behind a glass case, the royal orb she cradles in her hands is exposed. Pilgrims touch the orb with one hand and hold their other hand up to show that they accept Jesus.

You'll leave by walking along the **Ave Maria Path** (along the outside of the church). Before you leave the inner courtyard to head out into the main square, pop into the little room with many unusual votive offerings, which serve as prayer requests or thanks for divine intercession.

MUSEUM OF MONTSERRAT
Wander past antiquities and fine art, mostly donated by devout Catalan Catholics. On the main floor, you'll see ecclesiastical gear, a good icon collection, and paintings, including—at the very end—a Dalí painting, some Picasso sketches and prints, and a Miró. Upstairs are lesser-known works by El Greco, Caravaggio, Monet, Renoir, and more.

Cost and Hours: €7, covered by Tot Montserrat combo-ticket, daily July-Aug 10:00-18:45, Sept-June 10:00-17:45, tel. 938-777-745.

▲SANT JOAN FUNICULAR AND HIKES
This funicular climbs 820 feet above the monastery in five minutes. At the top is the starting point of a 20-minute walk to Sant Joan Chapel (follow sign for *Ermita de St. Joan*). Other hikes also begin at the trailhead by the funicular (details at TI; map at upper funicular station). The most popular is a 45-minute mostly downhill loop back to the monastery (go left from funicular station, the trail—marked

Monestir de Montserrat—will first go up to a rocky crest then downhill).

Cost and Hours: Funicular—€6.20 one-way, €9.50 round-trip, covered by Trans Montserrat and Tot Montserrat combo-tickets, goes every 20 minutes.

Rick's Tip: *If you're here late in the afternoon, check the* **funicular schedule** *before heading up to Sant Joan Chapel or down to the Sacred Cave to make sure you'll get back in time. You wouldn't want to miss the final ride (by cable car or rack railway) down the mountain to* **catch the train to Barcelona.**

SACRED CAVE (SANTA COVA) FUNICULAR
The Moreneta was originally discovered in the Sacred Cave, a 40-minute hike down from the monastery (another 50 minutes back up). The path (c. 1900), designed by Modernista architects, including Gaudí and Josep Puig i Cadafalch, is lined with statues. While the original Black Virgin statue is now in the basilica, a replica sits in the cave. A three-minute funicular ride cuts 20 minutes off the hike.

Cost and Hours: Funicular—€2.40 one-way, €3.70 round-trip, covered by Trans Montserrat and Tot Montserrat combo-tickets, goes every 20 minutes.

Eating and Sleeping
Near the basilica, a cafeteria is across from the rack railway station, and there's a grocery store and bar (with simple sandwiches) where the road curves on its way up to the hotel. In the other direction, follow the covered walkway below the basilica to **Mirador dels Apòstols,** with a bar, cafeteria, restaurant, and picnic area.

$$ Hotel Abat Cisneros, a three-star hotel, is low-key and appropriate for a pilgrimage site (Db-€80-120, www.montserratvisita.com, reserves@larsa-montserrat.com).

Figueres

An easy day trip from Barcelona, Figueres (feeg-YEHR-ehs) is of interest only for its Salvador Dalí Theater-Museum. In fact, the entire town is Dalí-dominated.

Orientation

Getting There: Take a regional train to Figueres Station—they depart from Barcelona's Sants Station or from the RENFE station at Metro: Passeig de Gràcia (hourly, 2 hours; the slightly pricier *media distancia* trains are 20 minutes faster than *regional* trains). The priciest option, the high-speed train, cuts your travel time in half (departs Sants Station; hourly, 1 hour).

Arrival in Figueres: From Figueres Station, simply follow *Museu Dalí* signs (and the crowds) for the 15-minute walk to the museum. From Figueres-Vilafant Station, it's about a 20-minute walk.

Sights

▲▲▲DALÍ THEATER-MUSEUM (TEATRE-MUSEU DALÍ)

Inaugurated in 1974, this is *the* essential Dalí sight. Ever the entertainer, Dalí per-

sonally conceptualized, designed, decorated, and painted it to showcase his life's work. Even the building's exterior—painted pink, studded with golden loaves of bread, and topped with monumental eggs—exudes Dalí's outrageous persona. The museum fills a former theater and is the artist's mausoleum (his tomb is in the crypt below center stage). It's also a kind of mausoleum to Dalí's creative spirit.

Dalí had his first public art showing at age 14 here in this building when it was a theater. After the theater was destroyed in the Spanish Civil War, Dalí struck a deal with the mayor: Dalí would rebuild the theater as a museum, Figueres would be put on the sightseeing map...and the money's been flowing in ever since.

Rick's Tip: *Much of Dalí's art is movable and* **coin-operated**—*bring a few €1 coins.*

Cost and Hours: €12; July-Sept daily 9:00-20:00; March-June and Oct Tue-Sun 9:30-18:00, closed Mon; Nov-Feb Tue-Sun 10:30-18:00, closed Mon; last entry 45 minutes before closing, tel. 972-677-500, www.salvador-dali.org. No flash

Dalí Theater-Museum

Salvador Dalí (1904-1989)

When Salvador Dalí was asked, "Are you on drugs?" he replied, "I am the drug... take me."

Labeled by various critics as sick, greedy, paranoid, arrogant, and a clown, Dalí produced some of the most thought-provoking art of the 20th century. His erotic, violent, disjointed imagery continues to disturb and intrigue today.

Born in Figueres to a well-off family, Dalí showed talent early. He was expelled from Madrid's prestigious art school—twice. After a breakthrough art exhibit in Barcelona in 1925, Dalí moved to Paris. He hobnobbed with fellow Spaniards Pablo Picasso and Joan Miró, along with a group of artists exploring Sigmund Freud's theory that we all have a hidden part of our mind, the unconscious "id," that surfaces when we dream. Dalí became the best-known spokesman for this group of Surrealists, channeling his id into bizarre dream images (melting watches, burning giraffes).

His life changed forever in 1929, when he met an older, married Russian woman named Gala who became his wife, muse, model, manager, and emotional compass. Dalí's popularity spread to the US, where he (and Gala) weathered the WWII years. In the prime of his career, Dalí's work became more classical. He produced large-scale paintings of historical events that were collages of realistic scenes floating in surrealistic landscapes, peppered with symbols.

Dalí mastered many media, including film. *An Andalusian Dog* (1929, with Luis Buñuel) was a cutting-edge montage of disturbing, eyeball-slicing images. He designed Alfred Hitchcock's big-eye backdrop for the dream sequence of *Spellbound* (1945). He made jewels for the rich and clothes for Coco Chanel.

Today, the waxed-mustached artist is remembered for his self-marketing persona, his provocative pairing of symbols, and his sheer creative drive.

photography. The free bag check has your belongings waiting for you at the exit.

Visiting the Museum: The museum has two parts—the theater-mausoleum and the "Dalí's Jewels" exhibit in an adjacent building. There's no logical order for a visit (that would be un-Surrealistic), and naturally, no audioguide. Dalí said there are two kinds of visitors: those who don't need a description, and those who aren't worth a description.

Stepping through the courtyard, go into the **theater** (with its audience of statues) and face the stage—and Dalí's unmarked crypt. You know how you can never get a cab when it's raining? Pop a coin into Dalí's personal 1941 Cadillac and it rains

inside the car. Look above, atop the tire tower: That's the boat Dalí enjoyed with his soulmate, Gala—his emotional life preserver, who kept him from going overboard. When she died, so did he (for his last seven years). Blue tears made of condoms drip below the boat.

Up on the **stage,** squint at the big digital Abraham Lincoln, and the 16th president comes into focus. Approach the painting to find that Abe's facial cheeks are Gala's butt cheeks. Under the painting, a door leads to the **Treasures Room,** with the greatest collection of original Dalí oil paintings in the museum. (Many of the other artworks are prints.) You'll see Cubist visions of the town of Cadaqués and dreamy portraits of Gala. Crutches—a recurring Dalí theme—represent Gala, who kept him supported whenever a meltdown threatened.

The famous **Homage to Mae West room** is a tribute to the sultry seductress. Saying things like, "Why marry and make one man unhappy, when you can stay single and make so many so happy?," Mae West was to conventional morality what Dalí was to conventional art. Climb to the vantage point where the sofa lips, fireplace nostrils, painting eyes, and drapery hair come together to make the face of Mae West.

The former theater's **smoking lounge** displays portraits of Gala and Dalí book-ending a Roman candle of creativity. The fascinating ceiling painting shows the feet of Gala and Dalí as they bridge earth and the heavens. Dalí's drawers are empty—he gave everything to his art.

Leaving the theater, keep your ticket and pop into the adjacent **"Dalí's Jewels"** exhibit. It shows sketches and paintings of jewelry Dalí designed, and the actual pieces jewelers made from his surreal visions: a mouth full of pearly whites, a golden finger corset, a fountain of diamonds, and the breathing heart. Explore the ambiguous perception worked into the big painting titled *Apotheosis of the Dollar*.

BEST OF THE REST

BASQUE COUNTRY

Stretching about 100 miles from Bilbao, Spain, north to Bayonne, France, lies the ancient, free-spirited land of the Basques. The region is famous for its beaches, modern architecture, distinctive towns, and feisty, industrious natives.

Fun-loving San Sebastián is the heart of the tourist's *País Vasco,* with its sparkling, picturesque beach framed by looming green mountains and a charming Old Town with gourmet *pintxos* (tapas) spilling out of every bar. On-the-rise Bilbao is worth a look for its landmark Guggenheim and its atmospheric Old Town. The thriving town of Pamplona hosts the world-famous Running of the Bulls.

I'd suggest two or three days for a visit to Basque Country. Allow one day per town: Spend one day relaxing in San Sebastián and the second day for a side-trip to Bilbao. For a third day, add Pamplona. For efficiency, you could home-base in San Sebastián for three days, and do Bilbao and Pamplona as two separate day trips.

In the Basque Country, everything is connected by good roads and public transportation. Buses generally run faster and more frequently than trains. Drivers favor the speedy toll roads; the free, but slower, back roads come with lots of twists and turns.

San Sebastián

Shimmering above the breathtaking Concha Bay, elegant and prosperous San Sebastián (in Euskara, it's Donostia, or Donosti for short) has golden beaches, twin peaks at either end, and a soaring statue of Christ. A promenade runs the length of the bay, with a lively, late-night Old Town at one end. It's also one of Spain's culinary capitals.

Orientation

San Sebastián can be divided into three areas: **Playa de la Concha** (best beaches); the **shopping district** (called Centro); and the grid-planned **Old Town** (called Parte Vieja, to the north of the shopping

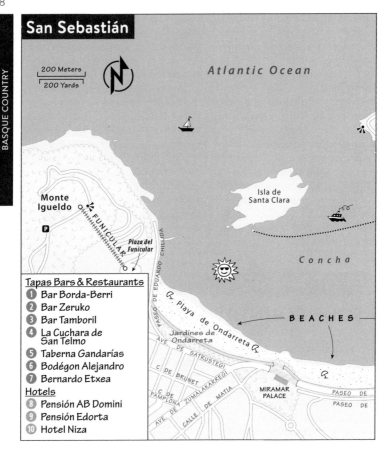

San Sebastián

200 Meters
200 Yards

Atlantic Ocean

Monte Igueldo

FUNICULAR

P

Plaza del Funicular

PASEO DE EDUARDO CHILLIDA

Isla de Santa Clara

Concha

Tapas Bars & Restaurants
1. Bar Borda-Berri
2. Bar Zeruko
3. Bar Tamboril
4. La Cuchara de San Telmo
5. Taberna Gandarías
6. Bodégon Alejandro
7. Bernardo Etxea

Hotels
8. Pensión AB Domini
9. Pensión Edorta
10. Hotel Niza

R. *Playa de Ondarreta*

BEACHES

Jardines de Ondarreta

AVE. DE SATRUSTEGI

C. DE BRUNET

C. DE PAMPLONA

AVE. DE ZUMALAKARREGI

CALLE DE MATIA

MIRAMAR PALACE

PASEO DE

PASEO DE

district). Centro, just east of Playa de la Concha, has beautiful architecture, but no sights. Standing where the city wall once ran, Alameda del Boulevard (or just "Boulevard") separates the Centro from the Old Town. It's bookended by Monte Urgull to the east, and Monte Igueldo to the west. The river (Río Urumea) divides the city center from the Gros district, with a lively night scene and surfing beach.

Day Plan: San Sebastián is a great place for a lazy day. Stroll the two-mile-long promenade and scout the best spot to work on a tan. Explore the Old Town, especially the tapas bars. Visit whatever interests you: the Museum of San Telmo, the castle at Monte Urgull, or the aquarium.

Getting to San Sebastián: You'll likely be coming from **Barcelona** (2 trains/day, 6 hours; 2 buses/day and 1 at night, 7 hours), **Madrid** (4 trains/day, 6-7 hours; 8 buses/day, 6-7 hours), **Bilbao** (2 buses/hour, hourly on weekends, 1.5 hours), **Pamplona** (8-10 buses/day, 1 hour), or maybe even **Santiago de Compostela** (1 direct train/day, 10.5 hours). To add it to my recommended two-week itinerary, splice it between Barcelona (fly or take the train to San Sebastián) and Madrid.

Arrival in San Sebastián: Trains stop at the main **RENFE station,** just across the river from the Centro shopping district—to get to the Old Town, catch a

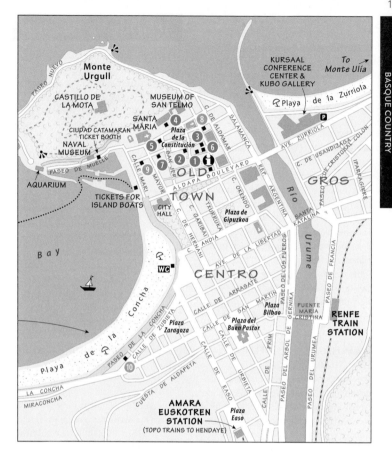

taxi (€6.20 to downtown) or **walk** (about 10-15 minutes)—beyond the tree-lined plaza, cross the fancy dragon-decorated bridge (María Cristina), turn right onto the busy avenue called Paseo de los Fueros, and follow the Urumea River to the last bridge. The new **bus station** is located by the RENFE train station.

Drivers take the Amara freeway exit, follow *Centro Ciudad* signs into the city center, and park in a pay lot (the Kursaal underground lot is the most central). If picking up or returning a rental car, Europcar is at the RENFE station (tel. 943-322-304).

From **San Sebastián Airport** (airport code: EAS), catch bus #E21 to San

Sebastián's Plaza de Gipuzkoa (www.ekialdebus.net) or a taxi (€35).

Tourist Information: The TI offers a variety of English-language walking tours (June-Sept Mon-Sat 9:00-20:00, Sun 10:00-19:00; Oct-May Mon-Sat 9:00-19:00, Sun 10:00-14:00; on the Boulevard at #8, tel. 943-481-166, www.sansebastianturismo.com).

Sightseeing Card: For most, the **San Sebastián Card** isn't worth the €16 fee. It gives you discounts, a free TI walking tour, and 12 shareable rides on public transit, but the city is walkable.

Guides: Consider **Gabriella Ranelli** for culinary tapas tours and more (prices vary per tour, about €85/person, roughly €185/

half-day, mobile 609-467-381, www.tene dortours.com, info@tenedortours.com).

San Sebastián Food does gastronomic tours, such as a €95 tapas tour, or making gourmet meals together (starting around €120/person), and more (tel. 943-421-143, www.sansebastianfood.com).

Sights

▲▲OLD TOWN (PARTE VIEJA)

Huddled in the shadow of Monte Urgull, the Old Town is where San Sebastián was born about 1,000 years ago. Because the town burned down in 1813, the architecture you see is generally Neoclassical. Still, the grid plan of streets hides heavy Baroque and Gothic churches, surprise plazas, and fun little shops. Its highlights are the lively bars for tapas—here called *pintxos* (PEEN-chohs). Bullfights were once held on Plaza de la Constitución; notice the seat numbering on the balconies.

▲▲MUSEUM OF SAN TELMO (SAN TELMO MUSEOA)

This museum, the largest on Basque culture in Spain, innovatively wraps a modern facade around a 16th-century Dominican convent. Its art collection features works by masters (El Greco, Rubens, Tintoretto) alongside 19th- and 20th-century paintings by Basque artists.

Cost and Hours: €6, free on Tue, open Tue-Sun 10:00-20:00, closed Mon, Plaza Zuloaga 1, tel. 943-481-580, www.san telmomuseoa.com.

▲BRETXA PUBLIC MARKET (MERCADO DE LA BRETXA)

Get in touch with Basque culture by wandering the public market. Although the sandstone market building and the large, former Pescadería have been converted into a modern shopping complex, the produce market (outside along the left side of the mall) still thrives, as does the underground fish and meat market. There's a free WC in the market—ask *"¿Dónde está el servicio, por favor?"*

Who Are the Basques?

Historically, Basques were some of the first and finest sailors in Europe, chasing whales a thousand miles from home by the year 1000. When the Spanish era of exploration began, Basques played a key role as sailors and shipbuilders. St. Ignatius of Loyola and St. Francis Xavier, known for their far-reaching missionary trips, were Basques.

Later, the Basques began using their rich iron deposits to make steel, and Basque industrialists dragged Spain into the modern world. Cities such as Bilbao were industrialized, sparking an influx of workers from around Spain.

Widespread Spanish and French immigration has made it difficult to know who actually has Basque ethnic roots. Today, anyone who speaks the Basque language, Euskara, is considered a Basque. Euskara is likely the oldest European language that's still spoken—used since Neolithic times. With its words filled with k's, tx's, and z's (restrooms are *komunak: gizonak* for men and *emakumeak* for women), Euskara makes Spanish seem easy. Kept alive as a symbol of Basque cultural identity, Euskara typically is learned proudly as a second or third language.

In the last few decades, the separatist group ETA has given the Basque people an unwarranted reputation for terrorism; fortunately, the ETA recently renounced its campaign of violence. While many Basques would like more autonomy from Madrid, the vast majority want to pursue it through peaceful means.

Hours: Mon-Fri 8:00-14:00 & 17:00-20:00, Sat 8:00-14:00, closed Sun, Bretxa Plaza.

THE PORT

At the west end of the Old Town, protected by Monte Urgull, is the port. Take the passage through the wall at Calle Puerto, and jog right along the portside promenade, Paseo del Muelle. You'll pass sailors' pubs and boats unloading the catch of the day. For trails to the top of Monte Urgull, climb the stairs next to the aquarium.

▲▲AQUARIUM

At this surprisingly good aquarium, you'll see a huge whale skeleton, an illuminated tank of jellyfish, and a 45-foot-long tunnel through a wet world of floppy rays and menacing sharks.

Cost and Hours: €13, €6.50 for kids under 13; daily 10:00-21:00, closes at 20:00 off-season; at the end of Paseo del Muelle, tel. 943-440-099, www.aquarium ss.com.

▲MONTE URGULL

The once-mighty castle (Castillo de la Mota) atop the hill deterred most attackers, allowing the city to prosper in the Middle Ages. Inside, the free **Casa de la Historia** museum covers the city's history. It has access to the statue of Christ's viewpoint over the city—but the best views are from the **Battery of Santiago** ramparts (to Christ's far right). Bring a picnic or stop by Café El Polvorín.

▲▲LA CONCHA BEACH AND PROMENADE

Shell-shaped Playa de la Concha is a lovely stretch of sand lined with a two-mile-long promenade. Sunbathers pack its shores in summer (it's empty off-season). *Cabinas* provide lockers, showers, and shade for a fee; showers are free. **Café de la Concha** serves reasonably priced, mediocre food from its terrace overlooking the beach.

Eating

Hop from pub to pub in the Old Town. If you want a meal instead of *pintxos,* some bars—even ones that look only like bars from the street—have attached dining rooms, usually in the back. Local brews include *sidra* (hard apple cider) and *txakolí* (chah-koh-LEE, a sparkling white wine

San Sebastián's beach and Monte Urgull

often theatrically poured from high above the glass for aeration).

Tapas are best, freshest, and accompanied by the most vibrant crowd from 12:00 to 14:00 and from 20:00 to 22:30. Watch what's being served—the locals know each bar's specialty. No matter how much you like a place, just order one dish; you want to be mobile. Some tapas bars lay out big platters of help-yourself goodies. Point to—or simply take—what looks good. You pay when you leave, on the honor system; keep a mental note of the tapas you've eaten.

Calle Fermín Calbetón has the most options; San Jerónimo and 31 de Agosto are also good. Try **Bar Borda-Berri** for beef cheeks (*carrillera de tenera;* closed Mon, Calle Fermín Calbetón 12); award-winning **Bar Zeruko** for cod (*hoguera;* closed Mon, Calle Pescadería 10); **Bar Tamboril** for seafood, mushrooms, and hot *pintxos* (Calle Pescadería 2); **La Cuchara de San Telmo** for adventurous gourmet plates (closed Mon and Thu night, 31 de Agosto #28); and **Taberna Gandarías** for savory *pinxtos* in an easygoing atmosphere (31 de Agosto #23).

For restaurants, try **Bodégon Alejandro** for modern Basque cuisine (closed Sun night and Mon, Calle Fermín Calbetón 4, tel. 943-427-158) or **Bernardo Etxea** for grilled seafood and meat (Wed eve and Thu, Puerto 7, tel. 943-422-055).

Sleeping

In the Old Town, try delightful **$$$ Pensión AB Domini** (San Juan 8, tel. 943-420-431, www.abpensiones.es, reservas@abpensiones.es) or stylish **$$ Pensión Edorta** (Calle Puerto 15, tel. 943-423-773, www.pensionedorta.com, info@pensionedorta.com). **$$$ Hotel Niza** is on the beach (Zubieta 56, tel. 943-426-663, www.hotelniza.com, reservas@hotelniza.com).

Bilbao

Bilbao (bil-BOW, rhymes with "now") enjoys a vitality and well-worn charm. The stunning Guggenheim Museum points the city toward an exciting new future, although there are eyesore apartment blocks that are reminders of its grimy industrial past.

Orientation

Bilbao hugs the Nervión River as it curves through town. The Guggenheim is centrally located near the top of that curve; the bus station is to the west; the Old Town (Casco Viejo) and train stations are to the east. The green tram called the EuskoTran ties it all together.

Day Plan: The Guggenheim is the main draw. With more time, hop on a tram to explore the Old Town (Casco Viejo).

*Rick's Tip: If you're visiting Bilbao outside of July and August, **don't come on Monday, when the Guggenheim is closed.***

Getting to Bilbao: You'll probably come from **San Sebastián** (2 buses/hour, hourly on weekends, 1.5 hours) or **Madrid** (2 trains/day, 6 hours).

Arrival in Bilbao: You'll want to go straight to the Guggenheim, which is easy to do thanks to the **tram system** (EuskoTran). At nearly any tram stop, simply buy a €1.50 single-ride ticket at a user-friendly green machine (€4.40 for an all-day pass). Activate your ticket or card at the machine just before boarding (follow the red arrow). Hop on a green-and-gray tram and head for the Guggenheim stop (there's only one line, 4/hour). Don't confuse the green tram (Eusko*Tran*) with the blue train to San Sebastián (Eusko*Tren*).

Trains coming from San Sebastián arrive at the riverside **Atxuri Station.** From here the tram (direction: La Casilla) follows the river to the Guggenheim stop. The **RENFE station,** in the city center, is atop a small mall; the tram stop nearest this station has no ticket machine—to board here you'll need to buy a shareable *Barik* card in the RENFE office before leaving the train station (€3/card, top-up in increments of €5). To reach the tram, descend into the stores. Leave from *Hurtado de Amézaga* exit, and go right to find the Abando tram stop (direction: La Casilla).

Buses stop at the **Termibús Station,** about a mile southwest of the Guggenheim. The tram (San Mamés Station) is on the road just below the station—look for the steel *CTB* sign or follow the *Tran* signs. Buy and validate a ticket at the machine, and hop on the tram (direction: Atxuri) to the Guggenheim or Old Town. The **best luggage storage** in town is at this Termibús Station.

Drivers should take the exit marked *Centro* (with bull's-eye symbol), follow signs to *Guggenheim* (you'll see the museum), and look for the big *P* that marks the big underground parking garage near the museum.

Tourist Information: The handiest TI, which offers walking tours, is near the main entrance of the Guggenheim (daily 10:00-19:00, off-season Sun until 15:00; Alameda Mazarredo 66, tel. 944-795-760, www.bilbaoturismo.net). A second TI is next to the RENFE station at Plaza Circular (daily 9:00-21:00, free Wi-Fi).

The TI runs a hop-on, hop-off **bus tour** (€14, ticket valid 24 hours, only runs 1/hour, July-Aug daily 11:00-18:00, April-June and Sept-Dec shorter hours and not on Tue, Jan-March Sat-Sun only, tel. 696-429-848, www.busturistikoa.com).

Sightseeing Card: The cheap **Bilbao Card** isn't worth it for day-trippers here to see the Guggenheim; it offers unlimited use of public transit, a free TI walking tour, and discounts on museums—except the Guggenheim (€6/1 day, €10/2 days).

Guide: Try **Iratxe Muñoz** for tours of the city and Guggenheim (mobile 607-778-072, www.apite.eu/iratxemunoz, iratxe.m@apite.eu).

Sights

▲▲▲GUGGENHEIM BILBAO

Even if you're not into contemporary art, the Guggenheim is a must-see. Its 20 galleries, on three floors, are full of surprises.

Guggenheim Bilbao

Bilbao

M Deusto

AVENIDA DE MADARIAGA

LUIS POWER

PEOTA BLAS DE OTERO

MORGAN RIBERA DE BOTICA

RIBERA DE DEUSTO

Plaza
San Pío

UNIVERSIDAD
DE DEUSTO

AVENIDA DE LAS UNIVERSIDADES

Nervión River

DEUSTO BRIDGE

Abandoibarra T

GUGGENHEIM
BILBAO

Guggenheim T 1

CONVENTION
CENTER

T Euskalduna

EUSKALDUNA
BRIDGE

A. DE MAZARREDO

IPARRAGUIRRE

Plaza
del Museo

HENAO

Parque Iturriza

Doña Casilda

PASEO JOSE ANSELMO CLAVE

FINE
ARTS
MUSEUM

P

CALLE DE ELCANO

LARREATEGUI

Sabino
Arana T

SAN MAMÉS
STADIUM

To T
La Casilla

M
San T
Mamés T

RODRIGUEZ ARIAS

LICENCIADO POZO

JOSE MARIA ESCUZA

Plaza
Teófilo
Guiard

COLON DE LARREATEGUI

GRAN VIA DE DON

ALAMEDA DOCTOR AREILZA

Plaza
Moyúa

RODRIGUEZ ARIAS

ERCILLA

IPARRAGUIRRE

ALAMEDA RECALDE

TERMIBUS
BUS
STATION

LUIS BRIÑAS

AVENIDA DE SABINO ARANA

MARIA DIAZ DE HARO

ALAMEDA DE URQUIJO

M
Indautxu

SIMON BOLIVAR

DOCTOR AREILZA

MANUEL ALLENDE

GREGORIO DE LA REVILLA

Plaza
Indautxu

Plaza
del
Bombero
Echaniz

GORDONIZ

Plaza
Bizkaia

IPARRAGUIRRE

Plaza de
Arriquibar

AZKUNA
ZENTROA

GENERAL CONCHA

FERNANDEZ DE CAMPO

ALAMEDA DE SAN MAMES

EGAÑA

Plaza
Zabálburu

AUTONOMIA

AUTONOMIA

LABAYRU

GENERAL SALAZAR

GORDONIZ

Parque
Ametzola

DOCTOR DIAZ EMPARANZA

AUTOPISTA SOLUCION SUR

To A-8 Freeway
& Santander

Plaza
Ametzola

PLAZA DE
TOROS

IRALA

AVENIDA KIRIKIÑO

To A-8 Freeway
& San Sebastián

DI

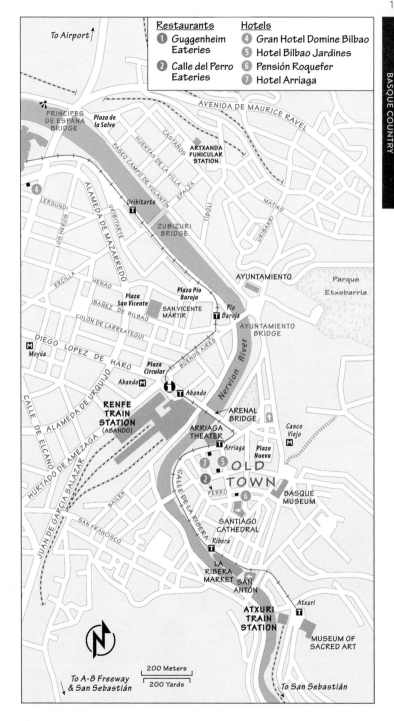

Restaurants
① Guggenheim Eateries
② Calle del Perro Eateries

Hotels
④ Gran Hotel Domine Bilbao
⑤ Hotel Bilbao Jardines
⑥ Pensión Roquefer
⑦ Hotel Arriaga

To Airport

AVENIDA DE MAURICE RAVEL

PRÍNCIPES DE ESPAÑA BRIDGE

Plaza de la Salve

PASEO CAMPO DE VOLANTÍN

HUERTAS DE LA VILLA

CASTAÑOS

ARTXANDA FUNICULAR STATION

EPALZA

TÍBOLI

MATIKO

Uribitarte

URIBARRI

ALAMEDA DE MAZARREDO

LERSUNDI

LOS HEROS

ZUBIZURI BRIDGE

AYUNTAMIENTO

Parque Etxebarria

ERCILLA

HENAO

IBÁÑEZ DE BILBAO

Plaza San Vicente

Plaza Pío Baroja

SAN VICENTE MÁRTIR

Pío Baroja

AYUNTAMIENTO BRIDGE

COLÓN DE LARREATEGUI

DIEGO LÓPEZ DE HARO

Moyúa

ALAMEDA DE URQUIJO

BUENOS AIRES

Plaza Circular

Abando

Nervión River

RENFE TRAIN STATION (ABANDO)

CALLE DE ELCANO

HURTADO DE AMÉZAGA

Abando

ARENAL BRIDGE

ARRIAGA THEATER

Arriaga

Casco Viejo

⑦ ⑤ OLD TOWN

JUAN DE GARCÍA SALAZAR

BAILÉN

SAN FRANCISCO

Plaza Nueva

② PERRO

⑥

BASQUE MUSEUM

CALLE DE LA RIBERA

SANTIAGO CATHEDRAL

Ribera

LA RIBERA MARKET

SAN ANTÓN

Atxuri

ATXURI TRAIN STATION

MUSEUM OF SACRED ART

N

200 Meters
200 Yards

To A-8 Freeway & San Sebastián

To San Sebastián

The building by Frank Gehry is a masterpiece in itself. It's reason enough to splice Bilbao into your itinerary.

Cost and Hours: €13; July-Aug daily 10:00-20:00; Sept-June Tue-Sun 10:00-20:00, closed Mon; same-day reentry allowed—get wristband on your way out; café, no photos inside galleries, Avenida Abandoibarra 2, tram stop: Guggenheim, Metro stop: Moyúa, tel. 944-359-080, www.guggenheim-bilbao.es.

Tours: Free audioguide included with entry. Free, 1-hour guided tours in English run once a day at 12:20; arrive 30 minutes earlier to sign up at the info desk.

Visiting the Museum: Study the exterior. Using cutting-edge technologies, unusual materials, and daring forms, Frank Gehry created a sculptural building that smoothly integrates with its environment. Gehry meshed many visions: The building is inspired by a silvery fish, but also evokes wind-filled sails.

Guarding the main entrance is artist Jeff Koons' 42-foot-tall **West Highland Terrier,** also known as "Puppy." The **atrium** acts as the heart of the building, pumping visitors from various rooms on three levels out and back, always returning to this central area before moving on to the next. There are virtually no straight lines. The sheets of glass that make up the elevator shaft overlap like fish scales.

From the atrium, step out onto the riverside **terrace.** The "water garden" is home to a five-part "fire fountain"; a "fog sculpture" that billows up from below; another piece by Jeff Koons, *Tulips;* and *Tall Tree and the Eye* by Anish Kapoor. On the right, a grand **staircase** leads under a big green bridge to a tower. The 30-foot-tall **spider,** called *Maman* ("Mommy"), is by Louise Bourgeois.

Gehry designed the vast **ground floor** to house huge installations. While most come and go, Richard Serra's *Matter of Time* in the largest gallery (#104) is permanent. Who would want to move its massive metal coils?

Take a circular stroll up and down each side of the river and over the two modern **pedestrian bridges.** Look out over the city and consider this: Gehry designed his building to reflect Bilbao.

Leaving the Museum: To get to the Old Town, take the tram that leaves from the river level beside the museum, just past the fountain (toward Atxuri). Hop off at the Arriaga stop, near the theater of the same name. Cross the street to enter the Old Town.

OLD TOWN
Bilbao's Old Town, with tall, narrow lanes lined with thriving shops and tapas bars, is worth a stroll.

Whether you're intending to or not, you'll eventually wind up at Old Bilbao's centerpiece, the **Santiago Cathedral,** a 14th-century Gothic church with a tranquil interior (free, €2 to dip into cloister and tiny museum featuring a smiling Jesus—pay the nun; Mon-Sat 10:00-13:00 & 17:00-19:30, closed Sun; tel. 944-153-627).

Or you might enjoy the **Basque Museum,** housed in a 16th-century convent, displaying artifacts of Basque heritage, described by English pamphlets (€3, Mon and Wed-Fri 10:00-19:00, Sat 10:00-13:30 & 16:00-19:00, Sun 10:00-14:00, closed Tue, Miguel de Unamuno Plaza 4, tel. 944-155-423, www.euskal-museoa.org/es).

Picnickers like the **La Ribera Market.** Stroll the stalls for the freshest fish, shop for produce, and admire a series of Art Deco stained-glass panels on the top floor (Mon and Sat 8:00-15:00, Tue-Fri 8:00-14:30 & 17:00-20:00, closed Sun).

Eating

Inside the Guggenheim, you'll find a **cafeteria** (Tue-Sun 9:30-20:30, also open Mon July-Aug) and a chic **Bistro** (open for dinner Thu-Sat, tel. 944-239-333). Outside by the playgrounds is a pleasant **outdoor café.** In the Old Town, good options are on **Calle del Perro,** including

Xukela Bar for tasty tapas (Calle del Perro 2), and three sit-down restaurants virtually next door to each other: **Egiluz, Río-Oja,** and **Rotterdam.**

Sleeping

$$$ Gran Hotel Domine Bilbao, near the Guggenheim, is a splurge for modern-art fans (Alameda Mazarredo 61, tel. 944-253-300, www.granhoteldominebilbao. com, recepcion.domine@hoteles-silken. com).

In the Old Town, try **$$ Hotel Bilbao Jardines** (Calle Jardines 9, tel. 944-794-210, www.hotelbilbaojardines.com, info@ hotelbilbaojardines.com), **$$ Pensión Roquefer** (Lotería 2, tel. 944-159-755, www.pensionroquefer.com, info@pension roquefer.com), or **$ Hotel Arriaga** (Ribera 3, tel. 944-790-001, www.hotelarriaga.es, info@hotelarriaga.es).

Pamplona

Proud Pamplona is best known for the Running of the Bulls (during the Fiesta de San Fermín, July 6-14), made famous by Ernest Hemingway. Unless you're looking for a constant party atmosphere, you'll find Pamplona more welcoming, sane, and enjoyable outside of the festival.

Rick's Tip: *Visit the last weekend in September for* **a festival with no bull: San Fermín Txikito** *is lively but practically tourist-free. The church of San Fermín de Aldapa is the heart of a celebration involving concerts, brass-band and food competitions, and parades of giant mannequins.*

Orientation

Everything of interest is in the tight, twisting lanes of the Old Town, centered on the main square, Plaza del Castillo. The newer Ensanche ("Expansion") neighborhood just to the south—with a sensible grid plan—holds the bus station.

Day Plan: Take my "Walking of the

Tourists" stroll, then visit the cathedral.

Getting to Pamplona: The town has good connections with **San Sebastián** (8-10 buses/day, 1 hour), **Madrid** (4 trains/ day direct, 3 hours), and **Barcelona** (6 trains/day, 3 direct, 4 hours).

Arrival in Pamplona: You can store bags at the bus station, but not at the train station. The sleek, user-friendly **bus station** is underground in Ensanche, about a 10-minute walk from the Old Town. On arrival, go up the escalators, cross the street, turn left, and walk a half-block, where you can turn right down the busy Conde Oliveto street. Walk two blocks to the big traffic circle called Plaza Príncipe de Viana. From here, turn left up Avenida de San Ignacio to reach the Old Town.

The **RENFE train station** is farther from the center, across the river to the northwest. It's easiest to hop on public bus #9 (€1.50, every 15 minutes), which drops you at the big Plaza Príncipe de Viana traffic circle south of the Old Town—look for a square with a fountain in the center.

Drivers should follow the bull's-eyes to the center of town. There's also handy parking right at Plaza del Castillo and Plaza de Toros (bullring).

Tourist Information: The TI is located next to City Hall (daily 10:00-20:00 in summer, shorter hours and closed Mon off-season, closed during Fiesta de San Fermín, on Plaza Consistorial at Calle San Saturnino 2, tel. 948-420-700, www. turismodepamplona.es).

Guides: Try **Francisco Glaría** (€140/ half-day up to 4 hours, mobile 629-661-604, www.novotur.com, francisco@novo tur.com).

The Walking of the Tourists

Follow the signs labeled *El Encierro,* which marks the route of the Running of the Bulls through the town center. Begin by the river, at the **Bull Corral,** where the bulls are released during the festival (the rest of the year, it's a parked-car

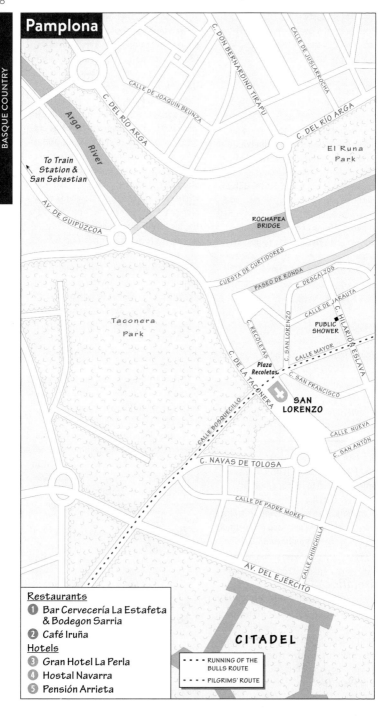

Pamplona

CALLE C. DON BERNARDINO TIRAPU
CALLE DE JUSLARROCHA
CALLE DE JOAQUIN BEUNZA
C. DEL RÍO ARGA
C. DEL RÍO ARGA

Arga River

El Runa Park

To Train Station & San Sebastian

AV. DE GUIPÚZCOA

ROCHAPEA BRIDGE

CUESTA DE CURTIDORES

PASEO DE RONDA
C. PESCALZOS

Taconera Park

CALLE DE JARAUTA
C. HILARION ESLAVA

C. RECOLETAS
C. SAN LORENZO

PUBLIC SHOWER

CALLE MAYOR

C. DE LA TACONERA

Plaza Recoletas

C. SAN FRANCISCO

SAN LORENZO

CALLE BOSQUECILLO

CALLE NUEVA

C. SAN ANTÓN

C. NAVAS DE TOLOSA

CALLE DE PADRE MORET

CALLE CHINCHILLA

AV. DEL EJÉRCITO

Restaurants
1. Bar Cervecería La Estafeta & Bodegon Sarria
2. Café Iruña

Hotels
3. Gran Hotel La Perla
4. Hostal Navarra
5. Pensión Arrieta

CITADEL

- - - - RUNNING OF THE BULLS ROUTE
- - - - PILGRIMS' ROUTE

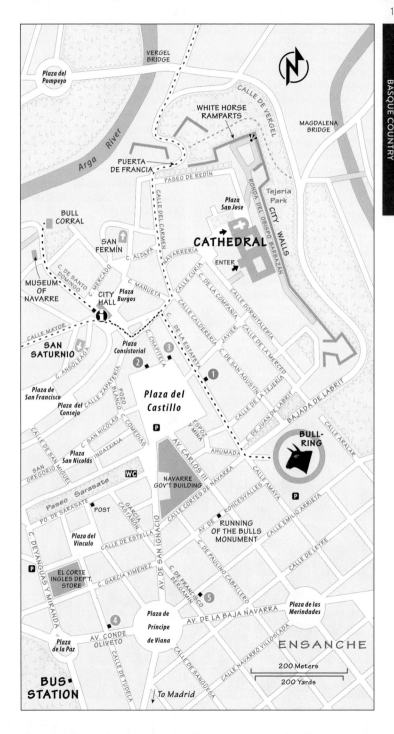

corral). They first run up Cuesta de Santo Domingo; follow their route.

A few blocks ahead on the right is the **Museum of Navarre** (Museo de Navarra), with four floors celebrating local art, including Goya's *Retrato de Marques de San Adrian* (€2, free Sat afternoons and all day Sun, open Tue-Sat 9:30-14:00 & 17:00-19:00, Sun 11:00-14:00, closed Mon, Santo Domingo 47, tel. 848-426-492, www.cfnavarra.es/cultura/museo). The **adjoining church** (on the left as you exit, show museum ticket) has an impressive golden Baroque-Rococo altarpiece depicting the Annunciation.

Continue along Cuesta de Santo Domingo. Embedded in the wall on the right is a small shrine with an image of San Fermín. Farther up on the left is the **food market of Santo Domingo,** handy for picnic supplies (Mon-Sat 8:00-14:00, closed Sun). Ahead in the square is **City Hall** (Ayuntamiento), built in 1423 to unite the community. The Baroque decoration is symbolic: Hercules demonstrates the city's strength, while the horn-blower trumpets its greatness.

The festival of San Fermín begins and ends on the balcony of this building (with the flags). Look in the direction you just came (also the route of the bulls). The line of metal squares in the pavement is used to secure barricades for the run. The inner space is for journalists and emergency medical care; spectators line up along the outer barrier.

Follow the route of the bulls two blocks down Calle de Mercaderes (next to Alexander Jewelry). Turn right onto **Calle de La Estafeta.** At this turn, the bulls—now going downhill—can lose their balance, sliding into the barricade. (The cathedral is dead ahead, three blocks up the lane called "Curia" from this corner.)

The bulls charge up narrow street La Estafeta. No room for barricades...no escape from the bulls! On days that the bulls aren't running, La Estafeta is home to the best tapas bars in town. Down the first block on the right, look for the hole-in-the-wall **Ultramarinos Beatriz** shop (at #22), makers of the best treats in town

Pamplona's Running of the Bulls

(Mon-Fri 9:00-14:00 & 16:30-20:00, Sat 9:00-14:00, closed Sun, tel. 948-220-618). Halfway down the street, notice the alley on the right leading to the main square. Farther down, near the very end of La Estafeta (on the right, at #76), look for the shop called **Kukuxumusu.** The giant clock outside the shop counts down to the next Running of the Bulls.

La Estafeta eventually leads you right to the **bullring,** used only during the festival. At the end of the run, the bulls charge down the ramp and through the red door. Built in 1923, the arena was expanded in the 1960s, doubling its capacity and halving its architectural charm. Bullfights start at 18:30. Pamplona's spectators are notorious for their raucous behavior.

Look for the big bust of **Ernest Hemingway,** celebrated by Pamplona as if he were a native son. Hemingway first came here during the 1923 Running of the Bulls. He wrote about the event in *The Sun Also Rises,* putting Pamplona on the map. At the beginning of the annual festival, young people tie a red neckerchief around this statue, so Hemingway can be properly outfitted for the occasion. Walk 20 yards, keeping the bullring on your left, then cross the street and walk a block into the pedestrian zone to the **Running of the Bulls Monument** (Monumento al Encierro), showing 6 bulls, 2 steer, and 10 runners.

From here you can turn right and walk two blocks up the street to the main square, **Plaza del Castillo.** Several Hemingway sights surround this square. The Gran Hotel La Perla was his favorite place to stay. His other haunts included Bar Txoko (top of the square) and Café Iruña

(bottom of the square). You've survived the run! Now enjoy Pamplona!

Sights

▲▲CATHEDRAL (CATEDRAL)

Even after an expensive makeover, Pamplona's cathedral—a Gothic core wrapped in a Neoclassical interior—remains dark and mysterious. The prominent tomb in the nave holds Charles III (the king of Navarre who united the disparate groups of Pamplona).

Cost and Hours: Cathedral and museum—€5, daily 10:30-19:00, until 17:00 in winter, museum closed Sun and during church services, tel. 948-212-594.

Eating

Head for the tapas bars on La Estafeta. Try **Bar Cervecería La Estafeta,** whose specialty is *gulas*—baby eels (#54, tel. 948-222-157), or **Bodegon Sarria,** for *escombro,* a hot sandwich with ham and chorizo (#52, tel. 948-227-713). For a restaurant, try **Café Iruña,** a favorite of Hemingway's (Plaza del Castillo 44, tel. 948-222-064, www.cafeiruna.com).

Sleeping

$$$ Gran Hotel La Perla is Hemingway's favorite splurge (Plaza del Castillo 1, tel. 948-223-000, www.granhotellaperla.com, informacion@granhotellaperla.com). **$$ Hostal Navarra** offers the best value in town (Calle Tudela 9, tel. 948-225-164, www.hostalnavarra.com, info@hostal navarra.com). **$ Pensión Arrieta** is the budget option (Calle Emilio Arrieta 27, tel. 948-228-459, www.pensionarrieta.net, pensionarrieta@pensionarrieta.net).

BEST OF THE REST

SANTIAGO DE COMPOSTELA

Santiago de Compostela has a powerful and mysterious draw on travelers: More than a thousand years' worth of Christian pilgrims have trod the desolate trail across northern Spain just to peer at the facade of its glorious cathedral. Today, they're joined by happy hippies finding themselves while hiking the ancient Camino de Santiago.

As a pilgrim mecca, the city's services are geared toward low-budget travelers. Its biggest downside is its location: Except by air (consider flying), it's a long trip from anywhere else in Spain. You can see Santiago in a day.

Orientation

You can walk across the city center in about 15 minutes. Known as Zona Monumental, it's a maze of squares centered around the cathedral. It's circled by a busy street that marks the former location of the town wall. Outside of that is the modern Céntrico district. A 10-minute walk through Céntrico takes you to the train station.

Day Plan: The cathedral is the city's top sight. The highlight of a visit is hanging out on the cathedral square at about 10:00 to welcome tired, happy pilgrims finishing their trek. Spend time visiting the museums, pilgrim-watching, and browsing the market, streets, and squares around the cathedral.

Rick's Tip: Skip the tourist train, *which does a pointless little loop around the outskirts of the city.*

Getting to Santiago de Compostela: Except by air, it's a long journey from any other notable stop in Spain. Here are sample times by train from **Madrid** (4/day, 5.5-8.5 hours), **Salamanca** (1/day, 6.5

hours), and **San Sebastián** (1-2/day, 10.5 hours). Allow a bit longer if you go by bus instead (Alsa bus company, www.alsa.es).

To add Santiago to my recommended two-week itinerary (see page 26), splice it after Madrid and Toledo (take the fast train or fly from Madrid to Santiago, then fly to Granada to continue the itinerary).

Arrival in Santiago de Compostela: The **train station** is on the southern edge of the modern Céntrico district. To reach the center of town, leave the station and walk up the grand granite staircase, jog right, cross the busy Avenida de Lugo, and walk uphill for 10 minutes on Rúa do Hórreo to Praza de Galicia, a few steps from the historical center. A **taxi** will cost you about €9.

From the **bus station,** northeast of the cathedral, it's about a 15-minute, mostly downhill walk to the center: Exit the station straight ahead on Rúa de Ánxel Casal and go to Praza da Paz. Turn left here onto Rúa da Pastoriza; follow it as it changes its name to Basquiños and Santa Clara before becoming Rúa de San Roque, which will bring you into town. Or take bus #5 to Praza de Galicia (to reach the historical center from here, walk uphill to cross busy Rúa da Senra—the Alameda park will be on your left). **Taxis** whisk you to the center for about €6. Only the bus station has **luggage storage.**

The **airport** is about six miles from the city center (airport code: SCQ). A bus connects the airport to the bus station, train station, and then to Praza de Galicia at the south end of the historical center (€3, catch bus at exit by car rentals, 2/hour, 6:15-24:35, 35 minutes, www.empresafreire.com). A **taxi** into town costs €21.

Drivers should take the north exit (#67) toward the airport and the old cen-

The Camino de Santiago

The Camino de Santiago—the "Way of St. James"—is Europe's ultimate pilgrimage route. Since the Middle Ages, pilgrims have trod hundreds of miles across northern Spain to pay homage to the remains of St. James in his namesake city, Santiago de Compostela (Santiago is Spanish for St. James).

The first person to undertake the Camino was...Santiago himself. After the death of Christ, the apostles scattered to the corners of the earth to spread the Word of God. Supposedly, St. James went on a missionary trip all the way to the northwest corner of Spain, then the end of the known world. According to legend, St. James' remains were discovered in 813 in the town that would soon bear his name. This put Santiago de Compostela on the map. In 951, the bishop of Le Puy in France walked to Santiago to pay homage to the relics. As other pilgrims followed his example, the Camino de Santiago informally began. In the 12th century, Pope Callistus II decreed that any person who walked to Santiago in a Holy Year, confessed their sins, and took communion at the cathedral would be forgiven. This opportunity made the Camino de Santiago one of the most important pilgrimages in the world.

By 1130 the trek was so popular that it prompted French monk Aimery Picaud to pen a chronicle of his journey, including tips on where to eat, where to stay, and how to pack light and use a money belt. This *Codex Calixtinus* (Latin for "Camino Through the Back Door") was the world's first guidebook—the great-great-granddaddy of the one you're holding now.

In the age of Columbus, the Renaissance, and the Reformation, interest in the Camino dissipated. The discovery of the New World led the Church and the monarchy to focus on the Americas, and the pilgrimage began to wane.

In the late 1960s, parish priests along the Camino who wanted to revitalize the route received help from an unusual source—Spain's dictator Franco—who decided that Catholicism and nationalism went hand-in-hand. Pope John Paul II visited Santiago twice in the 1980s, reminding the world of its historic significance. In 1987, the European Union designated the route Europe's first Cultural Itinerary. The Galician government has poured funds into reviving the tradition of the Camino. Today, the route attracts more than 200,000 pilgrims each year.

ter. The parking lot closest to the cathedral is 400 yards up Avenida de Xoán XXIII.

Tourist Information: The TI offers two-hour walking tours of the cathedral and surrounding plazas on most weekend afternoons in summer (June-Sept daily 9:00-21:00; Oct-May Mon-Fri 9:00-19:00, Sat-Sun 9:00-14:00 & 16:00-19:00; Rúa do Vilar 30, tel. 981-555-129, www.santiago turismo.com).

Local Guides: Try **Patricia Furelos** (mobile 630-781-795, patriciafurelos@ yahoo.es) or **Manuel Ruzo** (mobile 639-888-064, manuel@artnaturagalicia.com).

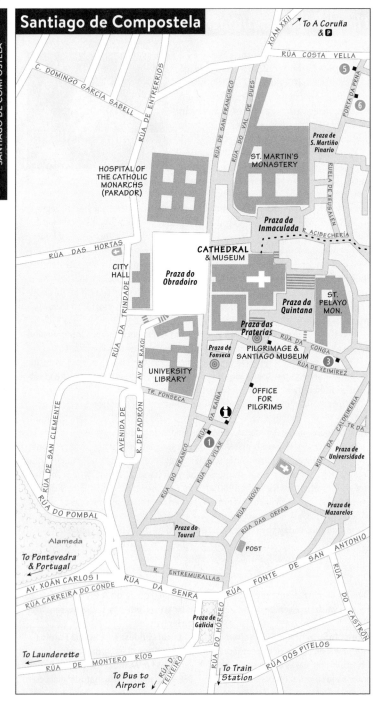

Santiago de Compostela

To A Coruña & P

RÚA COSTA VELLA

XOÁN XXII

C. DOMINGO GARCÍA SABELL

RÚA DE ENTRERRÍOS

RÚA DE SAN FRANCISCO

RÚA DO VAL DE DUES

5

PORTA DA PEÑA

6

Praza de S. Martiño Pinario

ST. MARTIN'S MONASTERY

RUELA DE XEUSALEN

HOSPITAL OF THE CATHOLIC MONARCHS (PARADOR)

Praza da Inmaculada

R. ACIBECHERÍA

RÚA DAS HORTAS

CITY HALL

CATHEDRAL & MUSEUM

Praza do Obradoiro

Praza da Quintana

ST. PELAYO MON.

RÚA DA TRINDADE

Praza das Praterías

RÚA DA CONGA

AV. DE RAXOI

Praza de Fonseca

PILGRIMAGE & SANTIAGO MUSEUM

3

RÚA DE XEIMÍREZ

UNIVERSITY LIBRARY

TR. FONSECA

OFFICE FOR PILGRIMS

RÚA DE SAN CLEMENTE

AVENIDA DE R. DE PADRÓN

RÚA DO VILAR

RÚA DA RAIÑA

1

Praza de Universidade

RÚA DA CALDEIRERÍA

TR DA

RÚA DO FRANCO

RÚA DO POMBAL

RÚA NOVA

Praza de Mazarelos

Alameda

To Pontevedra & Portugal

Praza do Toural

RÚA DAS ORFAS

POST

R. ENTREMURALLAS

AV. XOÁN CARLOS I

RÚA DA SENRA

RÚA FONTE DE SAN ANTONIO

RÚA DO CASTRÓN

RÚA CARREIRA DO CONDE

Praza de Galicia

RÚA DO HÓRREO

To Launderette

RÚA DE MONTERO RÍOS

RÚA DOS PITELOS

To Bus to Airport

RÚA D TEIXEIRO

To Train Station

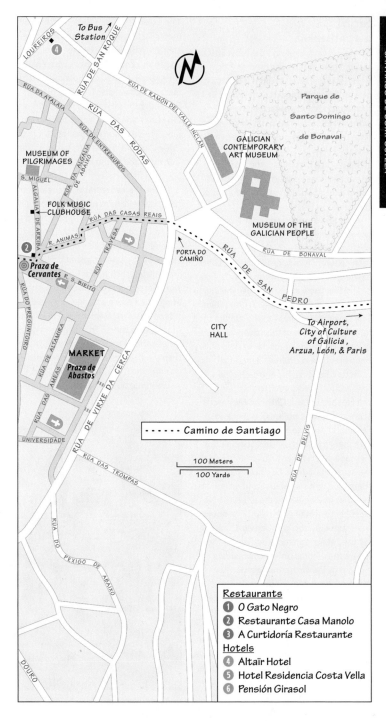

To Bus Station

LOUREIROS

RÚA DE SAN ROQUE

RÚA DE RAMÓN DEL VALLE INCLÁN

Parque de Santo Domingo de Bonaval

RÚA DA ATALAIA

RÚA DAS RODAS

RÚA DE ENTREMUROS

RÚA DA ALGALIA DE ABAIXO

GALICIAN CONTEMPORARY ART MUSEUM

MUSEUM OF PILGRIMAGES

S. MIGUEL

ALGALIA DE ARRIBA

FOLK MUSIC CLUBHOUSE

RÚA DAS CASAS REAIS

RÚA TRAVESA

MUSEUM OF THE GALICIAN PEOPLE

RÚA DE BONAVAL

R. ANIMAS

2 Praza de Cervantes

R.S. BIEITO

PORTA DO CAMIÑO

RÚA DE SAN PEDRO

RÚA DO PREGUNTOIRO

RÚA DE ALTAMIRA

MARKET
Praza de Abastos

RÚA DE VIRXE DA CERCA

CITY HALL

To Airport, City of Culture of Galicia, Arzua, León, & Paris

RÚA DAS ANEAS

UNIVERSIDADE

RÚA DE BELVIS

· · · · · Camino de Santiago

RÚA DAS TROMPAS

100 Meters
100 Yards

RÚA DO PEXIGO DE ABAIXO

DOURO

Restaurants
1 O Gato Negro
2 Restaurante Casa Manolo
3 A Curtidoría Restaurante
Hotels
4 Altaïr Hotel
5 Hotel Residencia Costa Vella
6 Pensión Girasol

Sights

▲▲CATHEDRAL

Santiago's cathedral isn't the most impressive in Spain, but it's the most mystical, with a spiritual magnetism that makes it one of the most important churches in Christendom. Put yourself in the well-worn shoes of millions of pilgrims who have trekked many miles to this powerful place.

If a service is going on, the front entrance is likely closed—enter around either side, about 100 yards to the left or the right.

Cost and Hours: Free, daily 7:00-20:30, www.catedraldesantiago.es.

Backpacks: Backpacks aren't allowed in the church; free baggage storage is next to the Office for Pilgrims on Rúa do Vilar.

Visiting the Cathedral: Begin facing the main facade, on Praza do Obradoiro. The pavement stone with the scallop shell right in the middle of this square is where millions of tired pilgrims have taken a deep breath and exulted: "I made it!"

Before heading into the cathedral, look around the square. To your left is the **Hospital of the Catholic Monarchs** (Hostal dos Reis Católicos). Isabel and Ferdinand came to Santiago in 1501 to give thanks for forcing the Moors out of Granada. Seeing many sick pilgrims, they decided to build this free hospital for them. Today, it's a parador and restaurant. Another 90 degrees to the left is the Neoclassical **City Hall** (Concello). The equestrian statue up top is St. James. Completing the square (90 more degrees to the left) is the original **university** building.

Look at the **cathedral facade.** Twelve hundred years ago, a monk followed a field of stars to the village of San Fiz de Solovio and discovered the lost tomb of St. James. On July 25, 813, the local bishop declared that St. James' remains had been found. They began building a church and named the place Santiago (St. James) de Compostela ("field of stars"). Construction of a larger cathedral began in 1075.

The exterior you see today is not what medieval pilgrims saw. In the mid-18th century, a Baroque exterior was added and the interior stonework was replaced with gaudy gold. Atop the middle steeple is St. James, dressed like a pilgrim. Beneath him is his tomb, marked by a star. On either side of the tomb are his disciples, Theodorus and Athanasius. On the side pillars are, to the left, James' father, Zebedee; and to the right, his mother, Salomé.

Inside the cathedral, at the rear of the nave, is the **Portico of Glory,** the original facade sculpted around 1180. Walk to the column in the middle of the entryway. (Squint down the nave to see the stone statue of St. James marking his tomb.) Pilgrims put their hands into the well-worn finger holes on the column, thanking St. James for safe passage. On the other side of the post, at knee level, is Maestro Mateo, who carved this facade. People tapped their heads against his to improve their intelligence—until a metal barrier was erected. (Grades have dropped.)

Continue up the nave to the big gold

Santiago's cathedral

altar, with three representations of St. James: On a white horse is James the Moor-Slayer; below that is pilgrim James; and below that is the original Apostle James by Maestro Mateo. Down the little stairway (see the green light, on your right) is the level of the 10th-century church and the **Tomb of St. James,** marked by a star. Pilgrims kneel and pray here, making requests or giving thanks. Behind the altar is the **Holy Door**, open only during Holy Years, when pilgrims use it to access the tomb and statue of the apostle. Near the exit from the tomb, find a little door (10 yards away, by another green light, closed 13:30-16:00 and after 20:00); climb the stairs to find a stone statue of St. James, gilded and caked with gems. Embrace him from behind and enjoy a saint's-eye view.

▲▲CATHEDRAL MUSEUM (MUSEO DA CATEDRAL)

The cathedral's museum shows off interesting pieces from the fine treasury collection and artifacts from the cathedral's history.

Cost and Hours: €6, daily April-Oct 9:00-20:00, Nov-March 10:00-20:00, last entry one hour before closing, ticket office in crypt under main stairs into cathedral, tel. 902-557-812, www.catedraldesantiago.es.

▲MUSEUM OF PILGRIMAGES (MUSEO DAS PEREGRINACIÓNS)

This well-presented museum examines various aspects of the pilgrimages around the world, including Santiago's, giving a historical context to all of those backpackers in the streets. Info sheets in English are available throughout.

Cost and Hours: Free, Tue-Fri 10:00-20:00, Sat 10:30-13:30 & 17:00-20:00, Sun 10:30-13:30, closed Mon, Praza de San Miguel dos Agros 4.

▲▲MARKET (MERCADO DE ABASTOS)

This wonderful market, housed in Old World stone buildings, offers a good opportunity to shop for a picnic while doing some serious people-watching. You're sure to see seafood, including *percebes*—gooseneck barnacles (Mon-Sat 8:00-14:00, closed Sun).

Eating

With the coast just 20 miles away, the city is swimming in fresh seafood. Rúa do Franco is lined with eateries, including the no-frills seafood tapas bar, **O Gato Negro** (Tue-Sat 12:30-15:00 & 19:00-late, Sun 12:30-15:00, closed Mon, near Rúa do Franco on side street Rúa da Raíña, tel. 981-583-105). The popular **Restaurante Casa Manolo** is cheap, classy, and fast (€9 fixed-price meal, Mon-Sat lunch 13:00-16:00, dinner 20:00-23:30, Sun lunch only, at the bottom of Praza de Cervantes, tel. 981-582-950). **A Curtidoría Restaurante** offers a €12 lunch special in a romantic setting (€20-33 paella and fish plates, Rúa da Conga 2).

Sleeping

High season is roughly Easter through September. The trickiest dates to book are Easter Sunday weekend and the Feast of St. James (July 24-25). Try rustic **$$$ Altaïr Hotel** (Rúa dos Loureiros 12, www.altairhotel.net); lovely **$$ Hotel Residencia Costa Vella,** which has a nice garden café open to nonguests, too (Rúa Porta da Pena 17, www.costavella.com); or decent **$ Pensión Girasol** (Rúa Porta da Pena 4, www.hgirasol.com).

Madrid

Madrid is upbeat and vibrant. You'll feel it the moment you set foot in the city. Even the living-statue street performers have a twinkle in their eyes.

Like its people, the city is relatively young. In medieval times, it was just another village, wedged between the powerful kingdoms of Castile and Aragon. When newlyweds Ferdinand and Isabel united those kingdoms in 1469, Madrid—at the center of Spain—became the focal point of a budding nation. By 1561, Spain ruled the world's most powerful empire, and Madrid was transformed into a European capital. By 1900, Madrid had 500,000 people.

Today, the hub of Spain—with a population of 3.3 million—is working to make itself more livable with urban improvements such as pedestrianized streets, parks, and commuter lines. Fortunately, the historic core is still intact and easy to navigate.

So dive into the city's grandeur as well as its intimate charms. Feel the vibe in Puerta del Sol, the pulsing heart of Spain itself. The lavish Royal Palace, with its gilded rooms and frescoed ceilings, rivals Versailles. The Prado has Europe's top collection of paintings, and nearby hangs Picasso's chilling masterpiece, *Guernica*. Retiro Park invites you to take a shady siesta. Save time for Madrid's elegant shops and pedestrian zones. After dark, take to the streets for an evening paseo that can continue past midnight. Lively Madrid has enough street-singing, bar-hopping, and people-watching for everyone.

MADRID IN 2 DAYS

Day 1: Take a brisk 20-minute walk along the pedestrianized Calle de las Huertas, from Puerta del Sol to the Prado. Spend the morning at the Prado (reserve in advance). Enjoy an afternoon siesta—or rent a rowboat—in nearby Retiro Park. Then tackle modern art at the Reina Sofía museum (closed Tue), which displays Picasso's *Guernica*.

On any evening: Have a progressive tapas dinner at a series of characteristic bars. Join the evening paseo; my favorite time is right before sunset, when beautifully lit people fill the city. Take in a flamenco or zarzuela performance.

Day 2: Follow my self-guided walk—a loop from Puerta del Sol—and break it up midway to tour the Royal Palace. Linger in Madrid's grand public spaces: Puerta del Sol, Plaza Mayor, and Gran Vía (take my self-guided walk). With extra time, try a walking or food-tasting tour, visit more museums, or do some shopping.

Day Trips: Toledo works as a day trip, but is worth two days and nights if you have more time. Allow a half-day to see El Escorial (Inquisition palace), and one day to visit small-town Segovia (ancient Roman aqueduct). Add the lively university town of Salamanca to a Segovia excursion to make a pleasant two- or three-day loop.

ORIENTATION

Puerta del Sol marks the center of Madrid. No major sight is more than a 20-minute walk or a €7 taxi ride from this central square. Get out your map and frame off Madrid's historic core: To the west of Puerta del Sol is the Royal Palace. To the east, you'll find the Prado Museum, along with the Reina Sofía museum. North of Puerta del Sol is Gran Vía, a broad east-west boulevard bubbling with shops and cinemas. Between Gran Vía and Puerta del Sol is a bustling pedestrian shopping zone. And southwest of Puerta del Sol is Plaza Mayor, the center of a 17th-century, slow-down-and-smell-the-cobblestones district.

This entire historic core around Puerta del Sol—Gran Vía, Plaza Mayor, the Prado, and the Royal Palace—is easily covered on foot. A wonderful chain of pedestrian streets crosses the city east to west, from the Prado to Plaza Mayor (along Calle de las Huertas) and from Puerta del Sol to the Royal Palace (on Calle del Arenal). Stretching north from Gran Vía, Calle de Fuencarral is a trendy shopping and strolling pedestrian street.

Tourist Information

Madrid's city-run TIs share a website, a central phone number, and hours (generally daily 9:30-20:30, tel. 914-544-410, www.esmadrid.com). The best and most central city TI is on **Plaza Mayor.** Oth-

ers are at **Plaza de Colón** (in the underground passage accessed from Paseo de la Castellana and Calle de Goya), **Palacio de Cibeles** (closed Mon, inside, up the stairs and to the right), **Plaza de Cibeles** (at Paseo del Prado), **Paseo del Arte** (on Plaza Sánchez Bustillo, near the Reina Sofía museum), and at the **airport** (Terminals 2 and 4). In summer, the city sends mobile TIs to major sites around town.

Madrid also has regional TIs, privately run by Turismo Madrid (and therefore profit-motivated), with branches near the **Prado Museum** (daily 8:00-15:00, on Duque de Medinaceli, across from Palace Hotel), at **Chamartín train station** (Mon-Sat 8:00-15:00, Sun 9:00-14:00, near track 20), at the **Atocha train station** (daily 8:00-20:00, AVE arrivals side), and at the **airport** (Mon-Sat 9:00-20:00, Sun 9:00-14:00, Terminals 1 and 4, www.turismo madrid.es).

Pick up and use the free, well-designed *Public Transport* map, which includes detailed transportation routes throughout the city center.

At most TIs, you can get the *Es Madrid* English-language monthly, which lists events around town.

For arts and culture listings, pick up the Spanish-language weekly entertainment guide **Guía del Ocio,** which lists daily live music *("Conciertos"),* museum exhibits, and restaurants (€1, sold at newsstands, sometimes free at TI or hotels, www.guiadelocio.com).

Rick's Tip: You'll find **one-stop shopping** *at the department store* **El Corte Inglés,** *which takes up several buildings in the pedestrian zone a block off Puerta del Sol (Mon-Sat 10:00-22:00, Sun 11:00-21:00, Preciados 3). The main (tallest) building gives out free city maps, hosts two* **travel agencies** *(both sell* **train tickets***), and has a top-floor* **cafeteria** *and a basement* **supermarket.** *The other branch has an electronics department for help with* **mobile devices** *and a top-floor* **box office.**

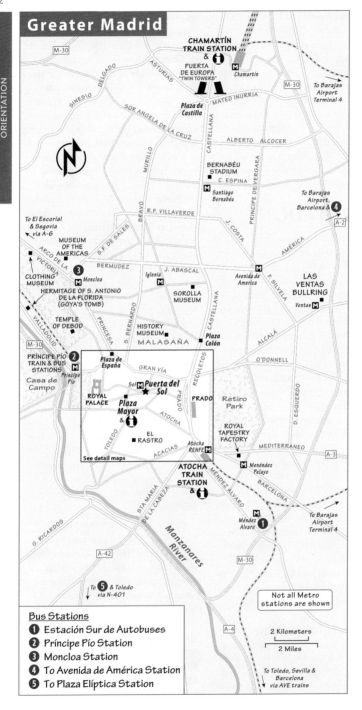

Greater Madrid

CHAMARTÍN
TRAIN STATION
& 🛈
PUERTA
DE EUROPA
"TWIN TOWERS"

M Chamartín

M-30

M-30

To Barajas
Airport
Terminal 4

DELGADO

SINESIO

ASTURIAS

Plaza de
Castilla

MATEO INURRIA

SOR ANGELA DE LA CRUZ

CASTELLANA

ALBERTO ALCOCER

MURILLO

BRAVO

BERNABÉU
STADIUM

C. ESPINA

M Santiago
Bernabéu

PRÍNCIPE DE VERGARA

To Barajas
Airport,
Barcelona & 4

A-2

R.F. VILLAVERDE

J. COSTA

AMÉRICA

To El Escorial
& Segovia
via A-6

ARCO DE LA

VICTORIA

MUSEUM
OF THE
AMERICAS

S.F. DE SALES

BERMUDEZ

J. ABASCAL

Avenida de
América

M

F. SILVELA

LAS
VENTAS
BULLRING

3 Moncloa

Iglesia

CLOTHING
MUSEUM

HERMITAGE OF S. ANTONIO
DE LA FLORIDA
(GOYA'S TOMB)

S. BERNARDO

PRINCESA

SOROLLA
MUSEUM

CASTELLANA

Ventas M

TEMPLE
OF DEBOD

VALLADOLID

M-30

HISTORY
MUSEUM

Plaza
Colón

ALCALÁ

MALASAÑA

O'DONNELL

PRÍNCIPE PÍO
TRAIN & BUS
STATIONS

2 Plaza de
España

GRAN VÍA

RECOLETOS

Casa de
Campo

Príncipe
Pío

M Sol ★ Puerta del
Sol

D. ESQUERDO

ROYAL
PALACE

Plaza
Mayor
& 🛈

PRADO

ATOCHA

PRADO

Retiro
Park

TOLEDO

EL
RASTRO

ACACIAS

Atocha
RENFE M

ROYAL
TAPESTRY
FACTORY

MEDITERRANEO

A-3

See detail maps

ATOCHA
TRAIN
STATION
& 🛈

MÉNDEZ ALVARO

M Menéndez
Pelayo

STA. MARIA

DE LA CABEZA

BARCELONA

G. RICARDOS

M Méndez
Alvaro 1

To Barajas
Airport
Terminal 4

A-42

Manzanares
River

M-30

To 5 & Toledo
via N-401

Not all Metro
stations are shown

A-4

2 Kilometers

2 Miles

To Toledo, Sevilla &
Barcelona
via AVE trains

Bus Stations
1 Estación Sur de Autobuses
2 Príncipe Pío Station
3 Moncloa Station
4 To Avenida de América Station
5 To Plaza Elíptica Station

Daily Reminder

SUNDAY: The Prado Museum and Centro de Arte Reina Sofía close earlier than normal today (19:00), as does the National Archaeological Museum (15:00). The flea market at El Rastro is held today (9:00-15:00). Midday, Retiro Park erupts into a carnival-like atmosphere. Bullfights take place on some Sundays (March through mid-Oct). Some flamenco places are closed today.

MONDAY: The National Archaeological Museum is closed today, and the Thyssen-Bornemisza Museum has shorter hours (12:00-16:00).

TUESDAY: The Reina Sofía is closed today.

WEDNESDAY/THURSDAY/FRIDAY: All major sights are open.

SATURDAY: All major sights are open. Midday, enjoy the scene at Retiro Park.

LATE-HOURS SIGHTSEEING: Sights with evening hours (20:30 or later) include the Reina Sofía (Mon and Wed-Sat until 21:00) and the Thyssen-Bornemisza Museum (exhibits only, Sat until 21:00 in summer).

FREE SIGHTSEEING: The Prado is free every evening from 18:00 (17:00 on Sun), the Reina Sofía has free evening hours Mon and Wed-Sat from 19:00 (15:00 on Sun), and the Thyssen-Bornemisza is free on Mon. The National Archaeological Museum is free all day Sun and on Sat afternoon (Sat from 14:00).

Sightseeing Passes

Very energetic travelers can save a little money and some valuable sightseeing time by buying the **Madrid Card.** It covers more than 50 sights—including the Royal Palace, Prado, Thyssen-Bornemisza, and Centro de Arte Reina Sofía—and lets you skip lines, a definite plus in high season, especially at the palace and the Prado. Additionally, the pass covers all the Essential Madrid tours and it's good for a 10 percent discount at El Corte Inglés. The three-day card for €67 is the best deal (other options include €47/24 hours and €60/48 hours, online discounts available, www.madridcard.com). You can pay extra to add the hop-on, hop-off bus tour (saves a maximum of €2) or public transport (only worthwhile if you ride multiple times a day).

If you want to visit the Prado, Thyssen-Bornemisza, and Centro de Arte Reina Sofía during day-time hours, you can save a few euros by buying the **Paseo del Arte combo-ticket,** though keep in mind that the Prado and Reina Sofía are free in the evenings, and the Thyssen is free on Mondays (€25.60, sold at each museum, good for a year, allows you to skip lines).

Tours

Essential Madrid offers interesting tours in English that depart from the Plaza Mayor TI; book at least a few hours in advance (€17, 20 percent discount for booking three different tours, 2 hours, 902-221-424, www.esmadrid.com).

Madrid Tours & Tastings bring together Spanish history, food, and wine (walking tours €15/person, tapas tours from €75/person, wine tastings from €65/person, mobile 620-883-900, www.madridtandt.com, nmurrell@madridtandt.com).

Frederico and Cristina specialize in family tours. They also offer museum tours and excursions to nearby towns (prices per group: €155/2 hours, €195/4 hours, €235/6 hours, tel. 913-102-974, mobile 649-936-222, www.spainfred.com, info@spainfred.com).

MADRID AT A GLANCE

▲▲▲**Royal Palace** Spain's sumptuous, lavishly furnished national palace. **Hours:** Daily April-Sept 10:00-20:00, Oct-March 10:00-18:00. See page 171.

▲▲▲**Prado Museum** One of the world's great museums, loaded with masterpieces by Diego Velázquez, Francisco de Goya, El Greco, Hieronymus Bosch, Albrecht Dürer, and more. **Hours:** Mon-Sat 10:00-20:00, Sun 10:00-19:00. See page 181.

▲▲▲**Centro de Arte Reina Sofía** Modern-art museum featuring Picasso's epic masterpiece *Guernica*. **Hours:** Mon and Wed-Sat 10:00-21:00, Sun 10:00-19:00, closed Tue. See page 195.

▲▲▲**Paseo** Evening stroll among the Madrileños. **Hours:** Sundown until the wee hours. See page 201.

▲▲**Puerta del Sol** Madrid's lively central square. **Hours:** Always bustling. See page 158.

▲▲**Thyssen-Bornemisza Museum** A great complement to the Prado, with lesser-known yet still impressive works and an especially good Impressionist collection. **Hours:** Mon 12:00-16:00, Tue-Sun 10:00-19:00, Sat until 21:00 in summer (exhibits only). See page 194.

▲▲**National Archaeological Museum** Traces the history of Iberia through artifacts. **Hours:** Tue-Sat 9:30-20:00, Sun 9:30-15:00, closed Mon. See page 200.

▲▲**Bullfights** Spain's controversial pastime. **Hours:** Scattered Sundays and holidays March-mid-Oct, plus almost daily in May-early June. See page 203.

▲▲Flamenco Captivating music and dance performances, at various venues throughout the city. **Hours:** Shows every night, some places closed on Sun. See page 202.

▲Plaza Mayor Historic cobbled square. **Hours:** Always open. See page 162.

▲Retiro Park Festive green escape from the city, with rental rowboats and great people-watching. **Hours:** Closes at dusk. See page 199.

▲Royal Botanical Garden A relaxing museum of plants from around the world. **Hours:** Daily 10:00-21:00, shorter hours off-season. See page 200.

▲El Rastro Europe's biggest flea market, filled with bargains and pick-pockets. **Hours:** Sun 9:00-15:00, best before 11:00. See page 200.

▲Zarzuela Madrid's delightful light opera. **Hours:** Evenings. See page 203.

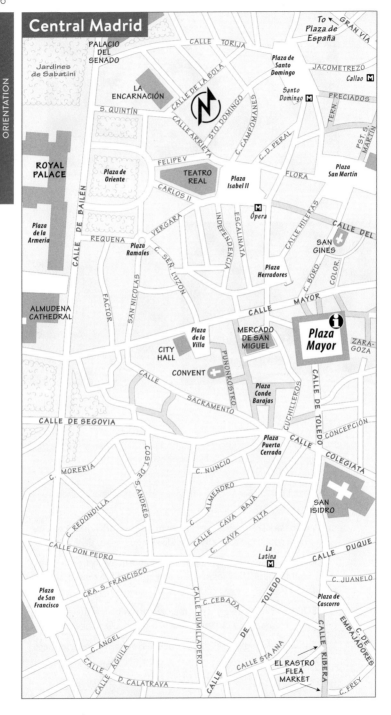

Central Madrid

To
Plaza de
España

GRAN VÍA

CALLE TORIJA

PALACIO
DEL
SENADO

Jardines
de Sabatini

Plaza de
Santo
Domingo

JACOMETREZO

Callao

LA
ENCARNACIÓN

S. QUINTÍN

CALLE DE LA BOLA

STO. DOMINGO

C. CAMPOMANES

Santo
Domingo

PRECIADOS

CALLE ARRIETA

C. D. PERAL

TERN.

PST. S. MARTÍN

ROYAL
PALACE

FELIPE V

CARLOS II

Plaza de
Oriente

TEATRO
REAL

Plaza
Isabel II

FLORA

Plaza
San Martín

Plaza
de la
Armería

CALLE DE BAILÉN

VERGARA

REQUENA

Plaza
Ramales

C. SEN. LUZÓN

INDEPENDENCIA

ESCALINATA

Ópera

CALLE HILERAS

CALLE DEL

SAN
GINES

C. BORD.

COLOR.

ALMUDENA
CATHEDRAL

FACTOR

SAN NICOLÁS

Plaza
Herradores

CALLE   MAYOR

Plaza
de la
Villa

MERCADO
DE SAN
MIGUEL

Plaza
Mayor

ZARA-
GOZA

CITY
HALL

CONVENT

PUÑONROSTRO

CALLE

SACRAMENTO

Plaza
Conde
Barajas

CUCHILLEROS

CALLE DE TOLEDO

CONCEPCIÓN

CALLE DE SEGOVIA

COSTA DE S. ANDRÉS

C. MORERIA

C. NUNCIO

C. ALMENDRO

Plaza
Puerta
Cerrada

CALLE

COLEGIATA

SAN
ISIDRO

C. REDONDILLA

CALLE CAVA BAJA

C. CAVA ALTA

La
Latina

CALLE DUQUE

CALLE DON PEDRO

C. JUANELO

Plaza
de San
Francisco

CRA. S. FRANCISCO

CALLE HUMILLADERO

C. CEBADA

TOLEDO

DE

Plaza de
Cascorro

C. DE EMBAJADORES

C. ÁNGEL

CALLE DE AGUILA

CALLE D. CALATRAVA

CALLE STA. ANA

CALLE RIBERA

EL RASTRO
FLEA
MARKET

C. FREY

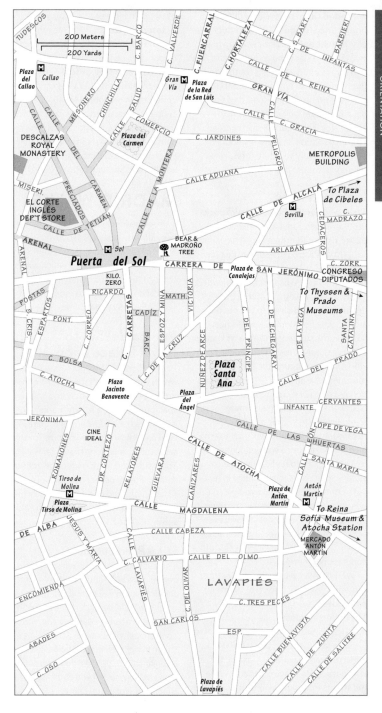

Madrid City Tour has two different hop-on, hop-off bus circuits through the city: historic and modern. You can hop from sight to sight and route to route. The two routes intersect at the south side of Puerta del Sol and in front of Starbucks across from the Prado (€21/1 day, €25/2 days, buy ticket on board; daily 9:30-22:00, Nov-Feb 10:00-18:00; recorded English narration, 15 stops, 1.5 hours, departures every 10-20 minutes, www. madridcitytour.es).

Helpful Hints

Theft and Safety: Beware of **pickpockets**—anywhere, anytime. Areas of particular risk are Puerta del Sol (the central square), El Rastro (the Sunday flea market), Gran Vía (the paseo zone: Plaza del Callao to Plaza de España), any crowded street, anywhere on the Metro, bus #27, and the airport. Be alert to the people around you: Someone wearing a heavy jacket in the summer is likely a pickpocket. Teenagers may dress like Americans and work the areas around the three big art museums. Assume any fight or commotion is a scam or a distraction.

Call the **SATE line** in an **emergency,** or for assistance in visiting a police station for any reason (24-hour tel. 902-102-112, English spoken once you get connected to a person). Help ranges from canceling stolen credit cards to assistance in reporting a crime. They can help you get to the police station (at Calle Leganitos 19 near Plaza de Santo Domingo) and will even act as an interpreter. You may see a police station in the Sol Metro station; this office handles only Metro theft.

While it's illegal to make money from someone else selling sex (i.e., pimping), **prostitutes** over 18 can solicit legally. They often frequent Calle de la Montera (leading north from Puerta del Sol to Plaza de la Red de San Luis). Don't stray north of Gran Vía around Calle de la Luna and Plaza Santa María Soledad—while the streets may look inviting, this area is a

meat-eating flower.

Internet Access: Plaza Mayor has free Wi-Fi, and more public spaces may offer it soon. You can get online on all Madrid buses and trains—look for *Wi-Fi gratis* signs. Most hotels offer Wi-Fi and a guest computer in the lobby. Any *locutorio* call center is generally the cheapest Internet option. Near the Puerta del Sol, **Workcenter** has plenty of terminals (Mon-Fri 8:00-21:00, Sat-Sun 10:00-14:30 & 17:00-20:30, Calle Sevilla 4, tel. 913-601-395).

MADRID WALKS

Two self-guided walks provide a look at two different sides of Madrid. For a taste of old Madrid, start with my "Puerta del Sol to Royal Palace Loop," which winds through the historic center. My "Gran Vía Walk" lets you glimpse a more modern side of Spain's capital.

Puerta del Sol to Royal Palace Loop

For a taste of old Madrid, follow this loop, which winds through the historic center. It's pedestrian-friendly and filled with spacious squares, a trendy market, bulls' heads in a bar, and a cookie-dispensing convent. Allow about two hours for this self-guided, mile-long triangular walk. You'll start and finish on Madrid's central square, Puerta del Sol (Metro: Sol).

• *Head to the middle of the square, by the equestrian statue of King Charles III, and survey the scene.*

❶ ▲▲Puerta del Sol

The bustling Puerta del Sol is Madrid's center. It's a hub for the Metro, local *cercanías* trains, revelers, and pickpockets. In recent years it has undergone a facelift to become a mostly pedestrianized, wide-open space...without a bench or spot of shade in sight. Nearly traffic-free, it's a popular site for political demonstrations. Don't be surprised if you come across a large, peaceful protest here.

The equestrian statue in the middle of the square honors **King Charles III** (1716-1788) whose enlightened urban policies earned him the affectionate nickname "the best mayor of Madrid." He decorated the city squares with beautiful fountains, got those meddlesome Jesuits out of city government, established the public school system, mandated underground sewers, opened his private Retiro Park to the general public, built the Prado, made the Royal Palace the wonder of Europe, and generally cleaned up Madrid.

Head to the slightly uphill end of the square and find the **statue of a bear** pawing a tree—a symbol of Madrid since medieval times. Bears used to live in the royal hunting grounds outside the city. And the *madroño* trees produce a berry that makes the traditional *madroño* liqueur. Near the statue, locate the Metro entrance and the glass-fish entrance to the *cercanías* trains.

Charles III faces a red-and-white building with a bell tower. This was Madrid's first post office, founded by Charles III in the 1760s. Today it's the **county governor's office** (Residencia de la Comunidad de Madrid), home to the president who governs greater Madrid. The building is notorious for having once been dictator Francisco Franco's police headquarters. An amazing number of those detained and interrogated by the Franco police "escaped" by jumping out its windows to their deaths. Notice the hats of the civil guardsmen at the entry. It's said the hats have square backs, cleverly designed so that the men can lean against the wall while enjoying a cigarette. On the opposite side of the square, look up to see the famous Tío Pepe sign, a neon advertisement from the 1950s for sherry wine.

Crowds fill the square on New Year's Eve as the rest of Spain watches the Times Square-style action on TV. The bell atop the governor's office chimes 12 times, while Madrileños eat one grape for each ring to bring good luck through each of the next 12 months.

• *Cross the square, walking to the governor's office.*

Puerta del Sol

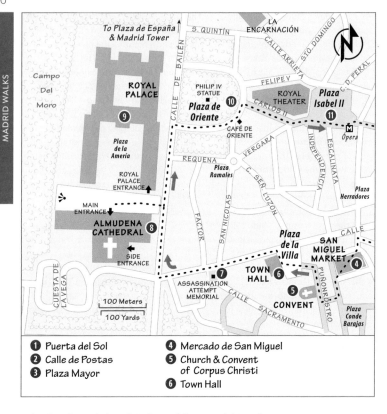

To Plaza de España ↑
& Madrid Tower

LA
ENCARNACIÓN
S. QUINTÍN
CALLE ARRIETA
STO. DOMINGO

Campo
Del
Moro

CALLE DE BAILÉN

ROYAL
PALACE

PHILIP IV
STATUE

FELIPE V

ROYAL
THEATER

Plaza
Isabel II

Plaza de
Oriente

⑩

C. D. PERAL

CARLOS II

Ⓜ
Ópera

❾

CAFÉ DE
ORIENTE

VERGARA

INDEPENDENCIA

ESCALINATA

⑪

Plaza
de la
Amería

REQUENA

Plaza
Ramales

C. SER. LUZON

Plaza
Herradores

ROYAL
PALACE
ENTRANCE

↑

SAN NICOLAS

↗
MAIN
ENTRANCE ↓

ALMUDENA
CATHEDRAL ❽

FACTOR

Plaza
de la
Villa

CALLE

SAN
MIGUEL
MARKET

❹

SIDE
ENTRANCE

CUESTA DE
LA VEGA

100 Meters

100 Yards

❼

ASSASSINATION
ATTEMPT
MEMORIAL

TOWN
HALL ❻

PUÑONROSTRO

CALLE
SACRAMENTO

❺
CONVENT

Plaza
Conde
Barajas

❶ Puerta del Sol
❷ Calle de Postas
❸ Plaza Mayor

❹ Mercado de San Miguel
❺ Church & Convent
   of Corpus Christi
❻ Town Hall

Look at the curb directly in front of the entrance to the governor's office. The marker is **"kilometer zero,"** the symbolic center of Spain (with its six main highways indicated). Standing on the zero marker with your back to the governor's office, get oriented visually: At twelve o'clock (straight ahead), notice how the pedestrian commercial zone (with the huge El Corte Inglés department store) is thriving. At two o'clock starts the seedier Calle de la Montera, a street with shady characters and prostitutes that leads to trendy, pedestrianized Calle de Fuencarral. At three o'clock is the biggest Apple store in Europe; the Prado is about a mile farther to your right. At 10 o'clock, you'll see the pedestrianized Calle del Arenal Street (which leads to the Royal Palace) dumping into this square...just where you will

end this walk.

On either side of the entrance to the governor's office are **two plaques** tied to important dates, expressing thanks from the regional government to its citizens for assisting in times of dire need. To the left of the entry, a plaque on the wall honors those who helped during the terrorist bombings of March 11, 2004 (we have our 9/11—Spain commemorates its 3/11). A similar plaque on the right marks the spot where the war against Napoleon started in 1808. When Napoleon invaded Spain and tried to appoint his brother (rather than the Spanish heir) as king of Spain, an angry crowd gathered outside this building. The French soldiers attacked and simply massacred the mob. Painter Francisco de Goya, who worked just up the street, observed the event and cap-

Puerta del Sol to Royal Palace Loop

❼ Assassination Attempt Memorial
❽ Almudena Cathedral
❾ Royal Palace
❿ Plaza de Oriente
⓫ Plaza de Isabel II
⓬ Calle del Arenal

tured the tragedy in his paintings *Second of May, 1808* and *Third of May, 1808,* now in the Prado.

On the corner of Puerta del Sol and Calle Mayor (downhill end of Puerta del Sol, across from McDonald's) is the busy *confitería* **La Mallorquina,** *"fundada en 1.894"* (daily 9:00-21:00, closed mid-July-Aug). Go inside for a tempting peek at racks with goodies hot out of the oven. Enjoy observing the churning energy at the bar lined with Madrileños popping in for a fast coffee and a sweet treat. The shop is famous for its cream-filled *Napolitana* pastry (€1.20). Or sample Madrid's answer to doughnuts, *rosquillas* (*tontas* means "silly"—plain, and *listas* means "all dressed up and ready to go"—with icing, about €1 each). The room upstairs is more genteel, with nice views of the square.

From inside the shop, look back toward the entrance and notice the tile above the door with the 18th-century view of Puerta del Sol. Compare this with today's view out the door. This was before the square was widened, when a church stood at its top end.

Puerta del Sol ("Gate of the Sun") is named for a long-gone gate with the rising sun carved onto it, which once stood at the eastern edge of the old city. From here, we begin our walk through the historic town that dates back to medieval times.

• *Head west on busy Calle Mayor, just past McDonald's, and veer left up the pedestrian alley called...*

❷ Calle de Postas

The street sign shows the post coach heading for that famous first post office.

Medieval street signs posted on the lower corners of buildings included pictures so the illiterate (and monolingual tourists) could "read" them. Fifty yards up the street on the left, at Calle San Cristóbal, is Pans & Company, a popular Catalan sandwich chain offering lots of healthy choices. While Spaniards consider American fast food unhealthy—both culturally and physically—they love it. McDonald's and Burger King are thriving in Spain.

• Continue up Calle de Postas, and take a slight right on Calle de la Sal through the arcade, where you emerge into...

❸ ▲Plaza Mayor

In medieval times, this was the city's main square; today it's a vast, cobbled, traffic-free chunk of 17th-century Spain. The equestrian statue (wearing a ruffled collar) honors Philip III, who (in 1619) transformed the medieval marketplace into a Baroque plaza. The square is 140 yards long and 102 yards wide, enclosed by three-story buildings with symmetrical windows, balconies, slate roofs, and steepled towers. Each side of the square is uniform, as if a grand palace were turned inside-out. This distinct look, pioneered by architect Juan de Herrera (who finished El Escorial), is found all over Madrid.

This site served as the city's 17th-century open-air theater. Upon this stage, much Spanish history has been played out: bullfights, fires, royal pageantry, and events of the gruesome Inquisition. Worn-down reliefs on the seatbacks under the lampposts tell the story. During the Inquisition, many were tried here—suspected heretics, Protestants, Jews, tour guides without a local license, and Muslims whose "conversion" to Christianity was dubious. The guilty were paraded around the square before their executions, wearing billboards listing their many sins. Bleachers were built for bigger audiences, while the wealthy rented balconies. The heretics were burned, and later, criminals were slowly strangled as they held a

crucifix, hearing the reassuring words of a priest as the life was squeezed out of them with a garrote.

The square's buildings are mainly private apartments. Want one? Costs run from €400,000 for a tiny attic studio to €2 million and up for a 2,500-square-foot flat. The square is painted a democratic shade of burgundy—the result of a citywide vote. Three different colors were painted as samples on the walls of this square, and the city voted for its favorite. Since the end of decades of dictatorship in 1975, there's been a passion for voting here.

A stamp-and-coin market bustles at Plaza Mayor on Sundays (10:00-14:00). The Casa Yustas shop at #30 (in the northeast corner) has been making hats here since 1894.

The building to Philip's left, on the north side beneath the twin towers, was once home to the baker's guild and now houses the TI. It's air-conditioned and offers daily walking tours with **Essential Madrid** (€17, 20 percent discount for booking three different tours, 2 hours, www.esmadrid.com). Consider reserving a spot now.

Day or night, Plaza Mayor is a colorful place to enjoy an affordable cup of coffee or overpriced food. Throughout Spain, lesser *plazas mayores* provide peaceful pools in the whitewater river of Spanish life.

For some interesting, if gruesome, bullfighting lore, drop by **La Torre del Oro Bar Andalú** (north side of the square at #26, a few doors to the left of the TI). With *Andalú* (Andalusian) ambience and an entertaining staff, this bar is a good place to end your Plaza Mayor visit. (Beware: They may push expensive tapas on tourists.) The price list posted outside the door makes your costs perfectly clear: "*barra*" indicates the price at the bar; "*terraza*" is the price at an outdoor table. Step inside, stand at the bar, and order a drink—a *caña* (small draft beer) shouldn't cost more than €2. At the outdoor tables, only larger size *cañas dobles* are available (for €4.50).

The interior is a temple to bullfighting, festooned with gory decor. Notice the breathtaking action captured in the many photographs. Look under the stuffed head of Barbero the bull. At eye level you'll see a *puntilla,* the knife used to put poor Barbero out of his misery at the arena. Just to the left of Barbero is a photo of longtime dictator Franco with the famous bullfighter Manuel Benítez Pérez—better known as El Cordobés, the Elvis of bullfighters and a working-class hero. At the top of the stairs to the WC, find the photo of El Cordobés and Robert Kennedy—looking like brothers. To the left of them (and elsewhere in the bar) is a shot of Che Guevara enjoying a bullfight. At the end of the bar, in a glass case, is the "suit of lights" that El Cordobés wore in an ill-fated 1967 fight in which the bull gored him. El Cordobés survived; the bull didn't. In the same case is the photo of a matador (not El Cordobés) hooked by a bull's horn.

Consider taking a break at one of the sidewalk tables of any café/bar terrace facing Madrid's grandest square. Nearby Cafetería Margerit occupies the sunniest corner of the square and is a good place to enjoy a coffee with the view. The scene is easily worth the extra euro you'll pay for the drink.

• *Leave Plaza Mayor on Calle de Ciudad Rodrigo (at the northwest corner of the square), passing a series of solid turn-of-the-20th-century storefronts and sandwich joints, such as Casa Rúa, famous for its cheap bocadillos de calamares—fried squid rings on a roll. Emerging from the arcade, turn left and head downhill toward the covered market hall.*

❹ Mercado de San Miguel

To wash down those *calamares* in a more refined setting, pop into this trendy market hall (daily 10:00-24:00). The historic iron-and-glass structure from 1916 stands on the site of an even earlier marketplace. Renovated in the 21st century, it now hosts some 30 high-end vendors of fresh produce, gourmet foods, wines by the glass, tapas, and full meals. Locals and tourists alike pause here for its food, natural-light ambience, and social scene.

Alongside the market, look down the street called Cava de San Miguel. If you like singing and sangria, come back after 22:00 on a Friday or Saturday night and visit one of the **mesones** that line the street. These cave-like bars, stretching far back from the street, get packed with Madrileños out on dates who—emboldened by sangria and the setting—are prone to suddenly breaking out in song. It's a lowbrow, electric-keyboard, karaoke-type ambience.

• *After you walk through the market and exit, continue west a few steps, then turn left, heading downhill on Calle del Conde de Miranda. At the first corner, turn right and cross the small plaza to the brick church in the far corner.*

Plaza Mayor

Mercado de San Miguel

❺ *Church and Convent of Corpus Christi*

The proud coats of arms over the main entry announce the rich family that built this Hieronymite church and convent in 1607. In 17th-century Spain, the most prestigious thing a noble family could do was build and maintain a convent. To harvest all the goodwill created in your community, you'd want your family's insignia right there for all to see. (You can see the donating couple, like a 17th-century Bill and Melinda Gates, kneeling before the communion wafer in the central panel over the entrance.) Inside is a quiet oasis with a Last Supper altarpiece.

Now for a unique shopping experience—buying goodies from cloistered nuns. A half-block to the right from the church entrance is its associated convent—it's the big brown door on the left, at Calle del Codo 3 (Mon-Sat 9:30-13:00 & 16:00-18:30, closed Sun). The sign reads: *Venta de Dulces* (Sweets for Sale). Buzz the *monjas* button, then wait patiently for the sister to respond over the intercom. Say *"dulces"* (DOOL-thays), and she'll let you in. When the lock buzzes, push open the door and follow the sign to the *torno,* the lazy Susan that lets the sisters sell their baked goods without being seen. Scan the menu, announce your choice to the sequestered sister (she may tell you she has only one or two of the options available), place your money on the *torno,* and your goodies (and change) will appear. *Galletas* (shortbread cookies) are the least expensive item (a *medio-kilo* costs about €9). Or try the *pastas de almendra* (almond cookies).

• *Continue uphill on Calle del Codo (where those in need of bits of armor shopped—see the street sign) and turn left, heading toward the Plaza de la Villa (pictured here). Before entering the square, notice an **old door** to the left of the **Real Sociedad Económica** sign, made of wood lined with metal. This is considered the oldest door in town on Madrid's oldest building—inhabited since 1480. It's set in a Moorish keyhole arch. Look up at what was a prison tower. Now continue into the square called Plaza de la Villa, dominated by Madrid's...*

❻ *Town Hall*

The impressive structure features Madrid's distinctive architectural style—symmetrical square towers, topped with steeples

Church and Convent of Corpus Christi

Town Hall

and a slate roof. The building still functions as Madrid's ceremonial Town Hall, though the city council and hands-on duties have moved elsewhere. Over the doorway, the three coats of arms sport many symbols of Madrid's rulers: Habsburg crowns, castles of Castile, and the city symbol—the berry-eating bear (the shield on the left). This square was the ruling center of medieval Madrid, a tiny remnant of the 14th-century town. Even before then, when Madrid was an Arab-Moorish community, this was the only square in town.

Imagine how Philip II took this city by surprise in 1651 when he decided to move the capital of Europe's largest empire (even bigger than ancient Rome at the time) from Toledo to humble Madrid. To better administer their empire, the Habsburgs went on a building spree. But because their empire was drained of its riches by prolonged religious wars, they built Madrid with cheap brick instead of elegant granite.

The statue in the garden is of Philip II's admiral, Don Alvaro de Bazán—mastermind of the Christian victory over the Turkish Ottomans at the naval battle of Lepanto in 1571. This pivotal battle, fought off the coast of Greece, slowed the Ottoman threat to Christian Europe. However, mere months after Bazán's death in 1588, his "invincible" Spanish Armada was destroyed by England...and Spain's empire began its slow fade.

• *From here, walk along busy Calle Mayor, which leads downhill toward the Royal Palace. A few blocks down Calle Mayor, on a tiny square, you'll find the...*

❼ Assassination Attempt Memorial

This statue memorializes a 1906 assassination attempt. The target was Spain's King Alfonso XIII and his bride, Victoria Eugenie, as they paraded by on their wedding day. While the crowd was throwing flowers, an anarchist (what terrorists used to be called) threw a bouquet lashed to a bomb from a balcony at #84 (across the street). He missed the royal newlyweds, but killed 23 people. Gory photos of the event hang inside the Casa Ciriaco restaurant, which now occupies #84 (photos to the right of the entrance). The king and queen went on to live to a ripe old age, producing many great-grandchildren, including the current king, Felipe VI.

Almudena Cathedral

• *Continue down Calle Mayor one more block to a busy street, Calle de Bailén. Take in the big, domed...*

❽ Almudena Cathedral (Catedral de la Almudena)

Madrid's massive, gray-and-white cathedral (110 yards long and 80 yards high) opened in 1993, 100 years after workers started building it. This is the side entrance for tourists (€1 donation requested). The main entrance (selling €6 museum-and-cupola tickets) is a block north, facing the Royal Palace. If you go inside, you'll see a refreshingly modern and colorful ceiling, a glittering 5,000-pipe organ, and a grand 15th-century painted altarpiece—striking in the otherwise Neo-Gothic interior. The highlight is the 12th-century coffin (empty, painted leather on wood, in a chapel behind the altar) of Madrid's patron saint, Isidro. A humble farmer, the exceptionally devout Isidro was said to have been helped by angels who did the plowing for him while he prayed. Forty years after he died, this coffin was opened, and his body was found to have been miraculously preserved. This convinced the pope to canonize Isidro as the patron

saint of Madrid and of farmers, with May 15 as his feast day.

Turn right on Calle de Bailén to reach the main entrance. The doors feature reliefs of the cathedral's 1993 consecration, including one with Pope John Paul II and former king and queen Juan Carlos I and his wife Sofía.

• *From the cathedral's front steps, face the imposing...*

❾ Royal Palace

Since the ninth century, this spot has been Madrid's center of power: from Moorish castle to Christian fortress to Renaissance palace to the current structure, built in the 18th century. With its expansive courtyard surrounded by imposing Baroque architecture, it represents the wealth of Spain before its decline. Its 2,800 rooms, totaling nearly 1.5 million square feet, make it Europe's largest palace.

• *You could visit the palace now, using my self-guided tour (page 173). To follow the rest of this walk back to Puerta del Sol, continue one long block north up Calle de Bailén (walking alongside the palace) to where the street opens up into...*

Plaza de Oriente

⑩ *Plaza de Oriente*

As its name suggests, this square faces east. The grand yet people-friendly plaza is typical of today's Europe, where energetic governments are converting car-congested wastelands into public spaces. A recent mayor of Madrid earned the nickname "The Mole" for all the digging he did. Where's the traffic? Under your feet.

Notice the quiet. You're surrounded by more than three million people, yet you can hear the birds, bells, and fountain. The park is decorated with statues of Visigothic kings who ruled from the third to seventh century. Romans allowed them to administer their province of Hispania on the condition that they'd provide food and weapons to the empire. The Visigoths inherited real power after Rome fell, but lost it to invading Moors in 711. The fine bronze equestrian statue honors King Philip IV; he faces Madrid's opera house, the 1,700-seat **Royal Theater** (Teatro Real). To your left, in the distance, the once-impressive **Madrid Tower** skyscraper (460 feet tall, built of concrete in

1957) marks Plaza de España (and the end of my "Gran Vía Walk").

• *Walk along the Royal Theater, on the right side, to the...*

⑪ *Plaza de Isabel II*

This square is marked by a statue of Isabel II, who ruled Spain in the 19th century. Although she's immortalized here, Isabel had a rocky reign, marked by uprisings and political intrigue. A revolution in 1868 forced her to abdicate, and she lived out her life in exile.

Evidence of Moorish walls turn up in this neighborhood and elsewhere in Madrid. Check out the tactile model in this square: The position of the old Moorish fortress and walls is outlined, with the modern city faintly depicted underneath. Notice also the grooved sidewalk you're standing on—designed for the white canes of people who can't see.

• *From here, follow Calle del Arenal, walking gradually uphill. You're heading straight to Puerta del Sol.*

Calle del Arenal

⑫ Calle del Arenal

As depicted on the tiled street signs, this was the "street of sand"—where sand was stockpiled during construction. Each cross street is named for a medieval craft that, historically, was plied along that lane (for example, "Calle de Bordadores" means "Street of the Embroiderers"). Wander slowly uphill. As you stroll, imagine this street as a traffic inferno—which it was until the city pedestrianized it a decade ago. Notice also how orderly the side streets are. Where a mess of cars once lodged chaotically on the sidewalks, bollards (bolardos) now keep vehicles off the walkways.

The brick **St. Ginés Church** (on the right) means temptation to most locals. From the uphill corner of the church, look to the end of the lane where—like a high-calorie red-light zone—a neon sign spells out Chocolatería San Ginés...every local's favorite place for hot chocolate and churros (always open). The charming bookshop clinging like a barnacle to the wall of the church has been selling books on this spot since 1650.

Next door is the **Joy Eslava disco,** a former theater famous for operettas in the Gilbert-and-Sullivan days and now a popular club. In Spain, when you're 18 you can do it all (buy tobacco, drink, drive, serve in the military). This place is an alcohol-free disco for the younger kids until midnight, when it becomes a thriving adult space, with the theater floor and balconies all teeming with clubbers. Their slogan: "Go big or go home."

Next, **Soccer Shop** (at #11) carries team regalia, postcards of today's stars, official mouth guards, etc., for soccer fans. Many Europeans come to Madrid primarily to see its 80,000-seat Bernabéu soccer stadium. The Starbucks on the next corner (opposite) is popular with young locals for its inviting ambience and American-style muffins, though the coffee is too tame for many Spaniards.

Kitty-corner from there is **Ferpal** (at #7), an old-school deli with an inviting bar and easy takeout options. Wallpapered with ham hocks, it's famous for selling the finest Spanish cheeses, hams, and other tasty treats. Spanish saffron costs half what you'd pay for it back in the US. While they sell quality sandwiches, cheap and ready-made, it's fun to buy some bread and—after a little tasting—choose a ham or cheese for a memorable picnic or snack. If you're lucky, you may get to taste a tiny bit of Spain's best ham (Ibérico de Bellota). Close your eyes and let the taste fly you to a land of happy acorn-fed pigs.

Across the street, in a little mall (at #8), a lovable mouse cherished by Spanish children is celebrated with a six-inch-tall bronze statue in the lobby. Upstairs is the fanciful **Casita Museo de Ratón Pérez** (€3, daily 11:00-14:00 & 17:00-20:00, Spanish only) with a fun window display. A steady stream of adoring children and their parents pour through here to learn about the wondrous mouse who is Spain's tooth fairy.

On the other side of the street is **Pronovias** (#3, opposite Burger King), a famous Spanish wedding-dress shop that attracts brides-to-be from across Europe. Computer terminals inside let young women virtual-shop for the dress of their dreams.

• You're just a few steps from where you started this walk, at Puerta del Sol. Back in the square, you're met by a statue popularly known as La Mariblanca. This mythological Spanish Venus—with Madrid's coat of arms at her feet—stands tall amid all the modernity, as if protecting the people of this great city.

Gran Vía Walk

This walk lets you glimpse a more modern side of Spain's capital.

Built primarily between 1900 and the 1950s, the Gran Vía is Spain's version of Fifth Avenue, affording a fun view of early-20th-century architecture and a chance to be on the street with workaday

Madrileños. I've broken this self-guided walk into five sections, each of which was the ultimate in its day.

• *Start at the skyscraper at Calle de Alcalá #42 (Metro: Banco de España).*

❶ *Circulo de Bellas Artes*

This 1920s skyscraper has a venerable café on its ground floor (free entry) and the best rooftop view around. Ride the elevator to the seventh-floor roof terrace (€4, daily 11:00-14:00 & 17:00-21:00), and stand under a black, Art Deco statue of Minerva, perhaps put here to associate Madrid with this mythological protector of culture and high thinking. Walk the perimeter of the rooftop from the far left for a clockwise tour.

Looking to the left, you'll see the gold-fringed dome of the landmark Metropolis building (inspired by Hotel Negresco in Nice), once the headquarters of an insurance company. It stands at the start of the Gran Vía and its cancan of proud facades

Circulo de Bellas Artes

celebrating the good times in pre-civil war Spain. On the horizon, the Guadarrama Mountains hide Segovia. Farther to the right, in the distance, skyscrapers mark the city's north gate, Puerta de Europa (with its striking slanted twin towers). The big traffic circle and fountain below are part of Plaza de Cibeles, with its ornate and bombastic cultural center and observation deck (Palacio de Cibeles). Behind that is the vast Retiro Park. Farther to the right, the big low-slung building surrounded by green is the Prado Museum. And, finally, at the far right (and hard to see) is the old town.

• *Descend the elevator and cross the busy boulevard immediately in front of Circulo de Belles Artes to reach the start of Gran Vía.*

❷ *1910s Gran Vía*

This first stretch, from the Banco de España Metro stop to the Gran Vía Metro stop, was built in the 1910s. While the people-watching and window-shopping can be enthralling, be sure to look up and enjoy the beautiful facades, too.

❸ *1920s Gran Vía*

The second stretch, from the Gran Vía Metro stop to the Callao Metro stop, starts where two recently pedestrianized streets meet. To the right, Calle de Fuencarral is the trendiest pedestrian zone in town, with famous brand-name shops and a young vibe (the 14-story 1920s Telefónica skyscraper at the corner was one of the city's first). To the left, Calle de la Montera is notorious for its prostitutes. The action pulses from the McDonald's down a block or so. Some find it an eye-opening detour.

❹ *1930s Gran Vía*

The final stretch, from the Callao Metro stop to Plaza de España, is considered the "American Gran Vía," built in the 1930s to emulate the buildings of Chicago and New York City. You'll even see the Nebraska Cafeteria restaurant—a

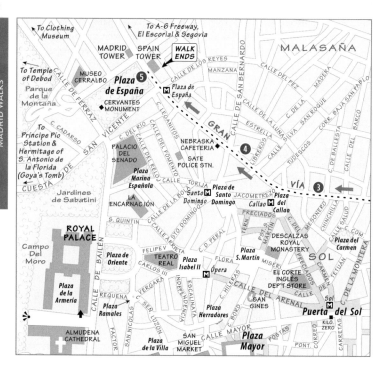

reminder that American food was trendy long before the advent of fast-food chains. This section is the Spanish version of Broadway, with all the big theaters and plays.

❺ Plaza de España

End your walk at Plaza de España (with a Metro station of the same name). Once the Rockefeller Plaza of Madrid, these days it's pretty tired. While statues of the

Gran Vía

Gran Vía Walk

1 Circulo de Bellas Artes
2 1910s Gran Vía (Banco de España to Gran Vía Metro)
3 1920s Gran Vía (Gran Vía to Callao Metro)
4 1930s Gran Vía (Callao to Plaza de España Metro)
5 Plaza de España

epic Spanish characters Don Quixote and Sancho Panza (part of a Cervantes monument) are ignored in the park, two Franco-era buildings do their best to scrape the sky above. Franco wanted to show he could keep up with America, so he had the Spain Tower (shorter) and Madrid Tower (taller) built in the 1950s. But they succeed in reminding people more of Moscow than the USA.

Plaza de España

SIGHTS

▲▲▲ROYAL PALACE (PALACIO REAL)

This is Europe's third-greatest palace, after Versailles and Vienna's Schönbrunn. It has arguably the most sumptuous original interior, packed with tourists and royal antiques.

The palace is the product of many kings over several centuries. Philip II (1527-1598) made a wooden fortress on this site his governing center when he established Madrid as Spain's capital. When that palace burned down, the current structure was built by King Philip V (1683-1746). Philip V wanted to make it his own private Versailles, to match his French upbringing; as the grandson of Louis XIV, he was born in Versailles—and ordered his tapas in French. His son, Charles III (whose statue graces Puerta del Sol), added interior decor in the Italian style, since he'd spent his formative years in Italy. These civilized Bourbon kings were trying to raise Spain to the cultural level of the rest of Europe. They hired foreign artists to oversee construction and established Spanish porcelain and tapestry factories to copy works done in Paris or Brussels. Over the years, the palace was expanded and enriched, as each Spanish king tried to outdo his predecessor.

Today's palace is ridiculously supersized—with 2,800 rooms, tons of luxurious tapestries, a king's ransom of chandeliers, frescoes by Tiepolo, priceless porcelain, and bronze decor covered in gold leaf. While these days the royal family lives in a mansion a few miles away, this place still functions as the ceremonial palace, used for formal state receptions, royal weddings, and tourists' daydreams.

Cost and Hours: €11; open daily April-Sept 10:00-20:00, Oct-March 10:00-18:00, last entry one hour before closing; from Puerta del Sol, walk 15 minutes down pedestrianized Calle del Arenal (Metro: Ópera); palace can close for royal functions—confirm in advance.

Crowd Control: The palace is most crowded on Wednesdays and Thursdays, when it's free for locals. On any day, arrive early or go late to avoid lines and crowds.

Madrid Card holders get to skip the line: Enter around the right side at the group entry point, a block down, along Calle de Bailén.

Information: Short English descriptions posted in each room complement what I describe in my tour. The museum guidebook demonstrates a passion for meaningless data. Tel. 914-548-800, www.patrimonionacional.es.

Tours: You can wander on your own or join a €4 **guided tour.** Check the time of the next English-language tour and decide as you buy your ticket; the tours are dry, depart sporadically, and aren't worth a long wait. The excellent €4 **audioguide** is much more interesting.

Services: Free lockers and a WC are just past the ticket booth. Upstairs you'll find a more serious bookstore with good books on Spanish history.

Photography: Not allowed.

Eating: Though the palace has a refreshing air-conditioned cafeteria upstairs (with a salad bar), I prefer to walk a few minutes and find a place near the Royal Theater or on Calle del Arenal. Another great option is **Café de Oriente,** boasting fin-de-siècle elegance immediately across the park from the Royal

Royal Palace

Palace. Its lunch special is good and reasonable—three courses for €15 (Mon-Fri 13:00-16:00)—but the restaurant and terrace menus are pricey (Plaza de Oriente 2, tel. 915-413-974, www.cafedeoriente.es).

⊙ SELF-GUIDED TOUR

You'll follow a simple one-way circuit on a single floor covering more than 20 rooms.

• *Buy your ticket, pass through the bookstore, stand in the middle of the vast open-air courtyard, and face the palace entrance.*

Palace Exterior: The palace sports the French-Italian Baroque architecture so popular in the 18th century—heavy columns, classical-looking statues, a balustrade roofline, and false-front entrance. The entire building is made of gray-and-white local stone (very little wood) to prevent the kind of fire that leveled the previous castle. Imagine the place in its heyday, with a courtyard full of soldiers on parade, or a lantern-lit scene of horse carriages arriving for a ball.

• *Enter the palace and show your ticket.*

Palace Lobby: In the old days, horse-drawn carriages would drop you off here. Today, stretch limos do the same thing for gala events. (If you're taking a guided palace tour, this is where you wait to begin.) The modern black bust in the corner is of Juan Carlos I, a "people's king," who is credited with bringing democracy to Spain after 36 years under dictator Franco. (Juan Carlos passed the throne to his son in 2014.)

Grand Stairs: Gazing up the imposing staircase, you can see that Spain's kings wanted to make a big first impression. Whenever high-end dignitaries arrive, fancy carpets are rolled down the stairs (notice the little metal bar-holding hooks). Begin your ascent, up steps that are intentionally shallow, making your climb slow and regal. Overhead, the white-and-blue ceiling fresco gradually opens up to your view. It shows the Spanish king, sitting on clouds, surrounded by female Virtues.

At the first landing, the burgundy coat of arms represents Felipe VI, Spain's current king and the son of Juan Carlos. J. C. knew Spain was ripe for democracy after Francisco Franco's dictatorial regime. Rather than become "Juan the Brief" (as some were nicknaming him), he returned real power to the parliament. You'll see his (figure) head on the back of the Spanish €1 and €2 coins.

Continue up to the top of the stairs. Before entering the first room, look to the right of the door to find a white marble bust of J. C.'s great-great-g-g-g-great-grandfather Philip V, who began the Bourbon dynasty in Spain in 1700 and had this palace built.

Guard Room: The palace guards used to hang out in this relatively simple room. Notice the two fake doors, added to give the room symmetry. The old clocks—still in working order—are part of a collection of hundreds amassed as a hobby by Spain's royal family. Throughout the palace, the themes chosen for the ceiling frescoes relate to the function of the room they decorate. In this room, the ceiling fresco is the first we'll see in a series by the great Venetian painter Giambattista Tiepolo. It depicts the legendary hero Aeneas (in red, with the narrow face of Charles III) standing in the clouds of heaven, gazing up at his mother Venus (with the face of Charles' own mother).

Notice the carpets in this room. Although much of what you see in the palace dates from the 18th century, the carpet on the left (folded over to show the stitching) is new, from 1991. It was produced by Madrid's royal tapestry factory, the same works that made the older original carpet. This new carpet was woven the traditional way—by hand. At the fine inlaid stone table in this room, the king signed the treaty finalizing Spain's entry into the European Union.

Hall of Columns: Originally a ballroom and dining room, today this space is used for formal ceremonies and intimate concerts. This is where Spain formally joined the European Union in 1985

Spain's Royal Families: From Habsburg to Bourbon

Spain as we know it was born when four long-established medieval kingdoms were joined by the 1469 marriage of Isabel, ruler of Castile and León, and Ferdinand, ruler of Aragon and Navarre. The "Catholic Monarchs" (Reyes Católicos) wasted no time in driving the Islamic Moors out of Spain (the Reconquista). By 1492, Isabel and Ferdinand conquered a fifth kingdom, Granada, establishing more or less the same borders that Spain has today.

This was an age when foreign policy was conducted, in part, by marrying royal children into other royal families. Among the dynastic marriages of their children, Isabel and Ferdinand arranged for their third child, Juana "the Mad," to marry the crown prince of Austria, Philip "the Fair." This was a huge coup for the Spanish royal family. A member of the Habsburg dynasty, Philip was heir to the Holy Roman Empire, which then encompassed much of today's Austria, Czech Republic, Hungary, Transylvania, the Low Countries, southern Italy, and more. And when Juana's brothers died, making her ruler of the kingdoms of Spain, it paved the way for her son, Charles, to inherit the kingdoms of his four grandparents—creating a vast realm and making him the most powerful man in Europe. He ruled as Charles I (king of Spain, from 1516) and Charles V (Holy Roman emperor, from 1519).

He was followed by Philip II, Philip III, Philip IV, and finally Charles II. Over this period, Spain rested on its laurels, eventually squandering much of its wealth and losing some of its holdings. Arguably the most inbred of an already very inbred dynasty (his parents were uncle and niece), Charles II was weak, sickly, and unable to have children, ending the 200-year Habsburg dynasty in Spain with his death in 1700.

Charles II willed the Spanish crown to the Bourbons of France, and his grand-nephew Philip of Anjou, whose granddaddy was the "Sun King" Louis XIV of

(the fancy table used to be in here) and honored its national soccer team after their 2010 World Cup victory. The tapestries (like most you'll see in the palace) are 17th-century Belgian, from designs by Raphael.

The central theme in the ceiling fresco (by Jaquinto, following Tiepolo's style) is Apollo driving the chariot of the sun, while Bacchus enjoys wine, women, and song with a convivial gang. This is a reminder that the mark of a good king is to drive the chariot of state as smartly as Apollo, while providing an environment where the people can enjoy life to the fullest.

• *The next several rooms were the living quarters of King Charles III (r. 1759-1788). First comes his* **lounge** *(with red walls), where the king would enjoy the company of a similarly great ruler—the Roman emperor Trajan—depicted "triumphing" on the ceiling. The heroics of Trajan, one of two Roman emperors born in Spain, naturally made the king feel good. Next, you enter the blue-walled...*

Antechamber: This was Charles III's dining room. The four paintings—all originals by Francisco de Goya—are of Charles III's son and successor, King Charles IV (looking a bit like a dim-witted George Washington), and his wife, María Luisa (who wore the pants in the palace). María

France, took the throne. But the rest of Europe feared allowing the already powerful Louis XIV to add Spain (and its vast New World holdings) to his empire. Austria, the Germanic States, Holland, and England backed a different choice (Archduke Charles of Austria). So began the War of Spanish Succession (1700-1714), involving all of Europe. The French eventually prevailed, but with the signing of the Treaty of Utrecht (1713), Philip had to give up any claim to the throne of France. This let him keep the Spanish crown but ensured that his heirs—the future Spanish Bourbon dynasty—couldn't become too powerful by merging with the French Bourbons.

In 1714, the French-speaking Philip became the first king of the Bourbon dynasty in Spain (with the name Philip V). He breathed new life into the monarchy, which had grown ineffectual and corrupt. When the wooden Habsburg royal palace burned on Christmas Eve of 1734, Philip (who was born at Versailles) built a spectacular late-Baroque-style palace as a bold symbol of his new dynasty. This is the palace that wows visitors to Madrid today. Construction was finished in 1764, and Philip V's son Charles III was the palace's first occupant. You'll see Charles III's decorations if you visit the palace's interior.

The Bourbon palace remained the home of Spain's kings from 1764 until 1931, when democratic elections led to the Second Spanish Republic and forced King Alfonso XIII into exile. After Francisco Franco took power in 1939, he sidelined the royals by making himself ruler-for-life. But later he handpicked as his successor Alfonso XIII's grandson, the Bourbon Prince Juan Carlos, whom Franco believed would continue his hard-line policies. When Franco died in 1975, Juan Carlos surprised everyone by voluntarily turning the real power back over to Spain's parliament. Juan Carlos abdicated the throne in 2014. Today, his son Felipe VI is a figurehead Bourbon king and Spain is a constitutional monarchy.

Luisa was famously hands-on, tough, and businesslike, while Charles IV was pretty wimpy as far as kings go. To meet the demand for his work, Goya made replicas of these portraits, which you'll see in the Prado.

The 12-foot-tall clock—showing Cronus, god of time, in porcelain, bronze, and mahogany—sits on a music box. Reminding us of how time flies, Cronus is shown both as a child and as an old man. The palace's clocks are wound—and reset—once a week (they grow progressively less accurate as the week goes on). The gilded decor you see throughout the palace is bronze with gold leaf. Velázquez's famous painting,

Las Meninas (which you'll marvel at in the Prado), originally hung in this room.

Gasparini Room: (Gasp!) The entire room is designed, top to bottom, as a single gold-green-pink ensemble: from the frescoed ceiling, to the painted stucco figures, silk-embroidered walls, chandelier, furniture, and multicolored marble floor. Each marble was quarried in, and therefore represents, a different region of Spain. Birds overhead spread their wings, vines sprout, and fruit bulges from the surface. With curlicues everywhere (including their reflection in the mirrors), the room dazzles the eye and mind. It's a triumph of the Rococo style, with

A *Grand Stairs*

B *Armory*

C *Gasparini Room*

D *Gala Dining Hall*

E *Porcelain Room*

F *Stradivarius Room*

G *Throne Room*

exotic motifs such as the Chinese people sculpted into the corners of the ceiling. (These figures, like many in the palace, were formed from stucco, or wet plaster.) The fabric gracing the walls was recently restored. Sixty people spent three years replacing the rotten silk fabric and then embroidering back on the silver, silk, and gold threads.

Note the micro-mosaic table—a typical royal or aristocratic souvenir from any visit to Rome in the mid-1800s. The chandelier, the biggest in the palace, is mesmerizing, especially with its glittering canopy of crystal reflecting in the wall mirrors.

The room was the king's dressing room. For a divine monarch, dressing was a public affair. The court bigwigs would assemble here as the king, standing on a platform—notice the height of the mirrors—would pull on his leotards and toy with his wig.

• In the next room, the silk wallpaper is from modern times—the intertwined "J. C. S." indicates the former monarchs Juan Carlos I and Sofía. Pass through the silk room to reach...

Charles III Bedroom: Charles III died here in his bed in 1788. His grandson, Ferdinand VII, redid the room to honor the great man. The room's blue color scheme recalls the blue-clad monks of Charles' religious order. A portrait of Charles (in blue) hangs on the wall. The ceiling fresco shows Charles establishing his order, with its various (female) Virtues. At the base of the ceiling (near the harp player) find the baby in his mother's arms—that would be Ferdy himself, the long-sought male heir, preparing to continue Charles' dynasty.

The chandelier is in the shape of the fleur-de-lis (the symbol of the Bourbon family) capped with a Spanish crown. As you exit the room, notice the thick walls between rooms. These hid service corridors for servants, who scurried about mostly unseen.

Porcelain Room: This tiny but lavish

room is paneled with green-white-gold porcelain garlands, vines, babies, and mythological figures. The entire ensemble was disassembled for safety during the civil war. (Find the little screws in the greenery that hides the seams between panels.) Notice the clock in the center with Atlas supporting the world on his shoulders.

Yellow Lounge: This was a study for Charles III. The properly cut crystal of the chandelier shows all the colors of the rainbow. Stand under it, look up, and sway slowly to see the colors glitter. This is not a particularly precious room, but its decor pops because the lights are generally left on. Imagine the entire palace as brilliant as this when fully lit. As you leave the room, look back at the chandelier to notice its design of a temple with a fountain inside.

• Next comes the...

Gala Dining Hall: Up to 12 times a year, the king entertains as many as 144 guests at this bowling lane-size table, which can be extended to the length of the room. The parquet floor was the preferred dancing surface when balls were held in this fabulous room. Note the vases from China, the tapestries, and the ceiling fresco depicting Christopher Columbus kneeling before Ferdinand and Isabel, presenting exotic souvenirs and his new friends. Imagine this hall in action when a foreign dignitary dines here. The king and queen preside from the center of the room. Find their chairs (slightly higher than the rest). The tables are set with fine crystal and cutlery (which we'll see a couple of rooms later). And the whole place glitters as the 15 chandeliers (and their 900 bulbs) are fired up. (The royal kitchens, where the gala dinners were prepared, may be open for viewing; ask the staff where to enter.)

• Pass through the next room of coins and medals, known as the **Cinema Room** *because the royal family once enjoyed Sunday afternoons at the movies here. The royal*

string ensemble played here to entertain during formal dinners. From here, move into the...

Silver Room: Some of this 19th-century silver tableware—knives and forks, bowls, salt and pepper shakers, and the big tureen—is used in the Gala Dining Hall on special occasions. If you look carefully, you can see quirky royal necessities, including a baby's silver rattle and fancy candle snuffers.

• *Head straight ahead to the...*

Crockery and Crystal Rooms: Philip V's collection of china is the oldest and rarest of the various pieces on display; it came from China before that country was opened to the West. Since Chinese crockery was in such demand, any self-respecting European royal family had to have its own porcelain works (such as France's Sèvres or Germany's Meissen) to produce high-quality knockoffs (and cutesy Hummel-like figurines). The porcelain technique itself was kept a royal secret. As you leave, check out Isabel II's excellent 19th-century crystal ware.

• *Exit to the hallway and notice the interior courtyard you've been circling one room at a time.*

Courtyard: You can see how the royal family lived in the spacious middle floor while staff was upstairs. The kitchens, garage, and storerooms were on the ground level. The new king, Felipe VI, married a commoner (for love) and celebrated their wedding party in this courtyard, which was decorated as if another palace room. Spain's royals take their roles and responsibilities seriously—making a point to be approachable and empathizing with their subjects—and are very popular.

• *Between statues of two of the giants of Spanish royal history (Isabel and Ferdinand), you'll enter the...*

Royal Chapel: This chapel is used for private concerts and funerals. The royal coffin sits here before making the sad trip to El Escorial to join the rest of Spain's past royalty. The glass case contains the

Tiepolo's Frescoes

In 1762, King Charles III invited Europe's most celebrated palace painter, Giambattista Tiepolo (1696-1770), to decorate three rooms in the newly built palace. Sixty-six-year-old Tiepolo made the trip from Italy with his two well-known sons as assistants. They spent four years atop scaffolding decorating in the fresco technique, troweling plaster on the ceiling and quickly painting it before it dried.

Tiepolo's translucent ceilings seem to open up to a cloud-filled heaven, where Spanish royals cavort with Greek gods and pudgy cherubs. Tiepolo used every trick to "fool the eye" (trompe l'oeil), creating dizzying skyscapes of figures tumbling at every angle. He mixes 2-D painting with 3-D stucco figures that spill over the picture frame. His colorful, curvaceous ceilings blend seamlessly with the flamboyant furniture of the room below. Tiepolo's Royal Palace frescoes are often cited as the final flowering of Baroque and Rococo art.

entire body of St. Felix, given to the Spanish king by the pope in the 19th century. Note the "crying room" in the back for royal babies. While the royals rarely worship here (they prefer the cathedral adjacent to the palace), the thrones are here just in case.

• *Pass through the* **Queen's Boudoir**—*where royal ladies hung out—and into the...*

Stradivarius Room: Of all the instruments made by Antonius Stradivarius (1644-1737), only 300 survive. This is the world's best collection and the only matching quartet set: two violins, a viola, and a cello. Charles III, a cultured man, fiddled around with these. Today, a single Stradivarius instrument might sell for $15 million.

• *Continue into the room at the far left.*

Crown and Scepter Room: The stunning crown and scepter of the last Habsburg king, Carlos II, are displayed in a glass case in the middle. Look for the 2014 proclamations of Juan Carlos' abdication of the crown and Felipe VI's acceptance as king of Spain. Notice which writing implement each man chose to sign with: Juan Carlos' traditional classic pen and Felipe VI's modern one.

• *Walk back through the Stradivarius Room and into the courtyard hallway. Continue your visit through the Antechamber, where ambassadors would wait to present themselves, and the Small Official Chambers, where officials are received by royalty and have their photos taken. Walk through two rooms, decorated in blue and red with tapestries and paintings, to the grand finale, the...*

Throne Room: This room, where the Spanish monarchs preside, is one of the palace's most glorious. And it holds many of the oldest and most precious things in the palace: silver-and-crystal chandeliers (from Venice's Murano Island), elaborate lions, and black bronze statues from the fortress that stood here before the 1734 fire. The 12 mirrors, impressively

Tiepolo ceiling fresco in the Throne Room

large in their day, each represent a different month.

The throne stands under a gilded canopy, on a raised platform, guarded by four lions (symbols of power found throughout the palace). The coat of arms above the throne shows the complexity of the Bourbon empire across Europe—which, in the 18th century, included Tirol, Sicily, Burgundy, the Netherlands, and more. Though the room was decorated under Charles III (late 18th century), the throne itself is modern. In Spain, a new throne is built for each king or queen, complete with a gilded portrait on the back.

Today, this room is where the king's guests salute him before they move on to dinner. He receives them relatively informally...standing at floor level, rather than seated up on the throne.

The ceiling fresco (1764) is the last great work by Tiepolo (see sidebar on page 178), who died in Madrid in 1770. His vast painting (88 × 32 feet) celebrates the vast Spanish empire—upon which the sun also never set. The Greek gods look down from the clouds, overseeing Spain's empire, whose territories are represented by the people ringing the edges of the ceiling. Find the Native American (hint: follow the rainbow to the macho red-caped conquistador who motions to someone he has conquered). From the near end of the room (where tourists stand), look up to admire Tiepolo's skill at making a pillar seem to shoot straight up into the sky. The pillar's pedestal has an inscription celebrating Tiepolo's boss, Charles III ("Carole Magna"). Notice how the painting spills over the gilded wood frame, where 3-D statues recline alongside 2-D painted figures. All of the throne room's decorations—the fresco, gold garlands, mythological statues, wall medallions—unite in a multimedia extravaganza.

• Exit the palace down the same grand stairway you climbed at the start. Cross the big courtyard, heading to the far-right corner to the...

Armory: Here you'll find weapons and armor belonging to many great Spanish historical figures. While some of it was actually for fighting, the great royal pastimes included hunting and tournaments, and armor was largely for sport or ceremony. Much of this armor dates from Habsburg times, before this palace was built. Circle the big room clockwise.

In the three glass cases on the left, you'll see the oldest pieces in the collection. In the central case (case III), the shield, sword, belt, and dagger belonged to Boabdil, the last Moorish king, who surrendered Granada in 1492. In case IV, the armor and swords belonged to Ferdinand, the husband of Isabel, and Boabdil's contemporary.

The center of the room is filled with knights in armor on horseback—mostly suited up for tournament play. Many of the pieces belonged to the two great kings who ruled Spain at its 16th-century peak, Charles I and his son Philip II.

The long wall on the left displays the personal armor wardrobe of Charles I (a.k.a. the Holy Roman emperor Charles V). At the far end, you'll meet Charles on horseback. The mannequin of the king wears the same armor and assumes the same pose as in Titian's famous painting of him (in the Prado).

The opposite wall showcases the armor and weapons of Philip II, the king who helped Spain start its long slide downward, impoverishing the country with his wars against the Protestants. Anticipating that debt collectors would ransack his estate after his death, he specifically protected his impressive collection of armor by founding this armory.

Downstairs is more armor, mostly from the 17th century. The pint-size armor wasn't for children to fight in. It's training armor for noble youngsters, who as adults would be expected to ride, fight, and play gracefully in these clunky getups. Before you leave, notice the life-saving breastplates dimpled with bullet dents (to the

right of exit door).
• *Climb the steps from the armory exit to the viewpoint.*

View of the Gardens: Looking down from this high bluff, it's clear why rulers have built on this strategically located spot since the ninth century. The vast palace backyard, once the king's hunting ground, is now a city park, dotted with fountains.
• *Walk to the center of the huge square and face the palace. Notice how the palace of the king faces the palace of the bishop (the cathedral). Whew. After all those rooms, frescoes, chandeliers, knickknacks, kings, and history, consider a final stop in the palace's upstairs café for a well-deserved rest.*

Madrid's Museum Neighborhood

Three great museums, all within a 10-minute walk of one another, cluster in east Madrid. The Prado is Europe's top collection of paintings. The Thyssen-Bornemisza sweeps through European art from old masters to moderns. And the Centro de Arte Reina Sofía has a choice selection of modern art, starring Picasso's famous *Guernica.*

Rick's Tip: *To really save money,* **visit when the sights are free:** *every evening for the Prado, every evening but Tuesday (when it's closed) for the Reina Sofía, and Mondays for the Thyssen-Bornemisza.*

Remember that the **Paseo del Arte** combo-ticket (€25.60, sold at the museums, allows line-skipping) is cheaper than paying admission.

▲▲▲PRADO MUSEUM (MUSEO NACIONAL DEL PRADO)

With more than 3,000 canvases, including entire rooms of masterpieces by superstar painters, the Prado (PRAH-doh) is my vote for the greatest collection anywhere of paintings by the European masters. The Prado is *the* place to enjoy the great Spanish painter Francisco de Goya, and

it's also the home of Diego Velázquez's *Las Meninas,* considered by many to be the world's finest painting, period. In addition to Spanish works, you'll find paintings by Italian and Flemish masters, including Hieronymus Bosch's fantastical *Garden of Earthly Delights* altarpiece.

Cost: €14, additional (obligatory) fee for occasional temporary exhibits, free Mon-Sat 18:00-20:00 and Sun 17:00-19:00, under age 18 always free.

Hours: Mon-Sat 10:00-20:00, Sun 10:00-19:00, last entry 30 minutes before closing.

Crowd Control and Avoiding Lines: It's generally less crowded at lunchtime (13:00-16:00), when there are fewer groups, and on weekdays. It can be busy on free evenings and weekends.

Ticket-buying lines can be long. Here are your time-saving options:

1. Use the ticket machines at the Goya entrance (credit cards only).

2. Book an entry time in advance online (www.museodelprado.es, print out ticket) or by phone (tel. 902-107-077, get a reference number). Same-day advance purchase is possible if space is available.

3. Buy a Paseo del Arte combo-ticket

Prado Museum

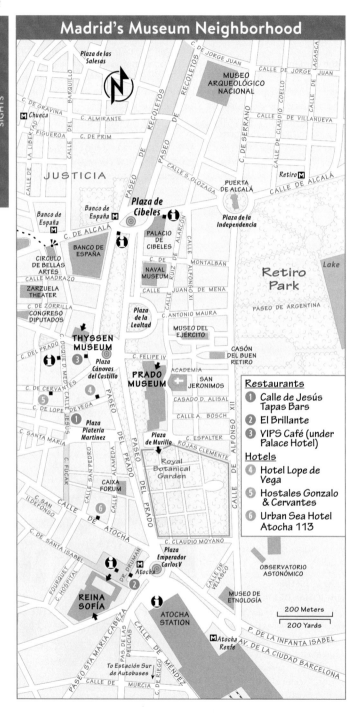

Madrid's Museum Neighborhood

Restaurants

1. Calle de Jesús Tapas Bars
2. El Brillante
3. VIPS Café (under Palace Hotel)

Hotels

4. Hotel Lope de Vega
5. Hostales Gonzalo & Cervantes
6. Urban Sea Hotel Atocha 113

(described earlier) at the less-crowded Thyssen-Bornemisza or Reina Sofía museums.

4. Get a Madrid Card beforehand (see page 153).

Getting There: It's at the Paseo del Prado. The nearest Metro stops are Banco de España (line 2) and Atocha (line 1), each a five-minute walk from the museum. It's a 15-minute walk from Puerta del Sol.

Getting In: While there are several entrances, you must buy tickets at the Goya (north) entrance. (Even at free-entry times, you need to pick up a gratis ticket at the Goya ticket window.) Once you have your ticket, you can enter at the Goya, Jerónimos, or Velázquez entrance. Those who book in advance or have a Madrid Card can pick up their tickets at the adjacent Jerónimos entrance, skipping the main line. The Murillo entrance is generally reserved for student groups. Your bags will be scanned as you enter.

Information: Tel. 913-302-800, www.museodelprado.es.

Tours: The €3.50 audioguide is a helpful supplement to my self-guided tour. Given the ever-changing locations of paintings (making my tour tough to follow), the audioguide is a good investment, allowing you to wander and dial up commentary on 250 masterpieces.

Services: The Jerónimos entrance has an information desk, bag check, audioguides, bookshop, WCs, and café. Larger bags must be checked. No drinks, food, backpacks, or large umbrellas are allowed inside.

Photography: Not allowed.

Eating: The self-service cafeteria and restaurant are open daily (€9 main dishes, €6 salads and sandwiches, Mon-Sat 10:00-19:30, Sun 10:00-18:30, hot dishes served only 12:30-16:00). A block west of the Prado, you'll find **VIPS,** a bright, popular chain restaurant, handy for a cheap and filling salad, engulfed in a shop selling books and candy (daily 9:00-24:00,

across boulevard from north end of Prado at Plaza de Canova del Castillo, under Palace Hotel). Next door is Spain's first Starbucks, opened in 2001. A strip of wonderful tapas bars is just a few blocks west of the museum, lining Calle de Jesús (see page 205). If you want to take a break outside the museum for lunch, you can reenter the museum on the same ticket as long as you get it stamped at a desk marked "*Educación*," near the Jerónimos entrance.

◑ SELF-GUIDED TOUR

Centuries of powerful kings (and lots of New World gold) funded the Prado, the greatest painting museum in the world. You'll see first-class Italian Renaissance art (especially Titian), Northern art (Bosch, Rubens, Dürer), and Spanish art (El Greco, Velázquez, Goya). This huge museum is not laid out chronologically, so this tour will not be chronological. Instead, we'll hit the highlights with a minimum of walking. Paintings are moved around frequently—if you can't find a particular one, ask a guard.

• *Pick up a museum map as you enter. Once inside, make your way to the main gallery on the ground floor. Plans are in the works to renumber the rooms. Compare the map in this book with the museum's printed map. Even if the room numbers are different, the paintings should be in the same physical locations. Follow your map and signs to Sala 49. Look for the following paintings in Room 49 and the adjoining galleries.*

ITALIAN RENAISSANCE

During its Golden Age (the 1500s), Spain may have been Europe's richest country, but Italy was still the most cultured. Spain's kings loved how Italian Renaissance artists captured a three-dimensional world on a two-dimensional canvas, bringing Bible scenes to life and celebrating real people and their emotions.

Raphael (1483-1520) was the undisputed master of realism. When he

painted *Portrait of a Cardinal* (*El Cardenal*, c. 1510), he showed the sly Vatican functionary with a day's growth of beard and an air of superiority, locking eyes with the viewer. The cardinal's slightly turned torso is as big as a statue. Nearby are Raphael's *Holy Family* and other paintings.

Fra Angelico's *The Annunciation* (*La Anunciación*, c. 1426) is in nearby Room 56b. It's half medieval piety, half Renaissance realism. In the crude Garden of Eden scene (on the left), a scrawny, sinful First Couple hovers unrealistically above the foliage, awaiting eviction. The angel's Annunciation to Mary (right side) is more Renaissance, both with its upbeat message (that Jesus will be born to redeem sinners like Adam and Eve) and in the budding photorealism, set beneath 3-D arches. (Still, aren't the receding bars of the porch's ceiling a bit off? Painting three dimensions wasn't that easy.)

Also in Room 56b, the tiny *Dormition of the Virgin* (*El Transito de la Virgen*), by **Andrea Mantegna** (c. 1431-1506), shows his mastery of Renaissance perspective. The apostles crowd into the room to mourn the last moments of the Virgin Mary's life. The receding floor tiles and open window in the back create the subconscious effect of Mary's soul finding its way out into the serene distance.

• *Find examples of Northern European art, including Dürer, in Room 55b.*

NORTHERN ART

Albrecht Dürer's *Self-Portrait* (*Autorretrato*), from 1498, is possibly the first time an artist depicted himself. The artist, age 26, is German, but he's all dolled up in a fancy Italian hat and permed hair. He'd recently returned from Italy and wanted to impress his countrymen with his sophistication. Dürer (1471-1528) wasn't simply vain. He'd grown accustomed, as an artist in Renaissance Italy, to being treated like a prince. Note Dürer's signature, the pyramid-shaped "A. D." (D inside the A), on the windowsill.

Dürer's 1507 panel paintings of Adam

❶ *Raphael,* Portrait of a Cardinal

❷ *Fra Angelico,* The Annunciation

❸ *Mantegna,* Dormition of the Virgin

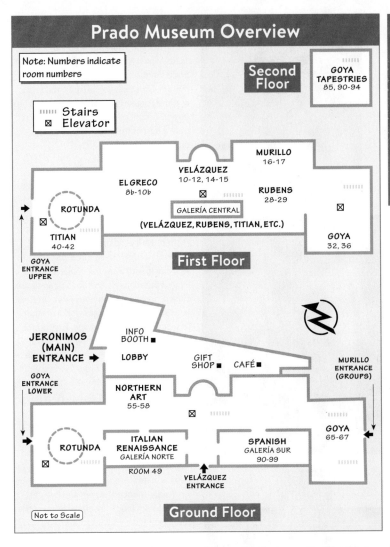

Prado Museum Overview

Note: Numbers indicate room numbers

Second Floor

GOYA TAPESTRIES
85, 90-94

▪▪▪▪ Stairs
⊠ Elevator

MURILLO
16-17

VELÁZQUEZ
10-12, 14-15

EL GRECO
8b-10b

RUBENS
28-29

ROTUNDA

GALERÍA CENTRAL
(VELÁZQUEZ, RUBENS, TITIAN, ETC.)

TITIAN
40-42

GOYA
32, 36

First Floor

GOYA ENTRANCE UPPER

JERONIMOS (MAIN) ENTRANCE ➔

INFO BOOTH ▪

LOBBY

GIFT SHOP ▪

CAFÉ ▪

MURILLO ENTRANCE (GROUPS)

GOYA ENTRANCE LOWER

NORTHERN ART
55-58

ROTUNDA

ITALIAN RENAISSANCE
GALERÍA NORTE

ROOM 49

SPANISH
GALERÍA SUR
90-99

GOYA
65-67

VELÁZQUEZ ENTRANCE

Not to Scale

Ground Floor

and Eve are the first full-size nudes in Northern European art. Like Greek statues, they pose in their separate niches, with three-dimensional, anatomically correct bodies. This was a bold humanist proclamation that the body is good, man is good, and the things of the world are good.

• Backtrack through Room 56b, and go through Rooms 57b and 57 to Room 58.

Descent from the Cross (El Descen-dimiento) by **Rogier van der Weyden** (c. 1399-1464) is a masterpiece. The Flemish painter reveals the psychological drama of this biblical event by placing the characters of real people in a contemporary (1435) scene. The Flemish were masters of detail, as you can see in the cloth, jewels, faces, and even tears. These effects are all enhanced by the artist's choice of oil paint, a relatively new and vibrant medium especially suited to conveying

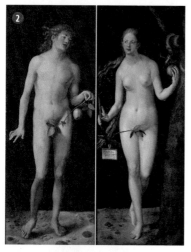

textural realism and intense color. The creative composition suggests that, in losing her son, Mary suffered along with Jesus, which is conveyed by showing their bodies in the same position. Note the realism, especially in the mournful faces, and the gorgeous arc of Mary Magdalene's pose (far right). As the Netherlands was then a part of the Spanish empire, this painting ended up in Madrid.

• Continue to Room 56a.

Hieronymus Bosch (c. 1450-1516), in his cryptic triptych *The Garden of Earthly Delights* (*El Jardín de las Delicias*, c. 1505), relates the message that the pleasures of life are fleeting, and we'd better avoid them or we'll wind up in hell.

This is a triptych—a three-paneled altarpiece, with a central image and two hinged outer panels. When the panels are closed, another image is revealed on their back side. All four images work together to teach a religious message. First notice the back side of this otherwise colorful work. It's a black-and-white scene depicting Creation on Day Three—before God added animals and humans to the mix. So, imagine the altarpiece closed. All is mellow. Then open it up, bring on the people, and splash into the colorful *Garden of Earthly Delights*.

On the left is Paradise, showing naked Adam and Eve before original sin. Everything is in its place, with animals behaving virtuously. Innocent Adam and Eve get married, with God himself performing the ceremony.

The central panel is a riot of hedonistic men and women on a perpetual spring break. Men on horseback ride round and round, searching for but never reaching the elusive Fountain of Youth. Others frolic in earth's "Garden," oblivious to where they came from (left) and where they may end up (exit...right).

Now, go to Hell (right panel). It's a burning Dante's Inferno-inspired wasteland where genetic-mutant demons torture sinners. Everyone gets their just des-

❶ *Dürer*, Self-Portrait
❷ *Dürer*, Adam and Eve
❸ *Van der Weyden*, Descent from the Cross

Bosch, The Garden of Earthly Delights

serts, like the glutton who is eaten and re-eaten eternally, the musician strung up on his own harp, and the gamblers with their table forever overturned. In the center, hell is literally frozen over. A creature with a broken eggshell body hosting a tavern, tree-trunk legs, and a hat featuring a bagpipe (symbolic of hedonism) stares out—it's the face of Bosch himself.

If you like this Bosch, you'll enjoy the others in this gallery. The table in the center features his *Seven Deadly Sins (Los Pecados Capitales,* late 15th century). Each of the four corners has a theme: death, judgment, paradise, and hell. The fascinating wheel, with Christ in the center, names the sins in Latin (lust, envy, gluttony, and so on), and illustrates each

with a vivid scene that works as a slice of 15th-century Dutch life.

Another triptych, *The Hay Wain (El Carro de Heno,* c. 1516), hangs nearby. Like *The Garden of Earthly Delights,* it teaches morality in what must have been an effective and frightening way back when Bosch painted it.

Nearby, **Pieter Bruegel** the Elder's (c. 1525-1569) work chronicles the 16th century's violent Catholic-Protestant wars in *The Triumph of Death (El Triunfo de la Muerte).* The painting is one big, chaotic battle, featuring skeletons attacking helpless mortals. Bruegel's message is simple and morbid: No one can escape death.

• *But you can escape this room. Continue through the next few galleries (55a and 55) and into the red lobby. Find the elevators on the right, and go up to level 1. Exiting the elevator, turn left into Room 11. This is one of several rooms with work by Velázquez, but Las Meninas is around the corner to the right in the large, lozenge-shaped Room 12.*

SPANISH MASTERS
Diego Velázquez (vel-LAHTH-keth, 1599-1660) was the photojournalist of court painters, capturing the Spanish king and his court in formal portraits that take on aspects of a candid snapshot. Room

Bruegel, The Triumph of Death

12 is filled with the portraits Velázquez was called on to produce. Kings and princes prance like Roman emperors. Get up close and notice that his remarkably detailed costumes are nothing but a few messy splotches of paint—the proto-Impressionism Velázquez helped pioneer.

The room's renowned centerpiece is Velázquez's *Las Meninas,* c. 1656. It's a peek at nannies caring for Princess Margarita and, at the same time, a behind-the-scenes look at Velázquez at work. One hot summer day in 1656, Velázquez (at left, with paintbrush and Dalí moustache) stands at his easel and stares out at the people he's painting—the king and queen. They would have been standing about where we are, and we see only their reflection in the mirror at the back of the room. Their daughter (blonde hair, in center) watches her parents being painted, joined by her servants *(meninas),* dwarves, and the family dog. At that very moment, a man happens to pass by the doorway at back and pauses to look in. Why's he there? Probably just to give the painting more depth.

This frozen moment is lit by the window on the right, splitting the room into bright and shaded planes that recede into the distance. The main characters look right at us, making us part of the scene, seemingly able to walk around, behind, and among the characters. Notice the exquisitely painted mastiff.

If you stand in the center of the room, the 3-D effect is most striking. This is art come to life.

• *Facing this painting, leave to the left and go back into Room 11.*

Look around this gallery and see how Velázquez enjoyed capturing light—and capturing the moment. *The Feast of Bacchus (Los Borrachos,* c. 1628) is a cell-phone snapshot in a blue-collar bar, with a couple of peasants mugging for a photo-op with a Greek god—Bacchus, the god of wine. This was an early work, before Velázquez got his court-painter gig. A personal homage to the hardworking farmers enjoying the fruit of their labor, it shows how Velázquez had a heart for real people and believed they deserved portraits, too. Notice the almost-sacramental presence of the ultrarealistic bowl of wine in the center, as Bacchus, with the honest gut, crowns a fellow hedonist.

• *Backtrack through the big gallery with Las Meninas to Room 14.*

Velázquez's boss, King Philip IV, had an affair, got caught, and repented by commissioning the *Crucified Christ (Cristo Crucificado,* c. 1632). Christ hangs his head, humbly accepting his punishment. Philip would have been left to stare at the slowly dripping blood, contemplating how long Christ had to suffer to atone for Philip's sins. This is an interesting death scene. There's no anguish, no tension, no torture. Light seems to emanate from Jesus as if nothing else matters. The crown of thorns and the cloth wrapped around his waist are particularly vivid. Above it all, a sign reads in three languages: "Jesus of Nazareth, King of the Jews."

• *The nearby rooms (16 and 17) are filled with Murillo paintings. Look for a couple of his immaculately conceived virgins.*

Velázquez, Las Meninas

Bartolomé Murillo (1618-1682) put a human face on the abstract Catholic doctrine that Mary was conceived and born free of original sin. Murillo painted several versions of the *Immaculate Conception,* of which the Prado has five that sometimes rotate. *The Immaculate Conception of Los Venerables* (*La Inmaculada Concepción de los Venerables,* c. 1678) hangs in Room 16, and another version is in Room 17. Murillo's "immaculate" virgin floats in a cloud of Ivory Soap cleanliness, radiating youth and wholesome goodness. She wears the usual colors of the Virgin Mary—white for purity and blue for divinity. Sweet and escapist, Murillo's work was a hit, and must have been comforting to the wretched people of post-plague Sevilla (his hometown was hit hard in 1647-1652).
• *Return to the main gallery (Rooms 28 and 29) for lots of fleshy excitement, courtesy of Peter Paul Rubens.*

NORTHERN BAROQUE

A native of Flanders, **Peter Paul Rubens** (1577-1640) painted Baroque-style art meant to play on the emotions, titillate the senses, and carry you away. His paintings surge with Baroque energy and ripple with waves of figures. Surveying his big, boisterous canvases, you'll notice his trademarks: sex, violence, action, emotion, bright colors, and ample bodies, with the wind machine set on full. Gods are melodramatic, and nymphs flee half-human predators. Rubens painted the most beautiful women of his day—well-fed, no tan lines, and very sexy.

Rubens' *The Three Graces* (*Las Tres Gracias,* c. 1630-1635) celebrates cellulite. The ample, glowing bodies intertwine as the women exchange meaningful glances. The Grace at the left is Rubens' young second wife, Hélène Fourment, who shows up regularly in his paintings.
• *From the main gallery with the Rubens, look to the near end of the hall, where Goya's royal portraits hang. We'll end up there. But first, head the other way to Titian and El Greco. Titians line the main gallery, and the El Grecos are in Rooms 8b, 9b, and 10b.*

SPANISH MYSTIC

El Greco (1541-1614) was born in Greece (his name is Spanish for "The Greek"), trained in Venice, then settled in Toledo—60 miles from Madrid. His paintings are like Byzantine icons drenched in Venetian color and fused in the fires of Spanish mysticism. The El Greco paintings displayed here rotate, but they all glow with his unique style.

Murillo, The Immaculate Conception of Los Venerables

Rubens, The Three Graces

In *Christ Carrying the Cross* (*Cristo Abrazado a la Cruz,* c. 1602), Jesus accepts his fate, trudging toward death with blood running down his neck. He hugs the cross and directs his gaze along the cross-bar. His upturned eyes (sparkling with a streak of white paint) lock onto his next stop—heaven.

The Adoration of the Shepherds (*La Adoración de los Pastores,* c. 1614), originally painted for El Greco's own burial chapel in Toledo, has the artist's typical two-tiered composition—heaven above, earth below. The long, skinny shepherds are stretched unnaturally in between, flickering like flames toward heaven.

The Nobleman with His Hand on His Chest (*El Caballero de la Mano al Pecho,* c. 1580) shows an elegant and somewhat arrogant man whose hand has the middle fingers touching—El Greco's trademark way of expressing elegance (or was it the 16th-century symbol for "Live long and prosper"?). The signature is on the right in faint Greek letters—"Doménikos Theotokópoulos," El Greco's real name.

• *Return to the main gallery. Spot several Titian paintings in Rooms 25-26, and meander through the Italian wing, including Venetian portraits in Rooms 40-44 (this collection may have moved into the main gallery—Rooms 24-27—by the time you visit). Continue down the main gallery to the center, under the dome (and opposite Las Meninas), where Charles I sits royally on horseback.*

VENETIAN PAINTER TO THE COURT

Spain's Golden Age kings Charles I (a.k.a. Charles V) and Philip II were both staunch Catholics, but that didn't stop them from amassing this sometimes surprisingly racy collection. Both kings sat for portraits by the Venetian master **Titian** (c. 1485-1576).

In *The Emperor Charles V at Mühlberg* (*Carlos V en la Batalla de Mühlberg,* 1548), the king rears on his horse, raises his lance, and rides out to crush an army of Lutherans. Charles, having inherited many kingdoms and baronies through his family connections, was the world's most powerful man in the 1500s. (You can see the suit of armor depicted in the painting in the Royal Palace.)

In contrast (just to the left), Charles I's son, *Philip II* (*Felipe II,* c. 1550-1551), looks pale, suspicious, and lonely—a scholarly and complex figure. He built the austere, monastic palace at El Escorial, but also indulged himself with Titian's bevy of Renaissance Playmates—a sampling of

El Greco, Christ Carrying the Cross

El Greco, The Nobleman with His Hand on His Chest

Titian, The Emperor Charles V at Mühlberg

which is here in the Prado.

These are the faces of the Counter-Reformation. While father and son ruled differently, both had underbites, a product of royal inbreeding (which Titian painted... but very delicately).

• *Now walk to the far end of the main gallery and enter the round Room 32, where you'll see royal portraits by Goya. The museum's exciting Goya collection is on three levels at this end of the building: classic Goya (royal portraits and La Maja), on this floor; early cartoons, upstairs; and his dark and political work, downstairs.*

PAINTER OF KINGS AND DEMONS

Follow the complex **Francisco de Goya** (1746-1828) through the stages of his life—from dutiful court painter, to political rebel and scandal maker, to the disillusioned genius of his "black paintings."

In the group portrait *The Family of Charles IV (La Familia de Carlos IV,* 1800), the royals are all decked out in their Sunday best. Goya himself stands at his easel to the far left, painting the court (a tribute to Velázquez in *Las Meninas*) and revealing the shallowness beneath the fancy trappings. Charles, with his ridiculous hairpiece and goofy smile, was a vacuous, henpecked husband. His toothless yet domineering queen upstages him, arrogantly stretching her swanlike neck. The other adults, with their bland faces, are bug-eyed with stupidity.

• *Exit to the right across a small hallway and enter Room 36, where you'll find Goya's most scandalous work.*

Rumors flew that Goya was fooling around with the vivacious Duchess of Alba, who may have been the model for two similar paintings, **Nude Maja** (*La Maja Desnuda,* c. 1800) and **Clothed Maja** (*La Maja Vestida,* c. 1808). A *maja* was a trendy, working-class girl. Whether she's a duchess or a *maja,* Goya painted a naked lady—an actual person rather than some mythic Venus. And that was enough to risk incurring the wrath of the Inquisition. In a Titian-esque pose, the nude stretches to display her charms, her pale body with realistic pubic hair highlighted by cool green sheets. (Notice the artist's skillful rendering of the transparent fabric on the pillow.) According to a believable legend, the two paintings were displayed in a double frame, with the *Clothed Maja* sliding over the front to hide the *Nude Maja* from Inquisitive minds.

• *Find the nearby staircase and elevator, and head up to level 2 to Rooms 85 and 90-94 for more Goya.*

These rooms display Goya's **designs for tapestries** (known as "cartoons") for nobles' palaces. As you stroll around, the scenes make it clear that, while revolution was brewing in America and France, Spain's lords and ladies were playing, blissfully ignorant of the changing times. Dressed in their "Goya-style" attire, they're picnicking, dancing, flying kites, playing paddleball and Blind Man's Bluff, or just relaxing in the sun—as in the well-known *The Parasol (El Quitasol,* Room 85).

• *For more Goya, take the stairs or elevator down to level 0. Room 66 leads into Goya's final paintings, with a darker edge. But first go to Room 65, which takes you to powerful military scenes.*

Goya became a political liberal, a champion of democracy. He was crushed when France's hero of the French Revolution, Napoleon, morphed into a tyrant and invaded Spain. In the **Second of May, 1808** (*El 2 de Mayo de 1808,* 1814), Madrid's citizens rise up to protest the occupation in Puerta del Sol, and the French send in their dreaded Egyptian mercenaries. They plow through the dense tangle of Madrileños, who have nowhere to run. The next day, the **Third of May, 1808** (*El 3 de Mayo de 1808,* 1814), the French rounded up ringleaders and executed them. The colorless firing squad—a faceless machine of death—mows them down, and they fall in bloody, tangled heaps. Goya throws a harsh prison-yard floodlight on the main victim, who spreads his arms Christ-like to ask, "Why?"

Politically, Goya was split—he was a Spaniard, but he knew France was leading Europe into the modern age. His art, while political, has no Spanish or French flags. It's a universal comment on the horror of war. Many consider Goya the last classical and first modern painter...the first painter with a social conscience.

• *About-face to the "black paintings" in Room 67.*

Depressed and deaf from syphilis, Goya retired to his small home and smeared its walls with his "**black paintings**"—dark in color and in mood. During this period in his life, Goya would paint his nightmares...literally. The style is considered Romantic—emphasizing emotion over beauty—but it foreshadows 20th-century Surrealism with its bizarre imagery, expressionistic and thick brushstrokes, and cynical outlook.

Stepping into Room 67, you are surrounded by art from Goya's dark period. These paintings are the actual murals from the walls of his house, transferred onto canvas. Imagine this in your living room. Goya painted what he felt with a radical technique unburdened by reality—a century before his time.

Dark forces convened continually in

❶ *Goya,* The Family of Charles IV
❷ *Goya,* Nude Maja
❸ *Goya,* Second of May, 1808
❹ *Goya,* Third of May, 1808

Goya's dining room, where *The Great He-Goat* (*El Aquelarre/El Gran Cabrón*, c. 1820-1823) hung. The witches, who look like skeletons, swirl in a frenzy around a dark, Satanic goat in monk's clothing who presides over the obscene rituals. The black goat represents the Devil and stokes the frenzy of his wild-eyed subjects. Amid this adoration and lust, a noble lady (far right) folds her hands primly in her lap ("I thought this was a Tupperware party!"). Or, perhaps it's a pep rally for her execution, maybe inspired by the chaos that accompanied Plaza Mayor executions. Nobody knows for sure.

In *Fight to the Death with Clubs* (*Duelo a Garrotazos*, c. 1820-1823), two giants stand face-to-face, buried up to their knees, and flail at each other with clubs. It's a standoff between superpowers in the never-ending cycle of war—a vision of a tough time when people on the streets would kill for a piece of bread.

In *Saturn* (*Saturno*, c. 1820-1823), the king of the Roman gods—fearful that his progeny would overthrow him—eats one of his offspring. Saturn, also known as Cronus (Time), may symbolize how time devours us all. Either way, the painting brings new meaning to the term "child's portion."

The Drowning Dog (*Perro Semihundido*, c. 1820-1823) is, according to some, the hinge between classical art and modern art. The dog, so full of feeling and sadness, is being swallowed by quicksand...much as, to Goya, the modern age was overtaking a more classical era. And look closely at the dog. It also can be seen as a turning point for Goya. Perhaps he's bottomed out—he's been overwhelmed by depression, but his spirit has survived.

• *Head back to Room 66, and look on the right.*

❶ *Goya,* The Great He-Goat

❷ *Goya,* Fight to the Death with Clubs

❸ *Goya,* Saturn

The last painting we have by Goya is *The Milkmaid of Bordeaux* (*La Lechera de Burdeos*, c. 1827). Somehow, Goya pulled out of his depression and moved to France, where he lived until his death at 82. While painting as an old man, color returned to his palette. His social commentary, his passion for painting what he felt (more than what he was hired to do), and, as you see here, the freedom of his brushstrokes explain why many consider Francesco de Goya to be the first modern artist.

• *There's lots more to the Prado, but there's also lots more to Madrid. The choice is yours.*

▲▲THYSSEN-BORNEMISZA MUSEUM

Locals call the stunning Museo del Arte Thyssen-Bornemisza simply the Thyssen (TEE-sun). It displays the impressive collection that Baron Thyssen (a wealthy German married to a former Miss Spain) sold to Spain for $350 million. The museum offers a unique chance to enjoy the sweep of all of art history—including a good sampling of the "isms" of the 20th century—in one collection. It's basically minor works by major artists and major works by minor artists. (Major works by major artists are in the Prado.) But art lovers appreciate how the good baron's art complements the Prado's collection by filling in where the Prado is weak—such as Impressionism, which is the Thyssen's forte.

Cost and Hours: €10, extra charge for special exhibits, free for kids under age 12, free on Mon; open Mon 12:00-16:00, Tue-Sun 10:00-19:00, Sat until 21:00 in summer (exhibits only), last entry 45 minutes before closing; audioguide-€4; kitty-corner from the Prado at Paseo del Prado 8 in Palacio de Villahermosa, Metro: Banco de España; tel. 902-760-511, www.museothyssen.org.

Services: The museum has free baggage storage (bags must fit through a small X-ray machine), a cafeteria and restaurant, and a shop/bookstore.

Visiting the Museum: After purchasing your ticket, continue down the wide main hall past larger-than-life paintings of former monarchs Juan Carlos I and Sofía, and then paintings of the baron (who died in 2002) and his art-collecting baroness, Carmen. At the info desk, pick up a museum map. Each of the three floors is divided into two separate areas: the permanent collection (numbered rooms)

Thyssen-Bornemisza Museum

and additions from the baroness since the 1980s (lettered rooms). Ascend to the top floor and work your way down, taking a delightful walk through art history. Visit the rooms on each floor in numerical order, from Primitive Italian (Room 1) to Surrealism and Pop Art (Room 45-47).

Rick's Tip: *If you're tired and want to* **get from the Thyssen to the Reina Sofía,** *hail a cab at the gate to zip straight there, or take bus #27.*

▲▲▲CENTRO DE ARTE REINA SOFÍA

Home to Picasso's *Guernica,* the Reina Sofía is one of Europe's most enjoyable modern art museums. Its exceptional collection of 20th-century art is housed in what was Madrid's first public hospital. The focus is on 20th-century Spanish artists—Picasso, Dalí, Miró, Gris, and Tàpies—but you'll also find plenty of works by Kandinsky, Braque, and many other giants of modern art.

The curator, who has a passion for cinema, has paired paintings with films from the same decade, which play continuously in nearby rooms. This provides a fascinating insight into the social context that inspired the art of Spain's tumultuous 20th century. Those with an appetite for modern and contemporary art can spend several delightful hours in this museum.

Cost: €8 (includes most temporary exhibits), €3 if you're under 18 or over 65, free Mon and Wed-Sat 19:00-21:00, Sun 15:00-19:00 (free times are often crowded, and you must pick up a ticket).

Hours: Mon and Wed-Sat 10:00-21:00, Sun 10:00-19:00 (fourth floor not accessible Sun after 15:00), closed Tue.

Getting There: It's a block from the Atocha Metro stop, on Plaza Sánchez Bustillo (at Calle de Santa Isabel 52). In the Metro station, follow signs for the Reina Sofía exit. Emerging from the Metro, walk straight ahead a half-block and look for an opening between the group of buildings. You'll see the tall, exterior glass elevators that flank the museum's main entrance.

A second entrance in the newer section of the building sometimes has shorter lines, especially during the museum's free hours. Facing the glass elevators, walk left around the old building to the large gates of the red-and-black Nouvel Building.

Information: Tel. 917-741-000, www.museoreinasofia.es.

Tours: The hardworking audioguide is €4.

Services: Bag storage is free. The *librería* just outside the Nouvel wing has a larger selection of Picasso and Surrealist reproductions than the main gift shop at the entrance.

Photography: Photos are not allowed in the room containing *Guernica* or in the surrounding rooms. Otherwise, photos without flash are OK.

Eating: The museum's café (a long block around the left from the main entrance) is a standout for its tasty cuisine. The square immediately in front of the museum is ringed by fine places for a simple meal or drink. My favorite is **El**

Centro de Arte Reina Sofía

Brillante, a classic dive offering pricey tapas and baguette sandwiches, but everyone comes for the fried squid sandwiches (evidenced by the older *señoras* with mouthfuls of *calamares*). Sit at the simple bar or at an outdoor table (long hours daily, two entrances—one on Plaza Sánchez Bustillo, the other at Plaza del Emperador Carlos V 8, tel. 915-286-966). Also nearby is my favorite strip of tapas bars, on Calle de Jesús (see page 205).

◉ SELF-GUIDED TOUR

Pick up a free map and use the good information sheets to supplement this tour.

The permanent collection is divided into three groups: art from 1900 to 1945 (second floor), art from 1945 to 1968 (fourth floor), and art from 1962 to 1982 (adjoining Nouvel wing, which also has space for bigger installations). Temporary exhibits are on the first and third floors.

While the collection is roughly chronological, it's displayed thematically. The second-floor grand hallway leads around a courtyard connecting a series of rooms, each clearly labeled with a theme. For a good first visit, ride the fancy glass elevator to level 2 and tour that floor clockwise (Goya, Surrealism, Cubism, Picasso's *Guernica*), and then finish with post-WWII art on level 4.

• *Begin in Room 201, with examples of...*

PROTO-MODERN GOYA

The wonderful curator insightfully begins your look at modern art with Goya engravings. That's because Goya is a proto-modernist—the first painter with a social conscience, the first to show inner feelings, and the first to deal with social reality. He painted because he had something to say, not just to get a paycheck.

• *Browse through the next rooms, whose underlying theme is the conflict between tradition (the powerful Church) and progress (social modernization). Find your way to Room 205 and...*

SURREALISM AND SALVADOR DALÍ

In 1914 a generation marched enthusiastically into combat, believing the Great War would be the "war to end all wars." Many artists embraced this fight, volunteered to serve, and died for the cause. But when it was over, it was clear: World War I brought no lasting change. Frustrated, many survivors turned their backs on society.

In the postwar years, a class of artists abandoned the outer world and looked inside (with inspiration from Freud). They painted mindscapes rather than landscapes. They had learned that reality is deeper than what you first "see." These were the Surrealists. To "see" their art, you need to vary your position: your physical perspective and your mental perspective. See it happy, sad, before coffee, after coffee.

In the Dalí room, you'll see the artist's distinct, Surrealist, melting-object style. Dalí places familiar items in a stark landscape, creating an eerie effect. Figures

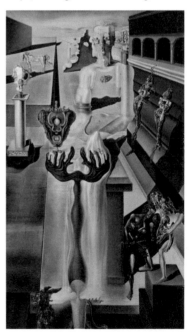

Dalí, The Invisible Man

morph into misplaced faces and body parts. Background and foreground play mind games—is it an animal (seen one way) or a man's face? A waterfall or a pair of legs? It's a wide shot...no, it's a close-up. Look long at paintings like Dalí's *Endless Enigma* (1938) and *The Invisible Man* (c. 1933); they take different viewers to different places.

The Great Masturbator (1929) is psychologically exhausting, depicting in its Surrealism a lonely, highly sexual genius in love with his muse, Gala (while she was still married to a French poet). This is the first famous Surrealist painting.

During this productive period, Dalí was working on the classic Surrealist film *Un Chien Andalou* (**The Andalusian Dog,** 1928) with his collaborator Luis Buñuel (the film plays in Room 203). Both men were members of the Generation of '27, a group of nonconformist Spanish bohemians whose creative interests had a huge influence on art and literature in their era.

• *Skirt back around the courtyard to find Room 210 and...*

CUBISM

Cubism was born in the first decade of the 20th century. You could make a good case that the changes in society in the year 1900 were more profound than those we lived through in 2000. Trains and cars brought speed to life. Electricity brought light. Einstein introduced us to abstract ideas. Photography captured reality. And art broke away. At the turn of the century there were two ways to express art: line (Picasso) and color (Matisse)—but it was still in two dimensions. With Cubism, three dimensions are shown in two. Imagine walking around a statue to take in all the angles, and then attempting to put it on a 2-D plane. With Cubism, everyone sees things differently. To appreciate it, take your time and free your imagination.

Room 210 shows the birth of Cubism—a movement in which Spaniards were at the forefront (with works by

Picasso, Braque, Léger, and Gris). To literally see a 2-D picture plane leap to life, watch the Lumière brothers' early film *Partie d'Écarté* (c. 1898).

• *In Room 206, you come to what is likely the reason for your visit...*

PICASSO'S *GUERNICA*

Perhaps the single most impressive piece of art in Spain is Pablo Picasso's *Guernica* (1937). The monumental canvas—one of Europe's must-see sights—is not only a piece of art but a piece of history, capturing the horror of modern war in a modern style.

While it's become a timeless classic representing all war, it was born in response to a specific conflict—the civil war (1936-1939), which pitted the democratically elected Second Republican government against the fascist general Francisco Franco. Franco won and ended up ruling Spain with an iron fist for the next 36 years. At the time Franco cemented his power, *Guernica* was touring internationally as part of a fund-raiser for the Republican cause. With Spain's political situation deteriorating and World War II looming, Picasso in 1939 named New York's Museum of Modern Art as the depository for the work. It was only after Franco's death, in 1975, that *Guernica* ended its decades of exile. In 1981 the painting finally arrived in Spain (where it had never before been), and it now stands as Spain's national piece of art.

Guernica—The Bombing: On April 26, 1937, Guernica—a Basque market town in northern Spain and an important Republican center—was the target of the world's first saturation-bombing raid on civilians. Franco gave permission to his fascist confederate Hitler to use the town as a guinea pig to try out Germany's new air force. The raid leveled the town, causing destruction that was unheard of at the time (though by 1944 it would be commonplace).

News of the bombing reached Picasso in Paris, where coincidentally he was just beginning work on a painting commission awarded by the Republican government. Picasso scrapped his earlier plans and immediately set to work sketching scenes of the destruction as he imagined it. In a matter of weeks he put these bomb-shattered shards together into a large mural (286 square feet). For the first time, the world could see the destructive force of the rising fascist movement—a prelude to World War II.

Guernica—The Painting: The bombs are falling, shattering the quiet village. A woman looks up at the sky (far right), horses scream (center), and a man falls from a horse and dies, while a wounded woman drags herself through the streets. She tries to escape, but her leg is too thick, dragging her down, like trying to run from something in a nightmare. On the left, a bull—a symbol of Spain—ponders it all, watching over a mother and her dead baby...a modern *pietà*. A woman in the center sticks her head out to see what's going on. The whole scene is lit from above by the stark light of a bare bulb. Picasso's painting threw a light on the brutality of Hitler and Franco, and suddenly the whole world was watching.

Picasso's abstract, Cubist style reinforces the message. It's as if he'd picked up the shattered shards and pasted them onto a canvas. The black-and-white tones are as gritty as the black-and-white newspaper photos that reported the bombing. The drab colors create a depressing,

almost nauseating mood.

Picasso chose images with universal symbolism, making the work a commentary on all wars. Picasso himself said that the central horse, with the spear in its back, symbolizes humanity succumbing to brute force. The fallen rider's arm is severed and his sword is broken, more symbols of defeat. The bull, normally a proud symbol of strength and independence, is impotent and frightened. Between the bull and the horse, the faint dove of peace can do nothing but cry.

The bombing of Guernica—like the entire civil war—was an exercise in brutality. As one side captured a town, it might systematically round up every man, old and young—including priests—line them up, and shoot them in revenge for atrocities by the other side.

Thousands of people attended the Paris exhibition, and *Guernica* caused an immediate sensation. They could see the horror of modern war technology, the vain struggle of the Spanish Republicans, and the cold indifference of the fascist war machine. Picasso vowed never to return to Spain while Franco ruled (the dictator outlived him).

With each passing year, the canvas seemed more and more prophetic—honoring not just those who died in Guernica, but also in Spain's bitter civil war (estimates range from 200,000 to 500,000) and the 55 million worldwide who perished

Picasso, Guernica

in World War II. Picasso put a human face on what we call "collateral damage."

• After seeing Guernica, view the additional exhibits that put the painting in its social context.

OTHER PICASSO EXHIBITS

On the back wall on the *Guernica* room is a line of **photos** showing the evolution of the painting, from Picasso's first concept to the final mural. The photos were taken in his Paris studio by Dora Maar, Picasso's mistress-du-jour (and whose portrait by Picasso hangs nearby). Notice how his work evolved from the defiant fist in early versions to a broken sword with a flower.

The room behind *Guernica* contains **studies** Picasso did for the painting. These studies are filled with motifs that turn up in the final canvas—iron-nail tears, weeping women, and screaming horses. Picasso returned to these iconic images in his work for the rest of his life. He believed that everyone struggles internally with aspects of the horse and bull: rationality vs. brutality. The Minotaur—half-man and half-bull—powerfully captures Picasso's poet/rapist vision of man. Having lived through World War I, the Spanish Civil War, and World War II, his outlook is understandable.

In the far end of this hall, you'll also find a **model of the Spanish Pavilion** at the 1937 Paris exposition where *Guernica* was first displayed (look inside to see Picasso's work). Because of this painting, the pavilion became a vessel for propaganda and a fund-raising tool against Franco.

Near the Spanish Pavilion are posters and political cartoons that are pro-communist and anti-Franco. Made the same year as *Guernica* and the year after, these touch on timeless themes related to rich elites, industrialists, agricultural reform, and the military industrial complex versus the common man, as well as promoting autonomy for Catalunya and the Basque Country.

• Head up to level 4, where the permanent collection continues.

POST-WWII ART

After World War II, the center of the art world moved from Paris to New York City. The organizing theme in this part of the museum is "Art in a Divided World." On this floor especially, you'll want to take full advantage of the English info sheets in each room and the narration provided by your audioguide.

You'll see Kandinsky as a bridge into abstract art and the Abstract Expressionism of Jackson Pollock and company. Room 419 is particularly interesting, with late works by Picasso and Miró (from the 1960s and 1970s). On this floor, you can see photographs and watch films documenting Spain's slow recovery from its devastating civil war.

• End your visit in the...

NOUVEL WING

The newest wing of the museum features art from the 1960s through the 1980s, with a thematic focus on the complexity of modern times. While these galleries have fewer household names, the pieces displayed demonstrate the many aesthetic directions of more recent modern art.

Near the Prado

▲RETIRO PARK

Once the private domain of royalty, the majestic Parque del Buen Retiro has been a favorite of Madrid's commoners since Charles III decided to share it with his subjects in the late 18th century. Siesta in this 300-acre green-and-breezy escape from the city. At midday on Saturday and Sunday, the area around the lake becomes a street carnival, with jugglers, puppeteers, and lots of local color. These peaceful gardens offer great picnicking and people-watching (closes at dusk). From the Retiro Metro stop, walk to the big lake (El Estanque), where you can rent a rowboat. Past the lake, a grand boulevard of statues leads to the Prado.

▲ROYAL BOTANICAL GARDEN

After your Prado visit, you can take a lush and fragrant break in the sculpted Real Jardín Botánico. Wander among trees from around the world, originally gathered by the enlightened King Charles III. This garden was established when the Prado's building housed the natural science museum. A flier in English explains that this is actually more than a park—it's a museum of plants.

Cost and Hours: €3, daily 10:00-21:00, shorter hours off-season, last entry 30 minutes before closing, entrance is opposite the Prado's Murillo/south entry, Plaza de Murillo 2, tel. 914-203-017.

▲▲NATIONAL
ARCHAEOLOGICAL MUSEUM

The Museo Arqueológico Nacional (MAN) takes you on a chronological walk through the story of Iberia. With a well-curated, rich collection of artifacts and tasteful multimedia displays, the museum shows off the wonders of each age: Celtic pre-Roman, Roman, a fine and rare Visigothic section, Moorish, Romanesque, and beyond. A highlight is the Lady of Elche (Room 13), a prehistoric Iberian female bust and a symbol of Spanish archaeology. You may also find underwhelming replica artwork from northern Spain's Altamira Caves (big on bison), giving you a faded peek at the skill of the cave artists who created the originals 14,000 years ago.

Cost and Hours: €3, free on Sat 14:00-20:00 and all day Sun; open Tue-Sat 9:30-20:00, Sun 9:30-15:00, closed Mon; €2 multimedia guide (also available as mobile app—MAN Museo Arqueológico Nacional); 20-minute walk north of the Prado at Calle Serrano 13, Metro: Serrano or Colón, tel. 915-777-912, www.man.es.

EXPERIENCES

Shopping

Madrileños have a passion for shopping. It's a social event, often incorporated into their afternoon paseo, which eventually turns into drinks and dinner. Most shoppers focus on the colorful pedestrian area between and around Gran Vía and Puerta del Sol. The fanciest big-name shops (Gucci, Prada, etc.) tempt strollers along Calle Serrano, northwest of Retiro Park. For trendier chain shops and local fashion, head to pedestrian Calle Fuencarral, Calle Augusto Figueroa, and the streets surrounding Plaza Chueca (north of Gran Vía, Metro: Chueca).

The giant El Corte Inglés, a block off Puerta del Sol, is a handy place to pick up just about anything you need (Mon-Sat 10:00-22:00, Sun 11:00-21:00).

▲EL RASTRO FLEA MARKET

Europe's biggest flea market is a field day for shoppers, people-watchers, and pickpockets. It's best before 11:00, though bargain shoppers like to go around 14:00, when vendors are more willing to strike

Retiro Park

National Archaeological Museum

end-of-day deals. Thousands of stalls titillate more than a million browsers with mostly new junk. Locals have lamented the tackiness of El Rastro—on the main drag, you'll find cheap underwear and bootleg CDs, but no real treasures (Sun only, 9:00-15:00, Metro: Tirso de Molina).

Rick's Tip: *El Rastro offers a fascinating chance to see gangs of young* **thieves** *overwhelming and ripping off naive tourists with no police anywhere in sight. Seriously:* **Don't even bring a wallet.** *The pickpocket action is brutal, and tourists are targeted.*

For an interesting market day (Sun only), start at Plaza Mayor, where Europe's biggest stamp and coin market thrives. Enjoy this genteel delight as you watch old-timers paging lovingly through one another's albums, looking for win-win trades. When you're done, head south or take the Metro to Tirso de Molina for El Rastro. Walk downhill, wandering off on the side streets to browse antiques, old furniture, and garage-sale-style sellers who often simply throw everything out on a sheet.

A typical Madrileño's Sunday could involve a meander through the Rastro streets with several stops for *cañas* (small beers) at the gritty bars along the way.

Nightlife

Those into clubbing may have to wait until after midnight for the most popular places to even open, much less start hopping. Spain has a reputation for partying late into the night—not stopping until offices open in the morning. (Spaniards, often awake into the wee hours of the morning, have a special word for this time of day: *la madrugada.*) If you're out early in the morning, it's actually hard to tell who is finishing their day and who's just starting it. Even if you're not an after-midnight party animal, make a point to be out with the happy masses, luxuriating in the cool evening air between 22:00 and midnight. The scene is unforgettable.

▲▲▲PASEO

Just walking the streets seems to be the way the Madrileños spend their evenings. Even past midnight on a hot summer night, entire families with little kids are strolling, licking ice cream, enjoying small beers and tapas in a series of bars, and greeting their neighbors. Good areas to wander include along Gran Vía (from about Plaza de Callao to Plaza de España;

El Rastro flea market

you could try my "Gran Vía Walk"); from Puerta del Sol to Plaza Mayor and down Calle del Arenal until you hit Plaza de Isabel II; the pedestrianized Calle de las Huertas from Plaza Mayor to the Prado; and, to window shop with the young and trendy, from Gran Vía up Calle de Fuen-carral (keep going until you hit traffic).

▲▲FLAMENCO

Although Sevilla is the capital of fla-menco, Madrid has a few easy and afford-able options. And on summer evenings, Madrid puts on live flamenco events in the Royal Palace gardens (ask TI for details). Among the listings below, Casa Patas is grumpy, while Carboneras is friendlier—but Casa Patas has better-quality artists and a riveting seriousness. Considering that prices are compara-ble, Casa Patas is the better value. And regardless of what your hotel reception-ist may want to sell you, flamenco places other than the ones I recommend are filled with tourists and pushy waiters.

Taberna Casa Patas attracts big-name flamenco artists. You'll quickly under-stand why this intimate venue (30 tables, 120 seats) is named "House of Feet."

Since this is for locals as well as tour groups, the flamenco is contemporary and may be jazzier than your notion—it depends on who's performing (€36 includes cover and first drink, Mon-Thu at 22:30, Fri-Sat at 21:00 and 24:00, closed Sun, 1.25-1.5 hours, reservations smart, no flash cameras, Cañizares 10, tel. 913-690-496, www.casapatas.com). Its restau-rant is a logical spot for dinner before the show (€30 dinners, Mon-Sat from 20:00). Or, since it's three blocks south of the tapas bars on Plaza Santa Ana, this could be your pre- or post-tapas-crawl entertainment.

Las Carboneras, more downscale, is an easygoing, folksy little place a few steps from Plaza Mayor with a nightly hour-long flamenco show. Dinner is served one hour before showtime (€36 includes entry and a drink, €69 gets you a table up front with dinner and unlimited cheap drinks if you reserve ahead, daily at 20:30, also Mon-Thu at 22:30 and Fri-Sat at 23:00, reserva-tions recommended, Plaza del Conde de Miranda 1, tel. 915-428-677, www.tablao lascarboneras.com).

Las Tablas Flamenco offers a less expensive nightly show respecting the

Madrid offers plenty of intimate flamenco venues.

traditional art of flamenco. You'll sit in a plain room with a mix of tourists and cool, young Madrileños in a modern, nondescript office block just over the freeway from Plaza de España (€27 with drink, reasonable drink prices, shows daily at 20:00 and 22:00, 1.25 hours, corner of Calle de Ferraz and Cuesta de San Vicente at Plaza de España 9, tel. 915-420-520, www.lastablasmadrid.com).

▲ZARZUELA

For a delightful look at Spanish light opera that even English speakers can enjoy, try zarzuela. Guitar-strumming Napoleons in red capes; buxom women with masks, fans, and castanets; Spanish-speaking pharaohs; melodramatic spotlights; and aficionados clapping and singing along from the cheap seats, where the acoustics are best—this is zarzuela...the people's opera. Originating in Madrid, zarzuela is known for its satiric humor and surprisingly good music. Performances occur evenings at Teatro de la Zarzuela, which alternates between zarzuela, ballet, and opera throughout the year. The TI's monthly guide has a special zarzuela section.

Getting Tickets: Prices range from €16-40, 50 percent off for Wed shows and anytime for those over 65, Teatro de la Zarzuela box office open Mon-Fri 12:00-18:00 and Sat-Sun 15:00-18:00 for advance tickets or until show time for same-day tickets, near the Prado at Jovellanos 4, Metro: Sevilla or Banco de España, tel. 915-245-400, http://teatrodelazarzuela.mcu.es. To purchase tickets online, go to www.entradasinaem.es and click on *"Espacios"* ("Spaces") to find Teatro de la Zarzuela; you will receive an email with your tickets, which you need to print before you arrive at the theater.

▲▲BULLFIGHTS

Madrid's Plaza de Toros hosts Spain's top bullfights on some Sundays and holidays from March through mid-October, and nearly every day during the San Isidro festival (May-early June—but often sold out long in advance). Fights start between 17:00 and 21:00 (early in spring and fall, late in summer). The bullring is at the Ventas Metro stop (a 25-minute Metro ride from Puerta del Sol, tel. 913-562-200, www.las-ventas.com).

Madrid hosts Spain's top bullfights.

Getting Tickets: Bullfight tickets range from €5 to €150. There are no bad seats at Plaza de Toros; paying more gets you in the shade and/or closer to the gore. (The action often intentionally occurs in the shade to reward the expensive-ticket holders.) To be close to the bullring, choose areas 8, 9, or 10; for shade: 1, 2, 9, or 10; for shade/sun: 3 or 8; for the sun and cheapest seats: 4, 5, 6, or 7. Note these key words: *corrida*—a real fight with professionals; *novillada*—rookie matadors, younger bulls, and cheaper tickets.

Getting tickets through your hotel or a booking office is convenient, but they add 20 percent or more and don't sell the cheap seats. There are two booking offices; call both before you buy: at Plaza del Carmen 1 (Mon-Sat 9:00-13:00 & 16:30-19:00, Sun 9:30-14:00, tel. 915-319-131, or buy online at www.bullfight ticketsmadrid.com), run by José and his English-speaking son, also José, who also sells soccer tickets; and at Calle Victoria 3 (Mon-Fri 10:00-14:00 & 17:00-19:00, Sat-Sun 10:00-13:00, tel. 915-211-213).

To save money, you can stand in the ticket line at the bullring. Except for important bullfights—or during the San Isidro festival—there are generally plenty of seats available. About a thousand tickets are held back to be sold in the five days leading up to and on the day of a fight. Scalpers hang out before the popular fights at the Calle Victoria booking

office. Beware: Those buying scalped tickets are breaking the law and can lose the ticket with no recourse.

For a dose of the experience, you can buy a cheap ticket and just stay to see a couple of bullfights. Each fight takes about 20 minutes, and the event consists of six bulls over two hours.

EATING

In Spain, only Barcelona rivals Madrid for taste-bud thrills. Note that many restaurants close in August.

For maximum fun, go mobile for dinner: Do the *tapeo*, going from one bar to the next, munching, drinking, and socializing. Rather than tapas plates, most of Madrid's bars offer bigger plates called *raciones* for around €6 (vegetables) to €15 (fish). The action begins late, around 21:00. But for beginners, an earlier start, with less commotion, can be easier.

In Madrid, any proper bar gives a free tapa to anyone ordering a drink. If you don't get one, ask, "Tapa?" After you get it, then order additional food as you like.

Two streets are particularly rewarding for a bar-crawl meal: **Calle de Jesús** (near the Prado) and **Calle Cava Baja** (fancier and energetic, with more bars). For a good, authentic Madrid dinner experience, survey the options and then choose your favorites. For a sit-down meal, pick one with tables in the back. Another good area for a tapas crawl (though a bit pricier) is **Plaza Santa Ana,** with inviting, trendy bars spilling out onto the square.

Budget Eats: Enjoy a quick bite on **Plaza Mayor,** where locals get take-out food from a nearby bar and plant themselves somewhere on the atmospheric square to eat. Tasty squid sandwiches, called *bocadillos de calamares*, are popular (€2.80 at Casa Rúa, at the square's northwest corner, a few steps up Calle Ciudad Rodrigo).

For cheap sandwiches and salads, look for **Rodilla** and **Pans & Company** on nearly every square (daily 9:00-23:00). Picnickers like **El Corte Inglés** for its supermarket (on lower level, Mon-Sat 10:00-22:00, Sun 11:00-21:00). You could gather a picnic at the produce stands in the touristy **Mercado de San Miguel,** which also has a food circus of eateries (daily 10:00-24:00, one block east of Plaza Mayor); it's fun to browse, hang out at the bars, or take a break at one of the market's tables.

If you like dunkable **churros con chocolate** for breakfast or anytime, try these places near Puerta del Sol: the classy **Chocolatería San Ginés** (open 24 hours, Pasadizo de San Ginés 5) and the modern **Chocolaterías Valor** (daily 8:00-22:30, Postigo de San Martín 7).

Tapas on Calle de Jesús

For locations, see map on page 182.

Cervecería Cervantes serves hearty *raciones,* specializes in octopus, and has both a fine bar and good restaurant seating (intersection of Plaza de Jesús and Calle de Cervantes, tel. 914-296-093).

Taberna de la Daniela Medinaceli has a lovely dining area. It's popular for its specialty *cocido madrileño,* a rich chickpea-based soup (Plaza de Jesús 7, tel. 913-896-238).

La Dolores, with a rustic little dining area, has been a hit since 1908 and is still extremely popular. Its canapés (€2.50 little sandwiches) are listed on the wall (Plaza de Jesús 4, tel. 914-292-243).

Cervezas La Fabrica packs in seafood lovers at the bar; there's a quieter back room with tables. Prices are the same in both spots (Calle de Jesús 2, tel. 913-690-671).

Cervecería Los Gatos is a kaleidoscope of Spanish culture, with chandeliers swinging above wine barrels in the bar area and characteristic tables below (Calle de Jesús 2, tel. 914-293-067).

La Anchoíta takes its name from its top-notch *anchoas* (cured anchovies) and *boquerones* (uncured anchovies). When these tasty little tidbits share a slice of bread, it's a *"matrimonio."* The three taps serve beer, "sin" (nonalcoholic) beer, and *vermut* (vermouth) from a tap shaped like a shrimp. If drinking white wine, get it in a frozen glass—ask for *"copa fría"* (Calle de Jesús 4, tel. 913-601-674).

Cervecería El Diario dates from 1879, yet today feels formulaic. It's known for *calamares* (intersection of Calle de las Huertas and Calle de Jesús, tel. 914-292-800).

Choosing tapas

Madrid Center Restaurants

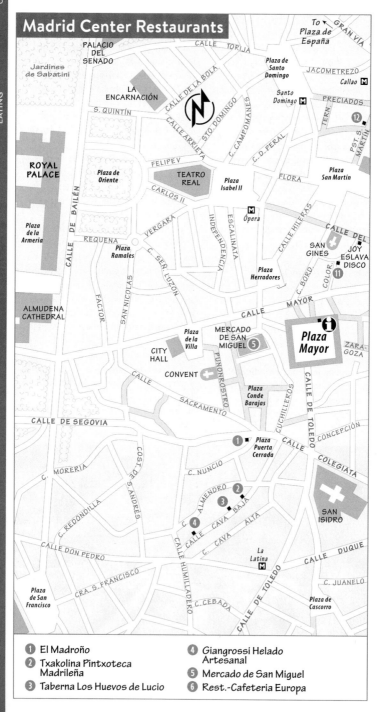

To Plaza de España

GRAN VIA

PALACIO DEL SENADO

CALLE TORIJA

Jardines de Sabatini

Plaza de Santo Domingo

JACOMETREZO

Callao Ⓜ

CALLE DE LA BOLA

LA ENCARNACIÓN

Santo Domingo Ⓜ

PRECIADOS

S. QUINTÍN

CALLE ARRIETA

STO. DOMINGO

C. CAMPOMANES

C. D. PERAL

TERN

PST. S. MARTÍN

⓬

ROYAL PALACE

FELIPE V

Plaza de Oriente

TEATRO REAL

Plaza Isabel II

FLORA

Plaza San Martín

CARLOS II

Plaza de la Armeria

CALLE DE BAILÉN

VERGARA

INDEPENDENCIA

ESCALINATA

Ⓜ Ópera

CALLE HILERAS

CALLE DEL

REQUENA

Plaza Ramales

C. SEN. LUZON

SAN GINES

JOY ESLAVA DISCO

Plaza Herradores

C. BORD

COLOR

⓫

ALMUDENA CATHEDRAL

FACTOR

SAN NICOLAS

CALLE MAYOR

CITY HALL

Plaza de la Villa

MERCADO DE SAN MIGUEL ⑤

Plaza Mayor ❶

ZARA-GOZA

CONVENT

PUNONROSTRO

CALLE

Plaza Conde Barajas

CUCHILLEROS

CALLE DE TOLEDO

SACRAMENTO

CONCEPCIÓN

CALLE DE SEGOVIA

COLEGIATA

C. MORERIA

COSTA DE S. ANDRÉS

C. NUNCIO

❶ Plaza Puerta Cerrada

CALLE

C. REDONDILLA

C. ALMENDRO

❷

C. CAVA BAJA

SAN ISIDRO

❸

❹

C. CAVA ALTA

CALLE DON PEDRO

CALLE HUMILLADERO

La Latina Ⓜ

CALLE DUQUE

CRA. S. FRANCISCO

C. JUANELO

Plaza de San Francisco

C. CEBADA

CALLE DE TOLEDO

Plaza de Cascorro

❶ El Madroño

❷ Txakolina Pintxoteca Madrileña

❸ Taberna Los Huevos de Lucio

❹ Giangrossi Helado Artesanal

❺ Mercado de San Miguel

❻ Rest.-Cafeteria Europa

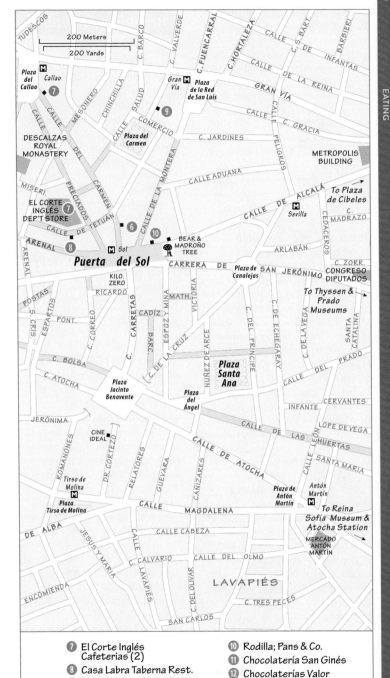

Map labels:

TUDESCOS
200 Meters
200 Yards
Plaza del Callao
Callao
CALLE DEL BARCO
C. VALVERDE
C. FUENCARRAL
C. HORTALEZA
CALLE DE S. BART.
BARBIERI
CALLE DE LAS INFANTAS
Gran Vía
Plaza de la Red de San Luis
GRAN VÍA
CALLE DE LA REINA
MESONERO
CHINCHILLA
CALLE SALUD
COMERCIO
CALLE C. GRACIA
CALLE PELIGROS
Plaza del Carmen
C. JARDINES
DESCALZAS ROYAL MONASTERY
METROPOLIS BUILDING
MISERI.
CALLE DEL CARMEN
PRECIADOS
CALLE ADUANA
CALLE DE LA MONTERA
CALLE DE ALCALÁ
To Plaza de Cibeles
EL CORTE INGLÉS DEP'T STORE
Sevilla
C. MADRAZO
CEDACEROS
CALLE DE TETUÁN
ARENAL
ARLABÁN
Sol
BEAR & MADROÑO TREE
C. ZORR.
Puerta del Sol
CARRERA DE SAN JERÓNIMO
CONGRESO DIPUTADOS
KILO. ZERO
Plaza de Canalejas
RICARDO
POSTAS
S. CRIS.
ESPARTOS
PONT.
C. CORREO
C. CARRETAS
CADIZ
BARC
MATH.
C. DE LA CRUZ
C. ESPOZ Y MINA
VICTORIA
NÚÑEZ DE ARCE
C. DEL PRÍNCIPE
C. DE ECHEGARAY
C. DE LA VEGA
SANTA CATALINA
To Thyssen & Prado Museums
C. BOLSA
C. ATOCHA
Plaza Jacinto Benavente
Plaza del Ángel
Plaza Santa Ana
CALLE DEL PRADO
CERVANTES
INFANTE
LOPE DE VEGA
JERÓNIMA
CINE IDEAL
DR. CORTEZO
RELATORES
GUEVARA
CAÑIZARES
CALLE DE LAS HUERTAS
CALLE LEÓN
SANTA MARIA
CALLE DE ATOCHA
ROMANONES
Tirso de Molina
Plaza Tirso de Molina
CALLE MAGDALENA
Plaza de Antón Martín
Antón Martín
To Reina Sofía Museum & Atocha Station
DE ALBA
JESUS Y MARIA
CALLE CABEZA
CALLE DEL OLMO
MERCADO ANTÓN MARTÍN
ENCOMIENDA
C. CALVARIO
CALLE LAVAPIÉS
C. DEL OLIVAR
LAVAPIÉS
C. TRES PECES
SAN CARLOS

Legend:

7 El Corte Inglés Cafeterias (2)
8 Casa Labra Taberna Rest.
9 Artemisia II Veggie Rest.
10 Rodilla; Pans & Co.
11 Chocolatería San Ginés
12 Chocolaterías Valor

Farther down the strip, **Taberna Maceira**, with a wonderfully woody and rustic energy, may become your favorite. It's a Galician restaurant (not a bar), specializing in octopus, codfish, *pimientos de Padrón* (green peppers), and *caldo Gallego* (white bean soup). Every day, the sign reads, *no hay Coca-Cola*—"no Coke" (Tue-Sun 13:00-16:00 & 20:30-24:00, closed Mon, cash only, Calle de Jesús 7, tel. 914-291-584). Taberna Maceira has two sister restaurants—Maceiras and Belesar—around the corner at Calle de las Huertas 64 and 66. Both are open long hours daily and accept credit cards.

Tapas on Calle Cava Baja

At the top of Calle Cava Baja, **El Madroño** is a cowboy bar that preserves a bit of old Madrid. A tile copy of Velázquez's famous *Drinkers* grins from its facade and photos of 1902 Madrid are above the stairs inside. Study the coats of arms of Madrid through the centuries as you try a *vermut* (vermouth) on tap and a €4 sandwich. Or ask to try the *licor de madroño;* a small glass *(chupito)* costs €2. Munch *raciones* at the bar or front tables to be in the fun scene, or have a quieter sit-down meal at the tables in the back. Sidewalk tables come with great people-watching (closed Mon, Plaza de la Puerta Cerrada 7, tel. 913-645-629).

Thriving **Txakolina Pintxoteca Madrileña** serves Basque-style fancy sandwiches (called *pintxos* in Basque) to a young crowd (generally €3/sandwich, Calle Cava Baja 26, tel. 913-664-877).

Jam-packed **Taberna Los Huevos de Lucio** serves good tapas, salads, *huevos estrellados* (scrambled eggs with fried potatoes), and wine. Head to the tables in the back for a sit-down meal. Their basement is much less atmospheric (Calle Cava Baja 30, tel. 913-662-984).

End your *tapeo* with ice cream at **Giangrossi Helado Artesanal**—it has great flavors (ask for a free taste) and

---

Breakfast in Madrid

Most hotels don't include breakfast (and many don't even serve it), so you may be out on the streets first thing looking for a place to eat. My typical breakfast, found at any corner bar, is *café con leche, tortilla española* (a slice of potato omelet), and *zumo de naranja natural* (fresh-squeezed orange juice). Bars offer pastries and sandwiches, too (toasted cheese, ham, or both). Touristy places will have a *desayuno* menu with various ham-and-eggs deals. Try *churros* once; if you're not in the mood for heavy chocolate in the morning, go local and dip your *churros* in a *café con leche.* Get advice from your hotel staff for their favorite breakfast place. If all else fails, a Starbucks is often nearby (just like home).

---

cocktails to boot (Calle Cava Baja 40, 50 yards from La Latina Metro stop).

Near Puerta del Sol

Restaurante-Cafeteria Europa is a fun, high-energy scene with a mile-long bar, old-school waiters, great people-watching, local cuisine, and a fine €11 fixed-price lunch (offered daily 13:00-16:00, inside only). The menu lists three price levels: bar (inexpensive), table (generally pricey), or terrace (sky-high but with good people-watching). Your best value is to stick to the lunch menu if you're sitting inside, or order off the plastic *barra* menu if you sit at the bar—the €3 ham-and-egg toast or the homemade *churros* make a nice breakfast (daily 7:00-24:00, next to Hotel Europa, 50 yards off Puerta del Sol at Calle del Carmen 4, tel. 915-212-900).

El Corte Inglés' top-floor cafeterias (in two of its buildings) are fresh, modern, and popular, though not particularly cheap.

The better one is near Plaza del Callao: Its snazzy Gourmet Experience houses a specialty grocery mart and 10 different mini-restaurants with cuisines ranging from Mexican to Chinese. The lunch hour is busy, though it's worth the wait for its great views of Gran Vía and Plaza de España. Take a seat at any of the indoor tables, or out on the open terrace (Mon-Sat 10:00-24:00, Sun 11:00-24:00). The other cafeteria has shorter hours (just off Puerta del Sol at the intersection of Calle de Preciados and Calle de Tetuán).

Casa Labra Taberna Restaurante is famous as the birthplace of the Spanish Socialist Party in 1879...and as a spot for great cod. Packed with Madrileños, it manages to be both dainty and rustic. It's a wonderful scene with three distinct sections: the stand-up bar (cheapest, with two lines: one for munchies, the other for drinks), a peaceful little sit-down area in back (a little more expensive but still cheap; €6 salads), and a fancy restaurant (€20 fixed-price lunch). Their tasty little €1.40 *tajada de bacalao* cod dishes put them on the map. The waiters are fun to joke around with (daily 11:00-15:30 & 18:00-23:00, a block off Puerta del Sol at Calle Tetuán 12, tel. 915-310-081).

Artemisia II, a hit with vegetarians and vegans, serves good, healthy food without the typical hippie ambience that comes with most veggie places (great €12 three-course fixed-price lunch Mon-Fri only, open daily 13:30-16:00 & 21:00-24:00, north of Puerta del Sol at Tres Cruces 4, a few steps off Plaza del Carmen, tel. 915-218-721).

SLEEPING

Madrid has plenty of centrally located budget hotels and *pensiones*. Most of the accommodations I've listed are within a few minutes' walk of Puerta del Sol.

You should be able to find a sleepable double for €60, a good double for €90, and a modern, air-conditioned double

---

> ## Sleep Code
>
> **Abbreviations:** S=Single, D=Double/Twin, T=Triple, Q=Quad, b=bathroom
>   **Price Rankings for Double Rooms: $$$** Most rooms €120 or more, **$$** €70-120, **$** €70 or less
>   **Notes:** Some hotels include the 10 percent IVA tax in the room price; others add it to your bill. Prices change; verify rates online or by email. For the best prices, book directly with the hotel.

---

with all the comforts for €120. Prices vary throughout the year at bigger hotels, but remain about the same for the smaller hotels and *hostales*. Anticipate full hotels only during May (for the San Isidro festival, celebrating Madrid's patron saint with bullfights and zarzuelas—especially around his feast day on May 15) and September (when conventions can clog the city). During the hot months of July and August, prices can be soft—ask for a discount.

To avoid street noise, request the highest floor possible. Rooms with twin beds are generally larger than rooms with double beds for the same price. You may find good deals by emailing several hotels (including business-class hotels) to ask for their best price.

Hotels are still allowed to designate up to 10 percent of their rooms for smokers.

Mid-Range and Fancier Places

These mostly business-class hotels are good values. Their formal prices may be inflated, but most offer weekend and summer discounts when it's slow. Drivers pay about €24 a day for parking.

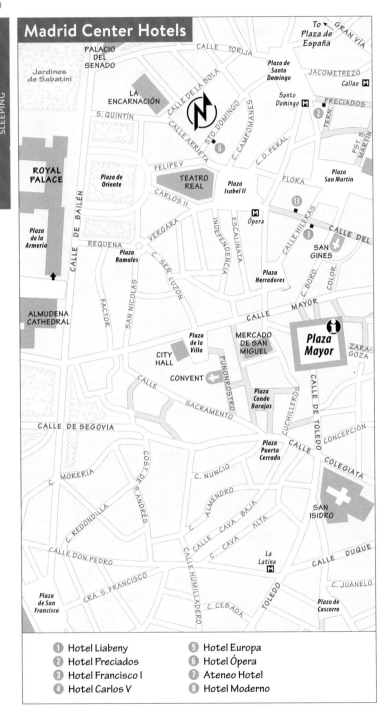

Madrid Center Hotels

1. Hotel Liabeny
2. Hotel Preciados
3. Hotel Francisco I
4. Hotel Carlos V
5. Hotel Europa
6. Hotel Ópera
7. Ateneo Hotel
8. Hotel Moderno

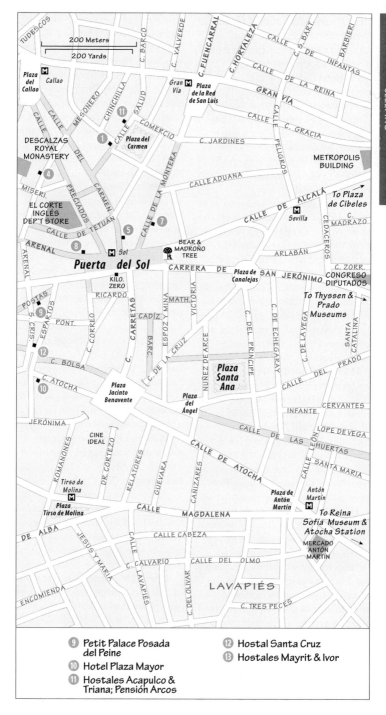

200 Meters
200 Yards

Plaza del Callao
Callao

Gran Vía

Plaza de la Red de San Luis

GRAN VÍA

CALLE DE LA REINA

CALLE DE INFANTAS

C. S. BART.

BARBIERI

C. DE

TUDESCOS

C. BARCO

C. VALVERDE

C. FUENCARRAL

C. HORTALEZA

CALLE

MESONERO

CHINCHILLA

SALUD

COMERCIO

CALLE

C. GRACIA

CALLE PELIGROS

CALLE

C. JARDINES

Plaza del Carmen

DESCALZAS ROYAL MONASTERY

MISERI.

EL CORTE INGLÉS DEP'T STORE

CALLE DEL CARMEN

PRECIADOS

CALLE DE TETUÁN

ARENAL

ARENAL

CALLE DE LA MONTERA

CALLE ADUANA

CALLE DE ALCALÁ

METROPOLIS BUILDING

To Plaza de Cibeles

C. MADRAZO

Sevilla

ARLABÁN

CEDACEROS

Sol

Puerta del Sol

BEAR & MADROÑO TREE

CARRERA DE SAN JERÓNIMO

Plaza de Canalejas

CONGRESO DIPUTADOS

C. ZORR.

KILO. ZERO

RICARDO

POSTAS

S. CRIS.

ESPARTOS

PONT.

C. CORREO

C. CARRETAS

CÁDIZ

BARC.

(C. DE LA CRUZ)

NÚÑEZ DE ARCE

ESPOZ Y MINA

VICTORIA

MATH.

C. DEL PRÍNCIPE

C. DE ECHEGARAY

C. DE LA VEGA

To Thyssen & Prado Museums

SANTA CATALINA

CALLE DEL PRADO

Plaza Santa Ana

Plaza del Ángel

Plaza Jacinto Benavente

C. BOLSA

C. ATOCHA

JERÓNIMA

CINE IDEAL

ROMANONES

DR. CORTEZO

RELATORES

GUEVARA

CANIZARES

CALLE DE ATOCHA

INFANTE

CERVANTES

LOPE DE VEGA

CALLE DE LAS HUERTAS

SANTA MARÍA

Tirso de Molina

Plaza Tirso de Molina

CALLE

MAGDALENA

Plaza de Antón Martín

Antón Martín

To Reina Sofía Museum & Atocha Station

DE ALBA

JESÚS Y MARÍA

CALLE CABEZA

C. CALVARIO

CALLE DEL OLMO

MERCADO ANTÓN MARTÍN

ENCOMIENDA

C. LAVAPIÉS

C. DE OLIVAR

LAVAPIÉS

C. TRES PECES

9 Petit Palace Posada del Peine

10 Hotel Plaza Mayor

11 Hostales Acapulco & Triana; Pensión Arcos

12 Hostal Santa Cruz

13 Hostales Mayrit & Ivor

Near Puerta del Sol and Gran Vía

These hotels are located in and around the pedestrian zone north and west of Puerta del Sol. Use Metro: Sol.

$$$ Hotel Liabeny rents 220 plush, spacious, business-class rooms offering all the comforts (Sb-€108, Db-€127, Tb-€165, 10 percent cheaper mid-July-Aug, prices vary widely according to demand, breakfast-€16, air-con, elevator, sauna, gym, off Plaza del Carmen at Salud 3, tel. 915-319-000, www.liabeny.es, reservas@hotelliabeny.com).

$$$ Hotel Preciados, a four-star business hotel, has 100 welcoming, sleek, and modern rooms as well as elegant lounges. It's well-located and reasonably priced for the luxury it provides (Db-€125-160, prices often soft, check Web specials in advance, breakfast-€18, free mini-bar, air-con, elevator, gym, parking-€21/day, just off Plaza de Santo Domingo at Calle Preciados 37, Metro: Callao, tel. 914-544-400, www.preciadoshotel.com, preciados hotel@preciadoshotel.com).

$$$ Hotel Francisco I is a big, quiet, and well-run place with 60 rooms, nicely situated midway between the Royal Theater and Puerta del Sol (Sb-€115, Db-€160, Tb-€200, breakfast-€8, prices fluctuate—book a month or more in advance to save 30-35 percent, air-con, showers only—no tubs, elevator, Calle del Arenal 15, tel. 915-480-204, www.hotel francisco.com, info@hotelfrancisco.com).

$$$ Hotel Carlos V is a Best Western with 67 high-ceilinged and somewhat worn-out rooms and a pleasant lounge (Sb-€80-120, standard Db-€100-173, Tb-€115-200, rates depend on demand and season, elegant breakfast-€10, air-con, nonsmoking floors, elevator, Maestro Victoria 5, tel. 915-314-100, www. hotelcarlosv.com, recepcion@hotelcarlos v.com).

$$ Hotel Europa, with sleek marble, red carpet runners along the halls, happy Muzak charm, and an attentive staff, is a tremendous value. It rents 100 squeaky-clean rooms, many with balconies overlooking the pedestrian zone or an inner courtyard. The hotel has an honest ethos and offers a straight price (Sb-€79, Db-€99, Db with view-€119, Tb-€142, Qb-€168, Quint/b-€190, sometimes cheaper with Web specials, air-con, elevator, gym, Calle del Carmen 4, tel. 915-212-900, www.hoteleuropa.eu, info@hotel europa.eu). The Europa cafeteria-restaurant next door is lively and convivial—fun for breakfast.

$$ Hotel Ópera, a serious and contemporary hotel with 79 classy rooms, is located just off Plaza Isabel II, a four-block walk from Puerta del Sol toward the Royal Palace (Db-€85-110 but prices spike wildly with demand, mentioning this book may get you a discount, includes breakfast, air-con, elevator, sauna and gym, ask for a higher floor—there are nine—to avoid street noise, Cuesta de Santo Domingo 2, Metro: Ópera, tel. 915-412-800, www.hotelopera.com, reservas@ hotelopera.com). Hotel Ópera's cafeteria is deservedly popular. Consider their **"singing dinners"**—great operetta music with a delightful dinner—offered nightly (around €60, reservations smart, call 915-426-382 or reserve at hotel).

$$ Ateneo Hotel, just steps off Puerta del Sol, lacks public spaces and character, but its 38 rooms are close to business-class (Db-€75-90, occasionally less or more, can be as high as €115, 5 percent discount if you book directly with the hotel with this year's book, air-con, elevator, Calle de la Montera 22, tel. 915-212-012, www.hotel-ateneo.com, info@ hotel-ateneo.com).

$$ Hotel Moderno, renting 97 rooms in a quiet, professional, and friendly atmosphere, has a comfy first-floor lounge and is just steps off Puerta del Sol (Db-€74-129, extra person-€25, breakfast-€11, air-con, Calle del Arenal 2, tel. 915-310-900, www.hotel-moderno.com, info@ hotel-moderno.com).

Near Plaza Mayor

Both of these are a block off Plaza Mayor.

$$$ Petit Palace Posada del Peine is part of a big, modern chain, but fills its well-located old building with fresh, efficient character. Behind the ornate Old World facade is a comfortable and modern business-class hotel with 67 rooms (Db-€80-160 depending on demand, breakfast-€10, air-con, free use of iPads, Calle Postas 17, tel. 915-238-151, www.petitpalace.com, posadadelpeine@petitpalace.com).

$$ Hotel Plaza Mayor, with 41 solidly outfitted rooms, is tastefully decorated and beautifully situated (Sb-€40-90, Db-€50-100, superior Db-€60-120, Tb-€80-140, breakfast-€8, air-con, elevator, Calle de Atocha 2, tel. 913-600-606, www.h-plazamayor.com, info@h-plaza mayor.com).

Near the Prado

$$ Hotel Lope de Vega is a good business-class hotel near the Prado. With 59 rooms, it feels cozy and friendly (Sb-€97, Db-€69-117, extra person-€20, rates vary wildly based on demand, cheaper July-Aug, one child under 12 sleeps free, air-con, elevator, limited parking-€25/day—request ahead, Calle Lope de Vega 49, tel. 913-600-011, www.accor.com, H9618@accor.com).

Cheap Sleeps
Near Plaza del Carmen

These three are all in the same building at Calle de la Salud 13, north of Puerta del Sol. The building overlooks Plaza del Carmen—a little square with a sleepy, almost Parisian ambience.

$ Hostal Acapulco rents 16 bright rooms with air-conditioning and all the big hotel gear. The neighborhood is quiet so a room with a balcony is worthwhile (Sb-€49-54, Db-€59-64, Tb-€77-80, elevator, fourth floor, reasonable laundry service, overnight luggage storage, limited parking available—ask when you reserve,

tel. 915-311-945, www.hostalacapulco.com, hostal_acapulco@yahoo.es).

$ Hostal Triana, also a good deal, is bigger—with 40 rooms—and offers a little less charm for a little less money (Sb-€38, Db-€53, Tb-€69, rooms facing the square have air-con and cost €3 extra, other rooms have fans, elevator and some stairs, first floor, tel. 915-326-812, www.hostal triana.com, triana@hostaltriana.com).

$ Pensión Arcos is tiny and old-fashioned—it's been in the Hernández family since 1936. You can reserve by phone (in Spanish), and must pay in cash. It has five clean, quiet rooms, an elevator, a tiny roof terrace, and a nice little lounge. For cheap beds in a great locale, it's unbeatable (D-€36, Db-€40, air-con, closed Aug, fifth floor, tel. 915-324-994).

Near Puerta del Sol

$ Hostal Santa Cruz, simple and well-located (but with a smoky office), has 16 rooms at a good price (Sb-€40, Db-€55, Tb-€70, air-con, elevator, Plaza de Santa Cruz 6, second floor, tel. 915-222-441, www.hostalsantacruz.com, info@hostal santacruz.com).

$ Hostal Mayrit and **Hostal Ivor** rent 28 rooms with thoughtful touches on a pedestrianized street (Sb-€40-55, Db-€55-65, air-con, elevator, near Metro: Ópera at Calle del Arenal 24, reception on third floor, tel. 915-480-403, www.hostal ivor.com, reservas@hostalivor.com).

Near the Prado

Two fine budget *hostales* are at Cervantes 34 (Metro: Antón Martín—but not handy to Metro). Both are homey, with inviting lounge areas; neither serves breakfast.

$ Hostal Gonzalo has 15 spotless, comfortable rooms on the third floor and is well-run by friendly and helpful Javier. Reserve in advance (Sb-€45, Db-€60, Tb-€75, air-con, elevator, tel. 914-292-714, www.hostalgonzalo.com, hostal@hostal gonzalo.com). Downstairs, the nearly as polished **$ Hostal Cervantes** also has 15 rooms (Sb-€35-40, Db-€45-50, Tb-€55-60, cheaper when slow and for longer stays, some rooms with air-con, tel. 914-298-365, www.hostal-cervantes.com, correo@hostal-cervantes.com).

$ Urban Sea Hotel Atocha 113 is a basic but contemporary option, nicely located between the Prado and the Reina Sofía, near Atocha Station (Sb-€40-45, Db-€50-75, rates vary on demand, includes self-service snacks, small rooftop terrace, Calle de Atocha 113, tel. 913-692-895, www.urbanseahotels.com, recepcion atocha@blueseahotels.es).

TRANSPORTATION

Getting Around Madrid
By Metro
Madrid's Metro is simple, cheap, and speedy (www.metromadrid.es). It costs €1.50 for a ride within zone A, which covers most of the city, but not trains out to the airport. The 10-ride, €12.20 Metrobus ticket can be shared by several travelers and works on both the Metro and buses. Buy tickets in the Metro (from easy-to-use machines or ticket booths), at newspaper stands, or at Estanco tobacco shops. Insert your ticket in the turnstile, then retrieve it and pass through. The Metro runs 6:00-1:30 in the morning. At all times, be alert to thieves, who thrive in crowded stations.

Study your Metro map. The lines are color-coded and numbered; use end-of-the-line station names to choose your direction of travel. Once in the Metro station, signs direct you to the train line and direction (e.g., Linea 1, *Valdecarros*). To transfer, follow signs in the station leading to connecting lines. Once you reach your final stop, look for the green *salida* signs pointing to the exits. Use the helpful neighborhood maps to choose the right *salida* and save yourself lots of walking.

By Bus
City buses, though not as easy as the Metro, can be useful. Find bus maps at the TI or info booth on Puerta del Sol; poster-size maps are usually posted at bus stops (€1.50 tickets sold on bus, €12.20 for a 10-ride Metrobus ticket, buses run 6:00-24:00, less frequent *Buho* buses run all night, www.emtmadrid.es).

By Taxi
Madrid's 15,000 taxis are reasonably priced and easy to hail. A green light on the roof indicates that a taxi is available. Foursomes travel as cheaply by taxi as by Metro. For example, a ride from the Royal Palace to the Prado costs about €6. After the drop charge (about €3, higher on weekends and late at night), the per-kilometer rate depends on the time: *Tarifa 1* (€1.05/kilometer) is charged Monday-Friday 6:00-21:00; *Tarifa 2* (€1.20/kilometer) is valid after 21:00 and on Saturdays, Sundays, and holidays. If your cabbie uses anything other than *Tarifa 1* on weekdays (shown as an isolated "1" on the meter), you're being cheated. Rates can be higher if you go outside Madrid. There is a flat rate of €30 between the city center and any of the airport terminals. Other legitimate charges include the €3 supplement for leaving any train or bus station, €20 per hour for waiting, and a few extra euros if you call to have the taxi come to you. Make sure the meter is turned on as soon as you get into the cab so the driver can't tack anything onto the official rate. If the driver starts adding up "extras," look for the sticker detailing all legitimate surcharges (which should be on the passenger window).

Arriving and Departing
By Plane
BARAJAS AIRPORT
Ten miles east of downtown, Madrid's modern airport has four terminals. Terminals 1, 2, and 3 are connected by long

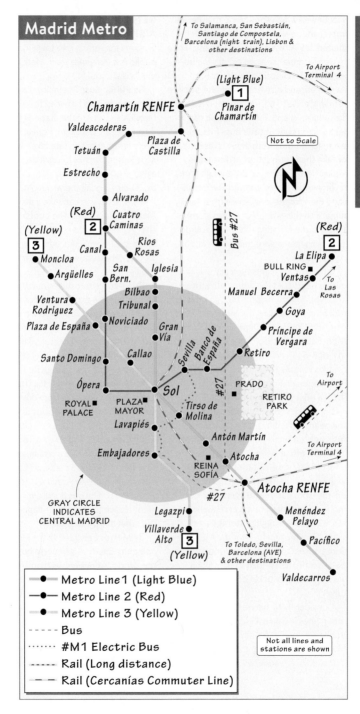

Madrid Metro

To Salamanca, San Sebastián, Santiago de Compostela, Barcelona (night train), Lisbon & other destinations

To Airport Terminal 4

(Light Blue) **1**

Chamartín RENFE

Pinar de Chamartín

Valdeacederas

Plaza de Castilla

Not to Scale

Tetuán

Estrecho

Alvarado

(Red) **2**

Cuatro Caminas

Canal

Rios Rosas

(Yellow) **3**

Moncloa

Argüelles

San Bern.

Iglesia

(Red) **2**

La Elipa

BULL RING

Ventas

To Las Rosas

Manuel Becerra

Ventura Rodriguez

Bilbao

Tribunal

Plaza de España

Noviciado

Gran Vía

Goya

Príncipe de Vergara

Santo Domingo

Callao

Sevilla

Banco de España

Retiro

Ópera

Sol

To Airport

ROYAL PALACE

PLAZA MAYOR

#27

PRADO

RETIRO PARK

Lavapiés

Tirso de Molina

Antón Martín

To Airport Terminal 4

Embajadores

REINA SOFÍA

Atocha

GRAY CIRCLE INDICATES CENTRAL MADRID

Atocha RENFE

#27

Legazpi

Menéndez Pelayo

Villaverde Alto **3**

(Yellow)

To Toledo, Sevilla, Barcelona (AVE) & other destinations

Pacífico

Valdecarros

Bus #27

—●— Metro Line 1 (Light Blue)
—●— Metro Line 2 (Red)
—●— Metro Line 3 (Yellow)
----- Bus
······· #M1 Electric Bus
----- Rail (Long distance)
— — Rail (Cercanías Commuter Line)

Not all lines and stations are shown

indoor walkways (about an 8-minute walk apart) and serve airlines including Delta, United, US Airways, and Air Canada. The newer Terminal 4 serves airlines including Iberia, Vueling, Ryanair, British, and American, and also has a separate satellite terminal called T4S. To transfer between Terminals 1-3 and Terminal 4, you can take a 10-minute shuttle bus (free, leaves every 10 minutes from departures level), or take the Metro (stops at Terminals 2 and 4). Make sure to allow enough time if you need to travel between terminals (and then for the long walk within Terminal 4 to the gates). For more information about navigating this massive airport, go to www.aena-aeropuertos.es (airport code: MAD).

International flights typically use Terminals 1 and 4. At the Terminal 1 arrivals area, you'll find a helpful, though privately run, English-speaking Turismo Madrid **TI** (marked *Oficina de Información Turística,* Mon-Sat 8:00-20:00, Sun 9:00-14:00, tel. 913-058-656), **ATMs,** a **flight info office** (marked simply *Information* in airport lobby, open daily 24 hours, tel. 902-353-570), a **post-office** window, a pharmacy, lots of phones (buy a phone card from the nearby machine), a few scattered **Internet** terminals (small fee), **eateries,** a **RENFE office** (where you can get train info and buy long-distance train tickets, long hours daily, tel. 902-320-320), and on-the-spot **car-rental agencies.** The modern Terminal 4 offers essentially the same services. **Luggage storage** *(con-signa)* is in Terminal 2, near the Metro exit. Some buses leave from the airport to far-flung destinations, such as Pamplona (see www.alsa.es; buy ticket online or from the driver).

Consider flying between Madrid and other cities in Spain. Domestic airline Vueling is popular for its discounts (e.g., Madrid-Barcelona flight as cheap as €30 if booked in advance, www.vueling.com).

GETTING BETWEEN THE AIRPORT AND DOWNTOWN

Options for getting into town include public bus, *cercanías* train, Metro, taxi, and minibus shuttle.

By Public Bus: The yellow **Exprés Aeropuerto** runs between the airport (all terminals) and Atocha Station (€5, pay driver in cash, departing from arrivals level every 15-20 minutes, ride takes about 40 minutes, runs 24 hours a day; from 23:30-6:00, the bus only goes to Plaza de Cibeles, not all the way to Atocha). From Atocha, you can take a taxi or the Metro to your hotel. The bus back to the airport leaves Atocha from near the taxi stand on the *cercanías* side (from 23:30-6:00, it departs downtown from Plaza de Cibeles).

Bus #200 (from all terminals) is less handy than the express bus because it leaves you farther from downtown (at the Metro stop at Avenida de América, northeast of the historical center). This bus departs from the arrivals level about every 10 minutes and takes about 20 minutes to reach Avenida de América (runs 6:00-24:00, buy €1.50 ticket from driver; or get a shareable 10-ride Metrobus ticket at a tobacco shop).

By Cercanías Train: From Terminal 4, passengers can ride a *cercanías* train to either of Madrid's stations (€2.60, 2/hour, 25 minutes to Atocha, 12 minutes to Chamartín). The bus is still a more convenient choice for arriving or departing from the other airport terminals.

By Metro: Considering the ease of riding the Exprés Aeropuerto bus in from the airport, I'd rather bus than Metro. The subway involves two transfers to reach the city; it's not difficult, but usually involves climbing some stairs (€4.50-6; or add a €3 supplement to your 10-ride Metrobus ticket). The airport's futuristic "Aeropuerto T-1, T-2, T-3" Metro stop (notice the ATMs, subway info booth, and huge lighted map of Madrid) is in Terminal 2. Access the Metro at the check-in level; to reach the Metro from Terminal 1's arrivals level, stand with your back to the baggage claim, then go to your far right, up the stairs, and follow red-and-blue Metro diamond signs to the station (8-minute walk). The Terminal 4 stop is the end of the line. To get to Puerta del Sol, take line 8 for 12 minutes to Nuevos Ministerios, then continue on line 10 to Tribunal, then line 1 to Puerta del Sol (30 minutes more total); or exit at Nuevos Ministerios and take a €5 taxi or bus #150 straight to Puerta del Sol.

By Taxi: With cheap and easy alternatives available, there's not much reason to take a taxi unless you have lots of luggage or just want to go straight to your hotel. If you do take a taxi between the airport and downtown, the flat rate is €30. There is no charge for luggage. Plan on getting stalled in traffic.

By Minibus Shuttle: The AeroCity shuttle bus provides door-to-door transport in a seven-seat minibus with up to three hotel stops en route. It's promoted by hotels, but if you want door-to-door service, simply taking a taxi generally offers a better value.

By Train

Madrid's two train stations, Chamartín and Atocha, are both on Metro lines with easy access to downtown Madrid. Both stations offer long-distance trains (*largo recorridos*) as well as smaller local trains (*regionales* and *cercanías*) to nearby destinations. Chamartín handles most international trains. Atocha generally covers southern Spain, as well as the AVE trains to and from Barcelona, Córdoba, Sevilla, and Toledo.

Buying Tickets: You can buy tickets at the stations, at travel agencies, or—not as easily—online (www.renfe.es). While travel agencies add a small fee, they can be worthwhile, especially during the high season or holidays, when the station's ticket counters have long lines. Convenient travel agencies include the El Corte

Inglés department store at Atocha (Mon-Fri 8:00-22:00, Sat-Sun 10:00-18:00, on ground floor of AVE side at the far end) and the El Corte Inglés a block off Puerta del Sol (Mon-Sat 10:00-22:00, Sun 11:00-21:00, Preciados 3, tel. 913-798-000).

Traveling Between Chamartín and Atocha Stations: You can take the Metro (line 1, 30-40 minutes, €1.50), but the *cercanías* trains are faster (6/hour, 13 minutes, €1.65)—and free with a rail pass or any regular train ticket to Madrid. Show it at ticket window in the middle of the turnstiles. Lines C3 and C4 are the most convenient; leave Atocha on track 6 or leave Chamartín from tracks 1, 3, 8, or 9—check the *Salidas Inmediatas* board to confirm.

CHAMARTÍN STATION

The TI is near track 20. The information, tickets, and customer-service office is at track 11. If you have a first-class rail pass and first-class seat or sleeper reservations, you can relax in the Sala VIP Club (between tracks 13 and 14, cooler of free drinks). Luggage storage (*consigna*) is across the street, opposite track 17. The station's Metro stop is also called Chamartín (not "Pinar de Chamartín").

ATOCHA STATION

The station is split in two: an AVE side (mostly long-distance trains) and a *cercanías* side (mostly local trains to the suburbs and the Metro for connecting into downtown). These two parts are connected by a corridor of shops. Each side of the station has separate schedules and customer-service offices. The TI, which is on the AVE arrivals side, offers tourist info, but no train info (Mon-Sat 8:00-20:00, Sun 9:00-14:00, tel. 915-284-630). To get to Atocha, use the "Atocha RENFE" Metro stop (not "Atocha").

Ticket Offices: The *cercanías* side has two offices—a small one for local trains and a big one for major trains (such as AVE). The AVE side sells tickets for AVE and other long-distance trains (two lines: "Tickets in Advance" or "Selling Out

Today"/"Departures Today"). A ticket counter will sometimes open up to sell tickets for trains departing soon—if you need to make a last-minute purchase, look for your destination and departure time, and get in line at that counter. If the line at one office is long, check the other offices. To secure your place in line, grab a number from a machine, usually located in the middle of the office by a sign with an image of a ticket. Ticket machines outside and around the office require a chip-and-PIN credit card.

AVE Side: Located in the towering old-station building, this half of the station boasts a lush, tropical garden filling its grand hall. It has the AVE trains, other fast trains (Grandes Líneas), a pharmacy (daily 8:00-22:00, facing garden), and Samarkanda—with both an affordable cafeteria (daily 13:00-20:00) and a pricey restaurant (daily from 21:00, tel. 915-309-746). Luggage storage (consigna, daily 6:00-22:20) is below Samarkanda. In the departure lounge on the upper floor, TV monitors announce track numbers. (A few trains, such as those for Toledo, depart from the lower floor.) For info, try the Información counter (daily 6:30-22:30), next to Centro Servicios AVE (which handles only AVE changes and problems). The Atención al Cliente office deals with problems on Grandes Líneas (daily 6:30-23:30). Also on the AVE side is the Club AVE/Sala VIP, a lounge reserved for AVE business-class travelers and for first-class ticket-holders or Eurailers with a first-class reservation (upstairs, past the security check on right; free drinks, newspapers, showers, and info service).

Cercanías Side: This is where you'll find the local cercanías trains, regionales trains, some eastbound faster trains, and the "Atocha RENFE" Metro stop. The Atención al Cliente office in the cercanías section has information only on trains to destinations near Madrid. During busy times, some AVE trains will pull in on this side—clearly marked signs lead you to the Metro, taxi stand, or back to the AVE side.

Terrorism Memorial: The terrorist bombings of March 11, 2004, took place in Atocha. Security is understandably tight here. A compelling memorial is in the cercanías part of the station near the Atocha RENFE Metro stop. Walk inside and under the cylinder to see thousands of condolence messages in many languages. The 36-foot-tall cylindrical glass memorial towers are visible from outside the station (daily 11:00-14:00 & 17:00-19:00).

AVE TRAINS

Spain's bullet train opens up some good itinerary options. You can get from Madrid's Atocha Station to **Barcelona** in about three hours, with trains running at least hourly. The AVE train is generally faster and easier than flying, but not necessarily cheaper. Basic second-class tickets are about €110-130 one-way for most departures; first-class tickets are €180. Advance purchase discounts (40-60 days ahead) are available through the national rail company (RENFE), but sell out quickly. Save by not traveling on holidays.

The AVE is also handy for visiting **Sevilla** (and, on the way, **Córdoba**). The basic Madrid-Sevilla second-class AVE fare is €75, depending upon departure time; first-class AVE costs €130 and comes with a meal. Consider this exciting day trip: 7:00-depart Madrid, 8:45-12:40-in Córdoba, 13:30-20:45-in Sevilla, 23:15-back in Madrid.

Other AVE destinations include **Toledo, Segovia,** and **Valencia.** Prices vary with times, class, date of purchase—RENFE discounts unsold AVE tickets as departure dates near. Eurail Pass holders pay a seat reservation fee (for example, Madrid to Sevilla is €13 second-class, but only at RENFE ticket windows—discount not available at ticket machines). Reserve each AVE segment ahead (tel. 902-320-320 for Atocha AVE info). For the latest, pick up the AVE brochure at the station, or check www.renfe.com.

TRAIN CONNECTIONS

Below I've listed both non-AVE and (where available) AVE trains to help you compare your options. General train info: tel. 902-320-320; international journeys: tel. 902-243-402; www.renfe.com.

From Madrid by Train to: Toledo (AVE or cheaper Avant: nearly hourly, 30 minutes, from Atocha); **El Escorial** (2/hour, but bus is better—see page 220); **Segovia** (AVE: 8-10/day, 30 minutes plus 20-minute shuttle bus into Segovia center, from Chamartín, take train going toward Valladolid; slower *cercanías* trains: 9/day, 2 hours, from both Chamartín and Atocha); **Salamanca** (7/day, 3 hours, from Chamartín); **Santiago de Compostela** (4/day, 5.5-8.5 hours, most transfer in Ourense, includes night train, from Chamartín); **Barcelona** (AVE: at least hourly, 2.5-3 hours from Atocha); **San Sebastián** (4/day, 5.5-7.5 hours, from Chamartín); **Bilbao** (2-3/day, 5-6.5 hours, some transfer in Zaragoza, from Chamartín); **Pamplona** (3/day direct, 3 hours, more with transfer in Zaragoza, from Atocha); **Granada** (2/day on Altaria, 4.5 hours; also 2/day with transfer to AVE in Málaga, 4 hours); **Sevilla** (AVE: hourly, 2.5 hours, departures from 16:00-19:00 can sell out far in advance, from Atocha); **Córdoba** (AVE: 2-3/hour, 2 hours; Altaria trains: 4/day, 2 hours; all from Atocha); **Málaga** (AVE: 9/day, 2.5-3 hours, from Atocha).

By Bus

Madrid has several major bus stations with good Metro connections. Multiple bus companies use these stations, including Alsa (tel. 902-422-242, www.alsa.es), Avanza and Auto-Res (tel. 902-020-052, www.avanzabus.com), and La Sepulvedana (tel. 901-119-699, www.lasepulvedana.es). If you take a taxi from any bus station, you'll be charged a legitimate €3 supplement (not levied for trips to the station).

Plaza Elíptica Station: Alsa buses to Toledo leave from here (2/hour, 1-1.5 hours, *directo* faster than *ruta*, Metro:

Plaza Elíptica).

Estación Sur de Autobuses (South Station): Served by Alsa, Socibus, and Avanza; buses go to **Ávila** (9/day, 6/day on weekends, 1.5 hours, Avanza), **Salamanca** (hourly express, 2.5-3 hours, Avanza), **León** (10/day, 3.5-4.5 hours, Alsa), **Santiago de Compostela** (5/day, 8-11 hours, includes 1 night bus, Alsa), **Granada** (nearly hourly, 5-6 hours, Alsa), and **Lisbon** (2/day, 9 hours, Avanza). The station sits squarely on top of the Méndez Álvaro Metro stop (has TI, tel. 914-684-200, www.estacionautobusesmadrid.com).

Príncipe Pío Station: Príncipe Pío, in a trendy mall, is a bus hub for local lines including Segovia (2/hour from platforms 6 or 7, 1.5 hours, runs from around 6:30-21:30, service starts later on Sat-Sun). From the Príncipe Pío Metro stop, follow signs to *terminal de autobuses* or follow pictures of a bus. Buy a ticket from the Sepulvedana window (platform 4). Reservations are rarely necessary.

Moncloa Station: This station, in the Moncloa Metro station, serves **El Escorial** (4/hour, fewer on weekends, 1 hour; for details, see page 220).

Avenida de América Station: Located at the Avenida de América Metro stop, Alsa buses go to **Burgos** (hourly, 3 hours) and **Pamplona** (7/day, 5-7.5 hours).

By Car

Avoid driving in Madrid. If you're planning to rent a car, do it when you depart the city.

Renting a Car: It's cheapest to make car-rental arrangements before you leave home. In Madrid, consider **Europcar** (central reservations tel. 902-105-030, San Leonardo 8 office tel. 915-418-892, Atocha Station tel. 902-105-055, Chamartín Station tel. 912-035-070, airport tel. 902-105-055), **Hertz** (central reservations tel. 902-402-405, Plaza de España 18 tel. 915-425-805, Chamartín Station tel. 917-330-400, airport tel.

913-228-331), **Avis** (central reservations tel. 933-443-700, Gran Vía 60 tel. 915-484-204, airport tel. 902-200-162), and **Enterprise Atesa** (central reservations tel. 902-100-101). Ask about free delivery to your hotel. At the airport, most rental cars are returned at Terminal 1.

Route Tips for Drivers: To leave Madrid from Gran Vía, simply follow signs for A-6 (direction *Villalba* or *A Coruña*) for Segovia or El Escorial.

NEAR MADRID

EL ESCORIAL, SEGOVIA, AND SALAMANCA

Consider several fine side-trips northwest of Madrid, all conveniently reached by car or public transit.

The formidable palace El Escorial was the headquarters of the Spanish Inquisition; allow a half-day to visit it (but avoid Monday when it's closed).

Nearby, and easiest for drivers to visit, is the somber Valley of the Fallen. Worth a day, the town of Segovia has a remarkable Roman aqueduct and a grand cathedral, plus a castle to boot. Lively Salamanca has a youthful vibe, a pair of conjoined cathedrals, and a marvelous town square. It's worth a day and an overnight (partly

because it's about 2.5 hours from Madrid).

Here's a possible two-day option for combining Salamanca and Segovia: Bus to Salamanca in the morning, spend the night (enjoying the nightlife), bus to Segovia the next morning, and return to Madrid that evening.

▲▲▲Monasterio de San Lorenzo de El Escorial

Thirty miles northwest of Madrid, the imposing Monasterio de San Lorenzo de El Escorial gives us a better sense of the Inquisition than any other site. A symbol of power rather than elegance, this

El Escorial

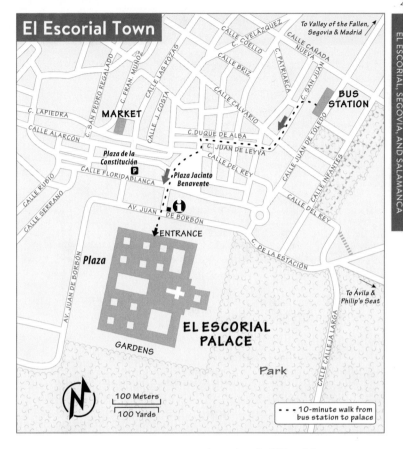

El Escorial Town

To Valley of the Fallen,
Segovia & Madrid

BUS
STATION

MARKET

Plaza de la
Constitución

Plaza Jacinto
Benavente

ENTRANCE

Plaza

EL ESCORIAL
PALACE

GARDENS

Park

To Ávila &
Philip's Seat

100 Meters
100 Yards

- - - 10-minute walk from
bus station to palace

16th-century palace was built at a time when Catholic Spain felt threatened by Protestant "heretics." Because of this bully in the national budget, Spain has almost nothing else to show from this period of history.

Getting There: Take the **bus** from Madrid; it's a quick one-hour trip and drops you closer to the palace than the train does (4 buses/hour, fewer on weekends, €4.20 one-way, buy ticket from driver; in Madrid take bus #664 or slower #661 from Moncloa's platform 11, Herranz Bus, tel. 918-969-028). Get off in San Lorenzo de El Escorial, a pleasant 10-minute stroll from the palace.

Coming by **car** from central Madrid, take A-6 (direction *Villalba* or *A Coruña*),

then exit 47 for El Escorial.

Cost and Hours: €10, April-Sept Tue-Sun 10:00-20:00, Oct-March Tue-Sun 10:00-18:00, closed Mon year-round, last entry one hour before closing.

Information: English descriptions are scattered within the palace. For more info, get the *Guide: Monastery of San Lorenzo El Real de El Escorial,* which follows the route you'll take (€9, sold at shops in palace).

Tours: For an extra €4, a guided 1.5-hour **tour** takes you through the complex, but there are so few tours in English that it generally isn't worth waiting around for one. You could rent the €4 **audioguide** instead.

Eating: There's no cafeteria on site, but restaurants serve fixed-price lunches two

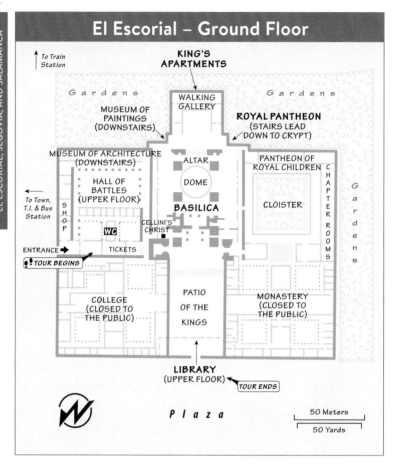

El Escorial – Ground Floor

To Train Station

KING'S APARTMENTS

Gardens

MUSEUM OF PAINTINGS (DOWNSTAIRS)

WALKING GALLERY

Gardens

ROYAL PANTHEON (STAIRS LEAD DOWN TO CRYPT)

MUSEUM OF ARCHITECTURE (DOWNSTAIRS)

ALTAR

PANTHEON OF ROYAL CHILDREN

HALL OF BATTLES (UPPER FLOOR)

DOME

To Town, T.I. & Bus Station

SHOP

BASILICA

CLOISTER

CHAPTER ROOMS

Gardens

CELLINI'S CHRIST

WC

ENTRANCE

TICKETS

TOUR BEGINS

COLLEGE (CLOSED TO THE PUBLIC)

PATIO OF THE KINGS

MONASTERY (CLOSED TO THE PUBLIC)

LIBRARY (UPPER FLOOR)

TOUR ENDS

N

Plaza

50 Meters

50 Yards

blocks north of the palace complex (on Plaza Jacinto Benavente and Plaza de la Constitución).

Visiting El Escorial: The giant, gloomy building made of gray-black stone looks more like a prison than a palace. About 650 feet long and 500 feet wide, it has 2,600 windows, 1,200 doors, more than 100 miles of passages, and 1,600 overwhelmed tourists.

Four hundred years ago, the enigmatic, introverted, and extremely Catholic King Philip II (1527-1598) ruled his empire and directed the Inquisition from here. To Philip, the palace embodied the wonders of Catholic learning. To 16th-century fol-

lowers of Martin Luther, it epitomized the evil of closed-minded Catholicism. Today it's a time capsule of Spain's "Golden Age," packed with history, art, and Inquisition ghosts. (And at an elevation of nearly 3,500 feet, it can be friggin' cold.)

As you tour the palace (following the *Visita* arrows on one continuous path), look for these highlights: The **Museum of Tapestries** has fascinating tapestry copies of Hieronymus Bosch's most famous and preachy paintings. Don't miss El Greco's towering *Martyrdom of St. Maurice*. The **Museum of Architecture** displays some of the actual machinery used to construct this immense palace (built 1563-1584).

Looking at the big model, you'll see the complex is shaped like a grill. San Lorenzo (St. Lawrence), martyred by pagan Romans in A.D. 258, was burned to death on a grill. Lorenzo reportedly told his executioners, "You can turn me over now— I'm done on this side." The **Hall of Battles** celebrates Spain's great military victories. After the royal apartments, containing some of the original furniture, you'll enter the **Royal Pantheon,** the gilded resting place of four centuries' worth of Spanish monarchy. In the basilica, find the flame-engulfed grill in the center of the altar wall that shows San Lorenzo meeting his death. The basilica's highlight is Benvenuto Cellini's marble sculpture, *The Crucifixion* (with your back to the altar, go to the right corner). The tour ends at the library; at the far end, the elaborate model of the solar system (looking like a giant gyroscope), revolves unmistakably around the Earth. As you leave, look back above the wooden door. The plaque warns *"Excomunión..."*—you'll be excommunicated if you take a book without checking it out properly. Who needs late fees when you hold the keys to hell?

Valley of the Fallen

Valley of the Fallen

Six miles from El Escorial is the Valley of the Fallen (Valle de los Caídos). A 500-foot-tall granite cross marks this immense, powerful underground basilica to the victims of Spain's 20th-century nightmare—the Spanish Civil War (1936-1939).

Getting There: Drivers find it easy to reach (take exit 47 off A-6; after one-half mile, it's on your right). Without wheels, negotiate a deal with a taxi to take you from El Escorial to Valley of the Fallen, wait 30-60 minutes, and then bring you back to El Escorial (about €45).

Cost and Hours: €9; April-Sept Tue-Sun 10:00-19:00, Oct-March Tue-Sun 10:00-18:00, closed Mon year-round; ask about audioguide, tel. 918-905-611, www. valledeloscaidos.es. During Mass the basilica is closed to sightseers (Tue-Sat at 11:00; Sun at 11:00, 13:00, and 17:30; one-hour service). A café and WC are near the parking lot.

Visiting the Basilica: The statue of the emotional pietà draped over the entrance is huge—you could sit in the palm of Christ's hand.

A solemn silence and a stony chill fill the huge basilica. After walking through the two long vestibules, stop at the iron gates of the actual basilica. The line of torch-like lamps adds to the shrine ambience. Franco's prisoners, the enemies of the right, dug this memorial out of solid rock from 1940 to 1950. The sides are lined with copies of 16th-century Brussels tapestries of the Apocalypse, and side chapels contain alabaster copies of Spain's most famous statues of the Virgin Mary.

Interred behind the high altar and side chapels (marked "RIP, 1936-1939, died for God and country") are the remains of approximately 34,000 people, both Franco's Nationalists and the anti-Franco Republicans (about 12,000), who lost their lives in the war. Today, families of the Republicans remain upset that their kin are lying with Franco and his Nation-alists. Franco takes center-stage here: His grave, strewn with flowers, lies behind the high altar.

When you leave, stare into the eyes of the angels with swords and two right wings and think about all the "heroes" who keep dying "for God and country," at the request of the latter.

Segovia

Fifty miles from Madrid, this town of 55,000 boasts a thrilling Roman aqueduct, a grand cathedral, and a historic castle. People come here for the cool mountain breezes and a break from the summer heat.

Orientation

Shaped like a boat, Segovia is ready for your inspection. The aqueduct is at the stern; Calle de Cervantes and Calle Juan Bravo lead to the prickly Gothic masts of the cathedral; and the Alcázar is at the bow.

Day Plan: On a day trip, marvel at the aqueduct, people-watch on the playful Plaza Mayor, and explore the Alcázar.

With more time, enjoy the charming evening scene and stay the night. You'll pay less for a hotel here than you would in Madrid.

Getting There: Easy AVE train and bus connections make Segovia a fine day trip from Madrid (30 minutes one-way by AVE train, 1.5 hours by bus).

Arrival in Segovia: If day-tripping from Madrid, check the return schedule (or get one at the TI). Only the bus station offers **luggage storage** (tokens sold daily 9:00-14:00 & 16:00-19:00, gives you access to locker until end of day).

It's a 10-minute walk from the **bus station** to the town center: Exit left out of the station, continue straight across the street, and follow Avenida Fernández Ladreda, passing San Millán church on the left, then San Clemente church on the right, before coming to the aqueduct.

From the **AVE train station** (called Guiomar), ride bus #11 for 20 minutes to the base of the aqueduct. To reach the center from the *cercanías* train station, you can catch bus #6 or #8, take a taxi, or walk 30 minutes (take Paseo del Conde de Sepulvedana—which becomes Paseo Ezequiel González—to the bus station,

Roman aqueduct at Segovia

turn right on Avenida Fernández Ladreda to the aqueduct).

Speedy **drivers** take A-6 out of Madrid, then AP-6 and AP-61 to Segovia (this toll route takes only one hour if traffic is light). At the aqueduct, follow *casco histórico* signs; the Alcázar's lot has free parking (move your car out by 19:00; 18:00 Oct-March).

Tourist Information: The TI on Plaza Mayor covers both Segovia and the surrounding region (daily July-mid-Sept 9:00-20:00, shorter hours off-season, at #10, tel. 921-460-334, www.turismo castillayleon.com). Other TIs are at Plaza del Azoguejo, at the base of the aqueduct—see wooden model of Segovia (daily 10:00-19:00, tel. 921-466-720, www.turismodesegovia.com); at the bus station (Wed-Sun 10:00-14:00, closed Mon-Tue, behind a window, tel. 921-436-569); and the AVE train station (Mon-Fri 8:15-15:15, Sat-Sun 10:00-14:15 & 16:00-17:45, tel. 921-447-262).

Guide: Consider **Elvira Valderrama Rascon** (€115/3 hours, mobile 636-227-949, elvisvalrras@yahoo.es).

Sights

▲ROMAN AQUEDUCT

When Segovia was a Roman military base, Emperor Trajan's engineers built a nine-mile aqueduct to channel water from the Río Frío to the city, culminating at the Roman castle (the Alcázar today). The exposed section of the 2,000-year-old *acueducto romano* is 2,500 feet long and 100 feet high, has 118 arches, was made from 20,000 granite blocks without any mortar, and can still carry a stream of water. On Plaza del Azoguejo, a grand stairway leads from the base of the aqueduct to the top—offering close-up looks at the remarkable work.

▲CATHEDRAL

Segovia's cathedral, built in Renaissance times, was Spain's last major Gothic building. Embellished to the hilt with pinnacles and flying buttresses, the exterior is a textbook example of the final, overripe stage of Gothic, called Flamboyant. The Renaissance arrived before it was finished, so the cathedral is crowned by a dome, not a spire.

Cost and Hours: €3, free Sun 9:30-13:15 (cathedral access only—no cloister),

Segovia's Alcázar

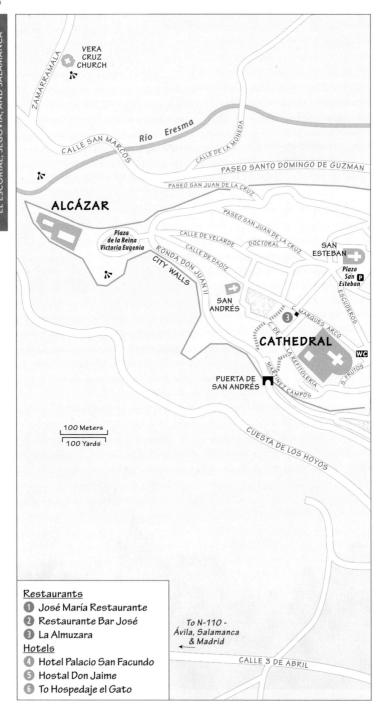

VERA
CRUZ
CHURCH

ZAMARRAMALA

Río Eresma

CALLE SAN MARCOS

CALLE DE LA MONEDA

PASEO SANTO DOMINGO DE GUZMAN

PASEO SAN JUAN DE LA CRUZ

ALCÁZAR

PASEO SAN JUAN DE LA CRUZ

CALLE DE VELARDE   DOCTORAL

Plaza
de la Reina
Victoria Eugenia

CALLE DE DAOIZ

RONDA DON JUAN II

CITY WALLS

SAN
ESTEBAN

Plaza
San
Esteban

ESCUDEROS

SAN
ANDRÉS

C. MARQUES ARCO

CATHEDRAL

C. DE LA RELLOLERIA

S. FRUTOS

WC

PUERTA DE
SAN ANDRÉS

MARTINEZ CAMPOS

CUESTA DE LOS HOYOS

100 Meters
100 Yards

Restaurants
1 José María Restaurante
2 Restaurante Bar José
3 La Almuzara
Hotels
4 Hotel Palacio San Facundo
5 Hostal Don Jaime
6 To Hospedaje el Gato

To N-110 -
Ávila, Salamanca
& Madrid

CALLE 3 DE ABRIL

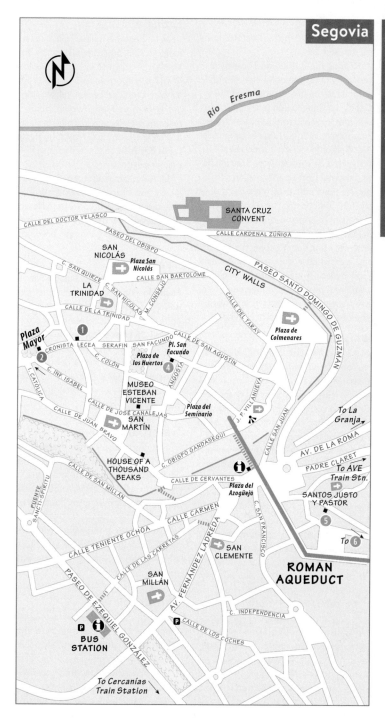

Segovia

Río Eresma

SANTA CRUZ CONVENT

CALLE DEL DOCTOR VELASCO

PASEO DEL OBISPO

CALLE CARDENAL ZÚÑIGA

SAN NICOLÁS

Plaza San Nicolás

C. SAN QUIRCE

CALLE SAN BARTOLOMÉ

CITY WALLS

PASEO SANTO DOMINGO DE GUZMÁN

LA TRINIDAD

C. SAN NICOLÁS

M. CONSEJO

CALLE DE LA TRINIDAD

CALLE DEL TARAY

Plaza de Colmenares

Plaza Mayor

CRONISTA LECEA SERAFIN SAN FACUNDO

CALLE DE SAN AGUSTÍN

Pl. San Facundo

C. COLÓN

Plaza de los Huertos

ANGOSTA

C. INF. ISABEL

C. CATÓLICA

MUSEO ESTEBAN VICENTE

Plaza del Seminario

J. P. VILLANUEVA

CALLE DE JOSÉ CANALEJAS

SAN MARTÍN

CALLE DE JUAN BRAVO

CALLE SAN JUAN

To La Granja

AV. DE LA ROMA

HOUSE OF A THOUSAND BEAKS

C. OBISPO GANDASÉGUI

PADRE CLARET

To AVE Train Stn.

PUENTE SANCTI-SPIRITU

CALLE DE SAN MILLÁN

CALLE DE CERVANTES

Plaza del Azoguejo

SANTOS JUSTO Y PASTOR

To 6

CALLE CARMEN

C. SAN FRANCISCO

CALLE TENIENTE OCHOA

CALLE DE LAS CARRETAS

SAN CLEMENTE

ROMAN AQUEDUCT

PASEO DE EZEQUIEL GONZÁLEZ

SAN MILLÁN

AV. FERNÁNDEZ LADREDA

C. INDEPENDENCIA

CALLE DE LOS COCHES

BUS STATION

To Cercanías Train Station

open daily 9:30-18:30, Oct-March until 17:30, last entry 30 minutes before closing, tel. 921-462-205.

Visiting the Cathedral: The elegant simplicity of the interior is a delightful contrast to the frilly exterior. Find the **Capilla La Concepción** (a chapel in the rear that looks like a mini-art gallery) and locate the painting *Tree of Life* by Ignacio Ries (left of the altar). It shows hedonistic mortals dancing atop the Tree of Life as a skeletal Grim Reaper prepares to receive them into hell (by chopping down the tree...timberrrr!). The center statue is Mary of the Apocalypse (as described in *Revelation*). Opposite from where you entered, a fine door (leading to the cloister) is crowned by a painted Flamboyant Gothic **pietà.** The museum in the **cloister** contains tapestries, paintings, and silver reliquaries. From the cloister courtyard, you can see the Renaissance dome.

▲**ALCÁZAR**

In the Middle Ages, this fortified palace was one of the favorite residences of the monarchs of Castile. As the Alcázar grew through the ages, its function changed: from a palace, to a prison, then a Royal Artillery School. After a fire in 1862, it was rebuilt and became a museum. Today's Alcázar is a Disney-esque exaggeration of the original. Still, its fine Moorish decor and historic furnishings are fascinating. The throne-room ceiling is the artistic highlight. The Hall of the Monarchs is lined with the busts of the 52 rulers who presided during the long, ultimately successful Reconquista (711-1492). Visit the tower afterward; its 152 steps up a tight spiral staircase reward you with the only 360-degree city view in town.

Cost and Hours: Palace—€5, daily 10:00-19:00, Oct-March until 18:00, €3 audioguide; tower—€2, same hours as palace except closed third Tue of month; tel. 921-460-759, www.alcazardesegovia. com. Buy your tickets at Real Laboratorio de Chimia, facing the palace on your left.

Eating

Look for Segovia's culinary claim to fame, roast suckling pig *(cochinillo asado).* **José María** is *the* place to pig out in the old town (daily 13:00-16:00 & 20:00-23:30, air-con, Cronista Lecea 11, tel. 921-466-017, www.restaurantejosemaria.com, reservas@restaurantejosemaria.com). For a filling lunch on Plaza Mayor, try **Restaurante Bar José,** (€16 three-course fixed-price meal).

La Almuzara is a garden of veggie delights (Tue 20:00-24:00, Wed-Sun 12:00-16:00 & 20:00-24:00, closed Mon, between cathedral and Alcázar at Marques del Arco 3, tel. 921-460-622).

Sleeping

Try luxurious **$$$ Hotel Palacio San Facundo** (Plaza San Facundo 4, tel. 921-463-061, www.hotelpalaciosanfacundo. com, info@hotelpalaciosanfacundo.com), friendly **$$ Hostal Don Jaime,** (Ochoa Ondategui 8, tel. 921-444-787, hostal donjaime@hotmail.com), or budget **$ Hospedaje el Gato** (Plaza del Salvador 10, tel. 921-423-244, www.hostalsegovia.es, hbarelgato@yahoo.es).

Salamanca

This sunny sandstone city boasts Spain's best Plaza Mayor and oldest university. Students congregate until late in the night, talking and singing. Another benefit of youthful exuberance: Students keep prices low.

Worth a day (and a night if you have time), Salamanca is feasible as a side-trip from Madrid (about 2.5 hours one-way by car, bus, or train).

Orientation

Salamanca's sights are like a barbell, with its magnificent town square on one end, and the cluster of cathedrals and the university at the other end—about five blocks south. The connecting streets are lively with eateries, shops, and people.

Day Plan: Head straight to Plaza Mayor

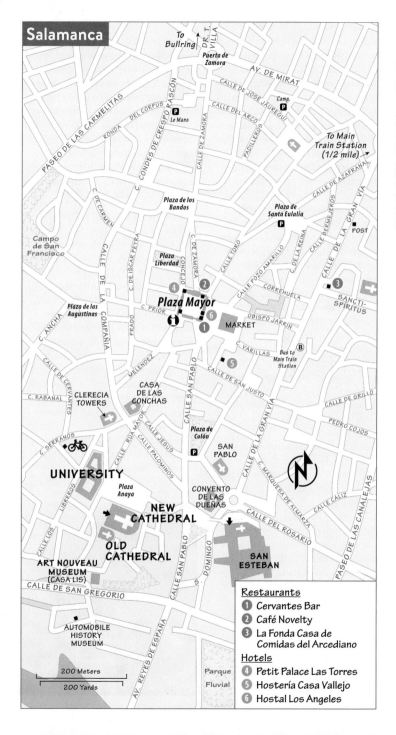

Salamanca

To Bullring

DR. T. VILLA

Puerta de Zamora

AV. DE MIRAT

CALLE DE JOSÉ JÁUREGU.

Camp. P

CALLE DEL ARCO

PASEO DE LAS CARMELITAS

RONDA DEL CORPUS

C. CONDES DE CRESPO RASCÓN

P Le Mans

CALLE DE ZAMORA

PADILLEROS

To Main Train Station (1/2 mile)

CALLE DE AZAFRANA.

C. DE CARMEN

Campo de San Francisco

CALLE DE LA COMPAÑIA

C. DE ISCAR PEYRA

Plaza de los Bandos

CONDEJO

Plaza de Santa Eulalia P

POST

Plaza Liberdad

Plaza de las Augustinas

C. DE ZAMORA

Plaza Mayor

CALLE TORO

CALLE POZO AMARILLO

C. DE LA REINA

CALLE BERMEJEROS

CALLE DE LA GRAN VÍA

CORREHUELA

SANCTI-SPIRITUS

C. ANCHA

PRADO

C. PRIOR

MARKET

OBISPO JARRÍN

C. VARILLAS

Bus to Main Train Station B

CALLE DE CERVANTES

C. RABANAL

CLERECIA TOWERS

CASA DE LAS CONCHAS

MELÉNDEZ

CALLE SAN PABLO

CALLE DE SAN JUSTO

CALLE DE GRILLO

PEDRO COJOS

C. SERRANOS

RÚA MAYOR

CALLE JESÚS

CALLE PALOMINOS

Plaza de Colón P

SAN PABLO

CALLE DE LA GRAN VÍA

C. MARQUESA DE ALMARZA

CALLE CALÍZ

UNIVERSITY

LIBREROS

Plaza Anaya

NEW CATHEDRAL

CONVENTO DE LAS DUEÑAS

CALLE DEL ROSARIO

PASEO DE LAS CANALEJAS

CALLE LOS

OLD CATHEDRAL

CALLE SAN PABLO

S. DOMINGO

SAN ESTEBAN

ART NOUVEAU MUSEUM (CASA LIS)

CALLE DE SAN GREGORIO

AUTOMOBILE HISTORY MUSEUM

AV. REYES DE ESPAÑA

200 Meters

200 Yards

Parque Fluvial

Restaurants

1 Cervantes Bar
2 Café Novelty
3 La Fonda Casa de Comidas del Arcediano

Hotels

4 Petit Palace Las Torres
5 Hostería Casa Vallejo
6 Hostal Los Angeles

and wander the square. Visit the cathedrals and university. Sample tapas at bars as needed. Visit the square again; linger over a drink or meal.

Getting There: From **Madrid,** you can take the bus (hourly express, 2.5-3 hours, from Madrid's Estación Sur, Avanza bus) or the train (7/day, 3 hours, Chamartín Station). Buses connect Salamanca with **Segovia** (2/day, 3 hours, Auto-Res bus) and **Santiago de Compostela** (1-2/day, 6-7.5 hours, Alsa bus; also 1 train/day, 6.5 hours).

Arrival in Salamanca: From either Salamanca's train or bus station to Plaza Mayor, it's an easy bus ride (€1.05, pay driver) or a €7 taxi trip. From Salamanca's main **train** station, take bus #1 into town; it lets you off just past Plaza del Mercado (the market), next to Plaza Mayor.

From the **bus station,** take bus #4 (exit station right, catch bus on same side of the street as the station) to the city center; the closest stop is on Gran Vía, about two blocks east of Plaza Mayor. Only the bus station offers luggage storage (*consignas*).

Drivers will find a handy underground parking lot at Plaza Santa Eulalia (€13/day, open 24 hours daily).

Tourist Information: It's on Plaza Mayor (Mon-Fri 9:00-14:00 & 16:30-20:00, Sat 10:00-20:00, Sun 10:00-14:00, shorter hours off-season, Plaza Mayor 19, tel. 923-218-342).

Sightseeing Pass: The **Salamanca Card,** which covers entry to the major sights, isn't quite worth it (€19/24 hours, www.salamancacard.com).

Guide: Try **Ines Criado Velasco** (€95-105/3 hours, €150/5 hours, mobile 609-557-528, inescriado@yahoo.es).

Sights

▲▲PLAZA MAYOR

Built from 1729 to 1755, this ultimate Spanish plaza is a good place to watch the world go by (have a coffee at Café Novelty). The town hall, with the clock, grandly overlooks the square. While most European squares honor a king or saint, this golden-toned square—ringed by famous Castilians—is for all the people. The square niches above the colonnade depict writers (Miguel de Cervantes), heroes and conquistadors (Christopher Columbus and Hernán Cortés), as well as numerous kings and dictators (Francisco Franco). Plaza Mayor is continually hosting a party or event; bullfights were held here until 1893. The best people-watching is Sunday after Mass (13:00-15:00).

▲▲CATHEDRALS, OLD AND NEW

These cool cathedrals share buttresses. The Old Cathedral is 12th-century Romanesque, while the "New" Cathedral, built from 1513 to 1733, is a towering mix of Gothic, Renaissance, and Baroque.

Before entering the **New Cathedral,** check out its ornate front door (west portal on Rúa Mayor). The facade is decorated Plateresque, Spain's version of Flamboyant Gothic. At the side door (around the corner to the left as you face the main entrance), look for the astronaut added by a capricious restorer in 1993. (Locals shrug and say, "He's the person closest to God.")

Head into the **Old Cathedral** (through the San Lorenzo Chapel near the ticket counter in the New Cathedral) to see the altarpiece's 53 scenes from the lives

Salamanca's Plaza Mayor

of Mary and Jesus (Florentino, 1445) surrounding a 12th-century statue of the Virgin. High above is a fresco of the Last Judgment. For a fantastic view of the upper floors and terraces of both cathedrals, visit the tower (marked *Jerónimos;* exit the cathedral to the left to the separate entrance around the corner).

Cost and Hours: Cathedrals—€4.75 for both, free Tue 10:00-12:00, open daily 10:00-19:30, Oct-March until 17:30, includes audioguide; tower—€3.75, free Tue 10:00-12:00, open daily 10:00-20:00, Jan-Feb until 18:00; last entry one hour before closing; cathedral tel. 923-217-476, tower tel. 923-226-701, www.catedral salamanca.org.

▲▲UNIVERSITY OF SALAMANCA

The University of Salamanca, the oldest in Spain (est. 1230), was one of Europe's leading centers of learning for 400 years. Columbus came here for travel tips. Today, it's popular with American exchange students. The old lecture halls around the cloister, where many of Spain's Golden Age heroes studied, are open to the public. To enter, buy a ticket (cash only at machine), or validate your Salamanca Card at the info counter.

Cost and Hours: Lecture halls—€10, Mon-Sat 10:00-20:00, Oct-March until 19:00, July-Sept closed midday (14:00-17:00), Sun 10:00-13:00 year-round, last entry 30 minutes before closing, audioguide—€2; museum—free, Tue-Sat 9:30-13:30 & 16:00-18:30, Sun 10:00-14:00, closed Mon, no photos allowed, tel. 923-294-400, ext. 1150.

Nightlife

Take a paseo with the local crowd down Calle de Rúa Mayor and through Plaza Mayor. Traditionally, Salamanca's poorer students earned money for their education by singing in the streets. This 15th- to 18th-century tradition survives today, as *tuna* **musical groups** serenade the public on and around Plaza Mayor. (The name has nothing to do with fish; it refers to a vagabond student lifestyle.) They sing for tips on summer weeknights (22:00 until after midnight).

Eating

Savor a meal on Plaza Mayor, the finest square in Spain with some of Europe's best people-watching. At one of the bars with little tables spilling out on the square, order a couple of *raciones* (ham and cheese, potatoes) and two glasses of wine, making a nice dinner for €25—one of the best eating values in all of Europe.

Good, inexpensive restaurants include these two on the square: the popular student hangout **Cervantes Bar** (daily 8:00-late, tel. 923-217-213) and **Café Novelty,** an Art Nouveau café dating from 1905 (daily 8:00-late, tel. 923-214-956).

At traditional **La Fonda Casa de Comidas del Arcediano,** you'll happily spend about €25 for dinner (daily 13:30-16:00 & 21:00-24:00, La Reja 2, tel. 923-215-712).

Picnickers like the covered **market** on Plaza Mercado, on the east side of Plaza Mayor (Mon-Sat 8:00-14:30, closed Sun).

Sleeping

Try modern **$$$ Petit Palace Las Torres** (Calle Concejo 4, tel. 923-212-100, www. petitpalace.com, lastorres@petitpalace. com); family-run **$$ Hostería Casa Vallejo** (San Juan de la Cruz 3, tel. 923-280-421, www.hosteriacasavallejo.com, info@hosteriacasavallejo.com); or budget **$ Hostal Los Angeles**—request a view, *"Con vista, por favor"* (Plaza Mayor 10, tel. 923-218-166, www.pensionlosangeles. com, info@pensionlosangeles.com).

Toledo

An hour south of Madrid by car, Spain's former capital crowds 2,500 years of tangled history—Roman, Jewish, Visigothic, Moorish, and Christian—onto a high, rocky perch protected on three sides by the Tajo River. Incredibly well preserved, the entire city has been declared a national monument. To keep its historic appearance intact, the Spanish government has forbidden any modern exteriors. The rich mix of Jewish, Moorish, and Christian heritages makes it one of Europe's cultural highlights.

Today, Toledo thrives as a provincial capital and a busy tourist attraction. Many of the town's sights were beautifully renovated in 2014 to mark the 400th anniversary of resident artist El Greco's death.

A high-speed AVE train connection makes Toledo a quick, 30-minute ride from Madrid. While locals worried that this link would turn their town into a bedroom community for wealthy Madrileños, high real-estate prices have minimized the impact. The convention center (Palacio de Congresos Miradero), with its huge underground parking garage and escalators into town, has made arrival by car and train easier and more efficient.

Despite its tourist vibe, this stony wonderland remains the historic, artistic, and spiritual center of Spain. Toledo sits enthroned on its history, much as it was when Europe's most powerful monarch, the Holy Roman Emperor Charles V (King Charles I in Spain), called it home.

TOLEDO IN 2 DAYS

You'll need at least two nights and a day to see Toledo's sights and experience its medieval atmosphere, especially after dark. Spending two days is more relaxing. Keep in mind that day-trippers and commuters from Madrid can fill up early and late trains; it's best to purchase tickets in advance.

Day 1: Upon arrival, take the Toledo City Tour bus to the viewpoint overlooking the town's impressive skyline, immortalized by El Greco in his art. Then head to the magnificent cathedral, the best in Spain. Don't rush this sight. Other top stops are the Santa Cruz Museum (for art lovers) and the Army Museum (for history aficionados). Fit in a siesta at your hotel during Toledo's notorious midday

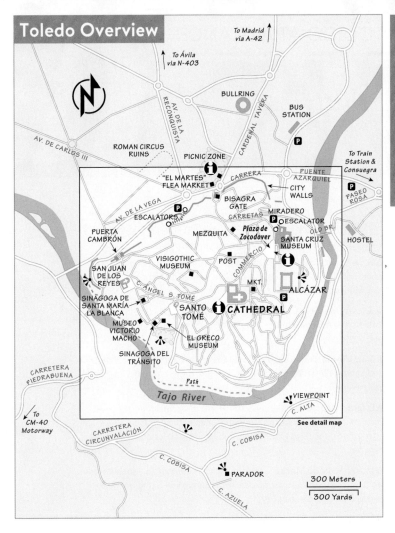

Toledo Overview

To Madrid via A-42

To Ávila via N-403

AV. DE LA RECONQUISTA

BULLRING

BUS STATION

CARDENAL TAVERA

AV. DE CARLOS III

ROMAN CIRCUS RUINS

PICNIC ZONE

To Train Station & Consuegra

PUENTE AZARQUIEL

"EL MARTES" FLEA MARKET

CARRERA

CITY WALLS

PASEO ROSA

BISAGRA GATE

AV. DE LA VEGA

CARRETAS

ESCALATORS

MIRADERO

ESCALATOR

OLD BR.

PUERTA CAMBRÓN

MEZQUITA

Plaza de Zocodover

SANTA CRUZ MUSEUM

HOSTEL

VISIGOTHIC MUSEUM

POST

COMMERCIO

SAN JUAN DE LOS REYES

C. ANGEL S. TOMÉ

MKT.

ALCÁZAR

SINÁGOGA DE SANTA MARÍA LA BLANCA

SANTO TOMÉ

CATHEDRAL

MUSEO VICTORIO MACHO

EL GRECO MUSEUM

CARRETERA PIEDRABUENA

SINÁGOGA DEL TRÁNSITO

Path

Tajo River

VIEWPOINT

C. ALTA

To CM-40 Motorway

CARRETERA CIRCUNVALACIÓN

See detail map

C. COBISA

C. COBISA

PARADOR

300 Meters

300 Yards

C. AZUELA

heat in summer. El Greco fans will enjoy seeing his art in chapels and museums around town.

Evening: Dine out (roast suckling pig, anyone?). Stroll the elegant former capital. You'll get goose bumps at sunset and twilight.

Day 2: Choose what appeals to you the most: Toledo has historic synagogues, a monastery, a Visigothic Museum, more art museums, and many shops. Wander the back lanes, sample sweet *mazapán*, and

people-watch in the main square, Plaza de Zocodover. If you want to cut your visit short, you could travel to your next destination later today (you'll likely transfer in Madrid, the nearest major hub).

ORIENTATION

Toledo sits atop a circular hill, with the cathedral roughly dead-center. Lassoed into a tight tangle of streets by the sharp bend of the Tajo River, Toledo has Spain's

TOLEDO AT A GLANCE

▲▲▲**Cathedral** One of Europe's best, with a marvelously vast interior and great art. **Hours:** Mon-Sat 10:00-18:30, Sun 14:00-18:30. See page 240.

▲▲**Santa Cruz Museum** Renaissance building housing wonderful artwork, including 15 El Grecos, but sections may be closed during your visit. **Hours:** Mon-Sat 10:00-19:00, Sun 10:00-14:30. See page 248.

▲▲**Army Museum** Covers all things military located in the imposing fortress, the Alcázar. **Hours:** Thu-Tue 11:00-17:00, closed Wed. See page 249.

▲**Santo Tomé** Simple chapel with El Greco's masterpiece, *The Burial of the Count of Orgaz.* **Hours:** Daily 10:00-18:45, until 17:45 mid-Oct-Feb. See page 250.

▲**El Greco Museum** Small collection of paintings, including the *View and Plan of Toledo,* El Greco's panoramic map of the city. **Hours:** Tue-Sat 9:30-20:00, until 18:30 Oct-March, Sun 10:00-15:00, closed Mon. See page 251.

▲**Museo Victorio Macho** Collection of 20th-century Toledo sculptor's works, with expansive river-gorge view. **Hours:** Mon-Sat 10:00-19:00, Sun 10:00-15:00. See page 253.

▲**San Juan de los Reyes Monasterio** Church/monastery intended as final resting place of Isabel and Ferdinand. **Hours:** Daily 10:00-18:45, until 18:00 mid-Oct-March. See page 254.

Visigothic Museum Romanesque church housing the only Visigothic artifacts in town. **Hours:** Tue-Sat 10:00-14:30 & 16:00-19:00, Sun 10:00-14:30, closed Mon. See page 250.

Sinagoga del Tránsito Museum of Toledo's Jewish past. **Hours:** Tue-Sat 9:30-20:00, Sun 10:00-15:00, shorter hours off-season, closed Mon year-round. See page 252.

Sinagoga de Santa María la Blanca Synagogue that harmoniously combines Toledo's three religious influences: Jewish, Christian, and Moorish. **Hours:** Daily 10:00-18:45, until 17:45 in winter. See page 254.

most confusing medieval street plan. But it's a small town within its walls, with only 10,000 inhabitants (84,000 live in greater Toledo, including its modern suburbs). The major sights are well-signed, and most locals will politely point you in the right direction if you ask. (You are, after all, the town's bread and butter.)

The top sights stretch from the main square, Plaza de Zocodover (zoh-koh-doh-VEHR), southwest along Calle del Comercio (a.k.a. Calle Ancha, "Wide Street") to the cathedral, and beyond that to Santo Tomé. The visitor's city lies basically along this small but central street and most tourists never stray from this axis. Give it a try; make a point to get lost. The town is compact. When it's time to return to someplace familiar, pull out the map or ask, *"¿Para Plaza de Zocodover?"* From the far end of town, handy bus #12 circles back to Plaza de Zocodover (see "Self-Guided Tour: Bus #12" on page 256).

While the city is very hilly (in Toledo, they say everything's uphill—it certainly feels that way), nothing is more than a short hike away.

Tourist Information

Toledo has four TIs: at the **train station** (daily 9:30-15:00, tel. 925-239-121), at **Bisagra Gate** (Mon-Sat 10:00-18:00, Sun 9:00-14:00, in freestanding building in park just outside gate, tel. 925-211-005), on **Plaza del Ayuntamiento** (daily 10:00-18:00, WC, near the cathedral), and on **Plaza de Zocodover** (Mon-Sat 10:00-18:00, Sun 10:00-14:00), which has a regional focus. At any TI, you can pick up the town map and the *Toledo Tourist and Cultural Guide*. The TIs share a website: www.toledo-turismo.com.

Sightseeing Passes

Skip Toledo's sightseeing passes. You'd pay more for any of the **Toledo Pass** or **Toledo Card** options than you would buying individual tickets, making either worth buying only if you want the included

guided tours to a handful of sights. Similarly, pass up the **Pulsera Turística** wristband, which covers six of the town's lesser sights, but not the top sights.

Tours

To get to the panoramic viewpoint across the gorge, where El Greco painted the famous portrait of Toledo, you have several options (the first two give you a five-minute photo-op stop).

The **Toledo City Tour** bus does a loop trip from Plaza de Zocodover, stopping at the bus station, train station, panorama viewpoint, and Bisagra Gate, before returning to the square (€5.50, pay driver; no need to pay €9 for hop-on, hop-off privileges; board at any stop, nearly hourly, daily 9:50-20:00, www.toledocitytour.es). If you're arriving in town by train or bus, I recommend taking the loop-trip bus (with your luggage) from the station to the viewpoint to Plaza de Zocodover, where you'd get off to find your hotel. That's more efficient and can be cheaper than taking separate trips (by bus or taxi) into town and to the viewpoint.

The cheesy **Tourist Train** leaves from Plaza de Zocodover for a 45-minute ride through town and along the gorge. Sit on the right side—not behind the driver—for the best views (€5.50, daily 1-2/hour 10:00-18:30, later in summer, www.bus vision.net).

Or consider hiring a **taxi.** There are three taxi stands in the old center: Plaza de Zocodover, Bisagra Gate, and Santo Tomé. Taxis routinely give visitors scenic circles around town with photo stops for around €15.

Try local guide **Juan José Espadas** (a.k.a. Juanjo; 3-hour tour-€150, tel. 667-780-475, juanjo@guiadetoledo.es).

Helpful Hints

Local Guidebook: Consider the readable *Toledo: Its Art and Its History* (€5-6 big version, €4 small version, same text and photos in both, sold all over town). It explains

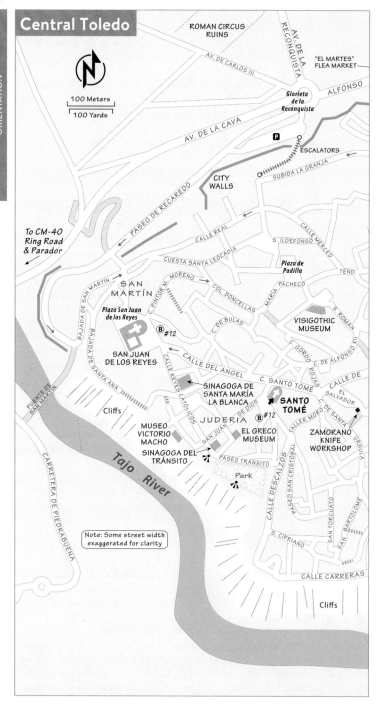

Central Toledo

ROMAN CIRCUS RUINS

AV. DE LA RECONQUISTA

AV. DE CARLOS III

"EL MARTES" FLEA MARKET

ALFONSO

Glorieta de la Reconquista

N

100 Meters

100 Yards

AV. DE LA CAVA

P

ESCALATORS

CITY WALLS

SUBIDA LA GRANJA

PASEO DE RECAREDO

CALLE REAL

S. ILDEFONSO

CALLE MERCED

To CM-40 Ring Road & Parador

CUESTA SANTA LEOCADIA

Plaza de Padilla

TEND.

C. PINTOR M. MORENO

COL. DONCELLAS

PACHECO

BAJADA DE SAN MARTÍN

SAN MARTÍN

MARÍA

S. ROMAN

Plaza San Juan de los Reyes

C. DE BULAS

VISIGOTHIC MUSEUM

B #12

C. GORDO

C. DE ALFONSO XII

BAJADA DE SANTA ANA

SAN JUAN DE LOS REYES

CALLE DEL ÁNGEL

ROJAS

CALLE REYES CATÓLICOS

C. SANTO TOMÉ

CALLE DE

PUENTE DE SAN MARTÍN

Cliffs

SINAGOGA DE SANTA MARÍA LA BLANCA

SANTO TOMÉ

EL SALVADOR

C. DE SANTA ÚRSULA

JUDERIA

DE DIOS

B #12

ZAMORANO KNIFE WORKSHOP

MUSEO VICTORIO MACHO

SAN JUAN

EL GRECO MUSEUM

TALLER MORO

SINAGOGA DEL TRÁNSITO

PASEO TRANSITO

CARRETERA DE PIEDRABUENA

Tajo River

Park

CALLE DESCALZOS

PASEO SAN CRISTOBAL

SAN TORCUATO

SAN BARTOLOME

Note: Some street width exaggerated for clarity

S. CIPRIANO

CALLE CARRERAS

Cliffs

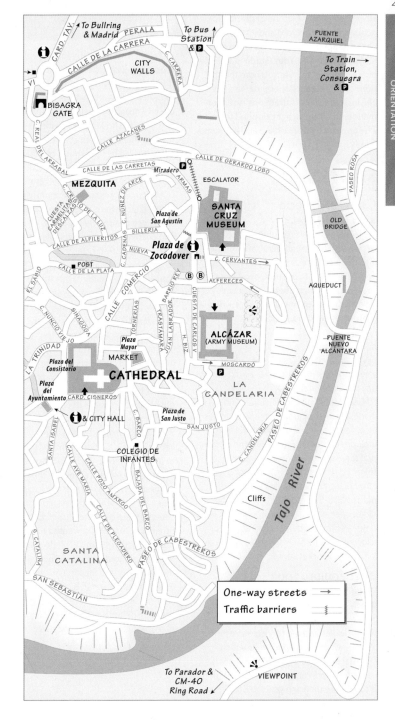

To Bullring
& Madrid
To Bus
Station
& P
PUENTE
AZARQUIEL
To Train
Station,
Consuegra
& P
CARD. TAV.
PERALA
CALLE DE LA CARRERA
CITY
WALLS
C. CARRERA
VI
BISAGRA
GATE
C. REAL DEL ARRABAL
CALLE AZACANES
PASEO ROSA
CALLE DE LAS CARRETAS
CALLE DE GERARDO LOBO
Miradero
P
ARMAS
ESCALATOR
OLD
BRIDGE
MEZQUITA
CUESTA
CARMELITAS
DESCALZOS
C. CRISTO DE LA LUZ
C. NÚÑEZ DE ARCE
Plaza de
San Agustín
SANTA
CRUZ
MUSEUM
SILLERIA
CALLE DE ALFILERITOS
C. CADENAS
NUEVA
Plaza de
Zocodover
AQUEDUCT
EL SABIO
POST
CALLE DE LA PLATA
C. CERVANTES
B B
ALFÉRECES
C. NUNCIO VIEJO
SINAGOGA
CALLE COMERCIO
TORNERÍAS
BARRIO REY
TRASTÁMARA
CUESTA DE CARLOS V
JUAN LABRADOR
H. BIZ
ALCÁZAR
(ARMY MUSEUM)
PUENTE
NUEVO
ALCÁNTARA
LA TRINIDAD
Plaza
Mayor
MARKET
Plaza del
Consistorio
Plaza
del
Ayuntamiento
CARD. CISNEROS
CATHEDRAL
MOSCARDÓ
P
LA
CANDELARIA
PASEO DE CABESTREROS
& CITY HALL
SANTA ISABEL
C. BARCO
Plaza de
San Justo
SAN JUSTO
C. CANDELARIA
COLEGIO DE
INFANTES
CALLE POZO AMARGO
BAJADA DEL BARCO
CALLE AVE MARÍA
CALLE DE PLEGADERO
PASEO DE CABESTREROS
Cliffs
Tajo River
S. CATALINA
SANTA
CATALINA
SAN SEBASTIÁN
To Parador &
CM-40
Ring Road
VIEWPOINT

One-way streets →
Traffic barriers

all of the sights (which generally provide no on-site information) and gives you a photo to point at and say, *"¿Dónde está...?"*

App: Toledo Be Your Guide is a simple but useful free travel app. Ignore the sections on restaurants, shopping, and nightlife; instead select "Attractions" for information on different sights around town. The app can be used offline and has some handy navigation links.

SIGHTS

Central Toledo

▲▲▲CATHEDRAL

Holy Toledo! Spain's leading Catholic city has a magnificent cathedral. Shoehorned into the old center, its exterior is hard to appreciate. (As is so typical of religious sites in hard-fought Iberia, it was built after the Reconquista on the spot where a mosque once stood.) But the interior is so lofty, rich, and vast that it'll have you wandering around like a Pez dispenser stuck open, whispering "Wow." The sacristy has a collection of paintings that would put any museum on the map.

Cost and Hours: €8 includes audioguide; €11 also includes trip up bell tower at assigned times; €12 combo-ticket includes cathedral, bell tower, and cathedral tapestry collection in Colegio de Infantes; tickets sold in shop opposite church entrance on Calle Cardenal Cisneros; Mon-Sat 10:00-18:30, Sun 14:00-18:30, open earlier for prayer only, last entry 30 minutes before closing; photos allowed without flash, tel. 925-222-241. A WC is in the ticket center.

❷ SELF-GUIDED TOUR

Wander among the pillars, thick and sturdy as a redwood forest. Sit under one and imagine a time when the light bulbs were candles and the tourists were pilgrims—when every window provided spiritual as well as physical light. The cathedral is primarily Gothic. But since it took more than 250 years to build

Toledo's History

Perched strategically in the center of Iberia, Toledo was a Roman transportation hub with a prospering Jewish population for centuries. After Rome fell, the city became a Visigothic capital (A.D. 554). In 711, the Moors (Muslims) made it a regional center. In 1085 the city was reconquered by Christians, but many Moors remained in Toledo, tolerated and respected as scholars and craftsmen.

Whereas Jews were commonly persecuted elsewhere in Europe, Toledo's Jewish community—educated, wealthy, and cosmopolitan—thrived from the city's earliest times. Jews of Spanish origin are called Sephardic Jews. The American expression "Holy Toledo" likely originated from the Sephardic Jews who eventually immigrated to America. To them, Toledo was the holiest Jewish city in Europe...Holy Toledo!

During its medieval heyday (c. 1350), Toledo was a city of the humanities, where God was known by many names. In this haven of cultural diversity, people of different faiths lived together in harmony.

Toledo remained Spain's political capital until 1561, when Philip II moved to more-spacious Madrid. Historians fail to agree on the reason for the move; some say that Madrid was the logical place for a capital in the geographic center of newly formed *España*, while others say that Philip wanted to separate politics from religion. (Toledo remained Spain's religious capital.) Whatever the reason, when the king moved out, Toledo was mothballed, only to be rediscovered by 19th-century Romantic travelers. They wrote of it as a mystical place, which it remains today.

Toledo's cathedral

(1226-1495)—with continuous embellishments after that (every archbishop wanted to leave his imprint)—it's a mix of styles, including Gothic, Renaissance, Baroque, and Neoclassical. Enjoy the elaborate wrought-iron work, lavish wood carvings, and window after colorful window of 500-year-old stained glass. Circling the interior are ornate chapels, purchased by the town's most noble families, and the sacristy, with its world-class collection of El Grecos and works by other famous painters.

This confusing collage of great Spanish art deserves a close look. Hire a private guide, discreetly freeload on a tour (they come by every few minutes during peak season), listen to the audioguide, or follow this quick tour.

• First, walk to the high altar.

High Altar: Climb two steps and grip the iron grille as you marvel at one of the most stunning altars in Spain. Real gold on wood, by Flemish, French, and local artists, it's one of the country's best pieces of Gothic art. Study the wall of scenes from the life of Christ, frame by frame. All of the images seem to celebrate the colorful Assumption of Mary in the center, with Mary escorted by six upwardly mobile angels. The crucified Christ on top is nine feet tall—taller than the lower statues— to keep this towering altar approachable. Don't miss the finely worked gold-plated iron grille itself—considered to be the best from the 16th century in Spain.

• About-face to the...

Choir: Facing the high altar, the choir is famous for its fine and richly symbolic carving. It all seems to lead to the archbishop's throne in the rear center. First, look carefully at the fine alabaster relief in the center (about where the bishop would rest his head on his throne): It shows a seventh-century Visigothic miracle, when Mary came down to give the local bishop the holy robe, legitimizing Toledo as the spiritual capital (and therefore political capital) of Spain.

Because of its primacy in Iberia, Toledo was the first city in the crosshairs of the Reconquista Christian forces. They recaptured the city in 1085 (over 400 years before they retook Granada). The fall of Toledo marked the beginning of the end of the Muslim domination of Iberia.

The cathedral entrance

High altar

Toledo's Cathedral

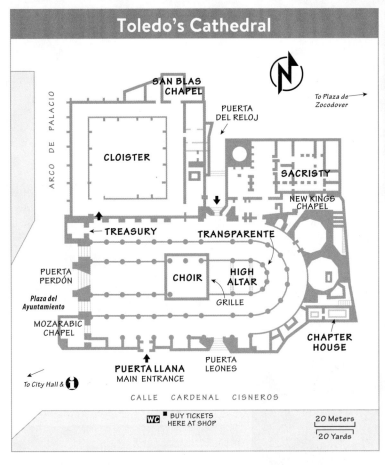

SAN BLAS CHAPEL

PUERTA DEL RELOJ

To Plaza de Zocodover →

ARCO DE PALACIO

CLOISTER

SACRISTY

NEW KINGS CHAPEL

← TREASURY

TRANSPARENTE

PUERTA PERDÓN

Plaza del Ayuntamiento

CHOIR

HIGH ALTAR

GRILLE

MOZARABIC CHAPEL

CHAPTER HOUSE

← To City Hall & 🛈

PUERTA LLANA
MAIN ENTRANCE

PUERTA LEONES

CALLE CARDENAL CISNEROS

WC ■ BUY TICKETS HERE AT SHOP

20 Meters

20 Yards

A local saying goes, "A carpet frays from the edges, but the carpet of Al-Andalus (Muslim Spain) frayed from the very center" (meaning Toledo).

The lower wooden stalls are decorated with scenes showing the steady one-city-at-a-time finale of the Christian Reconquista, when Muslims were slowly pushed back into Africa. Set in the last decade of the Reconquista, these images celebrate the retaking of the towns around Granada: Each idealized castle has the reconquered town's name on it, culminating in the final victory at Granada in 1492 (these two reliefs flank the archbishop's throne). Although the castles are roman-

ticized, the carvings of the clothing, armor, and weaponry are so detailed and accurate that historians have studied them to learn the evolution of weaponry.

The upper stalls feature Old Testament figures—an alabaster genealogy of the church—starting with Adam and Eve and working counterclockwise to Joseph and "S. M. Virgo Mater" (St. Mary the Virgin Mother). Notice how the statues on the Adam and Eve side (left) are more lifelike; they were done by Alonso Berruguete, nicknamed "the Michelangelo of Spain" for his realistic figures. All this imagery is designed to remind viewers of the legitimacy of the bishop's claims to religious

❶ *Transparente "skylight"*

❷ *Choir*

❸ *Chapter House*

power. Check out the seat backs, made of carved walnut and featuring New Testament figures—with Peter (key) and Paul (sword)—alongside the archbishop himself.

And, as is typical of choir decoration, the carvings on the misericords (the tiny seats that allowed tired worshippers to lean while they "stand") represent various sins and feature the frisky, folksy, sexy, profane art of the day. Apparently, since you sat on it, it could never be sacred.

Take a moment to absorb the marvelous complexity, harmony, and cohesiveness of the art around you. Look up. There are two fine pipe organs: one early 18th-century Baroque and the other late 18th-century Neoclassical. As you leave the choir, note the serene beauty of the 13th-century Madonna and child at the front (Virgin Blanca), thought to be a gift from the French king to Spain. Its naturalism and intimacy was proto-Renaissance—radical in its day.

• Face the altar, and go around it to your right to the...

Chapter House (Sala Capitular): Under its lavish ceiling, a fresco celebrates the humanism of the Italian Renaissance. There's a Deposition (taking crucified Jesus off the cross), a *pietà,* and a Resurrection on the front wall; they face a fascinating Last Judgment, where the seven sins are actually spelled out in the gang going to hell: arrogance (the guy striking a pose), avarice (holding his bag of coins), lust (the easy woman with the lovely hair and fiery crotch), anger (shouting at lust), gluttony (the fat guy), envy, and laziness. Think about how instructive this was in 1600.

Below the fresco, a pictorial review of 1,900 years of Toledo archbishops circles the room. The upper row of portraits dates from the 16th century. Except for the last two, these were not painted from life (the same face seems to be recycled over and over). The lower portraits were added one at a time from 1515 on and

are of more historic than artistic interest. Imagine sitting down to church business surrounded by all this tradition.

The current cardinal—whose portrait will someday grace the next empty panel—is the top religious official in Spain. He's conservative on issues unpopular with Spain's young: divorce, abortion, and contraception. When he speaks, it makes news all over Spain.

As you leave, notice the iron-pumping cupids carved into the pear-tree panels lining the walls.

• Go behind the high altar to find the...

Transparente: This is a unique feature of the cathedral. In the 1700s, a hole was cut into the ceiling to let a sunbeam brighten Mass. The opening faces east, and each morning the rising sun reminds all that God is light. Melding this big hole with the Gothic church presented a challenge: The result was a Baroque masterpiece. Gape up at this riot of angels doing flip-flops, babies breathing thin air, bottoms of feet, and gilded sunbursts. Carved out of marble from Italy, it's bursting with motion and full of energy. Appreciate those tough little cherubs who are supporting the whole thing—they've been waiting for help for about 300 years now.

Step back to study the altar, which looks chaotic, but is actually structured thoughtfully: The good news of salvation springs from Baby Jesus, up past the archangels (including one in the middle who knows how to hold a big fish correctly) to the Last Supper high above, and beyond into the light-filled dome. I like it, as did (I guess) the two long-dead cardinals whose faded red hats hang from the edge of the hole. (A perk that only a cardinal enjoys is to choose a burial place in the cathedral, and hang his hat over that spot until the hat rots.)

• Before entering the sacristy (to your right), peek into the...

Chapel of the New Kings (Capilla de Reyes Nuevos): In the 16th century, Emperor Charles V moved the tombs of eight kings who reigned before Ferdinand and Isabel to this spot.

• *Leaving this chapel, the next door on your right takes you into the...*

Sacristy: The cathedral's sacristy is a mini-Prado, with 19 El Grecos and masterpieces by Francisco de Goya, Titian, Diego Velázquez, Caravaggio, and Giovanni Bellini. First, notice the fine perspective work on the ceiling. It was painted by Neapolitan artist Lucca Giordano around 1690. (You can see the artist himself—with his circa-1690 spectacles—painted onto the door high above on the left; look for it at the base of the ceiling.) Then walk to the end of the room for the most important painting in the collection, El Greco's *The Spoliation* (a.k.a. *Christ Being Stripped of His Garments*).

Spain's original great painter was Greek, and this is his first masterpiece after arriving in Toledo. El Greco's painting from 1579 hangs exactly where he intended it to—in the room where priests prepared themselves for Mass. It shows Jesus surrounded by a sinister mob and suffering the humiliation of being stripped in public before his execution.

His scarlet robe is about to be yanked off, and the women (lower left) avert their eyes, turning to watch a carpenter at work (lower right) who bores the holes for nailing Jesus to the cross. While the carpenter bears down, Jesus—the other carpenter—looks up to heaven. The contrast between the motley crowd gambling for his clothes and Jesus' noble face underscores the quiet dignity with which he endures this ignoble treatment. Jesus' delicate white hand stands out from the flaming red tunic with an odd gesture that's common in El Greco's paintings. Some say this was the way Christians of the day swore they were true believers, not merely Christians-in-name-only, such as former Muslims or Jews who converted to survive.

On the right is a religious painting by Goya, the *Betrayal of Christ,* which shows Judas preparing to kiss Jesus, thus identifying him to the Roman soldiers. Across the room is a scene rarely painted: a touching El Greco portrait called *St. Joseph and the Christ Child.* Joseph is walking with Jesus, just as El Greco liked walking around the Toledo countryside with his sons. Notice Joseph's gentle expression—and the Toledo views in the background.

Enjoy the many other El Grecos here. Before exiting the sacristy, look for a glass case to the left of the door containing a small-but-lifelike 17th-century carving of St. Francis by Pedro de Mena (1628-1688).

• *As you step out of the sacristy, look high up to your right at the oldest stained glass in the church (from the 14th century). Then, passing a chapel reserved for worship, just before the treasury, you come to the...*

Cloister: The cloister is worth a stroll for its finely carved colonnade. Take a peaceful detour to the funerary **San Blas Chapel.** The ceiling over the marble tomb of a bishop is a fresco by a student of Giotto (a 14th-century Italian Renaissance master).

Cathedral cloister

Treasury: The *tesoro* is tiny but radiant with riches. The highlight is the 10-foot-high, 430-pound monstrance—the tower designed to hold the Holy Communion wafer (the host) during the festival of Corpus Christi ("body of Christ") as it's paraded through the city. Built in 1517 by Enrique de Arfe, it's made of 5,000 individual pieces held together by 12,500 screws. There are diamonds, emeralds, rubies, and 400 pounds of gold-plated silver. The inner part (which is a century older) is 35 pounds of solid gold. Yeow. The base is a later addition from the Baroque period.

To the right of the monstrance is a beautiful red-coral cross given by the Philippines. Below the cross is a facsimile of a 700-year-old Bible hand-copied and beautifully illustrated by French monks; it was a gift from St. Louis, the 13th-century king of France. Imagine looking on these lavish illustrations with medieval eyes—an exquisite experience. (The precious and fragile lambskin original is preserved out of public view.) The finely painted small crucifix on the opposite side in the corner (with the mirror behind it) is by the great Gothic Florentine painter Fra Angelico. It depicts Jesus alive on the back and dead on the front, and was a gift from Mussolini to Franco. Underneath, near the floor, you'll find Franco's rather plain sword. Hmmm. To the right of Fra Angelico's crucifix, find the gift (humble amid all this splendor) from Toledo's sister city: Toledo, Ohio.

Mozarabic Chapel: Before 10:00, the cathedral is open only for prayer (from north entrance). If you're here to worship at the 9:00 Mass (daily except Sun), you can peek into the otherwise-locked Mozarabic Chapel (Capilla Mozárabe). This Visigothic Mass (in Latin) is the oldest surviving Christian ritual in Western Europe. You're welcome to partake in this stirring example of peaceful coexistence of faiths. Toledo's proud Mozarabic community of 1,500 people traces its roots to Visigothic times.

Bell Tower: If you paid to climb the bell tower, meet just to the left of the San Blas Chapel at your assigned time. You'll climb up several sections of tight spiral staircases to reach panoramic views of Toledo and the largest (though cracked) bell in Spain.

PLAZA DE ZOCODOVER

The main square is Toledo's center and your gateway to the old town. The word "Zocodover" derives from the Arabic for "livestock market."

Because Toledo is the state capital of Castile-La Mancha, the regional government administration building overlooks Plaza de Zocodover. Look for the three flags: one for Europe, one for Spain, and one for Castile-La Mancha. And speaking of universal symbols—find the low-key McDonald's. A source of controversy, it was finally allowed...with only one small golden arch. Next came the bigger Burger King, which no one blinked at twice.

The square is a big local hangout and city hub. Once the scene of Inquisition

Bell tower

judgments and bullfights, today it's a lot more peaceful. Old people arrive in the morning, and young people come in the evening. The goofy tourist train leaves from here, as well as the Toledo City Tour bus and city buses #5, #11, #61, and #62, which lumber to the train station. Just uphill, near the taxi stand, is the stop for bus #12, which travels around the old town to Santo Tomé (and works as a good self-guided tour—described on page 256).

▲▲SANTA CRUZ MUSEUM (MUSEO DE SANTA CRUZ)

This stately Renaissance building was formerly an orphanage and hospital, funded by money left by the humanist and diplomat Cardinal Mendoza when he died in 1495. The cardinal, confirmed as Chancellor of Castile by Queen Isabel, was so influential that he was called "the third royal."

In 2014, the museum hosted an impressive gathering of paintings by El Greco to commemorate the 400th anniversary of the artist's death.

Cost and Hours: Likely €6, Mon-Sat 10:00-19:00, Sun 10:00-14:30; from Plaza de Zocodover, go through arch to Calle Miguel de Cervantes 3; www.patrimonio historicoclm.es. A WC is in the far corner of the lower cloister.

Visiting the Museum: The building's facade still wears bullet scars from the Spanish Civil War. The exterior, cloister arches, and stairway leading to the upper cloister are fine examples of the Plateresque style. This ornate strain of Spanish Renaissance is named for the fancy work of silversmiths of the 16th century. During this time (c. 1500-1550), the royal court moved from Toledo to Madrid—when Madrid was a village and Toledo was a world power. (You'll see no Plateresque work in Madrid.) Note the Renaissance-era mathematics, ideal proportions, round arches, square squares, and classic columns.

Look for the following artwork and exhibits:

The museum has 15 **El Greco** paint-

ings. A highlight is the impressive *Assumption of Mary,* a spiritual poem on canvas. This altarpiece, finished one year before El Greco's death in 1614, is the culmination of his unique style, combining all of his techniques to express an otherworldly event.

Study the *Assumption* (which some believe is misnamed, and actually shows the Immaculate Conception—the plaque describing the work entitles it *Inmaculada Concepción*). Bound to earth, the city of Toledo sleeps, but a vision is taking place overhead. An angel in a billowing robe, as if doing the breaststroke with his wings, flies up, supporting Mary, the mother of Christ. She floats up through warped space, to be serenaded by angels and wrapped in the radiant light of the Holy Spirit. Mary flickers and ripples, charged from within by her spiritual ecstasy, caught up in a vision that takes her breath away. No painter before or since has captured the supernatural world better than El Greco.

A beautiful collection of **tiles and**

Santa Cruz Museum

ceramics dates from the end of the Reconquista (1492). Each piece is categorized by the Spanish region where it was made. This may be the only place in Spain where you can compare regional differences in tile work and pottery.

You'll also see prehistoric pieces, some Roman artifacts, and a marble well bearing an Arabic inscription. If the well is on view, note the grooves in the sides made by generations of Muslims pulling their buckets up by rope. This well was once located in the courtyard of an 11th-century mosque, which stood where the cathedral does today.

▲▲ARMY MUSEUM (MUSEO DEL EJÉRCITO)

This museum features endless rooms of Spanish military collections of armor, uniforms, cannons, guns, paintings, and models. It tells the military history of Spain from 1492 to the 20th century. The displays are wonderfully explained in English, and the audioguide is excellent. If you like military history, allow at least three hours for one of Europe's top military museums. The museum has one major flaw: its skimpy coverage of the Spanish Civil War (1936-1939).

Cost and Hours: €5, €8 ticket includes superb 2-hour audioguide, free on Sun; open Thu-Tue 11:00-17:00, closed Wed; last entry 30 minutes before closing, café/restaurant where you can bump elbows with Spanish military, www.museo.ejercito.es.

Visiting the Museum: It's located in the Alcázar, the huge former imperial residence that dominates Toledo's skyline. It's built on the site of Roman, Visigothic, Moorish, and early Renaissance fortresses, the ruins of which (displayed just past the turnstile) are a poignant reminder of the city's strategic importance through the centuries.

Today's structure (originally built in the 16th century, then destroyed in the civil war and rebuilt) became a kind of right-wing Alamo. During the civil war, Franco's

Nationalists (and hundreds of hostages) were besieged here by Republican troops for two months in 1936. The Republicans took the son of the Alcázar's commander—Colonel José Moscardó—hostage and called Colonel Moscardó, threatening to execute his son if he didn't surrender in 10 minutes. Moscardó asked for his son to be put on the line, and told him that he would have to be a hero and die for Spain. Moscardó then informed the Republican leader that he would never give up the Alcázar. (While the Nationalists believed the son was shot immediately, he was actually executed with other prisoners weeks later in a reprisal for an air raid.)

Finally, after many fierce but futile Republican attacks that destroyed much of the Alcázar, Franco sent in an army that took Toledo, a major victory for the Nationalists. After the war, the place was rebuilt and glorified under Franco. Only one room on the sixth floor (labeled as *CM-Despacho del Coronel Moscardó* on the museum map) has been left in a tattered ruin since the siege: the office of Colonel Moscardó.

It's a confusing floor plan, but if you start at the top floor and follow the "historical round" arrows, you'll enjoy a roughly chronological sweep. Since so much of this country's history is military, this museum tells much of the story of Spain.

Look for special theme rooms (e.g., the use of photography in the army, and the evolution of Spain's flag). The main courtyard—Italian-inspired Renaissance in style—comes with a proud statue of Holy Roman Emperor Charles V (a.k.a. King Charles I of Spain), the ultimate military king and Europe's most powerful 16th-century leader.

The 20th-century section comes with some fascinating videos, but has just three small rooms of civil-war artifacts, including uniforms from both sides, Franco's cloak and cane, and posters. In addition there are photographs of the conflict and a small audiovisual slide show. As the museum was preparing to open, controversy broke out on how to handle the civil war. The curators dodged the issue by going light on *the* major event of 20th-century Spanish history; it's not even marked on the museum's map (look for *El Siglo XX*).

VISIGOTHIC MUSEUM IN THE CHURCH OF SAN ROMÁN

This 13th-century Mudejar church—with its rare, strangely modernist 13th-century Romanesque frescoes—provides an exquisite space for a small but interesting collection of Visigothic artifacts (Museo de los Concilios y de la Cultura Visigoda). The Visigoths were the Christian barbarian tribe who ruled Spain between the fall of Rome and the rise of the Moors. The only things Visigothic about the actual building are the few capitals topping its columns, recycled from a seventh-century Visigothic church. Though the elaborate crowns are copies (the originals are in Madrid), other glass cases show off metal and stone artifacts from the age when Toledo was the capital of the Visigoths. The items, while featur-

ing almost no human figures, are rich in symbolism. Their portability fits that society's nomadic heritage. Archaeologists have found almost no Visigothic artifacts within Toledo's fortified hill location. They lived in humble settlements along the river—apparently needing no defense system...until the Moors swept through in 711, ending two centuries of Visigothic rule in Iberia. Climb the steep stairs for a view of Toledo's rooftops from the church tower.

Cost and Hours: Likely €3, Tue-Sat 10:00-14:30 & 16:00-19:00, Sun 10:00-14:30, closed Mon, no English information, Plaza San Román.

Southwest Toledo

These sights cluster at the southwest end of town. For efficient sightseeing, visit them in this order, then zip back home on bus #12 (listed at the end of this section).

▲SANTO TOMÉ

A simple chapel on the Plaza del Conde holds El Greco's most beloved painting. *The Burial of the Count of Orgaz* couples heaven and earth in a way only The Greek could. It feels so right to see a painting in the same church where the artist placed it 400 years ago. It originally filled the space

Church of San Román

immediately to the right of where it is now, but as the popularity of this masterpiece was disturbing the main church, it was moved. Church officials even created a special entryway for viewing it.

Cost and Hours: €2.50, daily 10:00-18:45, until 17:45 mid-Oct-Feb, audioguide-€1, tel. 925-256-098. This sight often has a line; try going early or late to avoid tour groups.

Visiting Santo Tomé: Take this slow. Stay a while—let it perform. The year is 1323. Count Don Gonzalo Ruiz has died. You're at his burial right here in this chapel. The good count was so holy, even saints Augustine and Stephen have come down from heaven to lower his body into the grave. (The painting's subtitle is "Such is the reward for those who serve God and his saints.")

More than 250 years later, in 1586, a local priest (depicted on the far right, reading the Bible) hired El Greco to make a painting of the burial to hang over the count's tomb. The funeral is attended by Toledo's most distinguished citizens. (El Greco used local nobles as models.) The painting is divided in two by a serene line of noble faces—heaven above and earth below. Above the faces, the count's soul, symbolized by a little baby, rises up through a mystical birth canal to be reborn in heaven, where he's greeted by Jesus, Mary, and all the saints. A spiritual wind blows through as colors change and shapes stretch. This is Counter-Reformation propaganda—notice Jesus pointing to St. Peter, the symbol of the pope in Rome, who controls the keys to the pearly gates. Each face is a detailed portrait. It's clear that these portraits inspired the next great Spanish painter, Velázquez, a century later. El Greco himself (eyeballing you, seventh figure in from the left) is the only one not involved in the burial. The boy in the foreground—pointing to the two saints—is El Greco's son. On the handkerchief in the boy's pocket is El Greco's signature, written in Greek.

Don Gonzalo Ruiz's actual granite tombstone is at your feet. The count's two wishes upon his death were to be buried here and for his village to make an annual charity donation to feed Toledo's poor. Finally, more than two centuries later, the people of Orgaz said, "Enough!" and stopped the payments. The last of the money was spent to pay El Greco for this painting.

▲EL GRECO MUSEUM (MUSEO DEL GRECO)

This small museum, built near the site of El Greco's house, gives a look at the genius of his art and Toledo in his day. Its small collection of paintings is accompanied by interactive touch screens and videos.

A comfy little theater shows a fine 10-minute video on both the life of the artist and the story of this museum. You then proceed through halls that show the evolution of El Greco's art. While there aren't many great El Grecos here, you'll see a hall lined with his *Twelve Apostles*, *San Bernardino of Siena* (in a chapel), and the highlight of the museum—the *View and Plan of Toledo*. El Greco's panoramic map shows the city in 1614. Study the

El Greco, The Burial of the Count of Orgaz

El Greco (1541-1614)

Born on Crete and trained in Venice, Doménikos Theotokópoulos (tongue-tied friends just called him "The Greek") came to Spain to get a job decorating El Escorial. He failed there, but succeeded in Toledo, where he spent the last 37 years of his life. He mixed all three regional influences into his palette. From his Greek homeland, he absorbed the solemn, abstract style of icons. In Italy, he learned the bold use of color, elongated figures, twisting poses, and dramatic style of the later Renaissance. These elements were then fused in the fires of fanatic Spanish-Catholic devotion.

Not bound by the realism so important to his fellow artists, El Greco painted dramatic visions of striking colors and figures—bodies unnatural and lengthened as though stretched between heaven and earth. He painted souls, not faces. His work is on display at nearly every sight in Toledo. Thoroughly modern in his disregard for realism, he didn't impress the austere Philip II. But his art still seems as fresh as contemporary art does today. El Greco was essentially forgotten through the 18th and most of the 19th centuries. Then, with the Romantic movement (and the discovery of Toledo by Romantic-era travelers, artists, and poets), the paintings of El Greco became the hits they are today.

actual map and list of sights. It was commissioned to promote the city (suddenly a former capital) after the king moved to Madrid.

Cost and Hours: €3, €5 combo-ticket with Sinagoga del Tránsito, free Sat afternoon from 14:00 and all day Sun; open Tue-Sat 9:30-20:00, until 18:30 Oct-March, Sun 10:00-15:00, closed Mon; next to Sinagoga del Tránsito on Calle Samuel Leví, tel. 925-223-665.

SINAGOGA DEL TRÁNSITO (MUSEO SEFARDÍ)

Built in 1361, this is the best surviving slice of Toledo's Jewish past. Serving as Spain's national Jewish museum, it displays Jewish artifacts, including costumes, menorahs, and books. Your visit comes with three parts: the nave, a ground-floor exhibition space with a history of Spain's Jews, and the women's gallery upstairs, which shows lifestyles and holy rituals among Sephardic Jews. Though English sheets in each room explain the collection, rent the audioguide to get the most out of the exhibits.

Cost and Hours: €3, €5 combo-ticket with El Greco Museum, free Sat afternoon from 14:00 and all day Sun; open Tue-Sat 9:30-20:00, Sun 10:00-15:00, shorter

Sinagoga del Tránsito

Toledo's Muslim Legacy

You can see the Moorish influence in these sights:

- Sinagoga de Santa María la Blanca's mosque-like horseshoe arches and pinecone capitals
- Sinagoga del Tránsito's Mudejar plasterwork
- Mezquita del Cristo de la Luz, the last of the town's mosques
- Puerta del Sol (Gate of the Sun) and other surviving gates (with horseshoe arches) along the medieval wall
- The city's labyrinthine, medina-like streets

hours off-season, closed Mon year-round; near El Greco Museum on Calle de los Reyes Católicos.

Tours: You can rent an audioguide for €2, or connect to the synagogue's Wi-Fi with your mobile device for a free audioguide (starts automatically). You can also download the audioguide from www.audioviator.com (search for "Museo Sefardi").

Visiting the Synagogue: This 14th-century synagogue was built at the peak of Toledo's enlightened tolerance—constructed for Jews with Christian approval by Muslim craftsmen. Nowhere else in the city does Toledo's three-culture legacy shine brighter than at this place of worship. But in 1391, just a few decades after it was built, the Church and the Spanish kings began a violent campaign to unite Spain as a Christian nation, forcing Jews and Muslims to convert or leave. In 1492 Ferdinand and Isabel exiled Spain's remaining Jews. It's estimated that in the 15th century, while some of Spain's Jews were expelled, many others survived by converting to Christianity. A third left the country.

Surveying the synagogue from the back, its interior decor looks more Muslim than Jewish. After Christians reconquered the city in 1085, many Moorish workmen stayed on, beautifying the city with their unique style called Mudejar. The synagogue's intricate, geometrical carving in stucco—nearly all original, from 1360—features leaves, vines, and flowers; there are no human shapes, which are forbidden by the Torah—like the Quran—as being "graven images." In the frieze (running along the upper wall, just below the ceiling), the Arabic-looking script is actually Hebrew, quoting psalms (respected by all "people of the book"—Muslims, Jews, and Christians alike). The balcony was the traditional separate worship area for women.

Move up to the front. Stand close to the holy wall and study the exquisite workmanship (with reminders of all three religions: the coat of arms of the Christian king, Hebrew script, and Muslim decor). Look down. The small rectangular patch of the original floor only survived because the Christian altar table sat there. In the side room and upstairs, scale models of the development of the Jewish quarter and video displays give a picture of Jewish life in medieval Toledo.

▲MUSEO VICTORIO MACHO

Overlooking the gorge and Tajo River, this small, attractive museum—once the home and workshop of the early-20th-century sculptor Victorio Macho—offers a delightful collection of his bold Art Deco-inspired work. If you skip the museum, you can still enjoy the terrace view from its gate.

Cost and Hours: €3, Mon-Sat 10:00-19:00, Sun 10:00-15:00, between the two *sinagogas* at Plaza de Victorio Macho 2, tel. 925-284-225. A free audioguide is available for those with mobile devices (connect to museum Wi-Fi—audioguide starts automatically; or download from www.audioviator.com—search for "Victorio Macho").

Visiting the Museum: The house has four parts: ticket room with theater (showing a gimmicky Toledo Time Capsule multimedia show not worth the extra fee), lovely view terrace, a crypt, and the museum.

Macho was Spain's first great modern sculptor. When his left-wing politics made it dangerous for him to stay in Franco's Spain, he fled to the USSR, then Mexico and Peru, where he met his wife, Zoila. They later returned to Toledo, where they lived and worked until he died in 1966. Zoila eventually gave the house and Macho's art to the city.

Enjoy the peaceful, expansive view from the terrace. From here it's clear how the Tajo River served as a formidable moat protecting the city. Imagine trying to attack. The 14th-century bridge (on the right) connected the town with mansions of wealthy families, whose orchards of figs and apricots dot the hillside even today. To the left (in the river), look for the stubs of 15th-century watermills; directly below is a riverside trail that's delightful for a stroll or jog.

The door marked *Crypta* leads to *My Brother Marcelo*—the touching tomb Macho made for his brother. Eventually he featured his entire family in his art.

A dozen steps above the terrace, you'll find a single room marked *Museo* filled with Macho's art. A *pietà* is carved expressively in granite. Next to the *pietà,* several self-portrait sketches show the artist's genius. The bronze statue is a self-portrait at age 17. In the next section, exquisite pencil-on-paper studies illustrate how a sculptor must understand the body (in this case, Zoila's body). The sketch of Zoila from behind is entitled *Guitar* (Spaniards traditionally think of a woman's body as a guitar). Other statues show the strength of the peoples' spirit as leftist Republicans stood up to Franco's fascist forces, and Spain endured its 20th-century bloodbath. The highlight is *La Madre* (from 1935), Macho's life-size sculpture of his mother sitting in a chair. It illustrates the sadness and simple wisdom of Spanish mothers who witnessed so much suffering. Upon a granite backdrop, her white marble hands and face speak volumes.

SINAGOGA DE SANTA MARÍA LA BLANCA

This synagogue-turned-church has Moorish horseshoe arches and wall carvings. It's a vivid reminder of the religious cultures that shared (and then didn't share) this city. While it looks like a mosque, it never was one. Built as a Jewish synagogue by Muslim workers around 1200, it became a church in 1492 when Toledo's Jews were required to convert or leave—hence the mix-and-match name. After being used as horse stables by Napoleonic troops, it was further ruined in the 19th century. Today, it's an evocative space, beautiful in its simplicity.

Cost and Hours: €2.50, daily 10:00-18:45, until 17:45 in winter, Calle de los Reyes Católicos 4. Note the thirst-quenching bottled-water machine in the courtyard.

▲SAN JUAN DE LOS REYES MONASTERIO

"St. John of the Monarchs" is a grand Franciscan monastery, impressive church, and delightful "Isabeline" cloistered courtyard. The style is late Gothic, contemporaneous with Portugal's Manueline (c. 1500) and Flamboyant Gothic elsewhere in Europe. It was the intended burial site of the Catholic Monarchs, Isabel and Ferdinand. But after the Moors were expelled in 1492 from Granada, their royal bodies were planted there to show Spain's commitment to maintaining a Moor-free peninsula. Before entering and getting your ticket, take in the **facade.** It is famously festooned with 500-year-old chains. Moors used these to shackle Christians in Granada until 1492. It's said that the freed Christians brought these chains to the church, making them a symbol of their Catholic faith and a sign of victory.

Cost and Hours: €2.50, daily 10:00-18:45, until 18:00 mid-Oct-March, last entry 30 minutes before closing, San Juan de los Reyes 2, tel. 925-223-802.

Visiting the Sight: After buying your ticket, look up. A skinny monk welcomes you (and reminds us of our mortality). Enter the monastery at the side door. Even without the royal tombs that would have dominated the space, the glorious **chapel** gives you a sense of Spain when it was Europe's superpower. The monastery was built to celebrate the 1476 Battle of Toro, which made Isabel the queen of Castile. Since her husband, Ferdinand, was king of Aragon, this effectively created the Spain we know today. (You could say 1476 is to Spain what 1776 is to the US.) Now united, Spain was able to quickly finish the Reconquista, ridding Iberia of its Moors within the next decade and a half.

Sitting in the chapel, you're surrounded by propaganda proclaiming Spain's greatness. The coat of arms is repeated obsessively. The eagle with the halo disk represents St. John, protector of the royal family. The yoke and arrows are the symbols of Ferdinand and Isabel. The lions remind people of the power of the kingdoms joined together under Ferdinand and Isabel. The coat of arms is complex because of Iberia's many kingdoms (e.g., a lion for León, and a castle for Castile).

As you leave, look up over the door to see the Franciscan coat of arms—with the five wounds of the crucifixion (the stigmata—which St. Francis earned through his great faith) flanked by angels with dramatic wings.

Enjoy a walk around the **cloister.** Notice details of the fine carvings. Everything had meaning in the 15th century. In the corner (opposite the entry), just above eye level, find a small monkey—an insulting symbol of Franciscans—on a toilet reading the Bible upside-down. Perhaps a stone carver snuck in a not-too-subtle comment on Franciscan pseudo-intellectualism, with their big libraries and small brains.

Napoleon's troops are mostly to blame for the destruction of the church, a result of Napoleon's view that monastic power

Sinagoga de Santa María la Blanca

San Juan de los Reyes cloister

in Europe was a menace. While Napoleon's biggest error was to invade Russia, his second dumbest move was to alienate the Catholic faithful by destroying monasteries such as this one. This strategic mistake eroded popular support from people who might have seen Napoleon as a welcome alternative to the tyranny of kings and the Church.

If you're tired, skip going upstairs—if not, you can take a simple walk around the top level of the courtyard under a finely renovated Moorish-style ceiling.

▲ SELF-GUIDED TOUR: BUS #12

When you're finished with the sights at the Santo Tomé end of town, you can hike all the way back (not fun)—or simply catch **bus #12** (fun!) back to Plaza de Zocodover. The ride offers tired sightseers a sweat-free return trip—and a quick, interesting 15-minute look at the town walls. You can catch the bus from Plaza del Conde in front of Santo Tomé. This is the end of the line, so buses wait to depart from here twice hourly (at :25 and :55, until 21:25, pay driver €1.40). You can also catch the same bus across the street from the San Juan de los Reyes ticket entrance (at :28 and :58). Here's what you'll see on your way if you catch it from Santo Tomé:

Leaving Santo Tomé, you'll first ride through Toledo's Jewish section. On the right, you'll pass the El Greco Museum, Sinagoga del Tránsito, and Sinagoga de Santa María la Blanca, followed by—on your left—the ornate Flamboyant Gothic facade of San Juan de los Reyes Monasterio. After squeezing through the 16th-century city gate, the bus follows along the outside of the mighty 10th-century wall. Toledo was never conquered by force...only by siege.

Just past the big escalator (which brings people from parking lots up into the city) and Hotel Cardinal, the wall gets fancier, as demonstrated by the little old Bisagra Gate. Soon after, you see the big new Bisagra Gate, the main entry into the old town. While the city walls date from the 10th century, this gate was built as an arch of triumph in the 16th century. The massive coat of arms of Emperor Charles V, with the double eagle, reminded people that he ruled a unified Habsburg empire (successor of ancient Rome), and they were entering the capital of an empire that, in the 1500s, included most of Western Europe and much of America. (We'll enter the town through this gate in a couple minutes after a stop at the bus station.)

Just outside the big gate is a well-maintained and shaded park—a picnic-perfect spot and one of Toledo's few green areas. After a detour to the bus station basement to pick up people coming from Madrid, you swing back around Bisagra Gate. As an example of how things have changed in the last generation, as recently as 1960, all traffic into the city at this point had to pass through this gate's tiny original entrance.

As you climb back into the old town, you'll pass the fine, 14th-century Moorish Puerta del Sol (Gate of the Sun) on your right. Then comes the modern Palacio de Congresos Miradero convention center on your left, which is artfully incorporated into the more historic cityscape. Within moments you pull into the main square, Plaza de Zocodover. You can do this tour in reverse by riding bus #12 from Plaza de Zocodover to Plaza del Conde (departing at :25 and :55, same price and hours).

EXPERIENCES

Shopping

Toledo probably sells more souvenirs than any city in Spain. This is *the* place to buy medieval-looking swords, armor, maces, three-legged stools, lethal-looking letter-openers, and other nouveau antiques. It's also Spain's damascene center, where, for centuries, craftspeople have inlaid black steel with gold, silver, and copper wire. Spain's top bullfighters wouldn't have their swords made anywhere else.

Knives: At the workshop of English-speaking **Mariano Zamorano,** you can see swords and knives being made. His family has been putting its seal on handcrafted knives since 1890. Judging by what's left of Mariano's hand, his knives are among the sharpest (Mon-Fri 10:00-14:00 & 16:00-19:00, Sat-Sun 10:00-14:00—although you may not see work done on weekends, 10 percent discount with this book, behind Ayuntamiento/City Hall at Calle Ciudad 19, tel. 925-222-634, www.marianozamorano.com).

Damascene: You can find artisans all over town pounding gold and silver threads into a steel base to create shiny inlaid plates, decorative wares, and jewelry. The damascene is a real tourist racket, but it's fun to pop into a shop and see the intricate handiwork in action.

Nun-Baked Sweet Treats: Signs posted on convent doors all over town invite you in to buy *Dulces Artesanos* (sweets) including *mazapán.* Try the Santa Rita Convent—go in the main door to the left, press the buzzer, and a nun will appear in five minutes or so behind a turnstile window to take your order (small box—€6, Mon-Fri 9:00-13:00 & 15:00-16:15, Sat until 18:00, closed Sun, hours some-times vary, Calle Santa Ursula 3).

El Martes: Toledo's colorful outdoor market is a lively scene on Tuesdays at Paseo de Merchan, better known to locals as "La Vega" (9:00-14:00, outside Bisagra Gate near TI).

EATING

Typical Toledo dishes include partridge *(perdiz),* venison *(venado),* wild boar *(jabalí),* roast suckling pig *(cochinillo asado),* or baby lamb *(cordero*—similarly roasted after a few weeks of mother's milk). After dinner, find a *mazapán* place for dessert. Restaurants generally serve lunch from 13:00 to 16:00 and dinner from 20:00 until very late (Spaniards don't start dinner until about 21:00).

Fine Dining

Los Cuatro Tiempos Restaurante ("The Four Seasons") specializes in game and roasts, proficiently served in a tasteful, classy setting. They offer spacious dining with an extensive and inviting Spanish wine list. It's a good choice for a quiet, romantic dinner, and a good value for a midday meal (€19 weekend three-course lunches and dinners—drinks not included,

Toledo souvenirs

€35 à la carte dinners, Mon-Sat 13:00-16:00 & 20:30-23:00, Sun 13:00-16:00 only, at downhill corner of cathedral, Calle Sixto Ramón Parro 5, tel. 925-223-782, www.restauranteloscuatrotiempos.es).

Colección Catedral is the wine bar of the highly respected local chef Adolfo, who runs a famous gourmet restaurant nearby plus several eateries in Madrid. The bar offers up a pricey but always top-notch list of gourmet plates, including some traditional dishes like *carcamusas*—pork and vegetable stew (€7-19 each) and fine wines (about €3/glass), as well as a €15 three-course meal that includes wine. Sit next to the kitchen to be near the action. If the Starship *Enterprise* had a wine-and-tapas bar on its holodeck, this would be it. Wine is sold to take home or drink there for €3-8 more than the shop price (daily 12:00-23:30, across from cathedral at Calle Nuncio Viejo 1, tel. 925-224-244, Michael Angel takes good care of diners).

El Botero Taberna is a delightful little hideaway. The barman downstairs, who looks like a young Pavarotti, serves mojitos, fine wine, and exquisite tapas. Upstairs, there's an intimate, seven-table restaurant with romantic, white-table-cloth ambience and modern Mediterranean dishes (€29-48 fixed-price meals, €15 starters, €20 main courses, lunch only Sun-Tue, lunch and dinner Wed-Sat, a block below cathedral at Calle de la Ciudad 5, tel. 925-229-088, www.tabernaelbotero.com).

Restaurants with Character

These places are listed in geographical order from Plaza de Zocodover to Santo Tomé. Plaza de Zocodover is busy with eateries serving edible food at affordable prices, and its people-watching is great. But head off the main drag on side streets. It's worth a few extra minutes to find places where you'll be eating with locals as well as tourists. There's a lively midday tapas scene; almost every bar will offer a small nibble with a stand-up drink.

To dine with younger Spaniards, drop into **El Trébol,** tucked peacefully away just a short block off Plaza de Zocodover. Their €10 mixed grill can feed two. Locals enjoy their *pulgas* (€2.50 sandwiches). The seating inside is basic, but the outdoor tables are nice (daily 9:00-24:00, Calle de Santa Fe 1, tel. 925-281-297).

Restaurante Ludeña is a classic eatery with a bar, a well-worn dining room in back, and a handful of tables on a sunny courtyard. Locals duck in here to pretend there's no tourism in Toledo (Plaza de la Magdalena 10, tel. 925-223-384).

Madre Tierra Restaurante Vegetariano is Toledo's answer to a vegetarian's prayer, and is bright, spacious, and air-conditioned. Its appetizing, healthy dishes are based on both international and traditional Spanish cuisine (€8-13 main courses, €13.50 fixed-price weekday meal, good tea selection, great veggie pizzas, closed Mon night and all day Tue, 20 yards below La Posada de Manolo just before reaching Plaza de San Justo, Bajada de le Tripería 2, tel. 925-223-571).

Taberna La Flor de la Esquina is a rustic bar with a simple basement dining room and wonderful seating on a leafy square under a towering Jesuit church facade. It's part of a fun neighborhood scene (€10 lunch specials, basic *raciones,* open daily, Plaza Juan de Mariana 2, tel. 925-253-801).

Restaurante Placido, run by high-energy Anna and Abuela (grandma) Sagradio, serves traditional family-style cuisine on a leafy terrace or in a wonderful Franciscan monastery courtyard (€13, €15, and €22 fun fixed-price meals—more expensive option comes with partridge; open daily for lunch and dinner in summer, lunch only in winter; about a block uphill from Santo Tomé at Calle Santo Tomé 2, tel. 925-222-603).

Mercado San Agustín, a fancy food court, offers several different eateries.

You can taste gourmet cheeses, wines, hamburgers, Spanish delicacies, Japanese cuisine, fusion foods, and sweet delights. Explore the five levels before choosing, then find a table on any of the levels to dig in—or go to the top-floor terrace for a cocktail (Tue-Sun 10:00-24:00, closed Mon, at Calle Cuesta de Águila 1 right off of Plaza San Agustín, tel. 925-215-898, www.mercadodesanagustin.com).

Picnics are best assembled at the city market, **Mercado Municipal,** on Plaza Mayor (on the Alcázar side of cathedral, with a supermarket inside the market open Mon-Sat 9:00-15:00 & 17:00-20:00 and stalls open mostly in the mornings until 14:00, closed Sun). **Supermarket Coviran,** on Plaza de la Magdalena, has groceries and lots of other stuff at good prices (Mon-Sat 9:50-15:00 & 16:00-22:00, shorter hours on Sun, just below Plaza de Zocodover). For a picnic with people-watching, consider atmospheric Plaza de Zocodover or Plaza del Ayuntamiento.

Dessert

Toledo's famous almond-fruity-sweet *mazapán* is sold all over town. As you wander, keep a lookout for convents advertising their version, *Dulces Artesanos.* The big *mazapán* producer is **Santo Tomé** (daily 9:00-22:00, several outlets, including a handy one on Plaza de Zocodover). They sell *mazapán* goodies individually: *sin relleno*—without filling—is for purists; *de piñon* has pine nuts; *imperiales* is with almonds; others have fruit fillings (two for about €1.50). Boxes are good for gifts, but sampling is much cheaper when buying just a few pieces. Their *Toledana* is a nutty, crumbly, not-too-sweet cookie with a subtle thread of squash filling (€1.40 each).

Rick's Tip: *For a* **sweet, romantic evening dessert,** *pick up a few* mazapán *pastries and head down to the cathedral. Sit on the Plaza del Ayuntamiento's benches (or stretch out on the stone wall to the right of the TI). The fountain is on your right, Spain's best-looking City Hall is behind you, and her top cathedral is before you, shining brightly against the black night sky.*

Mazapán *confections*

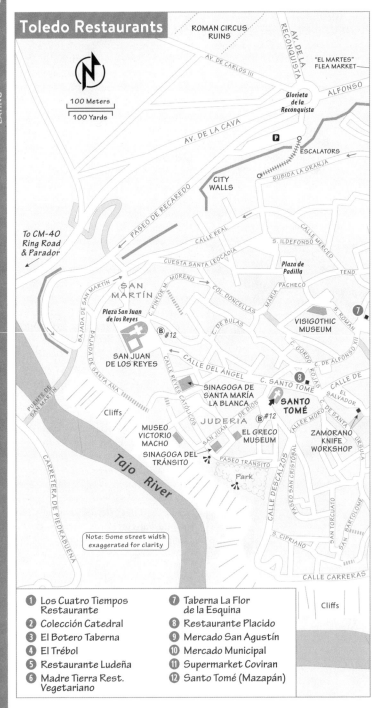

Toledo Restaurants

ROMAN CIRCUS RUINS

AV. DE LA RECONQUISTA

AV. DE CARLOS III

"EL MARTES" FLEA MARKET

ALFONSO

Glorieta de la Reconquista

N
100 Meters
100 Yards

AV. DE LA CAVA

P

ESCALATORS

SUBIDA LA GRANJA

CITY WALLS

PASEO DE RECAREDO

CALLE REAL

CALLE MERCED

S. ILDEFONSO

To CM-40 Ring Road & Parador

CUESTA SANTA LEOCADIA

Plaza de Padilla

TEND

PACHECO

SAN MARTÍN

C. PINTOR M. MORENO

COL. DONCELLAS

MARIA

S. ROMAN

Plaza San Juan de los Reyes

BAJADA DE SAN MARTÍN

C. DE BULAS

VISIGOTHIC MUSEUM

7

B #12

C. GORDO

C. DE ALFONSO III

SAN JUAN DE LOS REYES

CALLE DEL ÁNGEL

C. SANTO TOMÉ

8

CALLE DE

BAJADA DE SANTA ANA

CALLE REYES CATÓLICOS

SINAGOGA DE SANTA MARÍA LA BLANCA

SANTO TOMÉ

EL SALVADOR

C. DE SANTA URSULA

Cliffs

JUDERÍA

B #12

CALLER MORO

ZAMORANO KNIFE WORKSHOP

PUENTE DE SAN MARTÍN

MUSEO VICTORIO MACHO

SAN JUAN DE DIOS

EL GRECO MUSEUM

SINAGOGA DEL TRÁNSITO

PASEO TRANSITO

CALLE DESCALZOS

PASEO SAN CRISTÓBAL

Tajo River

Park

CARRETERA DE PIEDRABUENA

S. CIPRIANO

SAN TORCUATO

SAN BARTOLOMÉ

Note: Some street width exaggerated for clarity

CALLE CARRERAS

Cliffs

1 Los Cuatro Tiempos Restaurante

2 Colección Catedral

3 El Botero Taberna

4 El Trébol

5 Restaurante Ludeña

6 Madre Tierra Rest. Vegetariano

7 Taberna La Flor de la Esquina

8 Restaurante Placido

9 Mercado San Agustín

10 Mercado Municipal

11 Supermarket Coviran

12 Santo Tomé (Mazapán)

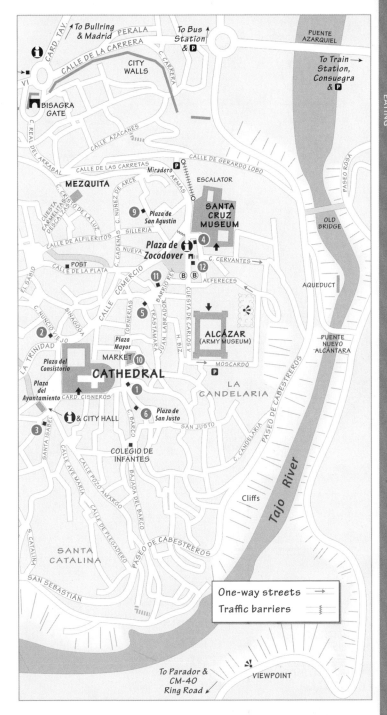

To Bullring & Madrid
To Bus Station & 🅿
PERALA
CARD. TAV.
CALLE DE LA CARRERA
C. CARRERA
VI
CITY WALLS
PUENTE AZARQUIEL
To Train → Station, Consuegra & 🅿

BISAGRA GATE

C. REAL DEL ARRABAL
CALLE AZACANES
CALLE DE LAS CARRETAS
Miradero
CALLE DE GERARDO LOBO
ESCALATOR
PASEO ROSA

MEZQUITA
CUESTA CARMELITAS DESCALZAS
C. CRISTO DE LA LUZ
C. NUÑEZ DE ARCE
Plaza de San Agustín 9
SANTA CRUZ MUSEUM
OLD BRIDGE

CALLE DE ALFILERITOS
SILLERIA
Plaza de Zocodover
4
C. CADENAS
NUEVA

EL SABIO
POST
CALLE DE LA PLATA
C. NUNCIO VIEJO
SINAGOGA
CALLE COMERCIO
TORNERIAS
BARRIO REY
B B 12
C. CERVANTES
ALFERECES
AQUEDUCT

2
11
5
TRASTAMARA
VIDA LABRADOR
H. BIZ.
CUESTA DE CARLOS V

LA TRINIDAD
Plaza Mayor
MARKET 10
ALCÁZAR (ARMY MUSEUM)
PUENTE NUEVO ALCÁNTARA

Plaza del Consistorio
CATHEDRAL
1
MOSCARDÓ
🅿

Plaza del Ayuntamiento
CARD. CISNEROS
& CITY HALL
6 Plaza de San Justo
SAN JUSTO
LA CANDELARIA

3
SANTA ISABEL
C. BARCO
COLEGIO DE INFANTES

CALLE AVE MARIA
CALLE POZO AMARGO
BAJADA DEL BARCO
CALLE DE PLEGADERO
PASEO DE CABESTREROS
C. CANDELARIA
PASEO DE CABESTREROS

S. CATALINA
SANTA CATALINA
Cliffs
Tajo River

SAN SEBASTIÁN

One-way streets →
Traffic barriers

To Parador & CM-40 Ring Road
VIEWPOINT

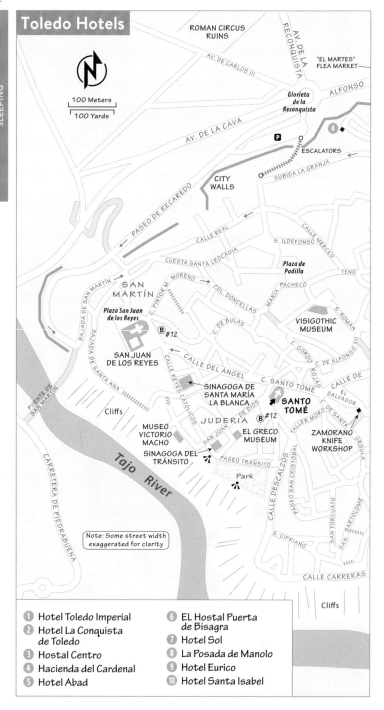

Toledo Hotels

1. Hotel Toledo Imperial
2. Hotel La Conquista de Toledo
3. Hostal Centro
4. Hacienda del Cardenal
5. Hotel Abad
6. EL Hostal Puerta de Bisagra
7. Hotel Sol
8. La Posada de Manolo
9. Hotel Eurico
10. Hotel Santa Isabel

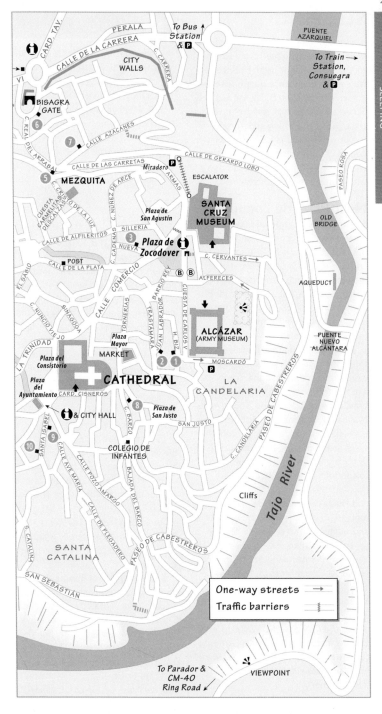

SLEEPING

Madrid day-trippers darken the sunlit cobbles, but few stay to see Toledo's medieval moonrise. Spend the night. Hotels often have a two-tiered price system, with prices 20 percent higher on Friday and Saturday. Spring and fall are high season; November through March and July and August are less busy. Fish around for deals and discounts. Most places have an arrangement with parking lots in town that can save you a few euros; ask when you reserve.

Near Plaza de Zocodover

$$ Hotel Toledo Imperial sits efficiently above Plaza de Zocodover, and rents 29 business-class rooms (Db-€50 Sun-Thu, Db-€85-100 Fri-Sat, higher rates with increased demand, breakfast-about €5, air-con, elevator, Calle Horno de los Bizcochos 5, tel. 925-280-034, www.hotel toledoimperial.com, reservas@hotel toledoimperial.com).

$ Hotel La Conquista de Toledo, a three-star hotel with 33 rooms, gleams with marble. It's so sleek and slick it almost feels more like a hospital than a hotel (Sb-€35, Db-€45-60, book directly by email and ask for their best Rick Steves price, skimpy breakfast-€8, air-con, elevator, near Alcázar at Juan Labrador 8, tel. 925-210-760, www.hotelconquistade toledo.com, conquistadetoeldo@git hoteles.com).

$ Hostal Centro rents 28 spacious rooms with sparse, well-worn furniture and a ramshackle feel. It's wonderfully central, with a third of its rooms overlooking the main square, though you may prefer to request a quiet room on the back side (Sb-€30-35, Db-€45-50, Tb-€60-65, book directly via email with hotel for a 10 percent weekday discount with this book, 50 yards off Plaza de Zocodover—take the first right off Calle del Comercio to Calle Nueva 13, tel. 925-257-091, www. hostalcentrotoledo.com, hostalcentro@ telefonica.net).

Near Bisagra Gate

$$$ Hacienda del Cardenal, a 17th-century cardinal's palace built into Toledo's wall, is quiet and elegant, with a cool garden, a less-than-helpful staff, and a stuffy restaurant. At the dusty old gate of Toledo, it's close to the station, but below all the old-town action (Sb-€59-91, Db-€75-118, Fri-Sat-€20-40 more, breakfast-€9, enter through town wall 100 yards below Bisagra Gate, Paseo de Recaredo 24, tel. 925-224-900, www. haciendadelcardenal.com, hotel@ haciendadelcardenal.com).

$$ Hotel Abad sits at the bottom of the old town's hill just a block inside the Bisagra Gate and offers 22 clean, rustic rooms with stone walls, wooden rafters, and contemporary furnishings (Db-€64-84 Sun-Thu, Db-€90-125 Fri-Sat, extra bed-€20, breakfast-€8, air-con, elevator, Real del Arrabal 1, tel. 925-283-500, www. hotelabadtoledo.com, reservas@hotel abad.com).

$ El Hostal Puerta Bisagra is in a sprawling old building that is fresh and modern inside. Located just across from Bisagra Gate, it's convenient for arrivals, but a long hike uphill to the action (hop on any bus). Its 38 comfortable rooms are rented at some of the best prices in town (Sb-€40-50, Db-€50-70, lower rates Sun-Thu, breakfast-€6, air-con, Calle del Potro

5, tel. 925-285-277, www.puertabisagra. com, elhostal@puertabisagra.com).

$ Hotel Sol has 15 nicely decorated pastel rooms. It's on a quiet, ugly side street between Bisagra Gate and Plaza de Zocodover (Sb-€32-48, Db-€43-58, Tb-€61-72, higher rates for Fri-Sat, slightly cheaper Nov-March, 10 percent discount with this book, breakfast-€4, air-con, private parking-€10/day; leave the busy main drag at Hotel Imperial and head 50 yards down the lane to Azacanes 8; tel. 925-213-650, www.hotelyhostalsol.com, info@ hotelyhostalsol.com). Their 11-room **$ Hostal Sol** annex across the street is just as comfortable, smoke-free, and cheaper (Sb-€30-39, Db-€39-48, Tb-€57-62, higher rates for Fri-Sat, slightly cheaper Nov-March, 10 percent discount with this book, breakfast-€4).

Deep in Toledo

$$ La Posada de Manolo rents 14 furnished rooms across from the downhill corner of the cathedral. Each of its three floors are themed differently—Moorish, Jewish, and Christian. It fills up quickly (Sb-€39, Db-€50 Sun-Thu, Db-€61 Fri, Db-€72 Sat, more for rooms with bigger beds, 10 percent discount with this book when you reserve directly with hotel, breakfast-€3, air-con, no elevator, two nice view terraces, Calle Sixto Ramón Parro 8, tel. 925-282-250, www.laposadademanolo.com, toledo@laposadademanolo. com).

$$ Hotel Eurico cleverly fits 23 sleek rooms and a friendly staff into a medieval building buried deep in the old town (Sb-€55-60, Db-€60-90, Tb-€70-120, higher rates for Fri-Sat, breakfast-€5-8, air-con, Calle Santa Isabel 3, tel. 925-284-178, www.hoteleurico.com, reservas@ hoteleurico.com).

$ Hotel Santa Isabel, in a 15th-century building two blocks from the cathedral, has 41 clean, modern, and comfortable rooms and squeaky tile hallways (Sb-€30-42, small old Db-€45-55, big new Db-€55-65, Db with view-€70-85, higher rates for Fri-Sat, extra bed-€10, 5 percent discount with this book, breakfast-€5, elevator, scenic roof terrace, parking-€12/day, buried deep in old town—take a taxi instead of the bus, drivers enter from Calle Pozo Amargo, Calle Santa Isabel 24, tel. 925-253-120, www.hotelsantaisabel.net, info@ hotelsantaisabel.net).

TRANSPORTATION

Getting Around Toledo

You can walk anywhere within the town walls in small, hilly Toledo, but buses can come in handy. Bus #12 gets you across town and back—running between Plaza de Zocodover and Santo Tomé (€1.40, pay driver; see my "Self-Guided Tour: Bus #12" on page 256). To get to the famous viewpoint across the gorge, see "Tours," near the beginning of this chapter. As for taxis, you'll find stands at the train station, bus station, and in the old town (Plaza de Zocodover, Bisagra Gate, and Santo Tomé).

Arriving and Departing

"Arriving" in Toledo means getting uphill to Plaza de Zocodover. As the bus and train stations are outside the town center and parking can be a challenge, this involves a taxi, a bus, or a walk plus a ride up a series of escalators.

Toledo and Madrid are easily and frequently connected by AVE train (30 minutes) and buses (1 hour).

By Train

Toledo's early-20th-century train station is Neo-Moorish and a national monument itself for its architecture and art, which both celebrate the three cultures that coexisted here.

Remember that early and late trains to/ from Madrid can sell out; reserve ahead. If you haven't yet bought a ticket for your departure from Toledo (even if it's for the next day), get it before you leave the Toledo station and choose a specific time rather than leave it open-ended. (If you prefer more flexibility, take the bus instead—see "By Bus" later.)

From Toledo's train station to Plaza de Zocodover, it's a €4.50 **taxi** ride (to hotels, the ride is metered), a 25-minute walk with the help of escalators, or an easy ride on various buses. You can take **city bus** #5, #11, #61, or #62; leaving the station, you'll see the bus stop 30 yards to the right (€1.40, pay on bus, confirm by asking, "*¿Para Plaza de Zocodover?*"). **Toledo City Tour** runs a *lanzadera* shuttle bus up to Plaza de Zocodover, but charges €1 more than the city buses; they also run a loop trip that stops at this train station, the famous city viewpoint, and Plaza de Zocodover (€5.50; see "Tours," page 237).

To **walk** into town, turn right as you leave the station and follow the fuchsia line on the sidewalk labeled *Up Toledo, Follow the Line.* Track this line (and periodic escalator symbols) past a bus stop, over the bridge, around the roundabout to the left, and into a bus parking area.

From here, go up a series of escalators that take you to the center of town: You'll emerge about a block from the Plaza de Zocodover.

From Toledo by Train to: Madrid (nearly hourly, 30 minutes by AVE or Avant to Madrid's Atocha Station, tel. 902-240-202, www.renfe.com).

To get to **Granada, Sevilla,** and elsewhere in Spain, assume you'll have to transfer in Madrid. See "Transportation" at the end of the Madrid chapter for information on reaching various destinations.

By Bus

At the bus station, buses park downstairs. Luggage lockers and a small bus-info office—where you can buy locker tokens—are upstairs opposite the cafeteria. From the bus station, Plaza de Zocodover is a 15-minute **hike,** a €4.50 **taxi** ride, or a short **bus** ride (catch #5 or #12 downstairs; €1.40, pay on bus). The **Toledo City Tour** shuttle bus and loop-trip bus also stop here and can also get you to Plaza de Zocodover (see mention in train info, above).

Toledo's train station

Before leaving the bus station, confirm your departure time. Unlike the trains, buses don't tend to get booked up. You can put off buying a return ticket for the bus until just minutes before you leave Toledo. Specify you'd like a *directo* bus (the *ruta* trip takes longer—1 hour versus 1.5 hours). But if you miss the *directo* bus (or if it's sold out), the *ruta* option offers a peek of off-the-beaten-path Madrid suburbia; you'll arrive at the same time as taking the next *directo* bus.

From Toledo by Bus to: Madrid (2/hour, 1-1.5 hours, *directo* faster than *ruta*, bus drops you at Madrid's Plaza Elíptica Metro stop, Alsa bus company, tel. 902-422-242, www.alsa.es).

By Taxi

While it may seem extravagant, if you have limited time, lots of luggage, and a small group, simply taking a taxi from your Toledo hotel to your Madrid hotel is breathtakingly efficient (€90, one hour door-to-door, tel. 925-255-050 or 925-227-070). You can ask several cabbies for their best "off the meter" rate. A taxi to the Madrid airport costs €110 (find one who will go "off the meter") and takes an hour.

By Car

A car is useless within Toledo's city walls, where the narrow, twisting streets are no fun to navigate. Ideally, see the old town outside of car-rental time.

But if you're arriving or leaving by car, enjoy a scenic big-picture view by taking a big circular (*Circunvalación*) drive around the city. You'll view Toledo from many angles across the Tajo Gorge. Stop at any viewpoint (best at sunset).

Here are two parking garages: the big **Miradero Garage** at the convention center (€16/day; drive through Bisagra Gate, go uphill half a mile, look for sign on the left directing you to *Plaza del Miradero*) and the **Alcázar Garage,** inside the city walls (just past the Alcázar—€1.80/hour, €20/day). Many hotels offer discounted parking rates at nearby garages; ask when making your reservation.

Granada

Granada was once the grandest city in Spain. Its magnificent Alhambra fortress represented the power of the Moorish kingdom—until it became its last stronghold. After the Christians retook Granada in 1492 and drove out the Moors, the city settled into a long slumber. Today, the city's evocative history and diverse North African-flavored culture make it worldly, while its large student population (80,000—including more than 10,000 from abroad) lends it a youthful zest.

A Spanish poet once wrote that "there is nothing worse in this life than to be blind in Granada." The city has much to see, and reveals itself in unpredictable ways. Peer through the intricate lattice of a Moorish window. Hear water burbling unseen among the labyrinthine hedges of the Generalife Gardens. Listen to a flute trilling deep in the swirl of alleys around the cathedral. Wander the angled Moorish quarter, the Albayzín. Don't be blind in Granada—open all your senses.

GRANADA IN 2 DAYS

Be sure to make reservations for the Alhambra fortress sight in advance; this plan assumes you're touring it on Day 2.

Day 1: Stroll the Alcaicería market streets and follow my self-guided tour of the old town, including a visit to the cathedral and its Royal Chapel. Enjoy the vibe at Plaza Nueva, the town's main square. Consider a city walking tour. Hike the hippie lane, stopping by a funky teahouse along the way, and wander into the Albayzín Moorish quarter. End your day at the San Nicolás viewpoint—the golden hour before sunset is best, when the Alhambra seems to glow with its own light.

On any evening, tapa-hop for dinner (consider Gayle's Granada Tapas Tours) or splurge on fine dining at a *carmen*. When the evening cools down, join the paseo. Take in a *zambra* dance in the Sacromonte district. Relax in an Arab bath (Hammam al Andalus) or a *tetería* (tea shop), or both. Slow down and smell the incense.

Day 2: Follow my self-guided tour of the Alhambra; you'll see the elaborate and many-roomed Palacios Nazaríes, Charles V's Palace, the refreshing Generalife Gardens, and more.

Rick's Tip: *If you're not prepared, you could become one of the untold number of tourists who show up in Granada and never see its main sight. To ensure that you can get into the Alhambra's* **Palacios Nazaríes** *during your stay, make an* **advance reservation**—*online or by phone.*

Granada Old Town Walk

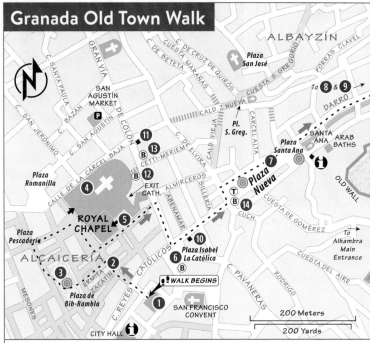

Walk
1 Corral del Carbón
2 Alcaicería
3 Plaza de Bib-Rambla
4 Cathedral
5 Royal Chapel Square
6 Plaza Isabel La Católica (Bus to Alhambra)
7 Plaza Nueva
8 To Paseo de los Tristes
9 To Hammam El Bañuelo

Other
10 Alhambra Bookstore, Info & ServiCaixa Machine (Alhambra Tickets)
11 ServiCaixa Machine
12 Gran Vía Cathedral Bus Stop (from Train & Bus Stations)
13 Gran Vía del Colón Bus Stop (to Train & Bus Stations)
14 Plaza Nueva Bus Stop (to Albayzín & Sacromonte)

to complement the romantic image of Granada popularized by the writings of Washington Irving.

Explore the mesh of tiny shopping lanes: overpriced trinkets, popcorn machines popping, men selling balloons, leather goods spread out on streets, kids playing soccer, barking dogs, dogged shoe-shine boys, and the whirring grind of bicycle-powered knife sharpeners.

• Turn left down Calle Ermita. After 50 yards, you'll leave the market via another fortified gate and enter a big square crowded with outdoor restaurants. Skirt around the tables to the Neptune fountain, which marks the center of the...

3 Plaza de Bib-Rambla

This exuberant square, just two blocks behind the cathedral (from the fountain you can see its blocky spire peeking above the big orange building) was once the center of Moorish Granada. While

❶ *Alcaicería entrance*
❷ *Plaza Isabel La Católica*
❸ *Plaza de Bib-Rambla*
❹ *Cathedral*

Moorish rule of Spain lasted 700 years, the last couple of those centuries were a period of decline as Muslim culture split under weak leadership and Christian forces grew more determined. The last remnants of the Moorish kingdom united and ruled from Granada. As Muslims fled south from reconquered lands, Granada was flooded with refugees. By 1400, Granada had an estimated 100,000 people—huge for medieval Europe. This was the main square, the focal point for markets and festivals, but it was much smaller than now, pushed in by the jam-packed city.

Under Christian rule, Moors and Jews were initially tolerated (as they were considered good for business), and this area became the Moorish ghetto. Then, with the Inquisition (under Philip II, c. 1550), ideology trumped pragmatism, and Jews and Muslims were evicted or forced to convert. The elegant square you see today was built, and built big. In-your-face Catholic processions started here. To assert Christian rule, all the trappings of Christian power were layered upon what had been the trappings of Moorish power. Between here and the cathedral were the Christian University (the big orange building) and the adjacent archbishop's palace.

Today Plaza de Bib-Rambla is good for coffee or a meal amid the color and fragrance of flower stalls and the burbling of its Neptune-topped fountain. It remains a multigenerational hangout, where it seems everyone is enjoying a peaceful retirement.

With Neptune facing you, leave the plaza by the left corner (along Calle Pescadería) to reach a smaller, similarly lively square—little Plaza Pescadería, where families spill out to enjoy its many restaurants. For a quick snack, drop into tiny **Cucini Pescadería**—next to its namesake restaurant—for a takeaway bite of *pescaito frito*—fried fish (€1-3.50).

• *Leave Plaza Pescadería on Calle Marqués de Gerona; within one block, you'll come to a small square fronting a big church.*

❹ Cathedral

Wow, the cathedral facade just screams triumph. That's partly because its design is based on a triumphal arch, built over a destroyed mosque. Five hundred yards away, there was once open space outside the city wall with good soil for a foundation. But the Christian conquerors said, "No way." Instead, they destroyed the mosque and built their cathedral right here on difficult, sandy soil. This was the place where the people of Granada traditionally worshipped—and now they would worship as Christians.

The church—started in the early 1500s and not finished until the late 1700s—has a Gothic foundation and was built mostly in the Renaissance style, with its last altars done in Neoclassical style. Hometown artist Alonso Cano (1601-1667) finished the building, at the king's request, in Baroque. Accentuating the power of the Roman Catholic Church, the emphasis here is on Mary rather than Christ. The facade declares *Ave Maria*. (This was Counter-Reformation time, and the Church was threatened by Protestant Christians. Mary was also more palatable to Muslim converts, as she is revered in the Quran.)

• *To tour the cathedral now, you can enter here (the interior is described in the self-guided cathedral tour on page 303). You'll exit on the far side, near the big street called Gran Vía de Colón.*

If you're skipping the cathedral interior for now, circle around the cathedral to the right, keeping the church on your left, until you reach the small square facing the Royal Chapel.

❺ Royal Chapel Square

This square was once ringed by important Moorish buildings. A hammam (public bath), a madrassa (school), a caravanserai (Day's Inn), the silk market, and the leading mosque were all right here. With Christian rule, the madrassa (the faux-gray-stone building with the walls painted in 3-D Baroque style) became Granada's first City Hall (€2, daily 10:00-20:00 for short guided tour of 14th-century *mihrab* and Mudejar-era annex). Here, too, is the entrance to the Royal Chapel, where the coffins of Ferdinand and Isabel were moved in 1521 from the Alhambra (see the self-guided tour of the Royal Chapel on page 300).

• *Continue up the cobbled, stepped lane to Gran Vía. With the arrival of cars and the modern age, the people of Granada wanted a Parisian-style boulevard. In the early 20th century, they mercilessly cut through the old town and created Gran Vía and its French-style buildings—in the process destroying everything in its path, including many historic convents.*

Turn right and walk down Gran Vía toward the big square just ahead (where minibus #C3 to the Alhambra stops). Face the statue above the fountain from across the busy intersection.

❻ Plaza Isabel La Católica

Granada's two grand boulevards, Gran Vía and Calle Reyes Católicos, meet here at Plaza Isabel La Católica. Above the fountain, a beautiful statue shows Columbus unfurling a long contract with Isabel. It lists the terms of Columbus' MCCCCLXXXXII voyage: "For as much as you, Columbus, are going by our command to discover and subdue some Islands and Continents in the ocean...." The two reliefs show the big events in Granada of 1492: Isabel and Ferdinand accepting Columbus' proposal and a stirring battle scene (which never happened) at the walls of the Alhambra.

Isabel was driven by her desire to spread Catholicism. Spain, needing an alternate trade route to the Orient's spices after the Ottoman Empire cut off the traditional overland routes, was driven by trade. And Columbus was driven by his

desire for money. As a reward for adding territory to Spain's Catholic empire, Isabel promised Columbus the ranks of Admiral of the Oceans and Governor of the New World. To sweeten the pot, she tossed in one-eighth of all the riches he brought home. Isabel died thinking that Columbus had found India or China. Columbus died poor and disillusioned.

Calle Reyes Católicos leads from this square downhill to the busy intersection called Puerta Real. From there, Acera del Darro takes you through modern Granada to the river, passing the huge El Corte Inglés department store and lots of modern commerce. This area erupts with locals out strolling each night. For one of the best Granada paseos, wander the streets here around 19:00.

• *Cross over Gran Vía on a green light (never go against the light at this odd intersection). Follow Calle Reyes Católicos to the left for a couple of blocks (if you need to pick up your Alhambra tickets, you'll pass its book shop, with a ServiCaixa machine, on the way) until you reach...*

❼ Plaza Nueva

Plaza Nueva is dominated at the far end by the Palace of Justice (grand Baroque facade with green Andalusian flag). The fountain is capped by a stylized pomegranate—the symbol of the city, always open and fertile. The main action here is the comings and goings of the busy little shuttle buses serving the Albayzín (#C1).

Plaza Nueva

The local hippie community, nicknamed the *pies negros* (black feet) for obvious reasons, hangs out here and on Calle de Elvira. They live—with their dogs and guitars—in abandoned caves above those the Gypsies occupy in Sacromonte. Many are the children of rich Spanish families from the north, hell-bent on disappointing their high-achieving parents.

• *Our tour continues with a stroll up Carrera del Darro. Leave Plaza Nueva opposite where you entered, on the little lane that runs alongside the Darro River. This is particularly enjoyable in the cool of the evening.*

❽ *Paseo de los Tristes*

This stretch of road—Carrera del Darro—is also called Paseo de los Tristes—"Walk of the Sad Ones." It was once the route of funeral processions to the cemetery at the edge of town. As you leave Plaza Nueva, notice the small Church of Santa Ana on your right. This was originally a mosque—the church tower replaced a minaret. Notice the ceramic brickwork. This is Mudejar art by Moorish craftsmen, whose techniques were later employed by Christians. If you happen to be on the square when the church is open (unpredictable hours), step inside to see its gilded chapels and a fine Alhambra-style cedar ceiling.

Follow Carrera del Darro along the Darro River, which flows around the base of the Alhambra. Six miles upstream, part of the Darro is diverted to provide water for the Alhambra's many fountains—a remarkable feat of Moorish engineering that allowed the grand fortress complex to be resistant to siege.

After passing two small, picturesque bridges, the road widens slightly for a bus stop. Here you'll see the broken nub of a once-grand 11th-century bridge that led to the Alhambra. Notice two slits in the column: One held an iron portcullis to keep bad guys from entering the town via the river. The second held a solid door that was lowered to build up water, then

released to flush out the riverbed and keep it clean.

• *Across from the remains of the bridge is the brick facade of an evocative Moorish bath.*

❾ *Hammam El Bañuelo (Moorish Baths)*

In Moorish times, hammams were a big part of the community (working-class homes didn't have bathrooms). Baths were strictly segregated and were more than places to wash: These were social meeting points where business was done. In Christian times it was assumed that conspiracies brewed in these baths—therefore, only a few of them survive. This place gives you the chance to explore the stark but evocative ruins of an 11th-century Moorish public bath (free, daily 9:30-14:30 & 17:00-21:00, Carrera del Darro 31, tel. 958-027-800).

Entering the baths, you pass the house of the keeper and the foyer, then visit the cold room, the warm room (where services like massage were offered), and finally the hot, or steam, room. Beyond that, you can see the oven that generated

Hammam El Bañuelo

the heat, which flowed under the hypo-caust-style floor tiles (the ones closest to the oven were the hottest). The romantic little holes in the ceiling once had stained-glass louvers that attendants opened and closed with sticks to regulate the heat and steaminess. Whereas Romans soaked in their pools, Muslims just doused. Rather than being totally immersed, people scooped and splashed water over them-selves. Imagine attendants stoking the fires under the metal boiler...while people in towels and wooden slippers (to protect their feet from the heated floors) enjoyed spa services as beams of light slashed through the mist.

This was a great social mixer. As all were naked, class distinctions disappeared—elites learned the latest from common-ers. Mothers found matches for their kids. A popular Muslim phrase sums up the attraction of the baths: "This is where any-one would spend their last coin."

• Just across from the baths is a stop for minibus #C1, if you want to head up to the Albayzín the easy way. Otherwise, continue straight ahead to Paseo de los Tristes, with its restaurant tables spilling out under the floodlit Alhambra.

SIGHTS

▲▲▲The Alhambra

This last and greatest Moorish palace is one of Europe's top sights. Attracting up to 8,000 visitors a day, it's the reason most tourists come to Granada. Nowhere else does the splendor of Moorish civilization shine so beautifully.

The last Moorish stronghold in Europe is, with all due respect, really a symbol of retreat. For centuries, Granada was merely a regional capital. Gradually the Christian Reconquista moved south, taking Córdoba (1237) and Sevilla (1248). The Nazarids, one of the many diverse ethnic groups of Spanish Muslims, held together the last Moorish kingdom, which they ruled from Granada until 1492. As you tour their grand

palace, remember that while Europe slum-bered through the Dark Ages, Moorish magnificence blossomed—ornate stucco, plaster "stalactites," colors galore, scal-loped windows framing Granada views, exuberant gardens, and water, water everywhere. Water—so rare and precious in most of the Islamic world—was the purest symbol of life to the Moors. The Alhambra is decorated with water: stand-ing still, cascading, masking secret conver-sations, and drip-dropping playfully.

Orientation

The Alhambra consists of four sights strung along the top of a hill:

Palacios Nazaríes: Elaborate Moorish palace, the Alhambra's most important sight (requiring a timed entry).

Charles V's Palace: A Christian Renaissance palace added after the Reconquista, with a worthwhile Alhambra Museum.

Generalife Gardens: Lush, sprawling but orderly gardens with a pool and small summer palace.

Alcazaba: Ruined fort with a tower and city views.

Cost and Hours

Cost: Various tickets cover the sights of the Alhambra. For many travelers, the first option is best.

• **€14 Alhambra General:** Covers the Alcazaba fort, Palacios Nazaríes, and Generalife Gardens. This is the only ticket that allows you to see Palacios Nazaríes during the day.

• **€8.40 Alhambra Gardens, Generalife, and Alcazaba:** Daytime admission to everything but Palacios Nazaríes

• **€9.40 Alhambra at Night—Palaces:** Nighttime visit to Palacios Nazaríes

• **€9.40 Alhambra at Night—General-ife:** Nighttime visit to the gardens and summer palace

• **€15.40 Alhambra Experiences:** Night-time visit to Palacios Nazaríes, then (the next morning) entry to the Alcaz-

aba and Generalife Gardens
- **Free:** A portion of the Alhambra grounds is free to visit, as is Charles V's Palace (and the Alhambra Museum inside it).

Hours: The whole Alhambra complex is open daily mid-March–mid-Oct 8:30-20:00, off-season 8:30-18:00; ticket office opens at 8:00, last entry one hour before closing, toll tel. 902-441-221, www.alhambra-patronato.es.

The Palacios Nazaríes and Generalife Gardens are also open most **evenings** mid-March–mid-Oct Tue-Sat 22:00-23:30 (ticket office open 21:30-22:30), closed Sun-Mon; and off-season Fri-Sat 20:00-21:30 (ticket office open 19:30-20:30), closed Sun-Thu.

Reservations

Reservations are essential to be assured of seeing the entire sight, because on most days, the highlight of the Alhambra, the popular Palacios Nazaríes, is sold out completely.

Make a Reservation: Reserve a specific entry time up to three months before your visit, and pick up your tickets in Spain (€1.40 surcharge). For most of the year, booking at least two weeks in advance is sufficient—but reserve farther out for Holy Week, weekends, and major holidays. Off-season (July-Aug and winter), you can generally book a few days ahead. Everyone who visits the palaces, even children, must have their own ticket (kids under 12 are free; 12-15-year-olds are discounted). Reserve online or by phone.

Rick's Tip: *If you don't mind seeing the* **Alhambra by moonlight,** *combining two separate tickets (daytime "Alhambra Gardens," evening "Alhambra at Night—Palaces") offers more flexibility than the "Alhambra Experiences" ticket, which locks you into a visit over two days. You can't see the Alcazaba fort at night, but Palacios Nazaríes provides 80 percent of the Alhambra's thrills. A few small sections of both the palace and the gardens are also closed at night, but some people find it magical—less crowded and beautifully lit.*

Order Tickets Online: Select the "Alhambra General" ticket on www.alhambra-tickets.es, then choose your

The Alhambra

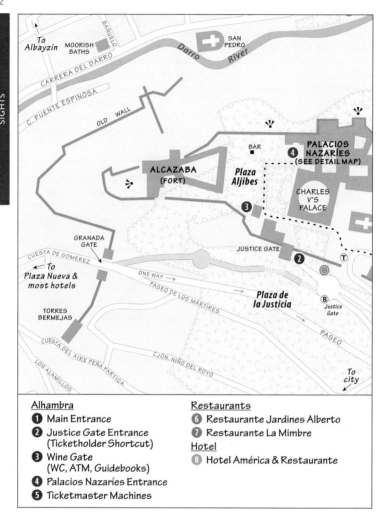

To Albayzín
MOORISH BATHS
BAÑUELO
Darro River
SAN PEDRO
CARRERA DEL DARRO
C. PUENTE ESPINOSA
OLD WALL
BAR ■
PALACIOS NAZARÍES
4 (SEE DETAIL MAP)
ALCAZABA (FORT)
Plaza Aljibes
3
CHARLES V'S PALACE
GRANADA GATE
JUSTICE GATE
CUESTA DE GOMEREZ
← To Plaza Nueva & most hotels
ONE WAY →
PASEO DE LOS MÁRTIRES
2
Ⓣ
Plaza de la Justicia
Ⓑ Justice Gate
TORRES BERMEJAS
PASEO
CUESTA DEL AIRE PEÑA PARTIDA
CJÓN. NIÑO DEL ROYO
LOS ALAMILLOS
To city

Alhambra
1 Main Entrance
2 Justice Gate Entrance (Ticketholder Shortcut)
3 Wine Gate (WC, ATM, Guidebooks)
4 Palacios Nazaríes Entrance
5 Ticketmaster Machines

Restaurants
6 Restaurante Jardines Alberto
7 Restaurante La Mimbre
Hotel
8 Hotel América & Restaurante

date and time period for entering the complex—morning (8:30-14:00) or afternoon (14:00-20:00, until 18:00 off-season), and then select the exact half-hour time slot for entry to Palacios Nazaríes (*agotado* means "sold out").

Order Tickets by Phone: An English-speaking operator will walk you through the process. Within Spain, dial 958-926-031 or 902-888-001. From the US, dial 011-34-958-926-031. The line is open Mon-Fri 8:00-24:00 Spanish time, closed Sat-Sun.

Pick Up Tickets: You'll need to convert your reservation to a printed ticket in Spain (bring the same credit card you used to reserve). Save time by retrieving your tickets before you reach the crowded Alhambra. You can print tickets at any yellow, ATM-like ServiCaixa terminal in Andalucía (there's one across from the cathedral at Gran Vía 16, and another in the official Alhambra bookstore in town at Calle Reyes Católicos 40). Picking up your

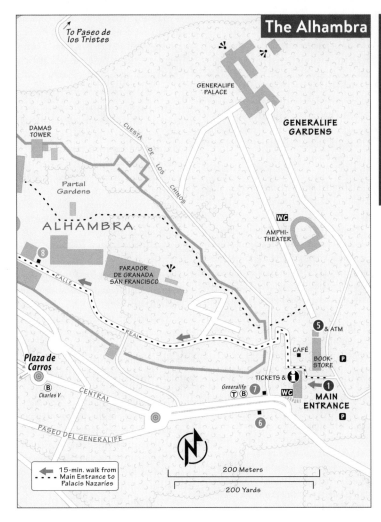

The Alhambra

To Paseo de
los Tristes

GENERALIFE
PALACE

GENERALIFE
GARDENS

DAMAS
TOWER

CUESTA DE LOS CHINOS

Partal
Gardens

ALHAMBRA

WC

AMPHI-
THEATER

PARADOR
DE GRANADA
SAN FRANCISCO

CALLE

REAL

5 & ATM

CAFÉ

BOOK-
STORE

P

Plaza de
Carros

TICKETS &

P

B
Charles V

CENTRAL

Generalife
T **B** **7**

WC

1

**MAIN
ENTRANCE**

P

PASEO DEL GENERALIFE

6

N

15-min. walk from
Main Entrance to
Palacis Nazaríes

200 Meters

200 Yards

---

ticket in advance lets you use the Justice Gate shortcut, avoiding the mob at the main entrance.

If your palace appointment is before 14:00, you can enter the Alhambra complex any time in the morning to visit the other sights before or after your appointment (you can linger past 14:00 at any sight, but you can't enter a sight after 14:00). If your palace appointment is for 14:00 or later, that's the earliest you can enter any sight.

Without Reservations

If you've arrived in Granada without an "Alhambra General" reservation, you have these options:

• Buy the **Bono Turístico city pass,** which even on late notice lets you choose virtually any entry time, even on the same day (see page 273).

• Take a **guided tour,** which admits you without reservations (see page 285).

• See if your **hotel** can wrangle a reservation.

• Try for a **last-minute reservation** online or by phone.

• **Be in line by 7:30** at the Alhambra's main entrance in the hopes of snaring a same-day ticket.

• Purchase a ticket online or at the main entrance to **visit everything except Palacios Nazaríes.** You can also stroll through the free parts (Charles V's Palace, Alhambra Museum, and the grounds) and enjoy the views.

Getting to the Alhambra

You have four options for getting to the Alhambra.

On Foot: From Plaza Nueva, hike 20-25 minutes up the street called Cuesta de Gomérez. Keep going straight—you'll see the Alhambra high on your left. Along the way, after about 10 minutes, you'll see the Justice Gate shortcut (which you can use if you already have your printed ticket). For the main entrance, keep going up. The ticket pavilion is on the far side of the Alhambra, near the entrance to the Generalife Gardens.

By Bus: From the bus stop at the cathedral or Plaza de Isabel La Católica, catch a red #C3 minibus, marked *Alhambra.* There are three Alhambra stops (all shown on the map on page 283): Justice Gate (best if you already have a printed ticket or are using a Bono Turístico card—described earlier), Charles V, and Generalife (main ticket office and the gardens).

By Taxi: It's a €6 ride from the taxi stand on Plaza Nueva.

By Car: If you're coming from outside the city by car, see the end of this chapter, which covers driving to the Alhambra's parking lot.

At the Main Entrance: Those with printed tickets can thread their way between the ticket pavilion and the bookstore to the entrance. The ticket pavilion has a cash-only line for same-day ticket purchases and a line for picking up reserved tickets. If these lines are long, or

if you want to pay with a credit card, head to the smaller pavilion just past the bookstore—you'll find a ServiCaixa ATM for printing reserved tickets as well as Ticketmaster machines for purchasing tickets.

Rick's Tip: *If you already have your printed ticket in hand (for example, if you picked it up in town), you can take a* **shortcut through the Justice Gate entrance,** *which is closer to town. If you're walking, this saves about 15 minutes of uphill climbing; you can also get off the minibus here. If you want to go to the Generalife Gardens first, or don't yet have a ticket in hand, use the upper, main entrance.*

Tours, Guidebooks, Photography

Tours: Various companies run tours that include transportation to the Alhambra and a guided tour of Palacios Nazaríes, including **Cicerone** (€55, 958-561-810 or mobile 607-691-676, www.cicerone granada.com, reservas@ciceronegranada.com). Ideally, reserve at least 3-4 days ahead.

Audioguides: The €6.50 "complete" audioguide brings the palace and grounds to life with a quality description of 50 stops throughout the complex. Rent it at the entrance or at Charles V's Palace; leave €40 cash deposit or your ID—you'll need to return the audioguide where you picked it up. Simpler €4 "garden" or "palace" audioguides cover just 15 stops each. Audioguides are not available for night visits.

Guidebooks: I recommend the slick and colorful *Alhambra and Generalife in Focus* (€9), sold at bookstores in town; to make the most of your visit, buy it and read it before you tour the site. Official Alhambra bookstores push the €18 *Official Guide,* a well-produced, scholarly tome—but it weighs a ton.

Photography: During the day, photos with flash are allowed everywhere except in the Alhambra Museum. For night visits, flash photography is prohibited.

Eating: Within the Alhambra walls, your choices are: the **parador** (cafeteria: €9-13 sandwiches, €12-20 light meals; restaurant terrace: €10-15 starters, €18-27 main dishes, €35 fixed-price meal); **Hotel América** (€6 sandwiches, €15-20 meals, Sun-Fri 12:30-16:30, closed Sat); a small **bar-café kiosk** in front of the Alcazaba fort (€3.50 sandwiches); and **vending machines** (next to the Wine Gate and WC, near Charles V's Palace). You're welcome to bring in a **picnic** as long as you eat it in a public area.

For better-value eateries, head outside at the top of the complex, where you'll find the charming **Restaurante Jardines Alberto** across from the main entrance (€14-17 *menú del día;* Tue-Sat 9:00-23:00, until 20:00 Sun-Mon; Paseo de la Sabica 1, enter up stairs from the street), and the breezy **Restaurante La Mimbre** by the #C3 bus stop (€8-12 salads, €11-16 main dishes, €15-18 fixed-price lunch, Tue-Sat 12:00-17:00 & 20:00-23:00, Sun-Mon 12:00-17:00, Paseo del Generalife 18).

● *Self-Guided Tour*

You can see the sights in any order. Where you start depends on where you enter (Justice Gate, if you have a printed ticket, or the main entrance on top) and when your Palacios Nazaríes appointment is. The Alhambra is a large complex. To minimize walking, try to see the sights in a linear fashion (from the main entrance down toward the Justice Gate, or vice versa).

Be sure to arrive at Palacios Nazaríes (which is a 15-minute walk from the main entrance) within your allotted entry time slot; ticket checkers are strict. If you have time to kill before your appointment, spend it luxuriously on the view terrace of the parador bar. Drinks, WCs, and guide-books are available at the Wine Gate, near the entrance of Palacios Nazaríes, but not inside the palace.

▲▲CHARLES V'S PALACE AND THE ALHAMBRA MUSEUM

While it's only natural for a conquering king to build his own palace over his foe's palace, the Christian Charles V (the Holy Roman Emperor, who ruled as Charles I over Spain) respected the splendid

Charles V's Palace and the Alhambra Museum

Moorish palace. And so, to make his mark, he built a modern Renaissance palace for official functions and used the existing Palacios Nazaríes as a royal residence. With a unique circle-within-a-square design by Pedro Machuca, a pupil of Michelangelo, this is Spain's most impressive Renaissance building. Stand in the circular courtyard surrounded by mottled marble columns, then climb the stairs. Perhaps Charles' palace was designed to have a dome, but it was never finished—his son, Philip II, abandoned it to build his own, much more massive palace outside Madrid, El Escorial (the final and most austere example of Spanish Renaissance architecture). Even without the dome, acoustics are perfect in the center—stand in the middle and sing your best aria. The palace doubles as a venue for the popular International Festival of Music and Dance.

The **Alhambra Museum** (Museo de la Alhambra, on the ground floor of Charles V's Palace), worth ▲, shows off some of the Alhambra's best surviving Moorish art. The museum's beautifully displayed and well-described artifacts—including tiles,

pottery, pieces of fountains, and a beautiful carved-wood door—help humanize the Alhambra (free, Wed-Sat 8:30-20:00, Sun and Tue 8:30-14:00, shorter hours off-season, closed Mon year-round). The **Fine Arts Museum** upstairs is of little interest to most.

• *From the front of Charles V's Palace (as you face the Alcazaba fort), the entrance to Palacios Nazaríes is to the right (look for the line snaking along the outside edge of the garden), while the Alcazaba is across a moat straight ahead (to get there, go through the keyhole-shaped Wine Gate—described in the sidebar on page 295—then hook right and walk up to the open area in front of the fort).*

ALCAZABA

This fort—the original "red castle" ("Alhambra")—is the oldest and most ruined part of the complex, offering exercise and fine city views. What you see is from the mid-13th century, but there was probably a fort here in Roman times. Once upon a time, this tower defended a medina (town) of 2,000 Muslims liv-

Alcazaba

ing within the Alhambra walls. It's a huge, sprawling complex—wind your way through passages and courtyards, over uneven terrain, to reach the biggest tower at the tip of the complex. Then climb stairs steeply up to the top. From there (looking north), find Plaza Nueva and the San Nicolás viewpoint in the Albayzín. To the south are the Sierra Nevada Mountains. Is anybody skiing today? Notice the tower's four flags: the blue of the European Union, the green and white of Andalucía, the red and yellow of Spain, and the red and green of Granada.

Imagine that day in 1492 when the Christian cross and the flags of Aragon and Castile were raised on this tower, and (according to a probably fanciful legend) the fleeing Moorish king Boabdil (Abu Abdullah, in Arabic) looked back and wept. His mom chewed him out, saying, "You weep like a woman for what you couldn't defend like a man." With this defeat, more than seven centuries of Muslim rule in Spain came to an end. Much later, Napoleon stationed his troops at the Alhambra, contributing substantially to its ruin when he left.

• *If you're going from the Alcazaba to Palacios Nazaríes, backtrack through the Wine Gate, then look for the people lined up along the gardens by Charles V's Palace.*

▲▲▲PALACIOS NAZARÍES

During the 30-minute entry time stamped on your ticket, enter the jewel of the Alhambra: the Moorish royal palace. Once you're in, you can relax—you're no longer under any time constraints. You'll walk through three basic sections: royal offices, ceremonial rooms, and private quarters. Built mostly in the 14th century, this palace offers your best possible look at the refined, elegant Moorish civilization of Al-Andalus (the Arabic word for the Moorish-controlled Iberian Peninsula).

You'll visit rooms decorated from top to bottom with carved wood ceilings, stucco "stalactites," ceramic tiles, molded-plaster walls, and filigree windows.

Open-air courtyards feature fountains with bubbling water, which give the palace a desert-oasis feel. A garden enlivened by lush vegetation and peaceful pools is the Quran's symbol of heaven. The palace is well-preserved, but the trick to fully appreciating it is to imagine it furnished and filled with Moorish life...sultans with hookah pipes lounging on pillows upon Persian carpets, heavy curtains on the windows, and ivory-studded wooden furniture. The whole place was painted with bright colors, many suggested by the Quran—red (blood), blue (heaven), green (oasis), and gold (wealth). Throughout the palace, walls, ceilings, vases, carpets, and tiles were covered with decorative patterns, mostly poems and verses of praise from the Quran written in calligraphy and from local poets. Much of what is known about the Alhambra is known simply from reading the inscriptions that decorate its walls.

As you wander, keep the palace themes in mind: water, a near absence of figural images (they're frowned upon in the Quran), "stalactite" ceilings—and few signs telling you where you are. As tempting as it might be to touch the stucco, don't—it is susceptible to damage from the oils from your hand. Use the map in this chapter to locate the essential stops listed below.

• *Begin by walking through a few administrative rooms (the mexuar) with a stunning Mecca-oriented prayer room (the oratorio, with a niche on the right facing Mecca) and a small courtyard with a round fountain, until you hit the big rectangular courtyard with a fish pond lined by a myrtle-bush hedge.*

❶ **Courtyard of the Myrtles** (Patio de Arrayanes): The standard palace design included a central courtyard like this. Moors loved their patios—with a garden and water, under the sky. In accordance with medieval Moorish mores, women rarely went out, so they stayed in touch with nature in courtyards like the

Courtyard of the Myrtles—named for the two fragrant myrtle hedges that added to the courtyard's charm. Notice the wooden screens (erected by jealous husbands) that allowed the cloistered women to look out without being clearly seen. The upstairs was likely for winter use, and the cooler ground level was probably used in summer.

• *Head left from the entry through gigantic wooden doors into the long narrow antechamber to the throne room, called the...*

❷ **Ship Room** (Sala de la Barca): It's understandable that many think the Ship Room is named for the upside-down-hull shape of its fine cedar ceiling. But the name is actually derived from the Arab word *baraka,* meaning "divine blessing and luck" (which was corrupted to *barca,* the Spanish word for "ship" or "boat"). As you passed through this room, blessings and luck are exactly what you'd need—because in the next room, you'd be face-to-face with the sultan.

• *Oh, it's your turn. Enter the ornate throne room.*

❸ **Grand Hall of the Ambassadors** (Gran Salón de los Embajadores): The palace's largest room functioned as the throne room. It was here that the sultan, seated on a throne opposite the entrance, received foreign emissaries. Ogle the room—a perfect cube—from top to bottom. The star-studded, domed wooden ceiling (made from 8,017 inlaid pieces, like a giant jigsaw puzzle) suggests the complexity of Allah's infinite universe. Wooden "stalactites" form the cornice, running around the entire base of the ceiling. The stucco walls, even without their original paint and gilding, are still glorious. The filigree windows once held stained glass and had heavy drapes to block out the heat. Some precious 16th-century tiles survive in the center of the floor.

A visitor here would have stepped from the glaring Courtyard of the Myrtles into this dim, cool, incense-filled world, to meet the silhouetted sultan. Imagine the alcoves functioning busily as work stations, and the light at sunrise or sunset, rich and warm, filling the room.

Let your eyes trace the finely carved Arabic script. One phrase—"only Allah is victorious"—is repeated 9,000 times throughout the palace. Find the charac-

Courtyard of the Myrtles, Palacios Nazaríes

The Alhambra's Palacios Nazaríes

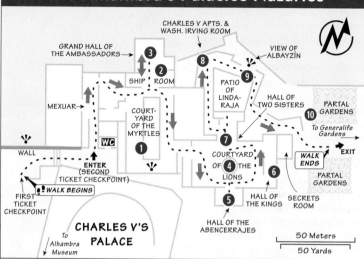

CHARLES V APTS. &
WASH. IRVING ROOM

GRAND HALL OF
THE AMBASSADORS →

VIEW OF
ALBAYZÍN

❸
❽
❷
❾

SHIP ROOM

PATIO
OF
LINDA-
RAJA

HALL OF
TWO SISTERS

PARTAL
GARDENS

MEXUAR →

COURT-
YARD
OF THE
MYRTLES

❿

To Generalife
Gardens →

WC
❶

❼

EXIT

WALL

ENTER
(SECOND
TICKET CHECKPOINT)

COURTYARD
OF ❹ THE
LIONS

❻

WALK
ENDS

FIRST
TICKET
CHECKPOINT

WALK BEGINS

❺

HALL OF
THE KINGS

SECRETS
ROOM

PARTAL
GARDENS

CHARLES V'S
PALACE

To
Alhambra
Museum

HALL OF THE
ABENCERRAJES

50 Meters

50 Yards

❶ Courtyard of the Myrtles
❷ Ship Room
❸ Grand Hall of the Ambassadors
❹ Courtyard of the Lions
❺ Hall of the Abencerrajes

❻ Hall of the Kings
❼ Hall of Two Sisters
❽ Washington Irving Room
❾ Hallway with a View
❿ Partal Gardens

---

ter for "Allah"—it looks like a cursive W with a nose on its left side. The swoopy toboggan blades underneath are a kind of artistic punctuation used to set off one phrase.

In 1492, two historic events likely took place in this room. Culminating a 700-year-long battle, the Reconquista was completed here as the last Moorish king, Boabdil, signed the terms of his surrender before eventually leaving for Africa.

And it was here that Columbus made one of his final pitches to Isabel and Ferdinand to finance a sea voyage to the Orient. Imagine the scene: The king, the queen, and the greatest minds from the University of Salamanca gathered here while Columbus produced maps and pie charts to make his case that he could sail west to reach the East. Ferdinand and the

professors laughed and called Columbus mad—not because they thought the world was flat (most educated people knew otherwise), but because they thought Columbus had underestimated the size of the globe, and thus the length and cost of the journey.

But Isabel said, *"Sí, señor."* Columbus fell to his knees (promising to pack light, wear a money belt, and use the most current guidebook available).

Opposite the Ship Room entrance, photographers pause for a picture-perfect view of the tower reflected in the Courtyard of the Myrtles pool. This was the original palace entrance before Charles V's Palace was built.

• *Continue deeper into the palace, to a courtyard where, 600 years ago, only the royal family and their servants could enter. It's the much-photographed...*

❹ Courtyard of the Lions (Patio de los Leones): This delightful courtyard is named for the famous fountain at its center with its ring of 12 marble lions—originals from the 14th century. Conquering Christians disassembled the fountain to see how it worked, rendering it nonfunctional; it finally flowed again in 2012. From the center of the courtyard, four channels carry water outward—figuratively to the corners of the earth and literally to various more private apartments of the royal family. The arched gallery that surrounds the courtyard is supported by 124 perfectly balanced columns. The craftsmanship is first-class. For example, the lead fittings between the precut sections of the columns allow things to flex during earthquakes, preventing destruction during shakes.

Six hundred years ago, the Muslim Moors could read the Quranic poetry that ornaments this court, and they could understand the symbolism of this lush, enclosed garden, considered the embodiment of paradise or truth. ("How beautiful is this garden/ where the flowers of Earth rival the stars of Heaven./ What can compare with this alabaster fountain, gushing crystal-clear water?/ Nothing except the fullest moon, pouring light from an unclouded sky.") They appreciated this part of the palace even more than we do today.

• On the right, off the courtyard, the only original door still in the palace leads into a square room called the...

❺ Hall of the Abencerrajes (Sala de los Abencerrajes): This was the sultan's living room, with an exquisite ceiling based on the eight-sided Muslim star. The name of the room comes from a legend of the 16th century. The father of Boabdil took a new wife and wanted to disinherit the children of his first marriage—one of whom was Boabdil. In order to deny power to Boabdil and his siblings, the sultan killed nearly all of the pre-Boabdil Abencerraje family members. He thought this would

Islamic Art

Rather than making paintings and statues, Islamic artists expressed themselves with beautiful but functional objects. Ceramics (most of them blue and white, or green and white), carpets, glazed tile panels, stucco-work ceilings, and glass tableware are covered with complex patterns. The intricate interweaving, repetition, and unending lines suggest the complex, infinite nature of God, known to Muslims as Allah.

You'll see few pictures of humans, since Islamic doctrine holds that the creation of living beings is God's work alone. However, secular art by Muslims for their homes and palaces was not bound by this restriction; you'll get an occasional glimpse of realistic art featuring men and women enjoying a garden paradise, a symbol of the Muslim heaven.

Look for floral patterns (twining vines, flowers, and arabesques) and geometric designs (stars and diamonds). The decorative motifs (Arabic script, patterns, flowers, shells, and so on) that repeat countless times throughout the palace were made by pressing wet plaster into molds. The most common pattern is calligraphy—elaborate lettering of an inscription in Arabic, the language of the Quran. A quote from the Quran on a vase or lamp combines the power of the message with the beauty of the calligraphy.

pave the way for the son of his new wife to be the next sultan. He is said to have stacked 36 Abencerraje heads in the pool, under the sumptuous honeycombed stucco ceiling in this hall. But his scheme failed, and Boabdil ultimately assumed the throne. Bloody power struggles like this were the norm here in the Alhambra.

A *Courtyard of the Myrtles*

B *Courtyard of the Lions*

C *Alhambra tilework*

D *Grand Hall of the Ambassadors*

E *Washington Irving Room*

Hall of Two Sisters

• At the end of the court opposite where you entered is the...

❻ Hall of the Kings (Sala de los Reyes): This hall has been undergoing restoration for several years and will likely be closed during your visit. When it opens, you'll see paintings on the goat-leather ceiling depicting scenes of the sultan and his family. The center room's group portrait shows the first 10 of the Alhambra's 22 sultans. The scene is a fantasy, since these people lived over a span of many generations. The two end rooms display scenes of princely pastimes, such as hunting and shooting skeet. In a palace otherwise devoid of figures, these offer a rare look at royal life in the palace.

• Continue around the fountain. As you exit, you'll pass doors leading right and left to a 14th-century WC plumbed by running water and stairs up to the harem. Next is the...

❼ Hall of Two Sisters (Sala de Dos Hermanas): The Sala de Dos Hermanas—nicknamed for the giant twin slabs of white marble on the floor flanking the fountain—has another oh-wow stucco ceiling lit by clerestory windows. This is a typical royal bedroom, with alcoves for private use and a fountain. Running water helped cool and humidify the room but also added elegance and extravagance, as running water was a luxury most could only dream of.

The room features geometric patterns and stylized Arabic script quoting verses from the Quran. If the inlaid color tiles look "Escher-esque," you've got it backward: Escher is Alhambra-esque. M. C. Escher was inspired by these very patterns on his visit. The sitting room (farthest from the entry) has low windows, because Moorish people sat on the floor. Some rare stained glass survives in the ceiling. From here the sultana enjoyed a grand view of the medieval city (before the 16th-century wing was added, which blocks the view today).

• That's about it for the palace. From here, we enter the later, 16th-century Christian

section, and wander past the domed roofs of the old baths down a hallway to a pair of rooms decorated with mahogany ceilings. Marked with a large plaque is the...

❽ Washington Irving Room: While living in Spain in 1829, Washington Irving stayed in the Alhambra, and he wrote *Tales of the Alhambra* in this room. It was a romantic time, when the palace was home to Gypsies and donkeys. His "tales" rekindled interest in the Alhambra, causing it to be recognized as a national treasure. A plaque on the wall thanks Irving, who later served as the US ambassador to Spain (1842-1846). Here's a quote from Irving's *The Alhambra by Moonlight*: "On such heavenly nights I would sit for hours at my window inhaling the sweetness of the garden, and musing on the checkered fortunes of those whose history was dimly shadowed out in the elegant memorials around."

• As you leave, stop at the open-air...

❾ Hallway with a View: Here you'll enjoy the best-in-the-palace view of the labyrinthine Albayzín—the old Moorish town on the opposite hillside. Find the famous San Nicolás viewpoint (below where the white San Nicolás church tower breaks the horizon). Creeping into the mountains on the right are the Gypsy neighborhoods of Sacromonte. Still circling old Granada is the Moorish wall (built in the 1400s to protect the city's population, swollen by Muslim refugees driven south by the Reconquista).

The Patio de Lindaraja (with its maze-like hedge pattern garden) marks the end of the palace visit. Before exiting, you can detour right into the adjacent "Secrets Room"—stark brick rooms of the former bath with fun acoustics. Whisper into a corner, and your friend—with an ear to the wall—can hear you in the opposite corner. Try talking in the exact center.

• Step outside into our last stop...

❿ The Partal Gardens (El Partal): The Partal Gardens are built upon the ruins of the Partal Palace. Imagine a palace like the one you just toured, built around this reflecting pond. A fragment of it still stands—once the living quarters—on the cooler north side. The Alhambra was the site of seven different palaces in 150 years. You have toured parts of just two or three.

• *Leaving the palace, climb a few stairs, continue through the gardens, and follow signs directing you left to the Generalife Gardens or right to the Alcazaba (and the rest of the Alhambra grounds).*

The path to the Generalife Gardens is a delightful 15-minute stroll through lesser (but still pleasant) gardens, along a row of fortified towers—just follow signs for Generalife. Just before reaching the Generalife, you'll cross over a bridge and look down on the dusty lane called Cuesta de los Chinos (a handy shortcut for returning to downtown later).

▲▲GENERALIFE GARDENS

The sultan's vegetable and fruit orchards and summer palace retreat, called the Generalife (heh-neh-raw-LEE-fay), was outside the protection of the Alhambra wall—and, today, a short hike uphill past the ticket office. The thousand or so residents of the Alhambra enjoyed the fresh fruit and veggies grown here. But most important, this little palace provided the sultan with a cool and quiet summer escape.

Follow the simple one-way path through the sprawling gardens. You'll catch glimpses of a sleek, modern outdoor theater, built in the 1950s, and still very much in use today.

From the head of the theater, signs will lead you through manicured-hedge gardens, along delightful ponds and fountains, to the palace.

At the small palace, pass through the dismounting room (imagine dismounting onto the helpful stone ledge, and letting your horse drink from the trough here). Show your ticket and enter the most accurately re-created Arabian garden in Andalucía.

Here in the retreat of the Moorish kings, this garden is the closest thing on earth to the Quran's description of heaven. It was planted more than 600 years ago—that's remarkable longev-

The Generalife

The Alhambra Grounds

As you wander the grounds, remember that the Alhambra was once a city of a thousand people fortified by a 1.5-mile rampart and 30 towers. The zone within the walls was the **medina,** an urban town. As you stroll from the ticket booth down the garden-like road to the palace, you're walking through the ruins of the medina (destroyed by the French in 1812). In the distance are the snowcapped Sierra Nevada peaks—the highest mountains in Iberia. Unlike the Alhambra sights that charge admission, the medina—with Charles V's Palace, a church, a line of woodworking shops, and the fancy parador—is wide open to anyone.

It's fun to snoop around the historic **Parador de Granada San Francisco,** which—as a national monument—is open to the public. Formerly a Moorish palace, then a Franciscan monastery, its church was where the Catholic Monarchs (Ferdinand and Isabel) were originally buried. For a peek, step through the arch leading to a small garden and reception. Enter to see the burial place, located in the open-air ruins of the church (just before the reception desk and the "guests-only-beyond-this-point" sign; the history is described in English). The slab on the ground near the altar marks where the king and queen rested until 1521 (when they were moved to the Royal Chapel downtown). The next room is a delightful former cloister. Now a hotel, the parador has a restaurant and terrace café—with lush views of the Generalife—open to nonguests.

The medina's main road dead-ended at the **Wine Gate** (Puerta del Vino), which protected the fortress. When you pass through the Wine Gate, you enter a courtyard that was originally a moat, then a reservoir (in Christian times). The well—now encased in a bar-kiosk—is still a place for cold drinks. If you're done with your Alhambra visit, you can exit down to the city from the Wine Gate via the Justice Gate, immediately below.

ity for a European garden. While there were originally only eight water jets, most of the details in today's garden closely match those lovingly described in old poems. The flowers, herbs, aromas, and water are exquisite...even for a sultan.

Up the Darro River, the royal aqueduct diverted a life-giving stream of water into the Alhambra. It was channeled through this long decorative fountain to irrigate the bigger garden outside, then along an aqueduct into the Alhambra for its thirsty residents. The splashing fountains are a 19th-century addition. The Moors liked a peaceful pond instead.

At the end of the pond, you enter the sultan's tiny three-room summer

retreat. From the last room, climb 10 steps into the upper Renaissance gardens (c. 1600). The ancient tree rising over the pond inspired Washington Irving, who wrote that this must be the "only surviving witness to the wonders of that age of Al-Andalus."

Climbing up and going through the turnstile, you enter the Romantic 19th-century garden. When you're ready to leave, head to the right and follow *salida* signs toward the gardens' exit (next to the Alhambra's main entrance).

Your visit to the Alhambra is complete, and you've earned your reward. "Surely Allah will make those who believe and do good deeds enter gardens beneath which

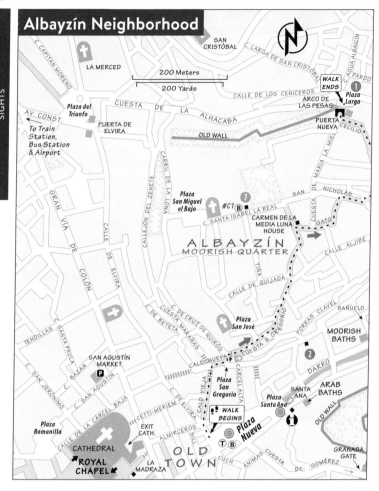

Albayzín Neighborhood

rivers flow; they shall be adorned therein with bracelets of gold and pearls, and their garments therein shall be of silk" (Quran 22.23).

Rick's Tip: *Return to town along the **Cuesta de los Chinos** footpath. It starts not far from the main entrance of the Alhambra, by Restaurante La Mimbre and the mini-bus stop—a sign just past the restaurant entrance will confirm you're on the right path. Walk downhill on a peaceful lane scented with lavender and rock rose for 10-15 minutes and you're back in town at*

Paseo de los Tristes. From here, you can stroll to Plaza Nueva or head up to the Albayzín district.

▲The Albayzín

This is Spain's best old Moorish quarter, with countless colorful corners, flowery patios, and shady lanes. Even the people of Granada recognize this hilltop neighborhood as a world apart.

Each of the district's 20 churches sits on a spot once occupied by a mosque. When the Reconquista arrived in

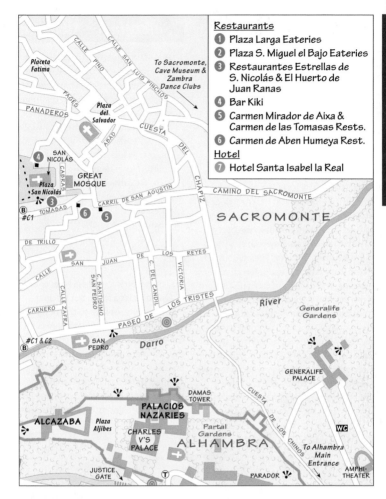

Restaurants
1 Plaza Larga Eateries
2 Plaza S. Miguel el Bajo Eateries
3 Restaurantes Estrellas de
   S. Nicolás & El Huerto de
   Juan Ranas
4 Bar Kiki
5 Carmen Mirador de Aixa &
   Carmen de las Tomasas Rests.
6 Carmen de Aben Humeya Rest.
Hotel
7 Hotel Santa Isabel la Real

Granada, the Christians attempted to coexist with the Muslims. But this idealistic attempt ended in failure. By 1567, tens of thousands of Muslims were expelled and many more suffered forced conversion, leading to 200 years of economic depression for the city. Eventually, large walled noble manor houses with private gardens were built here in the depopulated Albayzín. These survive today in the form of the characteristic *carmen* restaurants so popular with visitors.

Five centuries later, there are about 1 million Muslims in Spain. From their perspective, it's important for visitors to know that Muslims are as indigenous as any other cultural group in Spain. After living here for seven centuries, the Muslims of Granada and Andalucía are as Iberian as any other modern Spaniard.

You can't say you've really seen Granada until you've strolled at least a few of its twisty lanes. Climb high to the San Nicolás church for the best view of the Alhambra. Then wander through its mysterious back streets. For recommended eateries—good for lunch or dinner—see page 308.

Getting to the San Nicolás Viewpoint: Ride the minibus, hike up, or take a taxi.

By Minibus: The handy Albayzín minibus #C1 makes a 20-minute loop through the quarter, getting you scenically and sweat-free to the viewpoint (departs about every 10 minutes from Plaza Nueva). While good for a lift to the top of the Albayzín (buzz when you want to get off), I'd stay on for an entire circle for an orientation, and return to the Albayzín later for dinner—either on foot or by bus again. (Note: The less frequent minibus #C2, departing every 20 minutes, does a similar but longer route, with a side-trip up into Sacromonte—but it does not go past the San Nicolás viewpoint.)

Here's the #C1 route: The minibus leaves Plaza Nueva, heads along the Paseo de los Tristes, and turns up (left) to climb into the thick of the Albayzín, with stops below the San Nicolás church (with the famous viewpoint; the driver generally calls out this stop for tourists) and at Plaza San Miguel el Bajo (cute square with recommended eateries and another viewpoint). From here, you ride back down through residential neighborhoods before turning down the city's main drag, Gran

Safety in the Albayzín

While this charming Moorish district is certainly safe by day, it can be edgy after dark. Pickpocketing is common. Most of the area is fine to wander, though many streets are poorly lit, and the maze of lanes can make it easy to get lost. Don't avoid the Albayzín, or you'll miss out on its restaurants, ideal sunset views, and charming ambience. Just exercise normal precautions: Leave your valuables at your hotel, stick to better-lit streets, and take a minibus or taxi home if you're unsure of your route.

Vía, and returning to Plaza Nueva.

On Foot: It's a steep but fascinating 20-minute walk up to the viewpoint. Leave the west end of Plaza Nueva on Calle de Elvira. After about 50 yards, at the pharmacy and newsstand, bear right on Calle Calderería Vieja. Follow this stepped street past Moroccan eateries and pastry shops, vendors of imported North African goods, halal butchers, and

The Albayzín

teterías (Moorish tea rooms—have a look). The lane bears right, then passes to the left of the church (becoming Cuesta de San Gregorio), and slants, winds, and zigzags uphill. Cuesta de San Gregorio eventually curves left and is regularly signposted. When you reach the Moorish-style house, La Media Luna (with the tall trees and keyhole-style doorway), stop for a photo and a breather, then follow the wall, continuing uphill. At the next intersection (with the black cats), turn right on Aljibe del Gato. Farther on, this street takes a 90-degree turn to the right; at this point, turn left onto Calle Atarasana Vieja. It's not well signposted, but keep going up, up, up. At the crest (and the dead end), turn right on Camino Nuevo de San Nicolás, then walk 200 yards to the street that curves up left (look for a bus-stop sign—this is where the minibus would have dropped you off). Continue up the curve, and soon you'll see feet hanging from the plaza wall. Steps lead up to the viewpoint. Whew! You made it!

▲▲SAN NICOLÁS VIEWPOINT (MIRADOR DE SAN NICOLÁS)

For one of Europe's most romantic viewpoints, be here at sunset, when the Alhambra glows red and Albayzín widows share the benches with local lovers, hippies, and tourists. In 1997, President Clinton made a point to bring his family here—a favorite spot from a trip he made as a student. But this was hardly an original idea; generations of visitors have been drawn here. For an affordable drink with the same million-euro view, step into the **El Huerto de Juan Ranas Bar** (just below and to the left, at Calle de Atarazana 8). Enjoy the Roma (Gypsy) musicians who perform here for tips. Order a drink, tip them, settle in, and consider it a concert.

GREAT MOSQUE OF GRANADA

This striking mosque is just next to the San Nicolás viewpoint (to your left as you face the Alhambra). Built in 2003, it has a peaceful view courtyard and a minaret that comes with a live call to prayer five times a day. Visitors are welcome in the courtyard, which offers Alhambra views

San Nicolás viewpoint

without the hedonistic ambience of the more famous San Nicolás viewpoint (free, daily 11:00-14:00 & 18:00-21:00, shorter hours in winter, tel. 958-202-526, www.mezquitadegranada.com).

Royal Chapel and Cathedral

▲▲ROYAL CHAPEL (CAPILLA REAL)

Without a doubt Granada's top Christian sight, this lavish chapel in the old town holds the dreams—and bodies—of Queen Isabel and King Ferdinand. The "Catholic Monarchs" were all about the Reconquista. Their marriage united the Aragon and Castile kingdoms, allowing an acceleration of the Christian and Spanish push south. In its last 10 years, the Reconquista snowballed. This last Moorish capital—symbolic of their victory—was their chosen burial place. While smaller and less architecturally striking than the cathedral (described later), the chapel is far more historically significant.

Cost and Hours: €4, March-Sept daily 10:15-13:30 & 16:00-19:30 except opens at 11:00 on Sun, Oct-Feb closes daily at 18:30, no photos, entrance on Calle Oficios, just off Gran Vía del Colón—go through iron gate, tel. 958-227-848, www.capillarealgranada.com.

SELF-GUIDED TOUR

In the lobby, before you show your ticket and enter the chapel, notice the **painting of Boabdil** (on the black horse) giving the key of Granada to the conquering King Ferdinand. Boabdil wanted to fall to his knees, but the Spanish king, who had great respect for his Moorish foe, embraced him instead. They had fought a long and noble war (for instance, respectfully returning the bodies of dead soldiers). Ferdinand is in red, and Isabel is behind him wearing a crown. The painting is flanked high on the wall by portraits of Ferdinand and Isabel. Two small exhibits celebrate the 500th anniversaries of the death of Isabel in 2004 (with eight portraits) and of Philip the Fair (her son-in-law, a playboy who earned his nickname for his seductively good looks).

Isabel decided to make Granada the capital of Spain (and burial place for Spanish royalty) for three reasons: 1) With the conquest of this city, Christianity had finally overcome Islam in Europe; 2) her marriage with Ferdinand, fol-

Royal Chapel and Cathedral

lowed by the conquest of Granada, had marked the beginning of a united Spain; and 3) in Granada, she agreed to sponsor Columbus.

Show your ticket and step into the **chapel.** It's Plateresque Gothic—light and lacy silver-filigree style, inspired by the fine silverwork of the Moors. The chapel's interior was originally austere, with fancy touches added later by Ferdinand and Isabel's grandson, Emperor Charles V. Five hundred years ago, this must have been the most splendid space imaginable. Because of its speedy completion (1506-1521), the Gothic architecture is unusually harmonious.

Charles V thought it wasn't dazzling enough to honor his grandparents' importance, so he funded decorative touches like the iron screen and the Rogier van der Weyden painting *The Deposition* (to the left after passing through the screen; this is a copy—the original is at the Prado in Madrid). Immediately to the right, with the hardest-working altar boys in Christendom holding up gilded Corinthian columns, is a chapel with a locked-away relic (an arm) of John the Baptist.

In the center of the chapel (in front of the main altar), the **four royal tombs** are Renaissance-style. Carved in Italy in 1521 from Carrara marble, they were sent by ship to Spain. The faces—based on death masks—are considered accurate. **Ferdinand** and **Isabel** are the lower, more humble of the two couples. (Isabel fans

attribute the bigger dent she puts in the pillow to her larger brain.) Isabel's contemporaries described the queen as being of medium height, with auburn hair and blue eyes, and possessing a serious, modest, and gentle personality. (Compare Ferdinand and Isabel's tomb statues with the painted and gilded wood statues of them kneeling in prayer, flanking the altarpiece.)

Philip the Fair and **Juana the Mad** (who succeeded Ferdinand and Isabel) lie on the left. Philip was so "Fair" that it drove the insanely jealous Juana "Mad." Philip died young, and Juana, crazy like a fox, used her "grief" over his death to forestall a second marriage, thereby ensuring that their son Charles would inherit the throne. Charles was a key figure in European history, as his coronation merged the Holy Roman Empire (Philip the Fair's Habsburg domain) with Juana's Spanish empire. Charles V ruled a vast empire stretching from Holland to Sicily, from Bohemia to Bolivia (1519-1556). But today's Spaniards reflect that the momentous marriage that created their country also sucked them into centuries of European squabbling, eventually leaving Spain impoverished.

Granada lost power and importance when Philip II, the son of Charles V, built his El Escorial palace outside Madrid, establishing that city as the single capital of a single Spain. This coincided with the beginning of Spain's decline, as the country squandered her vast wealth trying

Painting of Boabdil

Royal tombs

to maintain an impossibly huge empire. Spain's rulers were defending the romantic, quixotic dream of a Catholic empire—ruled by one divinely ordained Catholic monarch—against an irrepressible tide of nationalism and Protestantism that was sweeping across the vast Habsburg holdings in Central and Eastern Europe. Spain's relatively poor modern history can be blamed, in part, on its people's stubborn unwillingness to accept the end of this old-regime notion. Even Franco borrowed symbols from the Catholic Monarchs to legitimize his dictatorship and keep the 500-year-old legacy alive.

Look at the intricate carving on the Renaissance tombs. It's a humanistic statement, with these healthy, organic, realistic figures rising out of the Gothic age.

From the feet of the marble tombs, step downstairs to see the actual **coffins.** They are plain. Ferdinand and Isabel were originally buried in the Franciscan monastery (in what is today the parador, up at the Alhambra). You're standing in front of the two people who created Spain. The fifth coffin (on right, marked *Príncipe Miguel*) belongs to a young Prince Michael, who would have been king of a united Spain and Portugal. (A sad—but too long—story...)

The **high altar** is one of the finest Renaissance works in Spain. It's dedicated to two Johns: the Baptist and the Evangelist. In the center you can see the Baptist and the Evangelist chatting as if over tapas—an appropriately humanistic scene. Scenes from the Baptist's life are on the left: John beheaded after Salomé's fine dancing, and (below) John baptizing Jesus. Scenes from the Evangelist's life are on the right: John's martyrdom (a failed attempt to boil him alive in oil), and (below) John on Patmos (where he may have written the last book of the Bible, *Revelation*). John is talking to the eagle that, according to tradition, flew him to heaven. A colorful series of reliefs

at the bottom level recalls the Christian conquest of the Moors (left to right): Ferdinand, Boabdil with army and key to Alhambra, Moors expelled from Alhambra (right of altar table), conversion of Muslims by monks, and Ferdinand again.

A finely carved Plateresque arch, with the gilded royal initials *F* and *Y,* leads to a small glass pyramid in the **treasury.** This holds Queen Isabel's silver crown ringed with pomegranates (symbolizing Granada), her scepter, and King Ferdinand's sword. Do a counterclockwise spin around the room to see it all, starting to the right of the entry arch. There you'll see the devout Isabel's prayer book, in which she followed the Mass. The book and its sturdy box date from 1496. According to legend, the fancy box on the other side of the door is supposedly the one that Isabel filled with jewels and gave to bankers as collateral for the cash to pay Columbus. In the corner (and also behind glass) is the ornate silver-and-gold cross that Cardinal Mendoza, staunch supporter of Queen Isabel, carried into the Alhambra on that historic day in 1492—and used as the centerpiece for the first Christian Mass in the conquered fortress. Next, the big silver-and-gold silk tapestry is the altar banner for the mobile campaign chapel of Ferdinand and Isabel, who always traveled with their army. In the case to its left, you'll see the original Christian army flags raised over the Alhambra in 1492.

The next zone of this grand hall holds the first great art collection ever established by a woman. Queen Isabel amassed more than 200 important paintings. After Napoleon's visit, only 31 remained. Even so, this is an exquisite collection, all on wood, featuring works by Sandro Botticelli, Pietro Perugino, the Flemish master Hans Memling, and some less-famous Spanish masters.

Finally, at the end of the room, the two carved sculptures of Ferdinand and Isabel were the originals from the high altar. Charles V considered these primitive (I disagree) and replaced them with the ones you saw earlier.

To reach the cathedral (described next), exit the treasury behind Isabel, and walk around the block to the right.

▲CATHEDRAL

One of only two Renaissance churches in Spain (the other is in Córdoba), Granada's cathedral is the second-largest church in Spain (after Sevilla's). While it was started as a Gothic church, it was built using Renaissance elements, and then decorated in Baroque style.

Cost and Hours: €4, Mon-Fri 10:15-18:45, Sat-Sun 16:00-18:45, audioguide-€3, tel. 958-222-959, www.catedraldegranada.com.

🡒 **Self-Guided Tour:** Enter the church from Plaza de las Pasiegas. Stand in the back of the nave for an overview.

Survey the church. It's huge. It was designed to be the national church when Granada was the capital of a newly reconquered-from-the-Muslims Spain.

High above the main altar are square niches originally intended for the burial of Charles V and his family. But King Philip II changed focus and abandoned Granada for El Escorial, so the niches are now plugged with paintings, including seven from the life of Mary by hometown great Alonso Cano (1601-1667).

The cathedral's cool, spacious interior is mostly Baroque—a refreshing break from the dark Gothic of so many Spanish churches. In a move that was modern back in the 18th century, the walls of the choir (the big, heavy wooden box that dominates the center of most Spanish churches) were taken out so that people could be involved in the worship. (Back when a choir clogged the middle of the church, regular people only heard the Mass.) At about the same time, a bishop ordered the interior painted with lime for hygienic reasons during a time of disease. People liked it white, and kept it that way.

Notice that the two rear chapels (on

Granada's cathedral

right and left) are Neoclassical in style—a reminder that the church took 300 years to finish.

As you explore, remember that the abundance of Marys is all part of the Counter-Reformation. Most of the side chapels are decorated in Baroque style.

Now, walk to the front for a closer look at the altar. You'll pass two fine organs with horizontal trumpet pipes, unique to Spain.

Standing before the altar, notice the abundance of gold leaf. It's from the local Darro River, which originally attracted Romans here for its gold. As this is a seat of the local bishop, there's a fine wooden bishop's throne on the right.

Between the slender Corinthian columns flanking the altar are paintings with a strong parenting theme: In the round frames are Adam and Eve, from whom came mankind. Around them are the four evangelists, who—with the New Testament—brought the Good News of salvation to believers. Completing the big parenting picture are Ferdinand and Isabel, who brought Catholicism to the land.

Their complex coat of arms celebrates how their marriage united two influential kingdoms to create imperial Spain.

To your right is the ornate carved stone Gothic door to the Royal Chapel, with a 15th-century facade that predates the cathedral. The chapel holds the most important historic relics in town—the tombs of the Catholic Monarchs. And, because the chapel and cathedral are run by two different religious orders, this door is always closed and there are separate admission fees for each. Immediately to the left of the door is a politically incorrect version of St. James the Moor-Slayer, with his sword raised high and an armored Moor trampled under his horse's hooves.

Strolling behind the altar, look for the giant music sheets: They're mostly 16th-century Gregorian chants. Notice the sliding C clef. Rather than a fixed G or F clef, the monks knew that this clef—which could be located wherever it worked best on the staff—marked middle C, and they chanted to notes relative to that. Go ahead—try singing a few verses of the Latin.

The cathedral's Baroque interior

The cathedral's little museum is tucked away back near the entrance, filling the ground floor of the big bell tower. Its highlight is a beautiful bust of San Pablo (Paul, with a flowing beard)—a self-portrait by Cano.

The sacristy (near the exit and the St. James altarpiece, in the right corner) is worth a look. It's lush and wide open; its gilded ceilings, mirrors, and wooden cabinets give it a light, airy feel. Two grandfather clocks made in London (one with Asian motifs) ensured that everyone got dressed on time. Enjoy Cano's small, delicate painted wood statue of the *Immaculate Conception*.

Exit the cathedral through its small shop (with a nicely curated selection of religious and secular souvenirs). If you walk straight out, you'll come directly to Gran Vía and the stop for minibus #C1 for the Albayzín (to walk to the Albayzín, head left up Gran Vía for two blocks, then turn right on Calle Cárcel Baja, just after the bank with the ServiCaixa machine). But first, for a fun detour, make a quick left into the little lane immediately upon exiting the cathedral—you'll be just steps from Medievo, a fine purveyor of bulk spices and teas.

EXPERIENCES

Arab Baths

For an intimate and subdued experience, consider some serious relaxation at **Hammam al Andalus,** near Plaza Nueva. At these Arab baths, you can enjoy three different-temperature pools and a steam room. A maximum of 35 people are allowed in the baths at one time. You'll need to reserve and pay in advance.

Cost and Hours: If you just want a 90-minute soak in the baths, the cost is €24; it costs more to add a 15-minute massage: a regular massage is €36, a traditional scrubbing massage is €43, and to have both costs €55. Open daily 10:00-24:00, appointments scheduled every even-numbered hour, coed with mandatory swimsuits, quiet atmosphere encouraged, free lockers and towels available, no loaner swimsuits but you can buy one for €12, just off Plaza Nueva—follow signs a few doors down from the TI to Santa Ana 16, paid reservation required (refunded if cancelled within 48 hours of appointment), tel. 958-229-978, http://granada.hammamalandalus.com.

Zambra Dance

A long flamenco tradition exists in Granada, and the Roma (Gypsies) of Sacromonte are credited with developing this city's unique style of this Andalusian art form. Sacromonte is a good place to see *zambra,* a flamenco variation in which the singer also dances. A half-dozen cave-bars offering *zambra* in the evenings line Sacromonte's main drag. Hotels are happy to book you a seat and arrange the included transfer. Two well-established venues are **Zambra Cueva de la Rocío** (€30, includes a drink and bus ride from and back to hotel, €25 without transport, daily show at 22:00, 1 hour, Camino del Sacromonte 70, tel. 958-227-129, www.cuevalarocio.com) and **María la Canastera,** an intimate venue where the Duke of Windsor came to watch *zambra* (€28, includes drink and bus ride, €22 without transport, daily show at 22:00, 1 hour, Camino del Sacromonte 89, tel. 958-121-183, www.granadainfo.com/canastera). The biggest operation here is the restaurant **Venta El Gallo,** which has performances of more straightforward flamenco—not specifically *zambra* (€30 with bus ride, €25 without transport, daily shows at 21:00 and 22:30, dinner possible beforehand on outdoor terrace, Barranco los Negros 5, tel. 958-228-476, www.ventaelgallo.com).

If you don't want to venture to Sacromonte, try **Casa del Arte Flamenco,** which performs one-hour shows just off Plaza Nueva (€18, at 19:30 and 21:00, Cuesta de Gomérez 11, tel. 958-565-767, www.casadelarteflamenco.com).

Festivals and Concerts

From late June to early July, the **International Festival of Music and Dance** offers classical music, ballet, flamenco, and zarzuela (light opera) nightly in the Alhambra and other historic venues at reasonable prices. This festival is one of the most respected and popular in Spain, and tickets for major performers typically sell out months in advance. The ticket office is located in the Corral del Carbón (open mid-April–Oct); beginning in February, you can also book tickets online at www.granadafestival.org. During the festival, flamenco is free every night at midnight; ask the ticket office or TI for the venue.

From fall through spring, the **City of Granada Orchestra** offers popular concerts—mostly on weekends—that generally sell out quickly (€6-23, late Sept–mid-May only, ticket office in Corral del Carbón, Mon-Fri 12:00–14:00 & 17:00–19:00, Sat 12:00–14:00, closed Sun, Auditorio Manuel de Falla, tel. 958-221-144, www.orquestaciudadgranada.es).

EATING

Along with the usual restaurants and tapas bar, Granada adds some spice: elegant *carmens* and hippie-style tea shops.

In search of an edible memory? A local specialty, *tortilla de Sacromonte,* is a spicy omelet with lamb's brain and other organs. *Berenjenas fritas* (fried eggplant) and *habas con jamón* (small green fava beans cooked with cured ham) are worth seeking out. *Tinto de verano*—a red-wine spritzer with lemon and ice—is refreshing on a hot evening.

Carmens: For a memorable splurge, consider fine dining with Alhambra views in a *carmen,* a typical Albayzín house with a garden. I recommend several: Carmen Mirador de Aixa, Carmen de las Tomasas, and Carmen de Aben Humeya.

Teterías: The trendy, laid-back tea shops are good places to linger, chat, and imagine you're in Morocco. They're open all day but are most interesting at tea time—17:00–19:30. Many offer the opportunity to rent a hookah (water pipe) to smoke fruit-flavored tobacco with friends. Some *teterías* are romantic, filled with

Zambra *dance*

Granada's Restaurants & Hotels

Restaurants

1. Bodegas Castañeda
2. Restaurante Carmela
3. La Cueva de 1900
4. Arrayanes Restaurante
5. Los Diamantes
6. Greens and Berries
7. Calle Calderería Nueva Tea Shops
8. Calle Navas Tapas Bars
9. Taberna La Tana & Bar Los Diamantes II
10. Café Futbol
11. Los Italianos Ice Cream
12. Mercado San Agustín
13. Pescadería Market Stalls

Hotels

14. Hotel Casa 1800 Granada
15. Hotel Maciá Plaza
16. Casa del Capitel Nazarí
17. Hotel Anacapri
18. Hotel Inglaterra
19. Hotel Puerta de las Granadas
20. Pensión Landazuri
21. Pensión Al Fin
22. Hotel Los Tilos
23. To Hotel Reina Cristina, Hostales Lima & Rodri; Pensión Zurita

incense, beaded cushions, African music, and effervescent youth. They sell light meals such as crêpes, and a worldwide range of teas. *Teterías* line Calle Calderería Nueva (from Plaza Nueva, walk two long blocks down Calle de Elvira and turn right onto the hip, Arabic-feeling Calle Calderería Nueva, leading uphill into the Albayzín).

Tapas Bars: Granada's **bars** pride themselves on serving a small tapas plate free with any beverage—a tradition that's dying out in most of Spain. If you do a tapas crawl (especially good along Calle Navas, right off Plaza del Carmen), order your drink and wait for the free tapa before ordering food. (If you order food with your drink, you likely won't get the freebie.)

Sweets: Café Fútbol is the best place for *chocolate con churros,* with a great scene on a lazy square (Plaza Mariana Pineda 6), though **Café Alhambra** is also good (on Plaza de Bib-Rambla). **Los Italianos** is popular for its ice cream, *horchata* (chufa-nut drink), and shakes (across the street from cathedral and Royal Chapel).

Picnics: The biggest supermarket is the basement of **El Corte Inglés** (Mon-Sat 10:00-21:30, closed Sun, Acera del Darro). The most central public market is **Mercado San Agustín,** with a cheap little eatery (Cafetería San Agustín) in the back that gives a small tapa free with each drink (Mon-Sat 9:00-15:00, closed Sun, a block north of cathedral and a half-block off Gran Vía on Calle Cristo San Agustín). The stalls around the market and at the **Pescadería** square (downhill from the market and a block from Plaza de Bib-Rambla) sell produce and more. Schlep your picnic supplies up into the Albayzín—this makes for a great cheap date at the San Nicolás viewpoint.

In the Albayzín

Many interesting meals hide out deep in the Albayzín. To find a particular square, ask any local, or follow my directions (see page 296). If dining late, take the minibus or a taxi back to your hotel; Albayzín back streets can be poorly lit and confusing to follow. Part of the charm of the quarter is the lazy ambience on its squares. My two favorites are Plaza Larga and Plaza San Miguel el Bajo.

Plaza Larga is extremely characteristic, with tapas bar tables spilling out onto the square, a morning market, and a much-loved pastry shop, **Casa Pasteles.**

Plaza San Miguel el Bajo boasts my favorite funky local scene—kids kicking soccer balls, old-timers warming benches, and women gossiping under the facade of a humble church. It's circled by half a dozen inviting little bars and restaurants—each competitive with cheap lunch deals, more expensive à la carte and evening meals, and good seating right on the square. Drop by for lunch or dinner and spend a few minutes surveying your options: **El Acebuche,** run with pride by friendly María, promises "Andalusian flavor with a light dash of the Orient" (open daily). **Rincón de la Aurora** feels more comfortable and has tapas (closed Wed and Sun afternoon). **El Ají** is a sit-down restaurant with a mod vibe and an Argentinian flair (closed Tue). And just down the street (beyond El Ají) is a little-hole-in-the-wall **takeaway shop** selling cheap empanadas and pizza by the slice to munch out on the square (closed Tue). Minibus #C1 rumbles by every few minutes, ready to zip you back to Plaza Nueva. And, a block west of the square is a viewpoint overlooking the modern city; it's a five-minute downhill walk to Plaza Nueva from here.

Near the San Nicolás Viewpoint

This area is thoroughly touristy, so don't expect any local hangouts here. The first two (both restaurants) are suitable for a good meal with an Alhambra view you'll never forget.

Restaurante Estrellas de San Nicolás, in the former home of a well-loved

Albayzín bigwig, is immediately next to the view terrace, with two floors of indoor seating. Serving a mix of French and Spanish cuisine, this splurge keeps its mostly tourist clientele happy (€11-22 starters, €20-26 main dishes, €31 fixed-price dinner, €27 fixed-price lunch, smart to reserve a view table, Atrazana Vieja 1, tel. 958-288-739, www.estrellasdesannicolas. es).

El Huerto de Juan Ranas Restaurante is a high-priced venue immediately below the San Nicolás viewpoint, but at their simple terrace bar you can order off their "casual" menu at half the price (€9 dish of the day, €15 *raciones,* Calle de Atarazana 8, tel. 958-286-925).

Bar Kiki, a laid-back and popular bar-restaurant on an unpretentious square with no view but plenty of people-watching, serves both simple and updated tapas, including tasty fried eggplant (Thu-Tue 9:00-24:00, closed Wed, just behind viewpoint at Plaza de San Nicolás 9, tel. 958-276-715).

Carmens *in the Albayzín*

For an upscale, romantic splurge, dine at a *carmen,* in an Albayzín house with a garden (buzz to get in) and unforgettable views.

Carmen Mirador de Aixa, small and elegant, has the dreamiest Alhambra views among the *carmens.* You'll pay a little more, but the food is exquisitely presented and the view makes the splurge worthwhile. Try the codfish or ox (€14-25 starters, €22-28 main dishes; closed Sun dinner, all day Mon, and Tue lunch; Carril de San Agustín 2, tel. 958-223-616, www. miradordeaixa.com).

Carmen de las Tomasas, next door, serves seasonal, gourmet Andalusian cuisine with killer views in a dressy/stuffy atmosphere (expect to spend €50 with wine; July-Sept Tue-Sat 20:30-24:00, closed Sun-Mon; Oct-June also open for lunch Wed-Sun 13:30-16:00 and closed Sun dinner; reservations required, Carril

de San Agustín 4, tel. 958-224-108, www. lastomasas.com, Joaquim and Cristina).

Carmen de Aben Humeya is the least expensive, least stuffy, and least romantic. Its outdoor-only seating lets you enjoy a meal or just a long cup of coffee while gazing at the Alhambra. This is a rare place enthusiastic about dinner salads (€10-20 starters and nicely presented main dishes, Mon-Tue and Thu-Fri 13:00-17:00 & 20:00-24:00, Sat-Sun 13:00-24:00, closed Wed, Cuesta de las Tomasas 12, tel. 958-226-665, www.abenhumeya. com).

Near Plaza Nueva

For people-watching, consider the many restaurants on Plaza Nueva or Plaza de Bib-Rambla. For a happening scene, check out the bars on and around Calle de Elvira. It's best to wander and see where the biggest crowds are.

Bodegas Castañeda, just a block off Plaza Nueva, is the best lively, central, and cheap tapas bar I found. When it's crowded, you need to power your way to the bar to order. When it's quiet, you can order at the bar and grab a little table (same budget prices). Consider their *tablas combinadas*—variety plates of cheese, meat, and *ahumados* (four different kinds of smoked fish)—and tasty *croquetas* (breaded and fried mashed potatoes and ham). Order a glass of their gazpacho. Their €12 *plato Casteñeda* feeds two. The big kegs tempt you with different local vermouths, and the €1.70 glasses of wine come with a free tapa (€2-3 tapas, €6-16 half-*raciones,* €8-20 *raciones,* daily 11:30-16:30 & 19:00-24:00, Calle Almireceros 1, tel. 958-215-464). They've added extra tables across the alley, but don't be confused by the neighboring "Antigua Bodega Castañeda" restaurant (run by a relative and not as good).

Restaurante Carmela is owned by a local culinary star who consistently participates in annual tapas contests. The flavors are complex, while the presentation is kept clean and simple. You can dine on the outside terrace or take a table in the fresh, modern interior. If breakfast isn't included at your hotel, consider starting your day here (€7 starters, €15 main courses, daily 8:00-24:00, just up from Plaza Isabel La Católica at Calle Colcha 13, tel. 958-225-794).

La Cueva de 1900, a family-friendly deli on the main drag, is appreciated for its simple dishes and quality ingredients. Though it lacks character, it's reliable and low-stress. They're proud of their homemade hams, sausages, and cheeses—sold in 100-gram lots and served on greaseproof paper. Their fixed-price lunch is €10, but if you've had enough meat, try one of their good €5-7 salads (€3-4 *boca-dillo* sandwiches, €8-17 meaty meals, open long hours daily, Calle Reyes Católicos 42, tel. 958-229-327).

Arrayanes is a good Moroccan restaurant a world apart from anything else listed here. Mostafa will help you choose among the many salads, appetizers, couscous, and *tajin* dishes. He treats his guests like old friends...especially the ladies (€4-10 starters, €10-16 main dishes, Wed-Mon 13:30-16:30 & 19:30-23:30, closed Tue, Cuesta Marañas 4, where Calles CaldererÍa Nueva and Vieja meet, tel. 958-228-401, mobile 619-076-862).

Los Diamantes is a modern, packed, high-energy local favorite for fresh seafood (free tapa with drink, but only *raciones* and half-*raciones* on the menu, prices the same at outside table as at the bar, Mon-Fri 12:00-18:00 & 20:00-24:00, Sat-Sun 11:00-24:00, facing Plaza Nueva at #13, tel. 958-075-313).

Greens and Berries anchors Plaza Nueva, serving fresh salads, sandwiches, and real fruit smoothies to go (no seating). Try one of their €7 combos—such as the *queso de cabra y tomate* sandwich (goat cheese and tomato with caramelized onions) paired with a Caribbean smoothie—and enjoy it on a sunny plaza bench (€3-6 salads and sandwiches,

daily 9:00-23:00, Plaza Nueva 1, tel. 633-895-086).

Tapas Beyond Plaza del Carmen

Granada is a wonderland of happening little tapas bars. As the scene changes from night to night, it's best to simply wander and see what appeals. You'll be amazed at how the vibe changes when you venture just five minutes from the historic and touristic center. Everything mentioned below lies within a few neighboring, parallel streets.

From Plaza del Carmen, wander down **Calle Navas** for a tight little gauntlet of competing tapas joints—try the bright and busy **Fogón de Galicia** (just off Plaza del Carmen), which specializes in seafood. If you want something quieter, try Calle San Matías. Another good street to explore is the arcaded Ángel Ganivet, off Puerta Real (stop at any of the wine bars, such as **Tinta Fina** at #8).

Don't miss my favorite stretch, where Calle Navas becomes Calle Virgen del Rosario. Consider **Taberna La Tana** (for fine wine, funky decor, and large raciones) and **Bar Los Diamantes II** (across the street, for seafood).

Head to **Café Fútbol** for chocolate and churros on Plaza Mariana Pineda. Two blocks away (to the southwest) is a good paseo street, Carrera de la Virgen, leading to the river.

Rick's Tip: *To enjoy an evening paseo without tourists, start with a tapas crawl (at any of the pubs or any of the streets mentioned in "Tapas Beyond Plaza del Carmen"), then stroll down Carrera de la Virgen, off Plaza del Campillo. This is the town's mini-Ramblas, leading gracefully down to the Paseo del Salón riverbank park (and passing the useful* **El Corte Inglés** *department store).*

SLEEPING

In July and August, when Granada's streets are littered with sunstroke victims, rooms are plentiful and prices soft. In the crowded months of April, May, September, and October, prices can spike up 20 percent. If you see a price range below, it indicates low- to high-season rates (excluding Holy Week and other pricier times).

If you're staying in the city center and traveling by car, you're free to drive into the prohibited center zone, but be sure your hotel registers you immediately with the traffic police (see arrival info on page 315).

(see arrival info on page 315).

On or near Plaza Nueva

Each of these is located within a 5-to-10-minute walk of Plaza Nueva.

$$$ Hotel Casa 1800 Granada sets the bar for affordable class. Its 25 rooms face the beautiful, airy courtyard of a 17th-century mansion, located just steps above Plaza Nueva in the lower part of the Albayzín. Tidy, well-run, and friendly, it offers a complimentary tea and coffee bar each afternoon (standard Db-€145, pricier "superior" and "deluxe" rooms not much different except for Alhambra views and patios, big buffet breakfast-€9.50, air-con, elevator, Benalúa 11, tel. 958-210-700, www.hotelcasa1800granada.com, info@hotelcasa1800granada.com).

$$$ Hotel Maciá Plaza, right on Plaza Nueva, has 44 smallish, clean, modern, and classy rooms. Choose between an on-the-square view or a quieter interior room (Sb-€60-100, Db-€140, square view-€20 extra, extra bed-€25; reserve by email, request Rick Steves discount, and show this book at check-in; buffet breakfast-€8.50, air-con, elevator, Plaza Nueva 5, tel. 958-227-536, www.maciahoteles.com, maciaplaza@maciahoteles.com).

$$ Casa del Capitel Nazarí, just off the church end of Plaza Nueva, is a restored 16th-century Renaissance palace transformed into 18 small but tastefully decorated rooms, all facing a courtyard that hosts art exhibits (Sb-€60-103, Db-€65-125, extra bed-€36, apartments available, breakfast-€10, includes afternoon tea/coffee, air-con, loaner laptop, parking-€19.50/day, Cuesta Aceituneros 6, tel. 958-215-260, www.hotelcasacapitel.com, info@hotelcasacapitel.com).

$$ Hotel Anacapri is a bright, cool marble oasis with 49 modern rooms and a quiet lounge (Sb-€59-85, Db-€59-118, Tb-€84-143, extra bed-€25; generally if book direct, breakfast is included; air-con, elevator, parking-€17/day, 2 blocks toward Gran Vía from Plaza Nueva at Calle Joaquín Costa 7, just a block from cathedral bus stop, tel. 958-227-477, www.hotelanacapri.com, reservas@hotelanacapri.com, helpful Kathy speaks Iowan).

$$ Hotel Inglaterra is a modern and peaceful hotel, with 36 rooms offering all the comforts (Db-€70-120, extra bed-€20-30, buffet breakfast-€9, air-con, elevator to third floor only, parking-€16/day, Cetti Merien 6, tel. 958-221-559, www.hotelinglaterragranada.com, info@hotel-inglaterra.es).

Cheap Sleeps on Cuesta de Gomérez

These lodgings, all inexpensive and some ramshackle, are on this street leading from Plaza Nueva up to the Alhambra. Sprinkled among the knickknack stores are the storefront workshops of several guitar makers, who are renowned for their hand-crafted instruments.

$$ Hotel Puerta de las Granadas has 16 crisp, clean rooms with an Ikea vibe, an inviting and peaceful courtyard, and a handy location (basic patio-view Db-€54-89, more for street view, cathedral view, or Alhambra view; book directly with hotel and ask for Rick Steves discount—can't combine with other discounts offered online, breakfast-€8, air-con, elevator, free tea and coffee in cafeteria all day, parking-€17/day, Cuesta de Gomérez 14, tel. 958-216-230, www.hotel puertadelasgranadas.com, reservas@ hotelpuertadelasgranadas.com).

$ Pensión Landazuri is run by friendly English-speaking Matilde Landazuri, her son Manolo, and daughters Margarita and Elisa. Their characteristic old house has 18 rooms—some are well-worn, while others are renovated. It boasts hardworking, helpful management and a great roof garden with an Alhambra view (S-€24-29, Sb-€28-39, D-€28-45, Db-€38-59, Tb-€60-74, Qb-€70-89, eggs-and-bacon breakfast-€3, no elevator or air-con, parking-€12/day, Cuesta de Gomérez 24, tel. 958-221-406, www.pensionlandazuri.com, info@pensionlandazuri.com). The Landazuris also run a good, cheap café open for breakfast and lunch.

$ Pensión Al Fin is located just up the street from Pensión Landazuri and run by the same family. Its five rooms feature antique wooden beams and marble columns with sultry, Moorish-style decor. A glass floor in the lobby lets you peer into a well from an ancient house (Db-€55, Tb-€70, some with balconies, parking-€12/day, reception and €3 breakfast at Pensión Landazuri, Cuesta de Gomérez 31, tel. 958-228-172, www.pensionalfin.com, info@pensionalfin.com).

Near the Cathedral

$$ Hotel Los Tilos offers 30 comfortable, business-like rooms (some with balconies) on the charming traffic-free Plaza de Bib-Rambla. Guests are welcome to use the fourth-floor terrace with views of the cathedral and the Alhambra (Sb-€45-55, Db-€55-80, Tb-€77-100, may be cheaper if you reserve online, free breakfast when you reserve via the hotel's website and show the latest edition of this book at check-in, air-con, parking-€18/day, Plaza de Bib-Rambla 4, tel. 958-266-712, www. hotellostilos.com, clientes@hotellostilos. com).

On or near Plaza de la Trinidad

The charming, park-like square called Plaza de la Trinidad, just a short walk west of the cathedral area (Pescadería and Bib-Rambla squares), is home to several good accommodations.

$$ Hotel Reina Cristina has 55 quiet, homey rooms a few steps off Plaza de la Trinidad. Check out the great Mudejar ceiling at the top of the stairwell (Sb-€48-81, Db-€58-134, Tb-€99-137, includes breakfast, ask for the rate without breakfast to save a few euros, air-con, elevator, parking-€18/day, Tablas 4, tel. 958-253-211, www.hotelreinacristina.com, clientes@ hotelreinacristina.com). They also rent 10 rooms, including family suites, in a location across from the cathedral (www. catedral-suites.com, reservas@catedral-suites.com).

$ Hostal Lima, run with class by Manolo and Carmen, has 25 well-appointed rooms (some small) in two buildings a block off the square. The public areas and rooms are flamboyantly decorated with medieval flair—colorful tiles, wood-carved life-sized figures, and swords (Sb-€33, Db-€48, Tb-€67, breakfast-€7, home-cooked dinner available—book in advance, air-con, elevator in one building only, parking-€14/day, Laurel de las Tablas 17, tel. 958-295-029, www. hostallimagranada.eu, info@hostallima granada.eu).

$ Hostal Rodri, run by Manolo's brother José, has 10 similarly good rooms a few doors down from Hostal Lima that feel new and classy for their price range. Take in the sun on the terrace (Sb-€26-34, Db-€38-52, air-con, elevator, parking-€14/day, Laurel de las Tablas 9, tel. 958-288-043, www.hostalrodri.com, info@hostalrodri.com).

$ Pensión Zurita, well-run by Francisco and Loli, faces Plaza de la Trinidad. Eight of the 14 rooms have small exterior balconies. Even with their double-paned windows, some rooms may come with night noise from cafés below. Request an updated bathroom for a little more luxury (S-€21, D-€34, Db-€42, Tb-€63, air-con, kitchen nook available for guest use, parking-€14/day, Plaza de la Trinidad 7, tel. 958-275-020, mobile 685-437-745, www. pensionzurita.es, pensionzurita@gmail. com).

In the Albayzín

$$ Hotel Santa Isabel la Real, a handsome 16th-century edifice, has 11 rooms ringing a charming courtyard. Each room is different; basic rooms look to the patio, while pricier rooms have better exterior views. With an old Moorish Granada ambience, it offers a warm welcome and rich memories (Db-€85-109 with breakfast, bigger and view rooms are €20 more and up, air-con, elevator, parking-€19/day, midway between San Nicolás viewpoint and Plaza San Miguel el Bajo on Calle Santa Isabel la Real, minibus #C1 stops in front, tel. 958-294-658, www.hotelsanta isabellareal.com, info@hotelsantaisabella real.com).

On the Alhambra Grounds

$$ Hotel América is classy and cozy, with 17 rooms in an early-19th-century house next to the parador (Sb-€75-80, Db-€99-118, superior Db-€140-150, €20 extra for terrace room, breakfast-€8.50, parking-€15/day, closed Dec-Feb, Calle Real de la Alhambra 53, a half-mile up the hill from Plaza Nueva, tel. 958-227-471, www. hotelamericagranada.com, reservas@ hotelamericagranada.com).

TRANSPORTATION

Getting Around Granada

With cheap taxis, frisky minibuses, good city buses, and nearly all points of interest an easy walk from Plaza Nueva, you'll get around Granada easily.

Tickets for minibuses and city buses cost €1.20 per ride. Buy tickets from the driver, except when riding the articulated LAC bus (for these, get tickets at machines at any LAC stop, change given). **Credibús cards** save you money if you'll be riding often, or if you're part of a group, since they're shareable (per-ride price drops to €0.79; can be loaded with €5, €10 or €20; plus refundable €2 card fee). Purchase the card from minibus drivers or from machines at any LAC bus stop (choose "contactless card," then "create card" options). To get a €5 card, ask for *"un bono de cinco."* For a €10 card, request *"un bono de diez."* These are valid on all buses (no fee for connecting bus if you transfer within 45 minutes). For schedules and routes, see www.transportesrober. com.

Handy little made-for-tourists red **minibuses,** which cover the city center, depart every few minutes from Plaza Nueva, Plaza Isabel La Católica, and Gran Vía ("Catedral" stop) until late in the evening. Here are several handy minibus routes:

Bus #C1 departs from Plaza Nueva and winds around the Albayzín quarter (every 8-10 minutes, 7:00-23:00; see page 298).

Bus #C2 follows a similar route as #C1 (although not to the San Nicolás viewpoint), delves deeper into the Albayzín, and also makes a side-trip into Sacromonte (every 20 minutes, 8:00-22:00).

Bus #C3 goes up to the Alhambra, departing from the "Catedral" stop and Plaza Isabel La Católica, and making Alhambra stops at the main entrance and the shortcut Justice Gate (Puerta de la Justicia) entrance (every 6-8 minutes, 7:00-23:00).

Other Bus Lines: If you're heading beyond the tourist core, you'll likely ride the articulated LAC bus. This high-capacity bus runs a circuit through the center of town and connects to outbound routes. The train station sits right on the circular LAC route.

Rick's Tip: Mega-chain **El Corte Inglés** sells plane, train, and bus tickets (Mon-Sat 10:00-21:30, closed Sun, ticket desk in basement level near supermarket, Acera del Darro, tel. 958-282-612).

Arriving and Departing
By Plane
Granada's sleepy airport, which serves only a dozen or so planes a day, is about 10 miles west of the city center (airport code: GRX, tel. 958-245-223—press "2" for English, www.aena-aeropuertos.es). To get between the airport and downtown, you can take a taxi (€35) or, much cheaper, the airport bus, timed to leave from directly outside the terminal when flights arrive and depart (€3, 12/day, 40 minutes). Get off at the "Catedral" stop. To reach the airport from the town center, use the bus stop at the end of Gran Vía del Colón, near the Jardines del Triunfo.

By Train
Granada's modest train station lacks luggage storage. Train info: tel. 902-320-320, www.renfe.com.

Getting Downtown: The station is well-connected to the center by frequent buses, a €7 taxi ride (taxis wait out front), or a 30-minute walk down Avenida de la

Constitución and Gran Vía.

To reach the **bus** stop, it's a three-minute walk: Exiting the train station, walk straight ahead up tree-lined Avenida Andaluces. At the first major intersection, turn right onto Avenida de la Constitución. Within a block you'll see a series of bus stops with routes marked on signposts. Look for the articulated LAC bus, which will head down Avenida de la Constitución to Gran Vía and stop at the cathedral (Catedral)—the nearest stop to Plaza Nueva and most of my recommended hotels. Before boarding, buy a €1.20 ticket from a machine at the stop. When you leave the bus, cross the busy Gran Vía and walk three short blocks to Plaza Nueva.

TRAIN CONNECTIONS
Most of the connections listed below have a more frequent (and sometimes faster) bus option.

From Granada by Train to: Barcelona (1/day, 7.5 hours on regional train and AVE, transfer in Antequera); **Madrid** (2/day on Altaria, 4.5 hours, also 2/day with transfer to AVE in Málaga, 4 hours); **Toledo** (all service is via Madrid, with nearly hourly AVE connections to Toledo); **Ronda** (3/day, 2.5 hours), **Sevilla** (4/day, 3 hours); **Córdoba** (2/day, 2.5 hours); **Málaga** (6/day, 2.5 hours with 1 transfer—bus is better).

By Bus
Located on the city outskirts, Granada's bus station (estación de autobuses) has a good and cheap cafeteria, ATMs, luggage lockers, and a privately run tourist agency masquerading as a TI. All of these services are downstairs, where you exit the buses.

Upstairs is the main arrivals hall with ticket windows, ticket machines, and a helpful info counter in the main hall that hands out printed schedules for each route.

If you want to buy a ticket for your next destination but there's a long line at the ticket windows, try using the machines (press the flag for English)—though these only sell tickets for some major routes (such as Málaga), and sometimes eat credit cards like a Spaniard eats *jamón*. There is almost always an Alsa representative at the machines to help and answer questions. All buses are operated by Alsa (tel. 902-422-242, www.alsa.es; bus station tel. 913-270-540).

Getting Downtown: To get from the bus station to the city center, it's either a 10-minute taxi ride (€8) or a 25-minute bus ride (€1.20, pay driver, change given). Take either bus #SN2 or #N4 until you reach the Cruz del Sur stop on Avenida de la Constitución, where you'll transfer to the articulated LAC bus. The transfer is free, but keep your ticket handy in case the bus driver or inspector asks for it. For Plaza Nueva, get off on Gran Vía at the "Catedral" stop (cathedral not visible from bus; ask, *"¿Catedral?"*—kah-tay-DRAHL), a half-block before the grand square called Plaza Isabel La Católica. From here, it's a short three-block walk to Plaza Nueva and most of my recommended hotels.

BUS CONNECTIONS
From Granada by Bus to: Nerja (6/day, 2-2.5 hours, more with transfer in Motril); **Sevilla** (to Plaza de Armas Station: 7/day, 3 hours *directo,* 3.5-4.5 hours *ruta;* to El Prado Station: 2/day, 3-3.5 hours); **Córdoba** (3/day *directo,* 2.75 hours; 2/day *ruta,* 4 hours); **Málaga** (hourly, 1.5-2 hours; if heading to **Ronda,** transfer here); **La Línea de la Concepción/Gibraltar** (3/day, 6-7 hours, change in Algeciras); **Jerez** (1/ day, 5 hours); **Madrid** (hourly, 5-6 hours; one direct to Barajas Airport); **Barcelona** (5/day, 13-14 hours).

By Car

With all the one-way streets, GPS can be frustrating for tourists driving into Granada. And driving in Granada's historic center is restricted to buses, taxis, and tourists with hotel reservations. Signs are posted to this effect, and entrances are strictly controlled. Hidden cameras snap a photo of your license plate as soon as you enter the restricted zone. If you have a reservation, simply drive past the sign, check in, and make sure your hotel registers you with the local traffic police (this is routine for them, but if they don't do it within 48 hours, you'll be stuck with a steep ticket). Hotels provide parking or have a deal with a central-zone garage (such as Parking San Agustín, just off Gran Vía del Colón, €25/day).

If you're driving and don't have a hotel reservation in the center, find a place to park outside the prohibited zone. The Alhambra, above the old town, has a huge public parking lot. You can drive directly to the Alhambra without passing through the city's historic, restricted center; from the freeway, take the exit marked *Ronda Sur-Alhambra*. Signs will lead you to the parking lot, located near the Alhambra's main entrance (€2.70/hour, €18/24 hours, guarded at night). To get into town, you can walk, catch the minibus, or take a taxi. When you leave Granada, be careful to drive out the same way you came in, avoiding the center.

There are also garages just outside the restricted zone: the Triunfo garage to the east (€23/day, Avenida de la Constitución 5) or the Neptune garage (Centro Comercial Neptuno) to the south (€15/day, Calle Neptuno). To reach the city center from either parking garage, catch the articulated LAC bus nearby (on Avenida de la Constitución) and get off at the "Catedral" stop.

Andalucía's
White Hill Towns

The American image of Spain is Andalucía. This is the home of bullfights, flamenco, gazpacho, and a charm bracelet of pristine whitewashed villages perched in the sierras.

Following the Route of the White Hill Towns (Ruta de los Pueblos Blancos) gives you wonderfully untouched Spanish culture. Spend a night in the romantic queen of the white towns, tiny Arcos de la Frontera. (Towns with "de la Frontera" in their names were established on the front line of the centuries-long fight to recapture Spain from the Muslims, who were slowly pushed back into Africa.) Farther east, the larger town of Ronda stuns visitors with its breathtaking setting—straddling a gorge that thrusts deep into the Andalusian bedrock.

Between Arcos and Ronda is the Pileta Cave, with prehistoric art, and two cute hill towns—Zahara and Grazalema. As a whole, the hill towns—no longer strategic, no longer on any frontier—are now just passing time peacefully. Join them.

Nearby is the workaday town of Jerez, a transit hub for the region; it's easy to visit on your way to or from the hill towns. Jerez is known for horse shows and sherry tastings; a well-timed visit can include both.

WHITE HILL TOWNS IN 2 DAYS

Andalucía's idyllic hill towns are experienced best not as a sightseeing destination but as a stroll in a historic, cultural park. **Arcos** is a tiny town perched on a cliff-top ledge; the highlight is simply walking through town (and not falling off). Arcos, best early or late in the day, makes a good overnight stop.

Ronda, with more to do, has a monumental bridge, a venerable bullring, a smattering of sights, and a thriving tapas scene. A taxi ride away is Pileta Cave; allow a half-day for a visit.

Unlike most hill towns, Arcos and Ronda are conveniently reached by public transportation: They have bus connections with surrounding towns, and Ronda is on a train line.

With or without a car, here's how you could spend two days—devoting most of it to Ronda, with an overnight for Arcos:

Arrive in Ronda early in the morning (or settle in the night before). Spend the day enjoying Ronda, stay overnight, linger in the morning, and head to Arcos in the mid-afternoon for an overnight stop there. After leaving Arcos, you could visit

ANDALUCÍA'S WHITE HILL TOWNS AT A GLANCE

▲▲▲**Arcos** My favorite Andalusian village, with a cliff-top old town that meanders down to a vibrant modern center. See page 322.

▲▲**Ronda** Bigger town, dramatically hanging over a deep gorge, and home to Spain's oldest bullring, with nearby prehistoric paintings at Pileta Cave. See page 333.

▲**Jerez de la Frontera** Proud equestrian mecca, birthplace of sherry, and relatively urban gateway to the hill towns. See page 345.

Zahara de la Sierra Tiny whitewashed village scenically set between a rocky Moorish castle and a turquoise lake. See page 332.

Grazalema Bright white town nestled in the green hills of Sierra de Grazalema Natural Park. See page 332.

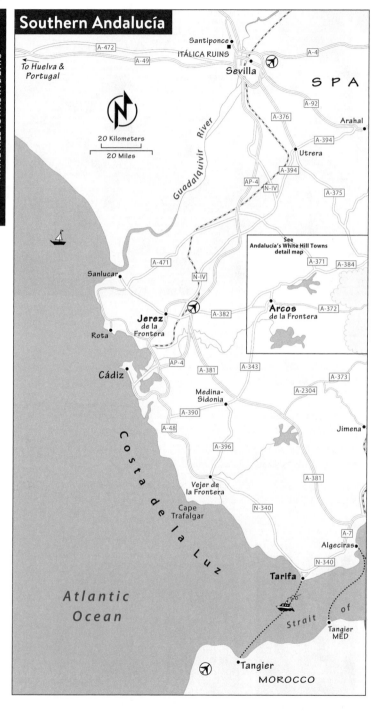

Southern Andalucía

To Huelva &
Portugal

A-472
A-49

Santiponce
ITÁLICA RUINS
Sevilla

S P A

A-4

A-92

A-376

A-394

Arahal

Utrera

N

20 Kilometers
20 Miles

Guadalquivir River

AP-4
N-IV
A-394

A-375

A-471

Sanlucar

N-IV

See
Andalucía's White Hill Towns
detail map

A-371
A-384

Jerez
de la
Frontera

Rota

A-382

Arcos
de la Frontera

A-372

Cádiz

AP-4

A-381
A-343

A-373

A-2304

Medina-
Sidonia

A-390

A-48

Jimena

A-396

Vejer de
la Frontera

A-381

Cape
Trafalgar

N-340

Costa de la Luz

Atlantic
Ocean

Algeciras

N-340

A-7

Tarifa

Strait of

Tangier
MED

Tangier

MOROCCO

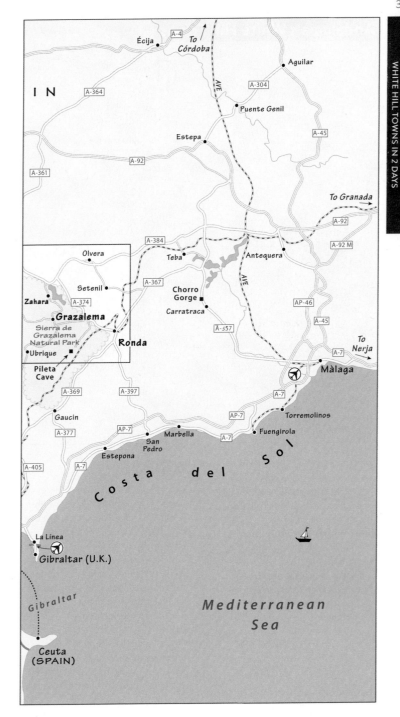

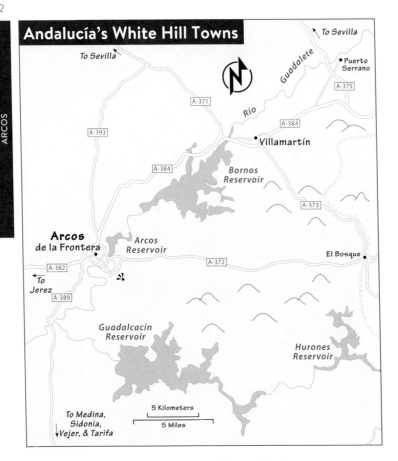

Andalucía's White Hill Towns

To Sevilla

To Sevilla

Guadalete

Puerto
Serrano

A-375

A-371

Río

A-384

A-393

Villamartín

A-384

Bornos
Reservoir

A-373

Arcos
de la Frontera

Arcos
Reservoir

A-372

El Bosque

A-382

To
Jerez

A-389

Guadalcacín
Reservoir

Hurones
Reservoir

To Medina,
Sidonia,
Vejer, & Tarifa

5 Kilometers

5 Miles

Jerez (for horse and sherry action around noon on weekdays), or go to Sevilla.

If you're driving between Ronda and Arcos, you could stop at Pileta Cave, Grazalema, and Zahara en route. The hill towns of Andalucía are a pleasure to tour by car with Michelin map 578 or any good map or app.

If you want to explore this region further, visit www.andalucia.com for more information on hotels, festivals, museums, and nightlife.

ARCOS

Arcos, rated ▲▲▲, smothers its long, narrow hilltop and tumbles down the back of the ridge like the train of a wedding dress. It consists of the fairy-tale old town on top of the hill and the fun-loving lower, or new, town. The old center is a labyrinthine wonderland, a photographer's feast. Arcos doesn't have much to offer other than its basic whitewashed self. Viewpoint-hop through town. Feel the wind funnel through the narrow streets as cars inch around tight corners. Join the kids' soccer game on the churchyard patio. Enjoy the moonlit view from the main square. You can arrive late and leave early and still see it all.

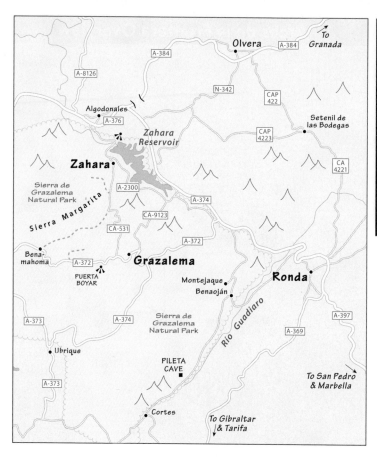

Orientation
Tourist Information
The **main TI** is on the skinny one-way road leading up into the old town—park up top or down below and walk to it (Mon-Sat 9:30-14:00 & 15:00-19:30, Sun 10:00-14:00, Cuesta de Belén 5, tel. 956-702-264, www.turismoarcos.es). A **TI kiosk** is on Plaza de España in the new town (Mon-Sat 9:30-13:30 & 18:00-20:00, Sun 10:00-14:00).

Rick's Tip: There are **no ATMs in the old town,** but you'll find several along Calle Corredera, between Plaza de España and the old town.

Arcos Old Town Walk
This self-guided walk will introduce you to everything worth seeing in Arcos. It's best early or late in the day; avoid it during the hot midday siesta.

• Start at the top of the hill, in the main square dominated by the church.

PLAZA DEL CABILDO
Stand at the viewpoint opposite the church on the town's main square. Survey the square, which in the old days doubled as a bullring. On your right is the parador, a former palace of the governor. It flies three flags: green for Andalucía, red-and-yellow for Spain, and blue-and-yellow for the European Union. On your left is City Hall, below the 11th-century Moorish

Arcos de la Frontera Overview

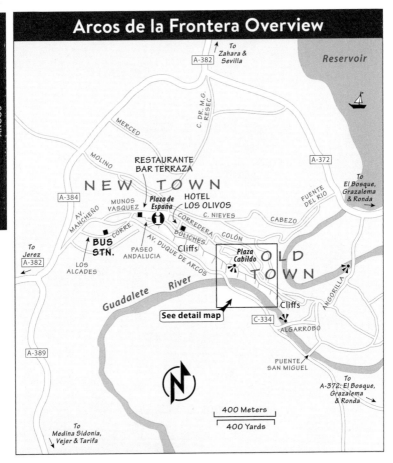

- To Zahara & Sevilla
- A-382
- Reservoir
- C. DR. M.G. RESEC
- MERCED
- MOLINO
- A-372
- RESTAURANTE BAR TERRAZA
- **N E W   T O W N**
- To El Bosque, Grazalema & Ronda
- A-384
- MUNOS VASQUEZ
- *Plaza de España*
- HOTEL LOS OLIVOS
- FUENTE DEL RIO
- AV. MANCHEÑO
- C. NIEVES
- CORREDERA
- CABEZO
- CORRE
- **BUS STN.**
- BOLICHES
- COLÓN
- PASEO ANDALUCIA
- AV. DUQUE DE ARCOS
- Cliffs
- *Plaza Cabildo*
- **O L D   T O W N**
- To Jerez
- A-382
- LOS ALCADES
- ANGORILLA
- Guadalete   River
- **See detail map**
- C-334
- Cliffs
- ALGARROBO
- A-389
- PUENTE SAN MIGUEL
- To A-372: El Bosque, Grazalema & Ronda
- N
- 400 Meters
- 400 Yards
- To Medina Sidonia, Vejer & Tarifa

Arcos

castle where Ferdinand and Isabel held Reconquista strategy meetings (castle privately owned and closed to the public).

Now belly up to the railing and look down. The people of Arcos boast that only they see the backs of the birds as they fly. Ponder the parador's erosion concerns—in the 1990s, part of its lounge dropped right off. You'll see orderly orange groves below and fine views toward the southernmost part of Spain. You're 330 feet above the Guadalete River. This is the town's suicide departure point for men (women jump from the other side).

• *Looming over the square is the...*

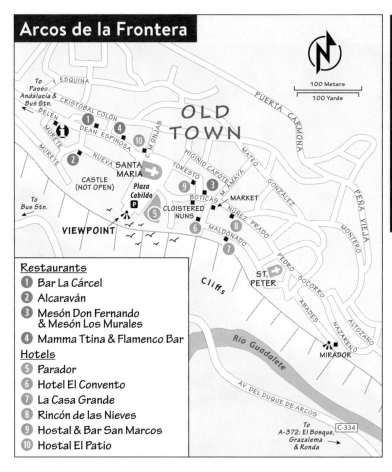

Arcos de la Frontera

OLD TOWN

100 Meters
100 Yards

To Paseo
Andalucía &
Bus Stn.

ESQUINA

CRISTÓBAL COLÓN

BELÉN

MURETE

DEAN ESPINOSA

MURETE

NUEVA

SANTA
MARIA

CASTLE
(NOT OPEN)

Plaza
Cabildo

To
Bus Stn.

VIEWPOINT

C. MONJAS

HIGINIO CAPOTE

TORESTO

BOTICAS

CLOISTERED
NUNS

PUERTA CARMONA

MATEO

M. AMAYA

GONZÁLEZ

MARKET

NÚÑEZ PRADO

MALDONADO

PEÑA VIEJA

MONTERO

Cliffs

**ST.
PETER**

PEDRO SOCORRO

ABADES

NAZARENO

ALTOZANO

Río Guadalete

MIRADOR

AV. DEL DUQUE DE ARCOS

To
A-372: El Bosque,
Grazalema
& Ronda

C-334

Restaurants
1 Bar La Cárcel
2 Alcaraván
3 Mesón Don Fernando
   & Mesón Los Murales
4 Mamma Ttina & Flamenco Bar

Hotels
5 Parador
6 Hotel El Convento
7 La Casa Grande
8 Rincón de las Nieves
9 Hostal & Bar San Marcos
10 Hostal El Patio

CHURCH OF SANTA MARÍA

After Arcos was retaken from the Moors in the 13th century, this church was built atop a mosque. Notice the church's fine but chopped-off bell tower. The old one fell in the earthquake of 1755. The replacement was intended to be the tallest in Andalucía after Sevilla's—but money ran out. The church guardian resides on an upper floor in a room strewn with bell-ringing ropes.

Cost and Hours: €2, Mon-Fri 10:00-13:00 & 15:30-18:30, Sat 10:00-14:00, shorter hours in winter, closed Sun and Jan-Feb.

Visiting the Church: Buy a ticket and step into the center, where you can see the beautifully carved choir. The organ was built in 1789 with that many pipes. At the front of the church, the fine Renaissance high altar—carved in wood—covers up a Muslim prayer niche that survived from the older mosque. The altar shows God with a globe in his hand (on top), and scenes from the life of Jesus (on the right) and Mary (left).

Circle the church counterclockwise and notice the elaborate chapels. Although most of the architecture is Gothic, the chapels are decorated in the Baroque and Rococo styles that were popular when the post-earthquake

Church of Santa María

remodel began. The ornate statues are used in Holy Week processions. Sniff out the "incorruptible body" (miraculously never rotting) of St. Felix—a third-century martyr (directly across from the entry). Felix may be nicknamed "the incorruptible," but take a close look at his knee. He's no longer skin and bones...just bones and the fine silver mesh that once covered his skin. Rome sent his body here in 1764 after recognizing this church as the most important in Arcos.

• Back outside, examine the...

CHURCH EXTERIOR

Circle clockwise around the church, down four steps, to find the third-century Roman votive altar with a carving of the palm tree of life directly in front of you. Though the Romans didn't build this high in the mountains, they did have a town and temple at the foot of Arcos. This carved stone was discovered in the foundation of the original Moorish mosque that stood here.

Head down a few more steps and come to the main entrance (west portal) of the church (closed for restoration). This is a good example of Plateresque Gothic—Spain's last and most ornate kind of Gothic.

In the pavement, notice the 15th-century magic circle with 12 red and 12 white stones—the white ones are marked with "constellations" (which don't resemble any of today's star charts). When a child would come to the church to be baptized, the parents stopped here first for a good Christian exorcism. The exorcist would stand inside the protective circle and cleanse the baby of evil spirits. While locals no longer do this (and a modern rain drain now marks the center), many Sufi Muslims still make pilgrimages every November.

Go down the next few stairs to the street (the route of a public minibus that does a circular joyride through town), and continue along to the right under the **flying buttresses.** Notice the scratches of innumerable car mirrors on each wall (be glad you're walking). The buttresses were built to shore up the church when it was damaged by an earthquake in 1699 (and helped it survive the bigger earthquake of 1755). The security grille (over the window above) protected cloistered nuns when this building was a convent. Look at the arches that prop up the houses downhill on the left; all over town, arches support earthquake-damaged structures.

• Now make your way...

FROM THE CHURCH TO THE MARKET

Completing your circle around the church (back uphill), turn left under more arches built to repair earthquake damage and walk east down the bright, white Calle Escribanos. From now to the end of this walk, you'll basically follow this lane until you come to the town's second big church (St. Peter's). After a block, you hit Plaza Boticas.

On your right is the last remaining **convent** in Arcos. Notice the no-nunsense, spiky window grilles high above, with tiny peepholes in the latticework for the cloistered nuns to see through. If you're hungry, check out the list of treats the nuns provide. Then step into the lobby under the fine portico to find their one-way mirror and a spinning cupboard that hides the nuns from view. Push the buzzer, and one of the eight sisters (several are from Kenya and speak English well) will spin out some boxes of excellent, freshly baked cookies (€6-8, open daily but not reliably 8:30-14:30 & 17:00-19:00). If you stand big and tall to block out the light, you may actually see the sister through the glass. If you ask for *magdalenas,* bags of cupcakes will swing around (€3). Buy some treats to support their church work, and give them to kids as you complete your walk.

The **covered market** (*mercado*) at the other end of the plaza (down from the convent) resides in an unfinished church. At the entry, notice half of a church wall. The church was being built for the Jesuits, but construction stopped in 1767 when

King Charles III, tired of the Jesuit appetite for politics, expelled them from Spain. The market is closed on Sunday and Monday—they rest on Sunday, so there's no produce, fish, or meat ready for Monday. Poke inside. It's tiny but has everything you need. Pop into the *servicio público* (public WC)—no gender bias here.

• *As you exit the market, turn right and continue straight down Calle Botica...*

FROM THE MARKET TO THE CHURCH OF ST. PETER

As you walk, peek discreetly into private patios. The wonderful, cool-tiled courtyards filled with plants, pools, and furniture are typical of Arcos. Except in the mansions, these patios are generally shared by several families. Originally, each courtyard served as a catchment system, funneling rainwater to a drain in the middle, which filled the well. You can still see tiny wells in wall niches with now-decorative pulleys for the bucket.

At the next corner (Calle Platera), look back and up at the corner of the tiled rooftop on the right. You may be able to make out a tiny stone where the corner

A typical Arcos side street

hits the sky; it's an eroded mask, placed here to scare evil spirits from the house. This is Arcos' last surviving mask from a tradition that lasted until the mid-19th century.

Also notice the ancient columns on each corner. All over town, these columns—many appropriated from the ancient Roman settlement at the foot of the hill—protect buildings from reckless donkey carts and tourists in rental cars.

As you continue straight, notice that the walls are scooped out on either side of the windows. These are a reminder of the days when women stayed inside but wanted the best possible view of any action in the streets. These "window ears" also enabled boys to lean inconspicuously against the wall to chat up eligible young ladies.

Across from the old chapel facade ahead, find the **Association of San Miguel.** Duck right, past a bar, into the oldest courtyards in town—you can still see the graceful Neo-Gothic lines of this noble home from 1850. The bar is a club for retired men—always busy when a bull-fight's on TV or during card games. The guys are friendly, and drinks are cheap. You're welcome to flip on the light and explore the old-town photos in the back room.

Just beyond, facing the elegant front door of that noble house, is Arcos' second church, **St. Peter's** (€1 donation, Mon-Fri 9:00-14:00 & 15:30-18:30, Sat 10:00-14:00, closed Sun). You know it's St. Peter's because St. Peter, mother of God, is the centerpiece of the facade. Let me explain. It really is the second church, having had an extended battle with Santa María for papal recognition as the leading church in Arcos. When the pope finally favored Santa María, St. Peter's parishioners changed their prayers. Rather than honoring "María," they wouldn't even say her name. They prayed "St. Peter, mother of God." Like Santa María, it's a Gothic structure, filled with Baroque decor, many Holy Week procession statues, humble English descriptions, and relic skeletons in glass caskets (two from the third century A.D.).

In the cool of the evening, the tiny square in front of the church—about the only flat piece of pavement around—serves as the old-town soccer field for neighborhood kids. Until a few years ago, this church also had a resident bellman—notice the cozy balcony halfway up. He was a basket-maker and a colorful character, famous for bringing a donkey into his quarters that grew too big to get back out. Finally, he had no choice but to kill and eat the donkey.

FROM THE CHURCH TO THE MAIN SQUARE

Twenty yards beyond the church, step into the nice **Galería de Arte San Pedro,** featuring artisans in action and their reasonably priced paintings and pottery. Walk inside. Find the water drain and the well.

Across the street, a sign directs you to a **mirador**—a tiny square 100 yards downhill that affords a commanding view of Arcos. The reservoir you see to the east of town is used for water sports in the summertime and forms part of a power plant that local residents protested—to no avail—based on environmental concerns.

From the Church of St. Peter, circle down and around back to the main square, wandering the tiny neighborhood lanes. Just below St. Peter's (on Calle Maldonado) is a delightful little Andalusian garden laid out in formal Arabic style, with aromatic plants and water in the center. Farther along on Maldonado, peek into **Belén Artístico,** a quirky, little cave-like museum, featuring miniatures of favorite Nativity scenes (free, but donations accepted). The lane called Higinio Capote, below the Church of Santa María, is particularly picturesque with its many geraniums. Peek into patios, kick a few soccer balls, and savor the views.

Eating
View Dining

The **Parador de Arcos de la Frontera** has a restaurant with a cliff-edge setting. Its tapas and *raciones* are reasonably priced but mediocre; still, a drink and a snack on the million-dollar-view terrace at sunset is a memorable experience (€3 tapas, €6-14 *raciones*, €25 three-course fixed-price meal at lunch or dinner, daily 12:00-16:00 & 20:30-23:00, shorter hours off-season, Plaza del Cabildo, on main square).

Cheaper Eating in the Old Town

Several decent, rustic bar-restaurants are within a block or two of the old town's main square and church. Most serve tapas at the bar and *raciones* at their tables. Prices are fairly consistent (€2.50 tapas, €5-7 *media-raciones,* €8-10 *raciones*).

Bar La Cárcel ("The Prison") is run by a hardworking family that brags about its exquisite tapas and small open-faced sandwiches. I would, too. The menu is accessible, prices are the same at the bar or at the tables, and the place has a winning energy (Tue-Sun 12:00-16:00 & 20:00-24:00, closed Mon—except open Mon and closed Sun July-Aug, Calle Deán Espinosa 18, tel. 956-700-410).

Alcaraván tries to be trendy yet *típico.* A flamenco ambience fills its medieval vault in the castle's former dungeon. This place attracts French and German tourists who give it a cool vibe (closed Mon, Calle Nueva 1, tel. 956-703-397).

Bar San Marcos is a tiny, homey bar with five tables, an easy-to-understand menu offering hearty, simple home cooking, including cheap plates and a variety of fixed-price meals (€8 plates, €15 fixed-price meals, kitchen open long hours Mon-Sat, closed Sun, Marqués de Torresoto 6, tel. 956-700-721).

Mesón Don Fernando gives rustic an inviting twist, with a nice bar and both indoor and great outdoor seating on the square just across from the little market

(Tue-Thu 13:30-16:00 & 20:15-23:00 for food, closed Wed, longer hours for drinks on the square, Plaza Boticas 5, tel. 956-717-326).

Mesón Los Murales serves tasty, affordable tapas, *raciones,* and fixed-price meals in their rustic bar or at tables in the square outside (€2.50 tapas and *montaditos,* €9-12 *raciones,* fixed-price meals from €9, Fri-Wed 10:00-24:00, closed Thu, at Plaza Boticas 1, tel. 956-700-607).

Mamma Ttina gives you a break from Andalucía, with Italian fare to go along with the Italian pop music and Italian staff (€7-12 pizzas and pastas, Thu-Mon 12:00-16:00 & 18:30-24:00, Tue-Wed 18:30-24:00 only, Deán Espinosa 10, tel. 956-703-937). Right next door, the same owners run bar **El Tablao de Manuela,** which has flamenco, tapas, and homemade sangria most nights (€5 cover, 21:00-late, Deán Espinosa 1, tel. 671-176-851).

Tapas in the New Town

Plaza de España, in the lower new town, is lined with tapas bars and restaurants. For a great perch while enjoying the local family scene, consider busy **Restaurante Bar Terraza** (€12 plates) at the end of Plaza de España.

Sleeping

Hotels in Arcos consider April, May, August, September, and October to be high season. Note that some hotels double their rates during the motorbike races in nearby Jerez (usually April or May, varies yearly, call TI or ask your hotel) and during Holy Week (the week leading up to Easter); these spikes are not reflected in the prices below.

In the Old Town

If traveling by car, be sure to obtain a parking pass (€5) from your hotel if you want to park overnight on the main square. (The pass does not exempt you from daytime rates.) Otherwise, park in the lot at Plaza de España, and catch a taxi

or the shuttle bus up to the old town.

$$$ Parador de Arcos de la Frontera is royally located, with 24 elegant, refurbished, and reasonably priced rooms (eight have balconies). If you want to experience a parador, this is a good one (Sb/Db-€90-170, Db with terrace-€39 extra, prices fluctuate considerably with season and demand, breakfast-€16, air-con, elevator, Plaza del Cabildo, tel. 956-700-500, www.parador.es, arcos@parador.es).

$$ Hotel El Convento, deep in the old town just beyond the parador, is the best value in town. Run by a hardworking family and their wonderful staff, this cozy hotel offers 13 fine rooms—all with great views, most with balconies. Enjoy an à la carte breakfast on their terrace, with all of Andalucía spreading beyond your *café con leche* (Sb with balcony-€45-62, Sb with terrace-€55-65, Db with balcony-€65-82, Db with terrace-€75-97, extra person-€15; ask for Rick Steves discount if you book directly with hotel, pay in cash, and show this book; usually closed Nov-Feb, Maldonado 2, tel. 956-702-333, www.hotelelconvento.es, reservas@hotelelconvento.es).

$$ La Casa Grande is a lovingly appointed *Better Homes and Moroccan Tiles* place that rents eight rooms with big-view windows. As in a B&B, you're free to enjoy its fine terrace, homey library, and atrium-like patio, where you'll be served a traditional breakfast. They also offer guided visits and massage services (Db-€74-90, junior suite Db-€90-121, Tb-€111-121, Qb-€125-140, email them directly for best prices, generous breakfast-€9, air-con, Wi-Fi in public areas only, Maldonado 10, tel. 956-703-930, www.lacasa grande.net, info@lacasagrande.net).

$$ Rincón de las Nieves, with simple Andalusian style, has a cool inner courtyard surrounded by three rooms. Two of the rooms have their own outdoor terraces with obstructed views, but all have access to the rooftop terrace (Db-€50-60, higher for Holy Week and Aug, air-con, Boticas 10, tel. 956-701-528, mobile 656-886-256, www.rincondelasnieves. com, info@rincondelasnieves.com).

$ Hostal San Marcos, above a neat little bar in the heart of the old town, offers four air-conditioned rooms and a great sun terrace with views of the reservoir (Sb-€25, Db-€35, Tb-€45, air-con, best to reserve by phone, Marqués de Torresoto 6, tel. 956-105-429, mobile 664-118-052, sanmarcosdearcos@hotmail. com, José speaks some English).

$ Hostal El Patio offers the best cheap beds in the old town. With a tangled floor plan and nine simple rooms, it's on a noisy street behind the Church of Santa María. The bar-restaurant in the cellar serves an affordable breakfast, tapas, and several fixed-priced meals (Sb-€23, Db-€35, Db with terrace-€45, Tb-€60, air-con, Calle Callejón de las Monjas 4, tel. 956-702-302, mobile 605-839-995, www.mesonel patio.com, padua@mesonelpatio.com, staff speak a bit of English).

In the New Town
$$ Hotel Los Olivos is a bright, cool, and airy place with 19 rooms, an impressive courtyard, roof garden, generous public spaces, bar, view, friendly folks, and easy parking. The five view rooms can be noisy in the afternoon, but—with double-paned windows—are usually fine at night (Sb-

€51-56, Db-€82-97, Tb-€97-112, extra bed-€15, includes buffet breakfast; ask for Rick Steves discount when you book directly with hotel, pay in cash, and show this book; Paseo de Boliches 30, tel. 956-700-811, www.hotel-losolivos.es, reservas@hotel-losolivos.es, Raquel, Marta, and Miguel Ángel).

Transportation
Getting Around Arcos
The old town is easily walkable, but it's fun and relaxing to take a circular **minibus** joyride. The little shuttle bus constantly circles through the town's one-way system and around the valley. For a 30-minute tour, hop on. You can catch it just below the main church in the old town, near the mystical stone circle (generally departs roughly at :20 and :50 past the hour). Sit in the front seat for the best view of the tight squeezes as you wind through the old town. After passing under a Moorish gate, you enter a modern residential neighborhood, circle under the eroding cliff, and return to the old town by way of the bus station and Plaza de España.

Arriving and Departing
BY BUS
The bus station is on Calle Corregidores, at the foot of the hill. Here are three ways to get up to the old town: Catch the **shuttle bus** marked *Centro* from the bus stalls behind the station (€1, pay driver, 2/hour, runs roughly Mon-Fri 8:00-21:00, Sat 9:00-21:00, none on Sun; this bus does the joyride just mentioned); hop a **taxi** (€5 fixed rate; if there are no taxis waiting, call 956-704-640), or **hike** 20 uphill minutes.

Leaving Arcos by bus can be frustrating, especially if you're going to Ronda. Buses generally leave late, the schedule information boards are often inaccurate, and the ticket window usually isn't open (luckily, you can buy your tickets on the bus). But buses do give you a glimpse at

España profunda ("deep Spain"), where everyone seems to know each other, no one's in a hurry, and despite any language barriers, people are quite helpful when approached.

Two bus companies share the Arcos bus station: Los Amarillos (tel. 902-210-317, www.losamarillos.es) and Comes (tel. 956-291-168, www.tgcomes.es). For bus schedules and routes, ask the TI, your hotelier, or check the bus websites and www.movelia.es. Buses run less frequently on weekends. The closest train station to Arcos is Jerez.

From Arcos by Bus to: Jerez (hourly, 30 minutes); **Ronda** (1-2/day, 2 hours); **Sevilla** (1-2/day, 2 hours, more departures with transfer in Jerez).

BY CAR

Avoid driving in the old town. Navigating the narrow lanes is like threading needles (many drivers pull in their side-view mirrors to buy a few extra precious inches). Turns are tight, parking is frustrating, and congestion can lead to long jams.

It's best to park in the modern underground pay lot at Plaza de España in the new town (€15/day). Many hotels offer discounts at this lot; inquire when booking your room. From this lot, **hike** 15 minutes, or catch a **taxi** or the *Centro* **shuttle bus** up to the old town (2/hour; as you're looking uphill, the bus stop is to the right of the traffic circle).

ZAHARA AND GRAZALEMA

If you're connecting Arcos and Ronda by car, you'll drive through Zahara de la Sierra and Grazalema, two of my favorite white hill towns. Either or both villages make a pleasant stop for a meal or a stroll. Public transportation is frustrating, so I'd only visit these villages by car.

Zahara de la Sierra

This tiny town in a tingly setting under a Moorish castle has a spectacular view over a turquoise lake. While the big church facing the town square is considered one of the richest in the area, the smaller church has the most-loved statue. The Virgin of Dolores is Zahara's answer to Sevilla's Virgin of Macarena (and is similarly paraded through town during Holy Week).

Park for free in the main plaza, or continue up the hill to the parking lot at the base of the castle. It's one way up and one way down, so follow *salida* signs to depart.

Tourist Information

The TI is located in the main plaza (Tue-

Zahara de la Sierra

Sun 9:00-14:00 & 16:00-19:00, closed Mon, guest computer, gift shop, Plaza del Rey 3, tel. 956-123-114). Upstairs from the TI are Spanish-only displays about the flora and fauna of nearby Sierra de Grazalema Natural Park.

Sights

During Moorish times, Zahara lay within the fortified castle walls above today's town. It was considered the gateway to Granada and a strategic stronghold for the Moors by the Christian forces of the Reconquista. Locals tell of the Spanish conquest of the Moors' castle (in 1482) as if it happened yesterday.

Skip the church, but it's a fun 15-minute hike up to the remains of the **castle** (free, tower always open). Start at the paved path across from the town's upper parking lot.

Eating and Sleeping

$$ Hotel Arco de la Villa is the town's only real hotel. Its very good restaurant offers a €10 *menú del día,* along with reservoir and mountain views (16 small modern rooms, Sb-€36, Db-€60, breakfast-€3, Wi-Fi in common areas, tel. 956-123-230, www.tugasa.com, arco-de-lavilla@tugasa.com).

Grazalema

Postcard-pretty Grazalema offers a royal balcony for a memorable picnic and plenty of quiet whitewashed streets to explore. Situated within Sierra de Grazalema Natural Park, it's graced with scenery and greenery.

A tiny lane leads a block from the center rear of the square to Plaza de Andalucía (filled by the tables of tapas bars). Shops sell the town's beautiful and famous handmade wool blankets. A block farther uphill takes you to the main square with the church, Plaza de España. A coffee on the square is a joy. Small lanes stretch from here into the rest of the town.

Tourist Information

The TI is located at the car park at the cliffside viewpoint, Plaza de los Asomaderos. It has WCs and a small gift shop featuring locally produced products (daily 10:00-14:00 & 15:30-19:00, tel. 956-132-052, www.grazalemaguide.com). Enjoy the view, then wander into the town.

Eating

Tiny Plaza de Andalucía has several good bars for tapas, including **Zulema, La Posadilla,** and **La Cidulia.** To pick up picnic supplies, head to the **Día** supermarket (Mon-Sat 9:00-14:00 & 17:00-21:00, Sun 9:00-14:00, on Calle Corrales Terceros 3).

RONDA

Ronda, rated ▲▲▲, is one of the largest white hill towns, with more than 35,000 people. It's also one of the most spectacular, thanks to its gorge-straddling setting. Approaching the town from the train or bus station, it seems flat...until you reach the New Bridge and realize that it's clinging to the walls of a canyon. The cliffside setting, dramatic today, was practical back in its day. For the Moors, it provided a tough bastion, taken by the Spaniards only in 1485, seven years before Granada fell.

Ronda's main attractions are its gorge-spanning bridges and the oldest bullring in Spain (it's known as the cradle of modern bullfighting and the home of 19th-century *bandoleros*). But the real joy of Ronda is in wandering its back streets and taking in its beautiful balconies, exuberant flowerpots, and panoramic views.

Day-trippers clog Ronda's streets during the day, but locals retake the town in the early evening, making nights peaceful. If you liked Toledo at night, you'll love evenings in Ronda. Since it's served by train and bus, Ronda makes a relaxing break for nondrivers traveling between Granada and Sevilla. Drivers can use Ronda as a convenient base from which to explore many of the other *pueblos blancos.*

Orientation

Ronda's breathtaking ravine divides the town's labyrinthine Moorish quarter and its new, noisier, sprawling Mercadillo quarter. A powerful 18th-century bridge sturdily connects these two neighborhoods. Most things of interest to tourists (TI, hotels, bullring) are clustered within a few blocks of the bridge. The paseo (early evening stroll) happens in the new town, on Ronda's major pedestrian and shopping street, Carrera Espinel.

Tourist Information

Ronda's TI, across the square from the bullring, covers not only the town but all of Andalucía. It gives out good, free maps of the town, Andalusia's roads, Granada, Sevilla, and the Route of the White Towns (Mon-Fri 10:00-19:00, Sat 10:00-17:00, Sun 10:00-14:30, shorter hours Oct-late March, Paseo Blas Infante, tel. 952-187-119, www.turismoderonda.es). It also organizes two-hour walking tours (generally

daily at 14:30 for €18—includes bullring, in summer also Thu-Sat at 20:00 for €15—no bullring, language used on tour depends on guide, 4-person minimum).

For a short visit, you won't need the €10 **Bono Turístico** city pass sold at the TI, which doesn't cover all of the sights.

Sights

Ronda's New Town

▲▲▲ THE GORGE AND NEW BRIDGE (PUENTE NUEVO)

The ravine, called El Tajo—360 feet down and 200 feet wide—divides Ronda into the whitewashed old Moorish town (La Ciudad) and the new town (El Mercadillo) that was built after the Christian reconquest in 1485. The New Bridge, built from 1751 to 1793, mightily spans the gorge. Look down...carefully.

An earlier bridge was built here in 1735, but fell after six years. You can see its foundations—along with a super view of the New Bridge—from the Jardines de Cuenca park. To reach the park from Plaza de España, walk down Calle Rosario, turn right on Calle Los Remedios, and

Ronda's gorge and New Bridge

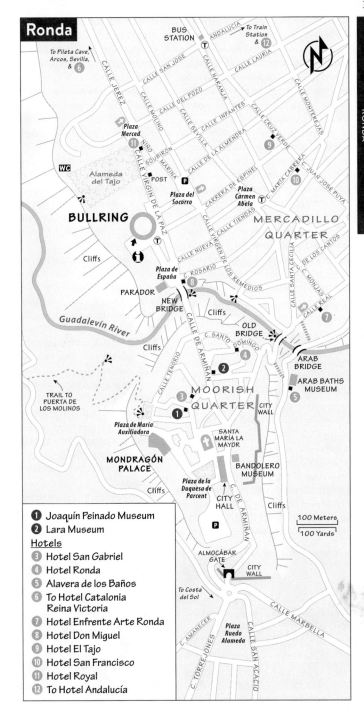

Ronda

BUS STATION
To Pileta Cave, Arcos, Sevilla, & ❻

CALLE JEREZ
CALLE SAN JOSE
ANDALUCÍA
To Train Station & ⓬
CALLE LAURIA
CALLE NARANJA
CALLE MOLINO
CALLE DEL POZO
CALLE SEVILLA
CALLE INFANTES
CALLE CRUZ VERDE
CALLE MONTEREJAS

Plaza Merced ⓫
NIÑO SOUBIRON
CALLE VIRGEN DE LA PAZ
CALLE MARINA
CALLE DE LA ALMENDRA
C. MARÍA CABRERA
C. JUAN-JOSÉ PUYA

WC
Alameda del Tajo
POST
P
Plaza del Socorro
CARRERA DE ESPINEL
Plaza Carmen Abela T
❾

❿

BULLRING
T
ℹ ❶
Cliffs

CALLE TIENDAS
CALLE NUEVA
VIRGEN DE LOS REMEDIOS
MERCADILLO QUARTER
CALLE SANTA CECILIA
C. DE LOS CANTOS
C. C. MONJAS

Plaza de España ❽
C. ROSARIO
PARADOR
NEW BRIDGE
CALLE DE ARMIÑAN
Cliffs
CALLE REAL
❼

Guadalevín River
OLD BRIDGE
C. SANTO DOMINGO
❹
ARAB BRIDGE

Cliffs
CALLE TENORIO
❷
ARAB BATHS MUSEUM
❺

TRAIL TO PUERTA DE LOS MOLINOS
❸
❶
MOORISH QUARTER
CITY WALL

Plaza de María Auxiliadora
SANTA MARÍA LA MAYOR
T

MONDRAGÓN PALACE
BANDOLERO MUSEUM
Cliffs
Plaza de la Duquesa de Parcent
CITY HALL
Cliffs

P
C. DE ARMIÑAN
100 Meters
100 Yards

ALMOCÁBAR GATE
CITY WALL
To Costa del Sol

CALLE MARBELLA

C. AMANECER
Plaza Ruedo Alameda
CALLE SAN ACACIO
C. TORREJONES

❶ Joaquín Peinado Museum
❷ Lara Museum

Hotels
❸ Hotel San Gabriel
❹ Hotel Ronda
❺ Alavera de los Baños
❻ To Hotel Catalonia Reina Victoria
❼ Hotel Enfrente Arte Ronda
❽ Hotel Don Miguel
❾ Hotel El Tajo
❿ Hotel San Francisco
⓫ Hotel Royal
⓬ To Hotel Andalucía

then take another right at the sign for the park (daily 9:30-21:30, until 18:30 in winter). There are also good views from the walkway that skirts the parador, which overlooks the gorge and bridge from the new-town side. For the price of a drink, you can enjoy the view from the parador's lobby bar or its terrace.

From the new-town side of the bridge, just outside the parador on the right, you'll see the entrance to the **New Bridge Interpretive Center,** where you can pay to climb down and enter the structure of the bridge itself (€2, Mon-Fri 10:00-19:00, Sat-Sun 10:00-15:00, closes earlier off-season, mobile 649-965-338). Inside are modest audiovisual displays about the bridge's construction and its famous visitors—worth a quick look only if you have the Bono Turístico pass.

▲▲▲BULLRING (REAL MAESTRANZA DE CABALLERÍA DE RONDA)

Ronda is the birthplace of modern bullfighting, and this was the first great Spanish bullring. Philip II initiated bullfighting as war training for knights in the 16th century. Back then, there were two kinds of bullfighting: the type with noble knights on horseback, and the coarser, man-versus-beast entertainment for the commoners (with no rules...much like when WWF wrestlers bring out the folding chairs). Ronda practically worships Francisco Romero, who melded the noble and chaotic kinds of bullfighting with rules to establish modern bullfighting here in the early 1700s. He introduced the scarlet

cape, held unfurled with a stick. His son Juan further developed the ritual, and his grandson Pedro was one of the first great matadors (killing nearly 6,000 bulls in his career).

Ronda's bullring and museum are Spain's most interesting (even better than Sevilla's). To tour the ring, stables, chapel, and museum, buy a ticket at the back of the bullring.

Cost and Hours: €6.50, daily April-Sept 10:00-20:00, March and Oct 10:00-19:00, Nov-Feb 10:00-18:00, no photography in museum, tel. 952-874-132, www.rmcr.org. The excellent €1.50 audioguide describes everything and is essential to fully enjoy your visit.

Bullfights: Bullfights are scheduled only for the first weekend of September during the *feria* (fair) and occur rarely in spring. Whereas every other *feria* in Andalucía celebrates a patron saint, the Ronda fair glorifies legendary bullfighter Pedro Romero. For September bullfights, tickets go on sale the preceding July. (As these sell out immediately, Sevilla and Madrid are more practical places for a tourist to see a bullfight.)

⊘ **Self-Guided Tour:** Visit in this order. Directly to the right as you enter is the bullfighters' **chapel.** Before going into the ring, every matador would stop here to pray to Mary for safety—and hope to see her again.

• *Just beyond the chapel are the doors to the museum exhibits: horse gear and weapons on the left, and the story of bullfighting on*

Ronda's historic bullring

Bullfighting Museum

the right, with English translations.

The **horse gear and guns exhibit** makes the connection with bullfighting and the equestrian upper class. As throughout Europe, "chivalry" began as a code among the sophisticated, horse-riding gentry. (In Spanish, the word for "gentleman" is the same as the word for "horseman" or "cowboy"—*caballero*.) And, of course, nobles are into hunting and dueling, hence the fancy guns. Don't miss the well-described dueling section with gun cases for two, as charming as a picnic basket with matching wine glasses.

Return to the hallway with the chapel to see Spain's best **bullfighting exhibit,** a shrine to bullfighting and the Romero family. First it traces the long history of bullfighting, going all the way back to the ancient Minoans on Crete. Historically, there were only two arenas built solely for bullfighting: in Ronda and Sevilla. Elsewhere, bullfights were held in town squares—you'll see a painting of Madrid's Plaza Mayor filled with spectators for a bullfight. (To this day, even a purpose-built bullring is generally called *plaza de toros*—"square of bulls.") You'll also see stuffed bull heads, photos, "suits of light" worn by bullfighters, and capes (bulls are actually colorblind, but the traditional red cape was designed to disguise all the blood). One section explains some of the dynasties of bullfighters. At the end of the hall are historical posters (all originals except the Picasso). Running along the left wall are various examples of artwork glorifying bullfighting, including original Goya engravings.

• *Exit at the far end of the bullfighting exhibit and take advantage of the opportunity to walk in the actual arena.*

Here's your chance to play *toro,* surrounded by 5,000 empty seats. The two-tiered **arena** was built in 1785—on the 300th anniversary of the defeat of the Moors in Ronda. Notice the 136 classy Tuscan columns, creating a kind of 18th-century Italian theater. Lovers of the "art" of bullfighting will explain that the event is much more than the actual killing of the bull. It celebrates the noble heritage and the Andalusian horse culture. When you leave the museum and walk out on the sand, look across to see the ornamental columns and painted doorway where the dignitaries sit (over the gate where the bull enters). On the right is the place for the band (marked *música*), which, in the case of a small town like Ronda, is most likely a high school band.

• *Just beyond the arena are more parts of the complex. Find the open gate beneath the dignitaries' seats.*

Walk through the bulls' entry into the bullpen and the **stables.** There are six bulls per fight (plus two backups)—and three matadors. The bulls are penned up here beforehand, and ropes and pulleys safely open the right door at the right time. Climb the skinny staircase and find the indoor arena (Picadero), where Spanish thoroughbred horses from the **Equestrian School** are trained (Mon-Fri). Explore the spectators' seating before exiting through the gift shop.

Nearby: One block away from the bullring, breezy **Alameda del Tajo Park** is a great place for a picnic lunch or people-watching. Don't miss its balcony overlooking the scenic Serranía de Ronda mountains.

Ronda's Old Town

▲CHURCH OF SANTA MARÍA LA MAYOR (IGLESIA DE SANTA MARÍA) This 15th-century church with a fine Mudejar bell tower shares a park-like square with orange trees and City Hall. It was built on and around the remains of Moorish Ronda's main mosque (which was itself built on the site of a temple to Julius Caesar). With an eclectic interior that features art with modern flair, and a good audioguide to explain it all, it's worth a visit.

Cost and Hours: €4.50, daily April-Sept 10:00-20:00, closed Sun 12:30-14:00

for Mass, closes earlier off-season, includes audioguide, Plaza Duquesa de Parcent in the old town.

Visiting the Church: In the room where you purchase your ticket, look for the only surviving mosque **prayer niche** (that's a mirror; look back at the actual mihrab, which faces not Mecca, but Gibraltar—where you'd travel to get to Mecca). Partially destroyed by an earthquake, the reconstruction of the church resulted in the Moorish/Gothic/Renaissance/Baroque fusion (or confusion) you see today.

The front of the church interior is dominated by a magnificent Baroque **Altar del Sagrario** with the statue of the *Immaculate Conception* in the center. The even more ornate chapel directly to the right is a good example of Churrigueresque architecture, a kind of Spanish Rococo in which the decoration obliterates the architecture—notice that you can hardly make out the souped-up columns. This chapel's fancy decor provides a frame for an artistic highlight of the town, the "Virgin of the Ultimate Sorrow." The big fresco of St. Christopher with Baby Jesus on his shoul-

ders (on the left, above the door where you entered) shows the patron saint both of Ronda and of travelers.

Facing the altar is an elaborately carved **choir** with a wall of modern bronze reliefs depicting scenes from the life of the Virgin Mary. Similar to the Via Crucis (Way of the Cross), this is the Via Lucis (Way of the Light), with 14 stations (such as #13—the Immaculate Conception, and #14—Mary's assumption into heaven) that serve as a worship aid to devout Catholics. The centerpiece is Mary as the light of the world, with the moon, stars, and sun around her.

Head to the left around the choir, noticing the bright **paintings** along the wall by French artist Raymonde Pagegie, who gave sacred scenes a fresh twist—like the Last Supper attended by female servants, or the scene of Judgment Day, when the four horsemen of the apocalypse pause to adore the Lamb of God.

The **treasury** (at the far-right corner, with your back to the high altar) displays vestments that look curiously like matadors' brocaded outfits—appropriate for this bullfight-crazy town.

Church of Santa María la Mayor

Mondragón Palace

MONDRAGÓN PALACE
(PALACIO DE MONDRAGÓN)

This beautiful, originally Moorish building was erected in the 14th century. At the entrance (free to view without a ticket) is a topographic model of Ronda, which helps you envision the fortified old town apart from the grid-like new one. The rest of the building houses Ronda's **Municipal Museum,** focusing on prehistory and geology. Wander through its many rooms to find the kid-friendly prehistory section, with exhibits on Neolithic toolmaking and early metallurgy (described in English). Panels describe the nearby Pileta Cave's formation and shape.

Cost and Hours: €3; Mon-Fri 10:00-19:00, Sat-Sun 10:00-15:00, closes earlier off-season; on Plaza Mondragón in old town, tel. 952-870-818.

Nearby Hike to View: Leaving the palace, wander left a few short blocks to the nearby Plaza de María Auxiliadora for more views. For an intense workout and a picture-perfect view, find the tiled *Puerta de los Molinos* sign and head down, down, down. (Just remember you have to walk back up, up, up.) Not for the faint of heart or in midday heat, this pathway leads down to the viewpoint where windmills once stood. Photographers go crazy reproducing the most famous postcard view of Ronda—the entirety of the New Bridge. Wait until just before sunset for the best light and cooler temperatures.

▲JOAQUÍN PEINADO MUSEUM
(MUSEO JOAQUÍN PEINADO)

Housed in an old palace, this fresh museum features an overview of the life's work of Joaquín Peinado (1898-1975), Ronda native and pal of Picasso. Because Franco killed creativity in Spain for much of the last century, nearly all of Peinado's work was created in Paris. His style evolved through the big "isms" of the 20th century, ranging from Expressionism to Cubism, and to eroticism. While Peinado's works may seem derivative, perhaps that's understandable as he was friends with one of the art world's biggest talents. The nine-minute movie that kicks off the display is only in Spanish, but there are good English explanations throughout the museum. It's fun to be exposed to a lesser-known but talented artist in his hometown.

Cost and Hours: €4, Mon-Fri 10:00-17:00, Sat 10:00-15:00, closed Sun, Plaza del Gigante, tel. 952-871-585, www.museojoaquinpeinado.com.

Near Ronda
PILETA CAVE

The Pileta Cave (Cueva de la Pileta) offers Spain's most intimate look at Neolithic and Paleolithic paintings up to 25,000 years old. Set in a dramatic, rocky limestone ridge at the eastern edge of Sierra de Grazalema Natural Park, Pileta Cave is 14 miles from Ronda, past the town of Benaoján, at the end of an access road. It's particularly handy to visit if you're driving between Ronda and Grazalema.

Cost and Hours: €8, one-hour tours generally depart daily at 13:00 & 16:00, additional tours go between 10:00-13:00 and 16:00-18:00 if enough people gather (Nov-mid-April until 17:00), closing times indicate last tour, €10 guidebook, no photos, tel. 952-167-343, www.cuevadelapileta.org.

Getting There: You can get from Ronda to the cave by taxi—it's about a half-hour drive on twisty roads—and have the driver wait (€60 round-trip). If you're driving, it's easy: Leave Ronda through the new part of town, and take A-374. After a few miles, passing Cueva del Gato, exit left toward Benaoján on MA-555. Go through Benaoján and follow the numerous signs to the cave. Leave nothing of value in your car.

Visiting the Cave: Farmer José Bullón and his family live down the hill from the cave, and because they strictly limit the

Aromatic spices and herbs are essential to Spain's cuisine.

number of visitors, Pileta's rare paintings are among the best preserved in the world. Señor Bullón and his son lead up to 25 people at a time through the cave, which was discovered by Bullón's grandfather in 1905. Call the night before to see if there's a tour and space available at the time you want. Note that if you simply show up for the 13:00 tour, you'll risk not getting a spot—and it'll be another three hours before the next one starts. Arrive early, and be flexible. Bring a sweater and good shoes. You need a good sense of balance to take the tour. The 10-minute hike—from the parking lot up a trail with stone steps to the cave entrance—is moderately steep. Inside the cave, there are no handrails, and it can be difficult to keep your footing on the slippery, uneven floor while being led single-file, with only a lantern light illuminating the way.

Señor Bullón is a master at hurdling the language barrier. As you walk the cool half-mile, he'll spend an hour pointing out lots of black, ochre, and red drawings, which are five times as old as the Egyptian pyramids. There are mostly just lines or patterns, with some horses, goats, cattle, and a rare giant fish, finger-painted with a mixture of clay and fat. The 200-foot main cavern is impressive, as are some weirdly recognizable natural formations such as the Michelin man and a Christmas tree.

Eating

Plaza del Socorro, a block in front of the bullring, bustles with tourists and local families enjoying the square and its restaurants. The pedestrian-only **Calle Nueva** is lined with hardworking eateries. To enjoy a drink or a light meal with the best view in town, consider the terraces of Hotel Don Miguel just under the bridge.

For coffee and pastries, locals like the elegant little **Confitería Daver** (café open daily 8:00-20:30, takeaway until 21:00, three locations—Calle Virgen de los Remedios 6, Calle Padre Mariano Soubiron 8, and Calle Espinel 58). At a bar or bakery, get your morning protein with a *mollete con jamón y aceite,* a soft bread roll with ham and olive oil (sometimes comes with cheese, too).

Picnic shoppers find the **Alameda Market** conveniently located next to Alameda del Tajo park, which has benches and a WC (Mon-Sat 8:30-21:00, Sun 9:00-15:00, Calle Virgen de La Paz 23). The **Día** supermarket, opposite Hotel El Tajo, is also central (Mon-Sat 9:15-21:15, closed Sun, Calle Cruz Verde 18).

Tapas in the City Center

Ronda has a fine tapas scene. You won't get a free tapa with your drink as in some other Spanish towns, but these bars have accessible tapas lists, and they serve bigger plates. Each of the following places could make a fine solo destination for a meal, but they're close enough that you can easily go tapa-hopping.

Tragatapas serves creative and always tasty tapas in a stainless-steel minimalist bar. There are just a handful of tall tiny tables and some bar space inside, with patio seating on the pedestrian street, and an enticing blackboard of the day's specials. You'll pay more for it, but if you want to sample Andalusian gourmet (e.g., a few €3 tapas such as asparagus on a stick sprinkled with grated manchego cheese), this is the place to do it (also €9-17 larger plates to share, daily 12:00-17:00 & 20:00-24:00, Calle Nueva 4, tel. 952-877-209).

Nueva 13, the latest entrant in the Calle Nueva tapa fest, serves up admirable €1.50 tapas and €6-14 *raciones*. Specials such as *rabo de toro* (bull's-tail stew) and *calamares* (squid) are listed on the giant blackboard inside (daily 13:00-17:00 & 20:00-24:00, Calle Nueva 13, tel. 952-190-090).

Bar Lechuguita, a hit with older locals early and younger ones later, serves a long and tasty list of tapas for a good price. Rip off a tapas inventory sheet and mark which ones you want (most cost €0.80; €5 plates also available). Be adventurous and don't miss the bar's namesake, *Lechuguita* (#15, a wedge of lettuce with vinegar, garlic, and a secret ingredient). The space has no chairs or tables, just a bar and tiny stand-up ledges. The order-form routine makes it easy to communicate and get exactly what you want, plus you know the exact price (Mon-Sat 13:00-15:15 & 20:15-23:30, closed Sun, Calle Virgen de los Remedios 35).

Café & Bar Faustino is a place Brueghel would paint—a festival of eating with a fun menu that works both at the bar and at tables. The atmosphere makes you want to stay, while the selection makes you wish you had a bigger appetite (lots of €1 tapas, €3 sandwiches, €5-8 *raciones*, Tue-Sun 12:00-24:00, closed Mon, just off Plaza Carmen Abela at Santa Cecilia 4, tel. 952-190-307).

Outside the Almocábar Gate

Leaving the old town and bustling city center—and the tourists—hike 10 minutes out to the far end of the old town, past City Hall, to a big workaday square that goes about life as if the world didn't exist outside Andalucía.

Bar-Restaurante Almocábar is a local favorite. Its restaurant—a cozy eight-table room with Moorish tiles and a window to the kitchen—serves up delicious, inventive meals from a menu that's well described in English (plus a handwritten list of the day's specials). Many opt for the good €8-15 salads—rare in Spain. At the busy bar up front, you can order anything from the dining room menu, or choose from the list of €2 tapas (€5-15 starters, €12-20 main dishes, closed Tue, Calle Ruedo Alameda 5, tel. 952-875-977).

Casa María is a small tapas bar offering typical Andalusian fare in a homey setting. In summer, their tables spill out onto the plaza (€1-3 tapas, €9-12 *raciones,* Wed-Mon 12:30-24:00, closed Tue, facing Plaza Ruedo Alameda at #27, tel. 676-126-822).

Bodega San Francisco is a rustic bar with tables upstairs, tables out front and on the square, and a homey restaurant across the street. They offer a list of €4-9 *raciones* and €1 tapas, as well as serious plates and big splittable portions (same menu in bar and restaurant). This place is great for people-watching and is a neighborhood favorite (closed Thu, Ruedo de Alameda 32, tel. 952-878-162).

Dining in the City Center

Ronda is littered with upscale restaurants that toe the delicate line between good dinner spots and tourist traps. Here are two of the better ones:

Restaurante Pedro Romero, though touristy and overpriced, is a venerable institution that gets good reviews. Rub elbows with the bullfighters or dine with

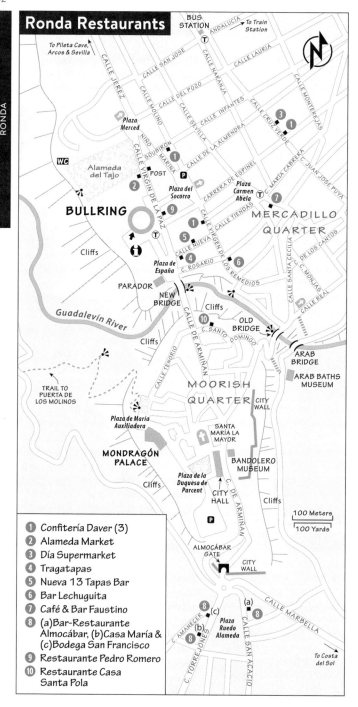

Ronda Restaurants

1 Confitería Daver (3)
2 Alameda Market
3 Día Supermarket
4 Tragatapas
5 Nueva 13 Tapas Bar
6 Bar Lechuguita
7 Café & Bar Faustino
8 (a)Bar-Restaurante Almocábar, (b)Casa María & (c)Bodega San Francisco
9 Restaurante Pedro Romero
10 Restaurante Casa Santa Pola

the likes (well, photographic likenesses) of Orson Welles, Ernest Hemingway, and Francisco Franco—if the shrine to bull-fighting doesn't ruin your appetite (€16 and €25 fixed-price meals, €7-12 starters, €16-20 main dishes, daily 12:00-16:00 & 19:30-23:00, air-con, across from bullring at Calle Virgen de la Paz 18, tel. 952-871-110).

Restaurante Casa Santa Pola offers gourmet versions of traditional food with professional service. It has several small dining rooms and a terrace perched on the side of the gorge—worth reserving ahead. They serve good oxtail stew, roasted lamb, and honey-tempura eggplant (pricey €12-18 starters, €17-24 main dishes, daily 12:30-16:30 & 19:00-22:30; after crossing New Bridge from bullring, take the first left downhill and you'll see the sign, Calle Santo Domingo 3; tel. 952-879-208, www.rsantapola.com).

Sleeping

Ronda has plenty of reasonably priced, decent-value accommodations. It's crowded only during Holy Week (before Easter) and the first week of September (for bullfighting season). Most of my recommendations are in the new town, a short stroll from the New Bridge and about a 10-minute walk from the train station. In the cheaper places, ask for a room with a *ventana* (window) to avoid the few interior rooms. Breakfast is usually not included. See map on page 335 for locations.

In the Old Town

As the best options in town, these hotels are worth reserving early. The first two are right in the heart of the Old Town, while the Alavera de los Baños is a steep 15- to 20-minute hike below, but still walkable to all the sights.

$$ Hotel San Gabriel has 22 pleasant rooms, a kind staff, public rooms filled with art and books, a wine cellar, and a garden terrace. The large 1736 townhouse, once the family's home, has been converted into a hotel marinated in history. If you're a cinephile, kick back in the charming TV room—with seats from Ronda's old theater and a collection of DVD classics. The breakfast room has photos of movie stars who have stayed here (Sb-€73, Db-€100, bigger superior Db-€111, Db junior suite-€120, breakfast-€6, air-con, incognito elevator, double-park in front and they'll direct you to a €10/day parking spot, follow signs on main street of old town to Calle Marqués de Moctezuma 19, tel. 952-190-392, www.hotelsangabriel.com, info@hotelsangabriel.com).

$$ Hotel Ronda provides an interesting mix of minimalist and traditional Spanish decor in a refurbished mansion, which is both quiet and homey. Although its five rooms lack views, the small, lovely rooftop deck overlooks the town (Sb-€53, Db-€70, extra bed-€22, breakfast-€4, air-con, ask for parking directions when you book, Ruedo Doña Elvira 12, tel. 952-872-232, www.hotelronda.net, laraln@tele fonica.net).

$$ Alavera de los Baños, a delightful oasis located next to ancient Moorish baths at the bottom of the hill, has nine small rooms, two spacious suites, and big inviting public places, with appropriately Moorish decor. Well run by personable Christian and Inma, the hotel has a swimming pool, a peaceful Arabic garden, and a selection of sandwiches for lunch. It's a bucolic setting: You're literally in the countryside, with sheep and horses outside (Sb-€60-70, Db-€85-97, Db with terrace-€95-107, Qb-€110-130, includes breakfast, free and easy parking, closed Jan, steeply below the heart of town at Calle Molino de Alarcón, tel. 952-879-143, www.alaveradelosbanos.com, hotel@alaveradelosbanos.com).

In the New Town

Located in the thriving new town, most of these hotels are more convenient than charming (except Hotel Enfrente Arte Ronda, which is in a class all its own).

$$$ Hotel Catalonia Reina Victoria hangs royally over the gorge at the edge of town and has a marvelous view—Hemingway loved it, and so does its well-dressed clientele. Its 89 renovated rooms are sleek and modern but lack character. Rooms with a gorge view cost €15 more—and they're worth it. A 10-minute walk from city center and easy to miss—it's set back from the street at the intersection of Avenida Victoria and Calle Jerez (Sb-€97-117, Db-€115-156—but check website for deals, breakfast-€13, air-con, elevator, pool, parking-€15/day, Jerez 25, tel. 952-871-240, www.hoteles-catalonia.com, reinavictoria@hoteles-catalonia.com).

$$ Hotel Enfrente Arte Ronda, a steep 10- to 15-minute walk below the heart of the new town, is relaxed and funky. The 12 rooms are spacious and exotically decorated, but dimly lit. It features a sprawling maze of public spaces with creative decor, a peaceful bamboo garden, a game and reading room, small swimming pool, sauna, and terraces with sweeping countryside views. Guests can help themselves to free drinks from the self-service bar or have their feet nibbled for free by "Dr. Fish." This place is one of a kind—Madonna even stayed here once—so reserve early (Db-€80-105, extra bed-€28-40, includes buffet breakfast, air-con, elevator, Real 40, tel. 952-879-088, www.enfrentearte.com, reservations@enfrentearte.com).

$$ Hotel Don Miguel, facing the gorge next to the bridge, can seem like staying in a cave, but it couldn't be more central. Of its 30 sparse but comfortable rooms, 20 have gorgeous views at no extra cost. Street rooms come with a little noise (Sb-€59-70, Db-€91-108, Tb-€110-135, free buffet breakfast, ask for Rick Steves discount if you book directly with the hotel via email and mention this book, air-con, elevator, Wi-Fi in lobby, parking garage a block away-€12/day, Plaza de España 4, tel. 952-877-722, www.dmiguel.com, reservas@dmiguel.com).

$$ Hotel El Tajo has 50 quiet rooms with updated bathrooms. You just have to get past the tacky faux-stone Moorish decoration in the foyer (Sb-€40-57, Db-€48-75, Tb-€75-99, breakfast-€6, air-con, elevator, parking-€11/day, Calle Cruz Verde 7, a half-block off the pedestrian street, tel. 952-874-040, www.hoteleltajo.com, reservas@hoteleltajo.com).

$$ Hotel San Francisco offers 27 small, nicely decorated rooms a block off the main pedestrian street in the town center (Sb-€40-55, Db-€48-60, Tb-€70-76, Qb-€85-106, breakfast-€5, air-con, elevator, parking-€9/day, María Cabrera 20, tel. 952-873-299, www.hotelsanfrancisco-ronda.com, recepcion@hotelsanfrancisco-ronda.com).

$ Hotel Royal has a dreary reception but friendly staff and 29 clean, spacious, simple rooms—many on the main street that runs between the bullring and bridge. Thick glass keeps out most of the noise, while the tree-lined Alameda del Tajo park across the street is a treat (Sb-€30-33, Db-€35-45, Tb-€50-60, breakfast-€4-5, air-con, parking-€10/day, 3 blocks off Plaza de España at Calle Virgen de la Paz 42, tel. 952-871-141, www.ronda.net/usuar/hotelroyal, hroyal@ronda.net).

$ Hotel Andalucía has 12 clean, comfortable rooms immediately across the street from the train station (Sb-€25, Db-€40, Tb-€53, breakfast-€2, air-con and TV in all rooms, easy street parking or €6/day in nearby garage, Martínez Astein 19, tel. 952-875-450, www.hotel-andalucia.net, info@hotel-andalucia.net).

Transportation
Arriving and Departing

Note that some destinations are linked with Ronda by both bus and train. Direct bus service to other hill towns can be sparse (as few as one per day), and train service usually involves a transfer in Bobadilla. It's worth spending a few minutes in the bus or train station on arrival to plan your departure.

BY TRAIN

The small station has ticket windows, a train info desk, and a café, but no baggage storage (there are lockers at the nearby bus station).

From the station, it's a 15- to 20-minute **walk** to the center: Turn right out of the station on Avenida de Andalucía, and go through the roundabout (you'll see the bus station on your right). Continue straight down the street (now called San José) until you reach Calle Jerez. Turn left and walk downhill past a church and the Alameda del Tajo park. Keep going down this street, passing the bullring, to get to the TI and the famous bridge. A **taxi** to the center costs about €7.

Transfers are a snap and time-coordinated in Bobadilla; with four trains arriving and departing simultaneously, double-check that you're jumping on the right one. Train info: tel. 902-320-320, www.renfe.com.

From Ronda by Train to: Bobadilla (4/day, 1 hour); **Málaga** (1/day, 2 hours, 2 more with transfer in Bobadilla; direct bus is better—see below); **Sevilla** (5/day, 3-4 hours, transfer in Bobadilla, Antequera, or Córdoba); **Granada** (3/day, 2.5 hours); **Córdoba** (2/day direct, 2 hours; more with transfer in Bobadilla or Antequera, 4 hours); **Madrid** (2/day, 4 hours).

BY BUS

To get to the center from the bus station, leave the station walking to the right of the roundabout, then follow the directions for train travelers described above. To use the station's baggage lockers, buy a token (*ficha*) at the kiosk by the exit.

For schedule info, you can compare schedules at the bus station on Plaza Concepción García Redondo (several blocks from train station), or pick up a bus timetable from the city TI. Bus info: Los Amarillos (tel. 902-210-317, www.losamarillos.es), Portillo (tel. 902-450-550, http://portillo.avanzabus.com), and Comes (tel. 956-291-168, www.tgcomes.es). If traveling to **Córdoba,** it's easiest

to take the train since there are no direct buses.

From Ronda by Bus to: Algeciras (1/day, 3.5 hours, Comes); **La Línea/Gibraltar** (1/day, transfer in Algeciras; Algeciras to Gibraltar—2/hour, 45 minutes, buy ticket on bus); **Arcos** (1/day, 2 hours, Comes); **Grazalema** (2/day, 45 minutes, Los Amarillos); **Zahara** (2/day, Mon-Fri only, 45 minutes, Comes); **Sevilla** (8/day, 2-2.5 hours, fewer on weekends, some via Villamartín, Los Amarillos; also see trains, above); **Málaga** (*directo* 6-10/day, 2 hours, Los Amarillos; access other Costa del Sol points from Málaga); **Nerja** (4 hours, transfer in Málaga; can take train or bus from Ronda to Málaga, bus is better).

BY CAR

In Ronda, street parking away from the center is often free. The handiest place to park in the city center is the underground lot at Plaza del Socorro (€18/24 hours, one block from bullring).

JEREZ DE LA FRONTERA

Jerez, rated ▲, is a flat big city with more than 200,000 people and two claims to fame: horses and sherry. It's ideal for a noontime visit on a weekday. See the famous horses, sip some sherry, wander through the old quarter, and swagger out. If arriving by bus or train, for the most efficient visit, taxi from the train station right to the Royal Andalusian School for the equestrian performance, then walk around the corner to the Sandeman winery for the next sherry tour.

Orientation

Thanks to its complicated, medieval street plan, there is no easy way to feel oriented in Jerez—so ask for directions liberally.

Tourist Information

The helpful TI is on Plaza del Arenal. If you're walking to see the horses, ask here

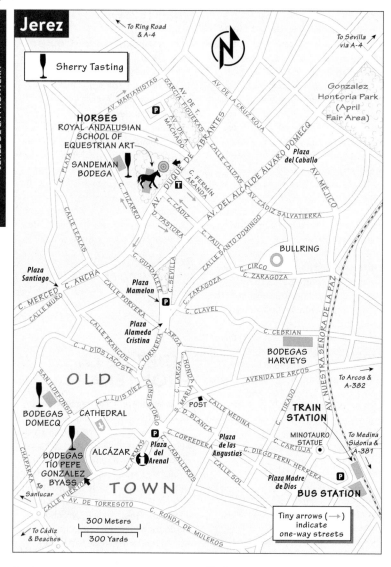

Jerez

To Ring Road & A-4

To Sevilla via A-4

Sherry Tasting

HORSES
ROYAL ANDALUSIAN
SCHOOL OF
EQUESTRIAN ART

SANDEMAN
BODEGA

Gonzalez
Hontoria Park
(April
Fair Area)

Plaza
del Caballo

AV. DE LA CRUZ ROJA

AV. MARIANISTAS

AV. DE I GARCÍA FIGUERAS

AV. DE A MACHADO

DUQUE DE ABRANTES

CALLE CALDAS

AV. DEL ALCALDE ÁLVARO DOMECQ

AV. MEJICO

C. PLATA

C. PIZARRO

CALLE LEALAS

C. FERMIN

C. ARANDA

AV. DEL ALCALDE ÁLVARO AV. CÁDIZ SALVATIERRA

C. CÁDIZ

P. PASTORA

C. PAULO SANTO DOMINGO

BULLRING

Plaza
Santiago

C. MERCED

C. MURO

C. ANCHA

Calle PORVERA

C. GUADALETE

C. SEVILLA

Plaza
Mamelon

C. ZARAGOZA

C. CIRCO

C. ZARAGOZA

Plaza
Alameda
Cristina

C. J. DIOS LACOSTE

Calle FRANCOS

LARGA

C. TORNERIA

C. CLAVEL

C. CEBRIAN

BODEGAS
HARVEYS

AVENIDA DE ARCOS

AV. NUESTRA SEÑORA DE LA PAZ

To Arcos & A-382

OLD

SAN ILDEFONSO

BODEGAS
DOMECQ

CATHEDRAL

C. J. LUIS DIEZ

CONSISTORIO

C. LARGA

C. HONDA

MARÍA

C. D. BLANCA

POST

CALLE MEDINA

C. TIRADO

TRAIN
STATION

*To Medina
Sidonia &
A-381*

BODEGAS
TÍO PEPE
GONZALEZ
BYASS

ALCÁZAR

Plaza
del
Arenal

C. ARMAS

C. CORREDERA

C. CABALLEROS

Plaza
de las
Angustias

MINOTAURO
STATUE

C. CARTUJA

C. DIEGO FERN. HERRERA

CALLE SOL

*To
Sanlucar*

CHAPARRA

CALLE PUERTO

AV. DE TORRESOTO

TOWN

Plaza Madre
de Dios

BUS STATION

*To Cádiz
& Beaches*

C. RONDA DE MULEROS

300 Meters

300 Yards

Tiny arrows (→)
indicate
one-way streets

---

for directions, as the route is confusing (Mon-Fri 9:00-15:00 & 17:00-19:00, Sat-Sun 9:30-14:30, shorter evening hours Oct-May, tel. 956-338-874, www.turismo jerez.com). They also offer free one-hour tours (Mon-Fri at 10:00, 12:00, and 17:00; Sat at 10:00 and 12:00; and Sun at 12:00).

Sights

▲▲ROYAL ANDALUSIAN SCHOOL OF EQUESTRIAN ART

If you're into horses, a performance of the Royal Andalusian School of Equestrian Art (Fundación Real Escuela Andaluza del Arte Ecuestre) is a must. Even if you're not, this is art like you've never seen.

Royal Andalusian School of Equestrian Art

Getting There: From the TI at Plaza del Arenal, it's about a half-hour walk down mostly pedestrianized shopping streets. Leave the plaza on Calle Lanceria, heading to the left of the rounded Fino La Ina Fundador building to Calle Larga. It will bend gently left, depositing you at the foot of a tree-lined boulevard (Plaza Alameda Christina/Plaza Memelon). From here, veer right and follow the *Real Escuela de Arte Ecuestre* signs.

From the bus or train stations to the horses, it's about a €6 **taxi** ride. Taxis wait at the exit of the school for the return trip.

One-way streets mean there is only one way to arrive by **car.** Follow signs to *Real Escuela de Arte Ecuestre.* Expect to make at least one wrong turn, so allow extra time. There's free parking behind the school.

PERFORMANCES

This is an equestrian ballet with choreography, music, and costumes from the 19th century. Stern riders and their talented, obedient steeds prance, jump, hop on their hind legs, and do-si-do in time to the music.

The riders cue the horses with subtle dressage commands, either verbally or with body movements. You'll see both purebred Spanish horses (with long tails and good jumping ability) and larger mixed breeds (with short tails and a walking—not prancing—gait). The horses must be three years old before their three-year training begins. Most performing horses are male (stallions or geldings), since mixing the sexes brings problems.

The equestrian school is a university. Professors often team with students and evaluate their performance during the show. Tightly fitted mushroom hats are decorated with different stripes to show each rider's level.

Cost and Hours: General seating-€21, "preference" seating-€27; 1.5-hour show runs Tue and Thu at 12:00 most of the year (also one Sat show per month year-round and on Fri in Aug and Sept, Jan-Feb Thu only); no photos allowed in show, stables, or museum; tel. 956-318-008, tickets available online at www.real escuela.org. General seating is fine; some "preference" seats are too close for good overall views. The show explanations are in Spanish.

TRAINING SESSIONS

The public can view training sessions on nonperformance days. Sessions can be exciting or dull, depending on what the trainers are working on. Afterward, take a 1.5-hour guided tour of the stables, horses, carriage museums, tack room, gardens, and horse health center. Sip sherry in the arena's bar to complete the experience.

Cost and Hours: €11; Mon, Wed, and Fri—except no Fri in Aug-Sept, also on Tue in Jan-Feb; arrive anytime between 10:00 and 14:00—they'll start a tour when they have a large-enough group (but avoid 11:00, when tour groups crowd in).

▲▲SHERRY BODEGA TOUR

Spain produces more than 10 million gallons per year of the fortified wine known as sherry. The name comes from English attempts to pronounce Jerez. Your tourist map of Jerez is speckled with *venen-*cia symbols, each representing a sherry bodega that offers tours and tasting. (*Venencias* are specially designed ladles for dipping inside the sherry barrel.) It's smart to confirm your tour time in advance.

Just around the corner from the equestrian school is the venerable **Sandeman** winery, founded in 1790 and the longtime choice of English royalty. This tour is the aficionado's choice for its knowledgeable guides and their quality explanations of the process. Each stage is explained in detail (€7.50 for regular sherries, more for rare sherries, €7.50 adds tapas to the tasting, tour/tasting lasts 1-1.5 hours; English tours Mon, Wed, and Fri at 11:30, 12:30, and 13:30 plus April-Oct also at 14:30; Tue and Thu at 10:30, 12:00, 13:00, and 14:15; Sat by appointment only, closed Sun; reservations not required, tel. 675-647-177, www.sandeman.eu).

Rick's Tip: *It looks tempting, but* **don't bother with Jerez's gutted Alcázar castle.**

Equestrian performance

Sherry bodega tour

Transportation
Arriving and Departing

The bus and train stations are located side by side, near Plaza del Minotauro (with enormous headless statue). Unfortunately, you can't store luggage at either one. Cheap and easy **taxis** wait in front of the train station (€4 to TI; about €6 to the horses).

Rick's Tip: *You can* **store luggage** *for free in the* **Royal Andalusian School's coat room** *while you attend an equestrian performance, but only for the duration of the show.*

From either station, it's a 20-minute **walk** to the center of town and the TI: Angle across the brick plaza (in front of the stations, with two black smokestacks) to find Calle Diego Fernández de Herrera (look for the awning for the *churros* bar). Follow this street for several blocks until you reach a little square (Plaza de las Angustias). Continue in the same direction, leaving the square at the far left side down Calle Corredera. In a few minutes you'll arrive at Plaza del Arenal (ringed with palm trees, with a large fountain in the center)—the TI is in the arcaded building across the plaza.

BY BUS

Bus Connections: Jerez's bus station is shared by six bus companies, each with its own schedule. The main companies serving most southern Spain destinations are Los Amarillos (tel. 902-210-317, www. losamarillos.es), Comes (tel. 956-291-

168, www.tgcomes.es), and Autocares Valenzuela (tel. 956-702-609, www.grupo valenzuela.com). Shop around for the best departure time and most direct route. While here, clarify routes for any further bus travel you may be doing in Andalucía—especially if you're going through Arcos de la Frontera, where the ticket office is often closed. Also check www. movelia.es for bus schedules and routes.

From Jerez by Bus to: **Arcos** (hourly, 30 minutes); **Ronda** (2/day, 2.5-3 hours); **Sevilla** (hourly, 1-1.5 hours); **Granada** (1/day, 5 hours).

BY TRAIN

From Jerez by Train to: Sevilla (nearly hourly, 1 hour); **Madrid** (3-4/day direct, 4 hours; nearly hourly with change in Sevilla, 4 hours);

Barcelona (nearly hourly, 7-9 hours, all with change in Sevilla and/or Madrid). **Train info:** tel. 902-320-320, www.renfe. com.

BY CAR

Driving in Jerez can be frustrating. The outskirts are filled with an almost endless series of roundabouts. Continue to follow traffic and signs to *centro ciudad*. The circuitous route should ultimately take you to Plaza Alameda Cristina; park in the underground garage (€1.30/hour) and catch a cab or walk to the equestrian school. Although you can park behind the school, it's easier to use the underground garage, given the confusing one-way and pedestrianized streets in the center.

Sevilla

lamboyant Sevilla (seh-VEE-yah) thrums with flamenco music, pulses with the passion of Don Juan and Carmen, and sizzles in the summer heat. It's a place where bullfighting is still politically correct and little girls still dream of growing up to become flamenco dancers.

The gateway to the New World in the 16th century, Sevilla boomed when Spain did. Explorers Amerigo Vespucci and Ferdinand Magellan sailed from its river harbor, discovering new trade routes and abundant sources of gold, silver, cocoa, and tobacco. By the 17th century, Sevilla was Spain's largest and wealthiest city. Local artists Diego Velázquez, Bartolomé Murillo, and Francisco de Zurbarán made it a cultural center. Sevilla's Golden Age—and its New World riches—ended when the harbor silted up and the Spanish empire crumbled.

Today, Spain's fourth-largest city (pop. 702,000) buzzes with guitars, castanets, and street life. Its impressive sights include Spain's largest cathedral and the Alcázar royal palace and garden, ornamented with Mudejar (Islamic) flair. But the real magic is the city itself, with its tangled former Jewish Quarter, riveting flamenco shows, and teeming evening paseo. James Michener wrote, "Sevilla doesn't *have* ambience, it *is* ambience." Sevilla has soul.

SEVILLA IN 2 DAYS

Day 1: Take Concepción Delgado's city walk. In the afternoon, tour the cathedral and climb its Giralda Bell Tower. With extra time, visit another sight, such as the Hospital de la Caridad nearby.

On any evening, take your pick: Take my Barrio Santa Cruz neighborhood walk (best about 18:00). Attend a riveting flamenco show. Stroll along the northern bank of the Guadalquivir River, or cross the river to explore the Triana neighborhood and savor cityscape views. Stay out late at least once to appreciate Sevilla on a warm night—one of its major charms.

Day 2: Tour the Royal Alcázar (before 13:30, if you want to see the Upper Royal Apartments); you can reserve an entry time online. In the afternoon, take your pick among the Bullfight Museum, Flamenco Dance Museum, Museo de Bellas Artes (Fine Arts Museum), or, farther from the center, the Basílica de la Macarena.

Day Trip: For Moorish sights, stay another day to make a quick trip to Córdoba (45 minutes on AVE high-speed train).

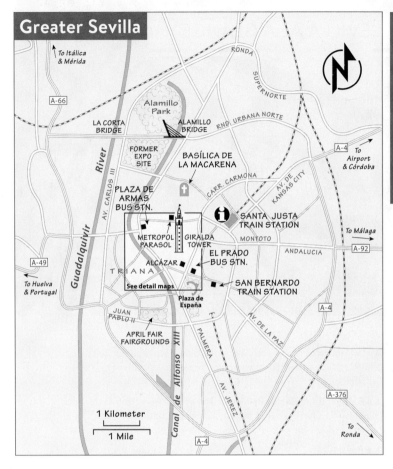

Greater Sevilla

To Itálica & Mérida

RONDA

SUPERNORTE

A-66

Alamillo Park

LA CORTA BRIDGE

ALAMILLO BRIDGE

RND. URBANA NORTE

FORMER EXPO SITE

BASÍLICA DE LA MACARENA

River

AV. CARLOS III

CARR. CARMONA

AV. DE KANSAS CITY

A-4 To Airport & Córdoba

PLAZA DE ARMAS BUS STN.

SANTA JUSTA TRAIN STATION

To Málaga

Guadalquivir

METROPOL PARASOL

GIRALDA TOWER

MONTOTO

ANDALUCIA

A-92

A-49

ALCÁZAR

EL PRADO BUS STN.

TRIANA

See detail maps

SAN BERNARDO TRAIN STATION

To Huelva & Portugal

Plaza de España

AV. DE LA PAZ

A-4

JUAN PABLO II

APRIL FAIR FAIRGROUNDS

PALMERA

Canal de Alfonso XIII

AV. DE JEREZ

A-376

1 Kilometer

1 Mile

A-4

To Ronda

ORIENTATION

For the tourist, this big city is small. The bull's-eye on your map should be the cathedral and its Giralda bell tower, which can be seen from all over town. Nearby are Sevilla's other major sights, the Alcázar palace and gardens and the lively Barrio Santa Cruz district. The central north-south pedestrian boulevard, Avenida de la Constitución, stretches north a few blocks to Plaza Nueva, gateway to the shopping district. A few blocks west of the cathedral are the bullring and the Guadalquivir River, while Plaza de España is a few blocks south. The colorful Triana neighborhood, on the west bank of the Guadalquivir River, has a thriving market and plenty of tapas bars, but no tourist sights. With most sights walkable, and taxis so friendly, easy, and affordable, you probably won't even bother with the bus.

Tourist Information

Sevilla has tourist offices at the **Santa Justa train station** (Mon-Fri 9:00-19:30, Sat-Sun 9:30-15:00, overlooking tracks 6-7, tel. 954-782-003), near the cathedral on **Plaza del Triunfo** (Mon-Fri 9:00-19:30, Sat-Sun 9:30-19:30, tel. 954-210-005), and at the **airport** (same hours as station TI).

SEVILLA AT A GLANCE

▲▲▲**Flamenco** Flamboyant, riveting music-and-dance performances, offered at clubs throughout town. **Hours:** Shows start as early as 19:00. See page 392.

▲▲**Cathedral and Giralda Bell Tower** The world's largest Gothic church, with Columbus' tomb, treasury, and climbable tower. **Hours:** Mon 11:00-16:30, Tue-Sat 11:00-18:00, Sun 14:30-19:00. See page 365.

▲▲**Royal Alcázar** Palace built by the Moors in the 10th century, revamped in the 14th century, and still serving as royal digs. **Hours:** Daily April-Sept 9:30-19:00, Oct-March 9:30-17:00. See page 372.

▲▲**Hospital de la Caridad** Former charity hospital with gorgeously decorated chapel. **Hours:** Mon-Sat 9:00-13:00 & 15:30-19:00, Sun 9:00-12:30. See page 381.

▲▲**Basílica de la Macarena** Church and museum with the much-venerated Weeping Virgin statue and two significant floats from Sevilla's Holy Week celebrations. **Hours:** Church daily 9:30-14:00 & 17:00-20:30, museum closes at 20:00. See page 385.

▲▲**Triana** Energetic, colorful neighborhood on the west bank of the river. **Hours:** Always strollable. See page 387.

▲▲**Bullring and Bullfight Museum** Guided tour of the bullring and its museum. **Hours:** Daily April-Oct 9:30-21:00, Nov-March 9:30-19:00, until 15:00 on fight days. See page 390.

▲▲**Evening Paseo** Locals strolling in the cool of the evening, mainly along Avenida de la Constitución, Barrio Santa Cruz, the Calle Sierpes and Tetuán shopping pedestrian zone, and the Guadalquivir River. (I also suggest a Shopping Paseo—see page 391.) **Hours:** Spring through fall; best paseo scene 18:00-20:00, until very late at night in summer. See page 392.

▲**Flamenco Dance Museum** High-tech museum explaining the history and art of Sevilla's favorite dance. **Hours:** Daily 10:00-19:00. See page 382.

▲**Museo de Bellas Artes** Andalucía's top paintings, including works by Spanish masters Murillo and Zurbarán. **Hours:** Tue-Sat 10:00-20:30, Sun 10:00-17:00, closed Mon. See page 383.

▲**Bullfights** Some of Spain's best bullfighting, held at Sevilla's arena. **Hours:** Fights generally at 18:30 on most Sun in May and June, on Easter and Corpus Christi, and daily through the April Fair and in late Sept. Rookies fight small bulls on Thurs in July. See page 389.

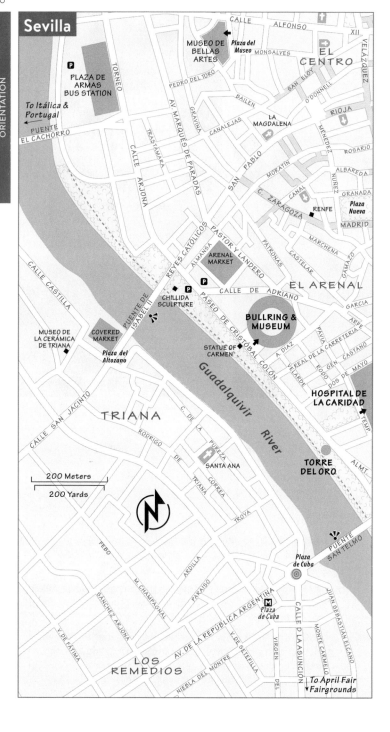

Sevilla

CALLE ALFONSO XII

Plaza del Museo

MUSEO DE BELLAS ARTES

MONSALVES

EL CENTRO

VELAZQUEZ

P

PLAZA DE ARMAS BUS STATION

TORNEO

PEDRO DEL TORO

SAN ELOY

O'DONNELL

To Itálica & Portugal

PUENTE EL CACHORRO

AV. MARQUÉS DE PARADAS

GRAVINA

BAILEN

CANALEJAS

LA MAGDALENA

SAN PABLO

MORATIN

RIOJA

MÉNDEZ

ROSARIO

ALBAREDA

NUÑEZ

GRANADA

CALLE ARJONA

TRASTAMARA

CALLE

C. ZARAGOZA

CANAL

RENFE

Plaza Nueva

MADRID

REYES CATÓLICOS

PASTOR Y LANDERO

ALMANSA

PATRONAS

CASTELAR

MARCHENA

GAMAZO

Arenal MARKET

CALLE DE ADRIANO

EL ARENAL

GARCIA

CALLE CASTILLA

PUENTE DE ISABEL II

CHILLIDA SCULPTURE

P

PASEO DE CRISTOBAL COLÓN

BULLRING & MUSEUM

ARFE

PAVIA

REAL DE LA CARRETERIA

GEN. CASTAÑO

MUSEO DE LA CERÁMICA DE TRIANA

COVERED MARKET

Plaza del Altozano

STATUE OF CARMEN

A. DIAZ

VELARDE

RODO

DOS DE MAYO

HOSPITAL DE LA CARIDAD

TEMP.

CALLE SAN JACINTO

TRIANA

RODRIGO

DE

C. DE LA

PUREZA

SANTA ANA

CORREA

TRIANA

Guadalquivir River

TORRE DEL ORO

ALMT.

200 Meters

200 Yards

N

TROYA

FEBO

M. CHAMPAGNAL

ARDILLA

PARAISO

PUENTE SAN TELMO

Plaza de Cuba

SANCHEZ ARJONA

Y. DE FATIMA

AV. DE LA REPÚBLICA ARGENTINA

Y. DE SEISEILLA

NIEBLA DEL MONTE

M

Plaza de Cuba

VIRGEN

CALLE P. LA ASUNCIÓN

JUAN SEBASTIAN ELCANO

MONTE CARMELO

LOS REMEDIOS

To April Fair Fairgrounds

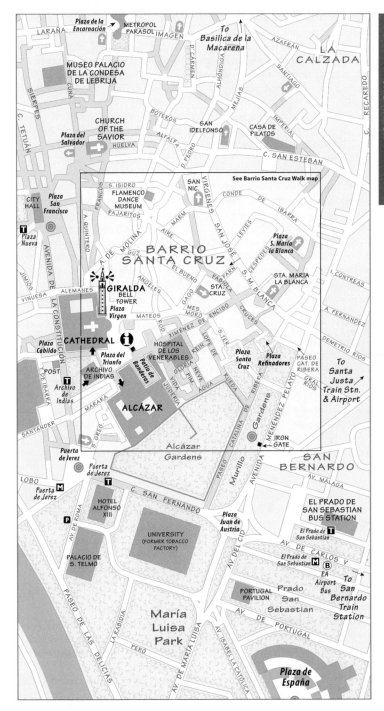

At any TI, ask for the city map, the English-language magazine *The Tourist* (also available online at www.thetourist sevilla.com), and a current listing of sights with opening times. The free monthly events guide—*El Giraldillo,* written in Spanish basic enough to be understood by travelers—covers cultural events throughout Andalucía, with a focus on Sevilla. At the TI, ask for information you might need for elsewhere in the region (for example, if heading south, pick up the free *Route of the White Towns* brochure and a Jerez map). Helpful websites are www.turismosevilla.org and www.anda lucia.org.

A small "visitors center" on Avenida de la Constitución (near the Archivo General de Indias) masquerades as a TI but is a private enterprise. Stick with the TIs listed above.

Sightseeing Pass

The **Sevilla Card** is unlikely to save you money (€30/24 hours—includes choice of 2 museums and river cruise, €48/48 hours—includes more sights and cruise or bus tour, sold at INFHOR at train station and near cathedral on Calle Fray Ceferino González, www.sevillacard.es).

Tours

Enthusiastic teacher Concepción Delgado takes small groups on English-only walks. Concepción has designed a fine two-hour **Sevilla Cultural Show & Tell** walk, sharing important insights most visitors miss. Her tour brilliantly complements your independent visits to major sights, and clues you in on what's going on around town during your visit (€15/person, 10:30 on Mon-Sat late Feb-Dec *except* no tours Aug 1-15; Mon, Wed, Fri only in Jan, early Feb, and late Aug; meet at statue in Plaza Nueva). Concepción also offers in-depth tours of the **cathedral** and the **Alcázar,** each lasting about 1.25 hours (€10 each plus entrance fees, €3 discount if you also take the Show & Tell tour; meet at

13:00 at statue in Plaza del Triunfo; cathedral tours—Mon, Wed, and Fri; Alcázar tours—Tue, Thu, and Sat; no cathedral tours Aug 1-15, no Alcázar tours Jan, Feb 1-15, and Aug). Although you can just show up for Concepción's tours, it's smart to confirm departure times and reserve a spot (4-person minimum, tel. 902-158-226, mobile 616-501-100, www.sevilla walkingtours.com, info@sevillawalking tours.com). Concepción does no tours on Sundays or holidays. Because she's a busy mom of two young kids, Concepción sometimes sends her colleague Alfonso (also excellent) to lead tours.

All Sevilla Guided Tours offers good, family-friendly private tours and day trips (€120/3 hours, €160/half-day, €22 monument tours leave Mon-Sat at 11:15 from Plaza del Triunfo, mobile 606-217-194, www.allsevillaguides.com, info@allsevilla guides.com).

Really Discover Seville hosts creative tours with a personal touch, including a 2.5-hour **bike tour** (€25, 2-10 people per group, includes bike, daily at 10:00, meet near cathedral by tall white monument in Plaza del Triunfo) and a two-hour **walking tour** (€20, 2-10 per group, daily at 10:00), with the option of lunchtime tapas for €35 more (tel. 955-113-912, www.really discover.com, davidcox@reallydiscover. com).

Rick's Tip: Skip the two hop-on, hop-off bus tours, *heavy on Expo '29 and Expo '92 neighborhoods—Sevilla is most interesting in places buses can't go. Leaving from the dock behind the Torre de Oro, the* **boat tours are boring***—there's little to see.*

Helpful Hints

Festivals: Sevilla's peak season is April and May. During two one-week festival periods, Holy Week and April Fair, the city is packed.

Holy Week (Semana Santa) is held the week between Palm Sunday and Eas-

Holy Week (Semana Santa) in Andalucía

Holy Week—the week between Palm Sunday and Easter—is a major holiday throughout the Christian world, but nowhere is it celebrated with as much fervor as in Sevilla. It's a remarkable spectacle: The intense devotion of the Andalusian people is an inspiration to behold.

Holy Week is all about the events of the Passion of Jesus Christ: his entry into Jerusalem, his betrayal by Judas and arrest, his crucifixion, and his resurrection. Each day throughout the week, 60 neighborhood groups parade from their neighborhood churches to the cathedral with floats depicting some aspect of the Passion story.

Visitors pour into town, grandstands are erected along parade routes, and TV stations anxiously monitor the weather report. The floats are so delicate that rain can force the processions to be called off—a crushing disappointment.

By midafternoon of any day during Holy Week, thousands line the streets. The parade begins with a line of penitents carrying a big cross, candles, and incense. The *penitentes* perform their penance publicly but anonymously, their identities obscured by pointy, hooded robes. (This white hooded garb has been worn for centuries—long before such hoods became associated with racism in the American South.) Some processions are silent, but others are accompanied by beating drums, brass bands, or wailing singers.

A hush falls over the crowd as the floats approach. First comes a Passion float, showing Christ in some stage of the drama—being whipped, appearing before Pilate, or carrying the cross to his execution. More penitents follow—with dozens or even hundreds of participants, a procession can stretch out over a half-mile. All this sets the stage for the finale—typically a float of the Virgin Mary, who represents the hope of resurrection.

The elaborate floats feature carved wooden religious sculptures, some embellished with gold leaf and silverwork. They can be adorned with fresh flowers, rows of candles, and even jewelry on loan from the congregation. Each float is carried by 30 to 50 men, who labor unseen (you might catch a glimpse of their shuffling feet). The bearers wear turban-like headbands to protect their heads and necks from the crushing weight of the floats, which can weigh up to three tons. Two "shifts" of float carriers rotate every 20 minutes.

As the slow-moving procession nears the cathedral, it passes through the square called La Campana, south along Calle Sierpes, and through Plaza de San Francisco. Some parades follow a parallel route a block or two east. If a procession blocks your way, look for a crossing point marked by a red-painted fence, or ask a guard where to find one.

Sevilla's Jews

In the summer of 1391, smoldering anti-Jewish sentiment flared up in Sevilla. On June 6, Christian mobs ransacked the city's Jewish Quarter (*Judería*). Around 4,000 Jews were killed, and 5,000 Jewish families were driven from their homes. Synagogues were stripped and transformed into churches. The former *Judería* eventually became the neighborhood of the Holy Cross—Barrio Santa Cruz. Sevilla's uprising spread through Spain (and Europe), the first of many nasty pogroms during the next century.

Before the pogrom, Jews had lived in Sevilla for centuries as the city's respected merchants, doctors, and bankers. They flourished under the Muslim Moors. After King Ferdinand III expelled the Moors from Sevilla in 1248, Jews were given protection by Spain's kings and allowed a measure of self-government, though they were confined to the Jewish neighborhood. But by the 14th century, Jews were increasingly accused of everything from poisoning wells to ritually sacrificing Christian babies. Mobs killed suspected Jews, and some of Sevilla's most respected Jewish citizens had their fortunes confiscated.

After 1391, Jews faced a choice: Be persecuted (even killed), relocate, or convert to Christianity. The newly Christianized—called *conversos* (converted) or *marranos* (swine)—were always under suspicion of practicing their old faith in private, and thereby undermining true Christianity. Longtime Christians were threatened by this new social class of converted Jews, who now had equal status, fanning the mistrust.

To root out the perceived problem of underground Judaism, the "Catholic Monarchs," Ferdinand and Isabel, established the Inquisition in Spain (1478). Under the direction of Grand Inquisitor Tomás de Torquemada, these religious courts arrested and interrogated *conversos* suspected of practicing Judaism. Using long solitary confinement and torture, they extracted confessions. Over the next three decades, thousands of *conversos* were tried and killed in Spain.

In 1492, the same year the last Moors were driven from Spain, Ferdinand and Isabel decreed that all remaining Jews convert or be expelled. Spain emerged as a nation unified under the banner of Christianity.

---

ter Sunday. What would normally be a five-minute walk can take an hour if a procession crosses your path. But any hassles become worthwhile as you listen to the *saetas* (spontaneous devotional songs) and let the spirit of the festival take over.

Two weeks later, Sevilla holds its **April Fair,** a celebration of all things Andalusian, with plenty of eating, drinking, singing, and merrymaking.

Book rooms well in advance for these festival times. Prices can go sky-high, many hotels have four-night minimums, and food quality at touristy restaurants can plummet.

Aggressive Fortune Tellers: In the city center, and especially near the cathedral, you may encounter women thrusting sprigs of rosemary into the hands of passersby. They want to read your fortune for a tip—at least €5. Don't make eye contact, don't accept a sprig, and say firmly but politely, *"No, gracias."*

Internet Access: You'll find free Wi-Fi on the tram, at Museo de Bellas Artes, and in Plaza de la Encarnación, among other public spaces.

Bike Rental: Sevilla is bike-friendly, with designated bike lanes. **BiciBike** rents bikes at the Santa Justa train station and will deliver them to your hotel at no charge (€8/3 hours, €10/6 hours, €15/24 hours, tel. 955-514-110, www.bicibike.es).

BARRIO SANTA CRUZ WALK

Of Sevilla's once-thriving Jewish Quarter, only the tangled street plan and a wistful Old World ambience survive. This classy maze of lanes, small plazas, tile-covered patios, and whitewashed houses with wrought-iron latticework draped in flowers is a great refuge from the summer heat and bustle of Sevilla. The streets are narrow—too narrow for cars, some with buildings so close they're called "kissing lanes." A happy result of the narrowness is shade: Locals claim the Barrio Santa Cruz is three degrees cooler than the rest of the city.

Orange trees abound—because they never lose their leaves, they provide constant shade. But forget about eating the oranges. They're bitter and used only to make vitamins, perfume, and marmalade. But when they blossom (usually in March), the aroma is heavenly.

The barrio is made for wandering. Getting lost is easy, and I recommend doing just that. But to get started, here's a self-guided plaza-to-plaza walk that loops you through the *corazón* (heart) of the neighborhood and back out again.

Tour groups often trample the barrio's charm in the morning. I find that early evening (around 18:00) is the ideal time to explore the quarter.

❶ Plaza de la Virgen de los Reyes

Start in the square in front of the cathedral, at the base of the Giralda bell tower.

This square is dedicated to the Virgin of the Kings—see her tile on the white wall facing the cathedral. She is one of several different versions of Mary you'll see in Sevilla, each appealing to a different type of worshipper. This particular one is big here because the Spanish king reportedly carried her image with him when he retook the town from the Moors in 1248. To the left of Mary's tiled plaque is a statue of sainted Pope John Paul II, who performed Mass here before a half-million faithful Sevillians during a 1982 visit. The central fountain dates from 1929. The reddish Baroque building on one side of the square is the Archbishop's Palace.

Notice the columns and chains that ring the cathedral, as if put there to establish a border between the secular and Catholic worlds. Many of these columns are far older than the cathedral, having originally been made for Roman and Visigothic buildings, and later recycled by medieval Catholics.

From this peaceful square, look up the street leading away from the cathedral and notice the characteristic (government-protected) 19th-century architecture. The ironwork, typical of Andalucía, is the pride of Sevilla. Equally ubiquitous is the traditional white-wash-and-goldenrod color scheme.

Another symbol you'll see throughout Sevilla is the city insignia: "NO8DO," the letters "NODO" with a figure-eight-like shape at their center. *Nodo* meant "knot" in Spanish, and this symbol evokes the strong ties between the citizens of Sevilla and King Alfonso X (during a succession dispute in the 13th century, the Sevillians remained loyal to their king).

• *Keeping the cathedral on your right, walk toward the next square.*

❷ Nun Goodies

The white building on your left was an Augustinian convent. At #3, step inside to meet (but not see) a cloistered nun behind a *torno* (the lazy Susan the nuns

Barrio Santa Cruz Walk

100 Meters

100 Yards

To Plaza Nueva

GUZMÁN EL BUENO

ANGELES

FABIOLA CRUCES

FARN.

SAN JOSE

S. M. BLANCA

CÉSPEDES

SANTA CRUZ

Plaza S. Maria la Blanca

GIRALDA BELL TOWER

WALK BEGINS

Plaza Virgen

GAGO

XIMÉNEZ DE ENCISO

CRUCES

CALLE MATEOS

MESON MORO

❶

CATHEDRAL ❷

WALK ENDS

Plaza Alianza

P. VILA

PASAJE ANDREU

CARO

JAMER.

REIN.

LOPE DE

S. TER.

❽

❼

Plaza Refinadores

❻

Plaza Santa Cruz

❶❶

HOSPITAL DE LOS VENERABLES

Plaza del Triunfo ❸

❹

Patio de Banderas

❿

GLORIA

SUS

❾

PIMIENTA

NEVE

AGUA

RUEDA

Murillo Gardens

ARCHIVO DE INDIAS

VIDA

JUDERÍA

❺

DE RIBERA

ALCÁZAR

MARARA

S. GREG.

Alcázar Gardens

Murillo Gardens

PASEO CATALINA

To San Telmo Bridge

To Plaza de España & El Prado de San Sebastian Bus Station

IRON GATE

AV. MEN. PELAYO

❶ Plaza de la Virgen de los Reyes
❷ Nun Goodies
❸ Plaza del Triunfo
❹ Patio de Banderas
❺ Calle Agua
❻ Plaza de la Santa Cruz
❼ Casa de Murillo

❽ Monasterio de San José del Carmen
❾ Plaza de los Venerables, Hospital de los Venerables & Centro Velazquez
❿ Plaza de Doña Elvira
❶❶ Plaza de la Alianza

spin to sell their goods while staying hidden). The sisters raise money by producing goodies—like tasty communion wafer *tabletas* (€1—eating them is like having sin-free cookies) and lovely rosaries (€4). Consider buying something here just as a donation. The sisters, who speak only Spanish, have a sense of humor

(Mon-Sat 9:00-13:00 & 16:45-18:15, Sun 10:00-13:00).

• *Then step into...*

❸ *Plaza del Triunfo*

The "Plaza of Triumph" is named for the 1755 earthquake that destroyed Lisbon, but only rattled Sevilla, leaving most of this city intact. A statue thanking the Virgin for protecting the city is at the far end of the square, under a stone canopy. That Virgin faces another one (closer to you), atop a tall pillar honoring Sevillian artists, including the painter Murillo.

• *Before leaving the square, consider stopping at the TI for a map or advice. Then pass through the arched opening in the Alcázar's crenellated wall. You'll emerge into a courtyard called the...*

❹ *Patio de Banderas*

The Banderas Courtyard (as in "flags," not Antonio) was once a military parade ground for the royal guard. The barracks surrounding the square once housed the king's bodyguards. Farther back, a Moorish palace stood on this spot; archaeologists are busy excavating what remains of it. Today, the far end of this square is a favorite spot for snapping a postcard view of the Giralda bell tower.

• *Exit the courtyard at the far corner, through the Judería arch. Go down the long, narrow passage. Emerging into the light, you'll be walking alongside the Alcázar wall.*

Take the first left at the corner lamppost, then go right, through a small square and follow the narrow alleyway called...

❺ *Calle Agua*

As you walk along the street, look to the left, peeking through iron gates for occasional glimpses of the flower-smothered patios of private residences. If the blue security gate for the patio at #2 is open, you'll see it's a delight—ringed with columns, filled with flowers, and colored with glazed tiles. The tiles are not merely decorative—they keep buildings cooler in the summer heat (if the gate is closed, the next door is often open; or just look up to get a hint of the garden's flowery bounty). Emerging at the end of the street, turn around and look back at the openings of two old pipes built into the wall. These 12th-century Moorish pipes once carried water to the Alcázar (and today give the street its name). You're standing at an entrance into the pleasant Murillo Gardens (through the iron gate), formerly the fruit-and-vegetable gardens for the Alcázar.

Plaza de la Virgen de Los Reyes

Ⓐ *Patio de Banderas*
Ⓑ *On the Calle Agua*
Ⓒ *Calle Reinosa*
Ⓓ *Side street off Plaza de la Alianza*

• Don't enter the gardens now, but instead cross the square diagonally to the left, and continue 20 yards down a lane to the...

❻ Plaza de la Santa Cruz

Arguably the heart of the barrio, this pleasant square, graced by orange trees and draping vines, was once the site of a synagogue (there used to be four in the barrio; now there are none), which Christians destroyed. They replaced the synagogue with a church, which the French (under Napoleon) later demolished. You'll see the oversized blue, white, and red French flag of the French consulate that overlooks this peaceful square. A fine 16th-century iron cross marks the center of the square and the site of the church the French destroyed. The Sevillian painter Murillo, who was buried in that church, lies somewhere below you.

At #9, you can peek into a lovely courtyard that's proudly been left open so visitors can enjoy it. The square is also home to the Los Gallos flamenco bar, which puts on nightly performances (see page 394).

• Go north on Calle Santa Teresa. At #8 (find the plaque on the left, near the big wooden doors) is...

❼ Casa de Murillo

One of Sevilla's famous painters, Bartolomé Esteban Murillo (1617-1682), lived here, soaking in the ambience of street life and reproducing it in his paintings of cute beggar children.

• Directly across from Casa de Murillo is the...

❽ Monasterio de San José del Carmen

This is where St. Teresa stayed when she visited from her hometown of Ávila. The convent (closed to the public) keeps artifacts of the mystic nun, such as her spiritual manuscripts.

Continue north on Calle Santa Teresa,

then take the first left on Calle Lope de Rueda (just before Las Teresas café), then left again, then right on **Calle Reinoso.** This street—so narrow that the buildings almost touch—is one of the barrio's "kissing lanes." This labyrinthine street plan goes back to Moorish times, when this area was a tangled market. Later, this was the Jewish ghetto, where all the city's Jews were forced to live in a very small area.

• *Just to the left, the street spills onto...*

❾ *Plaza de los Venerables*

This square is another candidate for "heart of the barrio." The streets branching off it ooze local ambience. When the Jews were expelled from Spain in 1492, this area became deserted and run-down. But in 1929, for its world's fair, Sevilla turned the plaza into a showcase of Andalusian style, adding the railings, tile work, orange trees, and other too-cute, Epcot-like adornments. A different generation of tourists enjoys the place today, likely unaware that what they're seeing in Barrio Santa Cruz is not as old as they imagine.

The large, harmonious Baroque-style Hospital de los Venerables (1675), once a retirement home for old priests (the "venerables"), is now a cultural foundation.

• *Continue west on Calle de Gloria, past an interesting tile map of the Jewish Quarter (on the right). You'll soon come upon...*

❿ *Plaza de Doña Elvira*

This small square—with orange trees, tile benches, and a stone fountain—sums up our barrio walk. Shops sell work by local artisans, such as ceramics, embroidery, and fans.

• *Cross the plaza and head north along Calle Rodrigo Caro; keep going until you enter the large...*

⓫ *Plaza de la Alianza*

Ever consider a career change? Gain inspiration at the site that once housed the painting studio of John Fulton (1932-

1998; find the small plaque on the other side of the square), an American who pursued two dreams: bullfighting and painting.

• *From Plaza de la Alianza, you can return to the cathedral by turning left (west) on Calle Joaquín Romero Murube (along the wall). Or, if you're ready for a bite, head northeast on Calle Rodrigo Caro, which intersects with Calle Mateos Gago, a street lined with tapas bars.*

SIGHTS

▲▲CATHEDRAL AND GIRALDA BELL TOWER

Sevilla's cathedral is the third-largest church in Europe (after St. Peter's at the Vatican in Rome and St. Paul's in London) and the largest Gothic church anywhere. When they ripped down a mosque of brick on this site in 1401, the Reconquista Christians announced their intention to build a cathedral so huge that "anyone who sees it will take us for madmen." They built for about a hundred years. Even today, the descendants of those madmen proudly display an enlarged photocopy of their *Guinness Book of Records* letter certifying, "Santa María de la Sede in Sevilla is the cathedral with the largest area: 126.18 meters x 82.60 meters x 30.48 meters high" (find the letter at the end of the following self-guided tour).

Cost and Hours: €9, €4 for students and those over age 65 (must show ID), kids under age 18 free; keep your ticket, which includes free entry to the Church of the Savior; Mon 11:00-16:30, Tue-Sat 11:00-18:00, Sun 14:30-19:00; closes one hour earlier in winter, last entry to cathedral one hour before closing, last entry to bell tower 30 minutes before closing; WC and drinking fountain just inside entrance and in courtyard near exit, tel. 954-214-971. Most of the website www.catedralde sevilla.es is in Spanish, but following the "vista virtual" links will take you to a virtual tour with an English option.

Rick's Tip: *Visit the* **cathedral** *later in the day to* **avoid the crowds** *of tour groups in the morning.*

Tours: My self-guided tour covers the basics. The €3 audioguide explains each side chapel for anyone interested in old paintings and dry details. For €10, you can enjoy Concepción Delgado's tour instead (see page 358).

⊃ SELF-GUIDED TOUR

Enter the cathedral at the south end (closest to the Alcázar, with a full-size replica of the Giralda's weathervane statue in the patio).

• *First, you pass through the...*

❶ Art Pavilion: Just past the turnstile, you step into a room of paintings that once hung in the church, including works by Sevilla's two 17th-century masters—Bartolomé Murillo (*St. Ferdinand,* depicting the king who freed Sevilla from the Moors) and Francisco de Zurbarán (*St. John the Baptist in the Desert*). Find a painting showing two of Sevilla's patron saints—Santa Justa and Santa Rufina,

killed in ancient Roman times for their Christian faith. Potters by trade, these two are easy to identify by their palm branches and their pots (at their feet or in their hands), and the bell tower symbolizing the town they protect. As you tour the cathedral, keep track of how many depictions of this dynamic and saintly duo you spot. They're everywhere.

• *Pick up a church map from the rack in this room, then enter the actual church (you'll pass a WC on the way). In the center of the church, sit down in front of the...*

❷ High Altar: Look through the wrought-iron Renaissance grille at what's called the largest altarpiece ever made— 65 feet tall, with 44 scenes from the life of Jesus and Mary carved from walnut and chestnut, blanketed by a staggering amount of gold leaf. The work took three generations to complete (1481-1564). The story is told left to right, bottom to top. Find Baby Jesus in the manger, in the middle of the bottom row, then follow his story through the miracles, the Passion, and the Pentecost. Look way up to the tippy-top, where a Crucifixion adorns the

Sevilla's cathedral

Sevilla's Cathedral

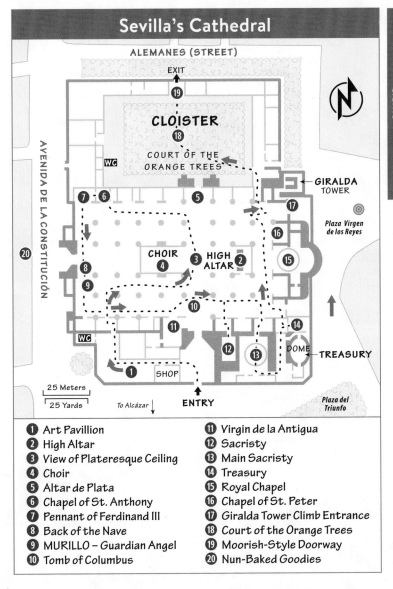

ALEMANES (STREET)

EXIT

⑲

CLOISTER

⑱

COURT OF THE
ORANGE TREES

WC

⑦ ⑥ ⑤

GIRALDA
TOWER

⑰

Plaza Virgen
de los Reyes

⑳

CHOIR
④

HIGH
ALTAR
③ ② ⑯

⑮

⑧

⑨

⑩

⑬

⑪

⑫ ⑬

⑭

WC

DOME

TREASURY

① SHOP

25 Meters

25 Yards

To Alcázar

ENTRY

Plaza del
Triunfo

AVENIDA DE LA CONSTITUCIÓN

N

① Art Pavillion
② High Altar
③ View of Plateresque Ceiling
④ Choir
⑤ Altar de Plata
⑥ Chapel of St. Anthony
⑦ Pennant of Ferdinand III
⑧ Back of the Nave
⑨ MURILLO – Guardian Angel
⑩ Tomb of Columbus

⑪ Virgin de la Antigua
⑫ Sacristy
⑬ Main Sacristy
⑭ Treasury
⑮ Royal Chapel
⑯ Chapel of St. Peter
⑰ Giralda Tower Climb Entrance
⑱ Court of the Orange Trees
⑲ Moorish-Style Doorway
⑳ Nun-Baked Goodies

dizzying summit. Now crane your neck skyward to admire the ❸ **Plateresque tracery** on the ceiling.

• *Turn around and check out the...*

❹ **Choir:** Facing the high altar, the choir features an organ of more than 7,000 pipes (played Mon-Fri at the 10:00

Mass, Sun at the 10:00 & 13:00 Mass, not in July-Aug, free for worshippers). A choir area like this one—enclosed within the cathedral for more intimate services—is common in Spain and England, but rare in churches elsewhere. The big, spinnable book holder in the middle

Ⓐ *High Altar*

Ⓑ *Nave and Plateresque ceiling*

Ⓒ *Chapel of St. Anthony*

Ⓓ *Tomb of Columbus*

Ⓔ *Virgen de la Antigua*

of the room held giant hymnals—large enough for all to chant from in a pre-Xerox age when there weren't enough books for everyone.

• *Now turn 90 degrees to the right to take in the enormous...*

❺ **Altar de Plata:** Rising up in what would be the transept, the gleaming silver altarpiece adorned with statues resembles an oversized monstrance (the vessel used during communion). Sevilla's celebration of La Macarena's "jubilee" year culminated here (to mark the 50th year of her canonical coronation), with the statue of the Virgin installed among the gleaming silver.

• *Go left, up the side aisle at the Altar de Plata, and head to the last chapel on the right.*

❻ **Chapel of St. Anthony** (Capilla de San Antonio): This chapel is used for baptisms. The Renaissance baptismal font has delightful carved angels dancing along its base. In Murillo's painting, *Vision of St. Anthony* (1656), the saint kneels in wonder as Baby Jesus comes down surrounded by a choir of angels. Anthony, one of Iberia's most popular saints, is the patron saint of lost things—so people come here to pray for his help in finding jobs, car keys, and life partners. Above the *Vision* is *The Baptism of Christ,* also by Murillo. You don't need to be an art historian to know that the stained glass dates from 1685. And by now you know who the women are.

Nearby, a glass case displays the ❼ **pennant of Ferdinand III,** which was raised over the minaret of the mosque on November 23, 1248, as Christian forces finally expelled the Moors from Sevilla. For centuries, it was paraded through the city on special days.

Continuing on, stand at the ❽ **back of the nave** (behind the choir) and appreciate the ornate immensity of the church. Can you see the angels trumpeting on their Cuban mahogany? Any birds? The massive candlestick holder to the right of

the choir dates from 1560. And before you is the gravestone of Ferdinand Columbus, Christopher's second son. Having given the cathedral his collection of 6,000 precious books, he was rewarded with this prime burial spot.

Turn around. To the left, behind an iron grille, is a niche with ❾ **Murillo's Guardian Angel** pointing to the light and showing an astonished child the way.

• *Now turn around and march down the side aisle to find the...*

❿ **Tomb of Columbus:** In front of the cathedral's entrance for pilgrims are four kings who carry the tomb of Christopher Columbus. His pallbearers represent the regions of Castile, Aragon, León, and Navarre (identify them by their team shirts). Notice how the cross held by Señor León has a pike end piercing an orb. Look closer: It's a pomegranate, the symbol of Granada—the last Moorish-ruled city to succumb to the Reconquista (in 1492).

Columbus didn't just travel a lot while alive—he even kept it up posthumously. He was buried first in northwestern Spain (in Valladolid, where he died), then moved to a monastery here in Sevilla, then to what's now the Dominican Republic (as he'd requested), then to Cuba. Finally—when Cuba gained independence from Spain and the US in 1902—his remains sailed home again to Sevilla. After all that, it's fair to wonder whether the remains in the box before you are actually his. Sevillians like to think so. (Columbus died in 1506. Five hundred years later, to help celebrate the anniversary of his death, DNA samples did indeed give Sevillians some evidence to substantiate their claim.)

On the left is a 1584 mural of St. Christopher, patron saint of travelers. The clock above has been ticking since 1788.

• *Facing Columbus, duck into the first chapel on your right to find the...*

⓫ **Virgen de la Antigua:** Within this chapel is a gilded fresco of the Virgin delicately holding a rose and the Christ Child, who's holding a bird. It's the oldest art here, even older than the cathedral itself: It was painted onto a horseshoe-shaped prayer niche of the mosque that formerly stood on this site. After Sevilla was re-conquered in 1248, the mosque served as a church for about 120 years—until it was torn down to make room for this huge cathedral. The Catholic builders, who were captivated by the fresco's beauty and well aware of the Virgen de la Antigua's status as protector of sailors (important in this port city), decided to save the fresco.

• *Exiting the Virgen de la Antigua chapel, return to Columbus. Walk through the chapel on the left into the...*

⓬ **Sacristy:** This space is where the priests get ready each morning before Mass. The Goya painting above the altar features another portrayal of Justa and Rufina with their trademark bell tower, pots, and palm leaves.

• *Two chapels down is the entrance to the...*

⓭ **Main Sacristy:** Marvel at the ornate, 16th-century dome of the main room, a grand souvenir from Sevilla's Golden Age. The intricate masonry, called Plateresque, resembles lacy silverwork (*plata* means "silver"). God is way up in the cupola. The three layers of figures below him show the heavenly host; relatives in purgatory—hands folded—looking to heaven in hope of help; and the wretched in hell, including a topless sinner engulfed in flames and teased cruelly by pitchfork-wielding monsters.

Dominating the room is a nearly 1,000-pound, silver-plated monstrance—a vessel for displaying the communion wafer. It's used to parade the holy host through town during Corpus Christi festivities.

• *The next door down, signed* Tesoro, *leads you to the...*

⓮ **Treasury:** This fills several rooms in the corner of the church. Wander deep into the treasury to find a unique oval dome. It's in the 16th-century chapter room (*sala capitular*), where monthly

Bartolomé Murillo (1617-1682)

The son of a barber of Seville, Bartolomé Murillo (mur-EE-oh) got his start selling paintings meant for export to the frontier churches of the Americas. In his 20s, he became famous after he painted a series of saints for Sevilla's Franciscan monastery. By about 1650, Murillo's sugary, simple, and accessible religious style was spreading through Spain and beyond.

Murillo painted street kids with cute smiles and grimy faces, and radiant young Marías with Ivory-soap complexions and rapturous poses (Immaculate Conceptions). His paintings view the world through a soft-focus lens, wrapping everything in warm colors and soft light, with a touch (too much, for some) of sentimentality.

Murillo became a rich, popular family man, and the toast of Sevilla's high society. In 1664, his wife died, leaving him heartbroken, but his last 20 years were his most prolific. At age 65, Murillo died after falling off a scaffold while painting. His tomb is lost somewhere under the bricks of Plaza de la Santa Cruz, where a church once stood.

meetings take place with the bishop (he gets the throne, while the others share the bench). The paintings here are by Murillo: a fine *Immaculate Conception* (1668, high above the bishop's throne) and portraits of saints important to Sevillians.

The wood-paneled Room of Ornaments shows off gold and silver reliquaries, which hold hundreds of holy body parts, as well as Spain's most valuable crown. This jeweled piece (the Corona de la Virgen de los Reyes, by Manuel de la Torre) sparkles with thousands of tiny precious stones, and the world's largest pearl—used as the torso of an angel. This amazing treasure was paid for by locals who donated their wealth to royally crown their Madonna.

• *Leave the treasury and cross through the church, passing the closed-to-tourists* ⑮ **Royal Chapel,** *the burial place of several kings of Castile (open for worship only—access from outside), then the also-closed* ⑯ **Chapel of St. Peter,** *with paintings showing scenes from the life of St. Peter.*

In the far corner—past the glass case displaying the Guinness Book certificate declaring that this is indeed the world's largest church by area—is the entry to the Giralda bell tower. It's time for some exercise.

⑰ **Giralda Bell Tower Climb:** Your church admission includes entry to the bell tower, a former minaret. Notice the beautiful Moorish simplicity as you climb to its top, 330 feet up (35 ramps plus 17 steps), for a grand city view. The graded ramp was designed to accommodate a donkey-riding muezzin, who clip-clopped up five times a day to give the Muslim call to prayer back when a mosque stood here. Along the way, stop at balconies for expansive views over the city.

• *Back on the ground, head outside. As you cross the threshold, look up. Why is a wooden crocodile hanging here? It's a replica of a taxidermied specimen, the original of which is said to have been a gift to King Alfonso X from the sultan of Egypt in 1260 (when the croc died, the king had him stuffed and hung here). You're now in the...*

⑱ **Court of the Orange Trees:** Today's cloister was once the mosque's Patio de los Naranjos. Twelfth-century Muslims stopped at the fountain in the middle to wash their hands, face, and feet before praying. The ankle-breaking lanes between the bricks were once irrigation streams—a reminder that the Moors introduced irrigation to Iberia. The mosque was made of bricks; the church is built of stone. The only large-scale remnants of the mosque today are the Court

ⓐ *Corona de la Virgen de los Reyes*
ⓑ *View from the Bell Tower*
ⓒ *Moorish-style doorway*
ⓓ *Court of the Orange Trees*

of the Orange Trees, the Giralda bell tower, and the site itself.

• *You'll exit the cathedral through the Court of the Orange Trees (WCs are at the far end of the courtyard, downstairs). As you leave, look back from the outside and notice the arch over the...*

⓳ Moorish-Style Doorway: As with much of the Moorish-looking art in town, this doorway is actually Christian—the two coats of arms are a giveaway. The relief above the door shows the Bible story of Jesus ridding the temple of the merchants...a reminder to contemporary merchants that there will be no retail activity in the church. The plaque on the right honors Miguel de Cervantes, the great 16th-century writer. It's one of many plaques scattered throughout town showing places mentioned in his books. (In this case, the topic was pickpockets.) The huge green doors predate the church. They are bits of the pre-1248 mosque—wood covered with bronze. Study the fine workmanship.

Giralda Bell Tower Exterior: Step across the street from the exit gate and look at the bell tower. Formerly a Moorish minaret from which Muslims were called to prayer, it became the cathedral's bell tower after the Reconquista. A 4,500-pound bronze statue symbolizing the Triumph of Faith (specifically, the Christian faith over the Muslim one) caps the tower and serves as a weather vane (in Spanish, *girar* means "to rotate"; a *giraldillo* is something that rotates). In 1356, the original top of the tower fell. You're looking at a 16th-century Christian-built top with a ribbon of letters proclaiming, "The strongest tower is the name of God" (you can see *Fortísima*—"strongest"—from this vantage point).

Now circle around for a close look at the corner of the tower at ground level. Needing more strength than their bricks could provide for the lowest section of the tower, the Moors used Roman-cut stones. You can actually read the Latin that was

chiseled onto one of the stones 2,000 years ago. The tower offers a brief recap of the city's history: It sits on a Roman foundation, has a long Moorish section, which is capped by the current Christian age.

Today, by law, no building in the center may be higher than the statue atop the tower. (But the new Cajasol Tower, just across the river, is by far the tallest erection in the greater city—and that offends locals in this conservative town. The fact that it's the headquarters of one of Spain's major banks, which many Spaniards blame for the economic crisis, hasn't helped its popularity.)

• *Your cathedral tour is finished. If you've worked up an appetite, get out your map and make your way a few blocks for some...*

⓴ Nun-Baked Goodies: Stop by the El Torno Pastelería de Conventos, a co-op where various orders of cloistered nuns send their handicrafts (such as baptismal dresses for babies) and baked goods to be sold. You won't actually see *el torno* (a lazy Susan), since this shop is staffed by non-nuns, but this humble little hole-in-the-wall shop is worth a peek, and definitely serves the best cookies, bar nun. It's located directly across from the cathedral's main front door; at Avenida de la Constitución 24, enter the passageway marked *Plaza del Cabildo,* which takes you into the quiet courtyard (Mon-Fri 10:00-13:30 & 17:00-19:30, Sat-Sun 10:30-14:00, closed Aug, Plaza del Cabildo 2, tel. 954-219-190).

**▲▲ROYAL ALCÁZAR
(REAL ALCÁZAR)**

Originally a 10th-century palace built for the governors of the local Moorish state, this building still functions as a royal palace—the oldest in Europe that's still in use. The core of the palace features an extensive 14th-century rebuild, done by Muslim workmen for the Christian king, Pedro I (1334-1369). Pedro was nicknamed either "the Cruel" or "the Just," depending on which end of his sword you were on.

Today, visitors can enjoy several sections of the Alcázar. Spectacularly decorated halls and courtyards have distinctive Islamic-style flourishes. Exhibits call up the era of Columbus and Spain's New World dominance. The lush, sprawling gardens invite exploration.

Cost and Hours: €9.50, €2 for students and seniors over 65—must show ID, free for children under age 16. To see the (optional) Upper Royal Apartments, add €4.50 for mandatory tour. Palace open daily April-Sept 9:30-19:00, Oct-March 9:30-17:00, apartments close at 13:30 year-round, tel. 954-502-324, www.alcazar sevilla.org.

Crowd-Beating Tips: To skip the ticket-buying line, reserve a time slot ahead online. Mornings are the busiest with tour groups, especially on Tuesdays. It's less crowded late in the day—but remember that the Upper Royal Apartments close at 13:30.

Tours: The fast-moving, €5 audioguide gives you an hour of information as you wander. My self-guided tour hits the highlights. Consider Concepción Delgado's Alcázar tour (see page 358).

The **Upper Royal Apartments** can only be visited with a separate tour (€4.50, includes separate audioguide, must check bags in provided lockers). For some, it's worth the extra time and cost just to escape the mobs in the rest of the palace. If you're interested, once inside the main courtyard go directly to the upstairs desk and reserve a spot. Groups of 15 leave every half-hour from 10:00 to 13:30, listening to the 30-minute audio tour while escorted by a security guard.

⊙ SELF-GUIDED TOUR

This royal palace is decorated with a mix of Islamic and Christian elements—a style called Mudejar. It offers a thought-provoking glimpse of a graceful Al-Andalus world that might have survived its Castilian conquerors...but didn't. The floor plan is intentionally confusing, to make experiencing the place more exciting and surprising. While Granada's

Alhambra was built by Moors for Moorish rulers, what you see here is essentially a Christian ruler's palace, built in the Moorish style by Moorish artisans.

• *Buy your ticket and enter through the turnstiles. Pass through the garden-like Lion Patio (Patio del León), with the rough stone wall of the older Moorish fortress on your left (c. 913), and through the arch into a courtyard called the...*

❶ Courtyard of the Hunt (Patio de la Montería): Get oriented. The palace's main entrance is directly ahead, through the elaborately decorated facade. WCs are in the far-left corner. In the far-right corner is the staircase and ticket booth for the Upper Royal Apartments—if you're interested, reserve an entry time now.

The palace complex was built over many centuries, with rooms and decorations from the various rulers who've lived here. Moorish caliphs first built the original 10th-century palace and gardens. Then, after Sevilla was Christianized in 1248, King Pedro I built the most

Courtyard of the Maiden

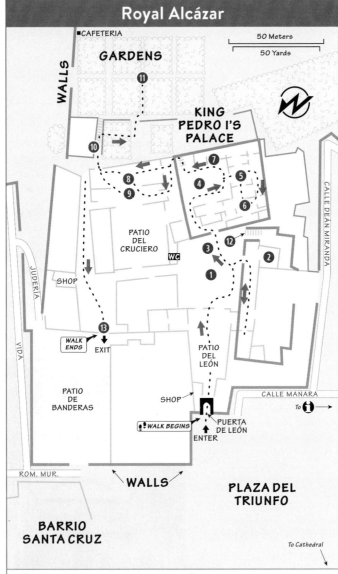

Royal Alcázar

1. Courtyard of the Hunt
2. Admiral's Hall
3. Palace Facade
4. Courtyard of the Maidens
5. Hall of the Ambassadors & Philip II Ceiling Room
6. Courtyard of the Dolls
7. Charles V Ceiling Room
8. Banquet Hall
9. Hall of Tapestries
10. Mercury Pool
11. Gardens
12. To Upper Royal Apartments (Ticket Res. Desk)
13. To Exit

famous part of the complex. During Spain's Golden Age, it was home to Ferdinand and Isabel and, later, their grandson Charles V; they all left their mark. Successive monarchs added still more luxury. And today's king and queen still use the palace's upper floor as one of their royal residences.

• *Before entering the heart of the palace, start in the wing to the right of the courtyard. Skip the large reception room for now and go directly to the...*

❷ **Admiral's Hall (Salón del Almirante):** When Queen Isabel debriefed Columbus here after his New World discoveries, she realized what he'd found could be big business. She created this wing in 1503 to administer Spain's New World ventures. In these halls, Columbus recounted his travels, Ferdinand Magellan planned his around-the-world cruise, and mapmaker Amerigo Vespucci tried to come up with a catchy moniker for that newly discovered continent.

In the pink-and-red Audience Chamber (once a chapel), the **altarpiece paint-**ing is of St. Mary of the Navigators (*Santa María de los Navegantes*, by Alejo Fernández, 1530s). The Virgin—the patron saint of sailors and a favorite of Columbus—keeps watch over the puny ships beneath her. Her cape seems to protect everyone under it—even the Native Americans in the dark background (the first time "Indians" were painted in Europe).

Standing beside the Virgin (on the right, dressed in gold, joining his hands together in prayer) is none other than Christopher Columbus. He stands on a cloud, because he's now in heaven (this was painted a few decades after his death). Notice that Columbus is blond. Columbus' son said of his dad: "In his youth his hair was blond, but when he reached 30, it all turned white." Many historians believe this to be the earliest known portrait of Columbus. If so, it's also likely to be the most accurate. The man on the left side of the painting, with the gold cape, is King Ferdinand.

Left of the painting is a **model** of Columbus' *Santa María,* his flagship and

Altarpiece painting in the Admiral's Hall

SEVILLA
SIGHTS

the only of his three ships not to survive the 1492 voyage. Columbus complained that the *Santa María*—a big cargo ship, different from the sleek *Niña* and *Pinta* caravels—was too slow. On Christmas Day it ran aground off present-day Haiti and tore a hole in its hull. The ship was dismantled to build the first permanent structure in America, a fort for 39 colonists. (After Columbus left, the natives burned the fort and killed the colonists.) Opposite the altarpiece (in the center of the back wall) is the family **coat of arms** of Columbus' descendants, who now live in Spain and Puerto Rico. Using Columbus' Spanish name, it reads: "To Castile and to León, Colón gave a new world."

Return to the still-used reception room, filled with big canvases. The **biggest painting** (and most melodramatic) shows a key turning point in Sevilla's history: King Ferdinand III humbly kneels before the bishop, giving thanks to God for helping him liberate the city from the Muslims (in 1248). Ferdinand promptly turned the Alcázar of the caliphs into the royal palace of Christian kings.

Pop into the room beyond the grand piano for a look at some ornate **fans** (mostly foreign and well-described in English). A long painting (designed to be gradually rolled across a screen and viewed like a primitive movie) shows 17th-century Sevilla during Holy Week. Follow the procession, which is much like today's, with traditional floats carried by teams of men and followed by a retinue of penitents.

• *Return to the Courtyard of the Hunt. Face the grand entrance in the...*

❸ **Palace Facade:** This is the entrance to **King Pedro I's Palace** (Palacio del Rey Pedro I), the Alcázar's 14th-century nucleus. The facade's elaborate blend of Islamic tracery and Gothic Christian elements introduces us to the Mudejar style seen throughout Pedro's part of the palace.

• *Enter the palace. Go left through the ves-*

tibule (impressive, yes, but we'll see better), and emerge into the big courtyard with a long pool in the center. This is the...

❹ **Courtyard of the Maidens (Patio de las Doncellas):** You've reached the center of King Pedro's palace. It's an open-air courtyard, surrounded by rooms. In the center is a long, rectangular reflecting pool. Like the Moors who preceded him, Pedro built his palace around water.

King Pedro cruelly abandoned his wife and moved into the Alcázar with his mistress, then hired Muslim workers from Granada to re-create the romance of that city's Alhambra in Sevilla's stark Alcázar. The designers created a microclimate engineered for coolness: water, sunken gardens, pottery, thick walls, and darkness. This palace is considered Spain's best example of the Mudejar style. Stucco panels with intricate designs, colorful ceramic tiles, coffered wooden ceilings, and lobed arches atop slender columns create a refined, pleasing environment. The elegant proportions and symmetry of this courtyard are a photographer's delight.

• *You'll explore the rooms branching off the*

King Pedro I's Palace

courtyard in the next few stops. Through the door at the end of the long reflecting pool is the palace's most important room, called the...

❺ Hall of the Ambassadors (Salón de Embajadores): Here, in his throne room, Pedro received guests and caroused in luxury. The room is a cube topped with a half-dome, like many important Islamic buildings. In Islam, the cube represents the earth, and the dome is the starry heavens. In Pedro's world, the symbolism proclaimed that he controlled heaven and earth. Islamic horseshoe arches stand atop recycled columns with golden capitals.

The stucco on the walls is molded with interlacing plants, geometrical shapes, and Arabic writing. Here, in a Christian palace, the walls are inscribed with unapologetically Muslim sayings: "None but Allah conquers" and "Happiness and prosperity are benefits of Allah, who nourishes all creatures." The artisans added propaganda phrases, such as "Dedicated to the magnificent Sultan Pedro—thanks to God!"

The Mudejar style also includes Christian motifs. Find the row of kings, high up

at the base of the dome, chronicling all of Castile's rulers from the 600s to the 1600s. Throughout the palace (as in the center of the dome above you), you'll see coats of arms—including the castle of Castile and the lion of León. There are also natural objects (such as shells and birds), which you wouldn't normally find in Islamic decor, as it traditionally avoids realistic images of nature.

Notice how it gets cooler as you go deeper into the palace. Straight ahead from the Hall of the Ambassadors, in the **Philip II Ceiling Room** (Salón del Techo de Felipe II), look above the arches to find peacocks, falcons, and other birds amid interlacing vines. Imagine day-to-day life in the palace—with VIP guests tripping on the tiny steps.

• *Make your way to the second courtyard nearby (in the Hall of the Ambassadors, face the Courtyard of the Maidens, then walk to the left). This smaller courtyard is the...*

❻ Courtyard of the Dolls (Patio de las Muñecas): This delicate courtyard was reserved for the king's private family life. Originally, the center of the courtyard had a pool, cooling the residents and reflecting decorative patterns that were

Hall of the Ambassadors ceiling

- **A** *Hall of Tapestries*
- **B** *Courtyard of the Dolls*
- **C** *Tilework detail*
- **D** *Gardens*

once brightly painted on the walls. The columns—recycled from ancient Roman and Visigothic buildings—are of alternating white, black, and pink marble. The courtyard's name comes from the tiny doll faces found at the base of one of the arches. Circle the room and try to find them. (Hint: While just a couple of inches tall, they're eight feet up.)

Pedro's original courtyard was a single story; the upper floors and skylight were added centuries later by Isabel's grandson, Charles V, in the 16th century. See the different styles: Mudejar below (lobed arches and elaborate tracery) and Renaissance above (round arches and less decoration).

• *The long adjoining room with the gilded ceiling, the* **Prince's Room** *(Cuarto del Príncipe), was Queen Isabel's bedroom, where she gave birth to a son, Prince Juan.*

Return to the Courtyard of the Maidens. As you stand in the courtyard with your back to the Hall of the Ambassadors, the door in the middle of the right side leads to the...

❼ **Charles V Ceiling Room (Salón del Techo del Carlos V):** Emperor Charles V, who ruled Spain at its peak of New World wealth, expanded the palace. The reason? His marriage to his beloved Isabel—which took place in this room—joined vast realms of Spain and Portugal. Devoutly Christian, Charles celebrated his wedding night with a midnight Mass, and later ordered the Mudejar ceiling in this room to be replaced with the less Islamic (but no less impressive) Renaissance one you see today.

• *We've seen the core of King Pedro's palace, with the additions by his successors. Return to the Courtyard of the Maidens, then turn right. In the corner, find the small staircase. Go up to rooms decorated with bright ceramic tiles and Gothic vaulting. Pass through the chapel (with its majestic mahogany altar on your left) and into a big, long, parallel room, the...*

❽ **Banquet Hall (Salón Gótico):** This big, airy banquet hall is where Charles and Isabel held their wedding reception. Tiles of yellow, blue, green, and orange line the room, some decorated with whimsical human figures with vase-like bodies. The windows open onto views of the gardens.

❾ **Hall of Tapestries (Salón Tapices):** Next door, the walls are hung with 18th-century Spanish copies of 16th-century Belgian tapestries showing the conquests, trade, and industriousness of Charles' prosperous reign. The map tapestry of the Mediterranean world has south pointing up. Find Genova, Italy, on the bottom; Africa on top; Lisbon *(Lisboa)* on the far right; and the large city of Barcelona in between. The artist included himself holding the legend—with a scale in both leagues and miles.

Facing the map, head to the far left end of the room, where the wall is filled by a dramatic portrayal of the Spanish Navy. Spain ruled the waves—and thereby an empire upon which the sun never set. Its reign lasted from 1492 until the Battle of Trafalgar in 1805; after that, Britannia's navy took the helm, and it was her crown that controlled the next global empire.

• *Return to the Banquet Hall, then head outside at the far end to the...*

❿ **Mercury Pool:** This pool, a reservoir fed by a 16th-century aqueduct, irrigated the palace's entire garden. As only elites had running water, the fountain was an extravagant show of power. Check out the bronze statue of Mercury, with his cute little winged feet. The wall defining the east side of the garden was part of the original Moorish castle wall. In the early 1600s, when fortifications were no longer needed here, that end was redesigned to be a grotto-style gallery.

• *From the Mercury Pool, steps lead into the formal gardens. Just past the bottom of the steps, a tunnel on the right leads under the palace to the coolest spot in the city. Finally, explore the...*

⓫ **Gardens:** The intimate geometric zone nearest the palace is the Moorish garden. The far-flung garden beyond that was the backyard of the Christian ruler.

Here in the gardens, as in the rest of the palace, the Christian and Islamic traditions merge. Both cultures used water and nature as essential parts of their architecture. The garden's pavilions and fountains only enhance this. Wander among palm trees, myrtle hedges, and fragrant roses. While tourists pay to be here, this is actually a public garden, and free to locals. It's been that way since 1931, when the king was exiled and Spanish citizens took ownership of royal holdings. In 1975, the Spanish people allowed the king back on the throne—but on their terms...which included keeping this garden.

• *Along the east wall is an air-conditioned* **cafeteria** *with a nice terrace overlooking the gardens. It's worth taking a few steps through the east wall to see the massive— and massively beautiful—bougainvillea that grows just on the other side of the wall.*

If you've booked a spot to visit the Upper Royal Apartments (see below), return to the Courtyard of the Hunt, and head upstairs.

❿ **Upper Royal Apartments** (Cuarto Real Alto): This is the royal palace of today's monarchs. Fifteen public reception rooms are open to visitors: the official dining room, Audience Hall, and so on. The rooms are amply decorated with Versailles-like furniture, chandeliers, carpets, and portraits of 19th-century nobility. The highlight is the Audience Room, a Mudejar-style room overlooking the Patio de la Montería.

• *Your Alcázar tour is over. From the Moors to Pedro I to Ferdinand and Isabel, and from Charles V to King Felipe VI, we've seen the home of a millennium of Spanish kings and queens. When you're ready to go, head out through the* **Patio de Banderas,** *once the entrance for guests arriving by horse carriage. Enjoy a classic Giralda bell tower view as you leave.*

Christopher Columbus (1451-1506)

This Italian wool-weaver ran off to sea, was shipwrecked in Portugal, married a captain's daughter, learned Portuguese and Spanish, and persuaded Spain's monarchs to finance his bold scheme to trade with the East by sailing west. On August 3, 1492, Columbus set sail from Palos (60 miles west of Sevilla) with three ships and 90 men, hoping to land in Asia, which Columbus estimated was 3,000 miles away. Ten weeks—and yes, 3,000 miles—later, with a superstitious crew ready to mutiny after they'd seen evil omens (including a falling meteor and a jittery compass), Columbus landed on an island in the Bahamas, convinced he'd reached Asia. He and his crew traded with the "Indians" and returned home to Palos harbor, where they were received as heroes.

Columbus made three more voyages to the New World and became rich with gold. But he gained a bad reputation among the colonists, was arrested, and returned to Spain in chains. Though pardoned, Columbus fell out of favor with the court. On May 20, 1506, he died in Valladolid. His son said he was felled by "gout and by grief at seeing himself fallen from his high estate," but historians speculate that diabetes or syphilis may have contributed. Columbus died thinking he'd visited Asia, unaware he'd opened up Europe to a New World.

Between the River and the Cathedral

▲▲HOSPITAL DE LA CARIDAD

This charity hospital, which functioned as a place of final refuge for Sevilla's poor and homeless, was founded in the 17th century by the nobleman Don Miguel Mañara. Your visit includes an evocative courtyard, his office, a chapel filled with powerful art, and a good audioguide that explains it all. This is still a working charity, so when you pay your entrance fee, you're advancing the work Mañara started back in the 17th century.

Cost and Hours: €5, includes audioguide, Mon-Sat 9:00-13:00 & 15:30-19:00, Sun 9:00-12:30, last entry 30 minutes before closing, Calle Temprado 3, tel. 954-223-232, www.santa-caridad.es.

Background: Don Miguel Mañara (1626-1679) was a big-time playboy and enthusiastic sinner who, late in life, had a massive change of heart. He spent his last years dedicating his life to strict worship and taking care of the poor. In 1674, Mañara acquired some empty warehouses and built this 150-ward "place of heroic virtues," called the Hospice and Hospital of the Holy Charity in Sevilla.

Mañara could well have been the inspiration for Don Juan, the character from a play set in 17th-century Sevilla, popularized later by Lord Byron's poetry and Mozart's opera *Don Giovanni* ("Don Juan" in Spanish). While no one knows for sure, it adds some fun to the visit.

One thing's for sure: Mañara is on the road to sainthood. His supporters request that you report any miraculous answers to prayers asking him to intercede—you need to perform miracles to become a saint.

Visiting the Hospital: The **courtyard** features statues from Genoa, Italy, as Mañara's family were rich Genovese merchants who moved to Sevilla to get in on the wealth from New World discoveries. The Dutch tiles (from Delft), depicting scenes from the Old and New Testament, are a reminder that the Netherlands was under Spanish rule in centuries past.

The **Sala de Cabildos,** a small room at the end of the courtyard, is Mañara's former office. Here you'll see his original desk, a painting of him at work (busy preaching against materialism and hedonism), a treasure box with an elaborate lock mechanism, his sword (he killed several people in his wilder days), a whip that was part of his austere style of worship, and his death mask.

Exit right and walk to the corner gift shop to reach the highlight—the **chapel,** which Mañara had built. On entering, you are greeted by Juan de Valdés Leal's *In the Blink of an Eye (In ictu oculi)*. In it, the Grim Reaper extinguishes the candle of life. Filling the canvas are the ruins of worldly goods, knowledge, power, and position. It's all gone in the blink of an eye—true in the 1670s...and true today.

Turn around to face the door you just entered and look up to find Leal's *The End of the Glories of the World*. The painting shows Mañara and a bishop decaying

Hospital de la Caridad

together in a crypt, with worms and assorted bugs munching away. Above, the hand of Christ—pierced by the nail—holds the scales of justice: sins (on the left) and good deeds (on the right). The placement of both paintings gave worshippers plenty to think about during and after their visit.

Sit in a pew and take it in: This is Sevillian Baroque. Seven original or replica Murillo paintings celebrate good deeds and charity: feeding the hungry, tending the sick, and so on. The altar is carved wood with gold leaf. A dozen hardworking cupids support the Burial of Christ. The duty of the order of monks here was to give a Christian burial to the executed and drowned. See the tombstone worked into the altar scene (on the right). Above are three female figures representing main Christian virtues (left to right): faith, charity, hope.

Before leaving the chapel, do Don Miguel Mañara a favor. Step on his **tombstone.** Located just outside the chapel's main entrance in the back, it's served as a welcome mat since 1679. He requested to be buried outside the chapel where everyone would step on him as they entered. It's marked "the worst man in the world."

Return to the courtyard, go straight across, and around to the left. Wander around, noticing the brick Gothic arches of the huge halls of the 13th-century **shipyards,** whose original floors are 15 feet below. Overlooking the courtyard, immediately behind the chapel's altar, were the rooms where Mañara spent his last years. Here he could be close to his charity work and his intensely penitent place of worship.

Across the street from the entry is a park. Pop in and see Don Juan—wracked with guilt—carrying a poor, sick person into his hospital.

North of the Cathedral

PLAZA NUEVA

This pleasant "New Square" is marked by a statue of King Ferdinand III, who liberated Sevilla from the Moors in the 13th century and was later sainted. For centuries afterward, a huge Franciscan monastery stood on this site; it was a spiritual home to many of the missionaries who colonized the California coast. (It was destroyed in 1840, following the disbanding of the monastic system under a government keen to take back power from the Church.) Plaza Nueva has been used for executions, bullfights, and—today—big city events. The modern City Hall runs along the bottom of the square. My "Shopping Paseo" starts at this square (see page 391).

▲FLAMENCO DANCE MUSEUM (MUSEO DEL BAILE FLAMENCO)

Though small and pricey, this museum is worthwhile for anyone who wants to understand more about the dance that embodies the spirit of southern Spain.

The main exhibition, on floor 1, takes about 45 minutes to see. It features well-produced videos, flamenco costumes, and other artifacts collected by the grande dame of flamenco, Christina Hoyos, including a collection of posters celebrating notable flamenco artists of yore (be sure to stand directly under the "sound showers"). The top floor and basement house temporary exhibits, mostly of photography and other artwork. On the ground floor and in the basement, you can watch flamenco lessons in progress—or even take one yourself (one hour, first person-€60, €20/person after that, shoes not provided).

Cost and Hours: €10, €24 combo-ticket includes evening concert, daily 10:00-19:00, pick up English booklet at front desk; hard to find—follow signs for *Museo del Baile Flamenco,* about 3 blocks east of Plaza Nueva at Calle Manuel Rojas Marcos 3; tel. 954-340-311, www.museo flamenco.com.

Performances: Live flamenco performances take place here nightly after the museum closes; see page 393.

▲MUSEO DE BELLAS ARTES

Sevilla's passion for religious art is preserved and displayed in its Museum of Fine Arts. While most Americans go for El Greco, Goya, and Velázquez (not a forte of this collection), this museum gives a fine look at other, less-appreciated Spanish masters: Zurbarán and Murillo. Rather than exhausting, the museum is enjoyable.

Cost and Hours: €1.50, Tue-Sat 10:00-20:30, Sun 10:00-17:00, closed Mon, tel. 955-542-942, www.museosdeandalucia. es.

Getting There: The museum is at Plaza Museo 9, a 15-minute walk from the cathedral, or a short ride on bus #C5 from Plaza Nueva. If coming from the Basílica de la Macarena, take bus #C4 to the Plaza de Armas bus station stop and walk inland four blocks. Pick up the English-language floor plan, which explains the theme of each room.

Background: Sevilla was once Spain's wealthy commercial capital (like New York City) at a time when Madrid was a newly built center of government (like Washington, DC). Spain's economic Golden Age (the 1500s) blossomed into the Golden Age of Spanish painting (the 1600s), especially in Sevilla. Several of Spain's top painters—Zurbarán, Murillo, and Velázquez—lived here in the 1600s. Like their contemporaries, they labored to make the spiritual world tangible, and forged the gritty realism that marks Spanish painting. You'll see balding saints and monks with wrinkled faces and sunburned hands.

In the early 1800s, Spain's government, in a push to take some power from the Church, began disbanding convents and monasteries. Secular fanatics had a heyday looting churches, but fortunately, much of Andalucía's religious art was rescued and hung safely here in this convent-turned-museum.

◐ **SELF-GUIDED TOUR**

The permanent collection features 20 rooms in neat chronological order. It's easy to breeze through once with my tour, then backtrack to what appeals to you.

• *Enter and follow signs to the permanent collection, which begins in Sala I (Room 1).*

Rooms 1-4: Medieval altarpieces of gold-backed saints, Virgin-and-babes, and Crucifixion scenes attest to the religiosity that nurtured Spain's early art. Spain's penchant for unflinching realism culminates in Room 2 with Pedro Torrigiano's 1525 statue of an emaciated San Jerónimo, and in Room 3 with the painted clay head of St. John the Baptist—complete with severed neck muscles, throat, and windpipe. This kind of warts-and-all naturalism would influence the great Sevillian painter Velázquez (one of his works is displayed in Room 4).

• *Continue through the pleasant outdoor courtyard to the former church that is now Room 5.*

Room 5: The far end of this room shows off the works of another home-town boy, **Bartolomé Murillo** (1617-1682). His signature subject is the Immaculate Conception, the doctrine that holds that Mary was exempt from original sin. Several *Inmaculadas* may be on display. Typically, Mary is depicted as young, dressed in white and blue, standing atop the moon (crescent or full). She clutches her breast and gazes up rapturously, surrounded by tumbling winged babies. Murillo's tiny *Madonna and Child* (*Virgen de la Servilleta*, 1665; at the end of the room in the center, where the church's altar would have been) shows the warmth and appeal of his work.

Murillo's sweetness is quite different from the harsh realism of his fellow artists, but his work was understandably popular. For many Spaniards, Mary is their main connection to heaven. They pray directly to her, asking her to intercede on their behalf with God. Murillo's Marys are always receptive and ready to help.

Besides his *Inmaculadas*, Murillo painted popular saints. They often carry sprigs of plants, and cock their heads upward, caught up in a heavenly vision of sweet Baby Jesus. Murillo is also known for his "genre" paintings—scenes of common folk and rascally street urchins—but the museum has few of these.

Also in Room 5 is *The Apotheosis of St. Thomas Aquinas (Apteosis de Santo Tomás de Aquino)* by Francisco de Zurbarán—considered to be Zurbarán's most important work. It was done at the height of his career, when stark realism was all the rage. In a believable, down-to-earth way, Zurbarán presents the pivotal moment when

An Immaculate Conception *by Murillo*

the great saint-theologian experiences his spiritual awakening. We'll see more of Zurbarán upstairs in Room 10.

• *Now head back outside and up the stairs to the first floor.*

Rooms 6-9: In Rooms 6 and 7, you'll see more Murillos and Murillo imitators. Room 8 is dedicated to another native Sevillian (and friend of Murillo), Juan de Valdés Leal (1622-1690). He adds Baroque motion and drama to religious subjects. His surreal colors and feverish, unfinished style create a mood of urgency.

Room 10: Francisco de Zurbarán (thoor-bar-AHN, 1598-1664) painted saints and monks, and the miraculous things they experienced, with an unblinking, crystal-clear, brightly lit, highly detailed realism. Monks and nuns could meditate upon Zurbarán's meticulous paintings for hours, finding God in the details.

In Zurbarán's *St. Hugo Visiting the Refectory (San Hugo en el Refectorio),* white-robed Carthusian monks gather together for their simple meal in a communal dining hall. Above them hangs a painting of Mary, Baby Jesus, and John the Baptist. Zurbarán created paintings for monks' dining halls like this. His audience: celibate men and women who lived in isola-

Zurbarán, Apotheosis of St. Thomas Aquinas

tion, as in this former convent, devoting their time to quiet meditation, prayer, and Bible study. Zurbarán shines a harsh spotlight on many of his subjects, creating strong shadows. They often stand starkly isolated against a single-color background—a dark room or the gray-white of a cloudy sky. He was the ideal painter for the austere religion of 17th-century Spain.

Find *The Virgin of the Caves (La Virgen de las Cuevas)* and study the piety and faith in the monks' weathered faces. Zurbarán's Mary is protective, with her hands placed on the heads of two monks. Note the loving detail on the cape embroidery, the brooch, and the flowers at her feet. But also note the angel babies holding the cape, with their painfully double-jointed arms. Zurbarán was no Leonardo.

The Rest of the Museum: Spain's subsequent art, from the 18th century on, generally followed the trends of the rest of Europe. Room 12 has creamy Romanticism and hazy Impressionism. You'll see typical Sevillian motifs such as matadors, cigar-factory girls, and river landscapes. Enjoy these painted slices of Sevilla, then exit to experience similar scenes today.

Far North of the Cathedral

▲▲BASÍLICA DE LA MACARENA

Sevilla's Holy Week celebrations are Spain's grandest. During the week leading up to Easter, the city is packed with pilgrims witnessing 60 processions carrying about 100 religious floats. If you miss the actual event, you can get a sense of it by visiting the Basílica de la Macarena and its accompanying museum to see the two most impressive floats and the darling of Semana Santa, the statue of the Virgen de la Macarena. Although far from the center, it's located on Sevilla's ring road and easy to reach.

Cost and Hours: Church-free, treasury museum-€5, audioguide-€1; church daily 9:30-14:00 & 17:00-20:30, treasury museum closes 30 minutes earlier. The museum closes a few weeks before Holy Week for float preparation.

Getting There: Wave down a taxi and say "Basílica Macarena" (about €6 from the city center). All the #C buses go there, including bus #C3 and #C4 from Puerta de Jerez (near the Torre de Oro) or Avenida de Menéndez Pelayo (the ring road east of the cathedral), tel. 954-901-800, www.hermandaddelamacarena.es.

SELF-GUIDED TOUR

Compared to the long history of the Macarena statue, the Neo-Baroque church is quite new, built in 1949 to give the oft-moved sculpture a permanent home.

• Grab a pew and study the…

Weeping Virgin: La Macarena is known as the "Weeping Virgin" for the five crystal teardrops trickling down her cheeks. She's like a Baroque doll with human hair and articulated arms, and is even dressed in underclothes. Sculpted in the late 17th century (probably by Pedro Roldán), she's

La Macarena

become Sevilla's most popular image of Mary.

Her beautiful expression—halfway between smiling and crying—is ambiguous, letting worshippers project their own emotions onto her. Her weeping can be contagious—look around you. She's also known as La Esperanza, the Virgin of Hope, and she promises better times after the sorrow.

Installed in a side chapel (on the left) is the **Christ of the Judgment** (from 1654), showing Jesus on the day he was condemned. This statue and La Macarena stand atop the two most important floats of the Holy Week parades.

• To see the floats and learn more, visit the treasury museum. (The museum entrance is on the church's left side; to reach it, either exit the church or go through a connecting door at the rear of the church.)

Treasury (Tesoro): This small three-floor museum tells the history of the Virgin statue and the Holy Week parades. Though rooted in medieval times, the current traditions developed around 1600, with the formation of various fraternities (hermandades). During Holy Week, they demonstrate their dedication to God by parading themed floats throughout Sevilla to retell the story of the Crucifixion and Resurrection of Christ. The museum displays ceremonial banners, scepters, and costumed mannequins; videos show the parades in action (some displays in English).

The three-ton float that carries the Christ of the Judgment is slathered in gold leaf and shows a commotion of figures acting out the sentencing of Jesus. (The statue of Christ—the one you saw in the church—is placed before this crowd for the Holy Week procession.) Pontius Pilate is about to wash his hands. Pilate's wife cries as a man reads the death sentence. During the Holy Week procession, pious Sevillian women wail in the streets while relays of 48 men carry this float on the backs of their necks—only their feet

Basílica de la Macarena

showing under the drapes—as they shuffle through the streets from midnight until 14:00 in the afternoon every Good Friday. The men rehearse for months to get their choreographed footwork in sync.

La Macarena follows the Christ of the Judgment in the procession. Mary's smaller 1.5-ton float seems all silver and candles—"strong enough to support the roof, but tender enough to quiver in the soft night breeze." Mary has a wardrobe of three huge mantles, worn in successive years; these are about 100 years old, as is her six-pound gold crown/halo. This float has a mesmerizing effect on the local crowds. They line up for hours, then clap, weep, and throw roses as it slowly sways along the streets, working its way through town. A Sevillian friend once explained, "She knows all the problems of Sevilla and its people; we've been confiding in her for centuries. To us, she is hope."

The museum collection also contains some matador paraphernalia. La Macarena is the patron saint of bullfighters, and they give thanks for her protection. Copies of her image are popular in

bullring chapels. In 1912, bullfighter José Ortega, hoping for protection, gave La Macarena the five emerald brooches she wears. It worked for eight years... until he was gored to death in the ring. For a month, La Macarena was dressed in widow's black—the only time that has happened.

West of the River
▲▲TRIANA

In Sevilla—as is true in so many other European cities that grew up in the age of river traffic—what was long considered the "wrong side of the river" is now the most colorful part of town. Sevilla's Triana is a proud neighborhood, famed for its flamenco soul (characterized by the statue that greets arrivals from across the river) and its independent spirit. Locals describe crossing the bridge toward the city center as "going to Sevilla."

Visiting Triana: From downtown Sevilla, head to the river and cross over Puente de Isabel II to enter Triana.

Just off the bridge is the **Castillo de San Jorge,** a 12th-century castle that in the 15th century was the headquarters for Sevilla's Inquisition (free small museum and TI kiosk). Next, on the right, is the neighborhood's covered **market.** Built in 2005 in the Moorish Revival style, it sits upon the ruins of the old castle (the scant remains of which you can see). The market bustles in the mornings and afternoons with traditional fruit and vegetable stalls as well as colorful tapas bars and cafés.

Calle San Jacinto, straight ahead just beyond the bridge, was recently liberated from car traffic. It's the hip center of a festival of life each evening. Venturing down side lanes, you find classic 19th-century facades with fine ironwork and colorful tiles. Long home to several tile factories, the district's crusty and flamenco-flamboyant character was shaped by its working-class industrial heritage and a sizeable Roma (Gypsy) population. You can still see a few flowery back courtyards that were once the *corrales* (communal patios) of Roma clans who shared one kitchen, bathroom, and fountain.

The first cross-street intersecting Calle San Jacinto, Calle Pureza, cuts (left) through the historic center of Triana, passing the **Church of Santa Ana,** nicknamed the "Cathedral of Triana." It's the home of the beloved Virgin statue called Nuestra Señora de la Esperanza de Triana (Our Lady of Hope of Triana). She's a big deal here—in Sevilla, upon meeting someone, it's customary to ask not only which football team they support, but which Virgin Mary they favor. The top two in town are the Virgen de la Macarena and La Esperanza de Triana. On the Thursday of Holy Week, it's a battle royale of the Madonnas, as Sevilla's two favorite Virgins are both in processions on the streets at the same time.

As you wander, pop into bars and notice how the decor mixes bullfighting lore with Virgin worship. Keep your eyes peeled for *abacerías,* traditional neighborhood grocers that also function as neighborhood bars (such as La Antigua Abacería, at Calle Pureza 12). And it's easy enough to follow your nose into Dulcería Manu Jara (at Calle Pureza 5), where tempting artisan pastries are made right on the spot.

Colorful Triana

To learn about the district's **ceramic history,** make an easy 10-minute loop walk to see some beautifully tiled ceramic workshops and a ceramics museum. From San Jacinto, with your back to Puente de Isabel II, go right on Calle San Jorge, left on Calle Antillano Campos, and left on Alfarería—which puts you right back on San Jacinto. The route is lined with old facades of the ceramic workshops that once populated this quarter (many have moved to the outskirts of town, where rent is cheaper). But a few stalwarts remain—look for the lavishly decorated Santa Ana (at the end of Calle San Jorge) and the still-bustling Santa Isabel (at Alfarería 12).

Along the way is the **Museo de la Cerámica de Triana,** which covers one of the city's most important artistic treasures: tile and pottery production. Located in the remains of a former riverside factory, the museum explains the entire process, from selecting the right type of earth to kiln firing, with a small collection of ceramics and well-produced videos and interviews with former workers (good English translations). A short video highlights Triana's neighborhood pride

(free, Tue-Sat 10:00-14:00 & 17:00-20:00, Sun 10:00-15:00, closed Mon, Calle Antillano Campos 14).

Be sure to pop into **Hermanos Cofrades** (Alfarería 27), a supply shop where the bearers of religious floats (the *costaleros*) get their matching shoes and padded "sausages" to protect their necks; this is also where members of the religious confraternities buy their penitent attire (in case you need a conehead hat).

EXPERIENCES

Bullfighting
▲BULLFIGHTS

Some of Spain's most intense bullfighting happens in Sevilla's 14,000-seat bullring, Plaza de Toros. Fights are held (generally at 18:30) on most Sundays in May and June; on Easter and Corpus Christi; daily during the April Fair; and at the end of September (during the Feria de San Miguel). These serious fights, with adult matadors, are called *corrida de toros* and often sell out in advance. On many Thursday evenings in July, the *novillada* fights take place, with teenage novices doing the killing and smaller bulls doing the dying.

The matador's capework

Corrida de toros seats range from €25 for high seats looking into the sun to €150 for the first three rows in the shade under the royal box; *novillada* seats are half that—and easy to buy at the arena a few minutes before showtime (ignore scalpers outside; get information at a TI, your hotel, by phone, or online; tel. 954-210-315, www.plazadetorosdelamaestranza.com).

▲▲BULLRING (PLAZA DE TOROS) AND BULLFIGHT MUSEUM (MUSEO TAURINO)

Follow a bilingual (Spanish and English) 40-minute guided tour through the bullring's strangely quiet and empty arena, its museum, and the chapel where the matador prays before the fight. (Thanks to readily available blood transfusions, there have been no deaths in nearly three decades.) The two most revered figures of Sevilla, the Virgen de la Macarena and the Jesús del Gran Poder (Christ of All Power), are represented in the chapel. In the museum, you'll see great classic scenes and the heads of a few bulls—awarded the bovine equivalent of an Oscar for a particularly good fight. The city was so appalled when the famous matador Manolete was killed in 1947 that even the mother of the bull that gored him was destroyed. Matadors—dressed to kill—are heartthrobs in their "suits of light." Many girls have their bedrooms wallpapered with posters of cute bullfighters.

Cost and Hours: €7, entrance with escorted tour only—no free time inside; 3/hour, daily April-Oct 9:30-21:00, Nov-March 9:30-19:00; until 15:00 on fight days, when chapel and horse room are closed. The last tour departs 15 minutes before closing. While they take groups of up to 50, it's still wise to call or drop by to reserve a spot in the busy season (tel. 954-224-577, www.realmaestranza.com).

April Fair

Two weeks after Easter, much of Sevilla packs into its vast fairgrounds for a grand party that brings all that's Andalusian together. The local passion for horses, flamenco, and sherry is clear—riders are ramrod straight, colorfully clad girls ride sidesaddle, and everyone's drinking sherry spritzers. Women sport outlandish dresses that would look clownish elsewhere, but are somehow brilliant here en masse. Horses clog the streets in an endless parade until about 20:00, when they clear out and the streets fill with exuberant locals. The party goes on literally 24 hours a day for six days.

Countless private party tents, called *casetas,* line the lanes. Each tent is the private party zone of a family, club, or association. You need to know someone in the group—or make friends quickly—to get in. In each *caseta,* everyone knows everyone. It's like a thousand wedding parties being celebrated at the same time.

Any tourist can have a fun and memorable evening by simply crashing the party. The city's entire fleet of taxis (who'll try to charge double) and buses seems dedicated to shuttling people from downtown to the fairgrounds. Given the traffic jams and inflated prices, you may be better off hiking: From the Torre del Oro, cross the San Telmo Bridge to Plaza de Cuba and hike down Calle Asunción. You'll see the towering gate to the fairgrounds in the distance. Just follow the crowds (there's no admission charge). Arrive before 20:00 to see the horses, but stay later, as the ambience improves after the *caballos* giddy-up on out. Some of the larger tents are sponsored by the city and open to the public, but the best action is in the streets, where party-goers from the livelier *casetas* spill out. Although private tents have bouncers, everyone is so happy that it's not tough to strike up an impromptu friendship, become a "special guest," and be invited in. The drink flows freely, and the food is fun and cheap.

Shopping

Popular souvenir items include ladies' fans, shawls, *mantillas* (ornate head scarves), other items related to flamenco (castanets, guitars, costumes), ceramics, and bullfighting posters.

The El Postigo **arts and crafts market** is in an architecturally interesting old building behind Hospital de la Caridad (Mon-Sat 11:00-14:00 & 16:00-20:00, Sun 16:00-20:00, at the corner of Calles de Arfe and Dos de Mayo, tel. 954-560-013). And only on Sundays, there's an art market on Plaza del Museo (by Museo de Bellas Artes).

▲▲*Shopping Paseo*

Although many tourists never get beyond the cathedral and Barrio Santa Cruz, the thriving pedestrianized shopping area north of the cathedral is well worth a wander. The best shopping streets—Calle Tetuán, Calle Sierpes, and Calle Cuna—also happen to be part of the oldest section of Sevilla. A walk here is a chance to join one of Spain's liveliest paseos—that bustling celebration of life that takes place before dinner each evening, when everyone is out strolling. This walk, if done between 18:00 and 20:00, gives you a chance to experience the paseo scene while getting a look at the town's most popular shops. You'll pass windows displaying the best in both traditional and trendy fashion.

Start on the pedestrianized **Plaza Nueva**—the 19th-century square facing the ornate City Hall—which features a statue of Ferdinand III, a local favorite because he freed Sevilla from the Moors in 1248.

From here wander the length of **Calle Tetuán,** where old-time standbys bump up against fashion-right boutiques. **Juan Foronda** (#28) has been selling flamenco attire and *mantillas* since 1926. A few doors down, you'll find the flagship store of **Camper** (#24), the proudly Spanish shoe brand that's become a worldwide favorite. The rest of the street showcases mainly Spanish brands, such as Massimo Dutti, Zara, and Mango. Calle Tetuán (which becomes Calle Velázquez) ends at La Campana, a big intersection and popular meeting point, with the super department store, El Corte Inglés, just beyond, on Plaza del Duque de la Victoria.

Turn right here. At the corner of **Calle Sierpes** awaits a venerable pastry shop, **Confitería La Campana,** with a fine 1885 interior...and Sevilla's most tempting sweets (take a break at the outdoor tables, or head to the back of the shop, where you can grab a coffee and pastry at the stand-up bar).

Now head down Calle Sierpes. This is a great street for strolling, despite some signs of *"la crisis económica"*—empty storefronts. If you've got time, drop by the clock-covered, wood-paneled **El Cronómetro** shop (#19), where master watchmakers have been doing business since 1901. It's just the place to fix your Rolex—they're an official retailer of all the luxury brands. Take a minute to set your watch by their precisely set display clocks. **Sombrereria Maquedano** (#40, at the corner of Calle Rioja) is a styling place

Hat shoppers in Sevilla

for hats—especially for men. They claim to be the oldest hat seller in Sevilla, and maybe in all of Spain. Check out the great selection of Panama hats, perfect for the Sevillian heat.

At the corner of Sierpes and Jovellanos/Sagasta, you'll find several fine shops featuring Andalusian accessories. Drop in to see how serious local women are about their fans, shawls, *mantillas,* and *peinetas* (combs designed to secure and prop up the *mantilla*). The most valuable *mantillas* are silk, and the top-quality combs are made of tortoiseshell (though most women opt for much more affordable polyester and plastic). Andalusian women accessorize with fans, matching them to different dresses. The *mantilla* comes in black (worn only on Good Friday and by the mother of the groom at weddings) and white (worn at bullfights during the April Fair).

From here turn left down **Calle Sagasta.** Notice that the street has two names—the modern version and a medieval one: Antigua Calle de Gallegos ("Former Street of the Galicians"). With the Christian victory in 1248, the Muslims were given one month to evac-

uate. To consolidate Christian control during that time, settlers from Galicia, the northwest corner of Iberia, were planted here; this street was the center of their neighborhood.

Just before you hit the charming **Plaza del Salvador,** stop for a peek into the windows at **BuBi** (#6). This *boutique infantil* displays pricey but exquisitely made baby clothes—knit, embroidered, starched, and beribboned. Tiny crocheted booties are just affordable (€20). Now jump in to Plaza del Salvador—it's teeming with life.

Nightlife

▲▲ *Evening Paseo*

Sevilla is meant for strolling. The paseo thrives every nonwinter evening in these areas: along either side of the river between the San Telmo and Isabel II bridges (Paseo de Cristóbal Colón and Triana district), up Avenida de la Constitución, around Plaza Nueva, at Plaza de España, and throughout the Barrio Santa Cruz. On hot summer nights, even families with toddlers are out past midnight. Spend some time rafting through this river of humanity.

A shopping street

▲▲▲ *Flamenco*

This music-and-dance art form has its roots in the Roma (Gypsy) and Moorish cultures. Even at a packaged "flamenco evening," sparks fly. The men do most of the flamboyant machine-gun footwork. The women often concentrate on the graceful turns and smooth, shuffling step of the *soleá* version of the dance. Watch the musicians. Flamenco guitarists, with their lightning-fast finger-roll strums, are among the best in the world. The intricate rhythms are set by castanets or the hand-clapping (called *palmas*) of those who aren't dancing at the moment. In the raspy-voiced wails of the singers, you'll hear echoes of the Muslim call to prayer.

Like jazz, flamenco thrives on improvisation. Also like jazz, good flamenco is more than just technical proficiency. A singer or dancer with "soul" is said to have *duende*. Flamenco is a happening, with bystanders clapping along and egging on the dancers with whoops and shouts. Get into it.

Hotels push tourist-oriented, nightclub-style flamenco shows, but they charge a commission. Fortunately, it's easy to book a place on your own.

Sevilla's flamenco offerings tend to fall into one of three categories: serious concerts (usually about €18 and about an hour long), where the singing and dancing take center stage; touristy dinner-and-drinks shows with table service (generally around €35—not including food—and two hours long); and—the least touristy option—casual bars with late-night performances, where for the cost of a drink you can catch impromptu (or semi-impromptu) musicians at play.

SERIOUS FLAMENCO CONCERTS

These concerts give you a good overview of the art form. It's hard to choose among these three nightly, one-hour flamenco concerts. Each company offers equal quality, and costs about the same; each venue is small, intimate, and air-conditioned. For many, the concerts are preferable to the shows (listed later) because they're half the cost, half the length, and generally start earlier in the evening.

At each venue, you can reserve by phone and pay upon arrival, or drop by early to pick up a ticket. While La Casa del Flamenco is the nicest and most central venue, the other two have exhibits that can add to the experience.

La Casa de la Memoria is a wide venue (just two rows deep), where everyone gets a close-up view and room to stretch out (€18, nightly at 19:30 and 21:00, no drinks, no children under age 6, 100 seats, Calle Cuna 6, tel. 954-560-670, www.casadelamemoria.es, flamencomemoria@gmail.com, run by Rosanna). They also have an exhibit on one easy, well-described floor, with lots of photos and a few artifacts (free with concert ticket, open 10:30-14:00 & 17:00-19:00).

With 115 tightly packed seats, the **Flamenco Dance Museum** is the most congested venue. It has a bar and allows

Spirited flamenco erupts nightly in Sevilla.

drinks. The doors open at 18:00, when you can grab the seat of your choice, then spend an hour touring the museum and enjoying a drink before the show (€20, nightly at 19:00 and 21:45, €24 combo-ticket includes the museum and a show, reservations smart, tel. 954-340-311, www.museoflamenco.com).

La Casa del Flamenco has 60 spacious seats in a delightful arcaded courtyard right in the Barrio Santa Cruz. Reception at adjacent Hotel Alcántara serves as the box office (€18, €2 discount for Rick Steves readers with this book who book direct and pay cash in 2016; shows nightly at 19:00 and 20:30 in April-May and Sept-Oct, one show rest of year, at 19:00 or 20:30—best check website for current times; no drinks, no kids under age 6, Calle Ximénez de Enciso 28, tel. 954-500-595, www.lacasadelflamencosevilla.com).

RAZZLE-DAZZLE FLAMENCO SHOWS

These packaged shows can be a bit sterile—and an audience of tourists doesn't help—but I find both Los Gallos and El Arenal entertaining and riveting. While El Arenal feels slicker and may have a slight edge on talent, Los Gallos has a cozier setting, with cushy rather than hard chairs—and it's cheaper.

Los Gallos presents nightly two-hour shows. Owners José and Blanca promise goose bumps (€35 ticket includes drink, €3/person discount with this book—limited to two people, nightly at 20:15 and 22:30, arrive 30 minutes early for best seats, noisy bar, no food served, Plaza de la Santa Cruz 11, tel. 954-216-981, www.tablaolosgallos.com).

Tablao El Arenal has arguably more professional performers and a classier setting, but dinner customers get the preferred seating, and waiters are working throughout the performance (€38 ticket includes drink, €60 includes tapas, €72 includes dinner, 1.5-hour shows at 20:00 and 22:00, 30 minutes earlier off-season, near bullring at Calle Rodó 7, tel. 954-216-492, www.tablaoelarenal.com).

FLAMENCO IN BARS

Spirited flamenco singing still erupts in bars throughout the old town—but you need to know where to look. Ask a local for the latest.

La Carbonería Bar, the sangria equivalent of a beer garden, is a few blocks north of the Barrio Santa Cruz, not far from most of my recommended hotels. Worth a visit if you're not quite ready to end the day, it's a sprawling place with a variety of rooms leading to a big, open tent filled with young locals, casual guitar strummers, and nearly nightly flamenco music from about 22:30 to 24:00 (no cover, €2.50 sangria, daily 20:00-very late; near Plaza Santa María—find Hotel Fernando III, the side alley Céspedes dead-ends at Calle Levies, head left to Levies 18; tel. 954-214-460, www.levies18.com).

A few bars in Triana host live dancing; **Lo Nuestro** and **Rejoneo** are favorites (at Calle Betis 31A and 31B).

EATING

Eating in Sevilla is fun and affordable. A clear dining trend is the rise of gourmet tapas bars, with spiffed-up decor and creative menus, at the expense of traditional restaurants. Old-school places survive, but they often lack energy, and it seems that their clientele is aging with them. My quandary: I like the classic *típico* places, but the lively atmosphere and the best food are in the new places. One thing's certain: your best value is a trendy tapas bar that offers good table seating.

For **supermarkets,** try the El Corte Inglés department stores on Plaza Duque de la Victoria and Plaza Magdalena (Mon-Sat 10:00-22:00, Sun 11:00-21:00). **Mercado del Arenal,** the covered fish-and-produce market, is perfect for hungry photographers, though it is the least lively on Mondays (Mon-Sat 9:00-14:30, closed Sun, on Calle Pastor y Landero at Calle Arenal, just beyond the bullring).

In Triana

Crusty and colorful Triana, across the river from the city center, offers a nice range of eating options. Its covered market is home to a world of tempting lunchtime eateries—take a stroll, take in the scene, and take your pick (busiest Tue-Sat morning through afternoon). Beyond the market, the neighborhood has three main restaurant zones to consider: trendy Calle San Jacinto, the neighborhood scene behind the Church of Santa Ana, and several riverside restaurants with views.

On or near Calle San Jacinto

The area's pedestrianized main drag is lined with the tables of several enjoyable restaurants.

Taberna Miami is a reliable bet for seafood. Grab a table with a good perch right on the street (€8 half-*raciones*, €11-12 *raciones*, daily 11:30-24:00, Calle San Jacinto 21, tel. 954-340-843).

Patio San Eloy, famous for its €2-3 *montaditos*, has two locations on the main drag: an old-fashioned bar at San Jacinto 29 (daily 8:00-24:00), and its modern cousin across the street at #16 (daily 12:00-24:00, tel. 954-501-070).

Blanca Paloma Bar is a classic that's a hit with the neighborhood crowd. It has small tables for a sit-down meal, a delightful bar, and a fine selection of good Spanish wines by the glass, listed on the blackboard. They serve tasty tapa standards such as *pisto con huevo frito* (ratatouille with fried egg) that look and taste homemade (tapas at bar only, €7 half-*raciones*, €12 *raciones*, open daily at 8:30 but food served Mon-Sat 12:00-16:00 & 20:00-24:00, Sun 12:00-16:00, at the corner of Calle Pagés del Corro, tel. 954-333-640).

Las Golondrinas Bar is the talk of Triana, with a wonderful list of cheap and tasty tapas. Try the pork *solomillo* (sirloin) and *champiñones* (mushrooms). Add a veggie plate from the *aliños* section of the menu. They serve plenty of nice wines by the glass. Cling to a corner of the bar and watch the amazingly productive little kitchen at work; you'll need to be aggressive to get an order in. For a sit-down meal, nab a table upstairs (Tue-Sun 13:00-16:00 & 20:00-24:00, may also be open Mon; one block down Calle San Jacinto from Isobel II Bridge—take the first right onto Calle Alfarería, then the first left onto Calle Antillano Campos to #26; tel. 954-331-626).

Behind the Church of Santa Ana

This is the best place in the area to take a break from the trendy dining scene. It offers a charming setting where you can sit down under a big tree to eat dinner along with local families.

Bar Bistec, with most of the square's tables, does grilled fish with gusto. They're enthusiastic about their cod fritters and calamari, and brag about their pigeon, quail, and snails in sauce. Before taking a seat out on the square, consider the indoor seating and the fun action at the bar (€8 half-*raciones*, €14 *raciones*, daily 11:30-16:00 & 20:00-24:00, Plazuela de Santa Ana, tel. 954-274-759). **Taberna La**

Eat afuera (outside) in Sevilla.

Plazuela, which shares the square, is simpler, serving fried fish, grilled sardines, and *caracoles* (tree snails).

Bar Santa Ana, just a block away alongside the church, is a rustic neighborhood sports-and-bull bar with great seating on the street. Peruse the interior, draped in bullfighting and Weeping Virgin memorabilia. It's always busy with the locals, who enjoy fun tapas like *delicia de solomillo* (tenderloin). The bar serves even cheap tapas at the outdoor tables. If you stand at the bar, they'll keep track of your bill by chalking it directly on the counter in front of you (facing the side of the church at Pureza 82, tel. 954-272-102).

Along the River

Kiosco de Las Flores, which started out in a simple green shack on the river in 1930, has become a Sevillian tradition. They serve up €8-10 *raciones* and €18 meat dishes, but most diners gobble down the €10 fried fish, either inside or on the terrace (Tue-Sat 12:00-16:00 & 20:00-24:00, Sun 12:00-16:00, closed Mon, on Calle Betis across from Torre del Oro, tel. 954-274-576).

Abades Triana Ristorante is a hit for special occasions and riverfront dining. It's a dressy restaurant with formal waiters serving modern Mediterranean cuisine. You'll sit in air-conditioned comfort behind a big glass wall facing the river or on a classy outdoor terrace (€3.50 cover, €15-24 starters, €20-30 fish and meat plates, daily 13:30-16:00 & 20:00-24:00, reservations smart but they don't reserve specific tables, directly across from Torre del Oro at Calle Betis 69, tel. 954-286-459, www.abadestriana.com).

In Barrio Santa Cruz
Tapas with the Tourists

For tapas, Barrio Santa Cruz is trendy and *romántico*. Plenty of atmospheric-but-touristy restaurants fill the neighborhood near the cathedral and along Calle Santa María la Blanca. From the

cathedral, walk up Calle Mateos Gago, where several classic old bars—with the day's tapas scrawled on chalkboards—keep tourists and locals well fed and watered.

Bodega Santa Cruz (a.k.a. **Las Columnas**) is a popular, user-friendly standby with cheap, unpretentious tapas. You're not coming here for the basic food, but for the bustling atmosphere, as locals and tourists crowd the place, inside and out, for hours on end. Keep an eye on the busy kitchen from the bar, or hang out like a cowboy at the tiny stand-up tables out front. There's no table service, so you need to find your way to the bar to order—a fun experience in itself. Separate chalkboards list €2 tapas and €2.50 *montaditos* (daily 11:30-24:00, Calle de Rodrigo Caro 1A, tel. 954-213-246).

Las Teresas is a characteristic small bar draped in fun photos. It serves good tapas from a tight little menu. Prices at the bar and outside tables (for fun tourist-watching) are the same, but they serve tapas only at the bar. The hams, with little upside-down umbrellas that catch the dripping fat, show Spaniards' enthusiasm for cured meat (€3-4 tapas, €8-10 half-*raciones*, €14-20 *raciones*, open daily, Calle Santa Teresa 2, tel. 954-213-069).

Restaurante San Marco serves basic, reasonably priced Italian cuisine under the arches of what was a Moorish bath in the Middle Ages. The air-conditioned atmosphere may feel upscale, but it's also easygoing and family-friendly, with live Spanish guitar every night (€8-10 salads, pizza, and pastas; €11-18 meat dishes, daily 13:00-16:15 & 20:00-24:00, Calle Mesón del Moro 6, tel. 954-214-390, staff speaks English, welcoming Ángelo).

Casa Roman Taberna has a classic bar and tavern interior, with good tables inside and a few more on a great little square outside. When it's quiet, ask if they serve tapas at the tables; otherwise, it's your standard *raciones*. They have an easy menu, with lots of wines by

the glass (Plaza de los Venerables 1, tel. 954-228-483).

On or near Calle Santa María la Blanca

This lively street, which defines the eastern boundary of the Barrio Santa Cruz, has an inviting concentration of eateries and is only slightly less touristy.

Tapas Restaurants on Paseo Catalina de Ribera: Three easy and good-value places are located next to each other; they have similar prices (€3-4 tapas, €8-10 plates), fine bars, good indoor seating, and wonderful tables outside on a busy sidewalk facing the Murillo Gardens. **Modesto Tapas** is old-fashioned, with standard tapas and a crowd that seems averse to trendiness (tel. 955-290-690). The other two are more creative. **Vinería San Telmo** specializes in meaty tapas (try the lamb and Argentine-style steak) and offers lots of wine by the glass (tel. 954-410-600). **Catalina Tapas Bar** is my favorite—like me, it's more up-to-date and inspired than Modesto, but less hip than San Telmo (tel. 954-412-412).

Restaurante Modesto is a local favorite serving pricey but top-notch Andalusian fare—especially fish—with a comfortable dining room and atmospheric

outdoor seating in the bright, bustling square just outside the Murillo Gardens. It offers creative, fun meals—look around before ordering—and a good €20 fixed-price lunch or dinner served by energetic, occasionally pushy waiters. The €9 house salad is a meal, and the €15.50 fried seafood plate—*fritura modesto*—is popular (€7-15 starters, €12-20 main dishes, daily 12:30-24:00, near Santa María la Blanca at Calle Cano y Cueto 5, tel. 954-416-811).

Between the Cathedral and the River

In the area between the cathedral and the river, just across Avenida de la Constitución, you can find tapas, cheap eats, and fine dining. Calle García de Vinuesa leads past several colorful and cheap tapas places to a busy corner (where Calle de Adriano meets Calle Antonia Díaz) surrounded with an impressive selection of happy eateries.

Bodeguita Casablanca is famously the choice of bullfighters, and even the king. Just steps from the touristy cathedral area, this classy place seems a world apart, with refined locals, a great menu, and interior decor complete with a stuffed bull's head. Sit inside for a serious meal of half-*raciones*. Be bold and experiment—

Sevilla Restaurants & Flamenco Bars

Plaza del Museo
MUSEO DE BELLAS ARTES
MONSALVES
EL CENTRO
VELAZQUEZ

PLAZA DE ARMAS BUS STATION
TORNEO
PEDRO DEL TORO
SAN ELOY
O'DONNELL
RIOJA

To Itálica & Portugal
PUENTE EL CACHORRO
AV. MARQUES DE PARADAS
GRAVINA
CANALEJAS
BAILEN
LA MAGDALENA
SAN PABLO
MENENDEZ
ROSARIO
ALBAREDA

CALLE ARJONA
TRASTAMARA
MORATIN
19
C. ZARAGOZA
CANAL
NUÑEZ
GRANADA
RENFE
Plaza Nueva
MADRID

200 Meters
200 Yards
20
MARCHENA
CASTELAR
GAMAZO

REYES CATÓLICOS
PASTOR Y LANDERO
ALMANSA
ARENAL MARKET
21
PATRONAS
EL ARENAL
GARCIA

CALLE CASTILLA
PUENTE DE ISABEL II
CHILLIDA SCULPTURE
PASEO DE CRISTOBAL COLÓN
CALLE DE ADRIANO
BULLRING & MUSEUM
PAVIA
AREF
REAL DE LA CARRETERIA

MUSEO DE LA CERÁMICA DE TRIANA
COVERED MARKET
Plaza del Altozano
STATUE OF CARMEN
A. DIAZ
VELARDE
RODO
GEN. CASTAÑO
26
16
DOS DE MAYO

4
2
1
2
TRIANA
C. DE LA PUREZA
28
Guadalquivir River
HOSPITAL DE LA CARIDAD
TEMP.

4
3
CALLE SAN JACINTO
RODRIGO
6
DE
5
SANTA ANA
TRIANA
CORREA
TORRE DEL ORO
ALMT.

FEBO
TROYA
7
PUENTE SAN TELMO

Plaza de Cuba

1. Taberna Miami
2. Patio San Eloy (2)
3. Blanca Paloma Bar
4. Las Golondrinas Bar (2)
5. Bar Bistec & Taberna La Plazuela
6. Bar Santa Ana
7. Kiosco de Las Flores, Abades Triana Ristorante
8. Bodega Santa Cruz
9. Las Teresas Bar
10. Restaurante San Marco
11. Casa Roman Taberna
12. Paseo Catalina de Ribera Tapas Trio
13. Restaurante Modesto
14. Bodeguita Casablanca

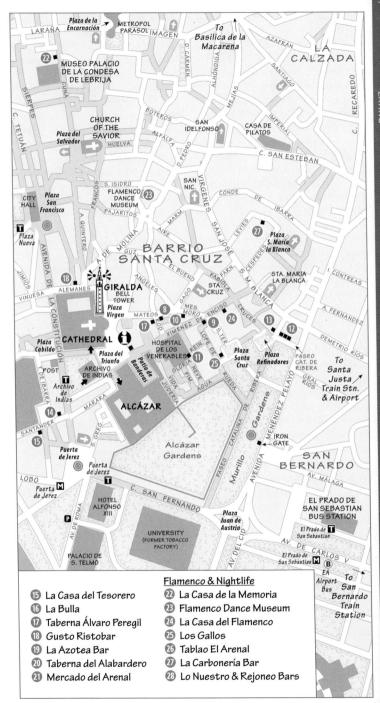

you can't go wrong here (€2.50 tapas, Mon-Fri 13:30-17:00 & 20:00-24:00, Sat 12:30-17:30 except closed Sat in July, closed Sun and Aug, Calle Adolfo Rodríguez Jurado 12, tel. 954-224-114).

La Casa del Tesoro, with mellow lighting and music, is a good, dressy Italian alternative to the tapas commotion. Below its calm, spacious interior are 12th-century Moorish ruins (look through the glass floor), and overhead are the historic arches of what used to be the city's treasury (€12 salads, pastas, and pizzas, €15 fixed-price dinner, Calle Santander 1, tel. 954-503-921).

La Bulla is intent upon mixing traditional dishes with an inventive international menu that's a welcome break from the usual fare. The place is bohemian-chic, with rickety tables gathered around a busy kitchen. The day's offerings are listed only on big chalkboards; ask for a stand-up English-language tour of what's available. You'll enjoy gourmet presentation, easy jazz ambience, a hip local crowd, and good-looking servers. There's no bar—only indoor table seating. The €5-12 dishes are easily splittable; three will stuff two people (daily 12:00-16:30 & 20:00-24:00, no reservations, midway between cathedral and Torre del Oro at Calle 2 de Mayo 26, tel. 954-219-262).

Near the Cathedral

I try to avoid the restaurants surrounding the cathedral, but if you can't take another step before finding a place to eat, here are a few decent options. The tiny **Taberna Álvaro Peregil** is mixed in with the tourist jumble, but their €2 small plates and €2.50 *montaditos* are the real thing (daily 12:00-24:00, Calle Mateos Gago 20, tel. 954-218-966). If you can't face one more tapa, **Gusto Ristobar,** just outside the cathedral's Court of the Orange Trees, has fresh-tasting €5-9 *panini*, pizza, and salads (daily 8:30-23:30, Calle Alemanes 3, tel. 954-500-923).

Near Plaza Nueva

La Azotea Bar is a modern place that makes up for its lack of traditional character with gourmet tapas—made with seasonal ingredients—that have earned it a loyal following. It's run by Juan Antonio and his partner from San Diego, Jeanine, who've taken care to make the menu easy and accessible for English speakers. Dine elegantly on tapas for reasonable prices (served only at the bar), or enjoy a sit-down meal at the tables (the big, €12 half-*raciones* feed two)—but you'll need to arrive early (Mon-Sat 13:30-16:30 & 20:30-24:00, closed Sun, Calle Zaragoza 5, tel. 954-564-316). They also have a little branch in Barrio Santa Cruz (long hours daily, Mateos Gago 8).

Taberna del Alabardero, one of Sevilla's finest restaurants, serves refined Spanish cuisine in chandeliered elegance just a couple of blocks from the cathedral. If you order à la carte, it adds up to about €45 a meal, but for €59 (or €74 with paired wine) you can have an elaborate, seven-course fixed-price meal with lots of little surprises from the chef. Or consider their €20/person (no sharing) starter sampler, followed by an entrée. The service in the fancy upstairs dining rooms gets mixed reviews (carefully read and understand your bill)...but the setting is stunning. Consider having tapas on their popular terrace while taking in views of the cathedral (daily 13:00-16:30 & 20:00-23:30, may be closed Aug, terrace closed in bad weather, air-con, reservations smart, Zaragoza 20, tel. 954-502-721, www.tabernadelalabardero.es). The ground-floor dining rooms (nice but nothing like upstairs) are popular with local office workers for a great-value, student-chef-prepared, fixed-price lunch sampler. To avoid a wait at lunch, arrive before 14:00 (three delightful courses-€13 Mon-Fri, €18 Sat-Sun; €20 dinner available daily, drinks not included, open daily 13:00-16:30 & 20:00-23:30, no reservations).

SLEEPING

All of my listings are centrally located, mostly within a five-minute walk of the cathedral. The first are near the charming but touristy Barrio Santa Cruz. The last group is just as central but closer to the river, across the boulevard in a more workaday, less touristy zone.

Room rates as much as double during the two Sevilla fiestas (Holy Week and the April Fair, held two weeks after Easter). In general, the busiest and most expensive months are April, May, September, and October. Hotels put rooms on the discounted push list in July and August—when people with good sense avoid this furnace—and from November through February. A price range indicates mid- to high-season prices (but I have not listed festival prices).

If you visit in July or August, you'll find the best deals in central, business-class places. They offer summer discounts and provide a (necessary) cool, air-conditioned refuge. Be aware that Spain's air-conditioning often isn't the icebox Americans might expect, especially in Sevilla.

Barrio Santa Cruz

These places are off Calle Santa María la Blanca and Plaza Santa María. The most convenient parking lot is the Cano y Cueto garage near the corner of Calle Santa María la Blanca and Avenida de Menéndez Pelayo (about €18/day, open daily 24 hours).

$$$ Hotel Casa 1800, well-priced for its elegance, is worth the extra euros. Located dead-center in Barrio Santa Cruz (facing a boisterous tapas bar that quiets down after midnight), it has 33 well-appointed rooms with high, beamed ceilings; a chandeliered patio lounge that hosts a daily free afternoon tea; and a rooftop terrace and swimming pool that offer an impressive cathedral view (Db-€165, deluxe Db with terrace and

> ## Sleep Code
>
> **Abbreviations:** S=Single, D=Double/Twin, T=Triple, Q=Quad, b=bathroom
> **Price Rankings for Double Rooms: $$$** Most rooms €110 or more, **$$** €60-110, **$** €60 or less
> **Notes:** Some hotels include the 10 percent IVA tax in the room price; others add it to your bill. Prices change; verify rates online or by email. For the best prices, book directly with the hotel.

outdoor Jacuzzi-€215, prices fluctuate with season, breakfast-€9.50, air-con, elevator, Calle Rodrigo Caro 6, tel. 954-561-800, www.hotelcasa1800.com, info@hotelcasa1800.com).

$$$ Casa del Poeta offers a tranquility that seems contrary to its location in the heart of Santa Cruz. At the end of a side-street, Trinidad and Ángelo have lovingly converted an old family mansion with 18 rooms surrounding a large central patio into a home away from home. Evening guitar concerts plus a fantastic view terrace make it a worthwhile splurge (Db-€120-300, about €60 more for private terrace or suite, prices fluctuate with season, breakfast-€9.50 or free if you reserve on their website, air-con, elevator, Calle Don Carlos Alonso Chaparro 3, tel. 954-213-868, www.casadelpoeta.es, direccion@casadelpoeta.es).

$$$ Hotel Las Casas de la Judería has 133 quiet, classic rooms and junior suites, most of them tastefully decorated with hardwood floors and a Spanish flair. The service can be a little formal, but the rooms, which surround a series of peaceful courtyards, are romantic (Sb-€110-160, Db-€125-250 depending on season, book directly with hotel and mention this book for 10 percent discount in low season,

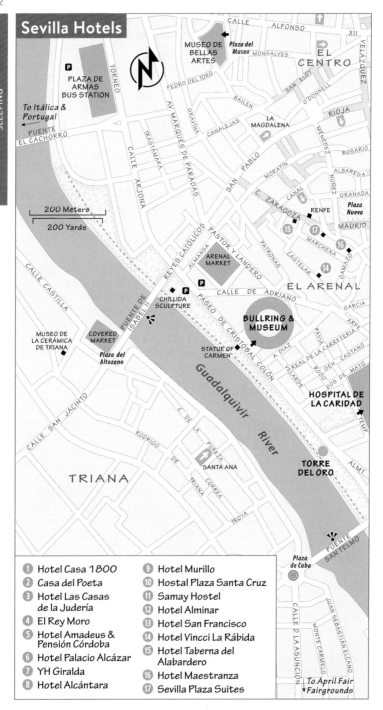

Sevilla Hotels

1. Hotel Casa 1800
2. Casa del Poeta
3. Hotel Las Casas de la Judería
4. El Rey Moro
5. Hotel Amadeus & Pensión Córdoba
6. Hotel Palacio Alcázar
7. YH Giralda
8. Hotel Alcántara
9. Hotel Murillo
10. Hostal Plaza Santa Cruz
11. Samay Hostel
12. Hotel Alminar
13. Hotel San Francisco
14. Hotel Vincci La Rábida
15. Hotel Taberna del Alabardero
16. Hotel Maestranza
17. Sevilla Plaza Suites

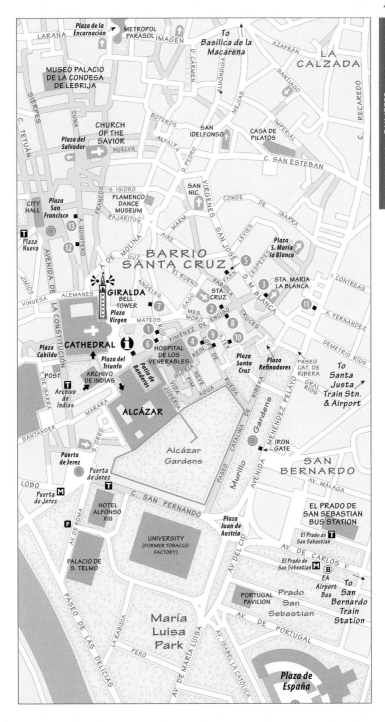

check website for even better rates, expensive but great buffet breakfast-€15, air-con, elevator, pool in summer, valet parking-€20/day, Plaza Santa María 5, tel. 954-415-150, www.casasypalacios.com, juderia@casasypalacios.com).

$$$ El Rey Moro encircles its spacious, colorful patio (which tourists routinely duck into for a peek) with 19 rooms. Dripping with quirky Andalusian character, and thoughtful about including extras (such as free loaner bikes, a welcome drink, and private rooftop Jacuzzi time), it's a class act (Sb-€79-99, Db-€100-129, Db suite-€129-199, breakfast-€9—or free if you reserve on their website, check their site for other specials, air-con, elevator, Calle Lope de Rueda 14, tel. 954-563-468, www.elreymoro.com, hotel@elreymoro. com).

$$$ Hotel Amadeus is a classy and comfortable gem, wonderfully run by María Luisa and her charming staff (Zaida and Cristina). The 30 rooms, lovingly decorated with a musical motif, are situated around small courtyards. Elevators take you to a roof terrace with an under-the-stars Jacuzzi. The €9 breakfast comes on a trolley—enjoy it in your room, in the lounge, or on a terrace. Welcoming public spaces include soundproof rooms with pianos—something I've seen nowhere else in Europe (Sb-€90, Db-€105-115, big Db-€115-137, Db suite-€165-195, cheaper July-Aug, air-con, elevator, iPads in every room, laundry-€16.50, parking-€22/day, Calle Farnesio 6, tel. 954-501-443, www. hotelamadeussevilla.com, reservas@ hotelamadeussevilla.com,).

$$$ Hotel Palacio Alcázar is the former home and studio of John Fulton, an American who moved here to become a bullfighter and painter. This charming boutique hotel has 12 crisp, modern rooms. Each soundproofed door is painted with a different scene of Sevilla. Triple-paned windows keep out the noise from the plaza (Sb-€85-120, Db-€95-130, Tb-€130-145, prices depend on room size

and season, breakfast-€9, air-con, elevator, rooftop terrace with bar and cathedral views, Plaza de la Alianza 11, tel. 954-502-190, www.hotelpalacioalcazar.com, hotel@palacioalcazar.com).

$$ YH Giralda, once an 18th-century abbots' house, is now a homey 14-room hotel tucked away on a little street right off Calle Mateos Gago, just a couple of blocks from the cathedral. The exterior rooms have windows onto a pedestrian street, and a few of the interior rooms have small windows that look into the inner courtyard. All rooms are basic but neatly appointed (Sb-€35-85, Db-€40-90, Tb-€55-105, no breakfast, air-con, Calle Abades 30, tel. 954-228-324, www. yh-hoteles.com, yhgiralda@yh-hoteles. com).

$$ Hotel Alcántara offers more no-nonsense comfort than character. Well situated, it rents 23 slick rooms at a good price (Sb-€57-90, twin Db-€68-120, fancy Db-€76-140, Tb-€94-175, breakfast-€6, air-con, elevator, rentable laptop and bikes, outdoor patio, Calle Ximénez de Enciso 28, tel. 954-500-595, www. hotelalcantara.net, info@hotelalcantara. net). The hotel also functions as the box office for the nightly La Casa del Flamenco show, next door (see page 394).

$$ Hotel Murillo enjoys one of the most appealing locations in Santa Cruz, along one of the narrow "kissing lanes." Above its antiques-filled lobby are 57 nondescript rooms with marble floors (Sb-€58-95, Db-€85-111, about €30 more for "superior" rooms with fancier decor, breakfast-€9, air-con, elevator, Calle Lope de Rueda 7, tel. 954-216-095, www. hotelmurillo.com, reservas@hotelmurillo. com). They also rent apartments with kitchens (Db-€90-120).

$$ Pensión Córdoba, a homier and cheaper option, has 12 tidy, quiet rooms, solid modern furniture, and a showpiece tiled courtyard (S-€35-45, Sb-€40-55, D-€50-65, Db-€60-75, no breakfast, cash only, air-con, on a tiny lane off Calle Santa

María la Blanca at Calle Farnesio 12, tel. 954-227-498, www.pensioncordoba.com, reservas@pensioncordoba.com).

$ Hostal Plaza Santa Cruz is charming and small, with thoughtful touches that you wouldn't expect in this price range. The 17 clean, basic rooms surround a bright little courtyard that's buried deep in the Barrio Santa Cruz, just off Plaza Santa Cruz (Sb-€39-55, Db-€45-60, Qb-€65-75, buffet breakfast-€5, air-con, Calle Santa Teresa 15, tel. 954-228-808, www.hostalplazasantacruz.com, info@hostal plazasantacruz.com).

$ Samay Hostel, on a busy street a block from the edge of the Barrio Santa Cruz, is a youthful, well-run slumber-mill with 80 beds in 17 rooms (bunk in dorm room-€15-20, Db-€50-64, includes linens, buffet breakfast-€2.50, shared kitchen, air-con, elevator, laundry service, 24-hour reception, rooftop terrace, Avenida de Menéndez Pelayo 13, tel. 955-100-160, www.samayhostels.com).

Near the Cathedral

$$$ Hotel Alminar, plush and elegant, is run by well-dressed, never-stressed Francisco and rents 11 fresh, slick, minimalist rooms (Sb-€60-95, Db-€95-125, superior Db with or without terrace-€115-155, extra bed-€20-25, breakfast-€8, air-con, elevator, loaner laptop-€2/hour, just 100 yards from cathedral at Calle Álvarez Quintero 52, tel. 954-293-913, www.hotelalminar.com, reservas@hotelalminar.com).

$ Hotel San Francisco may have a fancy facade, but inside, its 17 rooms are sparsely decorated, with metal doors. Carlos treats guests as part of the family. It's centrally located, clean, and quiet, except for the noisy ground-floor room next to the TV and reception (Sb-€40-55, Db-€50-68, Tb-€62-80, no breakfast, air-con, elevator, small rooftop terrace with cathedral view, located on pedestrian Calle Álvarez Quintero at #38, tel. 954-501-541, www.sanfranciscoh.com, info@sanfranciscoh.com).

West of Avenida de la Constitución

$$$ Hotel Vincci La Rábida, part of a big, impersonal hotel chain, offers four-star comfort with its 103 rooms, huge and inviting courtyard, and powerful air-conditioning. Its pricing is dictated by a computer that has it down to a science (see website—rates can spike to €400 with high demand and dip to €80 during slow times, when that air-con is most welcome; elevator, Calle Castelar 24, tel. 954-501-280, www.vinccihoteles.com, la rabida@vinccihoteles.com).

$$$ Hotel Taberna del Alabardero is unique, with only seven rooms occupying the top floor of a poet's mansion (above the classy Taberna del Alabardero). It's nicely located, a great value, and the ambience is perfectly circa-1900 (Db-€90-140, Db suite-€122-190, includes breakfast, air-con, elevator, parking-€20/day, may close in Aug, Zaragoza 20, tel. 954-502-721, www.tabernadelalabardero.es, rest.alabardero@esh.es).

$$ Hotel Maestranza, sparkling with loving care and charm, has 18 simple, small, clean rooms well-located on a street just off Plaza Nueva. It feels extra nice for its price. Double-paned windows help to cut down on noise from the tapas bars below (Sb-€40-59, Db-€50-95, Tb-€70-125, family suite-€89-155, extra bed-€20, 5 percent discount if you pay cash, no breakfast, air-con, elevator, Gamazo 12, tel. 954-561-070, www.hotelmaestranza.es, sevilla@hotelmaestranza.es).

$$ Sevilla Plaza Suites rents 10 self-catering apartments with kitchenettes. It's squeaky clean, family-friendly, and well-located—and comes with an Astroturf sun terrace offering a cathedral view. While service is scaled down, reception is open long hours (9:00-21:00) and rooms are cleaned daily (small Db-€60-120, big Db-€95-150, 2-bedroom apartment-€130-240, breakfast-€10, air-con, inside rooms are quieter, best deals though their website are nonrefundable, a block off Plaza Nueva at Calle Zaragoza 52, tel. 601-192-465, www.suitessevilla plaza.com, info@suitessevillaplaza.com).

TRANSPORTATION

Getting Around Sevilla

Most visitors have a full, fun experience in Sevilla without ever riding public transportation. The city center is compact, and most of the major sights are within easy walking distance (the Basílica de la Macarena is a notable exception). On a hot day, air-conditioned buses can be a blessing.

By Bus, Tram, and Metro

Thanks to ongoing construction projects in the city center, bus routes often change. It's best to check with your hotel or the TI for the latest updates.

A single trip on any form of city transit costs €1.40. A Tarjeta Turistica card is good for one (€5) or three (€10) days of unlimited rides (€1.50 deposit, buy at TUSSAM kiosks, airport, or Santa Justa Station; scan it on card reader as you board; www.tussam.es).

For any **bus,** you can buy a ticket from the driver. The various **#C buses,** handiest for tourists, make circular routes through town (all of them eventually wind up at Basílica de La Macarena). The #C3 stops at Murillo Gardens, Triana, then La Macarena. The #C4 goes the opposite direction, but without entering Triana. And the spunky little #C5 minibus winds through the old center of town, including Plaza del Salvador, Plaza de San Francisco, the bullring, Plaza Nueva, the Museo de Bellas Artes, La Campana, and La Macarena, providing a relaxing joyride that also connects some farther-flung sights.

A **tram** (tranvía) makes just a few stops in the heart of the city, but can save you a bit of walking. It makes five stops: San Bernardo (at the San Bernardo train sta-

tion—not the main Santa Justa Station), Prado San Sebastián (next to El Prado de San Sebastián bus station), Puerta Jerez (south end of Avenida de la Constitución), Archivo General de Indias (next to the cathedral), and Plaza Nueva. Buy your ticket at the machine on the platform before you board (runs about every 7 minutes until 1:45 in the morning).

Sevilla also has an underground, one-line **metro,** but it's designed to connect the suburbs with the center, and most tourists won't need it.

By Taxi

You can hail a taxi anywhere, or find a cluster of them parked by major intersections and sights (weekdays: €1.35 drop rate, €1/kilometer, €3.65 minimum; Sat-Sun, holidays, and after hours, 21:00-7:00: €2 drop rate, €1.40/kilometer, €4.50 minimum; calling for a cab adds about €3). A quick daytime ride in town will generally fall within the €3.65 minimum. Take advantage of taxis to avoid one-way streets and traffic congestion, but it's often just as fast to hoof it between central points.

Arriving and Departing

Note that many destinations are well served by both trains and buses.

By Train

Most trains arrive at sublime Santa Justa Station, with banks, ATMs, bike rental, and a TI. Baggage storage (cosigna) is below track 1, next to the bike-rental office (security checkpoint open 6:00-24:00). The TI overlooks tracks 6-7. If you don't have a hotel room reserved, INFHOR, the room-finding booth above track 11, can help; you can also get maps and other tourist info here—a good idea if the TI line is long (Mon-Sat 9:30-14:30 & 15:30-20:00, Sun 9:30-16:30). The plush little AVE Sala Club, designed for business travelers, welcomes those with a first-class AVE ticket and reservation (across the main hall from track 1).

Getting Downtown: Head for the ornate Giralda bell tower (visible from the front of the station—with your back to the tracks, it's at 1 o'clock); it's a flat and boring 25-minute walk. By city bus, it's a short ride on #C1 to the El Prado de San Sebastián bus station (find bus stop 100 yards in front of the train station, €1.40, pay driver), then a 10-minute walk or short tram ride to your hotel. Another option is taking a taxi (about €8).

TRAIN CONNECTIONS

For schedules and tickets, visit a RENFE Travel Center, either at the **train station** (daily 8:00-22:00, take a number and wait, tel. 902-320-320 for reservations and info) or near **Plaza Nueva** in the city center (Mon-Fri 9:30-14:00 & 17:30-20:00, Sat 10:00-13:30, closed Sun, Calle Zaragoza 29, tel. 954-211-455). You can also check schedules at www.renfe.com. Many travel agencies (including the El Corte Inglés department stores) sell train tickets; look for a train sticker in agency windows.

Most trains arriving and departing Sevilla, including all high-speed AVE trains, leave from the larger, more distant **Santa Justa Station.** But many *cercanías* and inter-regional trains heading south to Granada, Jerez, Cádiz, and Málaga also stop at the smaller **San Bernardo** station, which is connected to downtown by tram. Hourly *cercanías* trains connect both stations (about a 3-minute trip).

From Sevilla by AVE Train to Madrid: The AVE express train is expensive but fast. Departures between 16:00 and 19:00 can book up far in advance, but holidays and long weekends can totally jam up trains as well—reserve as far ahead as possible (2.5 hours to Madrid; hourly departures 7:00-23:00, see the end of the Madrid chapter for more on the Sevilla-Madrid route).

From Sevilla by Train to Córdoba: There are three options for this journey: slow and cheap **regional** trains (7/ day, 80 minutes), fast and cheap regional high-speed **Avant** trains (8/day, 45 minutes, requires reservation), and fast and expensive **AVE** trains en route to Madrid (2-3/hour, 45 minutes, requires reservation). Unless you must be on a particular departure, there's no reason to pay more for AVE; Avant is just as quick and a third of the price. (If you have a rail pass, you still must buy a reservation; Avant reservations are half the cost of the ones for AVE.)

From Sevilla by Train to: Málaga (6/ day, 2 hours on Avant; 5/day, 2.5 hours on slower regional trains); **Ronda** (5/day, 3-4 hours, transfer in Bobadilla, Antequera, or Córdoba); **Granada** (4/day, 3 hours); **Jerez** (nearly hourly, 1.25 hours); **Barcelona** (11/day, 6 hours; plus one overnight train, 13 hours).

By Bus

Sevilla's two major bus stations—El Prado de San Sebastián and Plaza de Armas—both have information offices, basic eateries, and baggage storage.

The **El Prado de San Sebastián bus station,** often called just "El Prado," covers most of Andalucía (daily 7:00-22:00, info tel. 954-417-111, generally no English spoken; baggage storage/*consigna* at far end of station daily 9:00-21:00). From the bus station to downtown (and Barrio Santa Cruz hotels), it's about a 10-minute **walk:** Exit the station straight ahead. When you reach the busy avenue (Menéndez Pelayo), turn right to find a crosswalk and cross the avenue. Enter the Murillo Gardens through the iron gate, emerging on the other side in the heart of Barrio Santa Cruz. Sevilla's **tram** connects the El Prado station with the city center (and many of my recommended hotels): Turn left as you exit the bus station and walk to Avenida de Carlos V (€1.40, buy ticket at machine before boarding; ride it two stops to Archivo General de Indias to reach the cathedral area, or three stops to Plaza Nueva).

The **Plaza de Armas bus station** serves long-distance destinations such as Madrid, Barcelona, Lagos, and Lisbon (located near the river and bullring, opposite Expo '92 site, info tel. 902-450-550). Ticket counters line one wall, an info kiosk is in the center, and at the end of the hall are pay luggage lockers (purchase tokens from info kiosk). **Taxis** to downtown cost around €7. Or, to take the **bus,** exit onto the main road (Calle Arjona) to find bus #C4 into the center (stop is to the left, in front of the taxi stand; €1.40, pay driver, get off at Puerta de Jerez).

BUS CONNECTIONS

It's easiest to go to the TI for the latest schedule info than to call for bus info (tel. 954-908-040, but rarely answered).

From Sevilla's El Prado de San Sebastián Station to Andalucía and the South Coast: Regional buses are operated by Comes (www.tgcomes.es), Los Amarillos (www.losamarillos.es), and Autocares Valenzuela (www.grupovalenzuela.com). Connections to **Jerez** are frequent, as many southbound buses head there first (7-10/day, 1.5 hours, run by all three companies; note that train is also possible—see earlier). Los Amarillos runs buses to some of Andalucía's hill towns, including **Ronda** (8/day, 2-2.5 hours, some via Villamartín, fewer on weekends) and **Arcos** (1-2/day, 2 hours; many more departures possible with transfer in Jerez). For Spain's South Coast, a handy Comes bus departs Sevilla for **La Línea/Gibraltar** (4/day, 4-4.5 hours). There are also buses from this station to **Granada** (2/day, 3-3.5 hours); the rest depart from the Plaza de Armas station.

From Sevilla's Plaza de Armas station to: Madrid (9/day, 6 hours, tel. 902-229-292, www.socibus.es); **Córdoba** (7/day, 1-2 hours); **Granada** (7/day, 3 hours *directo*, 3.5-4.5 hours *ruta*); **Málaga** (6/day direct, 2.5-3 hours); **Nerja** (2/day, 4-5 hours);

Barcelona (2/day, 16.5 hours, including one overnight bus).

By Car

To drive into Sevilla, follow *centro ciudad* (city center) signs. For simplicity, park at a garage (€15-22/day) on one of the major avenues and catch a taxi to your hotel. Try the big garage under the bus station at Plaza de Armas, the Cristóbal Colón garage by the Puente de Isabel II (near the bullring), or the one at Avenida Roma/Puerta de Jerez (cash only). For hotels in the Barrio Santa Cruz area, the handiest place to park is the Cano y Cueto underground garage near the corner of Calle Santa María la Blanca and Avenida de Menéndez Pelayo (about €18/day, open daily 24 hours, at edge of big park).

By Plane

Sevilla's San Pablo Airport sits about six miles east of downtown (airport code: SVQ, tel. 954-449-000, www.aena-aeropuertos.es).

The **airport bus,** Especial Aeropuerto (EA), connects the airport with both train stations, both bus stations, and several stops in the town center (2/hour, 30-45 minutes, €4, buy ticket from driver). The two most convenient stops downtown are south of the Alcázar gardens on Avenida de Carlos V, near the El Prado de San Sebastián bus station (close to my recommended Barrio Santa Cruz hotels); and on the Paseo de Cristóbal Colón, near the Torre del Oro. Look for the small *EA* sign at bus stops. (If you're going from downtown Sevilla *to* the airport, the bus stop is on the side of the street closest to Plaza de España.)

To **taxi** into town, go to one of the airport's taxi stands to ensure a fixed rate (€22 by day, €24 at night and on weekends, extra for luggage, confirm price with the driver before your journey).

BEST OF THE REST
CÓRDOBA

Straddling the Guadalquivir River, Córdoba has a glorious Roman and Moorish past as a one-time regional capital for both empires. An easy train ride from Sevilla, it's worth a day trip to see Córdoba's top sight—the mosque-turned-cathedral called the Mezquita. To this day, you'll hear the Muslim call to prayer in Córdoba.

Orientation

The Mezquita is buried in the characteristic medieval town, near the overrated Alcázar fortress, Renaissance triumphal arch, and pedestrian Roman bridge that leads to the Museum of Al-Andalus Life (Moorish culture).

Day Plan: On a quick day trip, focus on the Mezquita—take a taxi from the train station, spend two hours there, and explore the old town for an hour.

Getting to Córdoba: The city is an efficient stopover between Madrid and Sevilla on the slick AVE train, or an easy side-trip from Sevilla (frequent trains, 45-minute trip). The Avant line is cheaper and just as fast. The cheapest Media Distancia train doesn't require a reservation, but is slower (80 minutes).

Arrival in Córdoba: The **train** station is on Avenida de América, across from the **bus** station. Only the bus station has lockers (look for *consigna* sign and buy token at machine). To get to the Mezquita, hop a **taxi** (€8) or catch **bus** #3 (buy €1.20 ticket on board, ask driver for *"mezquita,"* get off at Calle San Fernando, and take Calle del Portillo, following twists, turns, and sporadic signs to the Mezquita). **Drivers** enter the city center from Madrid or Sevilla on A-4/E-5 (exit Plaza de Andalucía, following A-431, a.k.a. Avenida del Corregidor); a half-mile after crossing the river, veer right on Paseo de la Victoria, and look for the blue parking sign on the right.

Tourist Information: TIs are at the train station, Plaza de las Tendillas, and Plaza del Triunfo (open daily, tel. 902-201-774, www.turismodecordoba.org).

Guides: Consider **Isabel Richter** (€130/3 hours, mobile 669-369-645, isabmr@gmail.com) or **Ángel Lucena** (€100/3 hours, mobile 607-898-079, lucenaangel@hotmail.com).

Sights

▲▲▲MEZQUITA

This massive former mosque, which has a church (built later) rising up in the middle of it, was once the center of Western Islam. This wonder of the medieval world is well-preserved, giving you a chance to soak up the ambience of 10th-century Islamic Córdoba.

Cost: €8, cash only, ticket kiosk in courtyard; Mon-Sat free entry but restricted access 8:30-9:30; dry €3.50 audioguide (near ticket kiosk).

Hours: Mon-Sat 8:30-19:00, Sun 8:30-11:30 & 15:00-19:00. To avoid midday crowds (11:00-15:00), try to come early or late. Check for holiday closures at www.catedraldecordoba.es.

Visiting the Mezquita: At 600 feet by 400 feet, the Mezquita (for pronunciation ease, think female mosquito) dominates the medieval town. Its grand courtyard, Patio de los Naranjos, is free to enter. Walking from the patio into the former mosque, you'll pass from an orchard of orange trees to a forest of 800-plus delicate columns. The mosque is vast, but the low ceilings and dense columns create an intimate, worshipful atmosphere.

In the center of the 8th-century mosque sits the 16th-century cathedral, its nave extending far above the roofline of the mosque. Though it would

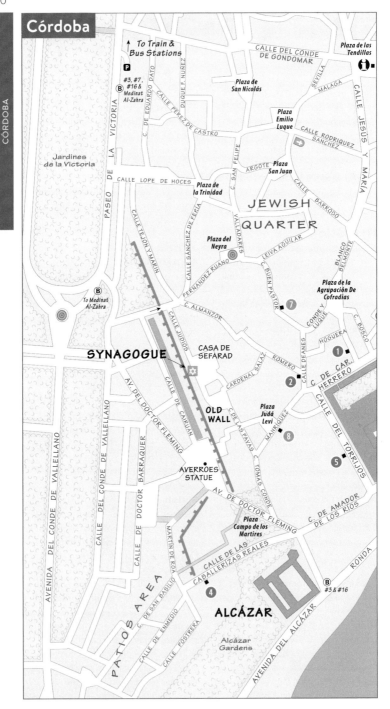

Córdoba

↑ To Train &
Bus Stations

P

#3, #7,
#16 &
Medinat
Al-Zahra

C. DE EDUARDO PATO

C. PÉREZ DE CASTRO

DUQUE NÚÑEZ

CALLE DEL CONDE
DE GONDOMAR

Plaza de las
Tendillas

CALLE JESÚS Y MARÍA

SEVILLA

MÁLAGA

PASEO DE LA VICTORIA

Jardines
de la Victoria

Plaza de
San Nicolás

Plaza
Emilio
Luque

CALLE RODRÍGUEZ
SÁNCHEZ

CALLE SAN FELIPE

ARGOTE

Plaza
San Juan

CALLE
BARROSO

CALLE LOPE DE HOCES

Plaza de
la Trinidad

JEWISH
QUARTER

CALLE SÁNCHEZ DE FERIA

VALLADARES

Plaza del
Neyra

LEIVA AGUILAR

C. BUEN PASTOR

BLANCO BELMONTE

CALLE TORNY MARÍN

FERNÁNDEZ RUANO

Plaza de la
Agrupación De
Cofradías

CONDE Y LUQUE

C. BOSCO

B
To Medinat
Al-Zahra

C. ALMANZOR

CALLE JUDÍOS

7

SYNAGOGUE

CASA DE
SEFARAD

CARDENAL SALAZ

ROMERO

CALLE DEANES

HOGUERA

1

C. DE CAR.
HERRERO

AV. DEL DOCTOR FLEMING

CALLE DE CAIRUÁN

OLD
WALL

C. DE LAS PAVAS

C. TOMÁS CONDE

2

Plaza
Judá
Levi

MAIMÓNIDES

8

CALLE DEL TORRIJOS

5

AVENIDA DEL CONDE DE VALLELLANO

CALLE DEL CONDE DE VALLELLANO

CALLE DE DOCTOR BARRAGUER

AVERROES
STATUE

AV. DE DOCTOR FLEMING

C. DE AMADOR
DE LOS RÍOS

Plaza
Campo de los
Mártires

RONDA

CALLE DE SAN BASILIO

MARTÍN DE ROA

CALLE DE LAS
CABALLERIZAS REALES

4

B
#3 & #16

PATIOS AREA

CALLE DE ENMEDIO

CALLE FOSTRERA

ALCÁZAR

Alcázar
Gardens

AVENIDA DEL ALCÁZAR

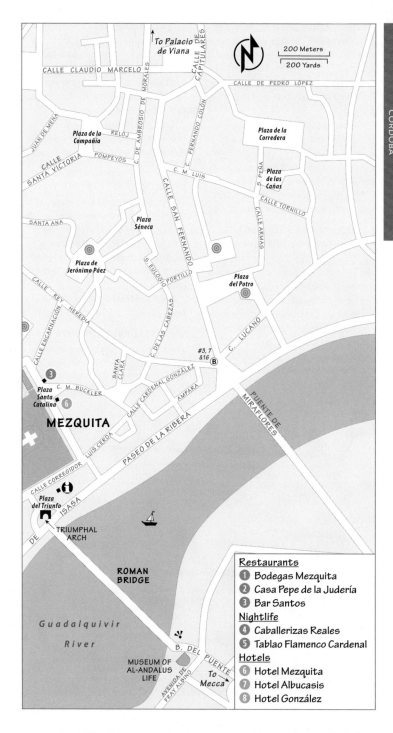

To Palacio de Viana

CALLE CLAUDIO MARCELO
CALLE DE CAPITULARES
CALLE DE PEDRO LÓPEZ

200 Meters
200 Yards

CALLE DE MORALES
CALLE FERNANDO COLÓN

Plaza de la Compañía
RELOJ
C. DE AMBROSIO DE

JUAN DE MENA
CALLE SANTA VICTORIA
POMPEYOS
C. M. LUIS

Plaza de la Corredera

S. PEÑA
Plaza de las Cañas

CALLE SAN FERNANDO
CALLE TORNILLO

SANTA ANA
Plaza Séneca

CALLE ARMAS

Plaza de Jerónimo Páez
S. EULOGIO PORTILLO

Plaza del Potro

CALLE REY HEREDIA
C. DE LAS CABEZAS

C. LUCANO

CALLE ENCARNACIÓN
SANTA CLARA
#3, 7 &16 B

❸
Plaza Santa Catalina ❻
C. M. BUCKLER
CALLE CARDENAL GONZÁLEZ
AMPARA

PUENTE DE MIRAFLORES

MEZQUITA
LUIS CERDA
PASEO DE LA RIBERA

CALLE CORREGIDOR
Plaza del Triunfo
DE ISASA

TRIUMPHAL ARCH

ROMAN BRIDGE

Guadalquivir River

MUSEUM OF AL-ANDALUS LIFE
B. DEL PUENTE
To Mecca
AVENIDA DE FRAY ALBINO

Restaurants
❶ Bodegas Mezquita
❷ Casa Pepe de la Judería
❸ Bar Santos
Nightlife
❹ Caballerizas Reales
❺ Tablao Flamenco Cardenal
Hotels
❻ Hotel Mezquita
❼ Hotel Albucasis
❽ Hotel González

have been quicker and cheaper for the Christian builders to destroy the mosque entirely, they respected its beauty and built their church inside it instead. The cathedral's highlight is the 18th-century choir, with 109 stalls featuring Bible scenes.

On the opposite wall from the mosque's entrance is the mihrab, a mosque's equivalent of a church's high altar. At this decorated niche, the prayer leader (imam) gave sermons. Facing the mihrab, the treasury is to your left, and a hidden WC is to your right in the corner.

▲MUSEUM OF AL-ANDALUS LIFE

The museum explains the thriving Muslim Moorish culture of 9th- to 12th-century Córdoba with fun scale models and dollhouse tableaus, though the obligatory one-hour audioguide system is clumsy. It's worth the climb to the rooftop terrace for the best panoramic view of Córdoba.

Cost and Hours: €4.50, daily May-Sept 10:00-14:00 & 16:30-20:30, Oct-April 10:00-18:00, Torre de la Calahorra.

CASA DE SEFARAD

This museum explores Córdoba's rich Jewish past, focusing on domestic life, celebrations, and holidays. Upstairs you'll see an exhibit about the synagogue (across the street) and rooms dedicated to the Inquisition.

Cost and Hours: €4, daily 10:00-18:00, corner of Calle de los Judíos and Calle Averroes, tel. 957-421-404, www.casa desefarad.es.

SYNAGOGUE

This small, beautiful 14th-century synagogue, across the street from Casa de Sefarad, is one of only three medieval synagogues still standing in Spain. Rich Mudejar decorations of intertwined flowers, arabesques, and Stars of David plaster the walls.

Cost and Hours: Free, Tue-Sun 9:00-14:45, closed Mon, Calle de los Judíos 20.

MUSEO TAURINO CÓRDOBA

This high-tech museum in a beautiful old palatial home examines the city's bull-fighting tradition.

Mezquita facade

Cost and Hours: €4, Sept-June Tue-Fri 8:30-20:45, Sat 8:30-16:30, Sun 8:30-14:30; July-Aug Tue-Sat closes at 15:00; closed Mon year-round; Plaza de Maimonides.

ARTISAN MARKET
The Zoco Municipal is a charming series of courtyards and studios off Calle Judíos, where artists make tiles, jewelry, and leather bracelets and bags (Mon-Fri 10:00-20:00, Sat-Sun 11:00-14:00).

Nightlife

The **Caballerizas Reales** equestrian show combines an artful demonstration of different riding styles with flamenco dance (€15, June-Aug 1-hour performances generally Wed, Fri, and Sat at 21:00, Sept-May only on Sun at noon, at royal stables, www.caballerizasreales.com). While flamenco is better in Sevilla, **Tablao Flamenco Cardenal** is popular in Córdoba (€23, 1.5-hour shows Mon-Sat, Calle de Torrijos 10, across from Mezquita, www.tablaocardenal.es).

Eating and Sleeping

Touristy **Bodegas Mezquita** is good, bright, and air-conditioned (Céspedes 12). At lively **Casa Pepe de la Judería,** happy eaters dig into tapas and *raciones* (Calle Romero 1). **Bar Santos** offers cheap, hearty takeout (Calle Magistral González Francés 3).

For an overnight, try modern **$$$ Hotel Mezquita** (www.hotelmezquita.com), cozy **$$ Hotel Albucasis** (hotelalbucasis@hotmail.com), or spartan **$ Hotel González** (www.hotelgonzalez.com).

BEST OF THE REST
SPAIN'S SOUTH COAST

Much of Spain's South Coast is so bad, it's interesting. Oblivious to the concrete, pollution, high prices, and traffic jams, tourists lie on the beach like game hens on skewers. But the coast holds a few gems. Unroll your beach towel at Nerja, the most appealing resort town on the coast. And jolly olde England beckons: The land of tea, scones, fish-and-chips, and pubs awaits you—in Gibraltar.

Allow a day apiece for Nerja (or more, to really relax) and Gibraltar.

Nerja

Despite cashing in on the fun in the sun, Nerja has kept its Old World charm. It has good beaches, a fun evening paseo, enough nightlife to keep you entertained, and locals who get more excited about their many festivals than the tourists do.

Orientation

The tourist center is right along the water, close to its famous bluff, the Balcony of Europe (Balcón de Europa). Fine beaches stretch in either direction. The old town is just inland from the Balcony, while the more modern section slopes up and away from the water.

Day Plan: It couldn't be easier—explore the old town, enjoy the views from the Balcony of Europe, and find your favorite beach.

Getting There: Nerja, which doesn't have a train station, has direct bus connections with **Granada** (6/day, 2.5 hours), **Sevilla** (2/day, 5 hours), and **Málaga,** the nearest major transit hub (1-2/hour, 1 hour *directo*). Málaga has train connections with all major cities in Spain, plus buses as well: to **Ronda** (6-10/day, 2 hours, Los Amarillos) and **La Línea de Concepción/Gibraltar** (4/day, 3 hours, Portillo bus

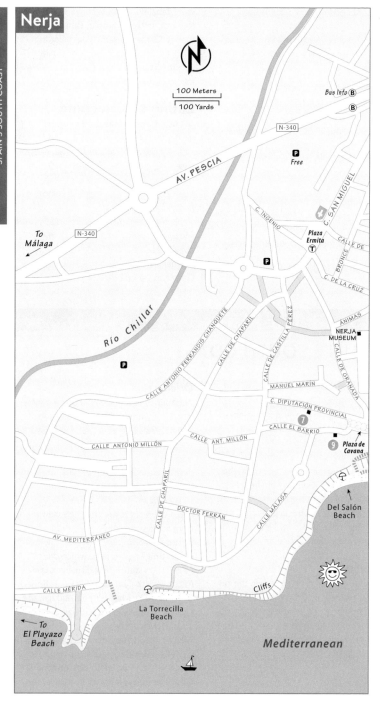

Nerja

100 Meters
100 Yards

Bus Info **B**
B

N-340

AV. PESCIA

P
Free

C. INGENIO

C. SAN MIGUEL

Plaza
Ermita
T

CALLE DE

BRONCE

To
Málaga

N-340

P

C. DE LA CRUZ

Río Chillar

ÁNIMAS

CALLE DE CASTILLA PEREZ

CALLE DE CHAPARIL

CALLE ANTONIO FERRANDIS CHANQUETE

P

NERJA
MUSEUM

CALLE DE GRANADA

MANUEL MARIN

C. DIPUTACIÓN PROVINCIAL

7

CALLE EL BARRIO

CALLE ANTONIO MILLÓN

CALLE ANT. MILLÓN

9 Plaza de
Cavana

Del Salón
Beach

CALLE DE CHAPARIL

DOCTOR FERRÁN

CALLE MÁLAGA

AV. MEDITERRÁNEO

CALLE MÉRIDA

Cliffs

To
El Playazo
Beach

La Torrecilla
Beach

Mediterranean

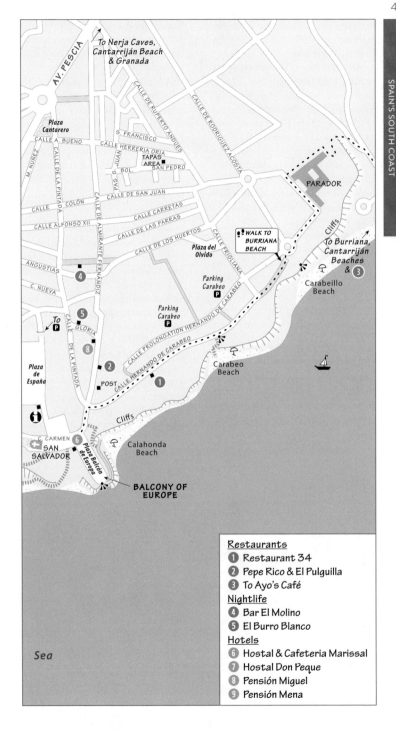

AV. PESCIA

To Nerja Caves,
Cantarriján Beach
& Granada

CALLE DE RUPERTO ANDUES

CALLE DE RODRIGUEZ ACOSTA

Plaza
Cantarero

CALLE A. BUENO

M. NÚÑEZ

CALLE DE LA PINTADA

S. FRANCISCO

CALLE HERRERIA ORIA

S. JUAN BOL.

TAPAS AREA

SAN PEDRO

CALLE COLÓN

CALLE DE SAN JUAN

PARADOR

CALLE ALFONSO XII

CALLE DE ALMIRANTE FERNÁNDIZ

CALLE CARRETAS

CALLE DE LAS PARRAS

CALLE DE LOS HUERTOS

CALLE FRIGILIANA

Plaza del
Olvido

WALK TO
BURRIANA
BEACH

Cliffs

To Burriana,
Cantarriján
Beaches
& 3

ANGUSTIAS

4

C. NUEVA

Parking
Carabeo
P

Carabeillo
Beach

To
P

5

GLORIA

8

CALLE DE LA PINTADA

Parking
Carabeo
P

CALLE PROLONGATION HERNANDO DE CARABEO

CALLE HERNANDO DE CARABEO

Plaza
de
España

2

POST

1

Carabeo
Beach

Cliffs

C. CARMEN

SAN
SALVADOR

6

Plaza Balcón de Europa

Calahonda
Beach

BALCONY OF
EUROPE

Sea

Restaurants
1 Restaurant 34
2 Pepe Rico & El Pulguilla
3 To Ayo's Café

Nightlife
4 Bar El Molino
5 El Burro Blanco

Hotels
6 Hostal & Cafeteria Marissal
7 Hostal Don Peque
8 Pensión Miguel
9 Pensión Mena

company). To fit Nerja into my recommended two-week itinerary, visit it (by bus) after Granada.

Arrival in Nerja: The **bus station** is actually just a bus stop with an info kiosk on Avenida de Pescia (Mon-Tue and Fri 6:00-20:15, Wed-Thu and Sat-Sun 7:00-12:15 & 14:45-19:00, schedules posted, Alsa tel. 902-422-242, www.alsa.es).

Drivers can find the old town center and parking by following *Balcón de Europa, Centro Urbano,* or *Centro Ciudad* signs; pull into the enormous above-ground Parking Carabeo, just east of the Balcony (€1.80/hour, €18/24 hours).

Tourist Information: The TI is 100 yards from the Balcony of Europe (Mon-Fri 10:00-14:00 & 17:00-20:30, Sat-Sun 10:00-14:00; longer in summer, mornings only off-season, tel. 952-521-531, www.nerja.es).

Sights

▲▲BALCONY OF EUROPE (BALCÓN DE EUROPA)

This bluff, jutting happily into the sea, is the center of Nerja's paseo and a magnet for street performers. The mimes, music, and puppets draw bigger crowds than the Balcony itself, which overlooks the Mediterranean. Walk out to the very tip to soak up the sun and the sound of the pounding surf.

A castle, and later a fort, occupied this spot from the ninth century until the earthquake of 1884. Nearby, a statue commemorates King Alfonso XII, who came here after the devastating earthquake. He mobilized the community and put things back together. Marveling at the view, he coined its now-famous name, Balcón de Europa.

BEACHES

The single best thing to do in Nerja is hit the beach. Many of the beaches are well-equipped with bars and restaurants, free showers, and rentable lounge chairs and umbrellas. During the summer, sun worshippers pack the beach from about 11:00 until around 13:30, when they move into the beach restaurants for relief from the heat. Red flags on the beach indicate rough seas unsafe for swimming. Don't take valuables to the beach, as thieves have fast fingers.

Directly beneath the Balcony of Europe is pebbly **Playa Calahonda,** with fun pathways, crags, and crannies. A 20-minute

Balcony of Europe

walk east is bustling **Playa de Burriana** (where Ayo's has cheap paella). West of the Balcony of Europe, a pleasant promenade connects sandy, crowded **Playa del Salón, Playa la Torrecilla,** and local favorite **El Playazo.**

▲NERJA CAVES (CUEVAS DE NERJA)
These caves (2.5 miles east of Nerja), with an impressive array of stalactites and stalagmites, are a classic roadside attraction. Take a 45-minute unguided ramble inside the cave, up and down 400 dark stairs. At the end is the Hall of the Cataclysm, with the world's largest stalactite column.

Cost and Hours: €9, daily 10:00-14:00 & 16:00-18:30, July-Aug until 20:00, easy parking—€1/day, restaurant on site, tel. 952-529-520, www.cuevadenerja.es.

Getting There: Catch a bus across the street from Nerja's main bus stop (€1.16, roughly 1/hour, 10-minute ride—get schedule at TI) or a taxi (€10 one-way). Drivers take A-7 (exit 295) and follow *Cueva de Nerja* signs.

Nightlife
Bar El Molino offers live Spanish folk singing (nightly from 22:00, Calle San José 4). **El Burro Blanco** hosts touristy flamenco shows (nightly from 22:30, corner of Calle Pintada and Calle de la Gloria). And there's always a party down at the beach.

Paella on the beach, Nerja

Eating
For a cheap breakfast with a front-row view of the promenade action on the Balcony of Europe, grab a wicker seat under palm trees at **Cafetería Marissal** (daily from 9:00, Balcón de Europa 3).

The old town is busy with lively restaurants. **Restaurant 34** manages both elegance and a relaxed atmosphere (Tue-Sun 12:30-15:30 & 19:00-late, closed Mon, Calle Hernando de Carabeo 34, tel. 952-525-444). On the touristy restaurant row, Calle Almirante Ferrándiz, **Pepe Rico** is the most romantic option (Mon-Sat 12:30-15:00 & 19:00-23:00, closed Sun, at #28, tel. 952-520-247), while the high-energy **El Pulguilla** has a tapas bar up front and sit-down meals on the terrace. Half-portions—*media-raciones*—are available for many items (closed Mon, at #26).

On Playa de Burriana, **Ayo's** serves up a €6.50 beachside all-you-can-eat paella feast (open daily "sun to sun," paella served only in afternoon, cash only, tel. 952-522-289).

Sleeping
The entire Costa del Sol is crowded during August and Easter Week, when prices are at their highest. **Hostal Marissal** has an unbeatable location next door to the fancy Balcón de Europa hotel (Balcón de Europa 3, reception at Cafetería Marissal, tel. 952-520-199, www.hostalmarissal. com, reservas@hostalmarissal.com).
$$ Hostal Don Peque has cheery rooms, some with sea views (Calle Diputación 13, tel. 952-521-318, www.hostaldonpeque. com, info@hostaldonpeque.com). **$ Pensión Miguel** offers sunny rooms in the heart of the restaurant row (Calle Almirante Ferrándiz 31, tel. 952-521-523, mobile 696-799-218, www.pensionmiguel.net, pensionmiguel@gmail.com). **$ Pensión Mena** rents 11 nice rooms—4 with seaview terraces (Calle el Barrio 15, tel. 952-520-541, www.hostalmena.es, info@ hostalmena.es).

Gibraltar

One of the last bits of the empire upon which the sun never set, Gibraltar is famous for its dramatic Rock, which rockets improbably into the air from an otherwise flat terrain. Britain has controlled this strategic spit of land since they took it by force in 1704. Locals speak English.

Orientation

Gibraltar is a narrow peninsula (three miles by one mile), dominated by the steep-faced Rock itself. The long, skinny town of Gibraltar is at the western base of the Rock. Just north of the border is the Spanish town, La Línea de la Concepción, which offers cheaper lodging than you'll find in Gibraltar.

Day Plan: Head for the Rock (by bus and cable car, or by taxi), then walk down, seeing the sights along the way, and explore the town. Avoid visiting on a Sunday, when nearly everything but the cable car is closed.

Getting There: The nearest bus station is in La Línea de la Concepción in Spain, a short walk across the border from Gibraltar. La Línea is connected by bus to **Málaga** (4/day, 3 hours), **Sevilla** (5/day, 4.5 hours), **Granada** (3/day, 7 hours, change

Rock of Gibraltar

in Algeciras), and **Algeciras** (8/day, less on weekends, 45 minutes). The nearest train station is in Algeciras, the region's transit hub.

To add Gibraltar to my recommended two-week itinerary (see page 26), visit in this order: Granada, Nerja (if you visit), Gibraltar, and **Ronda** (from Gibraltar, take short bus ride to Algeciras, then train to Ronda—5/day, 2 hours).

Arrival in Gibraltar: If you're arriving by **bus,** you'll get off at Spain's La Línea de la Concepción bus station, a five-minute walk from the Gibraltar border.

Drivers should park in La Línea and walk across the border. La Línea's main square—Plaza de la Constitución—covers a huge underground municipal parking lot; just look for the blue *"P"* signs (€18.20/day).

You'll need your **passport** to cross the border (also called the frontier). Before exiting the customs building, pick up a map at the TI window on your left (Mon-Fri 9:00-16:30, closed Sat-Sun).

Getting from the border to downtown, you have several options:

• It's a 20-minute **walk:** Go straight across the runway (look left, right, and up), then down Winston Churchill Avenue. Angle right at the second roundabout, then walk along the fortified Line Wall Road to Casemates Square (with TI).

• Catch red **bus** #5, and ride it to the Market Square stop near Casemates Square (with TI). From there, you could catch blue bus #2 to the cable-car station, and ride the cable car to the peak of the Rock. Frustratingly, the buses charge different rates (**red border buses**—€1.80/£1.30 one-way, €2.80/£2 round-trip, 4/hour; **blue city buses**—€2/£1.50 one-way, €3/£2.25 all-day), and tickets aren't transferable between them.

• Taking a **taxi** from the border is a little pricey (€9/£6 to cable-car station). If you plan to join a **taxi tour** to the Rock, you can book one right at the border.

Tourist Information: Gibraltar's helpful

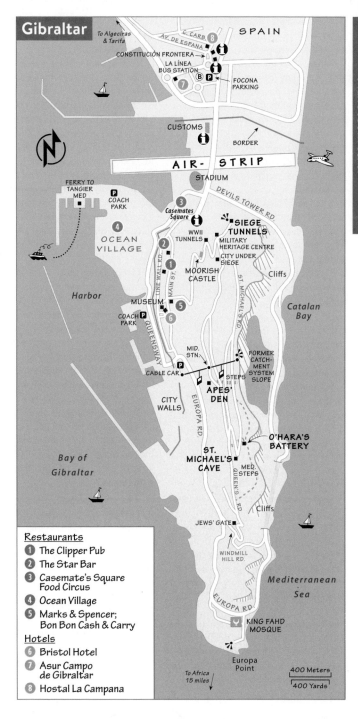

Gibraltar

To Algeciras & Tarifa

SPAIN

C. CARB.
AV. DE ESPANA
CONSTITUCIÓN FRONTERA
LA LÍNEA BUS STATION
FOCONA PARKING

CUSTOMS
BORDER

AIR- STRIP

STADIUM

FERRY TO TANGIER MED
COACH PARK

OCEAN VILLAGE

DEVILS TOWER RD.

Casemates Square
WWII TUNNELS
SIEGE TUNNELS
MILITARY HERITAGE CENTRE
CITY UNDER SIEGE
MOORISH CASTLE
Cliffs

Harbor

LINE WALL RD.
MAIN ST.

MUSEUM
COACH PARK

QUEENSWAY

Catalan Bay

ST. MICHAEL'S RD.

MID. STN.
CABLE CAR

FORMER CATCHMENT SYSTEM SLOPE
STEPS

CITY WALLS

EUROPA RD.

APES' DEN

Bay of Gibraltar

ST. MICHAEL'S CAVE

O'HARA'S BATTERY

MED. STEPS

QUEEN'S RD.

Cliffs

JEWS' GATE

WINDMILL HILL RD.

Mediterranean Sea

EUROPA RD.

To Africa 15 miles

KING FAHD MOSQUE

Europa Point

400 Meters
400 Yards

Restaurants
1 The Clipper Pub
2 The Star Bar
3 Casemate's Square Food Circus
4 Ocean Village
5 Marks & Spencer; Bon Bon Cash & Carry

Hotels
6 Bristol Hotel
7 Asur Campo de Gibraltar
8 Hostal La Campana

TI is at Casemates Square (Mon-Fri 9:00-17:30, Sat 10:00-15:00, Sun 10:00-13:00, tel. 74982, www.visitgibraltar.gi).

Money: Gibraltar uses the **British pound sterling** (£1 = about $1.60; a pound is broken into 100 pence). Businesses also accept euros, but at a 20 percent extra cost to you. Still, on a quick trip, or if you'll be making few purchases, don't bother withdrawing pounds from an ATM; you can buy things with your credit card or use euros (though you may get pounds back in change).

Phones: To phone Gibraltar from anywhere in Europe, dial 00-350-200 and the five-digit local number. To call Gibraltar from the US or Canada, dial 011-350-200-local number.

Baggage Storage: It's at Gibraltar's airport, at the border (go to airport info desk in departures hall).

Sights
THE ROCK OF GIBRALTAR

The actual Rock's attractions include the stupendous view from the very top, temperamental apes, St. Michael's Cave, and the impressive Siege Tunnels drilled for military purposes. Hikers can ride the cable car up and take a long, steep, scenic walk down, connecting the various sights by strolling along paved lanes (allow about 1.5 hours to walk down, not including sightseeing).

Cost: £0.50 fee to enter the grounds of the Rock, called the Upper Rock Nature Reserve. A £10 nature reserve ticket is required to enter St. Michael's Cave, the Siege Tunnels, small Military Heritage Centre, and hokey City Under Siege exhibit. If you take a taxi tour, all entry fees are included; if you ride the cable car, only the £0.50 grounds entry fee is included (and you'll need to purchase the £10 ticket separately). Two sights on the Rock have separate fees, and aren't covered by the nature reserve ticket: O'Hara's Battery (£3, gun emplacement atop Rock) and World War II Tunnels (£8).

Hours: Daily 9:30-19:15, until 18:15 late Oct-late March, last entry 30 minutes before closing.

Visiting the Rock: Here are two options for touring the Rock—using the cable car or taking a taxi tour:

The **cable car** takes you to the very top of the Rock (the taxi tours don't). You can still see the sights, but you'll have to pay for an entry ticket and connect them by foot (it's a pleasant walk down). The cable car runs every 10-15 minutes, or continuously in busy times (£8.50 one-way, £10.50 round-trip, daily from 9:30; April-Oct last ascent at 19:15, last descent at 19:45; Nov-March last ascent at 17:15, last descent at 17:45). Cable cars don't run in stormy weather.

Taxi tours and big buses do the same 1.5-hour loop tour with four stops: a Mediterranean viewpoint (called Pillar of Hercules), St. Michael's Cave, a viewpoint near the top of the Rock where you can get up close to the apes, and the Siege Tunnels (£22/person, 4-person minimum, or £65 for only 2 people in one taxi, includes reserve sights ticket, tel. 70027). Taxi minivans are standing by at the border and at various points in town. Because the cable car doesn't get you very close to the cave and tunnels (and doesn't cover their admission fees), take the taxi tour if you'll be visiting those sights and don't want to walk.

Rick's Tip: There's no reason to take a big-bus tour (advertised and sold all over town), considering how **fun and easy** *the* **taxi tours** *are. Private cars are not allowed high on the Rock.*

▲▲▲THE SUMMIT OF THE ROCK
The cable car takes you to the real highlight of Gibraltar: its summit. The limestone massif is nearly a mile long, rising 1,400 feet with very sheer cliffs. According to legend, this was one of the Pillars of Hercules, marking the edge of

the known world in ancient times. In A.D. 711, Muslim chieftain Tarik ibn Ziyad crossed over from Africa and landed on the Rock, beginning the Moorish conquest of Spain and naming the Rock after himself—Djebel-Tarik ("Rock of Tarik"), which became "Gibraltar." From here you can explore old ramparts and drool at the 360-degree views. The cable-car terminal has a terrace and café.

▲▲APES' DEN

The Rock is home to about 200 apes (actually tailless Barbary macaques—a type of monkey). Taxi tours stop at the Apes' Den, but you'll see them anywhere there are tourists who may have food. Legend says as long as the monkeys remain here, so will the Brits (when the ape population was waning, Churchill sent reinforcements!). Keep your distance from the monkeys. While guides may feed them, you shouldn't—it disrupts their diet and encourages aggressive behavior.

Rick's Tip: *Beware the* **monkeys' kleptomaniac tendencies.** *They associate plastic bags with food. Tourists who wander by, loosely clutching a bag, are apt to have it stolen.*

▲ST. MICHAEL'S CAVE

Studded with stalagmites and stalactites, eerily lit, and echoing with classical music, the cave is dramatic, corny, and slippery when wet. It's been considered a one-star sight since Neolithic times. All taxi tours stop here (and include cave entry); hikers need the £10 nature reserve ticket to enter. Walking through takes about 15 minutes; you'll pop out at the gift shop.

▲SIEGE TUNNELS

These chilly tunnels were blasted out of the rock by the Brits during the Great Siege (1779-1783). The British used gunpowder to carve out a network of tunnels for aiming artillery. During World War II, 30 more miles of tunnels were blasted

out. Hokey but fun dioramas help recapture a time when Brits were known more for conquests than for crumpets. All taxi tours stop here (entry included); hikers must have the £10 nature reserve ticket.

▲GIBRALTAR MUSEUM

This museum, in the town center, tells the story of a chunk of land that has been fought over for centuries—using video, artifacts, military memorabilia, models, old photos, and more.

Cost and Hours: £2, Mon-Fri 10:00-18:00, Sat 10:00-14:00, closed Sun, last entry 30 minutes before closing, no photos, on Bomb House Lane near cathedral, www.gibmuseum.gi.

Eating

Take a break from *jamón* and sample some English pub grub. **The Clipper** offers filling meals (Mon-Sat 9:30-22:00, Sun 10:30-22:00, on Irish Town Lane, tel. 79791). **The Star Bar** claims to be Gibraltar's oldest bar (Mon-Sat 7:00-23:30, Sun 7:00-22:00, on Parliament Lane off Main Street, tel. 75924). The **Casemates Square Food Circus** has a variety of eateries. The **Ocean Village** boardwalk, a five-minute walk from Casemates Square, is lined with bars and restaurants, and is fun for strolling. For picnics, try **Marks & Spencer** or **Bon Bon Cash & Carry** (both on Main Street).

Sleeping

In Gibraltar, try the **$$$ Bristol Hotel** (Cathedral Square 10, tel. 76800, www.bristolhotel.gi, reservations@bristolhotel.gi), though you'll find cheaper accommodations in La Línea de la Concepción, across the border: **$$ Asur Campo de Gibraltar** (at intersection of Avenida Príncipe de Asturias and Avenida del Ejército, tel. 956-691-211, www.campodegibraltarhotel.com, lalinea@asurhoteles.com) or **$ Hostal La Campana** (Calle Carboneros 3, tel. 956-173-059, www.hostalcampana.es, info@hostalcampana.es).

Spain: Past and Present

The distinctive Spanish culture has been shaped by the country's parade of rulers. Roman emperors, Muslim sultans, hard-core Christians, conquistadors, French dandies, and Fascist dictators have all left their mark on Spain's art, architecture, and customs. Start by understanding the country's long history of invasions and religious wars, and you'll better appreciate the churches, museums, and monuments you'll visit today.

The sunny weather, fertile soil, and Mediterranean ports of the Iberian Peninsula have long made it a popular place to call home. A mix from various migrations and invasions, the original "Iberians" crossed the Pyrenees around 800 B.C. The Phoenicians established the city of Cádiz around 1100 B.C., and Carthaginians settled around 250 B.C.

Romans
(C. 200 B.C.–A.D. 400)
The future Roman Emperor Augustus finally quelled the last Iberian resistance in 19 B.C., making the province of "Hispania" an agricultural breadbasket (olives, wine) to help feed the vast Roman Empire. The Romans brought the Latin language, a connection to the wider world, and (in the fourth century) Christianity. When the empire began crumbling around A.D. 400, Spain made a peaceful transition, ruled by Christian Visigoths from Germany who had strong Roman ties. Roman influence remained for centuries after, in the Latin-based Spanish language, irrigation methods, and building materials and techniques. The Romans' large farming estates would change hands over the years, passing from Roman senators to Visigoth kings to Islamic caliphs to Christian nobles.

Moors
(711-1492)
In A.D. 711, 12,000 zealous members of the world's newest religion—Islam—landed on the Rock of Gibraltar and, in three short years, conquered the Iberian Peninsula. These North African Muslims—generically called "Moors"—dominated Spain for the next 700 years. Though powerful, they were surprisingly tolerant

Six Dates That Changed Spain

711 Arab Muslims ("Moors") from North Africa invade and occupy Iberia.

1492 Christians finish their "reconquest" (Reconquista) of Iberia. Muslims and Jews who refuse to convert to Christianity are expelled from Spain. Columbus sails Spain into a century of wealth and power.

1588 Spain's Invincible Armada is routed by the British, and the country's slow decline begins.

1898 Spain is thrashed by the US in the Spanish-American War, losing its colonies in the Americas to the US, which greatly diminishes the extent and power of the Spanish empire.

1936 The Spanish Civil War begins, killing about 200,000 during its three-year span, and brings on more than three decades of Franco's fascist rule.

1975 After Franco's death, Juan Carlos I is crowned king; he later leads the nation to democracy and membership in the European Union.

of the people they ruled, allowing native Jews and Christians to practice their faiths, so long as the infidels paid extra taxes.

The Moors themselves were an ethnically diverse culture, including both simple Berber tribesmen from Morocco and sophisticated rulers from old Arab families. From their capital in Córdoba, various rulers of the united Islamic state of "Al-Andalus" pledged allegiance to foreign caliphs in Syria, Baghdad, or Morocco.

With cultural ties that stretched from Spain to Africa to Arabia to Persia and beyond, the Moorish culture in Spain (especially around A.D. 800-1000) was perhaps Europe's most advanced, a beacon of learning in Europe's so-called "Dark" Ages. Mathematics, astronomy, literature, and architecture flourished. Even winemaking was encouraged, though for religious reasons the Muslims didn't drink alcohol. The Moorish legacy lives on in Spain mainly in architecture (horseshoe arches, ceramic tiles, fountains, and gardens), of which Granada's Alhambra is an exquisite example.

Reconquista
(711-1492)

The Moors ruled for more than 700 years, but throughout that time they were a minority ruling a largely Christian populace. Pockets of independent Christians remained, particularly in the mountains in the peninsula's north. Local Christian kings fought against the Moors whenever they could, whittling away at the Muslim empire, "reconquering" more and more land in what's known as the Reconquista. The last Moorish stronghold, Granada, fell to the Christians in 1492.

The slow, piecemeal process of the Reconquista split the peninsula into many independent kingdoms and dukedoms, some Christian, some Moorish. The Reconquista picked up steam after A.D. 1000, when Al-Andalus splintered into smaller regional states—Granada, Sevilla, Valencia—ruled by local caliphs. Toledo fell to the Christians in 1085. By 1249 the neighboring Christian state of Portugal had the borders it does today, making it the oldest unchanged state in Europe. The rest of the peninsula was a battleground, a loosely knit collection of small kingdoms, some Christian, some Muslim. Heavy stone castles dotted the interior region of Castile, as lords and barons duked it out. Along the Mediterranean coast (from the Pyrenees to Barcelona to Valencia), three

Significant Spaniards

In Politics

Ferdinand (1452-1516) **and Isabel** (1451-1504)—Their marriage united much of Spain, ushering in its Golden Age. The Catholic Monarchs (Reyes Católicos) drove out Moors and Jews, and financed Columbus' lucrative voyages to the New World.

Charles V (1500-1558)— The Flanders-born grandson of Ferdinand and Isabel assumed the Spanish throne in 1516 (as King Charles I) and led the Holy Roman Empire from 1519 to 1555 (as Emperor Charles V), ruling over much of Western Europe, the Far East, and the Americas.

Francisco Franco (1892-1975)—This general led the military uprising against the elected Republic, sparking Spain's Civil War (1936-1939). After victory, he ruled Spain for nearly four decades as an absolute dictator, maintaining its Catholic, aristocratic heritage while slowly modernizing the country.

King Juan Carlos I (1938-?). Taking over Spain after the death of dictator Franco, Carlos turned Spain into a democracy in 1977. He abdicated in 2014 in favor of his son, now serving as King Felipe VI.

In Exploration

Juan Ponce de León (1460-1521)—He's primarily known for being the first European to explore Florida. His quest for the Fountain of Youth is a myth popularized by American author Washington Irving three centuries later.

Francisco Pizarro (1476-1541)—This conquistador vanquished the Incan Empire in the 1530s and founded Peru's current capital, Lima.

Hernán Cortés (1485-1547)—A Spanish nobleman seeking his fortune, Cortés conquered Mexico in 1521, explored the New World, and exploited its indigenous peoples.

Christian states united into a sea-trading power, the kingdom of Aragon.

In 1469, Isabel of Castile married Ferdinand II of Aragon. These so-called Catholic Monarchs (Reyes Católicos) united the peninsula's two largest kingdoms, instantly making Spain a European power. In 1492, while Columbus explored the seas under Ferdinand and Isabel's flag, the Catholic Monarchs drove the Moors out of Granada and expelled the country's Jews, creating a unified, Christian, militaristic nation-state, fueled by the religious zeal of the Reconquista.

The Golden Age
(1500-1600)

Spain's bold sea explorers changed the economics of Europe, opening up a New World of riches and colonies. The Spanish flag soon flew over most of South and Central America. Gold, silver, and agricultural products (grown on large estates with cheap labor) poured into Spain. In return, the stoked Spaniards exported Christianity, converting the American natives with persistent Jesuit priests and cruel conquistadors.

Ferdinand and Isabel's daughter (Juana the Mad) wed a German prince (Philip

In the Arts

El Greco (1541-1614)—Born in Greece, but an honorary Spaniard for spending nearly 40 years in Toledo, this artist created ethereal, spiritual paintings of elongated "flickering" saints, using bold colors and dramatic poses and settings.

Miguel de Cervantes (1547-1616)—Author of the classic satirical romance *Don Quixote*, Cervantes was also a poet and a playwright whose works shaped Spanish literature and the language itself.

Diego Velázquez (1599-1660)—His masterful royal court portraits were studies in camera-eye realism and cool detachment from his subjects.

Bartolomé Murillo (1617-1682)—He painted a dreamy, sentimental world of religious visions: pastel soft-focus works of cute Baby Jesuses and radiant Virgin Marys.

Francisco de Goya (1746-1828)—This artist's liberal tendencies shone through in unflattering portraits of royalty and in emotional scenes of abuse of power.

Antoni Gaudí (1852-1926)—A famous Catalan architect and a leader in the Modernista movement in Barcelona, he designed the astonishing Sagrada Família and other unusual buildings and public spaces (La Pedrera, Casa Batlló, Palau Güell, Park Güell, and more).

Pablo Picasso (1881-1973)—The 20th century's greatest artist explored Spanish themes, particularly in his inspirational antiwar *Guernica* mural, depicting the horrors of war.

Joan Miró (1893-1983)—This modern artist was known for his playful artistic compositions with a Surrealist bent.

Salvador Dalí (1904-1989)—The flamboyant, waxed-mustachioed painter created Surrealist, mind-bending art and installations.

---

the Fair), and their son Charles (1500-1558) inherited not only their crowns but that of his grandfather, the Holy Roman Emperor Maximilian I. Known as King Charles I of Spain, and as Emperor Charles V, he was the most powerful man in the world, ruling an empire that stretched from Holland to Sicily, from Bohemia to Bolivia. The aristocracy and the clergy were swimming in money. Art and courtly life flourished during this Golden Age, with Spain hosting the painter El Greco and the writer Miguel de Cervantes.

But Charles V's Holy Roman Empire was torn by different languages and ethnic groups, and by protesting Protestants. He spent much of the empire's energies at war with Protestants, encroaching Muslim Turks, and Europe's rising powers. When an exhausted Charles announced his abdication (1555) and retired to a monastery, his sprawling empire was divvied up among family members, with Spain and its possessions going to his son, Philip II (1527-1598).

Philip II inherited Portugal in 1581, moved Spain's capital to Madrid, built the palace of El Escorial, and continued fighting losing battles across Europe (the Netherlands, France) that drained the treasury of its New World gold. In the summer of 1588, Spain's seemingly unbeatable royal fleet of 125 ships—the Invincible Armada—sailed off to conquer England, only to be unexpectedly routed in battle by bad weather and Sir Francis Drake's cunning. Just like that, Britannia ruled the waves, and Spain spiraled downward, becoming a debt-ridden, overextended, flabby nation.

Slow Decline
(1600-1900)

Easy money from the colonies kept Spain from seeing the dangers at home. The country stopped growing its own wheat and neglected its fields. Great Britain and the Netherlands were the rising sea-trading powers in the new global economy. During the centuries when science and technology developed as never before in other European countries, Spain was preoccupied by its failed colonial politics.

By 1700, once-mighty Spain lay helpless while rising powers France, England, and Austria fought over the right to pick Spain's next king in the War of the Spanish Succession (1701-1714), which was fought partly on Spanish soil (Britain held out against the French in the Siege of Gibraltar). Spanish king Charles II didn't have an heir, so he willed his kingdom to Louis XIV's grandson, Philip of Anjou, who was set to inherit both France and Spain. But the rest of Europe didn't want powerful France to become even stronger. The war ended in compromise: Philip became king of Spain (Spain lost several possessions), but he had to renounce claims to any other thrones. The French-born, French-speaking Bourbon King Philip V (1683-1746) ruled Spain for 45 years. He and his heirs made themselves at home, building the Versailles-like Royal Palace in Madrid and La Granja near Segovia.

The French invaded Spain under Napoleon, who installed his brother as king in 1808. The Spaniards rose up (chronicled by Goya's paintings of the second and third of May 1808), sparking the Peninsular War—called the War of Independence by Spaniards—that finally won Spain's independence from French rule in 1814.

Nineteenth-century Spain was a backward nation, with internal wars over which noble family should rule (the Carlist Wars), liberal revolutions put down brutally, and political assassinations. Spain gradually lost its global possessions to other European powers and to South American revolutionaries. Spain hit rock bottom in 1898, when the upstart United States picked a fight and thrashed them in the Spanish-American War, taking away Spain's last major possessions: Cuba, Puerto Rico, and the Philippines.

The 20th Century

A drained and disillusioned Spain was ill-prepared for modern technology and democratic government.

The old ruling class (the monarchy, church, and landowners) fought new economic powers (cities, businessmen, labor unions) in a series of coups, strikes, and sham elections. In the 1920s, a military dictatorship under Miguel Primo de Rivera kept the old guard in power. In 1930 he was ousted and an open election brought a modern democratic Republic to power. But the right wing regrouped under the Falange (fascist) party, fomenting unrest and sparking a military coup against the Republic in 1936, supported by General Francisco Franco (1892-1975).

Thus began the bloody Spanish Civil War (1936-1939), fought between Franco's Nationalists (also called Falangists) and the Republic (called Loyalists). Adolf Hitler and Benito Mussolini sent troops and supplies to their fellow fascist Franco. It was Hitler's Luftwaffe that helped Franco bomb the town of Guernica (April 1937), an event famously captured on canvas by Pablo Picasso. On the Republican side, hundreds of Americans (including Ernest

Hemingway) steamed over to Spain to fight for democracy.

The civil war resulted in Franco's victory and thousands of deaths (estimates range from 200,000 to 500,000—the exact total will never be known). For nearly the next four decades, Spain was ruled by Franco, an authoritarian, church-blessed dictator who tried to modernize the backward country while shielding it from corrupting modern influences. Spain was officially neutral in World War II, and the country spent much of the postwar era as a world apart.

Before Franco died, he handpicked his protégé, King Juan Carlos I, to succeed him. But to everyone's surprise, the young, conservative, mild-mannered king stepped aside, settled for a figurehead title, and guided the country quickly and peacefully toward democratic elections (1977).

Spain had a lot of catching up to do. Culturally, the once-conservative nation exploded and embraced new ideas, even plunging to wild extremes. In the 1980s Spain flowered under left-leaning Prime Minister Felipe González. Spain showed the world a modern face in 1992, hosting both a World Exhibition at Sevilla and the Summer Olympics at Barcelona.

Spain Today

From 1996 to 2004, Spain was led by Prime Minister José María Aznar. He adopted conservative policies to minimize the stress on the country's young democracy, fighting problems such as unemployment and foreign debt with reasonable success. However, his support of the United States' war in Iraq was extremely unpopular. In spring of 2004, the retiring Aznar supported a similarly centrist successor, Mariano Rajoy, who seemed poised to win the election. On the eve of the election, on March 11, three Madrid train stations were bombed at the height of rush hour, killing 191 people. The terrorist group claiming responsibility denounced Spain's Iraq policy, and Aznar's party lost the election.

The new prime minister, left-of-center José Luis Rodríguez Zapatero, quickly began pulling Spain's troops out of Iraq, as well as enacting sweeping social changes. But Zapatero and his party were shown the door in 2011, a casualty of the economic crisis. The more-conservative Popular Party regained the majority, and Mariano Rajoy became prime minister.

Spain enjoyed a strong economy through the late 1990s and early 2000s, thanks in part to EU loans and subsidies, a thriving tourism industry, and a boom in housing construction. But the country was hit hard by the 2009 global economic downturn, and its economy entered a recession. Spain's banks stopped lending, many people lost homes to foreclosures, and by 2013 unemployment had soared to 27 percent. So many young Spaniards were out of work (one-fourth of those under 30, and nearly half of those under 25) that a new name was coined to describe them: *generación ni-ni* (the neither-nor generation).

Under pressure from the EU to cut its national debt, Spain's government has limited payouts to new parents, scaled back government pensions and salaries, and made cuts in education and health care. These austerity measures have drawn criticism from unions and the public, and Spain's mainstream politicians have become unpopular.

Even the once-admired King Juan Carlos lost popular support due to some ill-timed, expensive hijinks while Spain's economic woes mounted. After almost 40 years on the throne, he abdicated in 2014, turning over the crown to his well-respected son, who now reigns as King Felipe VI.

Practicalities

TOURIST INFORMATION

Spain's national tourist office **in the US** will answer your general travel questions by email (newyork.information@tour spain.es). Scan their website (www.spain. info) for information and sightseeing ideas; you can download many brochures free of charge. If you're going to Barcelona, also see www.barcelonaturisme.cat.

In Spain, your best first stop in a city is the *Turismo*, the tourist information office (abbreviated **TI** in this book). Prepare a list of questions and a proposed plan to double-check. Pick up a city map, confirm opening hours of sights, and get informa-tion on public transit (including bus and train schedules), walking tours, special events, and nightlife.

TRAVEL TIPS

Time Zones: Spain, like most of continental Europe, is generally six/nine hours ahead of the East/West coasts of the US. The exceptions are the beginning and end of Daylight Saving Time: Europe "springs forward" the last Sunday in March (two weeks after most of North America), and "falls back" the last Sunday in October (one week before North America). For an online time converter, try www.timeand date.com/worldclock.

Business Hours: Some businesses respect the afternoon siesta; when it's 100 degrees in the shade, you'll understand why. Shops are generally open from 9:00 to 13:00 and from 16:00 to 20:00 (and some close on Saturday afternoon and all day Sunday), though in touristy places, many stores stay open throughout the day. Banking hours are generally Monday through Friday from 9:00 to 14:00. Most museums stay open all day; smaller ones may close for a siesta.

On Sundays, sights are generally open, while some shops are closed, and public transportation options are fewer (for example, no bus service to or from smaller towns). Sunday evenings are usually quiet, compared to the liveliness of Friday and Saturday evenings.

Discounts: This book lists only the full adult price for sights. However, many sights offer discounts for youths (up to age 18), students (with proper identification cards, www.isic.org), families, and seniors (loosely defined as retirees or those willing to call themselves seniors). Always ask. Some discounts are available only for citizens of the European Union (EU).

Online Translation: The Google Translate app converts spoken English into most European languages (and vice versa) and can also translate text it "reads" with your mobile device's camera. To translate websites, use Google's free Chrome browser (www.google.com/chrome) or paste the URL of the site into the translation window at www.google.com/translate.

HELP!

Emergency and Medical Help

Dial 091 for police help and 112 in any emergency (medical or otherwise). Or ask your hotelier for help—they'll know of the nearest medical and emergency services. If you get a minor ailment, do as the locals do and go to a pharmacist for advice.

Avoiding Theft and Scams

Like anywhere in Europe, thieves target tourists, especially in Barcelona, Madrid, Granada, and Sevilla. Pickpockets often stage a commotion or a fight to enable them to work unnoticed. Someone in a small group pushing you as you enter or exit a crowded subway car may slip one hand in your pocket or daybag. Thieves snatch purses and break into cars. They've been known to zip by on motorbikes to grab handbags from pedestrians or even from cars in traffic.

Be on guard, and treat any disturbance around you as a smoke screen for theft. Remember to wear a money belt (tucked under your clothes) to keep your cash, credit cards, and passport secure; carry only the money you need for the day in your front pocket.

Don't believe any "police officers" looking for counterfeit bills—one of many creative scams that lowlifes dream up. When traveling by train, keep your luggage in sight and get a litera (berth in an attendant-monitored sleeping car) for safety on overnight trips. Drivers should read the tips on page 459.

Theft or Loss

To replace a passport, you'll need to go in person to an embassy or consulate office (listed later). If your credit and debit cards disappear, cancel and replace them. If your things are lost or stolen, file a police report, either on the spot or within a day or two; you'll need it to submit an insurance claim for rail passes and travel gear, and it can help with replacing your passport or credit and debit cards. For more information, see www.ricksteves.com/help.

Damage Control for Lost Cards

If you lose your credit, debit, or ATM card, you can stop people from using your card by reporting the loss immediately to your card company. Call these 24-hour US numbers collect: Visa (tel. 303/967-1096, toll-free number in Spain is 900-991-124), MasterCard (tel. 636/722-7111), and American Express (tel. 336/393-1111). In Spain, to make a collect call to the US, dial 900-990-011; press zero or stay on the line for an English-speaking operator. Visa's and MasterCard's websites list European toll-free numbers by country.

If you report your loss within two days, you typically won't be responsible for any unauthorized transactions on your account, although many banks charge a liability fee of $50. You can generally receive a temporary replacement card within two or three business days in Europe.

Embassies and Consulates

US Embassy in Madrid: Tel. 915-872-240, after-hours emergency tel. 915-872-200 (Calle Serrano 75, http://madrid.usembassy.gov)

US Consulate in Barcelona: Tel. 932-802-227, after-hours emergency tel. 915-872-200 (Paseo Reina Elisenda de Montcada 23, http://barcelona.usconsulate.gov)

Canadian Embassy in Madrid: Tel. 913-828-400 (Torre Espacio, Paseo de la Castellana 259D, in Torre Espacio skyscraper, www.espana.gc.ca)

MONEY

This section offers advice on how to pay for purchases on your trip (including getting cash from ATMs and paying with plastic), VAT (sales tax) refunds, and tipping.

What to Bring

Bring both a credit card and a debit card. You'll use the debit card at cash machines (ATMs) to withdraw local cash for most purchases, and the credit card to pay for larger items. Some travelers carry a third card, in case one gets demagnetized or eaten by a rogue machine.

For an emergency stash, bring several hundred dollars in hard cash in $20 bills. If you have to exchange the bills, go to a bank; avoid using currency-exchange booths because of their lousy rates and/or outrageous (and often hard-to-spot) fees.

Cash

Cash is just as desirable in Europe as it is at home. Small businesses (*pensiónes,* mom-and-pop cafés, shops, etc.) prefer that you pay your bills with cash. Some vendors will charge you extra for using a credit card; some won't accept foreign credit cards; and some won't take any credit cards at all. Cash is the best—and sometimes only—way to pay for cheap food, bus fares, taxis, and local guides.

Throughout Europe, ATMs are the standard way for travelers to get cash. They work just like they do at home. To withdraw money from an ATM (called a *cajero automático* in Spain), you'll need a debit card (ideally with a Visa or MasterCard logo for maximum usability), plus a PIN code (numeric and four digits). For increased security, shield the keypad when entering your PIN code.

Whenever possible, use ATMs located outside banks—a thief is less likely to target a cash machine near surveillance cameras, and if your card is munched by a machine, you can go inside for help.

Don't use an ATM if anything on the front of the machine looks loose or damaged (a sign that someone may have attached a "skimming" device to capture account information). If a cash machine eats your ATM card, check for a thin plastic insert with a tongue hanging out (thieves use these devices to extract cards).

Exchange Rate

1 euro (€)=about $1.10

To convert prices in euros to dollars, add about 10 percent: €20=about $22, €50=about $55. (Check www.oanda. com for the latest exchange rates.) Just like the dollar, one euro (€) is broken down into 100 cents. Coins range from €0.01 to €2, and bills range from €5 to €500 (though bills over €50 are rarely used).

Stay away from "independent" ATMs such as Travelex, Euronet, YourCash, Cardpoint, and Cashzone, which charge huge commissions, have terrible exchange rates, and may try to trick users with "dynamic currency conversion" (described at the end of "Credit and Debit Cards," next).

If you want to monitor your accounts online during your trip to detect any unauthorized transactions, be sure to use a secure connection (see page 448).

Although you can use a credit card to withdraw cash at an ATM, this comes with high bank fees and only makes sense in an emergency.

Credit and Debit Cards

For purchases, Visa and MasterCard are more commonly accepted than American Express. Just like at home, credit or debit cards work easily at larger hotels, restaurants, and shops. I typically use my debit card to withdraw cash to pay for most purchases.

I use my credit card sparingly: to book hotel reservations, to buy advance tickets for events or sights, to cover major expenses (such as car rentals or plane tickets), and to pay for things online or near the end of my trip (to avoid another visit to the ATM). While you could instead use a debit card to make these

purchases, a credit card offers a greater degree of fraud protection.

Ask Your Credit- or Debit-Card Company: Before your trip, contact the company that issued your debit or credit cards.

• Confirm that your **card will work overseas,** and alert them that you'll be using it in Europe; otherwise, they may deny transactions if they perceive unusual spending patterns.

• Ask for the specifics on transaction **fees.** When you use your credit or debit card—either for purchases or ATM withdrawals—you'll typically be charged additional "international transaction" fees of up to 3 percent (1 percent is normal) plus $5 per transaction. If your card's fees seem high, consider getting a different card just for your trip: Capital One (www. capitalone.com) and most credit unions have low-to-no international fees.

• Verify your daily ATM **withdrawal limit,** and if necessary, ask your bank to adjust it. I prefer a high limit that allows me to take out more cash at each ATM stop and save on bank fees; some travelers prefer to set a lower limit in case their card is stolen. Note that foreign banks also set maximum withdrawal amounts for their ATMs.

• Get your bank's emergency **phone**

ATMs work just like back home.

number in the US (but not its 800 number, which isn't accessible from overseas) to call collect if you have a problem.

• Ask for your credit card's **PIN** in case you need to make an emergency cash withdrawal or encounter Europe's chip-and-PIN system; the bank won't tell you your PIN over the phone, so allow time for it to be mailed to you.

Magnetic-Stripe versus Chip-and-PIN Credit Cards: Europeans are increasingly using chip-and-PIN credit cards embedded with an electronic security chip and requiring a four-digit PIN. Your American-style card (with just the old-fashioned magnetic stripe) will work fine in most places. But there could be minor inconveniences; it might not work at unattended payment machines, such as those at train and subway stations, toll plazas, parking garages, bike-rental kiosks, and gas pumps. If you have problems, try entering your card's PIN, look for a machine that takes cash, or find a clerk who can process the transaction manually.

No matter what kind of card you have, it pays to carry euros, and remember, you can always use an ATM to withdraw cash with your magnetic-stripe debit card.

Dynamic Currency Conversion: If merchants or hoteliers offer to convert your purchase price into dollars (called dynamic currency conversion, or DCC), refuse this "service." You'll pay even more in fees for the expensive convenience of seeing your transaction in dollars. If your receipt shows the total in dollars only, ask for the transaction to be processed in euros. If the clerk refuses, pay in cash. Similarly, if an ATM offers to "lock in" or "guarantee" your conversion rate, choose "proceed without conversion" and opt for euros over dollars.

Tipping

Tipping in Spain isn't as automatic and generous as it is in the US. For special service, tips are appreciated, but not expected. As in the US, the proper amount depends on your resources, tipping philosophy, and the circumstances, but some general guidelines apply.

Restaurants: If you order a meal at a counter—as you often will when sampling tapas at a bar—there's no need to tip (though if you buy a few tapas, you can round up the bill with a few small coins). At restaurants with table service, most Spaniards tip nothing or next to nothing; a service charge is generally included in the bill (servicio incluido). If you like to tip for good service, give up to 5 percent extra. If service is not included (servicio no incluido), you could tip up to 10 percent. It's best to tip in cash even if you pay with your credit card. Otherwise the tip may never reach your server.

Taxis: Locals usually don't tip cabbies, but you could round up the fare a bit if you like (for instance, if the fare is €4.85, pay €5). If the cabbie hauls your bags and zips you to the airport to help you catch your flight, you might want to toss in a little more. But if you feel like you're being driven in circles or otherwise ripped off, skip the tip.

Services: In general, if someone in the service industry does a super job for you, a small tip of a euro or two is appropriate...but not required. If you're not sure whether (or how much) to tip for a service, ask a local for advice.

Getting a VAT Refund

Wrapped into the purchase price of your Spanish souvenirs is a Value-Added Tax (VAT) of 21 percent (in Spain, it's called IVA—Impuesto sobre el Valor Añadido). You're entitled to get most of that tax back if you purchase more than €90.15 (about $100) worth of goods at a store that participates in the VAT-refund scheme. Typically, you must ring up the minimum at a single retailer—you can't add up your purchases from various shops to reach the required amount.

If the merchant ships the goods to your

home, the tax will be subtracted from your purchase price. Otherwise, you'll need to:

Get the paperwork. Have the merchant completely fill out the necessary refund document. You'll have to present your passport. Get the paperwork done before you leave the store to ensure you'll have everything you need (including your original sales receipt).

Get your stamp at the border or airport. Process your VAT document at your last stop in the European Union (usually an airport) with the customs agent who deals with VAT refunds. Arrive an additional hour early before you need to check in for your flight to allow time to find the local customs office—and to stand in line. It's best to keep your purchases in your carry-on. If they're too large or dangerous to carry on (such as knives), pack them in your checked bags and alert the check-in agent. You'll be sent (with your tagged bag) to a customs desk outside security, where an official will examine your bag, stamp your paperwork, and put your bag on the belt. You're not supposed to use your purchased goods before you leave. If you show up at customs wearing your flashy new flamenco outfit, officials might look the other way—or deny you a refund.

Collect your refund. You'll need to return your stamped document to the retailer or its representative. Many merchants work with services, such as Global Blue or Premier Tax Free, that have offices at major airports, ports, or border crossings (either before or after security, probably strategically located near a duty-free shop). These services, which extract a 4 percent fee, can refund your money immediately in cash or credit your card (within two billing cycles). If the retailer handles VAT refunds directly, it's up to you to contact the merchant for your refund. You can mail the documents from home or from your point of departure. You'll then have to wait—it can take months.

Customs for American Shoppers

You are allowed to take home $800 worth of items per person duty-free, once every 31 days. You can take home many processed and packaged foods: vacuum-packed cheeses, dried herbs, jams, baked goods, candy, chocolate, oil, vinegar, mustard, and honey. Fresh fruits and vegetables and most meats are not allowed, with exceptions for some canned items.

You can bring home one liter of alcohol duty-free. It can be packed securely in your checked luggage, along with any other liquid-containing items. But if you want to pack the alcohol (or any liquid-packed food) in your carry-on bag for your flight home, buy it at a duty-free shop at the airport.

For details on allowable goods, customs rules, and duty rates, visit http://help.cbp.gov.

SIGHTSEEING

Sightseeing can be hard work. Use these tips to make your visits to Spain's finest sights meaningful, fun, efficient, and painless.

Plan Ahead

Set up an itinerary that allows you to fit in all your must-see sights. For a one-stop look at opening hours, see the "At a Glance" sidebars in this book for each major destination. Most places keep stable hours, but you can confirm the latest at the TI or by checking museum websites. Many museums are closed or have reduced hours at least a few days a year, especially on major holidays. In summer, some sights stay open late. Off-season, many museums have shorter hours. Whenever you go, don't put off visiting a must-see sight—you never know if a place will close unexpectedly for a holiday, strike, or restoration.

Take advantage of the tips in this book

on avoiding lines. Sometimes you can make reservations for an entry time, such as for Granada's Alhambra or Barcelona's Sagrada Família. Specifics appear in the chapters. If you can't reserve a popular sight, try visiting very early or very late. Evening visits are usually peaceful, with fewer crowds.

At Sights

Here's what you can typically expect:

Entering: Be warned that you may not be allowed to enter if you arrive 30 to 60 minutes before closing time. And guards start ushering people out well before the actual closing time, so don't save the best for last.

Some important sights have a security check, where you must open your bag or send it through a metal detector. Some sights require you to check daypacks and coats. (If you'd rather not check your day-pack, try carrying it tucked under your arm like a purse as you enter.)

Photography: If the museum's photo policy isn't clearly posted, ask a guard. Generally, taking photos without a flash or tripod is allowed. Some sights ban photos altogether.

Temporary Exhibits: Museums may show special exhibits in addition to their permanent collection. Some exhibits are included in the entry price, while others come at an extra cost (which you may have to pay even if you don't want to see the exhibit).

Expect Changes: Artwork can be on tour, on loan, out sick, or shifted at the whim of the curator. Pick up a floor plan as you enter, and ask the museum staff if you can't find a particular item. Say the title or artist's name, or point to the photograph in this book, and ask, *"¿Dónde está?"* (DOHN-day ay-STAH; meaning, "Where is?").

Audioguides and Apps: Many sights rent audioguides, which generally offer dry-but-useful recorded descriptions (sometimes included with admission). If you bring your own earbuds, you can enjoy better sound. Increasingly, sights offer apps—often free—that you can download to your mobile device (check their websites).

Services: Major sights may have an on-site café or cafeteria, usually a handy place to rejuvenate during a long visit. The WCs at sights are free and generally clean.

Before Leaving: At the gift shop, scan the postcard rack or thumb through a

Granada's terrace eateries come with world-class views.

guidebook to be sure that you haven't overlooked something that you'd like to see.

EATING

Spanish cuisine is hearty, and meals are served in big, inexpensive portions. You can eat well in restaurants for about €15-20—or even more cheaply with more variety if you graze on tapas in bars.

The Spanish eating schedule—lunch from 13:00 to 16:00, dinner after 21:00—frustrates many visitors. Most Spaniards eat one major meal of the day—lunch (comida/almuerzo)—around 14:00, when stores close, schools let out, and people gather with their friends and family for the siesta. Because most Spaniards work until 19:30, supper (cena) is usually served at about 21:00 or 22:00. And, since few people want a heavy meal that late, many Spaniards build a light dinner out of appetizer portions called tapas.

Don't buck this system. Generally, no self-respecting restaurant serves meals at American hours. If you're looking for a nontouristy restaurant (such as a casa de comidas—"house of eating"—a good, traditional eatery), remember that a popular spot is often filled with tourists at 20:00; then at 22:00 the scene is entirely different—and more authentic.

Not only are mealtimes different—the portions are, too. It's unusual to find a restaurant with "starters" and "main dishes." Instead, most restaurants (like bars) serve their dishes in ample portions called raciones, or the smaller half-servings, media-raciones. (The smaller tapas are more commonly served at bars than at sit-down restaurants; for details, see later.) Enjoy this as an opportunity to explore the regional cuisine. Ordering media-raciones may cost a bit more per ounce, but you'll broaden your tasting experience. Two people can fill up on four media-raciones.

No matter where you eat, you'll encounter the cured ham called jamón. The cheapest meal is simply a bocadillo de jamón (sandwich of ham on a baguette), sold virtually everywhere.

The Spanish diet—heavy on jamón and deep-fried foods (usually fried in olive oil)—can be brutal on Americans more accustomed to salads, fruit, and grains. A few vegetarian and lighter options exist, but you'll have to seek them out. The secret to getting your veggies at restaurants is to order two courses, because the first course generally has a green option. Resist the cheese-and-ham appetizers and instead choose first-course menu items such as creamed vegetable soup, parrillada de verduras (sautéed vegetables), or ensalada mixta. Spaniards rarely eat only a salad, so salads tend to be small and simple—just iceberg lettuce, tomatoes, and maybe olives and tuna. Main courses such as meats or fish are usually served with only a garnish, not a side of vegetables. Fruit isn't normally served for breakfast or as a snack—it's a dessert. After-meal dessert menus usually have a fruit option.

Survival Tips: To get by in Spain, either adapt yourself to the Spanish schedule and cuisine, or scramble to get edible food in between. Have an early light lunch at a bar. Many Spaniards have a bocadillo (baguette sandwich) at about 11:00 to bridge the gap between their coffee-and-roll breakfast and lunch at 14:00 (hence the popularity of fast-food bocadillo chains such as Pans & Company).

Then, either have your main meal at a restaurant at 15:00, followed by a tapas snack for dinner later; or reverse it, having a tapas meal in the afternoon, followed by a late restaurant dinner (for more tips, see "Tapas Bars," later).

Breakfast

Hotel breakfasts are generally handy, optional, and pricey (about €6 and up). Start your day instead with a Spanish flair at a corner bar or at a colorful café near

Tasty Words for Breakfast

Here are some key words for breakfast:

café solo	shot of espresso
café con leche	espresso with hot milk
cortado	espresso with a little milk
café americano	you know it
té or infusión	tea
zumo	juice
zumo de naranja (natural)	orange juice (freshly squeezed)
pan (de molde / de barra)	bread (sandwich bread / baguette)
tostada con aceite (y tomate)	toasted bread with olive oil (and tomato)
sandwich (tostado)	white bread sandwich (toasted)
bocadillo	baguette sandwich
...con jamón / queso / mixto	...with ham / cheese / both
...mixto con huevo	...with ham, cheese, and an egg

the town market hall (and pay just €2-3). Ask for the *desayunos* (breakfast special, usually available until noon), which can include coffee, a roll (or sandwich), and juice for one price—much cheaper than ordering them separately. Sandwiches can either be on white bread (called "sandwich") or on a baguette (*bocadillo*).

A basic, standard savory breakfast item is *tostada con aceite,* toasted bread with olive oil (sometimes with tomato as well). For something more substantial any time of day, look for a *tortilla española*—an inexpensive potato omelet cooked fresh at bars every morning and served in slices.

You'll have many sweet rolls to choose from. But if you like a doughnut and coffee in American greasy-spoon joints, try the Spanish equivalent: greasy cigar-shaped fritters called *churros* (or the thicker *porras*) that you dip in warm chocolate pudding or your *café con leche.*

Restaurants

Avoid places with neon signs boasting, "We Speak English and Accept Credit Cards." Venturing even a block or two off the main drag leads to higher-quality food for cheaper prices. You'll eat better at lower-rent locales—and even better if you have *Rick Steves' Spanish Phrase Book & Dictionary.*

Paella

Sampling Jamón

The staple of Spanish cuisine, *jamón* (hah-MOHN) is prosciutto-like ham that's dry-cured and aged. It's generally sliced thin (right off the hock) and served at room temperature. *Jamón* can be eaten straight, served in a *bocadillo* (baguette sandwich), or mixed into a wide variety of dishes. Bars proudly hang ham hocks from the rafters as part of the decor.

Like connoisseurs of fine wine, Spaniards debate the merits of different breeds of pigs, the pig's diet, and the quality of the curing. The two major types of ham are *jamón serrano,* from white pigs whose meat is cured in the *sierras* (mountains) of Spain, and the higher-quality *jamón ibérico,* made with the back legs of black-hooved pigs (a.k.a. *pata negra,* "black foot").

To sample this delicacy without the high price tag you'll find in bars and restaurants, go to the local market. Ask for 100 grams of top-quality ham (*cien gramos de jamón ibérico extra;* about €70/kilo, so your portion will run about €7), and enjoy it as a picnic with red wine and a baguette. To round out your picnic, also pick up some cheese, olives, and pickles.

Although not fancy, Spanish cuisine comes with an endless variety of regional specialties. Two famous Spanish dishes are paella and gazpacho. Paella features saffron-flavored rice as a background for whatever the chef wants to mix in—seafood, sausage, chicken, peppers, and so on. While paella is heavy for your evening meal, jump (like everyone else in the bar) at the opportunity to snare a small plate of paella when it appears hot out of the kitchen in a tapas bar. Avoid the paella shown in pretty pictures on a separate menu—it's from the microwave. Gazpacho and *salmorejo,* Andalusian specialties, are chilled tomato-based soups, served with chunks of bread or *jamón* and chopped egg. Both are refreshing on a hot day and are commonly available as soon as the weather heats up. Spanish cooks love garlic and olive oil—many dishes are soaked in both.

For a budget meal in a restaurant, try a *plato combinado* (combination plate), which usually includes portions of one or two main dishes, a vegetable, and bread for a reasonable price. Another option is the *menú del día* (menu of the day, also known as *menú turístico*), a substantial three- to four-course meal that usually comes with a carafe of house wine.

Whether you go to a restaurant or bar, you won't be bothered by indoor smoke. Smoking has been banned in closed public spaces.

Tapas Bars

You can eat well any time of day in tapas bars. Tapas are small portions of seafood, salads, meat-filled pastries, deep-fried tasties, and on and on.

Tapas typically cost about €2-3 apiece.

Tapas Menu Decoder

You can often just point to what you want on the menu, say *por favor,* and get your food, but these words will help.

Tapas Terms

pincho	snack-size portion, like a tapa
tapa	snack-size portion
½ ración (media-ración)	half portion
ración	full portion
surtido (de)	assortment (of)
frito	fried
a la plancha / parrilla	grilled / barbecued
brocheta	shish kebab (on a stick)
¿Cuánto cuesta una tapa?	How much per tapa?

Sandwich Words

bocadillo	baguette sandwich, cheap and basic
canapé	tiny open-faced sandwich
flauta	sandwich made with flute-thin baguette
montadito	tapa "mounted" on bread
pulga, pulguita, pepito	a small, closed baguette sandwich

Typical Tapas

aceitunas	olives
albóndigas	spiced meatballs with sauce
almejas (a la marinera)	clams (in paprika sauce)
almendras	almonds (usually fried)
atún	tuna
bacalao	cod
banderilla	skewer of spicy, pickled veggies
bombas	fried meat-and-potato ball
cabrillas	snails
calamares fritos	fried squid rings
caracoles	tree snails (May-Sept)
champiñones	mushrooms
charcutería	cured meats
chorizo	spicy sausage

empanadillas	pastries stuffed with meat or seafood
ensaladilla rusa	potato salad with mayo
espinacas	spinach
gambas	shrimp
...a la plancha / al ajillo	...grilled / with garlic
...con cáscara / peladas	...with shell / peeled
gazpacho	cold tomato soup
guiso	stew
jamón	cured ham (like prosciutto)
judías (verdes)	(green) beans
lomo	pork tenderloin
mejillones	mussels
paella	saffron rice dish with seafood and meat
pan	bread
patatas bravas	fried potatoes with spicy tomato sauce
pescaditos fritos	assortment of little fried fish
picos	little breadsticks
pimiento (relleno)	pepper (stuffed)
pinchos morunos	skewer of spicy lamb or pork
pisto	mixed sautéed vegetables
pollo (alioli)	chicken (with garlic sauce)
pulpo	octopus
queso	cheese
rabo de toro	bull's-tail stew (fatty and oh so tender)
revuelto (de setas)	scrambled eggs (with wild mushrooms)
salchichón	salami-like sausage
tabla serrana	hearty plate of meat and cheese
tortilla española	potato omelet
tortilla de jamón / queso	potato omelet with ham / cheese
tortillitas de camarones	shrimp fritters (Andalucía)
variado fritos	mix of various fried fish

There are happy exceptions: A small, free tapa may be included with your drink in some cities, including Madrid, Salamanca, Santiago de Compostela, Granada, and Nerja. Order your drink first to get the freebie; then order additional food as you like.

Many bars push larger portions called *raciones* (dinner plate-sized portions). Ask for the smaller tapas portions or a *media-ración* (listed as ½ *ración* on a menu)—though some bars simply don't serve anything smaller than a *ración*.

Locate the price list (often posted in fine type on a wall somewhere) to know the menu options and price tiers. Eating and drinking at a bar is usually cheapest if you sit or stand at the counter (*barra*). You may pay a little more to eat sitting at a table (*mesa* or *salón*), and still more for an outdoor table (*terraza*). Traditionally, tapas are served at the bar, and *raciones* (and *media-raciones*) are served at tables. It's bad form to order food at the bar, then take it to a table. If you're standing and a table opens up, it's OK to move as long as you signal to the waiter; anything else you order will be charged at the higher *mesa/salón* price.

Bars can be extremely crowded with locals, and you might find it hard to get in an order—or even find a place to sit. You'll have more room, and get better service, by showing up before the local crowd. Try to be there by 13:30 for lunch, and 20:30-21:00 for dinner.

Hang back and observe before ordering. Sometimes the tapas are displayed under glass at the counter (you'll be able to point to what you want). Look around to see what appeals on other customers' plates. Use my "Tapas Menu Decoder" for ideas.

When you're ready to order, be assertive or you'll never be served. *Por favor* (please) grabs the server's attention. Then quickly rattle off what you'd like (pointing to other people's food if necessary). Don't worry about paying until you're ready to leave (he's keeping track of your tab). To get the bill, ask, "*¿La cuenta?*"

Chasing down a particular bar for tapas nearly defeats the purpose and spirit of tapas—they are impromptu. Just drop in at any lively place with lots of customers, a TV blaring, and crumpled napkins on the floor (it's considered unsanitary to put trash back on the bar).

Get a fun, inexpensive sampler plate. Ask for *una tabla de canapés variados* to get a plate of various little open-faced sandwiches. Or ask for a *surtido de charcutería* (an assortment of meat) or *queso* (cheese). *Un surtido de jamón y queso* means a mix of different hams and cheeses. Order bread and two glasses of red wine on the right square, and you've got a romantic (and €15) dinner for two.

Spanish Drinks

Spain is one of the world's leading producers of grapes, and that means lots of excellent wine: both red (*tinto*) and white (*blanco*). Major wine regions include Valdepeñas (both red and white wines made in Don Quixote country south of Toledo); Penedès (cabernet-style wines from near Barcelona); Rioja (spicy, lighter reds from the tempranillo grape, from the high plains of northern Spain); and Rib-

¡Salud!

Spanish Drinking Words

These words will help quench your thirst. *¡Salud!* (Cheers!)

Wine and Spirits

vino	wine
rojo / blanco	red / white
cava	sparkling wine (Spanish champagne)
un tinto / un blanco	glass of house red / white wine
un crianza	glass of aged, quality wine
un reserva / gran reserva	much higher-quality, pricier wine
tinto de verano	red wine with lemonade (like sangria)
seco / dulce	dry / sweet
mucho cuerpo	full-bodied
afrutado	fruity
vermú	vermouth
jerez	sherry (fortified wine from Jerez)
amontillado, fino, manzanilla	rich, dry sherries

Beer

cerveza	beer
caña	small glass of draft beer
clara con limón / con casera	shandy—beer with lemonade / soda
doble, tubo	tall glass of beer
sidra	hard, dry cider

Nonalcoholic

agua con / sin gas	water with / without bubbles
un vaso de agua (del grifo)	glass of (tap) water
una jarra de agua	pitcher of tap water
refresco	soft drink (Fanta—*limón* or *naranja,* and Schweppes—*limón* or *tónica*)
mosto	nonalcoholic grape juice—red or white—served where wine is served
una sin	nonalcoholic beer

era del Duero (reds from northwest of Madrid).

For a basic glass of red wine, you can order *un tinto*. But for quality wine, ask for *un crianza* (old), *un reserva* (older), or *un gran reserva* (oldest). The single most important tip for good, economical wine drinking is to ask for *un crianza*—for little or no extra money than a basic *tinto*, you'll get a quality, aged wine.

Sherry, a fortified wine from the Jerez region, is a shock to the taste buds if you're expecting a sweet dessert drink. Named for its city of origin, *jerez* ranges from dry (*fino*) to sweet (*dulce*)—Spaniards drink the *fino* and export the *dulce*. *Cava* is Spain's answer to champagne. Sangria (a punch of red wine mixed with fruit slices) is refreshing and popular with tourists; Spaniards generally prefer *tinto de verano* (wine with lemonade).

Most places just have the standard local beer—a light lager—on tap. The brand is determined by regional pride, rather than quality. (For instance, Cruzcampo—which is very light so that hot, thirsty drinkers can consume more—is big in the south, whereas San Miguel is big in the north.) To get a small draft beer, ask for a *caña*. Nonalcoholic beer is quite popular and often on tap. If you say *"una sin,"* which means "one without," it's assumed you want a nonalcoholic beer. While *sin* comes with less than 1 percent alcohol, you can get totally alcohol-free brew by asking for *"zero punto zero"* (0.0). If you'd prefer a grape juice alternative to wine, ask for *mosto* (it comes in red or white).

Spain's bars often serve fresh-squeezed orange juice (*zumo de naranja natural*). For something completely different, try *horchata*, a sweet, milky beverage extracted from *chufa* tubers. If ordering mineral water in a restaurant, request a *botella grande de agua* (big bottle). They push the more profitable small bottles. For a glass of tap water, specify *un vaso de agua del grifo*. The waiter may counter with *"Embotellada?"*—"Bottled?"—hoping to sell you something. Be strong and insist on tap water (*del grifo*), and you'll get it.

One challenge for tapas bar-hoppers is that you'll generally order a drink in each place. If you're visiting several different bars (as you should), this can add up. If you'd like to drink a lot without getting drunk, remember a few key terms: *caña* (small beer), *clara con limón* (small beer with lemonade) or *con casera* (with soda), *tinto de verano* (red wine with soda and often with a slice of lemon), and *una sin* (nonalcoholic beer, pronounced "seen").

Quick, Cheap Meals and Picnics

Located in most cities, sandwich shops such as the Pans & Company chain serve fresh, affordable sandwiches and salads. Try pizza shops for slices-to-go and empanadas (pastry turnovers filled with seasoned meat and veggies). Bakeries often sell sandwiches. Bigger cities have at least one El Corte Inglés department store, with a cafeteria and supermarket.

Picnicking saves lots of euros. At a *supermercado* or an open-air market (*mercado*), you can pick up cold cuts, cheese, rolls, yogurt, and other picnic treats. Ordering 100 grams of cheese (*cien gramos*) is about a quarter-pound, enough for two sandwiches.

Shopkeepers will sell small quantities of produce (like a couple of apples or some carrots), but it's customary to let the merchant choose for you; watch locals and imitate. Either say or indicate by gesturing how much you want.

For beverages, you can get juice (look for 100% on the label), beer, or wine. To save on drinks, I fill my water bottle with tap water.

Even on a budget, picnics can be an adventure in high cuisine. Be daring. It's fairly cheap to buy a little bit of anything.

SLEEPING

I favor hotels and restaurants that are handy to your sightseeing activities. Rather than list hotels scattered throughout a city, I choose hotels in my favorite neighborhoods.

Spain's high season (temporada alta), with the highest prices, is from July to September. Shoulder season (temporada media) is roughly April through June plus October. Low season (temporada baja) runs from November through March. Book your accommodations well in advance, particularly if you'll be traveling during busy times (such as Semana Santa—Holy Week—in Spain, especially in the south). See page 462 for a list of major holidays and festivals in Spain; for tips on making reservations, see page 445.

Rates and Deals

I've described my recommended accommodations using a Sleep Code (see sidebar). The prices I list are for one-night stays in peak season, and assume you're booking directly with the hotel (not through an online hotel-booking engine or TI). Booking services extract a commission from the hotel, which logically closes the door on special deals. Book direct.

My recommended hotels each have a website (often with a built-in booking form) and an email address; you can expect a response in English within a day (and often sooner).

If you're on a budget, it's smart to email several hotels to ask for their best price. Comparison-shop and make your choice. In general, prices can soften if you do any of the following: offer to pay cash, stay at least three nights, mention this book, or try asking for a cheaper room or a discount.

Types of Accommodations

Spanish hotels come with a handy government-regulated classification system. Look for a blue-and-white plaque by the hotel door indicating the category.

Hotel (H): The most comfortable and expensive accommodation option (rated with stars).

Hotel-Residencia (HR) and Hostal-Residencia (HsR): Hotels without restaurants.

Parador: A government-run inn, often in a refurbished castle or palace. These can be expensive unless you qualify for a discounted rate (check www.parador.es).

Hostal (Hs): Less expensive than a hotel, but still rated by stars. Don't confuse hostales with youth hostels.

Pensión (P), Casa de Huéspedes (CH), and Fonda (F): Cheaper, usually family-run places.

Albergue Juvenil: Basic hostel.

Casa Particular: Private home renting budget rooms.

Hotels

Spain offers some of the best accommodations values in Western Europe. Most places are government-regulated, with posted prices. Hoteliers are encouraged to quote prices with the 10 percent IVA tax included. If you have any doubts, ask.

Spain has stringent restrictions on smoking in public places. Smoking is not permitted in common areas, but hotels can designate 10 percent of their rooms for smokers.

Some hotels don't use central heat before November 1 and after April 1 (unless it's unusually cold); prepare for cool evenings if you travel in spring and fall. Summer can be extremely hot. Consider air-conditioning, fans, and noise (since you'll want your window open). Many rooms come with mini refrigerators.

Street noise in Spain is high (even late at night), and walls and doors tend to be thin—earplugs are a necessity. Always ask to see your room first. If you suspect night noise will be a problem, request a quiet (tranquilo) room in the back or on an upper floor (piso alto). In most cases, view rooms (con vista) come with street

Sleep Code

Price Rankings

To help you easily sort through my listings, I've divided the accommodations into three categories, based on the highest price for a basic double room with bath during high season:

$$$ **Higher Priced**

$$ **Moderately Priced**

$ **Lower Priced**

Prices can change without notice; verify the hotel's current rates online or by email. For the best prices, always book directly with the hotel.

Abbreviations

I use the following code to describe accommodations in this book. Prices listed are per room, not per person. When a price range is given for a type of room (such as double rooms listed for €100-150), it means the price fluctuates with the season, size of room, or length of stay; expect to pay the upper end for peak-season stays, especially in resort areas.

S= Single room (or price for one person in a double).

D= Double or twin room. "Double beds" can be two twins sheeted together and are big enough for nonromantic couples.

T= Triple (generally a double bed with a single).

Q= Quad (usually two double beds; adding an extra child's bed to a T is usually cheaper).

b= Private bathroom with toilet and shower or tub.

According to this code, a couple staying at a "Db-€140" hotel would pay a total of €140 for a double room with a private bathroom. Unless otherwise noted, breakfast is not included, hotel staff speak basic English, and credit cards are accepted. Some hotels include the 10 percent IVA tax in the room price; others tack it on to your bill. If the city adds a room tax on top of the national IVA tax, it generally isn't included in the rates I list.

There's almost always free Wi-Fi and/or a guest computer available.

noise. You'll often sleep better and for less money in a room without a view.

Hoteliers can be a great help and source of advice. Most know their city well, and can assist you with everything from public transit and airport connections to finding a good restaurant, the nearest launderette, or Wi-Fi hotspots.

Even at the best places, mechanical breakdowns occur: air-conditioning malfunctions, sinks leak, hot water turns cold, and toilets gurgle and smell. Report your concerns clearly and calmly at the front desk. For more complicated problems, don't expect instant results. Any legitimate place is legally required to have a complaint book (libro de reclamaciones). A request for this book will generally prompt the hotelier to solve your problem to keep you from writing a complaint.

To guard against theft in your room, keep valuables out of sight. Some rooms come with a safe, and other hotels have safes at the front desk, though I've never

Making Hotel Reservations

Reserve your rooms several weeks in advance—or as soon as you've pinned down your travel dates. Note that some national holidays merit your making reservations far in advance (see page 462).

Requesting a Reservation: It's easiest to book your room through the hotel's website. (For the best rates, always use the hotel's official site and not a booking agency's site.) If there's no reservation form, or for complicated requests, send an email (see below for a sample request). Most recommended hotels take reservations in English.

The hotelier wants to know:

- the number and type of rooms you need
- the number of nights you'll stay
- your date of arrival (use the European style for writing dates: day/month/year)
- your date of departure
- any special needs (such as bathroom in the room or down the hall, cheapest room, twin beds vs. double bed, and so on)

Sample Email Request

From:	rick@ricksteves.com
Sent:	Today
To:	info@hotelcentral.com
Subject:	Reservation request for 19-22 July

Dear Hotel Central,
I would like to reserve a room for 2 people for 3 nights, arriving 19 July and departing 22 July. If possible, I would like a quiet room with a double bed and private bathroom inside the room.

Please let me know if you have a room available and the price.

Thank you!
Rick Steves

Confirming a Reservation: Most places will request a credit-card number to hold your room. If they don't have a secure online reservation form—look for the https—you can email it (I do), but it's safer to share that confidential info via a phone call or two emails (splitting your number between them).

Canceling a Reservation: If you must cancel, it's courteous—and smart—to do so with as much notice as possible, especially for smaller family-run places. Be warned that cancellation policies can be strict; read the fine print or ask about these before you book. Internet deals may require prepayment, with no refunds for cancellations.

Reconfirming a Reservation: Always call or email to reconfirm your room reservation a few days in advance. For B&Bs or very small hotels, I call again on my day of arrival to tell my host what time I expect to get there (especially important if arriving late—after 17:00).

Phoning: For tips on how to call hotels overseas, see page 449.

The Good and Bad of Online Reviews

User-generated travel review websites—such as TripAdvisor, Booking.com, and Yelp—give you access to actual reports—good and bad—from travelers who have experienced the hotel, restaurant, tour, or attraction.

While these sites try hard to weed out bogus users, I've seen hotels "bribe" guests (for example, offer a free breakfast) in exchange for a positive review. Nor can you always give credence to negative reviews: Different people have different expectations.

A user-generated review is based on the experience of one person, who likely stayed at one hotel and ate at a few restaurants, and doesn't have much of a basis for comparison. A guidebook is the work of a trained researcher who visited many alternatives to assess their relative value. When I've checked out top-rated TripAdvisor listings in various towns, I've found that some are gems but just as many are duds.

Guidebooks and review websites both have their place, and in many ways, they're complementary. If a hotel or restaurant is well reviewed in a guidebook, and also gets good ratings on one of these sites, it's likely a winner.

bothered using one.

Checkout can pose problems if surprise charges pop up on your bill. If you settle your bill the afternoon before you leave, you'll have time to discuss and address any points of contention (before 19:00, when the night shift usually arrives).

Above all, keep a positive attitude. Remember, you're on vacation. If your hotel is a disappointment, spend more time out enjoying the city you came to see.

Hostels

A hostel (*albergue juvenil*) provides cheap dorm beds for about €20-30 per night. Family and double rooms may be available on request. Travelers of any age are welcome. Most hostels offer kitchen facilities, guest computers, Wi-Fi, and a self-service laundry. Most hostels provide all bedding, including sheets.

There are two kinds of hostels: **Independent hostels** tend to be easygoing,

colorful, and informal (no membership required); try www.hostelworld.com, www.hostelz.com, or www.hostels.com. **Official hostels** are part of Hostelling International (HI), share an online booking site (www.hihostels.com), and typically require that you either have a membership card or pay extra per night.

Other Accommodation Options

Renting an apartment, house, or villa can be a fun and cost-effective way to go local. Websites such as Booking.com, Airbnb, VRBO, and FlipKey let you browse properties and correspond directly with European property owners or managers.

Airbnb and Roomorama also list rooms in private homes. Beds range from air-mattress-in-living-room basic to plush-B&B-suite posh. If you want a place to sleep that's free, Couchsurfing.org is a vagabond's alternative to Airbnb. It lists millions of members who host fellow "surfers" in their homes.

STAYING CONNECTED

Staying connected in Europe gets easier and cheaper every year. The simplest solution is to bring your own device—mobile phone, tablet, or laptop—and use it just as you would at home (following the tips below, such as connecting to free Wi-Fi whenever possible). Another option is to buy a European SIM card for your mobile phone—either your US phone or one you buy in Europe. Or you can travel without a mobile device and use European landlines and computers to connect. Each of these options is described below, and you'll find even more details at www.ricksteves.com/phoning.

Using Your Mobile Device in Europe

Roaming with your mobile device in Europe doesn't have to be expensive. These budget tips and options will keep your costs in check.

Use free Wi-Fi whenever possible. You can access the Internet, send texts, and even make voice calls over Wi-Fi. It's smart to save most of your online tasks for Wi-Fi unless you have an unlimited-data plan.

Most accommodations in Europe offer free Wi-Fi (pronounced wee-fee in Spanish). Many cafés—including Starbucks and McDonald's—have hotspots for customers; look for signs offering it and ask for their Wi-Fi password when you buy something. You'll also often find Wi-Fi at TIs, city squares, major museums, public-transit hubs, airports, and aboard trains and buses.

Sign up for an international plan for your mobile phone. Most providers offer a global calling plan that cuts the per-minute cost of phone calls and texts, and a flat-fee data plan that includes a certain amount of megabytes. Your normal plan may already include international coverage (T-Mobile's does).

Before your trip, call your provider or check online to confirm that your phone will work in Europe, and research your provider's international rates. A day or two before you leave, activate the plan by calling your provider or logging on to your mobile phone account. Remember to cancel your plan (if necessary) when your trip's over.

Minimize the use of your cellular network. When you can't find Wi-Fi, you can use your cellular network—convenient but slower and potentially expensive—to connect to the Internet, text, or make voice calls. When you're done, avoid further charges by manually switching off "data roaming" or "cellular data" (in your device's Settings menu; if you don't know how to switch it off, ask your service provider or Google it). Another way to make sure you're not accidentally using data roaming is to put your device in "airplane" or "flight" mode (which also disables phone calls and texts, as well as data), and then turn on Wi-Fi as needed.

Don't use your cellular network for bandwidth-gobbling tasks, such as Skyping, downloading apps, and watching YouTube—save these for when you're on Wi-Fi. Using a navigation app such as Google Maps can take lots of data, so use this sparingly.

Limit automatic updates. By default, your device is constantly checking for a data connection and updating apps. It's smart to disable these features (in your device's Setting menu) so they'll only update when you're on Wi-Fi, and to change your device's email settings from "auto-retrieve" to "manual" (or from "push" to "fetch").

It's also a good idea to keep track of your data usage. On your device's menu, look for "cellular data usage" or "mobile data" and reset the counter at the start of your trip.

Use Skype or other calling/messaging apps for cheaper calls and texts. Certain apps let you make voice or video calls or send texts over the Internet for free or

Tips on Internet Security

Using the Internet while traveling brings added security risks, whether you're accessing the Internet with your own device or at a public terminal using a shared network.

First, make sure that your device is running the latest version of its operating system and security software. Next, ensure that your device is password- or passcode-protected, so thieves can't access your information if your device is stolen. For extra security, set passwords on apps that access key info (such as email or Facebook).

On the road, use only legitimate Wi-Fi hotspots. Ask the hotel or café staff for the specific name of their Wi-Fi network, and make sure you log on to that exact one. Hackers sometimes create a bogus hotspot with a similar or vague name (such as "Hotel Europa Free Wi-Fi"). The best Wi-Fi networks require entering a password.

Be especially cautious when checking your online banking, credit-card statements, or other personal-finance accounts. Internet security experts advise against accessing these sites while traveling. Even if you're using your own mobile device at a password-protected hotspot, any hacker who's logged on to the same network may be able see what you're doing. If you do need to log on to a banking website, use a hard-wired connection (such as an Ethernet cable in your hotel room) or a cellular network, which is safer than Wi-Fi.

Never share your credit-card number (or any other sensitive information) online unless you know that the site is secure. A secure site displays a little padlock icon, and the URL begins with https (instead of the usual http).

cheap. If you're bringing a tablet or laptop, you can also use them for voice calls and texts. All you have to do is log on to a Wi-Fi network, then contact any of your friends or family members who are also online and signed into the same service. You can make voice and video calls using Skype, Viber, FaceTime, and Google+ Hangouts. If the connection is bad, try making an audio-only call.

You can also make voice calls from your device to telephones worldwide for just a few cents per minute using Skype, Viber, or Hangouts if you pre-buy credit.

To text for free over Wi-Fi, try apps like Google+ Hangouts, What's App, Viber, and Facebook Messenger. Apple's iMessage connects with other Apple users, but make sure you're on Wi-Fi to avoid data charges.

Using a European SIM Card in a Mobile Phone

This option works well for those who want to make a lot of voice calls at cheap local rates. Either buy a phone in Europe (as little as $40 from mobile-phone shops anywhere), or bring an "unlocked" US phone (check with your carrier about unlocking it). With an unlocked phone, you can replace the original SIM card (the microchip that stores info about the phone) with one that will work with a European provider.

In Europe, buy a European SIM card. Inserted into your phone, this card gives you a European phone number—and European rates. SIM cards are sold at mobile-phone shops, department-store electronics counters, some newsstands,

Phoning Cheat Sheet

Calling from the US to Europe: Dial 011 (US access code), country code (34 for Spain), and phone number.* To call one of my recommended hotels in Madrid, I dial 011-34-915-212-900.

Calling from Europe to the US: Dial 00 (Europe access code), country code (1 for US), area code, and phone number. To call my office in Edmonds, Washington, I dial 00-1-425-771-8303.

Calling country to country within Europe: Dial 00, country code, and phone number.* To call the Madrid hotel from Germany, I dial 00-34-915-212-900.

Calling within Spain: Dial the entire phone number. To call the Madrid hotel from Barcelona, I dial 915-212-900 (Spain doesn't use area codes).

Calling with a mobile phone: The "+" sign on your mobile phone automatically selects the access code you need (for a "+" sign, press and hold "0").* To call the Madrid hotel from the US or Europe, I dial +34-915-212-900.

For more dialing help, see www.howtocallabroad.com.

If the phone number starts with zero, drop it for all countries except Italy.

Country	Country Code	Country	Country Code
Austria	43	Hungary	36
Belgium	32	Ireland/N Ireland	353/44
Czech Republic	420	Italy	39
Denmark	45	Netherlands	31
England	44	Norway	47
France	33	Portugal	351
Germany	49	Scotland	44
Gibraltar	350	Spain	34
Greece	30	Switzerland	41

and even vending machines. Costing about $5-10, they usually include about that much prepaid calling credit, with no contract and no commitment. You can still use your phone's Wi-Fi function to get online. To get a SIM card that also includes data costs (including roaming), figure on paying $15-30 for one month of data within the country you bought it. This can be cheaper than data roaming through your home provider. To get the best rates, buy a new SIM card whenever you arrive in a new country.

I like to buy SIM cards at a mobile-phone shop where there's a clerk to help explain the options and brands. Certain brands—including Lebara and Lycamobile, both of which operate in multiple European countries—are more reliable and economical. Ask the clerk to help you insert your SIM card, set it up, and show you how to use it. In some countries—

including Spain—you'll be required to register the SIM card with your passport as an antiterrorism measure (which may mean you can't use the phone for the first hour or two).

When you run out of credit, you can top it up at newsstands, tobacco shops, mobile-phone stores, or many other businesses (look for your SIM card's logo in the window), or online.

Using Landlines and Computers in Europe

Phones in your **hotel room** can be inexpensive for local calls and calls made with cheap international phone cards (*tarjetas telefónicas con códigos;* sold at many post offices, newsstands, street kiosks, tobacco shops, and train stations). You'll either get a prepaid card with a toll-free number and a scratch-to-reveal PIN code, or a code printed on a receipt; to make a call, dial the toll-free number, follow the prompts, enter the code, then dial your number.

Most hotels charge a fee for placing calls from your room—ask for rates. Since you're never charged for receiving calls, it's better to have someone from the US call you in your room.

You'll see **public pay phones** in post offices and train stations. The phones generally come with multilingual instructions, and most work with insertable phone cards (*tarjetas telefónicas;* sold at post offices, newsstands, etc.). To use the card, simply take the phone off the hook, insert the card, wait for a dial tone, and dial away. With the exception of Great Britain, European countries have their own insertable phone card—so your Spanish card won't work in an Italian phone.

Cheap **call shops** (*locutorios),* often located in train-station neighborhoods, advertise low international rates. Before making your call, be completely clear on the rates (e.g., if there's a charge per unit, find out how long a unit is).

It's always possible to find **public com-**

puters: at your hotel (many have one in their lobby for guests to use), at an Internet café, or a library (ask your hotelier or the TI for the nearest location). If typing on a European keyboard, use the "Alt Gr" key to the right of the space bar to insert the extra symbol that appears on some keys. If you can't locate a special character (such as @), simply copy it from a Web page and paste it into your email message.

Mail

You can mail one package per day to yourself worth up to $200 duty-free from Europe to the US (mark it "personal purchases"). If you're sending a gift to someone, mark it "unsolicited gift." For details, visit www.cbp.gov, and search for "Know Before You Go."

The Spanish postal service works fine, but for quick transatlantic delivery (in either direction), consider services such as DHL (www.dhl.com).

TRANSPORTATION

This section covers the basics on trains, buses, long-distance taxis, rental cars, and flights.

Choosing between public transit or driving? While a car gives you more freedom to explore the countryside, Spain's trains and buses take you effortlessly from city to city, usually dropping you in the center, often near a TI. Cars are worthless in big cities.

Trains

RENFE is the acronym for Spain's national train system. For information and reservations, dial RENFE's number (toll tel. 902-320-320) from anywhere in the country, or visit www.renfe.com.

Spain's fast trains are pricier than slow trains, but all are cheaper per mile than their northern European counterparts. As is usual in Europe, first-class tickets cost 50 percent more than second class—often as much as a domestic flight.

In general, if you're on a tight budget, go for second class and compare the different options (see "Types of Trains" below) before buying. Assume you'll need to make reservations for fast trains. Faster trains also offer significant discounts for advance booking, available starting about two months before your travel date (see "Buying Train Tickets/Online," later). Note that discounted tickets come with restrictions, such as being nonrefundable and nonchangeable. Be sure to read all the details carefully at time of purchase.

Types of Trains

Spain categorizes trains this way:

The high-speed train called the AVE (AH-vay, stands for *Alta Velocidad Española*) whisks travelers between Madrid and Toledo in 30 minutes, Madrid and Sevilla or Barcelona in three hours, and Madrid and Málaga in less than three hours. AVE trains can be priced differently according to their time of departure. Peak hours (*punta*) are most expensive, followed by *llano* and *valle* (quietest and cheapest times). AVE is almost entirely covered by the Eurail Pass (book ahead, seat reservation fee from Madrid to Sevilla costs Eurailers about $12 in second class; $29 for first class).

Other fast, pricey trains are the Alvia and Talgo. Avant, Euromed, and Altaria are generally as fast as AVE but cheaper. Intercity and Electro trains are a bit slower, cheaper, and less comfortable.

The slow trains are the Rápido, Tranvía,

Spain's trains are modern and efficient.

Semidirecto, and Expreso. Cercanías and Rodalies are commuter trains for big-city workers and small-town tourists. And the slowest trains are Regional and Correo. Spain loves to name trains, so you may encounter types of trains not listed here.

Salidas means "departures," and *llegadas* means "arrivals." On train schedules, "LMXJVSD" stands for the days of the week in Spanish, starting with Monday. A train that runs "LMXJV-D" doesn't run on Saturdays. *Laborables* can mean Monday through Friday or Monday through Saturday.

Overnight Trains: For long trips, you can go overnight on the train or consider flying (domestic shuttle flights are generally less than $100). Overnight trains (and buses) are usually cheaper and slower than the daytime rides, not counting sleeper fees. Most overnight trains have rental berths and beds, not included in the cost of your train ticket or rail pass. A sleeping berth (*litera*) costs extra. Night trains are popular, so it's smart to reserve in advance, even from home.

Rail Passes vs. Tickets

If you're traveling only in Spain or Iberia, buying tickets as you go, and using a combination of trains and buses, is generally cheaper than buying a rail pass. As an added plus, buying individual train tickets (either in advance or as you travel) gives you better access to seat reservations, which are limited for rail-pass holders. And individual ticket prices already include seat reservations when required (for instance, for fast trains and longer distances).

However, for multi-country trips to France and beyond, a rail pass can offer better value. For detailed advice on whether a rail pass makes sense for your trip, visit www.ricksteves.com/rail.

Buying Train Tickets

Trains can sell out, so it's smart to buy your tickets a day in advance, even for

Public Transportation Routes in Iberia

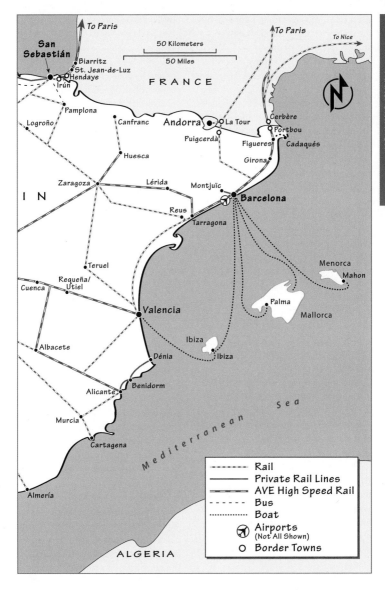

short rides. You have four options for buying train tickets: at a travel agency, at the station, by phone, or online.

Travel Agency: Most travelers find it easiest to go to an English-speaking travel agency, since train-station ticket offices can get very crowded. The El Corte Inglés department stores (with locations in most Spanish cities) often have travel agencies inside. Look for a train sticker in agency windows. Their service is worth the nominal service fee they charge.

At the Station: You will likely have to wait in a line to buy your ticket. First find the correct line—at bigger stations, there might be separate windows for short-distance, long-distance, advance, and "today" (para hoy) tickets. To avoid wasting time in the wrong line, read the signs carefully, and ask a local (or a clerk at an information window) which line you need. You might have to take a number—watch others and follow their lead. While clerks accept regular US credit cards, most RENFE ticket machines only take chip-and-PIN credit cards.

As another option, you could buy tickets or reservations at the RENFE offices located in more than 100 city centers. These are more central and multilingual—also less crowded and confusing—than the train station.

By Phone: You can purchase your ticket by phone (toll tel. 902-240-202), then pick it up at the station by punching your confirmation code (localizador) into one of the automated machines. Discounts up to 40 percent off are offered a week or more ahead by phone (and at stations).

You can also reserve tickets by phone, then buy them at the station, which you must do a few days before departure (at a ticket window, usually signed "venta anticipada"). You can't pay for reserved tickets at the station on your day of travel.

Online: Although the website www.renfe.com is useful for confirming schedules and prices, you cannot dependably buy tickets online unless you have a European credit card or use PayPal. The website rejects nearly every attempt to use a US card. With patience and enough Spanish language skill, you may be able to nab an online discount of up to 60 percent (available two weeks to two months ahead of travel). Online vendors based in the US include www.raileurope.com and www.petrabax.com (higher fees).

Rail Passes

You can buy a Eurail Spain "flexi" rail pass that allows train travel for a given number of days over a longer period of time, but you'll pay separately ($10-35) for seat reservations on all trains.

RENFE also offers their own eticketed "Renfe Spain Pass" that works entirely differently. It counts trips instead of calendar days, requires reservations to be made in chronological order, and is only sold on their website.

If your trip also includes a neighboring country, consider the Eurail France-Spain, Portugal-Spain, or Italy-Spain passes (see chart on page 455). A Eurail Select pass lets you travel even farther. These passes are sold only outside Europe. Even if you have a rail pass, use buses when they're more convenient and direct than the trains. Remember to reserve ahead for the fast AVE trains and overnight journeys.

Buses

Spain has a number of different bus companies (usually clustered within one main building in big cities), sometimes running buses to the same destinations and using the same transfer points. Bus service on holidays, Saturdays, and especially Sundays can be less frequent.

The larger stations have a consolidated information desk with all the schedules. In smaller stations, check the destinations and schedules posted on each office window. A good place to begin researching schedules and carriers online is www.movelia.es.

Rail Passes

Prices listed are subject to change. For the latest prices, details, and train schedules (and easy online ordering), see www.ricksteves.com/rail.

"Saver" prices are per person for two or more people traveling together. "Youth" means under age 26. Up to two kids age 4-11 travel free with each adult on any Eurail-brand pass. Addidional kids pay the youth rate. Kids under age 4 travel free.

SPAIN PASS

	1st Class	2nd Class
3 days in 1 month	$245	$197
4 days in 1 month	290	233
5 days in 1 month	328	264
8 days in 1 month	431	346

Map key:

Approximate point-to-point one-way second-class rail fares in US dollars. First class costs 50 percent more. Add up fares for your itinerary to see whether a rail pass will save you money. Dashed lines are buses and ferries (not covered by passes).

SPAIN-PORTUGAL PASS

	1st Class Adult	2nd Class Adult	1st Class Saver	2nd Class Saver
4 days in 2 months	$307	$247	$262	$211
5 days in 2 months	352	283	300	241
6 days in 2 months	392	315	334	268
8 days in 2 months	466	374	397	318
10 days in 2 months	532	427	453	364

SELECTPASS

This pass covers travel in four adjacent countries.

	Individual 1st Class	Saver 1st Class	Youth 1st Class	Youth 2nd Class
5 days in 2 months	$459	$391	$369	$301
6 days in 2 months	502	428	403	329
8 days in 2 months	584	498	469	383
10 days in 2 months	667	568	535	436

FRANCE–SPAIN PASS or ITALY–SPAIN PASS

Italy-Spain pass does not cover travel through France.

	1st Class Adult	2nd Class Adult	1st Class Saver	2nd Class Saver	1st Class Youth	2nd Class Youth
4 days in 2 months	$332	$267	$283	$228	$267	$218
5 days in 2 months	377	303	321	258	303	247
6 days in 2 months	418	336	356	286	336	274
8 days in 2 months	493	396	420	337	396	322
10 days in 2 months	559	449	476	382	449	365

If you'll need to transfer buses, make sure to look for a bus with the same name/logo as the company you bought the ticket from. If your connection requires a transfer to another company's bus in a different city, don't count on getting help from the originating clerk to figure out the onward connection.

If you arrive in a city by bus and plan to leave by bus, stick around the station upon your arrival to check your departure options and buy a ticket in advance if necessary (and possible). If you're downtown, need a ticket, and the bus station isn't central, save time by asking at the tourist office about travel agencies that sell bus tickets.

Drivers and station personnel rarely speak English. Buses generally lack WCs, but they stop every two hours or so for a break (usually 15 minutes, but can be up to 30). Drivers announce how long the stop will be, but if in doubt, ask the driver, "How many minutes here?" *("¿Cuántos minutos aquí?")* so you know if you have time to get out. Listen for the bus horn as a final call before departure. Bus stations have WCs (rarely with toilet paper) and cafés that offer quick and slightly overpriced food.

Taxis

Most taxis are reliable and cheap. Drivers generally respond kindly to the request, "How much is it to the Prado, more or less?" *("¿Cuánto cuesta a Prado, más o menos?")*. Spanish taxis have extra supplements (for luggage, nighttime, Sundays, train/bus-station or airport pickup, and so on). Locals generally don't tip cabbies, but you could round up the fare a bit if you're happy with the service. City rides cost €4-6. Keep a map in your hand so the cabbie knows (or thinks) you know where you're going. Big cities have plenty of taxis. In many cases, couples travel by cab for little more than the cost of two bus or subway tickets.

Renting a Car

If you're renting a car in Spain, bring your driver's license. You're also required to have an International Driving Permit—an official translation of your driver's license (sold at your local AAA office for $15 plus the cost of two passport-type photos; see www.aaa.com). While that's the letter of the law, I've rented cars without having this permit.

Research car rentals before you go. It's cheaper to arrange most car rentals from the US. Compare rates among several companies. Most of the major US rental agencies (including Avis, Budget, Enterprise, Hertz, and Thrifty) have offices throughout Europe. Also consider the two major Europe-based agencies, Europcar and Sixt. It can be cheaper to use a consolidator, such as Auto Europe/Kemwel (www.autoeurope.com) or Europe by Car (www.europebycar.com), which compares rates at several companies to get you the best deal—but because you're working with a middleman, it's especially important to ask in advance about add-on fees and restrictions.

Always read the fine print carefully for add-on charges—such as one-way drop-off fees (usually minimal within one country but high for dropping in a neighboring country), airport surcharges, or mandatory insurance policies—that aren't included in the "total price." You may need to query rental agents pointedly to find out your actual cost.

Figure on paying roughly $230 for a one-week rental. Allow extra for supplemental insurance, fuel, tolls, and parking. For the best deal, rent by the week with unlimited mileage. To save money on fuel, you can request a diesel car. I normally rent the smallest, least-expensive model with a stick shift (generally cheaper than an automatic). Almost all rentals are manual by default, so if you need an automatic, request one in advance; be aware that these cars are usually larger models and not as maneuverable on narrow, winding roads (such as in Andalucía's hill towns).

If you'll need a car for three weeks or more, look into leasing; you'll save money on insurance and taxes. Leasing, which has few age restrictions, can also be a good option for drivers that are younger (under age 21) or older (age 75 and up), who can be turned away by rental companies. See "Leasing," later.

Picking Up Your Car: Big companies have offices in most cities; ask whether they can pick you up at your hotel. Small local rental companies can be cheaper but aren't as flexible.

Compare pickup costs (downtown can be less expensive than the airport) and explore drop-off options. Always check the hours of the location you choose: Many rental offices close from midday Saturday until Monday morning and, in smaller towns, at lunchtime.

When you pick up the rental car, check it thoroughly and make sure any damage is noted on your rental agreement. Find out how your car's lights, turn signals, wipers, radio, and fuel cap function, and know what kind of fuel the car takes (diesel vs. unleaded).

Before returning a car at a big-city train station or downtown agency, get precise details on the drop-off location and hours, and allow ample time to find it. Make sure the agent verifies the car's condition with you. Some drivers take pictures of the returned vehicle as proof of its condition.

Car Insurance Options

When you rent a car, you are liable for a very high deductible, sometimes equal to the entire value of the car. Limit your financial risk with one of these three options: Buy Collision Damage Waiver (CDW) coverage with a low or zero deductible from the car-rental company, get coverage through your credit card (free, if your card automatically includes zero-deductible coverage), or get collision insurance as part of a larger travel-insurance policy.

Basic **CDW** includes a very high deductible (typically $1,000-1,500). Though each rental company has its own variation, basic CDW costs $10-30 a day (figure roughly 30 percent extra) and reduces your liability, but does not eliminate it. When you reserve or pick up the car, you'll be offered the chance to "buy

Traveling by car

down" the basic deductible to zero (for an additional $10-30/day; this is sometimes called "super CDW" or "zero-deductible coverage").

If you opt for **credit-card coverage,** there's a catch. You'll technically have to decline all coverage offered by the car-rental company, which means they can place a hold on your card (which can be up to the full value of the car). In case of damage, it can be time-consuming to resolve the charges with your credit-card company. Before you decide on this option, quiz your credit-card company about how it works.

If you're already purchasing a **travel-insurance policy** for your trip, adding collision coverage is an option. For example, Travel Guard (www.travelguard.com) sells affordable renter's collision insurance as an add-on to its other policies.

For more on car-rental insurance, see www.ricksteves.com/cdw.

Leasing

For trips of three weeks or more, consider leasing (which automatically includes zero-deductible collision and theft insurance). By technically buying and then selling back the car, you save lots of money on tax and insurance. Leasing provides you with a brand-new car with unlimited mileage and a 24-hour emergency assistance program. You can lease for as little as 21 days to as long as five and a half months. Car leases must be arranged from the US. One of many companies offering affordable lease packages is Europe by Car (www.europebycar.com/lease).

Driving

Driving in rural Spain is great—traffic is sparse and roads are generally good. But a car is a pain in big cities such as Madrid (park it). Drive defensively. If you're involved in an accident, you will be in for a monumental headache. Spaniards love to tailgate. Don't take it personally; let impatient drivers pass you so you can enjoy the drive.

Road Rules: Seatbelts are required by law. Children under 12 must ride in the back seat, and children up to age 3 must have a child seat. You must put on a reflective safety vest any time you get out of your car on the side of a highway or unlit road (most rental-car companies provide one—but check when you pick up the car). Those who use eyeglasses are required by law to have a spare pair in the car. It is illegal to talk on a cell phone while driving (unless using a fully hands-free system).

Drivers must turn on headlights during daylight hours if visibility is poor. Spain does not allow a right turn at a red light. On expressways it's illegal to pass drivers on the right. Ask your car-rental company about these rules, or check the US State Department website (www.travel.state. gov, search for your country in the "Learn about your destination" box, then click on

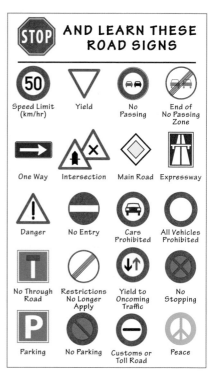

STOP AND LEARN THESE ROAD SIGNS

Speed Limit (km/hr)

Yield

No Passing

End of No Passing Zone

One Way

Intersection

Main Road

Expressway

Danger

No Entry

Cars Prohibited

All Vehicles Prohibited

No Through Road

Restrictions No Longer Apply

Yield to Oncoming Traffic

No Stopping

Parking

No Parking

Customs or Toll Road

Peace

Spain by Car

FRANCE

Santiago de Compostela · Comillas · Santillana del Mar · St-Jean-de-Luz
285M · 6H
Bilbao · 20M · .75H
80M · 1.5H
10M · .25H · Potes · 125M · 2.5H · San Sebastián
200M · 4.5H · 95M · 2.5H · 50M · 1.5H · 60M · 1.25H
270M · 5.5H · León · 120M · 2H · 55M · 1.5H · Barcelona to Cerbère (French border) 110m · 2h
140M · 2.5H · 125M · 2.25H (VIA VITORIA)
Porto · 220M · 4H · 210M · 3.5H · Burgos · Pamplona
75M · 1.25H · 150M · 3H · 150M · 3.5H · 115M 2H
Salamanca · 60M 1.5H · 55M 1H · Segovia · 115M · 3H
Coimbra · 185M · 4H · Ávila · 60M 1.25H · Zaragoza · Barcelona
520M · 9H · Madrid · 205M 3.5H · 220M · 3.5H
Lisbon · 315M · 5.5H · 70M · 1.5H · 45M 1H · Toledo · 225M · 3.5H
Évora · S P A I N
85M 1.5H · 200M · 3.5H · 220M 4H · Valencia
180M · 3H · 90M · 2H · Córdoba · 100M 3.5H · 330M · 5.5H
Salema · Sevilla · 155M · 3H · 225M 3H · Granada
55M · 1.5H · 80M · 2H · Ronda · 65M · 1.25H
Arcos · 120M · 2H
70M · 2H · Nerja
50M · 1.25H · 70M · 1.5H · 1H
Tarifa · 60M · 1.75H
.5H FERRY
Tangier · Gibraltar

m = miles
h = hours
···· = ferry

NOTE: YOUR TIMES MAY VARY BASED ON TRAFFIC, CONSTRUCTION & ROAD CONDITIONS.

"Travel and Transportation").

Navigation Apps: When driving in Europe, you can use the mapping app on your phone as long as you have an international data plan. Without a data plan (or to conserve data), you can rely on offline maps (via a mapping app or by downloading Google maps). As an alternative, you could rent a GPS device or bring your own GPS device from home (but you'll need to buy and download European maps before your trip).

A number of well-designed offline mapping apps allow you much of the convenience of online maps without any costly data demands. City Maps 2Go is popular; OffMaps and Navfree also offer good, zoomable offline maps—similar to Google Maps—for much of Europe.

Signs: In smaller towns, following signs to centro ciudad will get you to the heart of things. Learn the universal road signs (see illustration) and be ready to navigate by city and town names. Memorize some key road words: de sentido único (one way), despacio (slow), adelantamiento prohibido (no passing), and salida (exit). Mileage signs are in kilometers (to convert to miles, divide kilometers in half and add 10 percent of the original).

Freeways and Tolls: Spain's freeways come with tolls but save huge amounts of time. Each toll road (autopista de peaje) has its own pricing structure, so tolls vary (for example, Madrid-Toledo: €8.70; Bilbao-Irun/French border: €12.50). Near some major cities, you must prepay for each stretch of road you drive; on other routes, you take a ticket where you enter the freeway, and pay when you exit. Payment can be made in cash or by credit or debit card (credit-card-only lanes are labeled *"vias automáticas"*; cash lanes are *"vias manuales"*).

Traffic Cops: Watch for traffic radars and expect to be stopped for a routine check by the police; be sure your car-insurance form is up-to-date. Small towns come with speed traps and corruption. Tickets, especially for foreigners, are issued and paid for on the spot. Insist on a receipt *(recibo)*, so the money is less likely to end up in the cop's pocket.

Fuel: Gas and diesel prices are controlled and the same everywhere—about $6.50 a gallon for gas, and about $6 a gallon for diesel (gas is priced by the liter in Spain). Unleaded gas *(gasolina sin plomo)* is either *normal* or *super*. Note that diesel is called *diesel* or *gasóleo*—pay attention when filling your tank.

Theft and Parking: Choose parking places carefully. Stow valuables in the trunk during the day and leave nothing worth stealing in the car overnight. While you should avoid parking lots with twinkly asphalt, thieves break car windows anywhere, even at stoplights. If your car's a hatchback, take the trunk cover off at night so thieves can look in without breaking in. Try to make your car look locally owned by hiding the "tourist-owned" rental-company decals and putting a local newspaper in your front or back window. Parking attendants all over Spain holler, *"Nada en el coche"* ("Nothing in the car"). And they mean it. Ask your hotelier for advice on parking. In cities you can park safely but expensively in guarded lots.

Flights

The best comparison search engine for both international and intra-European flights is www.kayak.com. For inexpensive flights within Europe, try www.skyscanner.com or www.hipmunk.com; for inexpensive international flights, try www.vayama.com.

Flying to Europe: Start looking for international flights four to five months before your trip, especially for peak-season travel. Off-season tickets can be purchased a month or so in advance. Depending on your itinerary, it can be efficient to fly into one city and out of another.

Flying within Europe: If you're considering a train ride that's more than five hours long, a flight may save you both time and money. When comparing your options, factor in the time it takes to get to the airport and how early you'll need to arrive to check in.

These days you can fly within Europe on major airlines affordably for around $100 a flight. If you go instead with a budget airline such as easyJet or Ryanair, be aware of the potential drawbacks and restrictions: nonrefundable and non-changeable tickets, minimal or non-existent customer service, pricey and time-consuming treks to secondary airports, and stingy baggage allowances with steep overage fees. If you've got lots of luggage, a cheap flight can quickly become a bad deal. To avoid unpleasant surprises, read the small print before you book.

Flying to the US: Because security is extra tight for flights to the US, be sure to give yourself plenty of time at the airport. It's also important to charge your electronic devices before you board because security checks may require you to turn them on (see www.tsa.gov for latest rules).

RESOURCES FROM RICK STEVES

Books: *Rick Steves Best of Spain* is one of many books in my series on European travel, which includes country guidebooks, city guidebooks (Barcelona, Rome, Florence, Paris, London, etc.), Snapshot Guides (excerpted chapters from my country guides), Pocket Guides (full-color little books on big cities, including Barcelona), and my budget-travel skills handbook, *Rick Steves Europe Through the Back Door*. Most of my titles are available

Begin Your Trip at www.RickSteves.com

My mobile-friendly **website** is the place to explore Europe. You'll find thousands of fun articles, videos, photos, and radio interviews organized by country; a wealth of money-saving tips for planning your dream trip; monthly travel news dispatches; my travel talks and travel blog; my latest guidebook updates (www.ricksteves.com/update); and my free Rick Steves Audio Europe app. You can also follow me on Facebook and Twitter.

Our **Travel Forum** is an immense, yet well-groomed collection of message boards, where our travel-savvy community answers questions and shares their personal travel experiences (www.ricksteves.com/forums).

Our **online Travel Store** offers travel bags and accessories that will help you travel smarter and lighter. These include my popular bags (rolling carry-on and backpack versions, which I helped design...and live out of four months a year), money belts, totes, toiletries kits, adapters, other accessories, and a wide selection of guidebooks and planning maps.

Choosing the right **rail pass** for your trip—amid hundreds of options—can drive you nutty. Our website will help you find the perfect fit for your itinerary and your budget: We offer easy, one-stop shopping for rail passes, seat reservations, and point-to-point tickets.

Want to travel with greater efficiency and less stress? We organize **tours** with more than three dozen itineraries and more than 800 departures reaching the best destinations in this book...and beyond. Our Spain tours include Barcelona and Madrid in 8 days, the Basque Country of Spain and France in 9 days, a My Way: Spain "unguided" tour in 11 days, and Spain in 14 days. You'll enjoy great guides, a fun bunch of travel partners (with small groups of 24 to 28 travelers), and a roomy, comfortable bus. You'll find European adventures to fit every vacation length. For all the details, and to get our Tour Catalog and a free Rick Steves Tour Experience DVD (filmed on location during an actual tour), visit www.ricksteves.com or call us at 425/608-4217.

as ebooks. My phrase books—for Spanish, Italian, French, German, and Portuguese—are practical and budget-oriented. A more complete list of my titles appears near the end of this book.

Video: My public television series, *Rick Steves' Europe,* covers Europe from top to bottom with over 100 half-hour episodes. To watch full episodes online for free, see www.ricksteves.com/tv. Or to raise your travel I.Q. with video versions of our popular classes (including my talks on travel skills, packing smart, European art for travelers, travel as a political act, and individual talks covering most European countries), see www.ricksteves.com/travel-talks.

Audio: My weekly public radio show, *Travel with Rick Steves,* features interviews with travel experts from around the world. A complete archive of 10 years of programs (over 400 in all) is available in the radio section of www.ricksteves.com/radio. Most of this audio content is available for free through my **Rick Steves Audio Europe** app (see page 24).

HOLIDAYS AND FESTIVALS

This list includes selected festivals in major cities, plus national holidays (when banks and many sights close). Before planning your trip around a festival, verify its dates by checking the festival's website or TI sites (www.spain.info).

Jan 1	New Year's Day
Jan 6	Epiphany
Early Feb	La Candelaria (religious festival), Madrid
Feb 28	Day of Andalucía (some closures), Andalucía
Before Easter	Holy Week (Semana Santa)
March or April	Easter
After Easter	Easter Monday
April 12-17	April Fair (Feria de Abril), Sevilla
April 23	Sant Jordi (flowers and books), Barcelona
May 1	Labor Day (closures)
May 2	Dos de Mayo, Madrid
May 3	Fiesta de las Cruces (religious festival), Granada and Córdoba
Early May	Feria del Caballo (horse pageantry), Jerez
May 5	Ascension
May 15	San Isidro (religious festival), Madrid and Nerja
May or June	Pentecost and Whit Monday
May or June	Corpus Christi
June 24	Festival of St. John the Baptist (bonfires and fireworks)
June-July	International Festival of Music and Dance, Granada
July 6-14	Running of the Bulls (Fiesta de San Fermín), Pamplona
July 25	Feast Day of St. James, Santiago de Compostela
Aug	Gràcia Festival, Barcelona
Mid-Aug	Verbena de la Paloma (folk festival), Madrid
Aug 15	Assumption of Mary (religious festival)
Late Sept	La Mercé (parade), Barcelona
Late Sept	Feria de San Miguel (bullfights), Sevilla
Oct 12	Spanish National Day
Nov 1	All Saints' Day

Nov 9	Virgen de la Almudena, Madrid
Dec 6	Constitution Day
Dec 8	Feast of the Immaculate Conception
Dec 13	Feast of Santa Lucía
Dec 25	Christmas
Dec 31	New Year's Eve

CONVERSIONS AND CLIMATE

Numbers and Stumblers

- Europeans write a few of their numbers differently than we do. 1= *1*, 4 = *4*, 7 = *7*.
- In Europe, dates appear as day/month/year. Christmas is always 25/12.
- Commas are decimal points and decimals are commas. A dollar and a half is $1,50, and one thousand is 1.000.
- When counting with fingers, start with your thumb. If you hold up your first finger to request one item, you'll probably get two.
- What Americans call the second floor of a building is the first floor in Europe.
- On escalators and moving sidewalks, Europeans keep the left "lane" open for passing. Keep to the right.

Clothing and Shoe Sizes

Shoppers can use these US-to-European comparisons as guidelines.

Women: For clothing or shoe sizes, add 30 (US shirt size 10 = European size 40; US shoe size 8 = European size 38-39).

Men: For shirts, multiply by 2 and add about 8 (US size 15 = European size 38). For jackets and suits, add 10. For shoes, add 32-34.

Children: For clothing, subtract 1-2 sizes for small children and subtract 4 for juniors. For shoes up to size 13, add 16-18, and for sizes 1 and up, add 30-32.

Metric Conversions

A **kilogram** equals 1,000 grams and about 2.2 pounds. One hundred **grams** (a common unit of sale at markets) is about a quarter-pound.

One **liter** is about a quart, or almost four to a gallon.

A **kilometer** is six-tenths of a mile. To convert kilometers to miles, cut the kilometers in half and add back 10 percent of the original (120 km: 60 + 12 = 72 miles). One **meter** is 39 inches.

Using the **Celsius** scale, 0°C equals 32°F. To roughly convert Celsius to Fahrenheit, double the number and add 30. For weather, 28°C is 82°F—perfect. For health, 37°C is just right. At a launderette, 30°C is cold, 40°C is warm (default setting), and 60°C is hot.

Spain's Climate

First line, average daily high; second line, average daily low; third line, average days without rain. For worldwide weather statistics, see www.wunderground.com.

Madrid

J	F	M	A	M	J	J	A	S	O	N	D
47°	52°	59°	65°	70°	80°	87°	85°	77°	65°	55°	48°
35°	36°	41°	45°	50°	58°	63°	63°	57°	49°	42°	36°
23	21	21	21	21	25	29	28	24	23	21	21

Barcelona

J	F	M	A	M	J	J	A	S	O	N	D
55°	57°	60°	65°	71°	78°	82°	82°	77°	69°	62°	56°
43°	45°	48°	52°	57°	65°	69°	69°	66°	58°	51°	46°
26	23	23	21	23	24	27	25	23	22	24	25

Almería (Costa del Sol)

J	F	M	A	M	J	J	A	S	O	N	D
60°	61°	64°	68°	72°	78°	83°	84°	81°	73°	67°	62°
46°	47°	51°	55°	59°	65°	70°	71°	68°	60°	54°	49°
25	24	26	25	28	29	31	30	27	26	26	26

Packing Checklist

Clothing

- ☐ 5 shirts: long- & short-sleeve
- ☐ 2 pairs pants or skirt
- ☐ 1 pair shorts or capris
- ☐ 5 pairs underwear & socks
- ☐ 1 pair walking shoes
- ☐ Sweater or fleece top
- ☐ Rainproof jacket with hood
- ☐ Tie or scarf
- ☐ Swimsuit
- ☐ Sleepwear

Money

- ☐ Debit card
- ☐ Credit card(s)
- ☐ Hard cash ($20 bills)
- ☐ Money belt or neck wallet

Documents & Travel Info

- ☐ Passport
- ☐ Airline reservations
- ☐ Rail pass/train reservations
- ☐ Car-rental voucher
- ☐ Driver's license
- ☐ Student ID, hostel card, etc.
- ☐ Photocopies of all the above
- ☐ Hotel confirmations
- ☐ Insurance details
- ☐ Guidebooks & maps
- ☐ Notepad & pen
- ☐ Journal

Toiletries Kit

- ☐ Toiletries
- ☐ Medicines & vitamins
- ☐ First-aid kit
- ☐ Glasses/contacts/sunglasses (with prescriptions)
- ☐ Earplugs
- ☐ Packet of tissues (for WC)

Miscellaneous

- ☐ Daypack
- ☐ Sealable plastic baggies
- ☐ Laundry soap
- ☐ Clothesline
- ☐ Sewing kit
- ☐ Travel alarm/watch

Electronics

- ☐ Smartphone or mobile phone
- ☐ Camera & related gear
- ☐ Tablet/ereader/media player
- ☐ Laptop & flash drive
- ☐ Earbuds or headphones
- ☐ Chargers
- ☐ Plug adapters

Optional Extras

- ☐ Flipflops or slippers
- ☐ Mini-umbrella or poncho
- ☐ Travel hairdryer
- ☐ Belt
- ☐ Hat (for sun or cold)
- ☐ Picnic supplies
- ☐ Water bottle
- ☐ Fold-up tote bag
- ☐ Small flashlight
- ☐ Small binoculars
- ☐ Small towel or washcloth
- ☐ Inflatable pillow
- ☐ Tiny lock
- ☐ Address list (to mail postcards)
- ☐ Postcards/photos from home
- ☐ Extra passport photos
- ☐ Good book

Spanish Survival Phrases

Spanish has a guttural sound similar to the J in Baja California. In the phonetics, the symbol for this clearing-your-throat sound is the italicized *h*.

English	Spanish	Pronunciation
Good day.	*Buenos días.*	**bway**-nohs **dee**-ahs
Do you speak English?	*¿Habla Usted inglés?*	ah-blah oo-**stehd** een-**glays**
Yes. / No.	*Sí. / No.*	see / noh
I (don't) understand.	*(No) comprendo.*	(noh) kohm-**prehn**-doh
Please.	*Por favor.*	por fah-**bor**
Thank you.	*Gracias.*	**grah**-thee-ahs
I'm sorry.	*Lo siento.*	loh see-**ehn**-toh
Excuse me.	*Perdóneme.*	pehr-**doh**-nay-may
(No) problem.	*(No) problema.*	(noh) proh-**blay**-mah
Good.	*Bueno.*	**bway**-noh
Goodbye.	*Adiós.*	ah-dee-**ohs**
one / two	*uno / dos*	**oo**-noh / dohs
three / four	*tres / cuatro*	trays / **kwah**-troh
five / six	*cinco / seis*	**theen**-koh / says
seven / eight	*siete / ocho*	see-**eh**-tay / **oh**-choh
nine / ten	*nueve / diez*	**nway**-bay / dee-**ayth**
How much is it?	*¿Cuánto cuesta?*	**kwahn**-toh **kway**-stah
Write it?	*¿Me lo escribe?*	may loh ay-**skree**-bay
Is it free?	*¿Es gratis?*	ays **grah**-tees
Is it included?	*¿Está incluido?*	ay-**stah** een-kloo-**ee**-doh
Where can I buy / find...?	*¿Dónde puedo comprar / encontrar...?*	**dohn**-day **pway**-doh kohm-**prar** / ayn-kohn-**trar**
I'd like / We'd like...	*Quiero / Queremos...*	kee-**ehr**-oh / kehr-**ay**-mohs
...a room.	*...una habitación.*	**oo**-nah ah-bee-tah-thee-**ohn**
...a ticket to ___.	*...un billete para ___.*	oon bee-**yeh**-tay **pah**-rah ___
Is it possible?	*¿Es posible?*	ays poh-**see**-blay
Where is...?	*¿Dónde está...?*	**dohn**-day ay-**stah**
...the train station	*...la estación de trenes*	lah ay-stah-thee-**ohn** day **tray**-nays
...the bus station	*...la estación de autobuses*	lah ay-stah-thee-**ohn** day ow-toh-**boo**-says
...the tourist information office	*...la oficina de turismo*	lah oh-fee-**thee**-nah day too-**rees**-moh
Where are the toilets?	*¿Dónde están los servicios?*	**dohn**-day ay-**stahn** lohs sehr-**bee**-thee-ohs
men	*hombres, caballeros*	**ohm**-brays, kah-bah-**yay**-rohs
women	*mujeres, damas*	moo-**heh**-rays, **dah**-mahs
left / right	*izquierda / derecha*	eeth-kee-**ehr**-dah / day-**ray**-chah
straight	*derecho*	day-**ray**-choh
When do you open / close?	*¿A qué hora abren / cierran?*	ah kay **oh**-rah **ah**-brehn / thee-**ay**-rahn
At what time?	*¿A qué hora?*	ah kay **oh**-rah
Just a moment.	*Un momento.*	oon moh-**mehn**-toh
now / soon / later	*ahora / pronto / más tarde*	ah-**oh**-rah / **prohn**-toh / mahs **tar**-day
today / tomorrow	*hoy / mañana*	oy / mahn-**yah**-nah

In a Spanish Restaurant

English	Spanish	Pronunciation
I'd like / We'd like...	Quiero / Queremos...	kee-**ehr**-oh / kehr-**ay**-mohs
...to reserve...	...reservar...	ray-sehr-**bar**
...a table for one / two.	...una mesa para uno / dos.	oo-nah **may**-sah **pah**-rah oo-noh / dohs
Non-smoking.	No fumador.	noh foo-mah-**dohr**
Is this table free?	¿Está esta mesa libre?	ay-**stah** ay-stah **may**-sah lee-bray
The menu (in English), please.	La carta (en inglés), por favor.	lah **kar**-tah (ayn een-**glays**) por fah-**bor**
service (not) included	servicio (no) incluido	sehr-**bee**-thee-oh (noh) een-kloo-**ee**-doh
cover charge	precio de entrada	**pray**-thee-oh day ayn-**trah**-dah
to go	para llevar	**pah**-rah yay-**bar**
with / without	con / sin	kohn / seen
and / or	y / o	ee / oh
menu (of the day)	menú (del día)	may-**noo** (dayl **dee**-ah)
specialty of the house	especialidad de la casa	ay-spay-thee-ah-lee-**dahd** day lah **kah**-sah
tourist menu	menú turístico	meh-**noo** too-**ree**-stee-koh
combination plate	plato combinado	**plah**-toh kohm-bee-**nah**-doh
appetizers	tapas	**tah**-pahs
bread	pan	pahn
cheese	queso	**kay**-soh
sandwich	bocadillo	boh-kah-**dee**-yoh
soup	sopa	**soh**-pah
salad	ensalada	ayn-sah-**lah**-dah
meat	carne	**kar**-nay
poultry	aves	**ah**-bays
fish	pescado	pay-**skah**-doh
seafood	marisco	mah-**ree**-skoh
fruit	fruta	**froo**-tah
vegetables	verduras	behr-**doo**-rahs
dessert	postres	**poh**-strays
tap water	agua del grifo	**ah**-gwah dayl **gree**-foh
mineral water	agua mineral	**ah**-gwah mee-nay-**rahl**
milk	leche	**lay**-chay
(orange) juice	zumo (de naranja)	**thoo**-moh (day nah-**rahn**-hah)
coffee	café	kah-**feh**
tea	té	tay
wine	vino	**bee**-noh
red / white	tinto / blanco	**teen**-toh / **blahn**-koh
glass / bottle	vaso / botella	**bah**-soh / boh-**tay**-yah
beer	cerveza	thehr-**bay**-thah
Cheers!	¡Salud!	sah-**lood**
More. / Another.	Más. / Otro.	mahs / **oh**-troh
The same.	El mismo.	ehl **mees**-moh
The bill, please.	La cuenta, por favor.	lah **kwayn**-tah por fah-**bor**
tip	propina	proh-**pee**-nah
Delicious!	¡Delicioso!	day-lee-thee-**oh**-soh

INDEX

MAP INDEX

Start your trip at

Explore Europe

At ricksteves.com you can browse through thousands of articles, videos, photos and radio interviews, plus find a wealth of money-saving travel tips for planning your dream trip. And with our mobile-friendly website, you can easily access all this great travel information anywhere you go.

TV Shows

Preview the places you'll visit by watching entire half-hour episodes of Rick Steves' Europe (choose from all 100 shows) on-demand, for free.

ricksteves.com

your travel dreams into affordable reality

Radio Interviews

Enjoy ready access to Rick's vast library of radio interviews covering travel tips and cultural insights that relate specifically to your Europe travel plans.

Travel Forums

Learn, ask, share! Our online community of savvy travelers is a great resource for first-time travelers to Europe, as well as seasoned pros. You'll find forums on each country, plus travel tips and restaurant/hotel reviews. You can even ask one of our well-traveled staff to chime in with an opinion.

Travel News

Subscribe to our free Travel News e-newsletter, and get monthly updates from Rick on what's happening in Europe.

Audio Europe™

Rick's Free Travel App

Get your FREE Rick Steves Audio Europe™ app to enjoy…

- Dozens of self-guided tours of Europe's top museums, sights and historic walks
- Hundreds of tracks filled with cultural insights and sightseeing tips from Rick's radio interviews
- All organized into handy geographic playlists
- For Apple and Android

With Rick whispering in your ear, Europe gets even better.

Find out more at ricksteves.com

Pack Light and Right

Gear up for your next adventure at ricksteves.com

Light Luggage

Pack light and right with Rick Steves' affordable, custom-designed rolling carry-on bags, backpacks, day packs and shoulder bags.

Accessories

From packing cubes to moneybelts and beyond, Rick has personally selected the travel goodies that will help your trip go smoother.

Rick Steves has

Save time and energy

This guidebook is your independent-travel toolkit. But for all it delivers, it's still up to you to devote the time and energy it takes to manage the preparation and logistics that are essential for a happy trip. If that's a hassle, there's a solution.

Rick Steves Tours

A Rick Steves tour takes you to Europe's most

great tours, too!

with minimum stress

interesting places with great guides and small groups of 28 or less. We follow Rick's favorite itineraries, ride in comfy buses, stay in family-run hotels, and bring you intimately close to the Europe you've traveled so far to see. Most importantly, we take away the logistical headaches so you can focus on the fun.

nearly half of them repeat customers—along with us on four dozen different itineraries, from Ireland to Italy to Istanbul. Is a Rick Steves tour the right fit for your travel dreams? Find out at ricksteves.com, where you can also get Rick's latest tour catalog and free Tour Experience DVD.

Europe is best experienced with happy travel partners. We hope you can join us.

Join the fun
This year we'll take 25,000 free-spirited travelers—

See our itineraries at ricksteves.com

Nearly all Rick Steves guides are available as ebooks. Check with your favorite bookseller.
Rick Steves guidebooks are published by Avalon Travel, a member of the Perseus Books Group.

Maximize your travel skills with a good guidebook.

Photo © Patricia Feaster

RickSteves.com 📘🐦 **@RickSteves**

PHOTO CREDITS

Avalon Travel
a member of the Perseus Books Group
1700 Fourth Street
Berkeley, CA 94710

Text © 2016 by Rick Steves' Europe, Inc.

Maps © 2016 by Rick Steves' Europe, Inc. All rights reserved.

Printed in Canada by Friesens

First printing April 2016

ISBN 978-1-63121-315-1
ISSN 2470-1890

For the latest on Rick's lectures, guidebooks, tours, public radio show, and public television series, contact Rick Steves' Europe, 130 Fourth Avenue North, Edmonds, WA 98020, 425/771-8303, www.ricksteves.com, rick@ricksteves.com.

RICK STEVES' EUROPE
Special Publications Manager: Risa Laib
Managing Editor: Jennifer Madison Davis
Project Editor: Suzanne Kotz
Editorial & Production Assistant: Jessica Shaw
Maps & Graphics: David C. Hoerlein, Sandra Hundacker, Mary Rostad

AVALON TRAVEL
Editorial Director: Kevin McLain
Senior Editor and Series Manager: Madhu Prasher
Editor: Jamie Andrade
Associate Editor: Sierra Machado
Copy Editor: Naomi Adler Dancis
Proofreader: Kelly Lydick
Indexer: Stephen Callahan
Interior Design & Layout: McGuire Barber Design
Cover Design: Kimberly Glyder Design
Maps & Graphics: Kat Bennett, Mike Morgenfeld

Front Cover Photos: Top left: Park Güell, Barcelona, designed by the Catalan architect Antoni Gaudí, and part of the UNESCO World Heritage Sites Works of Antoni Gaudí. © Rui Caldeira | Dreamstime.com. Top middle: Sagrada Família Church in Barcelona © Yevgen Byelykh | Dreamstime.com. Top right: Spanish tapas © Ppy2010ha | Dreamstime.com. Bottom: view of the old city of Ronda, in the province of Málaga, Andalusia © minnystock | Dreamstime.com

Back Cover Photos: Left: Gaudí sculpture in Barcelona © portokalis/123rf.com; Middle: flamenco dresses in Malaga, Andalusia © Jorisvo | Dreamstime.com; Right: Plaza de España in Seville © Monysasi | Dreamstime.com

More for your Spain trip!
Maximize the experience with Rick Steves as your guide

Guidebooks
Rick's Barcelona and Portugal guides make side-trips smooth and affordable

Phrase Books
Rely on Rick's Spanish Phrase Book & Dictionary

Rick's TV Shows
Preview your destinations with 8 shows on Spain

Free! Rick's Audio Europe™ App
Hear Spain travel tips from Rick's radio shows

Small Group Tours
Take a lively Rick Steves tour through Spain

For all the details, visit ricksteves.com